MW01095036

BLACK
IN AMERICA

More Notes and Readings Online

The *Black in America* companion website offers dozens of recommended articles—as well as poems, artworks, and more—that have been selected for their relevance to the police murders of George Floyd and Breonna Taylor, and to the 2020 protests sparked by their deaths and the deaths of countless other Black Americans.

The website also provides a set of explanatory notes that go beyond the footnotes in the bound book. These notes are designed to be of particular help to students who have limited familiarity with American culture, and/or students who have learned English as an additional language—though the extra notes may offer support to any student. Words and phrases for which additional notes are provided on the website are marked with a small asterisk in these pages. The notes themselves may either be consulted online or be printed out and kept handy as you read.

Visit the website here:
https://sites.broadviewpress.com/blackinamerica/

BLACK
IN AMERICA

Advisory Editor
Jessica Edwards, University of Delaware

Textual Editors
Laura Buzzard
Don LePan
Nora Ruddock
Alexandria Stuart

broadview press

BROADVIEW PRESS – www.broadviewpress.com
Peterborough, Ontario, Canada

Founded in 1985, Broadview Press remains a wholly independent publishing house. Broadview's focus is on academic publishing; our titles are accessible to university and college students as well as scholars and general readers. With over 600 titles in print, Broadview has become a leading international publisher in the humanities, with world-wide distribution. Broadview is committed to environmentally responsible publishing and fair business practices.

© 2018 Broadview Press

All rights reserved. No part of this book may be reproduced, kept in an information storage and retrieval system, or transmitted in any form or by any means, electronic or mechanical, including photocopying, recording, or otherwise, except as expressly permitted by the applicable copyright laws or through written permission from the publisher.

Library and Archives Canada Cataloguing in Publication

Black in America / advisory editor, Jessica Edwards, University of Delaware ; editors, Laura Buzzard, Don LePan, Nora Ruddock, Alexandria Stuart.

ISBN 978-1-55481-428-2 (softcover)

1. American essays. 2. American literature—African American authors.
3. African Americans—Social conditions. I. Edwards, Jessica, 1984–, editor
II. Buzzard, Laura, editor III. LePan, Don, 1954–, editor IV. Ruddock, Nora, editor V. Stuart, Alexandria, editor

PS683.A35B53 2018   814'.0080352996073   C2018-901867-4

Broadview Press handles its own distribution in North America:
PO Box 1243, Peterborough, Ontario K9J 7H5, Canada
555 Riverwalk Parkway, Tonawanda, NY 14150, USA
Tel: (705) 743-8990; Fax: (705) 743-8353
email: customerservice@broadviewpress.com

Distribution is handled by Eurospan Group in the UK, Europe, Central Asia, Middle East, Africa, India, Southeast Asia, Central America, South America, and the Caribbean. Distribution is handled by Footprint Books in Australia and New Zealand.

Broadview Press acknowledges the financial support of the Government of Canada through the Canada Book Fund for our publishing activities.

Canada

Design and typeset by Alexandria Stuart
Cover design by Lisa Brawn

PRINTED IN CANADA

CONTENTS

CONTENTS BY SUBJECT

*Approaches to Activism / Artists and the Arts / Childhood and Education /
Civil Disobedience and Black Power Movements / Cultural Appropriation /
Economics and Social Class / Gender / Historical Analysis / International
Perspectives / Lynching and Police Brutality / Popular Culture / Prison and Mass
Incarceration / The Problem of White Liberalism / Religion / Segregation /
Self-help and Respectability Politics / Slavery / Sport / Urban Landscapes /
Visions of America / Voting and Democratic Representation*

International Perspectives

Lynching and Police Brutality

Popular Culture

Voting and Democratic Representation

CONTENTS BY GENRE AND RHETORICAL CATEGORY

Academic Writing / Blog Posts / Cause and Effect / Classification / Comparison and Contrast / Definition / Description / Journalism / Memoir, Biography, and Personal Experience / Narration / Poetry and Lyric Essays / Speeches and Lectures

Classification

Comparison and Contrast

Memoir, Biography, and Personal Experience

Narration

Poetry and Lyric Essays

Speeches and Lectures

SUGGESTED PAIRS AND GROUPS

Though it is by no means an exhaustive list of such combinations, the following list identifies pieces in this book that the editors suggest may be of interest to consider together:

PREFACE

When Broadview's editorial team began last year to think of publishing a series of themed readers, one topic in particular stood out—the lived experiences of African American people. Other publishers have issued readers for first-year students on a wide variety of topics, including Gender, Poverty, Happiness, Globalization, Monsters, Humor, Food, and Sustainability. But no themed reader existed on the topic that, so far as we could discern, was leading all others in interest as a focus for first-year courses at American colleges and universities. More resources were needed for such courses that sought to devote attention to the work of African American scholars, public intellectuals, and other writers whose varied examinations of Black history, politics, cultures, and identities are too often not centered in humanities education. Additionally, as Donald Trump succeeded Barack Obama and the nation continued to reel in the wake not only of the 2016 election but also of the Trayvon Martin shooting, of the Michael Brown shooting and the subsequent protests in Ferguson, of the Charleston church massacre, and of so many other disturbing developments, more and more national conversations have ignited, continuing and prompting conversations about Blackness. "Black in America" was clearly a theme that cried out for attention.

As it happened, Broadview included a considerable number of essays on this theme in the 2016 third edition of *The Broadview Anthology of Expository Prose*. The present volume incorporates fifteen of those selections—as well as over thirty-five selections for which headnotes, footnotes, and discussion questions have been prepared especially for *Black in America*.

It would not be possible for any one anthology, of course, to provide a comprehensive picture of African American lived experiences—and we do not attempt to do so in this volume. Our aim is rather to present a representative sampling of some important aspects of Black experiences, Black culture, Black history, and so on.

Initially, this book was conceived primarily as a reader for use in first-year writing courses in which the instructor chooses to focus the course on a single theme. But we have become increasingly aware as we have worked on the book that it may appeal just as widely to introductory courses offered in Black Studies, African American Studies, and other interdisciplinary programs—or even to certain sorts of courses offered in History departments. We have tried to keep in mind all these potential audiences as we have prepared the headnotes, the footnotes, and the questions at the end of each selection.

A central principle of the book is variety. A wide variety of analytical and persuasive essays are a central part of the anthology—but the reader will also find personal essays, occasional pieces, speeches, excerpts from biographies and autobiographies, and so on. A number of op-ed pieces are included, as are examples of blog posts, articles from online media, and film reviews. Selections range from more than twenty pages in length to less than a single page. The emphasis is on the twenty-first century, but a substantial representation of vitally important work from other eras is also included.

There is variety in level of difficulty, in type of audience, and in subject matter as well. In some selections the writing is almost transparent in its simplicity; in others the reader may be challenged by the inherent difficulty of the material. In many cases the intended audience is clearly the general reader, but some selections aim at a much narrower readership. Several selections are scholarly in nature, but these have been carefully selected on the basis of accessibility to a first-year undergraduate readership.

Any reader is bound to have written material at its core, but we are acutely aware as well of the importance of images in shaping history, culture, and experience. With that in mind we have included a color insert of visual material. Some of the selected images are mentioned specifically in one or more of the written pieces, while others have been chosen because they relate strongly to themes that recur throughout the anthology; all, we hope, will help to facilitate engaging discussion.

Another feature of the anthology is the inclusion of paired or grouped selections. In some cases, the pairings are of pieces that take directly opposing points of view on the same topic; such is the case with the two pieces on the NFL. In others, they treat a topic from complementary viewpoints. And in still others—notably the Alisha Knight and Pauline Hopkins selections—a piece from one era is the subject of academic analysis in another piece from a much later era. Although it is by no means exhaustive, a listing of articles that may usefully be taught in pairs or groups is provided in this anthology's prefatory material.

We have also aimed for what seems to us to be an appropriate balance so far as gender is concerned. What constitutes "appropriate balance" in this respect in 2018? To our minds for an anthology of this sort, it is a roughly fifty-fifty balance. In our draft table of contents, that balance was struck precisely. As frequently happens with anthologies, however, copyright issues prevented us from reprinting a few selections that we had wished to include; the result is that, so far as both the number of authors and the total number of selections are concerned, men slightly outnumber women in these pages—but only very slightly.

One issue in assembling almost any anthology is whether or not to excerpt. If the book is to be essentially an anthology of essays, does the integrity of the form demand that all essays selected for inclusion be included in their entirety? Should selections taken from full-length books be excluded on the grounds of their provenance? To both these questions we have answered in the negative. If an anthology such as this is to do the best possible job of presenting the widest possible range within a manageable compass, both practical and pedagogical concerns seem to us to justify the occasional decision to excerpt a very long essay, or to reprint a selection from a full-length book. We have, however, included a considerable number of longer essays in their entirety—including James Baldwin's "Stranger in the Village," Audre Lorde's "Uses of Anger," and Ta-Nehisi Coates's "The Case for Reparations."

Many themed readers designed for university use are arranged either by sub-themes or by rhetorical category. On the advice of the majority of academics we consulted on this matter, we have decided instead to use a chronological arrangement, in the interests both of simplicity and of flexibility. In an anthology where the grouping is by subject or by rhetorical category, each essay must of necessity appear as part of only one grouping—whereas in reality, of course, many of the finest and most interesting pieces will have more than one subject, many of the best persuasive essays also employ description or narration, and so on. A chronological approach allows the instructor to group the essays in whatever combinations seem most interesting or appropriate, and to change those groupings as desired each time a course is taught. Alternative tables of contents arranged by subject category and by rhetorical category—in both of which a given essay is quite likely to appear many times—appear following this preface.

The apparatus for the anthology is designed to provide substantial help to students, and to do so in ways that help them to engage actively with the material. Introductory headnotes are designed to fill in the context, not to provide a summary of each piece. Footnotes are there to assist students in understanding material that may be unfamiliar—but in every case the aim is to provide explanatory background rather than interpretation. Questions at the end of each selection are designed to provoke thought and discussion in a wide variety of areas.

We have also provided a set of additional notes on the anthology's companion website—notes designed to be of particular help to English as an Additional Language (EAL) students and/or students who have little familiarity with American history and culture. Phrases such as "X factor" or "tar and feather" are not likely to require glossing for the student who has just graduated from a high school in Chicago or Atlanta or San Francisco, but may seem obscure or confusing to a student who has recently arrived in the United States for the first time. And, of course, some students will always arrive at university with a larger vocabulary than others. These notes, then, offer additional support to any student who may wish to consult them. Words and phrases for which additional notes are provided are marked with a small asterisk in these pages. Students wishing to consult these additional notes may find them on the anthology's companion website; these notes may be read online or printed out and kept handy as the student reads the relevant selections.

•   •   •

We are indebted to a good many people for suggestions and guidance, and would like to thank the following for the advice they have provided to us along the way: Earl H. Brooks, University of Maryland, Baltimore County; Denise Burgher, University of Delaware; John Ernest, University of Delaware; Tiffany Gill, University of Delaware; Natasha N. Jones, University of Central Florida; Shirley Moody-Turner, Penn State University; Ebony R. Moore, Alcorn State University; Myrna Nurse, Delaware State University; Jeff Pruchnic, Wayne State University; Ken Rayes, University of New Orleans; Marc Robinson, Whitworth University; ReAnna S. Roby, University of Texas, San Antonio; Dara Rossman Regaignon, New York University; Jessica Rogers-Cerrato, Brooklyn Community College; Allison Tharp, University of Delaware; Sophie Weeks, Morehouse College; Dana A. Williams, Howard University; Délice Williams, University of Delaware; Craig Wynne, Hampton University.

•   •   •

We welcome the comments and suggestions of all readers—instructors or students—about any and all aspects of this book, from the selections themselves to the book's organization and ancillary material (both within these pages and on the companion website); please feel free to email the publishers at <broadview@broadviewpress.com>.We hope you will enjoy this book as it stands—but we also hope you will join us in thinking of possible improvements for future editions.

Jessica Edwards
Laura Buzzard
Don LePan
Nora Ruddock
Alexandria Stuart

OLAUDAH EQUIANO

from THE INTERESTING NARRATIVE OF THE LIFE OF OLAUDAH EQUIANO

The Interesting Narrative of the Life of Olaudah Equiano is widely considered the first autobiographical slave narrative. Published during the early years of the campaign to abolish slavery in Britain, Equiano's account of his experience of slavery and eventual conversion to Christianity was widely read.

In the chapters excerpted below, Equiano describes his childhood, capture, and transportation from Africa to the Americas. Unlike the rest of the autobiography, the chapters below may not be strictly true; many scholars now accept evidence, first advanced by the historian Vincent Carretta (1999), that Equiano was in fact born in Carolina. If it is not based on his own experience, however, this portion of the Interesting Narrative *represents research Equiano conducted through conversation with other slaves who had made the infamously grueling journey across the Atlantic, and can still be taken as broadly representative of that experience.*

CHAPTER 1

... That part of Africa, known by the name of Guinea, to which the trade for slaves is carried on, extends along the coast above 3400 miles, from the Senegal to Angola, and includes a variety of kingdoms. Of these the most considerable is the kingdom of Benin, both as to extent and wealth, the richness and cultivation of the soil, the power of its king, and the number and warlike disposition of the inhabitants. It is situated nearly under the line,[1] and extends along the coast about 170 miles, but runs back into the interior part of Africa to a distance hitherto I believe unexplored by any traveler; and seems only terminated at length by the empire of Abyssinia,[2] near 1500 miles from its beginning.

---

1   *under the line*   South of the equator.

2   *Abyssinia*   Also known as the Ethiopian Empire, a kingdom in what is today the northern portion of Ethiopia.

This kingdom is divided into many provinces or districts: in one of the most remote and fertile of which, called Eboe, I was born, in the year 1745, in a charming fruitful vale, named Effaka. The distance of this province from the capital of Benin and the sea coast must be very considerable; for I had never heard of white men or Europeans, nor of the sea: and our subjection to the king of Benin was little more than nominal; for every transaction of the government, as far as my slender observation extended, was conducted by the chiefs or elders of the place. The manners and government of a people who have little commerce with other countries are generally very simple; and the history of what passes in one family or village may serve as a specimen of a nation.

My father was one of those elders or chiefs I have spoken of, and was styled Embrenche; a term, as I remember, importing the highest distinction, and signifying in our language a *mark* of grandeur....

We are almost a nation of dancers, musicians, and poets. Thus every great event, such as a triumphant return from battle, or other cause of public rejoicing is celebrated in public dances, which are accompanied with songs and music suited to the occasion. The assembly is separated into four divisions, which dance either apart or in succession, and each with a character peculiar to itself. The first division contains the married men, who in their dances frequently exhibit feats of arms, and the representation of a battle. To these succeed the married women, who dance in the second division. The young men occupy the third; and the maidens the fourth. Each represents some interesting scene of real life, such as a great achievement, domestic employment, a pathetic[3] story, or some rural sport; and as the subject is generally founded on some recent event, it is therefore ever new. This gives our dances a spirit and variety which I have scarcely seen elsewhere.[4] We have many musical instruments, particularly drums of different kinds, a piece of music which resembles a guitar, and another much like a stickado.[5] These last are chiefly used by betrothed virgins, who play on them on all grand festivals.

5   As our manners are simple, our luxuries are few. The dress of both sexes is nearly the same. It generally consists of a long piece of calico, or muslin, wrapped loosely round the body, somewhat in the form of a highland plaid. This is usually dyed blue, which is our favorite color. It is extracted from a berry, and is brighter and richer than any I have seen in Europe. Besides this, our women of distinction wear golden ornaments; which they dispose with some profusion on their arms and legs....

---

3   *pathetic* Emotionally evocative.

4   [Equiano's note]   When I was in Smyrna I have frequently seen the Greeks dance after this manner.

5   *stickado* Percussion instrument that resembles a xylophone.

Our manner of living is entirely plain; for as yet the natives are unacquainted with those refinements in cookery which debauch the taste.... The head of the family usually eats alone; his wives and slaves have also their separate tables. Before we taste food we always wash our hands: indeed our cleanliness on all occasions is extreme; but on this it is an indispensable ceremony. After washing, libation is made, by pouring out a small portion of the drink, in a certain place, for the spirits of departed relations, which the natives suppose to preside over their conduct, and guard them from evil. They are totally unacquainted with strong or spirituous liquors; and their principal beverage is palm wine. This is gotten from a tree of that name by tapping it at the top, and fastening a large gourd to it; and sometimes one tree will yield three or four gallons in a night. When just drawn it is of a most delicious sweetness; but in a few days it acquires a tartish and more spirituous flavor: though I never saw any one intoxicated by it. The same tree also produces nuts and oil. Our principal luxury is in perfumes; one sort of these is an odoriferous wood of delicious fragrance.... We beat this wood into powder, and mix it with palm oil; with which both men and women perfume themselves.

In our buildings we study* convenience rather than ornament. Each master of a family has a large square piece of ground, surrounded with a moat or fence, or enclosed with a wall made of red earth tempered; which, when dry, is as hard as brick. Within this are his houses to accommodate his family and slaves; which, if numerous, frequently present the appearance of a village. In the middle stands the principal building, appropriated to the sole use of the master, and consisting of two apartments; in one of which he sits in the day with his family, the other is left apart for the reception of his friends. He has besides these a distinct apartment in which he sleeps, together with his male children. On each side are the apartments of his wives, who have also their separate day and night houses. The habitations of the slaves and their families are distributed throughout the rest of the enclosure. These houses never exceed one story in height: they are always built of wood, or stakes driven into the ground, crossed with wattles,[6] and neatly plastered within, and without. The roof is thatched with reeds....

As we live in a country where nature is prodigal of her favors, our wants are few and easily supplied; of course we have few manufactures. They consist for the most part of calicoes, earthen ware, ornaments, and instruments of war and husbandry. But these make no part of our commerce, the principal articles of which, as I have observed, are provisions. In such a state money is of little use; however we have some small pieces of coin, if I may call them such. They are made something like an anchor; but I do not remember either their value or

---

6   *wattles*   Woven sticks.

denomination. We have also markets, at which I have been frequently with my mother. These are sometimes visited by stout mahogany-colored men from the south west of us: we call them Oye-Eboe, which term signifies red men living at a distance. They generally bring us fire-arms, gunpowder, hats, beads, and dried fish. The last we esteemed a great rarity, as our waters were only brooks and springs. These articles they barter with us for odoriferous woods and earth, and our salt of wood ashes. They always carry slaves through our land; but the strictest account is exacted of their manner of procuring them before they are suffered to pass. Sometimes indeed we sold slaves to them, but they were only prisoners of war, or such among us as had been convicted of kidnapping, or adultery, and some other crimes, which we esteemed heinous. This practice of kidnapping induces me to think, that, notwithstanding all our strictness, their principal business among us was to trepan[7] our people. I remember too they carried great sacks along with them, which not long after I had an opportunity of fatally seeing applied to that infamous purpose.

Our land is uncommonly rich and fruitful, and produces all kinds of vegetables in great abundance. We have plenty of Indian corn,[8] and vast quantities of cotton and tobacco. Our pine apples grow without culture; they are about the size of the largest sugar-loaf, and finely flavored. We have also spices of different kinds, particularly pepper; and a variety of delicious fruits which I have never seen in Europe; together with gums of various kinds, and honey in abundance. All our industry is exerted to improve those blessings of nature. Agriculture is our chief employment; and every one, even the children and women, are engaged in it. Thus we are all habituated to labor from our earliest years. Every one contributes something to the common stock; and as we are unacquainted with idleness, we have no beggars. The benefits of such a mode of living are obvious. The West India planters prefer the slaves of Benin or Eboe to those of any other part of Guinea, for their hardiness, intelligence, integrity, and zeal. Those benefits are felt by us in the general healthiness of the people, and in their vigor and activity; I might have added too in their comeliness. Deformity is indeed unknown amongst us, I mean that of shape. Numbers of the natives of Eboe now in London might be brought in support of this assertion: for, in regard to complexion, ideas of beauty are wholly relative. I remember while in Africa to have seen three negro children, who were tawny, and another quite white, who were universally regarded by myself, and the natives in general, as far as related to their complexions, as deformed. Our women too were in my eyes at least uncommonly graceful, alert, and modest to·

7   *trepan* Capture.

8   *Indian corn* I.e., corn or maize. (In British English, "corn" refers to any type of grain; the adjective "Indian" here indicates that the grain is what North Americans call corn.)

a degree of bashfulness; nor do I remember to have ever heard of an instance of incontinence[9] amongst them before marriage. They are also remarkably cheerful. Indeed cheerfulness and affability are two of the leading characteristics of our nation.

Our tillage is exercised in a large plain or common,[10] some hours walk from our dwellings, and all the neighbors resort thither in a body. They use no beasts of husbandry; and their only instruments are hoes, axes, shovels, and beaks, or pointed iron to dig with. Sometimes we are visited by locusts, which come in large clouds, so as to darken the air, and destroy our harvest. This however happens rarely, but when it does, a famine is produced by it. I remember an instance or two wherein this happened. This common is often the theater of war; and therefore when our people go out to till their land, they not only go in a body, but generally take their arms with them for fear of a surprise; and when they apprehend an invasion they guard the avenue to their dwellings, by driving sticks into the ground, which are so sharp at one end as to pierce the foot, and are generally dipped in poison. From what I can recollect of these battles, they appear to have been irruptions of one little state or district on the other, to obtain prisoners or booty. Perhaps they were incited to this by those traders who brought the European goods I mentioned amongst us. Such a mode of obtaining slaves in Africa is common; and I believe more are procured this way, and by kidnapping, than any other.[11] When a trader wants slaves, he applies to a chief for them, and tempts him with his wares. It is not extraordinary, if on this occasion he yields to the temptation with as little firmness, and accepts the price of his fellow creature's liberty with as little reluctance as the enlightened merchant. Accordingly he falls on* his neighbors, and a desperate battle ensues. If he prevails and takes prisoners, he gratifies his avarice by selling them; but, if his party be vanquished, and he falls into the hands of the enemy, he is put to death: for, as he has been known to foment their quarrels, it is thought dangerous to let him survive, and no ransom can save him, though all other prisoners may be redeemed. We have fire-arms, bows and arrows, broad two-edged swords and javelins: we have shields also which cover a man from head to foot. All are taught the use of these weapons; even our women are warriors, and march boldly out to fight along with the men....

As to religion, the natives believe that there is one Creator of all things, and that he lives in the sun, and is girted round with a belt that he may never eat or drink; but, according to some, he smokes a pipe, which is our own favorite luxury. They believe he governs events, especially our deaths or captivity; but,

---

9 *incontinence* Unchastity.

10 *common* Area of land belonging to the whole community.

11 [Equiano's note] See Benezet's "Account of Africa" throughout.

as for the doctrine of eternity, I do not remember to have ever heard of it: some however believe in the transmigration of souls in a certain degree. Those spirits, which are not transmigrated, such as our dear friends or relations, they believe always attend them, and guard them from the bad spirits or their foes....

I was very fond of my mother, and almost constantly with her. When she went to ... her mother's tomb, which was a kind of small solitary thatched house, I sometimes attended her. There she made her libations, and spent most of the night in cries and lamentations. I have been often extremely terrified on these occasions. The loneliness of the place, the darkness of the night, and the ceremony of libation, naturally awful and gloomy, were heightened by my mother's lamentations; and these, concurring with the cries of doleful birds, by which these places were frequented, gave an inexpressible terror to the scene.

We compute the year from the day on which the sun crosses the line,[12] and on its setting that evening there is a general shout throughout the land; at least I can speak from my own knowledge throughout the vicinity....

We practiced circumcision like the Jews, and made offerings and feasts on that occasion in the same manner as they did. Like them also, our children were named from some event, some circumstance, or fancied foreboding at the time of their birth. I was named *Olaudah*, which, in our language, signifies vicissitude or fortunate, also, one favored, and having a loud voice and well spoken. I remember we never polluted the name of the object of our adoration; on the contrary, it was always mentioned with the greatest reverence; and we were totally unacquainted with swearing, and all those terms of abuse and reproach which find their way so readily and copiously into the languages of more civilized people. The only expressions of that kind I remember were "May you rot, or may you swell, or may a beast take you." ...

15 Such is the imperfect sketch my memory has furnished me with of the manners and customs of a people among whom I first drew my breath....

CHAPTER 2

... I have already acquainted the reader with the time and place of my birth. My father, besides many slaves, had a numerous family, of which seven lived to grow up, including myself and a sister, who was the only daughter. As I was the youngest of the sons, I became, of course, the greatest favorite with my mother, and was always with her; and she used to take particular pains to form my mind. I was trained up from my earliest years in the art of war; my daily exercise was shooting and throwing javelins; and my mother adorned me with emblems, after the manner of our greatest warriors. In this way I grew up till I was turned the age of eleven, when an end was put to my happiness in the

---

12 *the day on ... line* I.e., the vernal equinox.

following manner: Generally when the grown people in the neighborhood were gone far in the fields to labor, the children assembled together in some of the neighbors' premises to play; and commonly some of us used to get up a tree to look out for any assailant, or kidnapper, that might come upon us; for they sometimes took those opportunities of our parents' absence to attack and carry off as many as they could seize. One day, as I was watching at the top of a tree in our yard, I saw one of those people come into the yard of our next neighbor but one, to kidnap, there being many stout young people in it. Immediately on this I gave the alarm of the rogue, and he was surrounded by the stoutest of them, who entangled him with cords, so that he could not escape till some of the grown people came and secured him. But alas! ere long it was my fate to be thus attacked, and to be carried off, when none of the grown people were nigh. One day, when all our people were gone out to their works as usual, and only I and my dear sister were left to mind the house, two men and a woman got over our walls, and in a moment seized us both, and, without giving us time to cry out, or make resistance, they stopped our mouths, and ran off with us into the nearest wood. Here they tied our hands, and continued to carry us as far as they could, till night came on, when we reached a small house, where the robbers halted for refreshment, and spent the night. We were then unbound, but were unable to take any food; and, being quite overpowered by fatigue and grief, our only relief was some sleep, which allayed our misfortune for a short time.

The next morning we left the house, and continued traveling all the day. For a long time we had kept the woods, but at last we came into a road which I believed I knew. I had now some hopes of being delivered; for we had advanced but a little way before I discovered some people at a distance, on which I began to cry out for their assistance: but my cries had no other effect than to make them tie me faster and stop my mouth, and then they put me into a large sack. They also stopped my sister's mouth, and tied her hands; and in this manner we proceeded till we were out of the sight of these people. When we went to rest the following night they offered us some victuals; but we refused it; and the only comfort we had was in being in one another's arms all that night, and bathing each other with our tears. But alas! we were soon deprived of even the small comfort of weeping together.

The next day proved a day of greater sorrow than I had yet experienced; for my sister and I were then separated, while we lay clasped in each other's arms. It was in vain that we besought them not to part us; she was torn from me, and immediately carried away, while I was left in a state of distraction not to be described. I cried and grieved continually; and for several days I did not eat any thing but what they forced into my mouth. At length, after many days traveling, during which I had often changed masters, I got into the hands of a chieftain, in a very pleasant country. This man had two wives and some children, and they all used me* extremely well, and did all they could to comfort me; particularly the first wife, who was something like my mother. Although I was a great many days' journey from my father's house, yet these people spoke exactly the same language with us. This first master of mine, as I may call him, was a smith, and my principal employment was working his bellows, which were the same kind as I had seen in my vicinity....

... I was again sold, and carried through a number of places, till, after traveling a considerable time, I came to a town called Tinmah, in the most beautiful country I had yet seen in Africa. It was extremely rich, and there were many rivulets which flowed through it, and supplied a large pond in the center of the town, where the people washed.... Here I also saw and tasted for the first time sugar-cane.

Their money consisted of little white shells, the size of the finger nail. I was sold here for one hundred and seventy-two of them by a merchant who lived and brought me there. I had been about two or three days at his house, when a wealthy widow, a neighbor of his, came there one evening, and brought with her an only son, a young gentleman about my own age and size. Here they saw me; and, having taken a fancy to me, I was bought of the merchant, and went home with them. Her house and premises were ... very extensive, and she had a number of slaves to attend her. The next day I was washed and perfumed, and when meal-time came I was led into the presence of my mistress, and ate and drank before her with her son. This filled me with astonishment; and I could scarce help expressing my surprise that the young gentleman should suffer me, who was bound,[13] to eat with him who was free; and not only so, but that he would not at any time either eat or drink till I had taken first, because I was the eldest, which was agreeable to our custom. Indeed every thing here, and all their treatment of me, made me forget that I was a slave. The language of these people resembled ours so nearly, that we understood each other perfectly. They had also the very same customs as we. There were likewise slaves daily to attend us, while my young master and I with other boys sported with our darts and bows and arrows, as I had been used to do at home. In this resemblance to my former happy state I passed about two months; and I now began to think I was to be adopted into the family, and was beginning to be reconciled to my situation, and to forget by degrees my misfortunes, when all at once the delusion vanished; for, without the least previous knowledge, one morning early, while my dear master and companion was still asleep, I was wakened out of my reverie to fresh sorrow, and hurried away....

Thus, at the very moment I dreamed of the greatest happiness, I found myself most miserable; and it seemed as if fortune wished to give me this taste

---

13 *bound* Enslaved.

of joy, only to render the reverse more poignant. The change I now experienced was as painful as it was sudden and unexpected. It was a change indeed from a state of bliss to a scene which is inexpressible by me, as it discovered to me an element I had never before beheld, and till then had no idea of, and wherein such instances of hardship and cruelty continually occurred as I can never reflect on but with horror.

All the nations and people I had hitherto passed through resembled our own in their manners, customs, and language: but I came at length to a country, the inhabitants of which differed from us in all those particulars.... Thus I continued to travel, sometimes by land, sometimes by water, through different countries and various nations, till, at the end of six or seven months after I had been kidnapped, I arrived at the sea coast....

The first object which saluted my eyes when I arrived on the coast was the sea, and a slave ship, which was then riding at anchor, and waiting for its cargo. These filled me with astonishment, which was soon converted into terror when I was carried on board. I was immediately handled and tossed up to see if I were sound by some of the crew; and I was now persuaded that I had gotten into a world of bad spirits, and that they were going to kill me. Their complexions too differing so much from ours, their long hair, and the language they spoke, (which was very different from any I had ever heard) united to confirm me in this belief. Indeed such were the horrors of my views and fears at the moment, that, if ten thousand worlds had been my own, I would have freely parted with them all to have exchanged my condition with that of the meanest[14] slave in my own country. When I looked round the ship too and saw a large furnace of copper boiling, and a multitude of black people of every description chained together, every one of their countenances expressing dejection and sorrow, I no longer doubted of my fate; and, quite overpowered with horror and anguish, I fell motionless on the deck and fainted. When I recovered a little I found some black people about me, who I believed were some of those who brought me on board, and had been receiving their pay; they talked to me in order to cheer me, but all in vain....

I was soon put down under the decks, and there I received such a salutation in my nostrils as I had never experienced in my life: so that, with the loathsomeness of the stench, and crying together, I became so sick and low that I was not able to eat, nor had I the least desire to taste any thing. I now wished for the last friend, death, to relieve me; but soon, to my grief, two of the white men offered me eatables; and, on my refusing to eat, one of them held me fast by the hands, and laid me across I think the windlass, and tied my feet, while the other flogged me severely. I had never experienced any thing of

---

14 *meanest* Lowest in status.

this kind before; and although, not being used to the water, I naturally feared that element the first time I saw it, yet nevertheless, could I have got over the nettings, I would have jumped over the side, but I could not; and, besides, the crew used to watch us very closely who were not chained down to the decks, lest we should leap into the water: and I have seen some of these poor African prisoners most severely cut for attempting to do so, and hourly whipped for not eating. This indeed was often the case with myself.

25   In a little time after, amongst the poor chained men, I found some of my own nation, which in a small degree gave ease to my mind. I inquired of these what was to be done with us; they gave me to understand we were to be carried to these white people's country to work for them. I then was a little revived, and thought, if it were no worse than working, my situation was not so desperate: but still I feared I should be put to death, the white people looked and acted, as I thought, in so savage a manner; for I had never seen among any people such instances of brutal cruelty; and this not only shown towards us blacks, but also to some of the whites themselves. One white man in particular I saw, when we were permitted to be on deck, flogged so unmercifully with a large rope near the foremast, that he died in consequence of it; and they tossed him over the side as they would have done a brute. This made me fear these people the more; and I expected nothing less than to be treated in the same manner.

I could not help expressing my fears and apprehensions to some of my countrymen: I asked them if these people had no country, but lived in this hollow place (the ship): they told me they did not, but came from a distant one. "Then," said I, "how comes it in all our country we never heard of them?" They told me because they lived so very far off. I then asked where their women were. Had they any like themselves? I was told they had. "And why," said I, "do we not see them?" They answered, because they were left behind. I asked how the vessel could go. They told me they could not tell; but that there were cloths put upon the masts by the help of the ropes I saw, and then the vessel went on; and the white men had some spell or magic they put in the water when they liked in order to stop the vessel. I was exceedingly amazed at this account, and really thought they were spirits. I therefore wished much to be from amongst them, for I expected they would sacrifice me: but my wishes were vain; for we were so quartered that it was impossible for any of us to make our escape....

One day, when we had a smooth sea and moderate wind, two of my wearied countrymen who were chained together (I was near them at the time), preferring death to such a life of misery, somehow made through the nettings and jumped into the sea: immediately another quite dejected fellow, who, on account of his illness, was suffered to be out of irons, also followed their example; and I believe many more would very soon have done the same if they had not been prevented by the ship's crew, who were instantly alarmed. Those of us that were the most active were in a moment put down under the deck, and there was such a noise and confusion amongst the people of the ship as I never heard before, to stop her, and get the boat out to go after the slaves. However two of the wretches were drowned, but they got the other, and afterwards flogged him unmercifully for thus attempting to prefer death to slavery.

In this manner we continued to undergo more hardships than I can now relate, hardships which are inseparable from this accursed trade. Many a time we were near suffocation from the want of fresh air, which we were often without for whole days together. This, and the stench of the necessary tubs, carried off many. During our passage I first saw flying fishes, which surprised me very much: they used frequently to fly across the ship, and many of them fell on the deck....

At last we came in sight of the island of Barbadoes, at which the whites on board gave a great shout, and made many signs of joy to us. We did not know what to think of this; but as the vessel drew nearer we plainly saw the harbor, and other ships of different kinds and sizes; and we soon anchored amongst them off Bridge Town. Many merchants and planters now came on board, though it was in the evening. They put us in separate parcels, and examined us attentively. They also made us jump, and pointed to the land, signifying we were to go there....

What struck me first was that the houses were built with stories, and in every other respect different from those in Africa: but I was still more astonished on seeing people on horseback. I did not know what this could mean; and indeed I thought these people were full of nothing but magical arts.... We were not many days in the merchant's custody before we were sold after their usual manner, which is this: On a signal given, (as the beat of a drum) the buyers rush at once into the yard where the slaves are confined, and make choice of that parcel they like best. The noise and clamor with which this is attended, and the eagerness visible in the countenances of the buyers, serve not a little to increase the apprehensions of the terrified Africans, who may well be supposed to consider them as the ministers of that destruction to which they think themselves devoted. In this manner, without scruple, are relations and friends separated, most of them never to see each other again. I remember in the vessel in which I was brought over, in the men's apartment, there were several brothers, who, in the sale, were sold in different lots; and it was very moving on this occasion to see and hear their cries at parting.

O, ye nominal Christians! might not an African ask you, learned you this from your God, who says unto you, Do unto all men as you would men should do unto you? Is it not enough that we are torn from our country and friends to toil for your luxury and lust of gain? Must every tender feeling be likewise

30

sacrificed to your avarice? Are the dearest friends and relations, now rendered more dear by their separation from their kindred, still to be parted from each other, and thus prevented from cheering the gloom of slavery with the small comfort of being together and mingling their sufferings and sorrows? Why are parents to lose their children, brothers their sisters, or husbands their wives? Surely this is a new refinement in cruelty, which, while it has no advantage to atone for it, thus aggravates distress, and adds fresh horrors even to the wretchedness of slavery....

CHAPTER 3

I now totally lost the small remains of comfort I had enjoyed in conversing with my countrymen; the women too, who used to wash and take care of me, were all gone different ways, and I never saw one of them afterwards.

I stayed in this island for a few days; I believe it could not be above a fortnight; when I and some few more slaves, that were not saleable amongst the rest, from very much fretting, were shipped off in a sloop for North America. On the passage we were better treated than when we were coming from Africa, and we had plenty of rice and fat pork. We were landed up a river a good way from the sea, about Virginia county, where we saw few or none of our native Africans, and not one soul who could talk to me.

I was a few weeks weeding grass, and gathering stones in a plantation; and at last all my companions were distributed different ways, and only myself was left. I was now exceedingly miserable, and thought myself worse off than any of the rest of my companions; for they could talk to each other, but I had no person to speak to that I could understand. In this state I was constantly grieving and pining, and wishing for death rather than any thing else.

35   While I was in this plantation the gentleman, to whom I suppose the estate belonged, being unwell, I was one day sent for to his dwelling house to fan him; when I came into the room where he was I was very much affrighted at some things I saw, and the more so as I had seen a black woman slave as I came through the house, who was cooking the dinner, and the poor creature was cruelly loaded with various kinds of iron machines; she had one particularly on her head, which locked her mouth so fast that she could scarcely speak; and could not eat nor drink. I was much astonished and shocked at this contrivance, which I afterwards learned was called the iron muzzle. Soon after I had a fan put into my hand, to fan the gentleman while he slept; and so I did indeed with great fear.

While he was fast asleep I indulged myself a great deal in looking about the room, which to me appeared very fine and curious. The first object that engaged my attention was a watch which hung on the chimney, and was going. I was quite surprised at the noise it made, and was afraid it would tell the gentleman any thing I might do amiss: and when I immediately after observed a picture hanging in the room, which appeared constantly to look at me, I was still more affrighted, having never seen such things as these before. At one time I thought it was something relative to magic; and not seeing it move I thought it might be some way the whites had to keep their great men when they died, and offer them libation as we used to do to our friendly spirits.

In this state of anxiety I remained till my master awoke, when I was dismissed out of the room, to my no small satisfaction and relief; for I thought that these people were all made up of wonders. In this place I was called Jacob; but on board the African snow I was called Michael. I had been some time in this miserable, forlorn, and much dejected state, without having any one to talk to, which made my life a burden, when the kind and unknown hand of the Creator (who in very deed leads the blind in a way they know not) now began to appear, to my comfort; for one day the captain of a merchant ship, called the *Industrious Bee*, came on some business to my master's house. This gentleman, whose name was Michael Henry Pascal, was a lieutenant in the royal navy, but now commanded this trading ship, which was somewhere in the confines of the county many miles off. While he was at my master's house it happened that he saw me, and liked me so well that he made a purchase of me. I think I have often heard him say he gave thirty or forty pounds sterling for me; but I do not now remember which. However, he meant me for a present to some of his friends in England: and I was sent accordingly from the house of my then master, one Mr. Campbell, to the place where the ship lay; I was conducted on horseback by an elderly black man, (a mode of traveling which appeared very odd to me). When I arrived I was carried on board a fine large ship, loaded with tobacco, etc., and just ready to sail for England. I now thought my condition much mended; I had sails to lie on, and plenty of good victuals to eat; and every body on board used me very kindly, quite contrary to what I had seen of any white people before; I therefore began to think that they were not all of the same disposition. A few days after I was on board we sailed for England....

(1789)

Questions

1. What is/are Equiano's purpose(s) in writing the *Interesting Narrative*? How does he achieve it/them in these chapters?

2. In paragraph 14, Equiano highlights similarities between the Igbo and the Jews of the Old Testament. Why do you think he does this?

3. At the time of Equiano's writing, his British audience's perception of African people was influenced by two major stereotypes: that of the "noble savage" and that of the uncivilized brute. How does Equiano engage with these stereotypes in his depiction of Igbo life?

4. Compare and contrast Equiano's portrayal of slavery within Africa with his portrayal of slavery as practiced by Europeans. What reasons might there be for the similarities and differences in his depictions? Is Equiano's attitude toward each form of slavery reasonable?

5. Discuss the arguments and rhetorical strategies used in paragraph 31 (beginning "O, ye nominal Christians").

6. What are the rhetorical effects of Equiano presenting his arguments in the form of an autobiography, as opposed to a fictional work or a non-narrative essay?

7. Recently, scholars have found inconclusive evidence suggesting that Equiano might not have been born in Africa. If this is so, then the first two chapters of Equiano's book are not based on personal experience, but instead on research and the firsthand accounts of other slaves. Does this knowledge affect your experience of the chapters? Why or why not?

8. How does Equiano portray his own race in the text? How and to what extent does he portray himself as possessing Black/African characteristics? White/British characteristics?

Speech Delivered at the Akron, Ohio, Convention on Women's Rights, 1851

Born into slavery in Ulster County, New York, Sojourner Truth (then Isabella Bomfree) escaped in 1827, a year before a law was passed in the state that would have secured her freedom. She began her public speaking career as a preacher in the religious revival movement of the 1830s and went on to become a prominent speaker and activist for abolition, women's suffrage, and other causes.

The speech reproduced below, among the most famous of the American abolition movement, was delivered at a Women's Convention in Ohio before a primarily white audience. Truth could not read or write as a result of the institution of slavery, and this speech survives only as reported by others. Two surviving records, both of which appeared in abolitionist newspapers of the era, are reprinted below.

As Reported by the *Anti-Slavery Bugle*, 21 June 1851

One of the most unique and interesting speeches of the Convention was made by Sojourner Truth, an emancipated slave. It is impossible to transfer it to paper, or convey any adequate idea of the effect it produced upon the audience. Those only can appreciate it who saw her powerful form, her whole-souled, earnest gestures, and listened to her strong and truthful tones. She came forward to the platform and addressing the President said with great simplicity:

May I say a few words? Receiving an affirmative answer, she proceeded; I want to say a few words about this matter. I am a woman's rights. I have as much muscle as any man, and can do as much work as any man. I have plowed and reaped and husked and chopped and mowed, and can any man do more than that? I have heard much about the sexes being equal; I can carry as much as any man, and can eat as much too, if I can get it. I am as strong as any man that is now. As for intellect, all I can say is, if woman have a pint and man a quart—why can't she have her little pint full? You need not be afraid to give us our rights for fear we will take too much—for we can't take more than our pint'll hold. The poor men seem to be all in confusion, and don't know what to do. Why children, if you have woman's rights give it to her and you will feel better. You will have your own rights, and they won't be so much trouble. I can't read, but I can hear. I have heard the bible and have learned that Eve caused man to sin. Well if woman upset the world, do give her a chance to set it right side up again. The Lady has spoken about Jesus, how he never spurned woman from him, and she was right. When Lazarus died, Mary and Martha came to him with faith and love and besought him to raise their brother. And Jesus wept—and Lazarus came forth.[1] And how came Jesus into the world? Through God who created him and woman who bore him. Man, where is your part? But the women are coming up blessed be God and a few of the men are coming up with them. But man is in a tight place, the poor slave is on him, woman is coming on him, and he is surely between a hawk and a buzzard.

(1851)

AS REPORTED BY FRANCES DANA GAGE IN THE
NATIONAL ANTI-SLAVERY STANDARD, 2 MAY 1863

"Well, chillen, what dar's so much racket dar must be som'ting out o'kilter. I tink dat 'twixt de niggers of de South and de women at de Norf, all a-talking 'bout rights, de white men will be in a fix pretty soon. But what's all this here talking 'bout? Dat man ober dar say dat woman needs to be helped into carriages, and lifted ober ditches, and to have de best place eberywhar. Nobody eber helps me into carriages, or ober mud-puddles, or gives me any best place"; and, raising herself to her full height, and her voice to a pitch like rolling thunder, she asked, "And ar'n't I a woman? Look at me. Look at my arm," and she bared her right arm to the shoulder, showing its tremendous muscular power. "I have plowed and planted and gathered into barns, and no man could head[2] me—and ar'n't I a woman? I could work as much and eat as much as a man (when I could get it) and bear de lash as well—and ar'n't I a woman? I have borne thirteen chillen, and seen 'em mos' all sold off to slavery, and when I cried out with a mother's grief, none but Jesus heard—and ar'n't I a woman? Den dey talks 'bout dis ting in de head. What dis dey call it?" "Intellect," whispered some one near. "Dat's it, honey. What's dat got to do with woman's rights or niggers' rights? If my cup won't hold but a pint, and youm

---

1   *Jesus wept ... forth*   See John 11.1–44, in which Jesus brings the deceased Lazarus back to life.
2   *head*   Outdo.

holds a quart, wouldn't ye be mean not to let me have my little half-measure full?" and she pointed her significant finger and sent a keen glance at the minister who had made the argument. The cheering was long and loud. "Den dat little man in black dar, he say woman can't have as much rights as man, 'cause Christ wa'n'n't a woman. *Whar did your Christ come from?*"

Rolling thunder could not have stilled that crowd as did those deep, wonderful tones, as she stood there with outstretched arms and eye of fire. Raising her voice still louder, she repeated,

"Whar did your Christ come from? From God and a woman. Man had not'ing to do with him." Oh, what a rebuke she gave the little man. Turning again to another objector, she took up the defense of Mother Eve. I cannot follow her through it all. It was pointed and witty and solemn, eliciting at almost every sentence deafening applause, and she ended by asserting: "that if de fust woman God ever made was strong enought to turn de world upside down all her one lone, all dese togeder," and she glanced her eye over us, "ought to be able to turn it back, and git it right side up again, and now dey is asking to, de men better let 'em." (Long and continued cheering). "Bleeged[3] to ye for hearin' on me, and now ole Sojourner ha'n't got nothing more to say."

(1863)

Questions

1. What concepts from Truth's speech stand out to you? How does she use descriptive language to convey her ideas?

2. Compare and contrast these version of Truth's speech in terms of the following:

   a. Accent. Truth had a Dutch accent, which is not reflected in either account. What choices regarding accent does each reporter make, and how does this affect the impact of the speech? What do you think might have motivated these choices?

   b. Rhetorical style. How is Truth's way of speaking represented in each speech, and what impression of her does each rhetorical style create?

   c. Argument. What aspects of Truth's argument does each report emphasize? How (if at all) does this alter the impact of her speech?

---

3 *Bleeged* Obliged.

    d.   Reliability. Does either version of this speech seem more likely to be reliable than the other? Is it possible to tell?

    e.   Persuasiveness. Does one report strike you as more persuasive than the other? Explain why.

3.   This speech was delivered to a primarily white audience. What rhetorical and argumentative strategies does Truth use to appeal to this audience?

4.   How might white suffragists have been challenged by the links Truth draws between her race and her gender in this speech? How might male abolitionists have been challenged by these links?

5.   Truth sold photographs of herself as a means of financing her speaking tours; one such photograph is reproduced in this anthology's color insert. How does Truth represent herself in this photograph? To what extent does her self-representation in the image align with—or contradict—her self-representation in the speech recounted here?

FREDERICK DOUGLASS

from FOURTH OF JULY ORATION[1]

While living as a free man in Rochester in the 1850s, Douglass had become the publisher and editor of a newspaper, founding the North Star *to advance the cause of abolition and the rights of the disenfranchised. He also became involved in the local community, working to end segregation in Rochester public schools, for example, and in 1852, he was invited to give a speech to the citizenry of Rochester as part of the local Independence Celebrations. A substantial excerpt from the address appears here; the full speech is over 10,000 words long.*

The papers and placards say that I am to deliver a 4th of July oration....

This, for the purpose of this celebration, is the 4th of July.[2] It is the birthday of your National Independence, and of your political freedom.... This celebration also marks the beginning of another year of your national life; and reminds you that the Republic of America is now 76 years old....

Fellow Citizens, I am not wanting in respect for the fathers of this republic. The signers of the Declaration of Independence were brave men. They were great men too—great enough to give fame to a great age.... The point from which I am compelled to view them is not, certainly, the most favorable; and yet I cannot contemplate their great deeds with less than admiration. They were statesmen, patriots and heroes, and for the good they did, and the principles they contended for, I will unite with you to honor their memory....

They were peace men; but they preferred revolution to peaceful submission to bondage. They were quiet men; but they did not shrink from agitating against oppression. They showed forbearance; but that they knew its limits.

---

1   *Fourth of July Oration*   Douglass did not give the speech a title; it is often referred to as "What to the Slave Is the Fourth of July," and often, in excerpted form, given the title "The Hypocrisy of American Slavery."

2   *for the purpose of this celebration, is the 4th of July*   Though the address was part of the Independence Day festivities, it was delivered on the 5th of July rather than the 4th.

They believed in order; but not in the order of tyranny. With them, nothing was "settled" that was not right. With them, justice, liberty and humanity were "final"; not slavery and oppression. You may well cherish the memory of such men. They were great in their day and generation....

5   Friends and citizens, I need not enter further into the causes which led to this anniversary. Many of you understand them better than I do.... The causes which led to the separation of the colonies from the British crown* have never lacked for a tongue. They have all been taught in your common schools, narrated at your firesides, unfolded from your pulpits, and thundered from your legislative halls, and are as familiar to you as household words. They form the staple of your national poetry and eloquence.

I remember, also, that, as a people, Americans are remarkably familiar with all facts which make in their own favor. This is esteemed by some as a national trait—perhaps a national weakness. It is a fact, that whatever makes for the wealth or for the reputation of Americans (and can be had cheap!) will be found by Americans. I shall not be charged with slandering Americans, if I say I think the American side of any question may be safely left in American hands.

I leave, therefore, the great deeds of your fathers to other gentlemen whose claim to have been regularly descended will be less likely to be disputed than mine!

My business, if I have any here to-day, is with the present. The accepted time with God and his cause is the ever-living now....

Fellow-citizens, pardon me, allow me to ask, why am I called upon to speak here to-day? What have I, or those I represent, to do with your national independence? Are the great principles of political freedom and of natural justice, embodied in that Declaration of Independence, extended to us? And am I, therefore, called upon to bring our humble offering to the national altar, and to confess the benefits and express devout gratitude for the blessings resulting from your independence to us?

10   Would to God, both for your sakes and ours, that an affirmative answer could be truthfully returned to these questions! Then would my task be light, and my burden easy and delightful....

But, such is not the state of the case. I say it with a sad sense of the disparity between us. I am not included within the pale* of this glorious anniversary! Your high independence only reveals the immeasurable distance between us. The blessings in which you, this day, rejoice, are not enjoyed in common.—The rich inheritance of justice, liberty, prosperity and independence, bequeathed by your fathers, is shared by you, not by me. The sunlight that brought life and healing to you, has brought stripes and death to me. This Fourth [of] July is yours, not mine. You may rejoice, I must mourn. To drag a man in fetters into the grand illuminated temple of liberty, and call upon him to join you in joyous anthems, were inhuman mockery and sacrilegious irony. Do you mean, citizens, to mock me, by asking me to speak to-day? ...

Fellow-citizens; above your national, tumultuous joy, I hear the mournful wail of millions! whose chains, heavy and grievous yesterday, are, to-day, rendered more intolerable by the jubilee shouts that reach them.... My subject, then fellow-citizens, is American slavery. I shall see, this day, and its popular characteristics, from the slave's point of view. Standing, there, identified with the American bondman, making his wrongs mine, I do not hesitate to declare, with all my soul, that the character and conduct of this nation never looked blacker to me than on this 4th of July! Whether we turn to the declarations of the past, or to the professions of the present, the conduct of the nation seems equally hideous and revolting. America is false to the past, false to the present, and solemnly binds herself to be false to the future....

But I fancy I hear some one of my audience say, it is just in this circumstance that you and your brother abolitionists fail to make a favorable impression on the public mind. Would you argue more, and denounce less, would you persuade more, and rebuke less, your cause would be much more likely to succeed. But, I submit, where all is plain there is nothing to be argued. What point in the anti-slavery creed would you have me argue? On what branch of the subject do the people of this country need light? Must I undertake to prove that the slave is a man? That point is conceded already. Nobody doubts it. The slaveholders themselves acknowledge it in the enactment of laws for their government. They acknowledge it when they punish disobedience on the part of the slave. There are seventy-two crimes in the State of Virginia, which, if committed by a black man, (no matter how ignorant he be), subject him to the punishment of death; while only two of the same crimes will subject a white man to the like punishment. What is this but the acknowledgement that the slave is a moral, intellectual and responsible being? The manhood of the slave is conceded. It is admitted in the fact that Southern statute books are covered with enactments forbidding, under severe fines and penalties, the teaching of the slave to read or to write. When you can point to any such laws, in reference to the beasts of the field, then I may consent to argue the manhood of the slave. When the dogs in your streets, when the fowls of the air, when the cattle on your hills, when the fish of the sea, and the reptiles that crawl, shall be unable to distinguish the slave from a brute, then will I argue with you that the slave is a man!...

Would you have me argue that man is entitled to liberty? That he is the rightful owner of his own body? You have already declared it.... What, am I to argue that it is wrong to make men brutes, to rob them of their liberty, to work them without wages, to keep them ignorant of their relations to their fellow men, to beat them with sticks, to flay their flesh with the lash, to load their limbs with irons, to hunt them with dogs, to sell them at auction, to sunder their families, to knock out their teeth, to burn their flesh, to starve them into obedience and submission to their masters? Must I argue that a system thus marked with blood, and stained with pollution, is wrong? No! I will not. I have better employments for my time and strength than such arguments would imply.

15   What, then, remains to be argued? Is it that slavery is not divine; that God did not establish it; that our doctors of divinity are mistaken? ... The time for such argument is passed.

At a time like this, scorching irony, not convincing argument, is needed. O! had I the ability, and could I reach the nation's ear, I would, to-day, pour out a fiery stream of biting ridicule, blasting reproach, withering sarcasm, and stern rebuke. For it is not light that is needed, but fire; it is not the gentle shower, but thunder. We need the storm, the whirlwind, and the earthquake. The feeling of the nation must be quickened; the conscience of the nation must be roused; the propriety of the nation must be startled; the hypocrisy of the nation must be exposed; and its crimes against God and man must be proclaimed and denounced.

What, to the American slave, is your 4th of July? I answer: a day that reveals to him, more than all other days in the year, the gross injustice and cruelty to which he is the constant victim. To him, your celebration is a sham; your boasted liberty, an unholy license; your national greatness, swelling vanity; your sounds of rejoicing are empty and heartless; your denunciations of tyrants, brass fronted impudence; your shouts of liberty and equality, hollow mockery; your prayers and hymns, your sermons and thanksgivings, with all your religious parade, and solemnity, are, to him, mere bombast, fraud, deception, impiety, and hypocrisy—a thin veil to cover up crimes which would disgrace a nation of savages. There is not a nation on the earth guilty of practices, more shocking and bloody, than are the people of these United States, at this very hour.

Go where you may, search where you will, roam through all the monarchies and despotisms of the old world, travel through South America, search out every abuse, and when you have found the last, lay your facts by the side of the everyday practices of this nation, and you will say with me, that, for revolting barbarity and shameless hypocrisy, America reigns without a rival.

Take the American slave-trade, which, we are told by the papers, is especially prosperous just now.... This trade is one of the peculiarities of American institutions. It is carried on in all the large towns and cities in one-half of this confederacy; and millions are pocketed every year, by dealers in this horrid traffic. In several states, this trade is a chief source of wealth. It is called (in contradistinction to the foreign slave-trade) "the internal slave trade." It is, probably, called so, too, in order to divert from it the horror with which the foreign slave-trade is contemplated. That trade has long since been denounced by this government, as piracy.... Everywhere, in this country, it is safe to speak of this foreign slave-trade, as a most inhuman traffic, opposed alike to the laws of God and of man.... It is, however, a notable fact that, while so much execration is poured out by Americans upon those engaged in the foreign slave-trade, the men engaged in the slave-trade between the states pass without condemnation, and their business is deemed honorable.

Behold the practical operation of this internal slave-trade, the American slave-trade, sustained by American politics and American religion. Here you will see men and women reared like swine for the market. You know what is a swine-drover? I will show you a man-drover. They inhabit all our Southern States. They perambulate the country, and crowd the highways of the nation, with droves of human stock. You will see one of these human flesh-jobbers, armed with pistol, whip and bowie-knife, driving a company of a hundred men, women, and children, from the Potomac* to the slave market at New Orleans. These wretched people are to be sold singly, or in lots, to suit purchasers. They are food for the cotton-field, and the deadly sugar-mill. Mark the sad procession, as it moves wearily along, and the inhuman wretch who drives them. Hear his savage yells and his blood-chilling oaths, as he hurries on his affrighted captives! There, see the old man, with locks thinned and gray. Cast one glance, if you please, upon that young mother, whose shoulders are bare to the scorching sun, her briny tears falling on the brow of the babe in her arms. See, too, that girl of thirteen, weeping, yes! weeping, as she thinks of the mother from whom she has been torn! The drove moves tardily. Heat and sorrow have nearly consumed their strength; suddenly you hear a quick snap, like the discharge of a rifle; the fetters clank, and the chain rattles simultaneously; your ears are saluted with a scream, that seems to have torn its way to the center of your soul! The crack you heard, was the sound of the slave-whip; the scream you heard, was from the woman you saw with the babe. Her speed had faltered under the weight of her child and her chains! that gash on her shoulder tells her to move on. Follow the drove to New Orleans. Attend the auction; see men examined like horses; see the forms of women rudely and brutally exposed to the shocking gaze of American slave-buyers. See this drove sold and separated forever; and never forget the deep, sad sobs that arose from that scattered multitude. Tell me citizens, *where*, under the sun, you can witness a spectacle more fiendish and shocking. Yet this is but a glance at the American slave-trade, as it exists, at this moment, in the ruling part of the United States....

But the church of this country is not only indifferent to the wrongs of the slave, it actually takes sides with the oppressors.... Many of its most eloquent Divines, who stand as the very lights of the church, have shamelessly given the sanction of religion and the Bible to the whole slave system. They have taught that man may, properly, be a slave; that the relation of master and slave is ordained of God; that to send back an escaped bondman to his master is clearly the duty of all the followers of the Lord Jesus Christ; and this horrible blasphemy is palmed off upon the world for Christianity.

For my part, I would say, welcome infidelity! welcome atheism! welcome anything! in preference to the gospel, as preached by those Divines! ... [It is] a religion which favors the rich against the poor; which exalts the proud above the humble; which divides mankind into two classes, tyrants and slaves; which says to the man in chains, stay there; and to the oppressor, oppress on; it is a religion which may be professed and enjoyed by all the robbers and enslavers of mankind; it makes God a respecter of persons,[3] denies his fatherhood of the race, and tramples in the dust the great truth of the brotherhood of man....

I have detained my audience entirely too long already. At some future period I will gladly avail myself of an opportunity to give this subject a full and fair discussion.

Allow me to say, in conclusion, notwithstanding the dark picture I have this day presented of the state of the nation, I do not despair of this country. There are forces in operation, which must inevitably work the downfall of slavery. "The arm of the Lord is not shortened,"* and the doom of slavery is certain. I, therefore, leave off where I began, with hope. While drawing encouragement from the Declaration of Independence, the great principles it contains, and the genius of American Institutions, my spirit is also cheered by the obvious tendencies of the age. Nations do not now stand in the same relation to each other that they did ages ago. No nation can now shut itself up from the surrounding world, and trot round in the same old path of its fathers without interference. The time was when such could be done. Long established customs of hurtful character could formerly fence themselves in, and do their evil work with social impunity. Knowledge was then confined and enjoyed by the privileged few, and the multitude walked on in mental darkness. But a change has now come over the affairs of mankind. Walled cities and empires have become unfashionable. The arm of commerce has borne away the gates of the strong city. Intelligence is penetrating the darkest corners of the globe. It makes its pathway over and under the sea, as well as on the earth. Wind, steam, and lightning are its chartered agents. Oceans no longer divide, but link nations together. From Boston to London is now a holiday excursion. Space is comparatively annihilated. Thoughts expressed on one side of the Atlantic, are distinctly heard on the other. The far off and almost fabulous Pacific rolls in grandeur at our feet....

(1852)

---

3   *respecter of persons*   In Acts 10.34, Peter claims that "God is no respecter of persons," i.e., that he does not favor people of higher status.

Questions

1. In addition to the title given here, Douglass's speech is sometimes referred to as "What to the Slave Is the Fourth of July?" or (in excerpted form) as "the Hypocrisy of American Slavery." What does each of these titles suggest? Which do you think is most appropriate for the speech?

2. Douglass claims that "[a]t a time like this, scorching irony, not convincing argument, is needed" (paragraph 16). What does this mean?

3. What are Douglass's major criticisms of America? To what extent (if at all) do the criticisms of America advanced by Douglass still apply in the present?

4. Douglass was invited by a women's anti-slavery society to deliver this speech, and his audience was composed primarily of white women abolitionists. How (if at all) is Douglass's speech tailored to this initial audience? What kind of response do you think Douglass's speech would have evoked in this audience?

5. Find a point in the speech where Douglass uses repetition for rhetorical effect. How effective is this use of repetition? What does it accomplish?

6. How does Douglass connect the Fourth of July celebration to the institution of slavery? What is his major premise? How does he insert himself into the conversation? What evidence does he give us?

HARRIET JACOBS

from INCIDENTS IN THE LIFE OF A SLAVE GIRL, SEVEN YEARS CONCEALED

Writer and abolitionist Harriet Jacobs's autobiography is significant not only for its rhetorical excellence but also for its direct treatment of the cruelties more frequently faced by women slaves; horrors such as rape by one's masters were rarely discussed in men's slave narratives or addressed by white abolitionists. Due to anti-literacy laws and other systemic barriers to education for Black women, autobiographical slave narratives by women were rare. Jacobs's book was published under the pseudonym Linda Brent, and many thought it to be a fictional account by a white writer until the late twentieth century, when scholars established Jacobs's authorship and confirmed the truth of her account.

Jacobs wrote her narrative in the 1850s, but could not immediately find a publisher; when at last she managed to do so, the company went bankrupt before the book appeared. Lydia Maria Child, a white abolitionist who also acted as Jacobs's editor, then arranged for publication with a second press, which prepared plates for printing but also went bankrupt before actually producing the book. Jacobs was then able to purchase the plates and self-publish with the help of the Antislavery Society. Incidents in the Life of a Slave Girl, Seven Years Concealed *finally appeared in 1861 and received wide distribution through anti-slavery groups in America; a British edition was also well received.*

PREFACE BY THE AUTHOR

Reader be assured this narrative is no fiction. I am aware that some of my adventures may seem incredible; but they are, nevertheless, strictly true. I have not exaggerated the wrongs inflicted by Slavery; on the contrary, my descriptions fall far short of the facts. I have concealed the names of places, and given persons fictitious names. I had no motive for secrecy on my own account, but I deemed it kind and considerate towards others to pursue this course.

I wish I were more competent to the task I have undertaken. But I trust my readers will excuse deficiencies in consideration of circumstances. I was born and reared in Slavery; and I remained in a Slave State twenty-seven years. Since I have been at the North, it has been necessary for me to work diligently for my own support, and the education of my children. This has not left me much leisure to make up for the loss of early opportunities to improve myself; and it has compelled me to write these pages at irregular intervals, whenever I could snatch an hour from household duties.

When I first arrived in Philadelphia, Bishop Paine[1] advised me to publish a sketch of my life, but I told him I was altogether incompetent to such an undertaking. Though I have improved my mind somewhat since that time, I still remain of the same opinion; but I trust my motives will excuse what might otherwise seem presumptuous. I have not written my experiences in order to attract attention to myself; on the contrary, it would have been more pleasant to me to have been silent about my own history. Neither do I care to excite sympathy for my own sufferings. But I do earnestly desire to arouse the women of the North to a realizing sense of the condition of two millions of women at the South, still in bondage, suffering what I suffered, and most of them far worse. I want to add my testimony to that of abler pens to convince the people of the Free States[2] what Slavery really is. Only by experience can any one realize how deep, and dark, and foul is that pit of abominations. May the blessing of God rest on this imperfect effort in behalf of my persecuted people!

Linda Brent

1. CHILDHOOD

I was born a slave; but I never knew it till six years of happy childhood had passed away. My father was a carpenter, and considered so intelligent and skillful in his trade, that, when buildings out of the common line were to be erected, he was sent for from long distances, to be head workman. On condition of paying his mistress two hundred dollars a year, and supporting himself, he was allowed to work at his trade, and manage his own affairs. His strongest

---

1 *Bishop Paine* Daniel Alexander Payne (1811–93) was an influential educator and founder of Wilberforce University. He was a bishop in the African Methodist Episcopal (AME) Church for over forty years, and he played an important role in shaping that institution, particularly the church's emphasis on education.

2 *Free States* States in which slavery was prohibited or being legally eliminated.

wish was to purchase his children; but, though he several times offered his hard earnings for that purpose, he never succeeded. In complexion my parents were a light shade of brownish yellow, and were termed mulattoes.[3] They lived together in a comfortable home; and, though we were all slaves, I was so fondly shielded that I never dreamed I was a piece of merchandise, trusted to them for safe keeping, and liable to be demanded of them at any moment. I had one brother, William, who was two years younger than myself—a bright, affectionate child. I had also a great treasure in my maternal grandmother, who was a remarkable woman in many respects. She was the daughter of a planter in South Carolina, who, at his death, left her mother and his three children free, with money to go to St. Augustine,[4] where they had relatives. It was during the Revolutionary War;[5] and they were captured on their passage, carried back, and sold to different purchasers. Such was the story my grandmother used to tell me; but I do not remember all the particulars. She was a little girl when she was captured and sold to the keeper of a large hotel. I have often heard her tell how hard she fared during childhood. But as she grew older she evinced so much intelligence, and was so faithful, that her master and mistress could not help seeing it was for their interest to take care of such a valuable piece of property. She became an indispensable personage in the household, officiating in all capacities, from cook and wet nurse[6] to seamstress. She was much praised for her cooking; and her nice crackers[7] became so famous in the neighborhood that many people were desirous of obtaining them. In consequence of numerous requests of this kind, she asked permission of her mistress to bake crackers at night, after all the household work was done; and she obtained leave to do it, provided she would clothe herself and her children from the profits. Upon these terms, after working hard all day for her mistress, she began her midnight bakings, assisted by her two oldest children. The business proved profitable; and each year she laid by a little, which was saved for a fund to purchase her children. Her master died, and the property was divided among his heirs. The widow had her dower[8] in the hotel which she continued to keep open. My

---

3   *mulattoes*   Term once used to refer to people with one Black and one white parent, or to children born to "mulatto" parents.

4   *St. Augustine*   City of the coast of Florida.

5   *Revolutionary War*   Conflict fought between 1775 and 1783 between Great Britain and the Thirteen Colonies. The Thirteen Colonies declared independence and became the United States of America.

6   *wet nurse*   Woman who breastfeeds another's child.

7   *nice crackers*   Thin, sweet biscuits.

8   *dower*   Property and other assets of a deceased husband that his widow is allowed to possess for her life.

grandmother remained in her service as a slave; but her children were divided among her master's children. As she had five, Benjamin, the youngest one, was sold, in order that each heir might have an equal portion of dollars and cents. There was so little difference in our ages that he seemed more like my brother than my uncle. He was a bright, handsome lad, nearly white; for he inherited the complexion my grandmother had derived from Anglo-Saxon[9] ancestors. Though only ten years old, seven hundred and twenty dollars were paid for him. His sale was a terrible blow to my grandmother, but she was naturally hopeful, and she went to work with renewed energy, trusting in time to be able to purchase some of her children. She had laid up three hundred dollars, which her mistress one day begged as a loan, promising to pay her soon. The reader probably knows that no promise or writing given to a slave is legally binding; for, according to Southern laws, a slave, *being* property, can *hold* no property. When my grandmother lent her hard earnings to her mistress, she trusted solely to her honor. The honor of a slaveholder to a slave!

To this good grandmother I was indebted for many comforts. My brother Willie and I often received portions of the crackers, cakes, and preserves, she made to sell; and after we ceased to be children we were indebted to her for many more important services.

Such were the unusually fortunate circumstances of my early childhood. When I was six years old, my mother died; and then, for the first time, I learned, by the talk around me, that I was a slave. My mother's mistress was the daughter of my grandmother's mistress. She was the foster sister of my mother; they were both nourished at my grandmother's breast. In fact, my mother had been weaned at three months old, that the babe of the mistress might obtain sufficient food. They played together as children; and, when they became women, my mother was a most faithful servant to her whiter foster sister. On her death-bed her mistress promised that her children should never suffer for any thing; and during her lifetime she kept her word. They all spoke kindly of my dead mother, who had been a slave merely in name, but in nature was noble and womanly. I grieved for her, and my young mind was troubled with the thought who would now take care of me and my little brother. I was told that my home was now to be with her mistress; and I found it a happy one. No toilsome or disagreeable duties were imposed on me. My mistress was so kind to me that I was always glad to do her bidding, and proud to labor for her as much as my young years would permit. I would sit by her side for hours, sewing diligently, with a heart as free from care as that of any free-born white child. When she thought I was tired, she would send me out to run and jump;

5

---

9   *Anglo-Saxon*   I.e., English, Caucasian.

and away I bounded, to gather berries or flowers to decorate her room. Those were happy days—too happy to last. The slave child had no thought for the morrow; but there came that blight, which too surely waits on every human being born to be a chattel.[10]

When I was nearly twelve years old, my kind mistress sickened and died. As I saw the cheek grow paler, and the eye more glassy, how earnestly I prayed in my heart that she might live! I loved her; for she had been almost like a mother to me. My prayers were not answered. She died, and they buried her in the little churchyard, where, day after day, my tears fell upon her grave.

I was sent to spend a week with my grandmother. I was now old enough to begin to think of the future; and again and again I asked myself what they would do with me. I felt sure I should never find another mistress so kind as the one who was gone. She had promised my dying mother that her children should never suffer for any thing; and when I remembered that, and recalled her many proofs of attachment to me, I could not help having some hopes that she had left me free. My friends were almost certain it would be so. They thought she would be sure to do it, on account of my mother's love and faithful service. But, alas! we all know that the memory of a faithful slave does not avail much to save her children from the auction block.

After a brief period of suspense, the will of my mistress was read, and we learned that she had bequeathed me to her sister's daughter, a child of five years old. So vanished our hopes. My mistress had taught me the precepts of God's Word: "Thou shalt love thy neighbor as thyself." "Whatsoever ye would that men should do unto you, do ye even so unto them." But I was her slave, and I suppose she did not recognize me as her neighbor. I would give much to blot out from my memory that one great wrong. As a child, I loved my mistress; and, looking back on the happy days I spent with her, I try to think with less bitterness of this act of injustice. While I was with her, she taught me to read and spell; and for this privilege, which so rarely falls to the lot of a slave, I bless her memory.

10　　She possessed but few slaves; and at her death those were all distributed among her relatives. Five of them were my grandmother's children, and had shared the same milk that nourished her mother's children. Notwithstanding my grandmother's long and faithful service to her owners, not one of her children escaped the auction block. These God-breathing machines[11] are no more, in the sight of their masters, than the cotton they plant, or the horses they tend.

10　*chattel*　Possession, property.

11　*God-breathing machines*　Human beings made by God but treated as machines.

2. THE NEW MASTER AND MISTRESS

Dr. Flint, a physician in the neighborhood, had married the sister of my mistress, and I was now the property of their little daughter....

Little attention was paid to the slaves' meals in Dr. Flint's house. If they could catch a bit of food while it was going, well and good. I gave myself no trouble on that score, for on my various errands I passed my grandmother's house, where there was always something to spare for me. I was frequently threatened with punishment if I stopped there; and my grandmother, to avoid detaining me, often stood at the gate with something for my breakfast or dinner. I was indebted to *her* for my comforts, spiritual or temporal. It was *her* labor that supplied my scanty wardrobe. I have a vivid recollection of the linsey-woolsey[12] dress given me every winter by Mrs. Flint. How I hated it! It was one of the badges of slavery.

While my grandmother was thus helping to support me from her hard earnings, the three hundred dollars she had lent her mistress were never repaid. When her mistress died, her son-in-law, Dr. Flint, was appointed executor. When grandmother applied to him for payment, he said the estate was insolvent, and the law prohibited payment. It did not, however, prohibit him from retaining the silver candelabra, which had been purchased with that money. I presume they will be handed down in the family, from generation to generation....

5. THE TRIALS OF GIRLHOOD

During the first years of my service in Dr. Flint's family, I was accustomed to share some indulgences with the children of my mistress. Though this seemed to me no more than right, I was grateful for it, and tried to merit the kindness by the faithful discharge of my duties. But I now entered on my fifteenth year—a sad epoch in the life of a slave girl. My master began to whisper foul words in my ear. Young as I was, I could not remain ignorant of their import. I tried to treat them with indifference or contempt. The master's age, my extreme youth, and the fear that his conduct would be reported to my grandmother, made him bear this treatment for many months. He was a crafty man, and resorted to many means to accomplish his purposes. Sometimes he had stormy, terrific ways, that made his victims tremble; sometimes he assumed a gentleness that he thought must surely subdue. Of the two, I preferred his stormy moods, although they left me trembling. He tried his utmost to corrupt the pure principles my grandmother had instilled. He peopled my young mind with unclean images, such as only a vile monster could think of. I turned from him with

---

12 *linsey-woolsey* Fabric often used to clothe slaves because it was durable and inexpensive.

disgust and hatred. But he was my master. I was compelled to live under the same roof with him—where I saw a man forty years my senior daily violating the most sacred commandments of nature. He told me I was his property; that I must be subject to his will in all things. My soul revolted against the mean tyranny. But where could I turn for protection? No matter whether the slave girl be as black as ebony or as fair as her mistress. In either case, there is no shadow of law to protect her from insult, from violence, or even from death; all these are inflicted by fiends who bear the shape of men. The mistress, who ought to protect the helpless victim, has no other feelings towards her but those of jealousy and rage. The degradation, the wrongs, the vices, that grow out of slavery, are more than I can describe. They are greater than you would willingly believe. Surely, if you credited one half the truths that are told you concerning the helpless millions suffering in this cruel bondage, you at the north would not help to tighten the yoke. You surely would refuse to do for the master, on your own soil, the mean and cruel work which trained bloodhounds and the lowest class of whites do for him at the south.[13] ...

> [Jacobs writes that she tried to protect herself from Flint by accepting the attentions of another white man, a lawyer by whom she bore two children. She eventually managed to escape and went into hiding.]

21. THE LOOPHOLE OF RETREAT

15 A small shed had been added to my grandmother's house years ago. Some boards were laid across the joists at the top, and between these boards and the roof was a very small garret, never occupied by any thing but rats and mice. It was a pent roof, covered with nothing but shingles, according to the southern custom for such buildings. The garret was only nine feet long and seven wide. The highest part was three feet high, and sloped down abruptly to the loose board floor. There was no admission for either light or air. My uncle Philip, who was a carpenter, had very skilfully made a concealed trap-door, which communicated with the storeroom. He had been doing this while I was waiting in the swamp. The storeroom opened upon a piazza. To this hole I was conveyed as soon as I entered the house. The air was stifling; the darkness total. A bed had been spread on the floor. I could sleep quite comfortably on one side; but the slope was so sudden that I could not turn on the other without hitting the

---

13 *you at the north ... the south*   Reference to the Fugitive Slave Act, enacted by U.S. Congress in 1850. The act, which applied even to states where slavery itself was illegal, mandated increased efforts to hunt down and arrest fugitive slaves, while also imposing fines and jail time on anyone who assisted a fugitive slave. Since the Act also made it almost impossible for accused fugitives to defend themselves in court, it placed both free and fugitive Black people at greater risk of enslavement.

roof. The rats and mice ran over my bed; but I was weary, and I slept such sleep as the wretched may, when a tempest has passed over them. Morning came. I knew it only by the noises I heard; for in my small den day and night were all the same. I suffered for air even more than for light. But I was not comfortless. I heard the voices of my children. There was joy and there was sadness in the sound. It made my tears flow. How I longed to speak to them! I was eager to look on their faces; but there was no hole, no crack, through which I could peep. This continued darkness was oppressive. It seemed horrible to sit or lie in a cramped position day after day, without one gleam of light. Yet I would have chosen this, rather than my lot as a slave, though white people considered it an easy one; and it was so compared with the fate of others. I was never cruelly over-worked; I was never lacerated with the whip from head to foot; I was never so beaten and bruised that I could not turn from one side to the other; I never had my heel-strings cut to prevent my running away; I was never chained to a log and forced to drag it about, while I toiled in the fields from morning till night; I was never branded with hot iron, or torn by bloodhounds. On the contrary, I had always been kindly treated, and tenderly cared for, until I came into the hands of Dr. Flint. I had never wished for freedom till then. But though my life in slavery was comparatively devoid of hardships, God pity the woman who is compelled to lead such a life! ...

[Jacobs spent seven years in hiding in her grandmother's attic; not until 1842, at the age of 29, was she able to make her way to relative safety in the Northern states. Her children also managed to escape to the North.]

38. Renewed Invitations to Go South

We had a tedious winter passage, and from the distance specters seemed to rise up on the shores of the United States. It is a sad feeling to be afraid of one's native country. We arrived in New York safely, and I hastened to Boston to look after my children. I found Ellen well, and improving at her school; but Benny[14] was not there to welcome me. He had been left at a good place to learn a trade, and for several months every thing worked well. He was liked by the master, and was a favorite with his fellow-apprentices; but one day they accidentally discovered a fact they had never before suspected—that he was colored! This at once transformed him into a different being. Some of the apprentices were Americans, others American-born Irish; and it was offensive to their dignity to have a "nigger" among them, after they had been told that he *was* a "nigger."

---

14 *Ellen* Pseudonym generally agreed to refer to Louisa Sawyer, the author's daughter; *Benny* Pseudonym used for Jacobs's son, Joseph Sawyer.

They began by treating him with silent scorn, and finding that he returned the same, they resorted to insults and abuse. He was too spirited a boy to stand that, and he went off. Being desirous to do something to support himself, and having no one to advise him, he shipped for a whaling voyage. When I received these tidings I shed many tears, and bitterly reproached myself for having left him so long. But I had done it for the best, and now all I could do was to pray to the heavenly Father to guide and protect him.

Not long after my return, I received the following letter from Miss Emily Flint,[15] now Mrs. Dodge:—

> In this you will recognize the hand of your friend and mistress. Having heard that you had gone with a family to Europe, I have waited to hear of your return to write to you. I should have answered the letter you wrote to me long since, but as I could not then act independently of my father, I knew there could be nothing done satisfactory to you. There were persons here who were willing to buy you and run the risk of getting you. To this I would not consent. I have always been attached to you, and would not like to see you the slave of another, or have unkind treatment. I am married now, and can protect you. My husband expects to move to Virginia this spring, where we think of settling. I am very anxious that you should come and live with me. If you are not willing to come, you may purchase yourself; but I should prefer having you live with me. If you come, you may, if you like, spend a month with your grandmother and friends, then come to me in Norfolk, Virginia. Think this over, and write as soon as possible, and let me know the conclusion. Hoping that your children are well, I remain your friend and mistress.

Of course I did not write to return thanks for this cordial invitation. I felt insulted to be thought stupid enough to be caught by such professions.

> "Come up into my parlor," said the spider to the fly;
> "'Tis the prettiest little parlor that ever you did spy."[16]

It was plain that Dr. Flint's family were apprised of my movements, since they knew of my voyage to Europe. I expected to have further trouble from them; but having eluded them thus far, I hoped to be as successful in future. The money I had earned, I was desirous to devote to the education of my children,

15 *Miss Emily Flint* The author's legal owner, Dr. Flint's daughter.
16 *"'Come up into my parlor ... ever you did spy'"* Lines loosely quoted from "The Spider and the Fly" (1829), a poem by Mary Howitt in which a spider tries to persuade a fly to enter his home. In the poem's conclusion, the spider captures the fly and eats her.

and to secure a home for them. It seemed not only hard, but unjust, to pay for myself. I could not possibly regard myself as a piece of property. Moreover, I had worked many years without wages, and during that time had been obliged to depend on my grandmother for many comforts in food and clothing. My children certainly belonged to me; but though Dr. Flint had incurred no expense for their support, he had received a large sum of money for them. I knew the law would decide that I was his property, and would probably still give his daughter a claim to my children; but I regarded such laws as the regulations of robbers, who had no rights that I was bound to respect.

The Fugitive Slave Law had not then passed. The judges of Massachusetts had not then stooped under chains to enter her courts of justice,[17] so called. I knew my old master was rather skittish of Massachusetts. I relied on her[18] love of freedom, and felt safe on her soil. I am now aware that I honored the old Commonwealth beyond her deserts.[19] ...

20

(1861)

Questions

1. What makes slavery intolerable for Jacobs? To what extent (if at all) does she link these intolerable elements to the immorality of specific masters, and to what extent (if at all) does she present them as being inherent to slavery itself?

2. How would you characterize Jacobs's attitude towards the individual slave-owners she describes?

3. Jacobs writes that her goal is "to arouse the women of the North to a realizing sense of the condition of two millions of women at the South" (paragraph 3).

   a. How (if at all) is the stated intent to persuade white Northern women reflected in this text?

   b. How might Black Northerners have interpreted this text differently from white ones?

---

17 *judges of ... justice* Reference to literal chains that were used to secure the Boston courthouse while an escaped slave was held inside to await his forcible return to a slave state under the Fugitive Slave Act. Abolitionist outrage regarding the 1851 return of Thomas Sims and the 1854 return of Anthony Burns was so intense that in both cases the chains were deemed necessary to prevent protesters from freeing the slaves.

18 *her* I.e., Massachusetts's.

19 *beyond her deserts* More than she (Massachusetts) deserves.

4. In American history, racism towards African Americans tends to be associated far more strongly with the South than with the rest of the country. To what extent does Jacobs's account support this notion, and to what extent does her account contradict it?

5. Much of the content of this narrative is provocative. In these selections, when (if ever) does Jacobs directly express outrage, anger, or sadness? When (if ever) does she deliver information dispassionately? Would her account be more or less persuasive if the telling of it were more directly emotional? Why or why not?

6. What does Jacobs suggest in this selection about the economics of slavery? How does this compare with the ideas advanced by Ta-Nehisi Coates in "The Case for Reparations"?

7. Read Alice Walker's essay, "In Search of Our Mothers' Gardens," also printed in this anthology. How does Walker imagine life was like for Black women artists in the South during slavery? Consider the descriptions of Jacobs's grandmother and of Jacobs herself. Are they examples of the women that Walker imagines? Why or why not?

8. Jacobs includes in her narrative the letter she received from her mistress, asking her to return to the South and to slavery.

   a. As a reader, how did you react to the letter? How does Jacobs react to it?

   b. Compare Jacobs's response to Jordan Anderson's "Letter from a Freedman to His Old Master," printed elsewhere in this anthology. How are the responses similar, and how different?

JORDAN ANDERSON

LETTER FROM A FREEDMAN TO HIS OLD MASTER

Born into slavery and sold away from his place of birth as a young boy, Jordan (or Jourdon) Anderson grew up to perform slave labor until 1864 for Patrick Henry Anderson on Anderson's Tennessee plantation. During that year—the middle of the Civil War—Union soldiers reached the Anderson plantation and gave Jordan and his wife paperwork certifying their freedom. The couple left the plantation immediately and at the end of the war settled in Dayton, Ohio, with their children. A few months after the war ended, Jordan received a letter from Henry asking him to return to work on the plantation as a free laborer; Jordan, who could not read or write, dictated the following response to his friend the abolitionist Valentine Winters. It was first published in The Cincinnati Commercial, *then widely reprinted.*

Dayton, Ohio, August 7, 1865
To My Old Master, Colonel P.H. Anderson, Big Spring, Tennessee

Sir: I got your letter, and was glad to find that you had not forgotten Jordan, and that you wanted me to come back and live with you again, promising to do better for me than anybody else can. I have often felt uneasy about you. I thought the Yankees would have hung you long before this, for harboring Rebs[1] they found at your house. I suppose they never heard about your going to Colonel Martin's to kill the Union soldier that was left by his company in their stable. Although you shot at me twice before I left you, I did not want to hear of your being hurt, and am glad you are still living. It would do me good to go back to the dear old home again, and see Miss Mary and Miss Martha and Allen, Esther, Green, and Lee. Give my love to them all, and tell them I hope we will meet in the better world, if not in this. I would have gone back to see

---

1   *Yankees*   Union soldiers;   *Rebs*   Confederate soldiers.

37

you all when I was working in the Nashville Hospital, but one of the neighbors told me that Henry intended to shoot me if he ever got a chance.

I want to know particularly what the good chance is you propose to give me. I am doing tolerably well here. I get twenty-five dollars a month, with victuals and clothing; have a comfortable home for Mandy—the folks call her Mrs. Anderson—and the children—Milly, Jane, and Grundy—go to school and are learning well. The teacher says Grundy has a head for a preacher. They go to Sunday school, and Mandy and mé attend church regularly. We are kindly treated. Sometimes we overhear others saying, "Them colored people were slaves" down in Tennessee. The children feel hurt when they hear such remarks; but I tell them it was no disgrace in Tennessee to belong to Colonel Anderson. Many darkeys would have been proud, as I used to be, to call you master. Now if you will write and say what wages you will give me, I will be better able to decide whether it would be to my advantage to move back again.

As to my freedom, which you say I can have, there is nothing to be gained on that score, as I got my free papers in 1864 from the Provost-Marshal-General of the Department of Nashville. Mandy says she would be afraid to go back without some proof that you were disposed to treat us justly and kindly; and we have concluded to test your sincerity by asking you to send us our wages for the time we served you. This will make us forget and forgive old scores, and rely on your justice and friendship in the future. I served you faithfully for thirty-two years, and Mandy twenty years. At twenty-five dollars a month for me, and two dollars a week for Mandy, our earnings would amount to eleven thousand six hundred and eighty dollars. Add to this the interest for the time our wages have been kept back, and deduct what you paid for our clothing, and three doctor's visits to me, and pulling a tooth for Mandy, and the balance will show what we are in justice entitled to. Please send the money by Adams's Express, in care of V. Winters, Esq., Dayton, Ohio. If you fail to pay us for faithful labors in the past, we can have little faith in your promises in the future. We trust the good Maker has opened your eyes to the wrongs which you and your fathers have done to me and my fathers, in making us toil for you for generations without recompense. Here I draw my wages every Saturday night; but in Tennessee there was never any pay day for the Negroes any more than for the horses and cows. Surely there will be a day of reckoning for those who defraud the laborer of his hire.

In answering this letter, please state if there would be any safety for my Milly and Jane, who are now grown up, and both good-looking girls. You know how it was with poor Matilda and Catherine. I would rather stay here and starve—and die, if it come to that—than have my girls brought to shame by the violence and wickedness of their young masters. You will also please state if there has been any schools opened for the colored children in your neighborhood. The great desire of my life now is to give my children an education, and have them form virtuous habits.

Say howdy to George Carter, and thank him for taking the pistol from you 5 when you were shooting at me.

From your old servant,

Jordan Anderson

(1865)

Questions

1. Anderson shares details of his treatment as a slave in Tennessee. What does he ask of his former slave owner? What is the significance of his questions?

2. Why would Anderson's former slave owner ask him to return? What does Anderson's response say about the quality of his new life (for both him and his family) in comparison to that of his former life?

3. What is the significance of Anderson asking for back pay for labor he provided while enslaved?

4. Although Anderson articulated the points provided in the letter, he had to have someone write the letter on his behalf. Why was it against the law for enslaved people to learn to write?

Anna Julia Cooper

from A Voice from the South

Anna Julia Cooper is considered by many the "mother of Black feminism." Speaking at the Chicago World Fair in 1893, she said: "I speak for the colored women of the South, because it is there that the millions of blacks in this country have watered the soil with blood and tears, and it is there too that the colored woman of America has made her characteristic history and there her destiny is evolving."

Cooper herself set an example of unwavering dedication to her work and activism. Born into slavery in 1858, she began to attend school shortly after the end of the Civil War. At the age of nine she successfully petitioned to take the classes reserved for boys at St. Augustine's Normal School and Collegiate Institute. At Oberlin College, she took the "gentleman's course" rather than the "ladies'," receiving her B.A. in 1884 and her M.A. in 1887. She was the fourth African American woman to earn a PhD, which she received from the University of Paris-Sorbonne in 1925. She was a teacher at M Street High School in Washington when she wrote her first book, A Voice from the South: By a Black Woman of the South *(1892). This book, excerpted below, articulates the challenges facing Black women in the decades following Emancipation and puts forward Cooper's vision for racial uplift, emphasizing the importance of Black women's voices to the future of America.*

... Today America counts her millionaires by the thousand; questions of tariff and questions of currency are the most vital ones agitating the public mind. In this period, when material prosperity and well earned ease and luxury are assured facts from a national standpoint, woman's work and woman's influence are needed as never before; needed to bring a heart power into this money getting, dollar-worshipping civilization; needed to bring a moral force into the utilitarian motives and interests of the time; needed to stand for God and Home and Native Land *versus gain and greed and grasping selfishness....*

Now the periods of discovery, of settlement, of developing resources and accumulating wealth have passed in rapid succession. Wealth in the nation as in the individual brings leisure, repose, reflection. The struggle with nature is over, the struggle with ideas begins. We stand then, it seems to me, in this last decade of the nineteenth century, just in the portals of a new and untried movement on a higher plain and in a grander strain than any the past has called forth. It does not require a prophet's eye to divine its trend and image its possibilities from the forces we see already at work around us; nor is it hard to guess what must be the status of woman's work under the new regime.

In the pioneer days her role was that of a camp-follower,[1] an additional something to fight for and be burdened with, only repaying the anxiety and labor she called forth by her own incomparable gifts of sympathy and appreciative love; unable herself ordinarily to contend with the bear and the Indian, or to take active part in clearing the wilderness and constructing the home.

In the second or wealth producing period her work is abreast of man's, complementing and supplementing, counteracting excessive tendencies, and mollifying over-rigorous proclivities.

In the era now about to dawn, her sentiments must strike the keynote and   5
give the dominant tone. And this because of the nature of her contribution to the world.

Her kingdom is not over physical forces. Not by might, nor by power can she prevail. Her position must ever be inferior where strength of muscle creates leadership. If she follows the instincts of her nature, however, she must always stand for the conservation of those deeper moral forces which make for the happiness of homes and the righteousness of the country. In a reign of moral ideas she is easily queen.

There is to my mind no grander and surer prophecy of the new era and of woman's place in it, than the work already begun in the waning years of the nineteenth century by the W.C.T.U.[2] in America, an organization which has even now reached not only national but international importance, and seems destined to permeate and purify the whole civilized world. It is the living embodiment of woman's activities and woman's ideas, and its extent and strength rightly prefigure her increasing power as a moral factor.

---

1   *camp-follower*   Person who follows an army as it travels. Camp-followers included the wives of children and soldiers, as well as workers (usually women) who provided services to the soldiers, such as laundry, nursing, and prostitution.

2   *W.C.T.U.*   Woman's Christian Temperance Union, an influential social reform organization established by evangelical women. In addition to promoting abstention from alcohol, the W.C.T.U. advocated for causes such as labor reform and women's voting rights.

The colored woman of today occupies, one may say, a unique position in this country. In a period of itself transitional and unsettled, her status seems one of the least ascertainable and definitive of all the forces which make for our civilization. She is confronted by both a woman question and a race problem, and is as yet an unknown or an unacknowledged factor in both. While the women of the white race can with calm assurance enter upon the work they feel by nature appointed to do, while their men give loyal support and appreciative countenance to their efforts, recognizing in most avenues of usefulness the propriety and the need of woman's distinctive co-operation, the colored woman too often finds herself hampered and shamed by a less liberal sentiment and a more conservative attitude on the part of those for whose opinion she cares most. That this is not universally true I am glad to admit. There are to be found both intensely conservative white men and exceedingly liberal colored men. But as far as my experience goes the average man of our race is less frequently ready to admit the actual need among the sturdier forces of the world for woman's help or influence. That great social and economic questions await her interference, that she could throw any light on problems of national import, that her intermeddling could improve the management of school systems, or elevate the tone of public institutions, or humanize and sanctify the far reaching influence of prisons and reformatories and improve the treatment of lunatics and imbeciles—that she has a word worth hearing on mooted questions in political economy, that she could contribute a suggestion on the relations of labor and capital, or offer a thought on honest money and honorable trade, I fear the majority of "Americans of the colored variety" are not yet prepared to concede. It may be that they do not yet see these questions in their right perspective, being absorbed in the immediate needs of their own political complications. A good deal depends on where we put the emphasis in this world; and our men are not perhaps to blame if they see everything colored by the light of those agitations in the midst of which they live and move and have their being. The part they have had to play in American history during the last twenty-five or thirty years has tended rather to exaggerate the importance of mere political advantage, as well as to set a fictitious valuation on those able to secure such advantage. It is the astute politician, the manager who can gain preferment for himself and his favorites, the demagogue known to stand in with the powers at the White House and consulted on the bestowal of government plums, whom we set in high places and denominate great. It is they who receive the hosannas[3] of the multitude and are regarded as leaders of the people. The thinker and the doer, the man who solves the problem by enriching his country with an

---

3   *hosannas*   Exclamations of praise and adoration. In the New Testament, the word "hosanna" is frequently used in praise of Jesus.

invention worth thousands or by a thought inestimable and precious is given neither bread nor a stone. He is too often left to die in obscurity and neglect even if spared in his life the bitterness of fanatical jealousies and detraction.

And yet politics, and surely American politics, is hardly a school for great minds. Sharpening rather than deepening, it develops the faculty of taking advantage of present emergencies rather than the insight to distinguish between the true and the false, the lasting and the ephemeral advantage. Highly cultivated selfishness rather than consecrated benevolence is its passport to success. Its votaries[4] are never seers. At best they are but manipulators—often only jugglers.[5] It is conducive neither to profound statesmanship nor to the higher type of manhood. Altruism is its *mauvais succes*[6] and naturally enough it is indifferent to any factor which cannot be worked into its own immediate aims and purposes. As woman's influence as a political element is as yet nil in most of the commonwealths of our republic, it is not surprising that with those who place the emphasis on mere political capital she may yet seem almost a nonentity so far as it concerns the solution of great national or even racial perplexities.

There are those, however, who value the calm elevation of the thoughtful spectator who stands aloof from the heated scramble; and, above the turmoil and din of corruption and selfishness, can listen to the teachings of eternal truth and righteousness. There are even those who feel that the black man's unjust and unlawful exclusion temporarily from participation in the elective franchise[7] in certain states is after all but a lesson "in the desert"[8] fitted to develop in him insight and discrimination against the day of his own appointed time. One needs occasionally to stand aside from the hum and rush of human interests and passions to hear the voices of God. And it not unfrequently happens that the All-loving gives a great push to certain souls to thrust them out, as it were, from the distracting current for awhile to promote their discipline and growth, or to enrich them by communion and reflection. And similarly

10

---

4   *votaries*   Worshippers.

5   *jugglers*   In this context, dishonest tricksters.

6   *mauvais succes*   French: wrong (because undesired) achievement.

7   *elective franchise*   Right to vote in elections. Though the federal Constitution had ostensibly guaranteed Black men voting rights since 1870, in the late nineteenth and early twentieth centuries many Southern states created new state constitutions that disenfranchised Black voters.

8   *in the desert*   Allusion to Jesus' 40-day fast in the desert, during which (according to several passages in the New Testament) he was tempted by Satan. This period is often interpreted as a means of preparation for Jesus' role as messiah.

it may be woman's privilege from her peculiar coigne of vantage[9] as a quiet observer, to whisper just the needed suggestion or the almost forgotten truth. The colored woman, then, should not be ignored because her bark[10] is resting in the silent waters of the sheltered cove. She is watching the movements of the contestants none the less and is all the better qualified, perhaps, to weigh and judge and advise because not herself in the excitement of the race. Her voice, too, has always been heard in clear, unfaltering tones, ringing the changes on those deeper interests which make for permanent good. She is always sound and orthodox on questions affecting the well-being of her race. You do not find the colored woman selling her birthright for a mess of pottage.[11] Nay, even after reason has retired from the contest, she has been known to cling blindly with the instinct of a turtle dove[12] to those principles and policies which to her mind promise hope and safety for children yet unborn. It is notorious that ignorant black women in the South have actually left their husbands' homes and repudiated their support for what was understood by the wife to be race disloyalty, or "voting away," as she expresses it, the privileges of herself and little ones....

Fifty years ago woman's activity according to orthodox definitions was on a pretty clearly cut "sphere," including primarily the kitchen and the nursery, and rescued from the barrenness of prison bars by the womanly mania for adorning every discoverable bit of china or canvass with forlorn looking cranes balanced idiotically on one foot. The woman of today finds herself in the presence of responsibilities which ramify through the profoundest and most varied interests of her country and race. Not one of the issues of this plodding, toiling, sinning, repenting, falling, aspiring humanity can afford to shut her out, or can deny the reality of her influence. No plan for renovating society, no scheme for purifying politics, no reform in church or in state, no moral, social, or economic question, no movement upward or downward in the human plane is lost on her. A man once said when told his house was afire: "Go tell my wife; I never meddle with household affairs." But no woman can possibly put herself or her sex outside any of the interests that affect humanity. All departments in the new era are to be hers, in the sense that her interests are in all and through all; and it is incumbent on her to keep intelligently and

---

9   *coigne of vantage*   Position from which one can observe effectively.

10   *bark*   Ship.

11   *selling ... pottage*   Allusion to Genesis 25.29–34, in which Esau sells his birthright (the property and wealth due to him as first son) for a meal of lentil stew (pottage). The story is told as a warning against the perils of gratifying a present need at the expense of future prosperity.

12   *turtle dove*   Bird known for its affectionate nature and strong bonds between mates.

sympathetically *en rapport*[13] with all the great movements of her time, that she may know on which side to throw the weight of her influence. She stands now at the gateway of this new era of American civilization. In her hands must be molded the strength, the wit, the statesmanship, the morality, all the psychic force, the social and economic intercourse of that era. To be alive at such an epoch is a privilege, to be a woman then is sublime.

In this last decade of our century, changes of such moment* are in progress, such new and alluring vistas are opening out before us, such original and radical suggestions for the adjustment of labor and capital, of government and the governed, of the family, the church and the state, that to be a possible factor though an infinitesimal in such a movement is pregnant with hope and weighty with responsibility. To be a woman in such an age carries with it a privilege and an opportunity never implied before. But to be a woman of the Negro race in America, and to be able to grasp the deep significance of the possibilities of the crisis, is to have a heritage, it seems to me, unique in the ages. In the first place, the race is young and full of the elasticity and hopefulness of youth. All its achievements are before it. It does not look on the masterly triumphs of nineteenth century civilization with that *blasé*, world-weary look which characterizes the old washed out and worn out races which have already, so to speak, seen their best days....

(1892)

Questions

1. Cooper describes the last decade of the nineteenth century as being "at the gateway of [a] new era of American civilization" (paragraph 11).

   a. What does she mean by this? What reasons does she give in support of this claim?

   b. Research the 1890s in the United States. Was Cooper right to characterize the decade in this way?

2. Cooper is often described as the mother of Black feminism. To what extent (if at all) would you describe the selection above as feminist? In what ways—if any—does the selection above contradict present-day feminist ideas?

---

13 *en rapport* French: in touch.

3. Cooper states that

> All departments in the new era are to be [black women's], in the sense that her interests are in all and through all.... In her hands must be moulded the strength, the wit, the statesmanship, the morality, all the psychic force, the social and economic intercourse of that era. To be alive at such an epoch is a privilege, to be a woman then is sublime.

What role does Cooper see for women in "statesmanship" and "social and economic intercourse"? What does she mean when she says that "her interests are in all and through all"?

4. Some critics suggest that Cooper's work engages with the idea of "True Womanhood," a set of virtues that were thought to be natural to women by many writers of the nineteenth century (and especially by white writers).

   a. What—if any—virtues does Cooper associate with women? To what extent does she present these virtues as inherent in women, and to what extent does she present them as products of women's historical and political circumstances?

   b. How—if at all—does she present Black women as different from white women?

5. Consider the argument that Cooper makes in Paragraph 10.

   a. What does this paragraph suggest about voting rights? Who is she suggesting should have them?

   b. Compare Cooper's views regarding the vote with those outlined by Booker T. Washington in his speech printed elsewhere in this anthology.

   c. Consider the critique of Washington's perspective that W.E.B. Du Bois advances in his piece "On Booker T. Washington," sections from which are also printed in this anthology. To what extent—if at all—does Du Bois's critique of Washington apply to Cooper's claims? To what extent—if at all—does Cooper avoid the pitfalls Du Bois identifies?

BOOKER T. WASHINGTON

SPEECH DELIVERED AT THE COTTON STATES AND INTERNATIONAL EXPOSITION, 18 SEPTEMBER 1895

The end of slavery in the South led to a prolonged economic downturn that continued even after Reconstruction.* In an attempt to gain economic momentum and to expand trade with Latin America, Atlanta hosted the "Cotton States" International Exposition in Atlanta in 1895. Over 2 million dollars was spent to showcase Southern innovation and manufacture, and to transform Piedmont Park—creating a lake and tropical garden as well as various pavilions to house the exhibits, including a separate "Negro" building and a women's building. The exhibition ran for 100 days, with 800,000 people attending.

On opening day, 18 September 1895, Booker T. Washington gave the following speech to a racially mixed—though predominantly white—audience. The speech is sometimes referred to as the Atlanta Exposition Address, or, as styled by W.E.B. Du Bois, the Atlanta Compromise. The unofficial "compromise" it announced was that, under Washington's de facto leadership, Black organizations would not combat disenfranchisement or segregation, and in return whites would support Black people's pursuit of economic advancement through technical and vocational education.

MR. PRESIDENT AND GENTLEMEN OF THE BOARD OF DIRECTORS AND CITIZENS:

One-third of the population of the South is of the Negro race. No enterprise seeking the material, civil, or moral welfare of this section can disregard this element of our population and reach the highest success. I but convey to you, Mr. President and Directors, the sentiment of the masses of my race when I say that in no way have the value and manhood of the American Negro been more fittingly and generously recognized than by the managers of this magnificent Exposition at every stage of its progress. It is a recognition that will do more to cement the friendship of the two races than any occurrence since the dawn of our freedom.

Not only this, but the opportunity here afforded will awaken among us a new era of industrial progress. Ignorant and inexperienced, it is not strange that in the first years of our new life we began at the top instead of the bottom; that a seat in Congress or the State Legislature was more sought than real estate or industrial skill; that the political convention or stump speaking[1] had more attraction than starting a dairy farm or truck garden.[2]

A ship lost at sea for many days suddenly sighted a friendly vessel. From the mast of the unfortunate vessel was seen a signal: "Water, water; we die of thirst!" The answer from the friendly vessel at once came back: "Cast down your bucket where you are." A second time the signal, "Water, send us water!" ran up from the distressed vessel, and was answered, "Cast down your bucket where you are." A third and fourth signal for water was answered, "Cast down your bucket where you are." The captain of the distressed vessel, at last heeding the injunction, cast down his bucket, and it came up full of fresh, sparkling water from the mouth of the Amazon River. To those of my race who depend on bettering their condition in a foreign land, or who underestimate the importance of cultivating friendly relations with the Southern white man who is their next-door neighbor, I would say: "Cast down your bucket where you are"—cast it down in making friends, in every manly way, of the people of all races by whom you are surrounded.

5 Cast it down in agriculture, mechanics, in commerce, in domestic service, and in the professions. And in this connection it is well to bear in mind that whatever other sins the South may be called to bear, when it comes to business, pure and simple, it is in the South that the Negro is given a man's chance in the commercial world, and in nothing is this Exposition more eloquent than in emphasizing this chance. Our greatest danger is that in the great leap from slavery to freedom we may overlook the fact that the masses of us are to live by the productions of our hands, and fail to keep in mind that we shall prosper in proportion as we learn to dignify and glorify common labor, and put brains and skill into the common occupations of life; shall prosper in proportion as we learn to draw the line between the superficial and the substantial, the ornamental gewgaws[3] of life and the useful. No race can prosper till it learns that there is as much dignity in tilling a field as in writing a poem. It is at the bottom of life we must begin, and not at the top. Nor should we permit our grievances to overshadow our opportunities.

To those of the white race who look to the incoming of those of foreign birth and strange tongue and habits for the prosperity of the South, were I

---

1   *stump speaking*   Political speaking during a campaign.
2   *truck garden*   Market garden; vegetables raised for sale at market.
3   *gewgaws*   Useless gaudy things.

permitted I would repeat what I have said to my own race, "Cast down your bucket where you are." Cast it down among the eight million Negroes whose habits you know, whose fidelity and love you have tested in days when to have proved treacherous meant the ruin of your firesides. Cast down your bucket among these people who have without strikes and labor wars tilled your fields, cleared your forests, builded your railroads and cities, and brought forth treasures from the bowels of the earth, and helped make possible this magnificent representation of the progress of the South. Casting down your bucket among my people, helping and encouraging them as you are doing on these grounds, and, with education of head, hand, and heart, you will find that they will buy your surplus land, make blossom the waste places in your fields, and run your factories. While doing this, you can be sure in the future, as in the past, that you and your families will be surrounded by the most patient, faithful, law-abiding, and unresentful people that the world has seen. As we have proved our loyalty to you in the past, in nursing your children, watching by the sick-bed of your mothers and fathers, and often following them with tear-dimmed eyes to their graves, so in the future, in our humble way, we shall stand by you with a devotion that no foreigner can approach, ready to lay down our lives, if need be, in defense of yours, interlacing our industrial, commercial, civil, and religious life with yours in a way that shall make the interests of both races one. In all things that are purely social we can be as separate as the fingers, yet one as the hand in all things essential to mutual progress.

There is no defense or security for any of us except in the highest intelligence and development of all. If anywhere there are efforts tending to curtail the fullest growth of the Negro, let these efforts be turned into stimulating, encouraging, and making him the most useful and intelligent citizen. Effort or means so invested will pay a thousand percent interest. These efforts will be twice blessed—"Blessing him that gives and him that takes."[4]

There is no escape through law of man or God from the inevitable:

The laws of changeless justice
Bind oppressor with oppressed;
And close as sin and suffering joined
We march to fate abreast.[5]

Nearly sixteen millions of hands will aid you in pulling the load upward, or they will pull, against you, the load downward. We shall constitute one-third and more of the ignorance and crime of the South, or one-third its intelligence

---

4   *twice blessed ... takes*   See Shakespeare's *The Merchant of Venice* 4.1.190–94: "The quality of mercy is not strained. / ... It is twice blest: / It blesseth him that gives and him that takes."
5   *The laws ... abreast*   From John Greenleaf Whittier, "At Port-Royal" (1862).

and progress; we shall contribute one-third to the business and industrial prosperity of the South, or we shall prove a veritable body of death, stagnating, depressing, retarding every effort to advance the body politic.

10   Gentlemen of the Exposition, as we present to you our humble effort at an exhibition of our progress, you must not expect overmuch. Starting thirty years ago with ownership here and there in a few quilts and pumpkins and chickens (gathered from miscellaneous sources), remember, the path that has led from these to the inventions and production of agricultural implements, buggies, steam-engines, newspapers, books, statuary carving, paintings, the management of drug stores and banks, has not been trodden without contact with thorns and thistles. While we take pride in what we exhibit as a result of our independent efforts, we do not for a moment forget that our part in this exhibition would fall far short of your expectations but for the constant help that has come to our educational life, not only from the Southern states, but especially from Northern philanthropists, who have made their gifts a constant stream of blessing and encouragement.

The wisest among my race understand that the agitation of questions of social equality is the extremist folly, and that progress in the enjoyment of all the privileges that will come to us must be the result of severe and constant struggle rather than of artificial forcing. No race that has anything to contribute to the markets of the world is long, in any degree, ostracized. It is important and right that all privileges of the law be ours, but it is vastly more important that we be prepared for the exercise of these privileges. The opportunity to earn a dollar in a factory just now is worth infinitely more than the opportunity to spend a dollar in an opera-house.

In conclusion, may I repeat that nothing in thirty years has given us more hope and encouragement, and drawn us so near to you of the white race, as this opportunity offered by the Exposition; and here bending, as it were, over the altar that represents the results of the struggles of your race and mine, both starting practically empty-handed three decades ago, I pledge that, in your effort to work out the great and intricate problem which God has laid at the doors of the South, you shall have at all times the patient, sympathetic help of my race; only let this be constantly in mind, that while, from representations in these buildings of the product of field, of forest, of mine, of factory, letters, and art, much good will come, yet far above and beyond material benefits will be that higher good, that, let us pray God, will come in a blotting out of sectional differences and racial animosities and suspicions, in a determination to administer absolute justice, in a willing obedience among all classes to the mandates of law. This, coupled with our material prosperity, will bring into our beloved South a new heaven and a new earth.

(1895)

Questions

1. Consider the context of this speech, as well as its intended audience. How do the occasion and audience shape the central concerns of the speech?

2. Effective speeches often use metaphors and symbols to illustrate their arguments. In this speech, Washington repeatedly uses the metaphor of "filling your bucket where you are." How does this metaphor embody the vision for the South that Washington sets forward in this speech? Consider the image from various perspectives—what does the water symbolize? What does the metaphor imply about the ones seeking water, or about those giving advice about where to find it?

3. Washington says that "In all things that are purely social we [both races] can be as separate as the fingers, yet one as the hand in all things essential to mutual progress." What does this image suggest about Washington's vision for racial relations in the South?

4. Washington's agenda focuses primarily on education for Black Southerners. What are his ideas about education, as outlined in this speech? Why might this vision of education for African Americans appeal to the white population—or to the African American population?

5. Find three quotations in this speech that might have been intended to calm the racist fears of white audience members. What do you think were Washington's motives in making such statements? Do you think he was right to make them?

6. Washington delivered this speech at a time when life for Black Southerners was worsening; many of the advances made during Reconstruction were being lost, and lynchings* were frequent. How does his speech reflect this historical context?

7. The following questions relate to W.E.B. Du Bois's discussion of Booker T. Washington's speech printed elsewhere in this anthology. Compare both writers' positions on the following:

    a. Education

    b. Political engagement, including protest for civil rights

    c. Ideal relationship to the white population

JAMES WELDON JOHNSON
WITH JOHN ROSAMOND JOHNSON

LIFT EVERY VOICE AND SING

In the 1920s, "Lift Every Voice and Sing" became the official song of the NAACP (National Association for the Advancement of Colored People), and it has continued to be sung throughout the twentieth and twenty-first centuries as an anthem of strength, celebration, and resistance. It is often heard at civil rights protests and, in 2009, was performed at the inauguration of Barack Obama.

"Lift Every Voice and Sing" was written for a celebration of Lincoln's birthday being held at the segregated Black school where its author, James Weldon Johnson, was principal. The first performance was given as an introduction for the educator Booker T. Washington, a guest at the celebration who was at the time arguably the most prominent Black person in American politics. Years later, Johnson recalled the origin and history of the piece:

A group of young men in Jacksonville, Florida, arranged to celebrate Lincoln's birthday in 1900. My brother, J. Rosamond Johnson, and I decided to write a song to be sung at the exercises. I wrote the words and he wrote the music ... and the song was taught to and sung by a chorus of five hundred colored school children. Shortly afterwards my brother and I moved away from Jacksonville to New York, and the song passed out of our minds. But the school children of Jacksonville kept singing it; they went off to other schools and sang it; they became teachers and taught it to other children. Within twenty years it was being sung over the South and in some other parts of the country.... The lines of this song repay me in an elation, almost of exquisite anguish, whenever I hear them sung by Negro children.

Lift every voice and sing
Till earth and heaven ring,
Ring with the harmonies of Liberty;
Let our rejoicing rise
High as the listening skies,
Let it resound loud as the rolling sea.
Sing a song full of the faith that the dark past has taught us,
Sing a song full of the hope that the present has brought us.
Facing the rising sun of our new day begun,
Let us march on till victory is won.

Stony the road we trod,
Bitter the chastening rod,
Felt in the days when hope unborn had died;
Yet with a steady beat,
Have not our weary feet
Come to the place for which our fathers sighed?
We have come over a way that with tears have been watered,
We have come, treading our path through the blood of the slaughtered,
Out from the gloomy past,
Till now we stand at last
Where the white gleam of our bright star is cast.

God of our weary years,
God of our silent tears,
Thou who has brought us thus far on the way;
Thou who has by Thy might
Led us into the light,
Keep us forever in the path, we pray.
Lest our feet stray from the places, Our God, where we met Thee;
Lest, our hearts drunk with the wine of the world, we forget Thee;
Shadowed beneath Thy hand,
May we forever stand.
True to our God,
True to our native land.

(1899)

Questions

1. "Lift Every Voice and Sing" includes 3 distinct stanzas. Which stanza stands out to you as most compelling? Why?

2. The first performance of "Lift Every Voice and Sing" was not only in celebration of Lincoln's birthday, but also an introduction for a special guest on the occasion, the influential Black leader Booker T. Washington. Read Washington's speech delivered at the Cotton States and International Exhibition, reprinted elsewhere in this anthology, for an articulation of his political position. In your opinion, do the lyrics of "Lift Every Voice and Sing" support Washington's vision? Why or why not?

3. How does the song depict the past, present, and future struggle of Black Americans? To what extent, in your view, are these depictions accurate?

4. Do you see this song as a symbol of unity? Why or why not?

5. This song is often described as the Black National Anthem. What are the characteristics of anthems? What (if any) of those characteristics does this song display?

6. Find a performance of the song online and listen to it. Was your experience of listening different than that of reading? If so, how?

IDA B. WELLS

from LYNCH LAW IN AMERICA

The American practice of lynching—execution without any pretense of due legal process—began with extralegal acts carried out under the authority of Judge Charles Lynch in Virginia in the 1780s. It was not until the years following the Civil War, however—and particularly in the post-1877 period (after federal troops had ceased to enforce civil rights laws and had been withdrawn from Southern states) that lynching became a truly widespread practice. In the 1880s and 1890s, between 100 and 230 Americans were lynched annually—the vast majority of them African Americans. Most victims faced unproven accusations of serious crimes such as murder or rape, but African Americans could also be lynched for violating racist social norms; in one 1918 lynching, for example, a Black man was murdered for failing to get out of the way of a white man's car.

In the 21 May 1892 issue of her newspaper Free Speech, *Mississippi-born Memphis journalist and activist Ida Wells expressed her outrage at the "the many inhuman and fiendish lynchings of Afro-Americans which have recently taken place"; as she noted, there had been eight such incidents in the South in the one week that had passed since the last issue of her paper. Two days later, the two leading Memphis dailies expressed outrage of their own that an African American would try the "patience" of the local white community with such "loathsome calumnies." Wells might have been lynched herself had she not by that time left town; as it was, her newspaper offices were completely destroyed by mob violence. For the next decade she dedicated herself to researching and publicizing the phenomenon of lynching in America. On 22 June 1892 she published a long piece on the subject in the* New York Age, *and soon afterwards issued an expanded version of the piece as a pamphlet under the title* Southern Horrors: Lynch Law in All Its Phases. *Three years later she published a much longer pamphlet on the same topic (* The Red Record*), and for many years thereafter she campaigned vigorously against lynching, delivering many speeches in both the United States and Europe.*

The speech excerpted here was delivered in January 1900 to a Chicago audience. Also excepted below is the final chapter of Southern Horrors: Lynch Law in All Its Phases; *in this chapter, which she entitled "Self-Help," Wells gives full expression to her view that African Americans are better served by active than by passive resistance to oppression by whites.*

Our country's national crime is *lynching*. It is not the creature of an hour, the sudden outburst of uncontrolled fury, or the unspeakable brutality of an insane mob. It represents the cool, calculating deliberation of intelligent people who openly avow that there is an "unwritten law" that justifies them in putting human beings to death without complaint under oath, without trial by jury, without opportunity to make defense, and without right of appeal....

Judge Lynch was original in methods but exceedingly effective in procedure. He made the charge, impaneled the jurors, and directed the execution. When the court adjourned, the prisoner was dead....

But the spirit of mob procedure seemed to have fastened itself upon the lawless classes, and the grim process that at first was invoked to declare justice was made the excuse to wreak vengeance and cover crime. It next appeared in the South.... There it has flourished ever since, marking the thirty years of its existence with the inhuman butchery of more than ten thousand men, women, and children by shooting, drowning, hanging, and burning them alive. Not only this, but so potent is the force of example that the lynching mania has spread throughout the North and middle West....

This is the work of the "unwritten law" about which so much is said, and in whose behest butchery is made a pastime and national savagery condoned. The first statute of this "unwritten law" was written in the blood of thousands of brave men who thought that a government that was good enough to create a citizenship was strong enough to protect it. Under the authority of a national law that gave every citizen the right to vote, the newly-made citizens chose to exercise their suffrage. But the reign of the national law was short-lived and illusionary. Hardly had the sentences dried upon the statute-books before one Southern State after another raised the cry against "negro domination" and proclaimed there was an "unwritten law" that justified any means to resist it.

5 ... Thus lynchings began in the South, rapidly spreading into the various States until the national law was nullified and the reign of the "unwritten law" was supreme. Men were taken from their homes by "red-shirt" bands[1] and stripped, beaten, and exiled; others were assassinated when their

---

1   *"red-shirt" bands*   Paramilitary groups of white supremacists.

political prominence made them obnoxious to their political opponents; while the Ku-Klux* barbarism of election days, reveling in the butchery of thousands of colored voters, furnished records in Congressional investigations that are a disgrace to civilization.

The alleged menace of universal suffrage having been avoided by the absolute suppression of the negro vote, the spirit of mob murder should have been satisfied and the butchery of negroes should have ceased. But men, women, and children continued to be the victims of murder by individuals and murder by mobs, just as they had been when killed at the demands of the "unwritten law" to prevent "negro domination." Negroes were killed for disputing over terms of contracts with their employers. If a few barns were burned, some colored man was killed to stop it. If a colored man resented the imposition of a white man and the two came to blows, the colored man had to die, either at the hands of the white man then and there or later at the hands of a mob that speedily gathered. If he showed a spirit of courageous manhood he was hanged for his pains, and the killing was justified by the declaration that he was a "saucy nigger." Colored women have been murdered because they refused to tell the mobs where relatives could be found for "lynching bees."* Boys of fourteen years have been lynched by white representatives of American civilization....

... During the last ten years a new statute has been added to the "unwritten law." This statute proclaims that for certain crimes or alleged crimes no negro shall be allowed a trial; that no white woman shall be compelled to charge an assault under oath or to submit any such charge to the investigation of a court of law. The result is that many men have been put to death whose innocence was afterward established; and to-day, under this reign of the "unwritten law," no colored man, no matter what his reputation, is safe from lynching if a white woman, no matter what her standing or motive, cares to charge him with insult or assault....

Not only are two hundred men and women put to death annually, on the average, in this country by mobs, but these lives are taken with the greatest publicity. In many instances the leading citizens aid and abet by their presence when they do not participate, and the leading journals inflame the public mind to the lynching point with scare-head articles and offers of rewards. Whenever a burning is advertised to take place, the railroads run excursions, photographs are taken, and the same jubilee is indulged in that characterized the public hangings of one hundred years ago. There is, however, this difference: in those old days the multitude that stood by was permitted only to guy[2] or jeer. The nineteenth century lynching mob cuts off ears, toes, and fingers, strips off flesh, and distributes portions of the body as souvenirs among the crowd. If the leaders of

---

2   *guy*   Mock.

the mob are so minded, coal-oil is poured over the body and the victim is then roasted to death. This has been done in Texarkana and Paris, Tex., in Bardswell, Ky., and in Newman, Ga. In Paris the officers of the law delivered the prisoner to the mob. The mayor gave the school children a holiday and the railroads ran excursion trains so that the people might see a human being burned to death. In Texarkana, the year before, men and boys amused themselves by cutting off strips of flesh and thrusting knives into their helpless victim. At Newman, Ga., of the present year, the mob tried every conceivable torture to compel the victim to cry out and confess, before they set fire to the faggots[3] that burned him. But their trouble was all in vain—he never uttered a cry, and they could not make him confess.....

... The negro has been too long associated with the white man not to have copied his vices as well as his virtues. But the negro resents and utterly repudiates the efforts to blacken his good name by asserting that assaults upon women are peculiar to his race. The negro has suffered far more from the commission of this crime against the women of his race by white men than the white race has ever suffered through *his* crimes. Very scant notice is taken of the matter when this is the condition of affairs. What becomes a crime deserving capital punishment when the tables are turned is a matter of small moment when the negro woman is the accusing party....

10 ... [T]his question affects the entire American nation, and from several points of view: First, on the ground of consistency. Our watchword has been "the land of the free and the home of the brave." Brave men do not gather by thousands to torture and murder a single individual, so gagged and bound he cannot make even feeble resistance or defense. Neither do brave men or women stand by and see such things done without compunction of conscience, nor read of them without protest....

Second, on the ground of economy.... It is generally known that mobs in Louisiana, Colorado, Wyoming, and other States have lynched subjects of other countries. When their different governments demanded satisfaction, our country was forced to confess her inability to protect said subjects in the several States because of our State-rights[4] doctrines, or in turn demand punishment of the lynchers. This confession, while humiliating in the extreme, was not satisfactory; and, while the United States cannot protect, she can pay. This she has done, and it is certain will have to do again....

---

3 *faggots* Bundle of sticks used as fuel.
4 *State-rights* Reference to the Tenth Amendment of the United States Constitution: "The powers not delegated to the United States by the Constitution, nor prohibited by it to the States, are reserved to the States respectively, or to the people."

Third, for the honor of Anglo-Saxon civilization. No scoffer at our boasted American civilization could say anything more harsh of it than does the American white man himself who says he is unable to protect the honor of his women without resort to such brutal, inhuman, and degrading exhibitions as characterize "lynching bees."... No nation, savage or civilized, save only the United States of America, has confessed its inability to protect its women save by hanging, shooting, and burning alleged offenders.

Finally, for love of country. No American travels abroad without blushing for shame for his country on this subject. And whatever the excuse that passes current in the United States, it avails nothing abroad. With all the powers of government in control; with all laws made by white men, administered by white judges, jurors, prosecuting attorneys, and sheriffs; with every office of the executive department filled by white men—no excuse can be offered for exchanging the orderly administration of justice for barbarous lynchings and "unwritten laws." ... Although lynchings have steadily increased in number and barbarity during the last twenty years, there has been no single effort put forth by the many moral and philanthropic forces of the country to put a stop to this wholesale slaughter. Indeed, the silence and seeming condonation grow more marked as the years go by....

(1900)

from SOUTHERN HORRORS: LYNCH LAW IN ALL ITS PHASES

SELF-HELP

In the creation of ... healthier public sentiment, the Afro-American can do for himself what no one else can do for him. The world looks on with wonder that we have conceded so much and remain law-abiding under such great outrage and provocation.

To Northern capital and Afro-American labor the South owes its rehabilitation. If labor is withdrawn capital will not remain. The Afro-American is thus the backbone of the South. A thorough knowledge and judicious exercise of this power in lynching localities could many times effect a bloodless revolution. The white man's dollar is his god, and to stop this will be to stop outrages in many localities.

The Afro-Americans of Memphis denounced the lynching of three of their best citizens, and urged and waited for the authorities to act in the matter and bring the lynchers to justice. No attempt was made to do so, and the black men left the city by thousands, bringing about great stagnation in every branch of business. Those who remained so injured the business of the street car company by staying off the cars, that the superintendent, manager and treasurer called personally on the editor of the *Free Speech*, asked them to urge our people to give them their patronage again. Other business men became alarmed over the situation and the *Free Speech* was run away that the colored people might be more easily controlled. A meeting of white citizens in June, three months after the lynching, passed resolutions for the first time, condemning it. *But they did not punish the lynchers.* Every one of them was known by name, because they had been selected to do the dirty work, by some of the very citizens who passed these resolutions. Memphis is fast losing her black population, who proclaim as they go that there is no protection for the life and property of any Afro-American citizen in Memphis who is not a slave....

The appeal to the white man's pocket has ever been more effectual than all the appeals ever made to his conscience. Nothing, absolutely nothing, is to be gained by a further sacrifice of manhood and self-respect. By the right exercise of his power as the industrial factor of the South, the Afro-American can demand and secure his rights, the punishment of lynchers, and a fair trial for accused rapists.

5   Of the many inhuman outrages of this present year, the only case where the proposed lynching did *not* occur, was where the men armed themselves in Jacksonville, Fla., and Paducah, Ky., and prevented it. The only times an Afro-American who was assaulted got away has been when he had a gun and used it in self-defense.

The lesson this teaches and which every Afro-American should ponder well, is that a Winchester rifle should have a place of honor in every black home, and it should be used for that protection which the law refuses to give. When the white man who is always the aggressor knows he runs as great risk of biting the dust every time his Afro-American victim does, he will have greater respect for Afro-American life. The more the Afro-American yields and cringes and begs, the more he has to do so, the more he is insulted, outraged and lynched.

The assertion has been substantiated throughout these pages that the press contains unreliable and doctored reports of lynchings, and one of the most necessary things for the race to do is to get these facts before the public. The people must know before they can act, and there is no educator to compare with the press.

The Afro-American papers are the only ones which will print the truth, and they lack means to employ agents and detectives to get at the facts. The race must rally a mighty host to the support of their journals, and thus enable them to do much in the way of investigation....

Nothing is more definitely settled than [that the Afro-American] must act for himself. I have shown how he may employ the boycott, emigration and the press, and I feel that by a combination of all these agencies can be effectually stamped out lynch law, that last relic of barbarism and slavery. "The gods help those who help themselves."

(1892)

Questions

1. How would you characterize Wells's argumentative style? Through what means does she most effectively persuade her audience?
2. Is it possible to infer from the style and content of the two selections here anything about the audience(s) to whom they were addressed?
3. What means of resistance to lynchings does Wells propose? Should any of them be employed by those resisting police brutality against Black people today? Why or why not?
4. Compare the approach to "self-help" recommended here by Wells with that put forward by Pauline Hopkins. (See Hopkins's profile of Frederick Douglass, as well as Alisha Knights's piece on Hopkins, both reprinted in this anthology.)
5. Consider the excerpts from Bryan Stevenson's *Just Mercy* that are reprinted in this anthology. What happened to what he calls the "violent energies of lynching" once the lynchings themselves diminished in the 1960s? How, if at all, do you see these energies at work in contemporary America?

PAULINE HOPKINS

from HON. FREDERICK DOUGLASS[1]

*Pauline Hopkins is perhaps best known for her work as a playwright
and novelist, but she was also a prolific and respected journalist
and editor. In 1900 she began to publish fiction and essays in* The
Colored American Magazine, *a Black-owned journal dedicated to
discussing topics of interest to the African American community. She
soon became editor of* Colored American's *women's department,
and then, in 1903, she became the magazine's literary editor. She
resigned in 1904, her politically driven approach having fallen out
of favor with the magazine;* Colored American *had taken on a white
investor who advocated that they not print anything "alienating" to
white readers.*

*What follows are excerpts from Hopkins's essay "Hon. Frederick
Douglass," published in* The Colored American Magazine *as part of
her biographical series entitled "Famous Men of the Negro Race."
Each entry in the series celebrated the achievements of a prominent
African American, most of them activists or politicians. Hopkins
followed the "Famous Men" articles with another biographical
series, "Famous Women of the Negro Race."*

One of the most remarkable things in the curriculum of life is the birth
and growth of a great mind. In times of social or political changes the
upheaval of civil strife bringing in its train the death of old institutions and
ideas, changes in government and in religion, the passing of mighty nations
or races to the rear while new leaders are destined to press onward with the
standard of advancement, then, when God stands with one foot on the sea and
one on the shore leading the march of human progress toward the perfection
that shall usher in the millennium on earth—at such times great men are born;
in obscurity, in degradation, under the law it may be, that ever in our earthly
pilgrimage the life of our clear Redeemer shall be reproduced while time still

---

1   *Frederick Douglass*   American abolitionist, orator, writer, editor, and political figure
(1818–95).

holds—at such periods a hero comes unheralded and unsung in the solitude of poverty and communes with nature.... So came into being the gift of God to the Black race in the United States at the darkest hour in its history. Suddenly, as the heavens hung in sullen blackness, from out the gloom of the south a star shot forth celestial radiance—Frederick Douglass was born....

We can imagine the slave child Fred rolling and tumbling over the grass with other slave children each in his tow shirt, fed on ash-cake,[2] and in spite of bad treatment and frequent whippings, thriving under the beating so freely administered by "old Aunt Kate," who was the foster mother of the small army of plantation pickaninnies on the Lloyd plantation.[3] ...

For ten years the child Fred lived this life, seeing the separation of families, listening to the shrieks and cries of men and women flogged at the quarters, hearing the prayer, "Oh, Lord, how long?" Until that age, though a remarkably bright boy, he had probably had no ambitious dreams, but in his mind uneasiness began to take the place of endurance as he asked himself "Why is it thus with my people alone?" "Is there no help?"

Then he was sent to Baltimore to his young mistress who was also a member of the influential Lloyd family. She taught him to read the Bible, and the first rays of knowledge illuminated his mind. He taught himself to write by the models in his young master's copy-book.[4] Then came that mental thirst which must be quenched and he soon secured the speeches of Sheridan, Lord Chatham William Pitt and Fox.[5] His wonderful mental powers were awakened, his superior natural gifts began to reveal themselves. We can easily believe that in the veins of this man ran the best blood of old Maryland families mingled with the noble blood of African princes.

With enlightenment came dissatisfaction. He grew morose and gloomy; voices and beckoning hands called him and pointed to freedom's land. He determined to escape from thralldom....[6]

5

---

2   *tow shirt* Shirt made from cloth so coarse that it was painful to wear; *ash-cake* Dough baked in the ashes of a fire; a food commonly made and eaten by slaves.

3   *pickaninnies* Young Black children. In most contexts, the term is considered a racial slur; *Lloyd plantation* Douglass grew up on the plantation of Colonel Edward Lloyd in Maryland.

4   *copy-book* Book of handwriting samples with blank practice space for students.

5   *Sheridan* Richard Brinsley Sheridan, Irish playwright and politician (1751–1816); *Lord Chatham William Pitt* English politician William Pitt, First Earl of Chatham (1708–78); *Fox* English politician Charles James Fox (1749–1806). Sheridan, Pitt, and Fox were all known for their oratorical skill.

6   .... In the text omitted here, Douglass escapes and settles in New Bedford, Massachusetts, where slavery was illegal. He also adopts the last name "Douglass."

He learned something outside of books in New Bedford; there he saw the colored people owning their comfortable little homes and farms, schooling their children and transacting their own business. A wonderful new world of thought and action stretched before his startled gaze....

White men and black men had spoken on slavery but never like Frederick Douglass. The newspapers were filled with sayings of the "eloquent fugitive." He made his audiences weep, laugh, swear. He opened the hearts of thousands to mercy and pity for the slave by his eloquence and pathos. Many kept away from his lectures lest they be converted against their will. He knew the gamut of the human heart and swept the strings* with a master hand.

In 1841 he accepted an agency as lecturer for the anti-slavery society[7] and became at once invaluable to its promoters.

He visited Europe in 1845. In that same year he published the story of his life,[8] by this act giving a forward movement to the progress of the black race. This book was a soul-stirring and thrilling memoir of his slave life and the heartrending scenes with which he was so closely connected. He was most kindly received abroad and he traveled the length and breadth of England advocating the cause of his brother in chains in such powerful and eloquent language that the very heart of the people was stirred to its secret depths. He spoke as one with authority—as one into whose soul the iron of unutterable sorrow had entered.

10   It is argued by some that Frederick Douglass's ability as an editor and publisher did more than all his platform eloquence to compass the freedom of his people; that, of course, is a question.

Previous to 1848 the colored people of this country had no literature. *The National Reformer*, the *Mirror of Liberty*, the *Colored American*, *The Mystery*, the *Disfranchised American*, the *Ram's Horn*, and other papers of smaller magnitude, had been in existence, and ceased to live. All of these journals had done something towards raising the black man's standard, but literary work of colored men was received with great allowance by the whites and they were considered out of their sphere when they meddled with journalism. But Mr. Douglass's well-earned fame gave his paper[9] at once a standing with the first journals in the country; and he drew around him a score of contributors and correspondents from Europe, as well as all parts of America and the West Indies, that made its columns rich with the current news of the world.

7   *agency ... society*   Position as a lecturer representing the anti-slavery society.

8   *story of his life*   Douglass's *Narrative of the Life of Frederick Douglass, an American Slave* was published in 1845.

9   *his paper*   Douglass's paper the *North Star*, which he began publishing in 1847; in 1851 the *North Star* became *Frederick Douglass's Paper*, which was published until 1860.

In appearance Mr. Douglass was tall and well-made with a grandly developed head stamped with the sign-manual of intellectual superiority—a head that delighted phrenologists.[10] His voice was full round, rich, clear, and his enunciation perfect. I remember well the sensations which filled my own breast the first time it was my privilege to listen to the "grand old man." Child as I was, I felt that I could listen to the mellow richness of those sonorous accents forever. His bearing full of simplicity, was the dignified bearing of a wealthy cosmopolitan, sure of himself and of the world's homage, master of himself, unpretentious yet brilliant as a star. He handled his subject well, with that soulful eloquence which like a pure spring issued from the spirit of the God-head within him, coming in a flood, sweeping away every obstacle of contradiction, overwhelming and swallowing every adversary....

What were the times and conditions which tended to produce this inspired enthusiast? ...

The enactment by Congress of the Fugitive Slave Law[11] caused the friends of freedom to feel that the General Government was fast becoming the bulwark of slavery. The rendition of Thomas Sims, and later that of Anthony Burns,[12] was humiliating to the friends of the Blacks.

The "Dred Scott Decision"[13] added to the smouldering fire. By this decision in the highest court of American law, it was affirmed that no free Negro could claim to be a citizen of the United States, but was only under the jurisdiction of the separate State in which he resided; that the prohibition of slavery in any Territory of the Union was unconstitutional; and that the slave-owner might go where he pleased with his property, throughout the United States, and retain his right. This decision created much discussion, both in America and in Europe, and injured the good name of the country abroad.

15

---

10 *phrenologists* Pseudo-scientists who studied the shape of the head and delineated character traits from their observations. Phrenological principles were often invoked to justify belief in the inherent superiority of white people.

11 *Fugitive Slave Law* Enacted by U.S. Congress in 1850, the Fugitive Slave Act mandated increased efforts to hunt down and arrest fugitive slaves, while also imposing fines and jail time on anyone who assisted a fugitive slave. Since the Act also made it almost impossible for accused fugitives to defend themselves in court, it placed both free and fugitive Black people at greater risk of enslavement.

12 *rendition* Return of a fugitive to the relevant jurisdiction; *Thomas Sims* ... *Burns* Massachusetts men whose re-enslavement under the provisions of the Fugitive Slave Act became rallying points for abolitionists.

13 *Dred Scott Decision* Infamous 1857 Supreme Court decision *Dred Scott v. Sandford* in which Chief Justice Roger B. Taney gave the opinion that African Americans "had no rights which the white man was bound to respect."

The Constitution thus interpreted by Judge Taney, became the winding sheet[14] of liberty, and gave boldness to the Southerners. The slave-holders in the cotton, sugar and rice growing states began to urge the re-opening of the slave-trade, and the driving out of all free colored people from Southern States. In the Southern Rights' Convention, Baltimore, June 8, 1860, a resolution was adopted calling on the Legislature to pass a law to that effect. Every speaker took the ground that such a law was necessary to preserve the obedience of the slaves. Judge Catron of the Supreme Court of the United States, opposed the law. He said the free colored people were among the best mechanics, artisans, and most industrious laborers in the States, and that to drive them out would be an injury to the State itself. (The governments of the Southern States in 1900, will please take notice.)

Yet these free colored people were driven out in many States, and those unable to go, were reduced to slavery. These free people had never been permitted by law to school their children, or to read books that treated against the institution of slavery. The Rev. Samuel Green, a colored Methodist preacher, was convicted and sent to the Maryland penitentiary, in 1858, for the offence of being found reading *Uncle Tom's Cabin*.[15] ...

Progress follows upon the heels of discontent. Discontent is abroad and people open their eyes to the wickedness going on about them. Knowledge brought discontent to the slave Fred, and with it the grand resolve—liberty or death....

Douglass was present, practically, at the birth of aggressive anti-slavery agitation; he watched with interest the birth of the "Free Soil" party, and when the "Republican party"[16] first saw the light of day, with its face set firmly against the further extension of slave territory and the insolent domination of the slave power, he clapped his hands for joy.

20   Those old days seem far away to us of the present generation; some of us may even wish to never recall the horrors of our past. But is there not cause for anxiety? Are things, in the main, very much different at this hour?

To-day we have again the rise of the slave-power, for the old spirit is not dead; the serpent was scorched, not killed; so we have lynch-law* and a black

---

14 *winding sheet* Burial shroud.

15 *Uncle Tom's Cabin* 1852 anti-slavery novel by Harriet Beecher Stowe. It was among the most widely read novels of the nineteenth century.

16 *"Free Soil" party* Political party that opposed the spread of slavery to the Western states. The party was active in the 1848 and 1852 elections; *"Republican party"* The Republican party was originally founded in 1854 by anti-slavery activists and ex-free soilers, and it too opposed the expansion of slavery.

Postmaster Baker murdered[17] in cold blood and neither redress nor protection from the Federal Government. We have the Convict-lease system[18] and the word of influential Southerners that in it they have "a better thing than slavery, for them." ...

Speaking of an article written by Mr. T. Thomas Fortune on "Southern Home Rule," [Douglass] said:

> It is thoroughly comprehensive in its treatment, and will strike the true patriots of the country with no little alarm at the condition that seems to surround us. The nation should find a remedy for all this wrong. Unless it does this, it cannot be regarded otherwise than as a foul curse upon the age in which we live—a sham, a delusion and a snare. The situation is full of argument. It is like Mr. Lincoln's favorite method. He simply made a statement of facts, and they in themselves constituted a sufficient argument. The bare statement of our wrongs is really the best argument that can be made. They exist. There is no denial of them, nor any palliation....

O, venerable and historic sage! ... In his old age, with his wife and children and grandchildren about him, he rested in the evening of his life from his labors. His villa was one of the finest and most desirable in the Republic, whose original proprietor stipulated in the deed of transfer that the property should never be owned by a descendant of the African race. This estate is situated just beyond the eastern branch on the outskirts of Washington, embowered in oaks, commanding a view of the Navy Yard and the shaft of the Washington Monument. It gives a magnificent view of the most magnificent city on this continent. Such was Cedar Hill, where Douglass closed his eyes in sleep after life's fitful fever in 1895.

He had lived in Washington over twenty years, fifteen at Cedar Hill; before that time he lived at New Bedford three years; at Lynn, five; at Rochester, N.Y., twenty-five. He twice married.

---

17 *Postmaster Baker murdered*   In 1897, Frazier B. Baker was appointed postmaster in Lake City, South Carolina. That a Black man was given this position of respect outraged the predominantly white community, and a lynch mob murdered Baker and his two-year old daughter, Julia, on 22 February 1898.

18 *Convict-lease system*   Under this penal system in the Southern United States, prisoners were leased to private businesses, such as plantations, to labor as punishment for their crimes. The lessee would pay for the prisoners' food and board. Because of discriminatory law enforcement and racist sentencing, the majority of prisoners were Black men, creating in effect a system that in part replaced slavery as a source of free labor.

25   Mr. Douglass loved music, and played the violin. When the young people of Washington visited him at the Cedar Hill home, he frequently accompanied some expert pianist among them with the violin. His grandson, Joseph, inherits Mr. Douglass's musical gifts, and is not only a professional violinist, but has written some excellent scores. Joseph was Mr. Douglass's favorite grandchild. He had a large and extensive library, where one might see splendid busts of Feuerbach and Strauss.[19] Fine engravings adorned the walls, a bas relief of Dante[20] overlooking the pictures on the wall.

Mr. Douglass may have had his faults; who on this earthly planet has not? But they were not such as would dim one page of his great career.

He presents to us in his life an example of possibilities which may be within the reach of many young men of the rising generation—a mission divinely given, grandly accomplished. An honored name is his bequest to the Negro of the United States....

(1900)

Questions

1. To whom does Hopkins compare Douglass in the first paragraph of this essay? What does that comparison say about Hopkins's view of Douglass's position in African American history?

2. In Hopkins's view, have conditions improved for her generation? Why or why not?

3. How, if at all, does Hopkins's description of Cedar Hill take on political significance? What details strike you as important?

4. Hopkins's style in her biographies has been described as "panegyric." Do you agree with this assessment? Why or why not?

5. Read the biography of Douglass on Wikipedia. How does it differ in tone from Hopkins's? How do these differences reflect the rhetorical purpose of each piece of writing?

6. According to Hopkins, how did Douglass pave the way for Black journalism? Why was the involvement of someone like Douglass necessary to Black journalism's development?

---

19 *Feuerbach and Strauss*   Ludwig Feuerbach (1804–72) and David Friedrich Strauss (1808–74) were both German philosophers.

20 *bas relief* Sculpture in low-relief, in which less than half of the figures' shapes project from the carved surface; *Dante* Dante Alighieri, an Italian poet (1265–1321) best known for the long narrative poem *The Divine Comedy* (1320).

7. Hopkins includes a discussion of Douglass's parentage: "His wonderful mental powers were awakened, his superior natural gifts began to reveal themselves. We can easily believe that in the veins of this man ran the best blood of old Maryland families mingled with the noble blood of African princes." To what extent does Hopkins's account of Douglass, in this passage and elsewhere in the text, reflect prejudice? If it does, what form or forms of prejudice do you see reflected in this piece?

8. Hopkins's "Famous Men" and "Famous Women of the Negro Race" series are the subject of Alisha Knight's scholarly article "'To Aid in Everyway Possible in Uplifting the Colored People of America': Hopkins's Revisionary Definition of African American Success," selections from which are reprinted elsewhere in this anthology. Consider each of the following passages from Knight's work; to what extent does each passage accurately describe Hopkins's biography of Douglass? Support your answer with evidence from the Hopkins text, making sure to reference passages other than those Knight cites in her article.

   a. "[N]ot only were [Hopkins's] articles intended as examples of black achievement for white readers; they were also motivators for black readers." (paragraph 15)

   b. "Although Hopkins deemphasized the importance of wealth, fame was a key factor in her version of success.... In addition to fame, another indication that a black man had achieved success was the extent to which he was socially accepted and could use his acquired power to influence others." (paragraph 17)

   c. "Like the [ideal men associated with the white] traditional success model, Hopkins's self-made men possessed natural intelligence, high ethical and moral standards, honor, determination, and self-reliance. Unlike the white model, Hopkins's model also had a strong commitment to racial uplift." (paragraph 21)

W.E.B. DU BOIS

OF OUR SPIRITUAL STRIVINGS
[from *THE SOULS OF BLACK FOLK*]

Before the publication of The Souls of Black Folk *cemented his reputation, W.E.B. Du Bois had already achieved prominence as an activist and intellectual; he was a professor of sociology at Atlanta University[1] and made frequent appearances in America's most widely read periodicals. As he writes in his "Forethought" to the book, the purpose of* The Souls of Black Folk *is to "show the strange meaning of being black here in the dawning of the Twentieth Century"—a matter he suggests is of interest to all, "for the problem of the Twentieth Century is the problem of the color-line." He explores his subject via a diverse range of connected chapters, from an analysis of religious institutions to an autobiographical essay on the death of his son. The resulting text has had a tremendous impact on Black culture and politics of the twentieth century and beyond: as the critic Arnold Rampersad has said, "If all of a nation's literature may stem from one book, as Hemingway implied about* Adventures of Huckleberry Finn, *then it can as accurately be said that all of Afro-American literature of a creative nature has proceeded from Du Bois's comprehensive statement on the nature of the people in* The Souls of Black Folk.*

Two selections from* The Souls of Black Folk *are reproduced here: The first chapter is reprinted in its entirety, followed by selections from Du Bois's politically influential critique of the politics of Booker T. Washington, which appears later in the text.*

---

1   *Atlanta University*   A historically Black college in Atlanta, Georgia founded in 1865. The college merged with Clark College in 1985 and is now called Clark Atlanta University.

O water, voice of my heart, crying in the sand,
All night long crying with a mournful cry,
As I lie and listen, and cannot understand
The voice of my heart in my side or the voice of the sea,
O water, crying for rest, is it I, is it I?
All night long the water is crying to me.

Unresting water, there shall never be rest
Till the last moon droop and the last tide fail,
And the fire of the end begin to burn in the west;
And the heart shall be weary and wonder and cry like the sea,
All life long crying without avail,
As the water all night long is crying to me.[2]

ARTHUR SYMONS.

[3]

Between me and the other world there is ever an unasked question: unasked by some through feelings of delicacy; by others through the difficulty of rightly framing it. All, nevertheless, flutter round it. They approach me in a half-hesitant sort of way, eye me curiously or compassionately, and then, instead of saying directly, How does it feel to be a problem? they say, I know an excellent colored man in my town; or, I fought at Mechanicsville;[4] or, Do not these Southern outrages make your blood boil? At these I smile, or am interested, or reduce the boiling to a simmer, as the occasion may require. To the real question, How does it feel to be a problem? I answer seldom a word.

And yet, being a problem is a strange experience—peculiar even for one who has never been anything else, save perhaps in babyhood and in Europe. It is in the early days of rollicking boyhood that the revelation first bursts upon one, all in a day, as it were. I remember well when the shadow swept across

2   *O water ... to me*   From *The Crying of Waters* (1903) by white British poet Arthur Symons.

3   These bars of music record the first line of "Nobody Knows the Trouble I've Seen," a classic African American spiritual (a genre of religious song associated with the era of slavery).

4   *Mechanicsville*   The Confederate Army took heavy casualties during the American Civil War (1861–65) at the Battle of Mechanicsville, June 26, 1862 in Hanover County, Virginia.

me. I was a little thing, away up in the hills of New England, where the dark Housatonic winds between Hoosac and Taghkanic to the sea. In a wee wooden schoolhouse, something put it into the boys' and girls' heads to buy gorgeous visiting-cards—ten cents a package—and exchange. The exchange was merry, till one girl, a tall newcomer, refused my card—refused it peremptorily, with a glance. Then it dawned upon me with a certain suddenness that I was different from the others; or like, mayhap, in heart and life and longing, but shut out from their world by a vast veil. I had thereafter no desire to tear down that veil, to creep through; I held all beyond it in common contempt, and lived above it in a region of blue sky and great wandering shadows. That sky was bluest when I could beat my mates at examination-time, or beat them at a foot-race, or even beat their stringy heads. Alas, with the years all this fine contempt began to fade; for the words I longed for, and all their dazzling opportunities, were theirs, not mine. But they should not keep these prizes, I said; some, all, I would wrest from them. Just how I would do it I could never decide: by reading law, by healing the sick, by telling the wonderful tales that swam in my head—some way. With other black boys the strife was not so fiercely sunny: their youth shrunk into tasteless sycophancy, or into silent hatred of the pale world about them and mocking distrust of everything white; or wasted itself in a bitter cry, Why did God make me an outcast and a stranger in mine own house? The shades of the prison-house[5] closed round about us all: walls strait and stubborn to the whitest, but relentlessly narrow, tall, and unscalable to sons of night who must plod darkly on in resignation, or beat unavailing palms against the stone, or steadily, half hopelessly, watch the streak of blue above.

After the Egyptian and Indian, the Greek and Roman, the Teuton and Mongolian,[6] the Negro is a sort of seventh son, born with a veil, and gifted with second-sight[7] in this American world—a world which yields him no true self-consciousness, but only lets him see himself through the revelation of the other world. It is a peculiar sensation, this double-consciousness, this sense of always looking at one's self through the eyes of others, of measuring one's

---

5   *shades   of   the   prison-house*   Cf.   Wordsworth's   "Ode: Intimations   of Immortality"(1807): "Heaven lies about us in our infancy! / Shades of the prison-house begin to close / Upon the growing Boy."

6   *Egyptian ... Mongolian*   This list roughly mirrors the list of "world-historical peoples" discussed by the German philosopher G.W.F. Hegel in his *Lectures on the Philosophy of History* (1822–30). Hegel explicitly excludes much of the southern hemisphere "from the drama of the World's history"; *Teuton* I.e., German.

7   *seventh son ... second-sight*   In folkloric tradition the seventh son whose father is also a seventh son possesses mystical powers; children born with their faces obscured by birth membrane are said to be "born with a veil," meaning they are prone to good luck and extrasensory perception.

soul by the tape of a world that looks on in amused contempt and pity. One ever feels his twoness—an American, a Negro; two souls, two thoughts, two unreconciled strivings; two warring ideals in one dark body, whose dogged strength alone keeps it from being torn asunder.

The history of the American Negro is the history of this strife—this longing to attain self-conscious manhood, to merge his double self into a better and truer self. In this merging he wishes neither of the older selves to be lost. He would not Africanize America, for America has too much to teach the world and Africa. He would not bleach his Negro soul in a flood of white Americanism, for he knows that Negro blood has a message for the world. He simply wishes to make it possible for a man to be both a Negro and an American, without being cursed and spit upon by his fellows, without having the doors of Opportunity closed roughly in his face.

This, then, is the end* of his striving: to be a co-worker in the kingdom of culture, to escape both death and isolation, to husband* and use his best powers and his latent genius. These powers of body and mind have in the past been strangely wasted, dispersed, or forgotten. The shadow of a mighty Negro past flits through the tale of Ethiopia the Shadowy and of Egypt the Sphinx. Through history, the powers of single black men flash here and there like falling stars, and die sometimes before the world has rightly gauged their brightness. Here in America, in the few days since Emancipation, the black man's turning hither and thither* in hesitant and doubtful striving has often made his very strength to lose effectiveness, to seem like absence of power, like weakness. And yet it is not weakness—it is the contradiction of double aims. The double-aimed struggle of the black artisan—on the one hand to escape white contempt for a nation of mere hewers of wood and drawers of water,[8] and on the other hand to plough and nail and dig for a poverty-stricken horde—could only result in making him a poor craftsman, for he had but half a heart in either cause. By the poverty and ignorance of his people, the Negro minister or doctor was tempted toward quackery and demagogy; and by the criticism of the other world, toward ideals that made him ashamed of his lowly tasks. The would-be black savant was confronted by the paradox that the knowledge his people needed was a twice-told tale[9] to his white neighbors, while the knowledge which would teach the white world was Greek to* his own flesh and blood. The innate love of harmony and beauty that set the ruder souls of his people a-dancing and a-singing raised but confusion and doubt in the soul of the black artist; for the beauty revealed to him was the soul-beauty of a race which his larger audience

5

---

8   *hewers of wood ... water*   Biblical reference to unskilled laborers in the book of Joshua 9.21.

9   *twice-told tale*   Knowledge familiar through frequent repetition.

despised, and he could not articulate the message of another people. This waste of double aims, this seeking to satisfy two unreconciled ideals, has wrought sad havoc with the courage and faith and deeds of ten thousand thousand people—has sent them often wooing false gods and invoking false means of salvation, and at times has even seemed about to make them ashamed of themselves.

Away back in the days of bondage they thought to see in one divine event the end of all doubt and disappointment; few men ever worshipped Freedom with half such unquestioning faith as did the American Negro for two centuries. To him, so far as he thought and dreamed, slavery was indeed the sum of all villainies, the cause of all sorrow, the root of all prejudice; Emancipation was the key to a promised land of sweeter beauty than ever stretched before the eyes of wearied Israelites.[10] In song and exhortation swelled one refrain—Liberty; in his tears and curses the God he implored had Freedom in his right hand. At last it came—suddenly, fearfully, like a dream. With one wild carnival of blood and passion came the message in his own plaintive cadences:—

"Shout, O children!
Shout, you're ree!
For God has bought your liberty!"[11]

Years have passed away since then—ten, twenty, forty; forty years of national life, forty years of renewal and development, and yet the swarthy specter sits in its accustomed seat at the Nation's feast. In vain do we cry to this our vastest social problem:—

"Take any shape but that, and my firm nerves
Shall never tremble!"[12]

The Nation has not yet found peace from its sins; the freedman has not yet found in freedom his promised land. Whatever of good may have come in these years of change, the shadow of a deep disappointment rests upon the Negro people—a disappointment all the more bitter because the unattained ideal was unbounded save by the simple ignorance of a lowly people.

The first decade was merely a prolongation of the vain search for freedom, the boon that seemed ever barely to elude their grasp—like a tantalizing

---

10 *promised land ... Israelites* Reference to the biblical history of the Israelites (ancient Hebrews), who wandered the desert for 40 years in search of freedom in a bountiful homeland that was promised to them by God.

11 *Shout ... liberty* From "Shout, O Children," an African American spiritual.

12 *Take any ... never tremble* See *Macbeth* 3.4.106–07. Macbeth speaks these lines when he sees the ghost of Banquo, a rival whose murder he ordered, in Macbeth's own seat at a banquet.

will-o'-the-wisp, maddening and misleading the headless host.[13] The holocaust of war, the terrors of the Ku-Klux Klan, the lies of carpet-baggers,[14] the disorganization of industry, and the contradictory advice of friends and foes, left the bewildered serf with no new watchword beyond the old cry for freedom. As the time flew, however, he began to grasp a new idea. The ideal of liberty demanded for its attainment powerful means, and these the Fifteenth Amendment[15] gave him. The ballot, which before he had looked upon as a visible sign of freedom, he now regarded as the chief means of gaining and perfecting the liberty with which war had partially endowed him. And why not? Had not votes made war and emancipated millions? Had not votes enfranchised the freedmen? Was anything impossible to a power that had done all this? A million black men started with renewed zeal to vote themselves into the kingdom. So the decade flew away, the revolution of 1876[16] came, and left the half-free serf weary, wondering, but still inspired. Slowly but steadily, in the following years, a new vision began gradually to replace the dream of political power—a powerful movement, the rise of another ideal to guide the unguided, another pillar of fire[17] by night after a clouded day. It was the ideal of "book-learning"; the curiosity, born of compulsory ignorance, to know and test the power of the cabalistic[18] letters of the white man, the longing to know. Here at last seemed to have been discovered the mountain path to Canaan;[19] longer than the highway of Emancipation and law, steep and rugged, but straight, leading to heights high enough to overlook life.

---

13 *will-o'-the-wisp* In folk tradition, a mischievous spirit that appears as a fluttering light and draws a traveler away from their path; *headless host* Multitude of people without a leader.

14 *carpet-baggers* Northerners who moved South to profit from instability during the post-Civil War Reconstruction era in the United States. The term implied they were transient, poor, and carried their possessions in bags made of scraps of carpeting.

15 *Fifteenth Amendment* Amendment to the United States Constitution that granted men the right to vote regardless of race.

16 *revolution of 1876* Events following the 1876 presidential election, whose results were contested by three Southern states; the conflict regarding the election was resolved by a compromise in which the Southern states accepted the election results and the Northern states agreed to cease their involvement in matters of Black rights in the South. The withdrawal of this protection significantly worsened conditions for Black Southerners.

17 *pillar of fire* Reference to the Bible, Exodus 13.21, where God is manifested as light given to aid travelers in the dark.

18 *cabalistic* Mystical, esoteric.

19 *Canaan* I.e., the Promised Land; rather than traveling the shortest way, along the coast, the Israelites took a longer route to the land God had promised them, passing through mountains.

Up the new path the advance guard toiled, slowly, heavily, doggedly; only those who have watched and guided the faltering feet, the misty minds, the dull understandings, of the dark pupils of these schools know how faithfully, how piteously, this people strove to learn. It was weary work. The cold statistician wrote down the inches of progress here and there, noted also where here and there a foot had slipped or some one had fallen. To the tired climbers, the horizon was ever dark, the mists were often cold, the Canaan was always dim and far away. If, however, the vistas disclosed as yet no goal, no resting-place, little but flattery and criticism, the journey at least gave leisure for reflection and self-examination; it changed the child of Emancipation to the youth with dawning self-consciousness, self-realization, self-respect. In those somber forests of his striving his own soul rose before him, and he saw himself—darkly as through a veil; and yet he saw in himself some faint revelation of his power, of his mission. He began to have a dim feeling that, to attain his place in the world, he must be himself, and not another. For the first time he sought to analyze the burden he bore upon his back, that dead-weight of social degradation partially masked behind a half-named Negro problem. He felt his poverty; without a cent, without a home, without land, tools, or savings, he had entered into competition with rich, landed, skilled neighbors. To be a poor man is hard, but to be a poor race in a land of dollars is the very bottom of hardships. He felt the weight of his ignorance—not simply of letters, but of life, of business, of the humanities; the accumulated sloth and shirking and awkwardness of decades and centuries shackled his hands and feet. Nor was his burden all poverty and ignorance. The red stain of bastardy, which two centuries of systematic legal defilement of Negro women had stamped upon his race, meant not only the loss of ancient African chastity, but also the hereditary weight of a mass of corruption from white adulterers, threatening almost the obliteration of the Negro home.

10   A people thus handicapped ought not to be asked to race with the world, but rather allowed to give all its time and thought to its own social problems. But alas! while sociologists gleefully count his bastards and his prostitutes, the very soul of the toiling, sweating black man is darkened by the shadow of a vast despair. Men call the shadow prejudice, and learnedly explain it as the natural defense of culture against barbarism, learning against ignorance, purity against crime, the "higher" against the "lower" races. To which the Negro cries Amen! and swears that to so much of this strange prejudice as is founded on just homage to civilization, culture, righteousness, and progress, he humbly bows and meekly does obeisance. But before that nameless prejudice that leaps beyond all this he stands helpless, dismayed, and well-nigh speechless; before that personal disrespect and mockery, the ridicule and systematic humiliation,

the distortion of fact and wanton[20] license of fancy, the cynical ignoring of the better and the boisterous welcoming of the worse, the all-pervading desire to inculcate disdain for everything black, from Toussaint[21] to the devil—before this there rises a sickening despair that would disarm and discourage any nation save that black host to whom "discouragement" is an unwritten word.

But the facing of so vast a prejudice could not but bring the inevitable self-questioning, self-disparagement, and lowering of ideals which ever accompany repression and breed in an atmosphere of contempt and hate. Whisperings and portents came home upon the four winds: Lo! we are diseased and dying, cried the dark hosts; we cannot write, our voting is vain; what need of education, since we must always cook and serve? And the Nation echoed and enforced this self-criticism, saying: Be content to be servants, and nothing more; what need of higher culture for half-men? Away with the black man's ballot, by force or fraud—and behold the suicide of a race! Nevertheless, out of the evil came something of good—the more careful adjustment of education to real life, the clearer perception of the Negroes' social responsibilities, and the sobering realization of the meaning of progress.

So dawned the time of Sturm und Drang:[22] storm and stress today rocks our little boat on the mad waters of the world-sea; there is within and without the sound of conflict, the burning of body and rending of soul; inspiration strives with doubt, and faith with vain questionings. The bright ideals of the past—physical freedom, political power, the training of brains and the training of hands—all these in turn have waxed and waned, until even the last grows dim and overcast. Are they all wrong—all false? No, not that, but each alone was over-simple and incomplete—the dreams of a credulous race-childhood, or the fond imaginings of the other world which does not know and does not want to know our power. To be really true, all these ideals must be melted and welded into one. The training of the schools we need today more than ever—the training of deft hands, quick eyes and ears, and above all the broader, deeper, higher culture of gifted minds and pure hearts. The power of the ballot we need in sheer self-defense—else what shall save us from a second slavery? Freedom, too, the long-sought, we still seek—the freedom of life and limb, the freedom to work and think, the freedom to love and aspire. Work, cul-ture, liberty—all these we need, not singly but together, not successively but

---

20 *wanton* Undisciplined, reckless.

21 *Toussaint* Toussaint Louverture (1743–1803), leader of the Haitian Independence during the French Revolution.

22 *Sturm und Drang* German: storm and stress. This term refers to a movement in German Romantic literature that placed particular emphasis on emotionally intense individual experience.

together, each growing and aiding each, and all striving toward that vaster ideal that swims before the Negro people, the ideal of human brotherhood, gained through the unifying ideal of Race; the ideal of fostering and developing the traits and talents of the Negro, not in opposition to or contempt for other races, but rather in large conformity to the greater ideals of the American Republic, in order that some day on American soil two world-races may give each to each those characteristics both so sadly lack. We the darker ones come even now not altogether empty-handed: there are today no truer exponents of the pure human spirit of the Declaration of Independence than the American Negroes; there is no true American music but the wild sweet melodies of the Negro slave; the American fairy tales and folklore are Indian and African; and, all in all, we black men seem the sole oasis of simple faith and reverence in a dusty desert of dollars and smartness. Will America be poorer if she replace her brutal dyspeptic blundering with light-hearted but determined Negro humility? or her coarse and cruel wit with loving jovial good-humor? or her vulgar music with the soul of the Sorrow Songs?[23]

Merely a concrete test of the underlying principles of the great republic is the Negro Problem, and the spiritual striving of the freedmen's sons is the travail of souls whose burden is almost beyond the measure of their strength, but who bear it in the name of an historic race, in the name of this the land of their fathers' fathers, and in the name of human opportunity.

And now what I have briefly sketched in large outline let me on coming pages tell again in many ways, with loving emphasis and deeper detail, that men may listen to the striving in the souls of black folk.

(1903)

Questions

1. What is the significance of Du Bois's title *The Souls of Black Folk*? What ideas does he evoke by use of the title?

2. How does Du Bois see the position of Black Americans in world history?

3. What is "double-consciousness," according to Du Bois, and how does it characterize the inner lives of Black Americans?

---

23 *Sorrow Songs* Lamentful subgenre of African American spirituals; they are the focus of a later chapter of Du Bois's book.

4. According to Du Bois, African Americans pursued the ideals of "physical freedom, political power, the training of brains and the training of hands" in the eighteenth and nineteenth centuries (paragraph 12). Why was this pursuit not fully effective—and what does Du Bois propose instead?

5. What, according to Du Bois, is the ideal relationship between Black and white Americans? Do you agree?

6. Du Bois opens each chapter of *The Souls of Black Folk* with an epigram from a poem (often by a European poet) followed by a few bars of music from a spiritual. What is communicated by the epigrams at the beginning of this chapter?

7. What kinds of texts does Du Bois allude to in this chapter? What rhetorical purpose(s) do these allusions serve?

8. Du Bois shares in paragraph 12 that "the power of the ballot we need in sheer self-defense—else what shall save us from a second slavery?" Unpack this sentence and note its meaning. What do you think Du Bois would say about the current voter laws in America?

9. Some critics have characterized Du Bois's philosophy as elitist. Do you see evidence of elitism in this chapter? Why or why not?

from OF MR. BOOKER T. WASHINGTON AND OTHERS
[from *THE SOULS OF BLACK FOLK*]

While the period spanning the late nineteenth and early twentieth centuries was a time of economic and territorial expansion for the United States, it was also a time of sharp regression in racial relations and civil rights. Increased segregation, lynchings,* and disenfranchisement marked this period, the beginning of what is known as the Jim Crow era. In the mid-1890s, African American leader Booker T. Washington achieved great political influence as the champion of a compromise with the white population of the South: in exchange for due process in the law and access to vocational education, Washington assured whites that African Americans would stop agitating for desegregation and political representation.

This compromise, which held at least some promise of improvement for a population in a state of terror and oppression, was greeted with enthusiasm by whites and was supported or tolerated by the African American population for some years, though there was always a core of resistance to Washington's ideas. Activist and intellectual W.E.B. Du Bois, along with others, grew increasingly critical of this approach. Du Bois assesses Washington's methods in the following excerpts from his foundational work The Souls of Black Folk, *published at a time when Washington was arguably the most prominent Black man in American politics.*

... Easily the most striking thing in the history of the American Negro since 1876[24] is the ascendancy of Mr. Booker T. Washington. It began at the time when war memories and ideals were rapidly passing; a day of astonishing commercial development was dawning; a sense of doubt and hesitation overtook the freedmen's sons—then it was that his leading began. Mr. Washington came, with a simple definite program, at the psychological moment when the nation was a little ashamed of having bestowed so much sentiment on Negroes, and was concentrating its energies on Dollars. His program of industrial education, conciliation of the South, and submission and silence as to civil and political rights, was not wholly original.... But Mr. Washington first indissolubly linked these things; he put enthusiasm, unlimited energy, and perfect faith into this program, and changed it from a by-path into a veritable Way of Life. And the tale of the methods by which he did this is a fascinating study of human life.

It startled the nation to hear a Negro advocating such a program after many decades of bitter complaint; it startled and won the applause of the South, it interested and won the admiration of the North; and after a confused murmur of protest, it silenced if it did not convert the Negroes themselves.

To gain the sympathy and cooperation of the various elements comprising the white South was Mr. Washington's first task; and this, at the time Tuskegee[25] was founded, seemed, for a black man, well-nigh impossible. And yet ten years later it was done in the word spoken at Atlanta: "In all things purely social

24   *1876*   The results of the 1876 presidential election were contested by three Southern states, and the conflict regarding the election was resolved by a compromise in which the Southern states accepted the election results and the Northern states agreed to cease their involvement in matters of Black rights in the South. The withdrawal of this protection significantly worsened conditions for Black Southerners.

25   *Tuskegee*   Booker T. Washington founded the Tuskegee Institute (initially called the Tuskegee Normal School for Colored Teachers), an educational institution for Black students, in Alabama in 1881. It became Tuskegee University in 1985.

we can be as separate as the five fingers, and yet one as the hand in all things essential to mutual progress." This "Atlanta Compromise" is by all odds the most notable thing in Mr. Washington's career. The South interpreted it in different ways: the radicals[26] received it as a complete surrender of the demand for civil and political equality; the conservatives, as a generously conceived working basis for mutual understanding....

So Mr. Washington's cult has gained unquestioning followers, his work has wonderfully prospered, his friends are legion, and his enemies are confounded. Today he stands as the one recognized spokesman of his ten million fellows, and one of the most notable figures in a nation of seventy millions. One hesitates, therefore, to criticize a life which, beginning with so little, has done so much. And yet the time is come when one may speak in all sincerity and utter courtesy of the mistakes and shortcomings of Mr. Washington's career, as well as of his triumphs, without being thought captious or envious, and without forgetting that it is easier to do ill than well in the world.

The criticism that has hitherto met Mr. Washington has not always been of   5
this broad character. In the South especially has he had to walk warily to avoid the harshest judgments—and naturally so, for he is dealing with the one subject of deepest sensitiveness to that section. Twice—once when at the Chicago celebration of the Spanish-American War[27] he alluded to the color-prejudice that is "eating away the vitals* of the South," and once when he dined with President Roosevelt[28]—has the resulting Southern criticism been violent enough to threaten seriously his popularity. In the North the feeling has several times forced itself into words, that Mr. Washington's counsels of submission overlooked certain elements of true manhood, and that his educational program was unnecessarily narrow.... While, then, criticism has not failed to follow Mr. Washington, yet the prevailing public opinion of the land has been but too willing to deliver the solution of a wearisome problem into his hands, and say, "If that is all you and your race ask, take it."

Among his own people, however, Mr. Washington has encountered the strongest and most lasting opposition, amounting at times to bitterness, and even today continuing strong and insistent even though largely silenced in outward expression by the public opinion of the nation. Some of this opposition is, of course, mere envy; the disappointment of displaced demagogues and the spite of narrow minds. But aside from this, there is among educated

---

26   *radicals*   I.e., radical white supremacists.
27   *the Chicago ... War*   The Chicago Peace Jubilee, held to celebrate the end of the Spanish-American War in 1898.
28   *he dined ... Roosevelt*   Washington had dinner with Theodore Roosevelt in 1901, an act which was met with vitriolic condemnation in the Southern media.

and thoughtful colored men in all parts of the land a feeling of deep regret, sorrow, and apprehension at the wide currency and ascendancy which some of Mr. Washington's theories have gained. These same men admire his sincerity of purpose, and are willing to forgive much to honest endeavor which is doing something worth the doing. They cooperate with Mr. Washington as far as they conscientiously can; and, indeed, it is no ordinary tribute to this man's tact and power that, steering as he must between so many diverse interests and opinions, he so largely retains the respect of all....

... Booker T. Washington arose as essentially the leader not of one race but of two—a compromiser between the South, the North, and the Negro. Naturally the Negroes resented, at first bitterly, signs of compromise which surrendered their civil and political rights, even though this was to be exchanged for larger chances of economic development. The rich and dominating North, however, was not only weary of the race problem, but was investing largely in Southern enterprises, and welcomed any method of peaceful cooperation. Thus, by national opinion, the Negroes began to recognize Mr. Washington's leadership; and the voice of criticism was hushed.

Mr. Washington represents in Negro thought the old attitude of adjustment and submission; but adjustment at such a peculiar time as to make his program unique. This is an age of unusual economic development, and Mr. Washington's program naturally takes an economic cast, becoming a gospel of Work and Money to such an extent as apparently almost completely to overshadow the higher aims of life.... In the history of nearly all other races and peoples the doctrine preached at such crises has been that manly self-respect is worth more than lands and houses, and that a people who voluntarily surrender such respect, or cease striving for it, are not worth civilizing.

In answer to this, it has been claimed that the Negro can survive only through submission. Mr. Washington distinctly asks that black people give up, at least for the present, three things—

First, political power,
Second, insistence on civil rights,
Third, higher education of Negro youth—

and concentrate all their energies on industrial education, the accumulation of wealth, and the conciliation of the South. This policy has been courageously and insistently advocated for over fifteen years, and has been triumphant for perhaps ten years. As a result of this tender of the palm-branch,[29] what has been the return? In these years there have occurred:

---

29 *tender of the palm-branch*   Offer of peace. Palm branches are symbols of victory, so to offer one to an enemy is to end a conflict by conceding victory to them.

1. The disfranchisement of the Negro.

2. The legal creation of a distinct status of civil inferiority for the Negro.

3. The steady withdrawal of aid from institutions for the higher training of the Negro.

These movements are not, to be sure, direct results of Mr. Washington's teachings; but his propaganda has, without a shadow of doubt, helped their speedier accomplishment. The question then comes: Is it possible, and probable, that nine millions of men can make effective progress in economic lines if they are deprived of political rights, made a servile caste, and allowed only the most meager chance for developing their exceptional men? If history and reason give any distinct answer to these questions, it is an emphatic *No*. And Mr. Washington thus faces the triple paradox of his career: 10

1. He is striving nobly to make Negro artisans business men and property-owners; but it is utterly impossible, under modern competitive methods, for workingmen and property-owners to defend their rights and exist without the right of suffrage.[30]

2. He insists on thrift and self-respect, but at the same time counsels a silent submission to civic inferiority such as is bound to sap the manhood of any race in the long run.

3. He advocates common-school[31] and industrial training, and depreciates institutions of higher learning; but neither the Negro common-schools, nor Tuskegee itself, could remain open a day were it not for teachers trained in Negro colleges, or trained by their graduates.

This triple paradox in Mr. Washington's position is the object of criticism by two classes of colored Americans. One class is spiritually descended from Toussaint the Savior, through Gabriel, Vesey, and Turner,[32] and they represent

---

30 *the right of suffrage* The right to vote.

31 *common-school* Public elementary school.

32 *Toussaint the Savior* Toussaint Louverture (1743–1803) was the leader of the Haitian Revolution from 1791 to 1802. The Haitian Revolution was the first successful slave insurrection, and it led to the foundation of Haiti, a Black state free from slavery, in 1804; *Gabriel* Gabriel (d. 1800) was the leader of a planned slave revolt in Richmond, Virginia, in 1800. He was hanged with 25 others when plans for the revolt were discovered by the plantation owners; *Vesey* Denmark Vesey (c. 1767–1822) was accused and convicted of being a leader in the slave uprising planned in Charleston, South Carolina, in 1822. They planned to kill the plantation owners and then sail to Haiti for refuge, but the plan was discovered and Vesey was executed along with 35 others; *Turner* Nat Turner (1800–31) led a slave insurrection in Southampton County, Virginia, in 1831. The revolt gathered strength and momentum, but white militias eventually stopped it, imposing harsh measures in the aftermath to prevent future uprisings. Turner was hanged along with 18 others.

the attitude of revolt and revenge; they hate the white South blindly and distrust the white race generally, and so far as they agree on definite action, think that the Negro's only hope lies in emigration beyond the borders of the United States. And yet, by the irony of fate, nothing has more effectually made this program seem hopeless than the recent course of the United States toward weaker and darker peoples in the West Indies, Hawaii, and the Philippines[33]—for where in the world may we go and be safe from lying and brute force?

The other class of Negroes who cannot agree with Mr. Washington has hitherto said little aloud. They deprecate the sight of scattered counsels, of internal disagreement; and especially they dislike making their just criticism of a useful and earnest man an excuse for a general discharge of venom from small-minded opponents. Nevertheless, the questions involved are so fundamental and serious that it is difficult to see how men like the Grimkes, Kelly Miller, J.W.E. Bowen,[34] and other representatives of this group, can much longer be silent. Such men feel in conscience bound to ask of this nation three things:

1. The right to vote.
2. Civic equality.
3. The education of youth according to ability....

This group of men ... do not expect that the free right to vote, to enjoy civic rights, and to be educated, will come in a moment; they do not expect to see the bias and prejudices of years disappear at the blast of a trumpet; but they are absolutely certain that the way for a people to gain their reasonable rights is not by voluntarily throwing them away and insisting that they do not want them; that the way for a people to gain respect is not by continually belittling and ridiculing themselves; that, on the contrary, Negroes must insist continually, in season and out of season, that voting is necessary to modern manhood, that color discrimination is barbarism, and that black boys need education as well as white boys....

---

33 *recent course of the United States ... Philippines* American foreign policy in the late 1890s was expansionist, with territorial acquisitions concentrated in areas predominantly populated by people of color. After the Spanish-American war in 1898, America took possession of the Philippine Islands, Puerto Rico, and Guam; it also annexed Hawaii in the same year.

34 *the Grimkes* Archibald H. Grimké (1849–1930) was an African American civil rights leader and lawyer; his brother, Francis J. Grimké (1850–1937) was also a civil rights activist, as well as a Presbyterian minister; *Kelly Miller* African American sociologist, mathematician, and writer (1863–1939) who edited the periodical *The Crisis* with Du Bois and was a leader in the NAACP (National Association for the Advancement of Colored People); *J.W.E. Bowen* John Wesley Edward Bowen (1855–1933) was a Methodist pastor and educator, as well as one of the first African American men to receive a PhD.

It would be unjust to Mr. Washington not to acknowledge that in several instances he has opposed movements in the South which were unjust to the Negro; he sent memorials to the Louisiana and Alabama constitutional conventions,[35] he has spoken against lynching, and in other ways has openly or silently set his influence against sinister schemes and unfortunate happenings. Notwithstanding this, it is equally true to assert that on the whole the distinct impression left by Mr. Washington's propaganda is, first, that the South is justified in its present attitude toward the Negro because of the Negro's degradation; secondly, that the prime cause of the Negro's failure to rise more quickly is his wrong education in the past; and, thirdly, that his future rise depends primarily on his own efforts. Each of these propositions is a dangerous half-truth. The supplementary truths must never be lost sight of: first, slavery and race-prejudice are potent if not sufficient causes of the Negro's position; second, industrial and common-school training were necessarily slow in planting because they had to await the black teachers trained by higher institutions—it being extremely doubtful if any essentially different development was possible, and certainly a Tuskegee was unthinkable before 1880; and, third, while it is a great truth to say that the Negro must strive and strive mightily, to help himself, it is equally true that unless his striving be not simply seconded, but rather aroused and encouraged, by the initiative of the richer and wiser environing group, he cannot hope for great success.

In his failure to realize and impress this last point, Mr. Washington is especially to be criticized. His doctrine has tended to make the whites, North and South, shift the burden of the Negro problem to the Negro's shoulders and stand aside as critical and rather pessimistic spectators; when in fact the burden belongs to the nation, and the hands of none of us are clean if we bend not our energies to righting these great wrongs.

The South ought to be led, by candid and honest criticism, to assert her better self and do her full duty to the race she has cruelly wronged and is still wronging. The North—her co-partner in guilt—cannot salve her conscience by plastering it with gold. We cannot settle this problem by diplomacy and suaveness, by "policy" alone. If worse come to worst, can the moral fiber of this country survive the slow throttling and murder of nine millions of men? ...

(1903)

---

35 *sent memorials to ... constitutional conventions* After Reconstruction Southern states such as Louisiana (in 1898) and Alabama (in 1901) passed new constitutions at conventions held with the explicit purpose of disenfranchising African American voters. The "memorials" that Washington sent to these conventions were letters requesting that, as Washington phrased it in his letter to the president of the Alabama convention, "[the Negro] have some share in choosing those who shall rule over him, especially when he has proven his worthiness by becoming a taxpayer and a worthy reliable citizen."

Questions

1. What were the historical circumstances that, according to Du Bois, made the time propitious for Washington's ideas to find acceptance in both the white and Black communities?

2. Du Bois talks about Washington's "cult" (paragraph 4). Why would he choose to describe Washington's followers this way? What does this descriptor suggest about Washington himself?

3. At the time *The Souls of Black Folk* was published, Du Bois's political prominence did not come close to Washington's; the latter was, as Du Bois writes elsewhere in the book, "the leader who bears the chief burden of his race." What rhetorical strategies does Du Bois use to criticize such a prominent leader?

4. What, according to Du Bois, are the things Washington asks African Americans to give up? What resulted from these concessions?

5. Many of Washington's enduring achievements were in the field of education. He succeeded in founding and funding schools for Black children in the South, as well as the Tuskagee Institute. What, according to Du Bois, is problematic about Washington's vision of education for African Americans?

6. Who, according to Du Bois, should be held responsible for improving the lives of African Americans? How is his vision different from Washington's?

7. Read Washington's Atlanta Exposition Address, printed elsewhere in this anthology.

    a. Do you agree with Du Bois that Washington's ideas for African American progress involve "the old attitude of adjustment and submission" (paragraph 8)? Provide citations from the speech that back up your opinion.

    b. Du Bois writes the following:

        on the whole the distinct impression left by Mr. Washington's propaganda is, first, that the South is justified in its present attitude toward the Negro because of the Negro's degradation; secondly, that the prime cause of the Negro's failure to rise more quickly is his wrong education in the past; and, thirdly, that his future rise depends primarily on his own efforts. Each of these propositions is a dangerous half-truth. (paragraph 14)

Why, according to Du Bois, are these propositions "half-truth[s]"? In your view, does the Atlanta Exposition Address advance these "half-truth[s]"?

c. Du Bois twice describes Washington's ideas as "propaganda" (paragraphs 10 and 14). What is propaganda? Is it accurate to describe the Atlanta Exposition Address as propaganda? Why or why not?

THE NIAGARA MOVEMENT'S DECLARATION OF PRINCIPLES, 1905

In 1905, W.E.B. Du Bois and newspaper editor William Monroe Trotter organized the first meeting of the Niagara Movement for civil rights in Niagara Falls, Ontario. The movement was created with the express purpose of opposing the widely accepted approach to improving the lives of African Americans that was associated with prominent educator and political figure Booker T. Washington.[1] In opposition to Washington's emphasis on vocational education and economic advancement, the Niagara Movement advocated instead for more direct political action to secure rights for African Americans. The original twenty-nine members included men from across the country, though representation was strongest in New England and the Midwest. (Trotter opposed the membership of women, but Du Bois supported it, and in 1906 women were admitted as members.)

The Niagara Movement grew to considerable size by 1907, but its membership began to diminish in 1908, when Trotter began a rival movement, and the final meeting was in 1909. At this time, a race riot in Springfield, Illinois prompted some white people to join Du Bois in forming the NAACP (National Association for the Advancement of Colored People). The Niagara Movement then disbanded, and most members followed Du Bois to the NAACP. Although it was only extant for five years, the Niagara Movement is recognized as a cornerstone of the Civil Rights Movement, and as instrumental in establishing a radical alternative for people seeking to assert their rights outside the moderate parameters of Washington's leadership.

The following document articulates the principles by which the organization governed itself.

---

1   Washington's approach to improving conditions for African Americans is set out in his speech delivered at the Cotton States and International Exposition, also published in this anthology.

Progress: The members of the conference, known as the Niagara Movement, assembled in annual meeting at Buffalo, July 11th, 12th and 13th, 1905, congratulate the Negro-Americans on certain undoubted evidences of progress in the last decade, particularly the increase of intelligence, the buying of property, the checking of crime, the uplift in home life, the advance in literature and art, and the demonstration of constructive and executive ability in the conduct of great religious, economic and educational institutions.

Suffrage:[2] At the same time, we believe that this class of American citizens should protest emphatically and continually against the curtailment of their political rights. We believe in manhood suffrage;[3] we believe that no man is so good, intelligent or wealthy as to be entrusted wholly with the welfare of his neighbor.

Civil Liberty: We believe also in protest against the curtailment of our civil rights. All American citizens have the right to equal treatment in places of public entertainment according to their behavior and deserts.[4]

Economic Opportunity: We especially complain against the denial of equal opportunities to us in economic life; in the rural districts of the South this amounts to peonage[5] and virtual slavery; all over the South it tends to crush labor and small business enterprises; and everywhere American prejudice, helped often by iniquitous laws, is making it more difficult for Negro-Americans to earn a decent living.

Education: Common school education should be free to all American children and compulsory. High school training should be adequately provided for all, and college training should be the monopoly of no class or race in any section of our common country. We believe that, in defense of our own institutions, the United States should aid common school education, particularly in the South, and we especially recommend concerted agitation to this end. We urge an increase in public high school facilities in the South, where the Negro-Americans are almost wholly without such provisions. We favor well-equipped trade and technical schools for the training of artisans, and the need

5

---

2   *Suffrage*   The right to vote in public political elections.

3   *manhood suffrage*   The right to vote for adult males.

4   *deserts*   What they deserve.

5   *peonage*   Debt slavery, in which an employer forces an employee to work to repay a debt.

of adequate and liberal endowment for a few institutions of higher education must be patent[6] to sincere well-wishers of the race.

Courts: We demand upright judges in courts, juries selected without discrimination on account of color and the same measure of punishment and the same efforts at reformation for black as for white offenders. We need orphanages and farm schools for dependent children, juvenile reformatories for delinquents, and the abolition of the dehumanizing convict-lease system.[7]

Public Opinion: We note with alarm the evident retrogression in this land of sound public opinion on the subject of manhood rights, republican government and human brotherhood, and we pray God that this nation will not degenerate into a mob of boasters and oppressors, but rather will return to the faith of the fathers,[8] that all men were created free and equal, with certain unalienable rights.

Health: We plead for health—for an opportunity to live in decent houses and localities, for a chance to rear our children in physical and moral cleanliness.

Employers and Labor Unions: We hold up for public execration the conduct of two opposite classes of men: The practice among employers of importing ignorant Negro-American laborers in emergencies, and then affording them neither protection nor permanent employment; and the practice of labor unions in proscribing and boycotting and oppressing thousands of their fellow-toilers, simply because they are black. These methods have accentuated and will accentuate the war of labor and capital, and they are disgraceful to both sides.

10 **Protest:** We refuse to allow the impression to remain that the Negro-American assents to inferiority, is submissive under oppression and apologetic before insults. Through helplessness we may submit, but the voice of protest of ten million Americans must never cease to assail the ears of their fellows, so long as America is unjust.

Color-Line: Any discrimination based simply on race or color is barbarous, we care not how hallowed it be by custom, expediency or prejudice. Differences

---

6   *patent*   Obvious.

7   *farm schools*   I.e., orphanages where children were taught agricultural and related skills;   *convict-lease system*   Prisoners were hired out to private businesses, such as plantations, at a very low cost.

8   *fathers*   Founding fathers, authors of the Constitution of the United States.

made on account of ignorance, immorality, or disease are legitimate methods of fighting evil, and against them we have no word of protest; but discriminations based simply and solely on physical peculiarities, place of birth, color or skin, are relics of that unreasoning human savagery of which the world is and ought to be thoroughly ashamed.

"Jim Crow" Cars:[9] We protest against the "Jim Crow" car, since its effect is and must be to make us pay first-class fare for third-class accommodations, render us open to insults and discomfort and to crucify wantonly our manhood, womanhood and self-respect.

Soldiers: We regret that this nation has never seen fit adequately to reward the black soldiers who, in its five wars, have defended their country with their blood, and yet have been systematically denied the promotions which their abilities deserve. And we regard as unjust, the exclusion of black boys from the military and naval training schools.

War Amendments: We urge upon Congress the enactment of appropriate legislation for securing the proper enforcement of those articles of freedom, the thirteenth, fourteenth and fifteenth amendments of the Constitution of the United States.[10]

Oppression: We repudiate the monstrous doctrine that the oppressor should be the sole authority as to the rights of the oppressed. The Negro race in America stolen, ravished and degraded, struggling up through difficulties and oppression, needs sympathy and receives criticism; needs help and is given hindrance, needs protection and is given mob-violence, needs justice and is given charity, needs leadership and is given cowardice and apology, needs bread and is given a stone. This nation will never stand justified before God until these things are changed. 15

---

9   *"Jim Crow" Cars*   Named for the Jim Crow laws which enforced segregation, certain railroad passenger cars were designated by law in 1900 for Black passengers only.
10   *thirteenth ... United States*   Amendments 13, 14, and 15 of the American Constitution were made following the Civil War in an attempt to ameliorate racial oppression in the South. Among other things, the amendments declare the abolishment of slavery; the extension of citizenship to "all persons born or naturalized in the United States"; the entitlement of all citizens to "equal protection under the law"; and the right to vote regardless "of race, color, or previous condition of servitude."

The Church: Especially are we surprised and astonished at the recent attitude of the church of Christ[11]—of an increase of a desire to bow to racial prejudice, to narrow the bounds of human brotherhood, and to segregate black men to some outer sanctuary.* This is wrong, unchristian and disgraceful to the twentieth-century civilization.

Agitation: Of the above grievances we do not hesitate to complain, and to complain loudly and insistently. To ignore, overlook, or apologize for these wrongs is to prove ourselves unworthy of freedom. Persistent manly agitation is the way to liberty, and toward this goal the Niagara Movement has started and asks the co-operation of all men of all races.

Help: At the same time we want to acknowledge with deep thankfulness the help of our fellowmen from the Abolitionist[12] down to those who today still stand for equal opportunity and who have given and still give of their wealth and of their poverty for our advancement.

Duties: And while we are demanding, and ought to demand, and will continue to demand the rights enumerated above, God forbid that we should ever forget to urge corresponding duties upon our people:

> The duty to vote.
> The duty to respect the rights of others.
> The duty to work.
> The duty to obey the laws.
> The duty to be clean and orderly.
> The duty to send our children to school.
> The duty to respect ourselves, even as we respect others.

20   This statement, complaint and prayer we submit to the American people, and Almighty God.

(1905)

---

11   *church of Christ*   The Church of Christ is a body of Evangelical churches that tend to share a set of beliefs and practices; it first emerged in America in the early nineteenth century. Though the Churches of Christ have no centralized leadership, they were generally consistent in practicing segregation during this period.

12   *Abolitionist*   Opponent of slavery.

Questions

1. What is a manifesto? What are the conventions of the genre? How does this document exemplify and/or diverge from these conventions?

2. Compare and contrast this manifesto with the speech by Booker T. Washington reprinted elsewhere in this anthology:

    a. How (if at all) do Washington's and the Niagara Movement's positions differ? What (if anything) do they have in common?

    b. If you lived during the late nineteenth and early twentieth century, which position would you be more likely to support—that of Washington or that of the Niagara Movement? Why?

    c. Du Bois critiques Washington's position in a chapter from *The Souls of Black Folk*, selections from which are reprinted in this anthology. How effectively does this manifesto address the concerns Du Bois raises in his essay?

3. What are the most important goals set by this Declaration of Principles? Have these goals been achieved?

4. What role does gender play in this document? How well does this Declaration of Principles represent the interests of African American women?

CLAUDE McKAY

IF WE MUST DIE

During the "Red Summer" of 1919, race riots occurred in dozens of cities and some rural areas across the United States. Hundreds of people, mostly Black, were killed, and in some cities Black people fought back. The riots were sparked by the return of soldiers from World War I, which caused competition for jobs; Black workers had also been hired as strikebreakers in some industries, which led to increased resentment in the white working class.

During this summer, writer and political activist Claude McKay was working as a waiter on the railways, and he later wrote that "our Negro newspapers were morbid, full of details of clashes between colored and white, murderous shootings and hangings. Traveling from city to city and unable to gauge the attitude and temper of each one, we Negro railroad men were nervous. We were less light-hearted.... We stuck together, some of us armed, going from the railroad station to our quarters. We stayed in our quarters all through the dreary ominous nights, for we never knew what was going to happen. It was during those days that the sonnet, 'If We Must Die,' exploded out of me. And for it the Negro people unanimously hailed me as a poet." This sonnet has long been considered to mark the beginning of the period of Black cultural flourishing known as the Harlem Renaissance. It was first published in the Liberator *in July 1919; it was then reprinted in many journals and magazines throughout the 1920s.*

If we must die, let it not be like hogs
Hunted and penned in an inglorious spot,
While round us bark the mad and hungry dogs,
Making their mock at our accursèd lot.
If we must die, O let us nobly die,
So that our precious blood may not be shed
In vain; then even the monsters we defy
Shall be constrained to honor us though dead!
O kinsmen! we must meet the common foe!
Though far outnumbered let us show us brave,
And for their thousand blows deal one death-blow!
What though before us lies the open grave?
Like men we'll face the murderous, cowardly pack,
Pressed to the wall, dying, but fighting back!

(1919)

Questions

1. Consider McKay's choice of form. Why (if at all) is it significant?

2. Consider the martial language used in the poem. How is this conflict depicted? Who is fighting? Who is excluded from the fight?

3. Who is the audience of this poem? What is the relationship between the language in this poem and the poem's audience?

4. Consider the use of animal imagery in this poem. What animals are depicted and in what way? How (if at all) do they represent humans and human behavior?

LANGSTON HUGHES

THE NEGRO ARTIST AND
THE RACIAL MOUNTAIN

The Harlem Renaissance, which flourished in the 1920s and 1930s, was a time of intense cultural production and social revolution; many artists, writers, and musicians were redefining and celebrating Black culture. The migration of African Americans from the South to Northern cities brought together a concentrated community of sophisticated, ambitious, and talented people in Harlem,* where they experimented with creative forms, from jazz and blues music, to jazz poetry—which Langston Hughes pioneered—to theater, visual art, and formally innovative literature. Though Harlem was the epicenter of these developments, the movement extended far beyond New York to other American cities, such as Chicago, and involved an exchange of art and ideas with Black diasporic communities in France, the Caribbean, and elsewhere.

The following is considered a landmark essay—a manifesto for the young artists of the Harlem Renaissance. In it, Hughes outlines some of the challenges facing Black artists as they begin their careers, particularly the way in which class can inflect those challenges. The essay was published in The Nation *magazine in 1926.*

One of the most promising of the young Negro poets said to me once, "I want to be a poet—not a Negro poet," meaning, I believe, "I want to write like a white poet"; meaning subconsciously, "I would like to be a white poet"; meaning behind that, "I would like to be white." And I was sorry the young man said that, for no great poet has ever been afraid of being himself. And I doubted then that, with his desire to run away spiritually from his race, this boy would ever be a great poet. But this is the mountain standing in the way of any true Negro art in America—this urge within the race toward whiteness, the desire to pour racial individuality into the mold of American standardization, and to be as little Negro and as much American as possible.

But let us look at the immediate background of this young poet. His family is of what I suppose one would call the Negro middle class: people who are by no means rich yet never uncomfortable nor hungry—smug, contented, respectable folk, members of the Baptist church. The father goes to work every morning. He is the chief steward at a large white club. The mother sometimes does fancy sewing or supervises parties for the rich families of the town. The children go to a mixed school. In the home they read white papers and magazines. And the mother often says, "Don't be like niggers" when the children are bad. A frequent phrase from the father is, "Look how well a white man does things." And so the word white comes to be unconsciously a symbol of all the virtues. It holds for the children beauty, morality, and money. The whisper of "I want to be white" runs silently through their minds. This young poet's home is, I believe, a fairly typical home of the colored middle class. One sees immediately how difficult it would be for an artist born in such a home to interest himself in interpreting the beauty of his own people. He is never taught to see that beauty. He is taught rather not to see it, or if he does, to be ashamed of it when it is not according to Caucasian patterns.

For racial culture the home of a self-styled "high-class" Negro has nothing better to offer. Instead there will be perhaps more aping of things white than in a less cultured or less wealthy home. The father is perhaps a doctor, lawyer, landowner, or politician. The mother may be a social worker, or a teacher, or she may do nothing and have a maid. Father is often dark but he has usually married the lightest woman he could find. The family attend a fashionable church where few really colored faces are to be found. And they themselves draw a color line. In the North they go to white theaters and white movies. And in the South they have at least two cars and a house "like white folks." Nordic manners, Nordic faces, Nordic hair, Nordic art (if any), and an Episcopal* heaven. A very high mountain indeed for the would-be racial artist to climb in order to discover himself and his people.

But then there are the low-down folks, the so-called common element, and they are the majority—may the Lord be praised! The people who have their nip of gin* on Saturday nights and are not too important to themselves or the community, or too well fed, or too learned to watch the lazy world go round. They live on Seventh Street in Washington or State Street in Chicago and they do not particularly care whether they are like white folks or anybody else. Their joy runs, bang! into ecstasy. Their religion soars to a shout. Work maybe a little today, rest a little tomorrow. Play awhile. Sing awhile. O, let's dance! These common people are not afraid of spirituals,[1] as for a long time their more intellectual brethren were, and jazz is their child. They furnish a wealth of colorful, distinctive material for any artist because they still hold their own individuality in the face of American standardization. And perhaps these common people will give to the world its truly great Negro artist, the one who is not afraid to be himself. Whereas the better-class Negro would tell the artist what to do, the people at least let him alone when he does appear. And they are not ashamed of him—if they know he exists at all. And they accept what beauty is their own without question.

5   Certainly there is, for the American Negro artist who can escape the restrictions the more advanced among his own group would put upon him, a great field of unused material ready for his art. Without going outside his race, and even among the better classes with their "white" culture and conscious American manners, but still Negro enough to be different, there is sufficient material to furnish a black artist with a lifetime of creative work. And when he chooses to touch on the relations between Negroes and whites in this country with their innumerable overtones and undertones, surely, and especially for literature and the drama, there is an inexhaustible supply of themes at hand. To these the Negro artist can give his racial individuality, his heritage of rhythm and warmth, and his incongruous humor that so often, as in the Blues, becomes ironic laughter mixed with tears. But let us look again at the mountain.

A prominent Negro clubwoman in Philadelphia paid eleven dollars to hear Raquel Meller sing Andalusian[2] popular songs. But she told me a few weeks before she would not think of going to hear "that woman," Clara Smith,[3] a great black artist, sing Negro folk songs. And many an upper-class Negro church, even now, would not dream of employing a spiritual in its services. The drab melodies in white folks' hymnbooks are much to be preferred. "We want to worship the Lord correctly and quietly. We don't believe in 'shouting.' Let's be dull like the Nordics," they say, in effect.

The road for the serious black artist, then, who would produce a racial art is most certainly rocky and the mountain is high. Until recently he received almost no encouragement for his work from either white or colored people. The

---

1   *spirituals*   African American religious songs associated with the era of slavery.

2   *Raquel Meller*   Internationally famous Spanish vaudeville singer (1888–1962);   *Andalusian*   From Andalusia, an autonomous region in Southern Spain.

3   *Clara Smith*   American Blues singer (1894–1935), known as "The World's Greatest Moaner" and "The Queen of the Moaners." Her bands featured other prominent jazz and blues musicians, including James P. Johnson, Louis Armstrong, and Don Redman.

fine novels of Chesnutt[4] go out of print with neither race noticing their passing. The quaint charm and humor of Dunbar's[5] dialect verse brought to him, in his day, largely the same kind of encouragement one would give a sideshow freak (A colored man writing poetry! How odd!) or a clown (How amusing!).

The present vogue in things Negro, although it may do as much harm as good for the budding colored artist, has at least done this: it has brought him forcibly to the attention of his own people among whom for so long, unless the other race had noticed him beforehand, he was a prophet with little honor. I understand that Charles Gilpin[6] acted for years in Negro theaters without any special acclaim from his own, but when Broadway gave him eight curtain calls, Negroes, too, began to beat a tin pan[7] in his honor. I know a young colored writer, a manual worker by day, who had been writing well for the colored magazines for some years, but it was not until he recently broke into the white publications and his first book was accepted by a prominent New York publisher that the "best" Negroes in his city took the trouble to discover that he lived there. Then almost immediately they decided to give a grand dinner for him. But the society ladies were careful to whisper to his mother that perhaps she'd better not come. They were not sure she would have an evening gown.

The Negro artist works against an undertow of sharp criticism and misunderstanding from his own group and unintentional bribes from the whites. "O, be respectable, write about nice people, show how good we are," say the Negroes. "Be stereotyped, don't go too far, don't shatter our illusions about you, don't amuse us too seriously. We will pay you," say the whites. Both would have told Jean Toomer not to write *Cane*.[8] The colored people did not praise it. The white people did not buy it. Most of the colored people who did read *Cane* hated it. They are afraid of it. Although the critics gave it good reviews the public remained indifferent. Yet (excepting the work of Du Bois[9])

---

4   *Chesnutt*   Charles Waddell Chesnutt (1858–1932) was an African American writer known for fiction exploring racial identity in the post-Civil War era South. His reputation waned in the 1920s, but his work's importance came to be appreciated once more in the latter half of the twentieth century.

5   *Dunbar*   Paul Laurence Dunbar (1872–1906) was an African American poet and lyricist who used both conventional and Black English in his poems.

6   *Gilpin*   Charles Gilpin (1878–1930) was a highly successful African American stage actor.

7   *beat a tin pan*   I.e., make a lot of noise.

8   *Toomer*   Jean Toomer (1894–1967) was an African American poet and novelist;   *Cane*   Title of Toomer's best-known novel, published in 1923.

9   *Du Bois*   W.E.B. Du Bois, a prominent and enormously influential African American writer and activist. Excerpts from his book *The Souls of Black Folk* (1903) are printed elsewhere in this anthology.

Cane contains the finest prose written by a Negro in America. And like the singing of Robeson,[10] it is truly racial.

10   But in spite of the Nordicized Negro intelligentsia and the desires of some white editors we have an honest American Negro literature already with us. Now I await the rise of the Negro theater. Our folk music, having achieved world-wide fame, offers itself to the genius of the great individual American Negro composer who is to come. And within the next decade I expect to see the work of a growing school of colored artists who paint and model the beauty of dark faces and create with new technique the expressions of their own soul-world. And the Negro dancers who will dance like flame and the singers who will continue to carry our songs to all who listen—they will be with us in even greater numbers tomorrow.

    Most of my own poems are racial in theme and treatment, derived from the life I know. In many of them I try to grasp and hold some of the meanings and rhythms of jazz. I am sincere as I know how to be in these poems and yet after every reading I answer questions like these from my own people: Do you think Negroes should always write about Negroes? I wish you wouldn't read some of your poems to white folks. How do you find any thing interesting in a place like a cabaret? Why do you write about black people? You aren't black. What makes you do so many jazz poems?

    But jazz to me is one of the inherent expressions of Negro life in America: the eternal tom-tom[11] beating in the Negro soul—the tom-tom of revolt against weariness in a white world, a world of subway trains, and work, work, work; the tom-tom of joy and laughter, and pain swallowed in a smile. Yet the Philadelphia clubwoman is ashamed to say that her race created it and she does not like me to write about it. The old subconscious "white is best" runs through her mind. Years of study under white teachers, a lifetime of white books, pictures, and papers, and white manners, morals, and Puritan standards made her dislike the spirituals. And now she turns up her nose at jazz and all its manifestations—likewise almost everything else distinctly racial. She doesn't care for the Winold Reiss[12] portraits of Negroes because they are "too Negro."

---

10 *Robeson* Paul Robeson (1898–1976) was an African American singer, actor, and activist. Though he would later record in a variety of genres, he established his singing career in the mid-1920s as a performer of spirituals and other African American traditional music.

11 *tom-tom* Low-toned drum, beaten by hand. Figuratively, to beat a tom-tom is to bring attention to something, or to express anticipation.

12 *Reiss* Winold Reiss (1886–1953) was a German-American artist. He was primarily a portraitist, and he painted many Native Americans, as well as African Americans. He illustrated Alain Locke's *The New Negro* (1925), a collection of work by artists involved in the Harlem Renaissance.

She does not want a true picture of herself from anybody. She wants the artist to flatter her, to make the white world believe that all Negroes are as smug and as near white in soul as she wants to be. But, to my mind, it is the duty of the younger Negro artist, if he accepts any duties at all from outsiders, to change through the force of his art that old whispering "I want to be white," hidden in the aspirations of his people, to "Why should I want to be white? I am a Negro—and beautiful!"

So I am ashamed for the black poet who says, "I want to be a poet, not a Negro poet," as though his own racial world were not as interesting as any other world. I am ashamed, too, for the colored artist who runs from the painting of Negro faces to the painting of sunsets after the manner of the academicians because he fears the strange un-whiteness of his own features. An artist must be free to choose what he does, certainly, but he must also never be afraid to do what he might choose.

Let the blare of Negro jazz bands and the bellowing voice of Bessie Smith[13] singing Blues penetrate the closed ears of the colored near-intellectuals until they listen and perhaps understand. Let Paul Robeson singing Water Boy, and Rudolph Fisher writing about the streets of Harlem, and Jean Toomer holding the heart of Georgia in his hands, and Aaron Douglas[14] drawing strange black fantasies cause the smug Negro middle class to turn from their white, respectable, ordinary books and papers to catch a glimmer of their own beauty. We younger Negro artists who create now intend to express our individual dark-skinned selves without fear or shame. If white people are pleased we are glad. If they are not, it doesn't matter. We know we are beautiful. And ugly too. The tom-tom cries and the tom-tom laughs. If colored people are pleased we are glad. If they are not, their displeasure doesn't matter either. We build our temples for tomorrow, strong as we know how, and we stand on top of the mountain, free within ourselves.

(1926)

---

13 *Smith* Bessie Smith (1894–1937) was an African American blues singer, nicknamed the "Empress of the Blues." She was highly influential, considered by most to be the foremost singer of the 20s and 30s.

14 *Rudolph Fisher* African American physician, writer, and activist (1897–1934) whose fiction is predominantly set in Harlem; *Douglas* Aaron Douglas (1899–1979) was an African-American artist and an important figure in the Harlem Renaissance.

Questions

1. What, according to Hughes, is the "mountain" that stands in the way of young Black artists?

2. For Hughes, what effect does class have on a young Black artist's self-perception and choice of subject? Answer this question with reference to each of the three classes Hughes discusses.

3. Hughes begins his essay with a quotation by a "young Negro poet" who had said to him that "I want to be a poet—not a Negro poet." How does Hughes interpret this statement? Do you agree with his interpretation? Why or why not?

4. This essay has been described as the manifesto for the Harlem Renaissance. List the traits that characterize what Hughes sees as the new generation of African American artist.

5. Hughes names many of his contemporaries in this essay.

   a. What role do these names play in this essay? What is the rhetorical effect of their inclusion?

   b. How many of these names are those of women? What role do women play in Hughes's portrayal of Harlem cultural life?

6. Who, for Hughes, are the "Nordicized Negro Intelligentsia"?

7. Hughes sets out a vision of "true Negro art." Does his idea of what constitutes this art—or even the idea that such a thing as "true Negro art" might exist—reflect any kind of prejudice? Why or why not?

8. Read Zora Neale Hurston's "How It Feels to Be Colored Me," also reprinted in this anthology. Compare Hurston's and Hughes's views of the relationship between race, identity, and artistic expression.

ALICE DUNBAR-NELSON

THE NEGRO WOMAN AND THE BALLOT

Black American men's right to vote was not constitutionally recognized until 1870; the same right for women of all races was constitutionally recognized even later, in 1920. Despite rampant racism within white women's suffrage organizations, Black leaders such as Sojourner Truth, Anna Julia Cooper, and Ida B. Wells played a crucial role in the fight to achieve the vote for women. The following article was published after this right had been recognized federally for six years—although actual access to the vote for Black people in general varied dramatically by state, as some states used methods such as poll taxes, egregiously unfair literacy tests, and police intimidation to prevent Black voters from exercising their rights.

Alice Dunbar-Nelson, a poet, teacher, fiction writer, activist, and political columnist, was, among her many other achievements, a significant contributor to the campaign for women's suffrage; she was also a prominent figure in the Harlem Renaissance, a Black cultural and intellectual movement that flourished in New York and other American cities in the 1920s and 30s. The following piece first appeared in The Messenger, *a magazine associated with the Harlem Renaissance.*

It has been six years since the franchise[1] as a national measure has been granted women. The Negro woman has had the ballot in conjunction with her white sister, and friend and foe alike are asking the question, What has she done with it?

Six years is a very short time in which to ask for results from any measure or condition, no matter how simple. In six years a human being is barely able to make itself intelligible to listeners; is a feeble, puny thing at best, with

---

1   *the franchise*   I.e., the right to vote.

undeveloped understanding, no power of reasoning, with a slight contributory value to the human race, except in a sentimental fashion. Nations in six years are but the beginnings of an idea. It is barely possible to erect a structure of any permanent value in six years, and only the most ephemeral trees have reached any size in six years.

So perhaps it is hardly fair to ask with a cynic's sneer, What has the Negro woman done with the ballot since she has had it? But, since the question continues to be hurled at the woman, she must needs be nettled[2] into reply.

To those colored women who worked, fought, spoke, sacrificed, traveled, pleaded, wept, cajoled, all but died for the right of suffrage for themselves and their peers, it seemed as if the ballot would be the great objective of life. That with its granting, all the economic, political, and social problems to which the race had been subject would be solved. They did not hesitate to say—those militantly gentle workers for the vote—that with the granting of the ballot the women would step into the dominant place, politically, of the race. That all the mistakes which the men had made would be rectified. The men have sold their birthright for a mess of pottage,[3] said the women. Cheap political office and little political preferment had dazzled their eyes so that they could not see the great issues affecting the race. They had been fooled by specious lies, fair promises and large-sounding works. Pre-election promises had inflated their chests, so that they could not see the post-election failures at their feet.

5 And thus on and on during all the bitter campaign of votes for women.

One of the strange phases of the situation was the rather violent objection of the Negro man to the Negro woman's having the vote. Just what his objection racially was, he did not say, preferring to hide behind the grandiloquent platitude of his white political boss. He had probably not thought the matter through; if he had, remembering how precious the ballot was to the race, he would have hesitated at withholding its privilege from another one of his own people.

But all that is neither here nor there. The Negro woman got the vote along with some tens of million other women in the country. And has it made any appreciable difference in the status of the race? … The Negro woman was going to be independent, she had averred. She came into the political game with a clean slate. No Civil War memories for her, and no deadening sense of gratitude to influence her vote. She would vote men and measures, not parties. She could scan each candidate's record and give him her support according to how he had stood in the past on the question of race. She owed no party

2   *nettled*   Irritated.
3   *sold … pottage*   Reference to Genesis 25.30–34, in which Esau sells his inheritance to his younger brother Jacob for a bowl of stew (pottage).

allegiance. The name of Abraham Lincoln was not synonymous with her for blind G.O.P. allegiance.[4] She would show the Negro man how to make his vote a power, and not a joke. She would break up the tradition that one could tell a black man's politics by the color of his skin.

And when she got the ballot she slipped quietly, safely, easily, and conservatively into the political party of her male relatives.

Which is to say, that with the exception of New York City, and a sporadic break here and there, she became a Republican. Not a conservative one, however. She was virulent and zealous. Prone to stop speaking to her friends who might disagree with her findings on the political issue, and vituperative in campaigns.

In other words the Negro woman has by and large been a disappointment in her handling of the ballot. She has added to the overhead charges of the political machinery, without solving racial problems.

One of two bright lights in the story hearten the reader. In the congressional campaign of 1922 the Negro woman cut adrift from party allegiance and took up the cudgel (if one may mix metaphors) for the cause of the Dyer Bill.[5] The Anti-Lynching Crusaders, led by Mrs. Mary B. Talbot, found in several states—New Jersey, Delaware, and Michigan particularly—that its cause was involved in the congressional election. Sundry gentlemen had voted against the Dyer Bill in the House and had come up for re-election. They were properly castigated by being kept at home.[6] The women's votes unquestionably had the deciding influence in the three states mentioned, and the campaign conducted by them was of a most commendable kind.

School bond issues here and there have been decided by the colored woman's votes—but so slight is the ripple on the smooth surface of conservatism that it has attracted no attention from the deadly monotony of the blind faith in the "Party of Massa Linkun."

As the younger generation becomes of age it is apt to be independent in thought and in act. But it is soon whipped into line by the elders, and by the promise of plums of preferment or of an amicable position in the community or

10

---

4   *G.O.P.*   Acronym that is used to refer to the Republican Party;   *Abraham Lincoln ... allegiance*   Before the mid-twentieth century, Black voters tended to vote for the Republican Party, which was more racially progressive than the Democratic Party during this period. A particularly powerful motivating factor was that the Republicans, under Lincoln's leadership, had ended slavery in the country.

5   *Dyer Bill*   Proposed bill making it a federal crime not only for any individual to participate in a lynching but also for law enforcement to fail to act to prevent or prosecute lynchings. The bill never became law; it passed in Congress in 1922, but did not make it through the Senate.

6   *kept at home*   I.e., not re-elected.

of easy social relations—for we still persecute socially those who disagree with us politically. What is true of the men is true of the women. The very young is apt to let father, sweetheart, brother, or uncle decide her vote....

Whether women have been influenced and corrupted by their male relatives and friends is a moot question. Were I to judge by my personal experience I would say unquestionably so. I mean a personal experience with some hundreds of women in the North Atlantic, Middle Atlantic, and Middle Western States. High ideals are laughed at, and women confess with drooping wings how they have been scoffed at for working for nothing, for voting for nothing, for supporting a candidate before having first been "seen." In the face of this sinister influence it is difficult to see how the Negro woman could have been anything else but "just another vote."

15   All this is rather a gloomy presentment of a well-known situation. But it is not altogether hopeless. The fact that the Negro woman CAN be roused when something near and dear to her is touched and threatened is cheering. Then she throws off the influence of her male companion and strikes out for herself. Whatever the Negro may hope to gain for himself must be won at the ballot box, and quiet "going along" will never gain his end. When the Negro woman finds that the future of her children lies in her own hands—if she can be made to see this—she will strike off the political shackles she has allowed to be hung upon her, and win the economic freedom of her race.

Perhaps some Joan of Arc[7] will lead the way.

(1927)

Questions

1. How does Dunbar-Nelson suggest that Black women can effect change through voting? What, in her view, has largely prevented Black women from doing so thus far?

2. In your view, how effective is voting as a means of achieving political change? Explain your reasoning.

3. Read Audra D.S. Burch's "The #MeToo Moment: After Alabama, Black Women Wonder, What's Next?" (also reprinted in this anthology). With that article in mind, consider how, if at all, the position of

---

7   *Joan of Arc* Jeanne D'Arc (1412–31), a young peasant woman who, guided by visions she believed came from God, became involved in military affairs. She led the French to several victories over English forces during the Hundred Years' War; she was eventually burned at the stake by the English Church and was later canonized as a saint.

Black women voters in general has changed since the 1920s. What is different? What is similar?

4. Dunbar-Nelson writes that "the Negro woman has by and large been a disappointment in her handling of the ballot. She has added to the overhead charges of the political machinery, without solving racial problems" (paragraph 10). Based on the content of the rest of the article, does this strike you as a fair assessment? Why or why not?

5. Depending on the state in which they lived, Black women in the 1920s could face tremendous barriers in exercising their right to vote. Research some of these barriers in your home state. Why do you think they are not discussed in this article?

6. In making her critique, Dunbar-Nelson writes that "What is true of the men is true of the women" (paragraph 13), but she titles this piece "The Negro Woman and the Ballot." To what extent does the critique advanced in this opinion piece apply only to Black women, and to what extent does it apply also to Black men? What is the rhetorical impact of Dunbar-Nelson's choice to frame this article in terms of Black women voters specifically?

ZORA NEALE HURSTON

HOW IT FEELS TO BE COLORED ME

Among leading figures of the Renaissance in African American literature and culture in the 1920s and 30s, there were often differences of opinion over the degree to which literature and the other arts should be political. Notables such as Langston Hughes and Richard Wright thought Black writers and artists had a responsibility to assist the African American struggle against oppression by celebrating African American identity and culture; in his essay "The Negro* Artist and the Racial Mountain," Hughes condemns any African American poet who says "I want to be a poet—not a Negro poet," arguing that such a desire to escape race in art is tantamount to a desire to be white. Some others—among them Hurston and Nella Larsen—resisted the sorts of identity politics that Hughes, Wright, and political figures such as W.E.B. Du Bois advocated.

"How It Feels to Be Colored Me" was first published in The World Tomorrow, *a magazine devoted to the causes of pacifism and Christian socialism.*

I am colored but I offer nothing in the way of extenuating circumstances except the fact that I am the only Negro in the United States whose grandfather on the mother's side was *not* an Indian chief.[1]

I remember the very day that I became colored. Up to my thirteenth year I lived in the little Negro town of Eatonville, Florida. It is exclusively a colored town. The only white people I knew passed through the town going to or coming from Orlando.* The native whites rode dusty horses, the Northern* tourists chugged down the sandy village road in automobiles. The town knew the Southerners and never stopped cane chewing when they passed. But the Northerners were something else again. They were peered at cautiously from

---

1   *I am ... Indian chief*   An improbably high number of African Americans claimed to have Native American heritage (considered prestigious in African American communities at this time).

behind curtains by the timid. The more venturesome would come out on the porch to watch them go past and got just as much pleasure out of the tourists as the tourists got out of the village.

The front porch might seem a daring place for the rest of the town, but it was a gallery[2] seat for me. My favorite place was atop the gate-post. Proscenium box for a born first-nighter.[3] Not only did I enjoy the show, but I didn't mind the actors knowing that I liked it. I usually spoke to them in passing. I'd wave at them and when they returned my salute, I would say something like this: "Howdy-do-well-I-thank-you-where-you-goin'?" Usually automobile or the horse paused at this, and after a queer exchange of compliments, I would probably "go a piece of the way" with them, as we say in farthest Florida. If one of my family happened to come to the front in time to see me, of course negotiations would be rudely broken off. But even so, it is clear that I was the first "welcome-to-our-state" Floridian, and I hope the Miami Chamber of Commerce* will please take notice.

During this period, white people differed from colored to me only in that they rode through town and never lived there. They liked to hear me "speak pieces" and sing and wanted to see me dance the parse-me-la,[4] and gave me generously of their small silver for doing these things, which seemed strange to me for I wanted to do them so much that I needed bribing to stop. Only they didn't know it. The colored people gave no dimes. They deplored any joyful tendencies in me, but I was their Zora nevertheless. I belonged to them, to the nearby hotels, to the county—everybody's Zora.

But changes came in the family when I was thirteen, and I was sent to   5
school in Jacksonville. I left Eatonville, the town of the oleanders,* as Zora. When I disembarked from the river-boat at Jacksonville, she was no more. It seemed that I had suffered a sea change.* I was not Zora of Orange County* any more, I was now a little colored girl. I found it out in certain ways. In my heart as well as in the mirror, I became a fast[5] brown—warranted not to rub nor run.

But I am not tragically colored. There is no great sorrow dammed up in my soul, nor lurking behind my eyes. I do not mind at all. I do not belong to the sobbing school of Negrohood who hold that nature somehow has given

---

2   *gallery*   Theater seating area situated in an elevated balcony.

3   *Proscenium box*   Theater seating area near the proscenium, the frame of the stage; *first-nighter*   Person who frequently appears in the audience of opening night performances.

4   *parse-me-la*   Dance common in African American communities in the American South in the early twentieth century.

5   *fast*   Adjective applied to dyes that will not run or change color.

them a lowdown dirty deal and whose feelings are all hurt about it. Even in the helter-skelter skirmish that is my life, I have seen that the world is to the strong regardless of a little pigmentation more or less. No, I do not weep at the world—I am too busy sharpening my oyster knife.*

Someone is always at my elbow reminding me that I am the granddaughter of slaves. It fails to register depression with me. Slavery is sixty years in the past.[6] The operation was successful and the patient is doing well, thank you. The terrible struggle that made me an American out of a potential slave said "On the line!" The Reconstruction[7] said "Get set!"; and the generation before said "Go!"* I am off to a flying start and I must not halt in the stretch to look behind and weep. Slavery is the price I paid for civilization, and the choice was not with me. It is a bully[8] adventure and worth all that I have paid through my ancestors for it. No one on earth ever had a greater chance for glory. The world to be won and nothing to be lost. It is thrilling to think—to know that for any act of mine, I shall get twice as much praise or twice as much blame. It is quite exciting to hold the center of the national stage, with the spectators not knowing whether to laugh or to weep.

The position of my white neighbor is much more difficult. No brown specter pulls up a chair beside me when I sit down to eat. No dark ghost thrusts its leg against mine in bed. The game of keeping what one has is never so exciting as the game of getting.

I do not always feel colored. Even now I often achieve the unconscious Zora of Eatonville before the Hegira.[9] I feel most colored when I am thrown against a sharp white background.

10   For instance at Barnard.[10] "Beside the waters of the Hudson"[11] I feel my race. Among the thousand white persons, I am a dark rock surged upon, and overswept, but through it all, I remain myself. When covered by the waters, I am; and the ebb but reveals me again.

---

6   *Slavery is ... the past*   In 1863, the Emancipation Proclamation legally ended slavery in America.

7   *Reconstruction*   Period (1865–77) after the Civil War during which federal troops occupied the former Confederacy and enforced federal laws, as the South tried to build a society without slavery. (With the withdrawal of those troops following the "compromise of 1877," conditions for African Americans in many Southern jurisdictions reverted for many decades to a state little better than slavery.)

8   *bully*   Merry, splendid.

9   *Hegira*   I.e., journey; refers to Mohammed's journey from Mecca to Medina, which marks the beginning of the current era in the Islamic calendar.

10   *Barnard*   Women's liberal arts college in New York City, affiliated with Columbia University.

11   *"Beside ... Hudson"*   Barnard school song.

Sometimes it is the other way around. A white person is set down in our midst, but the contrast is just as sharp for me. For instance, when I sit in the drafty basement that is The New World Cabaret with a white person, my color comes. We enter chatting about any little nothing that we have in common and are seated by the jazz waiters. In the abrupt way that jazz orchestras have, this one plunges into a number. It loses no time in circumlocutions, but gets right down to business. It constricts the thorax and splits the heart with its tempo and narcotic harmonies. This orchestra grows rambunctious, rears on its hind legs and attacks the tonal veil with primitive fury, rending it, clawing it until it breaks through to the jungle beyond. I follow those heathen—follow them exultingly. I dance wildly inside myself; I yell within, I whoop; I shake my assegai[12] above my head, I hurl it true to the mark yeeeeooww! I am in the jungle and living in the jungle way. My face is painted red and yellow and my body is painted blue. My pulse is throbbing like a war drum. I want to slaughter something—give pain, give death to what, I do not know. But the piece ends. The men of the orchestra wipe their lips and rest their fingers. I creep back slowly to the veneer we call civilization with the last tone and find the white friend sitting motionless in his seat smoking calmly.

"Good music they have here," he remarks, drumming the table with his fingertips.

Music. The great blobs of purple and red emotion have not touched him. He has only heard what I felt. He is far away and I see him but dimly across the ocean and the continent that have fallen between us. He is so pale with his whiteness then and I am *so* colored.

At certain times I have no race, I am *me*. When I set my hat at a certain angle and saunter down Seventh Avenue, Harlem City,* feeling as snooty as the lions in front of the Forty-Second Street Library, for instance. So far as my feelings are concerned, Peggy Hopkins Joyce on the Boule Mich[13] with her gorgeous raiment, stately carriage, knees knocking together in a most aristocratic manner, has nothing on me. The cosmic Zora emerges. I belong to no race nor time. I am the eternal feminine with its string of beads.

I have no separate feeling about being an American citizen and colored. I am merely a fragment of the Great Soul that surges within the boundaries. My country, right or wrong.*

Sometimes, I feel discriminated against, but it does not make me angry. It merely astonishes me. How *can* any deny themselves the pleasure of my company? It's beyond me. 15

---

12 *assegai* Spear made of a tree of the same name, used by people of southern Africa.
13 *Peggy Hopkins Joyce* White American actress (1893–1957) known for her extravagant lifestyle; *Boule Mich* Boulevard Saint-Michel, a major street in Paris.

But in the main, I feel like a brown bag of miscellany propped against a wall. Against a wall in company with other bags, white, red and yellow. Pour out the contents, and there is discovered a jumble of small things priceless and worthless. A first-water[14] diamond, an empty spool, bits of broken glass, lengths of string, a key to a door long since crumbled away, a rusty knife-blade, old shoes saved for a road that never was and never will be, a nail bent under the weight of things too heavy for any nail, a dried flower or two still a little fragrant. In your hand is the brown bag. On the ground before you is the jumble it held—so much like the jumble in the bags, could they be emptied, that all might be dumped in a single heap and the bags refilled without altering the content of any greatly. A bit of colored glass more or less would not matter. Perhaps that is how the Great Stuffer of Bags filled them in the first place—who knows?

(1928)

Questions

1. How does Hurston see her own generation in relation to the generations of African Americans before her? How does she see her position in comparison to that of white Americans of her own time?

2. When does Hurston feel most "colored"? How are her feelings connected to a larger history of American Americans in America?

3. Write a short essay reflecting on the relationship between your race and your identity.

4. What was the young Zora Neale Hurston like? What was her experience of race and racism in Eatonville?

5. What does Hurston mean when she says she is "too busy sharpening [her] oyster knife" to "weep at the world"?

6. What metaphor does Hurston use at the close of this essay to describe a human being? What does the metaphor suggest about race?

---

14 *first-water*   Best quality of diamond or other gem.

JAMES BALDWIN

STRANGER IN THE VILLAGE

*Perhaps no American essayist is better known for insight into the
nuances of race, class, nationality, and sexual orientation than
James Baldwin. In the face of persecution both as a Black man
and as a gay man, Baldwin left the United States for France in
1948, aged 24. The essay reprinted here, the occasion for which
is Baldwin's visit to the Swiss village of Leukerbad in 1951, first
appeared in the October, 1953 issue of* Harper's Magazine; *it was
then included in Baldwin's groundbreaking 1955 collection* Notes
of a Native Son. *Baldwin does not give the name of the village; nor
does he mention that he was there because the family of his lover
owned a nearby chalet where he could stay. But he provides a great
deal else that sheds light on what it meant to be an American—and
to be a Black American—in the middle of the twentieth century.*

From all available evidence no black man had ever set foot in this tiny Swiss
village before I came. I was told before arriving that I would probably be a
"sight" for the village; I took this to mean that people of my complexion were
rarely seen in Switzerland, and also that city people are always something of
a "sight" outside of the city. It did not occur to me—possibly because I am an
American—that there could be people anywhere who had never seen a Negro.

It is a fact that cannot be explained on the basis of the inaccessibility of
the village. The village is very high, but it is only four hours from Milan and
three hours from Lausanne. It is true that it is virtually unknown. Few people
making plans for a holiday would elect to come here. On the other hand, the
villagers are able, presumably, to come and go as they please—which they do:
to another town at the foot of the mountain, with a population of approximately
five thousand, the nearest place to see a movie or go to the bank. In the village
there is no movie house, no bank, no library, no theater; very few radios, one
jeep, one station wagon; and at the moment, one typewriter, mine, an invention
which the woman next door to me here had never seen. There are about six
hundred people living here, all Catholic—I conclude this from the fact that the
Catholic church is open all year round, whereas the Protestant chapel, set off on

113

a hill a little removed from the village, is open only in the summertime when the tourists arrive. There are four or five hotels, all closed now, and four or five bistros, of which, however, only two do any business during the winter. These two do not do a great deal, for life in the village seems to end around nine or ten o'clock. There are a few stores, butcher, baker, epicerie,[1] a hardware store, and a money-changer—who cannot change travelers' checks, but must send them down to the bank, an operation which takes two or three days. There is something called the Ballet Haus, closed in the winter and used for God knows what, certainly not ballet, during the summer. There seems to be only one school house in the village, and this for the quite young children; I suppose this to mean that their older brothers and sisters at some point descend from these mountains in order to complete their education—possibly, again, to the town just below. The landscape is absolutely forbidding, mountains towering on all four sides, ice and snow as far as the eye can reach. In this white wilderness, men and women and children move all day, carrying washing, wood, buckets of milk or water, sometimes skiing on Sunday afternoons. All week long boys and young men are to be seen shoveling snow off the rooftops, or dragging wood down from the forest in sleds.

The village's only real attraction, which explains the tourist season, is the hot spring water. A disquietingly high proportion of these tourists are cripples, or semi-cripples, who come year after year—from other parts of Switzerland, usually—to take the waters. This lends the village, at the height of the season, a rather terrifying air of sanctity, as though it were a lesser Lourdes.* There is often something beautiful, there is always something awful, in the spectacle of a person who has lost one of his faculties, a faculty he never questioned until it was gone, and who struggles to recover it. Yet people remain people, on crutches or indeed on deathbeds; and wherever I passed, the first summer I was here, among the native villagers or among the lame, a wind passed with me—of astonishment, curiosity, amusement and outrage. That first summer I stayed two weeks and never intended to return. But I did return in the winter, to work; the village offers, obviously, no distractions whatever and has the further advantage of being extremely cheap. Now it is winter again, a year later, and I am here again. Everyone in the village knows my name, though they scarcely ever use it, knows that I come from America though, this, apparently, they will never really believe: black men come from Africa—and everyone knows that I am the friend of the son of a woman who was born here, and that I am staying in their chalet. But I remain as much a stranger today as I was the first day I arrived, and the children shout *Neger! Neger!*[2] as I walk along the streets.

---

1   *epicerie*   Grocery store.
2   *Neger*   German: black, "negro."

It must be admitted that in the beginning I was far too shocked to have any real reaction. In so far as I reacted at all, I reacted by trying to be pleasant—it being a great part of the American Negro's education (long before he goes to school) that he must make people like him. This smile-and-the-world-smiles-with-you routine worked about as well in this situation as it had in the situation for which it was designed, which is to say that it did not work at all. No one, after all, can be liked whose human weight and complexity cannot be, or has not been, admitted. My smile was simply another unheard-of phenomenon which allowed them to see my teeth—they did not, really, see my smile and I began to think that, should I take to snarling, no one would notice any difference. All of the physical characteristics of the Negro which had caused me, in America, a very different and almost forgotten pain were nothing less than miraculous—or infernal*—in the eyes of the village people. Some thought my hair was the color of tar, that it had the texture of wire, or the texture of cotton. It was jocularly suggested that I might let it all grow long and make myself a winter coat. If I sat in the sun for more than five minutes some daring creature was certain to come along and gingerly put his fingers on my hair, as though he were afraid of an electric shock, or put his hand on my hand, astonished that the color did not rub off. In all of this, in which it must be conceded there was the charm of genuine wonder and in which there were certainly no element of intentional unkindness, there was yet no suggestion that I was human: I was simply a living wonder.

I knew that they did not mean to be unkind, and I know it now; it is necessary, nevertheless, for me to repeat this to my self each time that I walk out of the chalet. The children who shout *Neger!* have no way of knowing the echoes this sound raises in me. They are brimming with good humor and the more daring swell with pride when I stop to speak with them. Just the same, there are days when I cannot pause and smile, when I have no heart to play with them; when, indeed, I mutter sourly to myself, exactly as I muttered on the streets of a city these children have never seen, when I was no bigger than these children are now: Your mother was a nigger. Joyce is right about history being a nightmare[3]—but it may be the nightmare from which no one can awaken. People are trapped in history and history is trapped in them.

There is a custom in the village—I am told it is repeated in many villages—of buying African natives for the purpose of converting them to Christianity. There stands in the church all year round a small box with a slot for money, decorated with a black figurine, and into this box the villagers drop their francs.

5

---

3 *Joyce ... a nightmare* In James Joyce's novel *Ulysses*, the protagonist (Stephen Dedalus) at one point makes the following statement: "History is a nightmare from which I am trying to awake."

During the carnival which precedes Lent, two village children have their faces blackened—out of which bloodless darkness their blue eyes shine like ice—and fantastic horsehair wigs are placed on their blond heads; thus disguised, they solicit among the villagers for money for the missionaries in Africa. Between the box in the church and blackened children, the village "bought" last year six or eight African natives. This was reported to me with pride by the wife of one of the bistro owners and I was careful to express astonishment and pleasure at the solicitude shown by the village for the souls of black folks. The bistro owner's wife beamed with a pleasure far more genuine than my own and seemed to feel that I might now breathe more easily concerning the souls of at least six of my kinsmen.

I tried not to think of these so lately baptized kinsmen, of the price paid for them, or the peculiar price they themselves would pay, and said nothing about my father, who having taken his own conversion too literally never, at bottom, forgave the white world (which he described as heathen) for having saddled him with a Christ in whom, to judge at least from their treatment of him, they themselves no longer believed. I thought of white men arriving for the first time in an African village, strangers there, as I am a stranger here, and tried to imagine the astounded populace touching their hair and marveling at the color of their skin. But there is a great difference between being the first white man to be seen by Africans and being the first black man to be seen by whites. The white man takes the astonishment as tribute, for he arrives to conquer and to convert the natives, whose inferiority in relation to himself is not even to be questioned; whereas I, without a thought of conquest, find myself among a people whose culture controls me, has even, in a sense, created me, people who have cost me more in anguish and rage than they will ever know, who yet do not even know of my existence. The astonishment, with which I might have greeted them, should they have stumbled into my African village a few hundred years ago, might have rejoiced their hearts. But the astonishment with which they greet me today can only poison mine.

And this is so despite everything I may do to feel differently, despite my friendly conversations with the bistro owner's wife, despite their three-year-old son who has at last become my friend, despite the *saluts* and *bonsoirs*[4] which I exchange with people as I walk, despite the fact that I know that no individual can be taken to task for what history is doing, or has done. I say that the culture of these people controls me—but they can scarcely be held responsible for European culture. America comes out of Europe, but these people have never seen America, nor have most of them seen more of Europe than the hamlet at the foot of their mountain. Yet they move with an authority which I shall

4 *saluts and bonsoirs* Greetings.

never have; and they regard me, quite rightly, not only as a stranger in the village but as a suspect latecomer, bearing no credentials, to everything they have—however unconsciously—inherited.

For this village, even were it incomparably more remote and incredibly more primitive, is the West, the West on to which I have been so strangely grafted. These people cannot be, from the point of view of power, strangers anywhere in the world; they have made the modern world, in effect, even if they do not know it. The most illiterate among them is related, in a way that I am not, to Dante, Shakespeare, Michelangelo, Aeschylus, Da Vinci, Rembrandt, and Racine;* the cathedral at Chartres[5] says something to them which it cannot say to me, as indeed would New York's Empire State Building,* should anyone here ever see it. Out of their hymns and dances come Beethoven and Bach.* Go back a few centuries and they are in their full glory—but I am in Africa, watching the conquerors arrive.

The rage of the disesteemed is personally fruitless, but it is also absolutely inevitable: the rage, so generally discounted, so little understood even among the people whose daily bread it is, is one of the things that makes history. Rage can only with difficulty, and never entirely, be brought under the domination of the intelligence and is therefore not susceptible to any arguments whatever. This is a fact which ordinary representatives of the Herrenvolk,[6] having never felt this rage and being unable to imagine, quite fail to understand. Also, rage cannot be hidden, it can only be dissembled. This dissembling deludes the thoughtless, and strengthens rage and adds, to rage, contempt. There are, no doubt, as many ways of coping with the resulting complex of tensions as there are black men in the world, but no black man can hope ever to be entirely liberated from this internal warfare-rage, dissembling, and contempt having inevitably accompanied his first realization of the power of white men. What is crucial here is that since white men represent in the black man's world so heavy a weight, white men have for black men a reality which is far from being reciprocal; and hence all black men have toward all white men an attitude which is designed, really, either to rob the white man of the jewel of his naiveté, or else to make it cost him dear.

The black man insists, by whatever means he finds at his disposal, that the white man cease to regard him as an exotic rarity and recognize him as a human being. This is a very charged and difficult moment, for there is a great

10

---

5   *cathedral at Chartres*   Renowned as among the most impressive and beautiful Gothic cathedrals, Chartres has been described as one of the finest achievements of European civilization.

6   *Herrenvolk*   Nazi term meaning "master race," most often used in reference to peoples of Nordic/Aryan descent.

deal of will power involved in the white man's naiveté. Most people are not naturally reflective any more than they are naturally malicious, and the white man prefers to keep the black man at a certain human remove because it is easier for him thus to preserve his simplicity and avoid being called to account for crimes committed by his forefathers, or his neighbors. He is inescapably aware, nevertheless, that he is in a better position in the world than black men are, nor can he quite put to death the suspicion that he is hated by black men therefore. He does not wish to be hated, neither does he wish to change places, and at this point in his uneasiness he can scarcely avoid having recourse to those legends which white men have created about black men, the most usual effect of which is that the white man finds himself enmeshed, so to speak, in his own language which describes hell, as well as the attributes which lead one to hell, as being as black as night.

Every legend, moreover, contains its residuum of truth, and the root function of language is to control the universe by describing it. It is of quite considerable significance that black men remain, in the imagination, and in overwhelming numbers in fact, beyond the disciplines of salvation; and this despite the fact that the West has been "buying" African natives for centuries. There is, I should hazard, an instantaneous necessity to be divorced from this so visibly unsaved stranger, in whose heart, moreover, one cannot guess what dreams of vengeance are being nourished; and, at the same time, there are few things on earth more attractive than the idea of the unspeakable liberty which is allowed the unredeemed. When, beneath the black mask, a human being begins to make himself felt one cannot escape a certain awful wonder as to what kind of human being it is. What one's imagination makes of other people is dictated, of course, by the Master race laws of one's own personality and it's one of the ironies of black-white relations that, by means of what the white man imagines the black man to be, the black man is enabled to know who the white man is.

I have said, for example, that I am as much a stranger in this village today as I was the first summer I arrived, but this is not quite true. The villagers wonder less about the texture of my hair than they did then, and wonder rather more about me. And the fact that their wonder now exists on another level is reflected in their attitudes and in their eyes. There are the children who make those delightful, hilarious, sometimes astonishingly grave overtures of friendship in the unpredictable fashion of children; other children, having been taught that the devil is a black man, scream in genuine anguish as I approach. Some of the older women never pass without a friendly greeting, never pass, indeed, if it seems that they will be able to engage me in conversation; other women look down or look away or rather contemptuously smirk. Some of the men drink with me and suggest that I learn how to ski—partly, I gather, because they cannot imagine what I would look like on skis—and want to know if I am married, and ask questions about my *métier*.[7] But some of the men have accused *le sale negre*[8]—behind my back—of stealing wood and there is already in the eyes of some of them that peculiar, intent, paranoiac malevolence which one sometimes surprises in the eyes of American white men when, out walking with their Sunday girl,* they see a Negro male approach.

There is a dreadful abyss between the streets of this village and the streets of the city in which I was born, between the children who shout *Neger!* today and those who shouted Nigger! yesterday—the abyss is experience, the American experience. The syllable hurled behind me today expresses, above all, wonder: I am a stranger here. But, I am not a stranger in America and the same syllable riding on the American air expresses the war my presence has occasioned in the American soul. For this village brings home to me this fact: that there was a day, and not really a very distant day, when Americans were scarcely Americans at all but discontented Europeans, facing a great unconquered continent and strolling, say, into a marketplace and seeing black men for the first time. The shock this spectacle afforded is suggested, surely, by the promptness with which they decided that these black men were not really men but cattle. It is true that the necessity on the part of the settlers of the New World of reconciling their moral assumptions with the fact—and the necessity—of slavery enhanced immensely the charm of this idea, and it is also true that this idea expresses, with a truly American bluntness, the attitude which to varying extents all masters have had toward all slaves.

But between all former slaves and slave-owners and the drama which begins for Americans over three hundred years ago at Jamestown, there are at least two differences to be observed. The American Negro slave could not suppose, for one thing, as slaves in past epochs had supposed and often done, that he would ever be able to wrest the power from his master's hands. This was a supposition which the modern era, which was to bring about such vast changes in the aims and dimensions of power, put to death; it only begins in unprecedented fashion, and with dreadful implications, to be resurrected, today. But even had this supposition persisted with undiminished force, the American Negro slave could not have used it to lend his condition dignity, for the reason that this supposition rests on another: that the slave in exile yet remains related to his past, has some means—if only in memory—of revering and sustaining the forms of his former life, is able, in short, to maintain his identity.

This was not the case with the American Negro slave. He is unique among the black men of the world in that his past was taken from him, almost literally, at one blow. One wonders what on earth the first slave found to say to the first

15

---

7   *métier*   French: profession, set of skills.

8   *le sale negre*   French: the dirty Black [person].

dark child he bore. I am told that there are Haitians able to trace their ancestry back to African kings, but any American Negro wishing to go back so far will find his journey through time abruptly arrested by the signature on the bill of sale which served as the entrance paper for his ancestor. At the time—to say nothing of the circumstances—of the enslavement of the captive black man who was to become the American Negro, there was not the remotest possibility that he would ever take power from his master's hands. There was no reason to suppose that his situation would ever change, nor was there, shortly, anything to indicate that his situation had ever been different. It was his necessity, in the words of E. Franklin Frazier, to find a "motive for living under American culture or die." The identity of the American Negro comes out of this extreme situation, and the evolution of this identity was a source of the most intolerable anxiety in the minds and the lives of his masters.

For the history of the American Negro is unique also in this: that the question of his humanity, and of his rights therefore as a human being, became a burning one for several generations of Americans, so burning a question that it ultimately became one of those used to divide the nation. It is out of this argument that the venom of the epithet *Nigger!* is derived. It is an argument which Europe has never had, and hence Europe quite sincerely fails to understand how or why the argument arose in the first place, why its effects are frequently disastrous and always so unpredictable, why it refuses until today to be entirely settled. Europe's black possessions remained—and do remain—in Europe's colonies, at which remove they represented no threat whatever to European identity. If they posed any problem at all for the European conscience, it was a problem which remained comfortingly abstract: in effect, the black man, as a man, did not exist for Europe. But in America, even as a slave, he was an inescapable part of the general social fabric and no American could escape having an attitude toward him. Americans attempt until today to make an abstraction of the Negro, but the very nature of these abstractions reveals the tremendous effects the presence of the Negro has had on the American character.

When one considers the history of the Negro in America it is of the greatest importance to recognize that the moral beliefs of a person, or a people, are never really as tenuous as life—which is not moral—very often causes them to appear; these create for them a frame of reference and a necessary hope, the hope being that when life has done its worst they will be enabled to rise above themselves and to triumph over life. Life would scarcely be bearable if this hope did not exist. Again, even when the worst has been said, to betray a belief is not by any means to have put oneself beyond its power; the betrayal of a belief is not the same thing as ceasing to believe. If this were not so there would be no moral standards in the world at all. Yet one must also recognize that morality is based on ideas and that all ideas are dangerous—dangerous because ideas can only lead to action and where the action leads no man can say. And dangerous in this respect: that confronted with the impossibility of remaining faithful to one's beliefs, and the equal impossibility of becoming free of them, one can be driven to the most inhuman excesses. The ideas on which American beliefs are based are not, though Americans often seem to think so, ideas which originated in America. They came out of Europe. And the establishment of democracy on the American continent was scarcely as radical a break with the past as was the necessity, which Americans faced, of broadening this concept to include black men. This was, literally, a hard necessity. It was impossible, for one thing, for Americans to abandon their beliefs, not only because these beliefs alone seemed able to justify the sacrifices they had endured and the blood that they had spilled, but also because these beliefs afforded them their only bulwark against a moral chaos as absolute as the physical chaos of the continent it was their destiny to conquer. But in the situation in which Americans found themselves, these beliefs threatened an idea which, whether or not one likes to think so, is the very warp and woof[9] of the heritage of the West, the idea of white supremacy.

Americans have made themselves notorious by the shrillness and the brutality with which they have insisted on this idea, but they did not invent it; and it has escaped the world's notice that those very excesses of which Americans have been guilty imply a certain, unprecedented uneasiness over the idea's life and power, if not, indeed, the idea's validity. The idea of white supremacy rests simply on the fact that white men are the creators of civilization (the present civilization, which is the only one that matters; all previous civilizations are simply contributions to our own) and are therefore civilization's guardians and defenders. Thus it was impossible for Americans to accept the black man as one of themselves, for to do so was to jeopardize their status as white men. But not so to accept him was to deny his human reality, his human weight and complexity, and the strain of denying the overwhelmingly undeniable forced Americans into rationalizations so fantastic that they approached the pathological.

At the root of the American Negro problem is the necessity of the American white man to find a way of living with the Negro in order to be able to live with himself. And the history of this problem can be reduced to the means used by Americans—lynch law* and law, segregation and legal acceptance, terrorization and concession—either to come to terms with this necessity, or to find a way around it, or (most usually) to find a way of doing both these things at once. The resulting spectacle, at once foolish and dreadful, led someone to

20

---

9   *warp and woof*   Threads in any woven material; the "warp" threads run at a right angle to the "woof."

make the quite accurate observation that "the Negro-in-America is a form of insanity which overtakes white men."

In this long battle, a battle by no means finished, the unforeseeable effects of which will be felt by many future generations, the white man's motive was the protection of his identity; the black man was motivated by the need to establish an identity. And despite the terrorization which the Negro in America endured and endures sporadically until today, despite the cruel and totally inescapable ambivalence of his status in his country, the battle for his identity has long ago been won. He is not a visitor to the West, but a citizen there, an American; as American as the Americans who despise him, the Americans who fear him, the Americans who love him—the Americans who became less than themselves, or rose to be greater than themselves by virtue of the fact that the challenge he represented was inescapable. He is perhaps the only black man in the world whose relationship to white men is more terrible, more subtle, and more meaningful than the relationship of bitter possessed to uncertain possessors. His survival depended, and his development depends, on his ability to turn his peculiar status in the Western world to his own advantage and, it may be, to the very great advantage of that world. It remains for him to fashion out of his experience that which will give him sustenance, and a voice. The cathedral at Chartres, I have said, says something to the people of this village which it cannot say to me; but it is important to understand that, this cathedral says something to me which it cannot say to them. Perhaps they are struck by the power of the spires, the glory of the windows; but they have known God, after all, longer than I have known him, and in a different way, and I am terrified by the slippery bottomless well to be found in the crypt, down which heretics were hurled to death,* and by the obscene, inescapable gargoyles* jutting out of the stone and seeming to say that God and the devil can never be divorced. I doubt that the villagers think of the devil when they face a cathedral because they have never been identified with the devil. But I must accept the status which myth, if nothing else, gives me in the West before I can hope to change the myth.

Yet, if the American Negro has arrived at his identity by virtue of the absoluteness of his estrangement from his past, American white men still nourish the illusion that there is some means of recovering the European innocence, of returning to a state in which black men do not exist. This is one of the greatest errors Americans can make. The identity they fought so hard to protect has, by virtue of that battle, undergone a change: Americans are as unlike any other white people in the world as it is possible to be. I do not think, for example, that it is too much to suggest that the American vision of the world—which allows so little reality, generally speaking, for any of the darker forces in human life, which tends until today to paint moral issues in glaring black and white—owes a great deal to the battle waged by Americans to maintain between themselves and black men a human separation which could not be bridged. It is only now beginning to be borne in on us—very faintly, it must be admitted, very slowly, and very much against our will—that this vision of the world is dangerously inaccurate, and perfectly useless. For it protects our moral high-mindedness at the terrible expense of weakening our grasp of reality. People who shut their eyes to reality simply invite their own destruction, and anyone who insists on remaining in a state of innocence long after that innocence is dead turns himself into a monster.

The time has come to realize that the interracial drama acted out on the American continent has not only created a new black man, it has created a new white man, too. No road whatever will lead Americans back to the simplicity of this European village where white men still have the luxury of looking on me as a stranger. I am not, really, a stranger any longer for any American alive. One of the things that distinguishes Americans from other people is that no other people has ever been so deeply involved in the lives of black men, and vice versa. This fact faced, with all its implications, it can be seen that the history of the American Negro problem is not merely shameful, it is also something of an achievement. For even when the worst has been said, it must also be added that the perpetual challenge posed by this problem was always, somehow, perpetually met. It is precisely this black-white experience which may prove of indispensable value to us in the world we face today. This world is white no longer, and it will never be white again.

(1953)

Questions

1. How difficult is it for humans to separate our perceptions of culture from our perceptions of race? To what extent would living in a culture other than that in which a person was brought up help make perceptions clearer on these issues?

2. How was Baldwin a stranger in the village? How does he communicate being a stranger to his audience, which was mostly comprised of well-educated white Americans?

3. In what ways is Baldwin's argument about African Americans and their inability to trace their own history complicated by ancestry testing? What, do you think, would Baldwin say about this new technology and what it could offer African Americans?

4. To what extent (if at all) are Baldwin's observations of race relations in 1950s America still true of America in the present? What, if anything, has changed? What, if anything, remains the same?

5. In paragraph 5, Baldwin says the following: "I knew that they did not mean to be unkind, and I know it now; it is necessary, nevertheless, for me to repeat this to my self each time that I walk out of the chalet." Why must Baldwin repeat such a mantra to himself? In what ways is Baldwin commenting on a larger system of oppression, one that he chooses to negotiate with himself via language?

6. How does the tone of the essay change as Baldwin progresses from one topic to another?

IF BLACK ENGLISH ISN'T A LANGUAGE, THEN TELL ME, WHAT IS?

Although he spent most of his adult life in France, James Baldwin, born in Harlem,* made a profound intellectual contribution to the Civil Rights Movement through both fiction and nonfiction. From his position as an expatriate writer, Baldwin was able to give essential insight into the system of racial prejudice that shaped all aspects of life in his home country. The following essay, which Baldwin wrote at his home in the French village of St. Paul de Vence, was first published in the New York Times *Books section in 1979.*

The argument concerning the use, or the status, or the reality, of black English is rooted in American history and has absolutely nothing to do with the question the argument supposes itself to be posing. The argument has nothing to do with language itself but with the *role* of language. Language, incontestably, reveals the speaker. Language, also, far more dubiously, is meant to define the other—and, in this case, the other is refusing to be defined by a language that has never been able to recognize him.

People evolve a language in order to describe and thus control their circumstances, or in order not to be submerged by a reality that they cannot articulate. (And, if they cannot articulate it, they *are* submerged.) A Frenchman living in Paris speaks a subtly and crucially different language from that of the man living in Marseilles; neither sounds very much like a man living in Quebec; and they would all have great difficulty in apprehending what the man from Guadeloupe, or Martinique, is saying, to say nothing of the man from Senegal—although the "common" language of all these areas is French. But each has paid, and is paying, a different price for this "common" language, in which, as it turns out, they are not saying, and cannot be saying, the same things: They each have very different realities to articulate, or control.

What joins all languages, and all men, is the necessity to confront life, in order, not inconceivably, to outwit death: The price for this is the acceptance, and achievement, of one's temporal identity.[10] So that, for example, though it is not taught in the schools (and this has the potential of becoming a political issue) the south of France still clings to its ancient and musical Provençal, which resists being described as a "dialect." And much of the tension in the Basque countries, and in Wales,[11] is due to the Basque and Welsh determination not to allow their languages to be destroyed. This determination also feeds the flames in Ireland for among the many indignities the Irish have been forced to undergo at English hands is the English contempt for their language.

It goes without saying, then, that language is also a political instrument, means, and proof of power. It is the most vivid and crucial key to identity: It reveals the private identity, and connects one with, or divorces one from, the larger, public, or communal identity. There have been, and are, times, and places, when to speak a certain language could be dangerous, even fatal. Or, one may speak the same language, but in such a way that one's antecedents are revealed, or (one hopes) hidden. This is true in France, and is absolutely true in England: The range (and reign) of accents on that damp little island make England coherent for the English and totally incomprehensible for everyone else. To open your mouth in England is (if I may use black English) to "put your business in the street": You have confessed your parents, your youth, your school, your salary, your self-esteem, and, alas, your future.

Now, I do not know what white Americans would sound like if there had never been any black people in the United States, but they would not sound the way they sound. *Jazz*, for example, is a very specific sexual term, as in *jazz*

5

---

10   *temporal identity*   Identity as manifested in time (during earthly, rather than eternal, life).

11   *Basque countries*   Area in the western Pyrenees mountains made up of the Basque Country and Navarre in Spain and the Northern Basque Country in France;   *tension ... Wales*   The peoples of Wales and of the Basque Country have their own distinctive languages and cultures within the larger country that governs them (England and Spain, respectively). In both cases, political tension and conflict surrounds these peoples' efforts to achieve self-governance as a means of preserving cultural identities.

me, baby, but white people purified it into the Jazz Age. *Sock it to me,* which means, roughly, the same thing, has been adopted by Nathaniel Hawthorne's descendants[12] with no qualms or hesitations at all, along with *let it all hang out* and *right on! Beat to his socks* which was once the black's most total and despairing image of poverty, was transformed into a thing called the Beat Generation,[13] which phenomenon was, largely, composed of *uptight*, middle-class white people, imitating poverty, trying to *get down*, to get *with it*, doing their *thing*, doing their despairing best to be *funky*, which we, the blacks, never dreamed of doing—we *were* funky, baby, like *funk* was going out of style.

Now, no one can eat his cake, and have it, too,* and it is late in the day to attempt to penalize black people for having created a language that permits the nation its only glimpse of reality, a language without which the nation would be even more *whipped* than it is.

I say that the present skirmish is rooted in American history, and it is. Black English is the creation of the black diaspora.[14] Blacks came to the United States chained to each other, but from different tribes: Neither could speak the other's language. If two black people, at that bitter hour of the world's history, had been able to speak to each other, the institution of chattel slavery could never have lasted as long as it did. Subsequently, the slave was given, under the eye, and the gun, of his master, Congo Square,[15] and the Bible—or, in other words, and under these conditions, the slave began the formation of the black church, and it is within this unprecedented tabernacle that black English began to be formed. This was not, merely, as in the European example, the adoption of a foreign tongue, but an alchemy that transformed ancient elements into a new language: *A language comes into existence by means of brutal necessity, and the rules of the language are dictated by what the language must convey.*

---

12 *Nathaniel Hawthorne's descendants* Hawthorne (1804–64) was a nineteenth-century white American writer. He was descended from Puritans who immigrated to America in the early seventeenth century. His work explores themes of inherited guilt, sin, and evil.

13 *Beat Generation* Literary movement in the 1950s that rejected mainstream American culture, seeking to escape materialism and find spiritual and sexual liberation.

14 *black diaspora* People with ancestral roots in Africa who now live in other places.

15 *Congo Square* Open space in what is now Louis Armstrong Park in Tremé, New Orleans, where, in 1817, the mayor gave permission for slaves to gather on Sundays. Hundreds of slaves would come to dance, sing, make music, and attend voodoo ceremonies. The gatherings were notable for the bringing together of many traditional practices (and languages) of the various tribes from which the slaves had been taken. The meetings in Congo Square dwindled in the decade preceding Emancipation, but its dances, music, and rituals evolved into jazz and are still present in various forms in New Orleans today.

There was a moment, in time, and in this place, when my brother, or my mother, or my father, or my sister, had to convey to me, for example, the danger in which I was standing from the white man standing just behind me, and to convey this with a speed, and in a language, that the white man could not possibly understand, and that, indeed, he cannot understand, until today. He cannot afford to understand it. This understanding would reveal to him too much about himself, and smash that mirror before which he has been frozen for so long.

Now, if this passion, this skill, this (to quote Toni Morrison[16]) "sheer intelligence," this incredible music, the mighty achievement of having brought a people utterly unknown to, or despised by "history"—to have brought this people to their present, troubled, troubling, and unassailable and unanswerable place—if this absolutely unprecedented journey does not indicate that black English is a language, I am curious to know what definition of language is to be trusted.

A people at the center of the Western world, and in the midst of so hostile a population, has not endured and transcended by means of what is patronizingly called a "dialect." We, the blacks, are in trouble, certainly, but we are not doomed, and we are not inarticulate because we are not compelled to defend a morality that we know to be a lie.

10

The brutal truth is that the bulk of white people in America never had any interest in educating black people, except as this could serve white purposes. It is not the black child's language that is in question, it is not his language that is despised: It is his experience. A child cannot be taught by anyone who despises him, and a child cannot afford to be fooled. A child cannot be taught by anyone whose demand, essentially, is that the child repudiate his experience, and all that gives him sustenance, and enter a limbo in which he will no longer be black, and in which he knows that he can never become white. Black people have lost too many black children that way.

And, after all, finally, in a country with standards so untrustworthy, a country that makes heroes of so many criminal mediocrities, a country unable to face why so many of the nonwhite are in prison, or on the needle,* or standing, futureless, in the streets—it may very well be that both the child, and his elder, have concluded that they have nothing whatever to learn from the people of a country that has managed to learn so little.

(1979)

---

16 *Toni Morrison* Prominent African American writer and Nobel prize winner, best known for her novel *Beloved* (1998).

Questions

1. Look up how linguists define "dialect" and "language." Why does Baldwin view the label "dialect" as insulting when applied to the language spoken by African Americans? Do you agree with him?

2. Baldwin writes that Black language "permits the nation its only glimpse of reality" (paragraph 6). What does this mean?

3. Baldwin offers many reasons why African Americans developed a unique language in America. Summarize three of them. Are there others that you can think of that aren't mentioned here?

4. Research the Beat Generation. Why does Baldwin disapprove of this movement?

5. In the closing paragraphs of the essay, Baldwin moves from his discussion of language to that of education. What point does this essay make about the connection between the two?

6. According to Baldwin, how can language give power, and how can it limit power? How does this relate to its function as the "key to identity" (paragraph 4)?

7. Consider the last paragraph of this essay. Does this paragraph suggest that Baldwin is hopeful about the future of race relations in America? Why or why not?

8. Research a relatively recent borrowing from Black language into white speech (consider, for example, "to throw shade," "yas"/"yas queen," or "bae"). Given the history of the word you researched, do you think non-Black people ought not to use it? Why or why not?

FRANTZ FANON

from THE WRETCHED OF THE EARTH[1]

*Born to middle-class parents on the island of Martinique (then
a French colony), Frantz Fanon is one of the twentieth century's
most influential thinkers on the subjects of colonialism and racial
oppression. His work builds upon that of European political
philosophers such as Karl Marx and G.W.F. Hegel and that of
Black Francophone intellectuals such as Aimé Césaire; it also
draws upon Fanon's own experiences as a psychologist in Algeria,
where many of his patients were traumatized by fighting for or
against the colony's independence from France. His work has had
a global influence on anticolonial activists and intellectuals, and is
particularly important in the scholarly realms of postcolonial and
critical race theory, where his works such as* Black Skin, White
Masks *(1952) and* The Wretched of the Earth *(1961) are considered
foundational texts. The following selection is from the opening
pages of the latter, which is perhaps his best-known work.*

ON VIOLENCE

National liberation, national reawakening, restoration of the nation to the
people or Commonwealth, whatever the name used, whatever the latest
expression, decolonization is always a violent event. At whatever level we
study it—individual encounters, a change of name for a sports club, the guest
list at a cocktail party, members of a police force or the board of directors of
a state or private bank—decolonization is quite simply the substitution of one
"species" of mankind by another. The substitution is unconditional, absolute,
total, and seamless. We could go on to portray the rise of a new nation, the establishment of a new state, its diplomatic relations and its economic and political orientation. But instead we have decided to describe the kind of tabula rasa[2]
which from the outset defines any decolonization. What is singularly important

---

1   *The Wretched of the Earth*   Translated from the French by Richard Philcox, 2004.
2   *tabula rasa*   Latin: blank (or erased) slate.

is that it starts from the very first day with the basic claims of the colonized. In actual fact, proof of success lies in a social fabric that has been changed inside out. This change is extraordinarily important because it is desired, clamored for, and demanded. The need for this change exists in a raw, repressed, and reckless state in the lives and consciousness of colonized men and women. But the eventuality of such a change is also experienced as a terrifying future in the consciousness of another "species" of men and women: the colons, the colonists.

Decolonization, which sets out to change the order of the world, is clearly an agenda for total disorder. But it cannot be accomplished by the wave of a magic wand, a natural cataclysm, or a gentleman's agreement. Decolonization, we know, is an historical process: In other words, it can only be understood, it can only find its significance and become self coherent insofar as we can discern the history-making movement which gives it form and substance. Decolonization is the encounter between two congenitally antagonistic forces that in fact owe their singularity to the kind of reification secreted and nurtured by the colonial situation. Their first confrontation was colored by violence and their cohabitation—or rather the exploitation of the colonized by the colonizer—continued at the point of the bayonet and under cannon fire. The colonist and the colonized are old acquaintances. And consequently, the colonist is right when he says he "knows" them. It is the colonist who fabricated and continues to fabricate the colonized subject. The colonist derives his validity, i.e., his wealth, from the colonial system.

Decolonization never goes unnoticed, for it focuses on and fundamentally alters being, and transforms the spectator crushed to a nonessential state into a privileged actor, captured in a virtually grandiose fashion by the spotlight of History. It infuses a new rhythm, specific to a new generation of men, with a new language and a new humanity. Decolonization is truly the creation of new men. But such a creation cannot be attributed to a supernatural power: The "thing" colonized becomes a man through the very process of liberation.

Decolonization, therefore, implies the urgent need to thoroughly challenge the colonial situation. Its definition can, if we want to describe it accurately, be summed up in the well-known words: "The last shall be first." Decolonization is verification of this. At a descriptive level, therefore, any decolonization is a success.

5   In its bare reality, decolonization reeks of red-hot cannonballs and bloody knives. For the last can be the first only after a murderous and decisive confrontation between the two protagonists. This determination to have the last

move up to the front, to have them clamber up (too quickly, say some) the famous echelons of an organized society, can only succeed by resorting to every means, including, of course, violence.

You do not disorganize a society, however primitive it may be, with such an agenda if you are not determined from the very start to smash every obstacle encountered. The colonized, who have made up their mind to make such an agenda into a driving force, have been prepared for violence from time immemorial. As soon as they are born it is obvious to them that their cramped world, riddled with taboos, can only be challenged by out and out violence.

The colonial world is a compartmentalized world. It is obviously as superfluous to recall the existence of "native" towns and European towns, of schools for "natives" and schools for Europeans, as it is to recall apartheid in South Africa. Yet if we penetrate inside this compartmentalization we shall at least bring to light some of its key aspects. By penetrating its geographical configuration and classification we shall be able to delineate the backbone on which the decolonized society is reorganized.

The colonized world is a world divided in two. The dividing line, the border, is represented by the barracks and the police stations. In the colonies, the official, legitimate agent, the spokesperson for the colonizer and the regime of oppression, is the police officer or the soldier. In capitalist societies, education, whether secular or religious, the teaching of moral reflexes handed down from father to son, the exemplary integrity of workers decorated after fifty years of loyal and faithful service, the fostering of love for harmony and wisdom, those aesthetic forms of respect for the status quo, instill in the exploited a mood of submission and inhibition which considerably eases the task of the agents of law and order. In capitalist countries a multitude of sermonizers, counselors, and "confusion-mongers" intervene between the exploited and the authorities. In colonial regions, however, the proximity and frequent, direct intervention by the police and the military ensure the colonized are kept under close scrutiny, and contained by rifle butts and napalm.[3] We have seen how the government's agent uses a language of pure violence. The agent does not alleviate oppression or mask domination. He displays and demonstrates them with the clear conscience of the law enforcer, and brings violence into the homes and minds of the colonized subject.

---

3   *napalm* Flammable liquid treated with a gelling agent that causes it to stick to human skin. It was used by French forces to combat independence movements in Algeria (Algerian War of Independence, 1954–62) and Vietnam (First Indochina War, 1946–54); it would later become infamous in association with the Vietnam War (1955–75), where it was used extensively by American forces.

The "native" sector is not complementary to the European sector. The two confront each other, but not in the service of a higher unity. Governed by a purely Aristotelian logic,[4] they follow the dictates of mutual exclusion: There is no conciliation possible, one of them is superfluous. The colonist's sector is a sector built to last, all stone and steel. It's a sector of lights and paved roads, where the trash cans constantly overflow with strange and wonderful garbage, undreamed-of leftovers. The colonist's feet can never be glimpsed, except perhaps in the sea, but then you can never get close enough. They are protected by solid shoes in a sector where the streets are clean and smooth, without a pothole, without a stone. The colonist's sector is a sated, sluggish sector, its belly is permanently full of good things. The colonist's sector is a white folks' sector, a sector of foreigners.

10   The colonized's sector, or at least the "native" quarters, the shanty town, the Medina,[5] the reservation, is a disreputable place inhabited by disreputable people. You are born anywhere, anyhow. You die anywhere, from anything. It's a world with no space, people are piled one on top of the other, the shacks squeezed tightly together. The colonized's sector is a famished sector, hungry for bread, meat, shoes, coal, and light. The colonized's sector is a sector that crouches and cowers, a sector on its knees, a sector that is prostrate. It's a sector of niggers,* a sector of towelheads.* The gaze that the colonized subject casts at the colonist's sector is a look of lust, a look of envy. Dreams of possession. Every type of possession: of sitting at the colonist's table and sleeping in his bed, preferably with his wife. The colonized man is an envious man. The colonist is aware of this as he catches the furtive glance, and constantly on his guard, realizes bitterly that: "They want to take our place." And it's true there is not one colonized subject who at least once a day does not dream of taking the place of the colonist.

This compartmentalized world, this world divided in two, is inhabited by different species. The singularity of the colonial context lies in the fact that economic reality, inequality, and enormous disparities in lifestyles never manage to mask the human reality. Looking at the immediacies of the colonial context, it is clear that what divides this world is first and foremost what species,

4   *Aristotelian logic*   A western form of logic in which certain types of statements taken together lead to a logically necessary conclusion. Basic principles of this form of logic include that no mutually contradictory statements can be true at the same time (it cannot be true both that "it is raining" and that "it is not raining") and that, for any statement, either it is true or the negation of it is true (for example, it must be true either that "it is raining" or that "it is not raining").

5   *Medina*   Name historically given to the portion of a colonized North African city where the country's native inhabitants lived.

what race one belongs to. In the colonies the economic infrastructure is also a superstructure.[6] The cause is effect: You are rich because you are white, you are white because you are rich. This is why a Marxist analysis should always be slightly stretched when it comes to addressing the colonial issue. It is not just the concept of the precapitalist society, so effectively studied by Marx, which needs to be reexamined here. The serf is essentially different from the knight, but a reference to divine right[7] is needed to justify this difference in status. In the colonies the foreigner imposed himself using his cannons and machines. Despite the success of his pacification, in spite of his appropriation, the colonist always remains a foreigner. It is not the factories, the estates, or the bank account which primarily characterize the "ruling class." The ruling species is first and foremost the outsider from elsewhere, different from the indigenous population, "the others."

The violence which governed the ordering of the colonial world, which tirelessly punctuated the destruction of the indigenous social fabric, and demolished unchecked the systems of reference of the country's economy, lifestyles, and modes of dress, this same violence will be vindicated and appropriated when, taking history into their own hands, the colonized swarm into the forbidden cities. To blow the colonial world to smithereens is henceforth a clear image within the grasp and imagination of every colonized subject. To dislocate the colonial world does not mean that once the borders have been eliminated there will be a right of way between the two sectors. To destroy the colonial world means nothing less than demolishing the colonist's sector, burying it deep within the earth or banishing it from the territory....

(1961)

---

6   *economic ... superstructure*   Political theorist Karl Marx described societies as comprised of an economic base, here referred to as infrastructure (meaning the forces of production and division of labor) and a superstructure (meaning culture and political institutions). For Marx, while the superstructure might influence the base to some extent, the base shapes the superstructure much more strongly.

7   *divine right*   Reference to the "divine right of kings," a phrase reflecting the idea that monarchs received their political authority from God (and that therefore the feudal class hierarchy was divinely justified).

Questions

1. Fanon writes that "decolonization is always a violent event" (paragraph 1).

    a. Define "decolonization" and "violent" as they are used in this statement.

    b. What reasons does Fanon give to support his claim that decolonization is always a violent event?

    c. Do you agree with Fanon's characterization of decolonization and its relationship to violence? Why or why not?

2. According to Fanon, how does colonization shape the psyches of colonized individuals? How does it shape the psyches of colonizing individuals?

3. Fanon discusses the differences between the "European sector" and the "colonized's sector."

    a. To what extent are these "sectors" physical spaces, and to what extent are they psychological and/or cultural spaces?

    b. Can the United States today be understood in terms of "European" and "colonized's" sectors? If not, why not? If so, what do these sectors look like in present-day America?

4. What is the tone of this text? Who (if anyone) is this tone likely to appeal to? Who (if anyone) is it likely not to appeal to?

5. In this selection Fanon writes about colonization in general. To what extent do his claims apply to the colonization of Black Americans specifically?

6. Fanon refers to the Marxist concepts of infrastructure (also called economic base) and superstructure. Through your own research, define these concepts; then, explain Fanon's claim that "[i]n the colonies the economic infrastructure is also a superstructure" (paragraph 10).

MARTIN LUTHER KING JR.

LETTER FROM BIRMINGHAM JAIL

In the spring of 1963, Martin Luther King Jr. was among many civil rights activists leading protests against segregation in Birmingham, Alabama. In response to the protests, the city obtained an injunction, making "parading, demonstrating, boycotting," and other nonviolent forms of protest illegal. When King continued, undeterred, he was arrested within two days. The following essay, written during his eight days in jail in Birmingham, is a response to "A Call for Unity," a condemnation of the American Civil Rights Movement by a group of white clergy that had been published in the Birmingham News. *King's letter became perhaps the best known exposition of the principles of the Civil Rights movement.*

King's "Letter from Birmingham Jail" was published in 1963 in several newspapers and periodicals (including The New York Post, Christianity Today, *and* Ebony); *it was also included in his 1964 book,* Why We Can't Wait.

MY DEAR FELLOW CLERGYMEN:

While confined here in the Birmingham city jail, I came across your recent statement calling my present activities "unwise and untimely." Seldom do I pause to answer criticism of my work and ideas. If I sought to answer all the criticisms that cross my desk, my secretaries would have little time for anything other than such correspondence in the course of the day, and I would have no time for constructive work. But since I feel that you are men of genuine good will and that your criticisms are sincerely set forth, I want to try to answer your statement in what I hope will be patient and reasonable terms.

I think I should indicate why I am here in Birmingham, since you have been influenced by the view which argues against "outsiders coming in." I have the honor of serving as president of the Southern Christian Leadership Conference, an organization operating in every southern state, with headquarters in Atlanta, Georgia. We have some eighty-five affiliated organizations across the South, and one of them is the Alabama Christian Movement for

Human Rights. Frequently we share staff, educational, and financial resources with our affiliates. Several months ago the affiliate here in Birmingham asked us to be on call to engage in a nonviolent direct-action program if such were deemed necessary. We readily consented, and when the hour came we lived up to our promise. So I, along with several members of my staff, am here because I was invited here. I am here because I have organizational ties here.

But more basically, I am in Birmingham because injustice is here. Just as the prophets of the eighth century BC left their villages and carried their "thus saith the Lord"* far beyond the boundaries of their home towns, and just as the Apostle Paul left his village of Tarsus and carried the gospel of Jesus Christ to the far corners of the Greco-Roman world, so am I compelled to carry the gospel of freedom beyond my own home town. Like Paul, I must constantly respond to the Macedonian call for aid.[1]

Moreover, I am cognizant of the interrelatedness of all communities and states. I cannot sit idly by in Atlanta and not be concerned about what happens in Birmingham. Injustice anywhere is a threat to justice everywhere. We are caught in an inescapable network of mutuality, tied in a single garment of destiny. Whatever affects one directly, affects all indirectly. Never again can we afford to live with the narrow, provincial "outside agitator" idea. Anyone who lives inside the United States can never be considered an outsider anywhere within its bounds.

5   You deplore the demonstrations taking place in Birmingham. But your statement, I am sorry to say, fails to express a similar concern for the conditions that brought about the demonstrations. I am sure that none of you would want to rest content with the superficial kind of social analysis that deals merely with effects and does not grapple with underlying causes. It is unfortunate that demonstrations are taking place in Birmingham, but it is even more unfortunate that the city's white power structure left the Negro community with no alternative.

In any nonviolent campaign there are four basic steps: collection of the facts to determine whether injustices exist; negotiation; self-purification; and direct action. We have gone through all these steps in Birmingham. There can be no gainsaying the fact that racial injustice engulfs this community. Birmingham is probably the most thoroughly segregated city* in the United States. Its ugly record of brutality is widely known. Negroes have experienced grossly unjust treatment in the courts. There have been more unsolved bombings of Negro homes and churches in Birmingham than in any other city in the nation. These

---

1   *Macedonian call for aid*   According to the New Testament, the Apostle Paul went to preach in Macedonia in response to a vision of a man who said to him, "Come over into Macedonia, and help us" (Acts 16.9).

are the hard, brutal facts of the case. On the basis of these conditions, Negro leaders sought to negotiate with the city fathers. But the latter consistently refused to engage in good-faith negotiation.

Then, last September, came the opportunity to talk with leaders of Birmingham's economic community. In the course of the negotiations, certain promises were made by the merchants—for example, to remove the stores' humiliating racial signs. On the basis of these promises, the Reverend Fred Shuttlesworth and the leaders of the Alabama Christian Movement for Human Rights agreed to a moratorium on all demonstrations. As the weeks and months went by, we realized that we were the victims of a broken promise. A few signs, briefly removed, returned; the others remained.

As in so many past experiences, our hopes had been blasted, and the shadow of deep disappointment settled upon us. We had no alternative except to prepare for direct action, whereby we could present our very bodies as a means of laying our case before the conscience of the local and the national community. Mindful of the difficulties involved, we decided to undertake a process of self-purification. We began a series of workshops on nonviolence, and we repeatedly asked ourselves: "Are you able to accept blows without retaliating?" "Are you able to endure the ordeal of jail?" We decided to schedule our direct-action program for the Easter season, realizing that except for Christmas, this is the main shopping period of the year. Knowing that a strong economic-withdrawal program would be the by-product of direct action, we felt that this would be the best time to bring pressure to bear on the merchants for the needed change.

Then it occurred to us that Birmingham's mayoral election was coming up in March, and we speedily decided to postpone action until after election day. When we discovered that the Commissioner of Public Safety, Eugene "Bull" Connor, had piled up enough votes to be in the run-off, we decided again to postpone action until the day after the run-off so that the demonstrations could not be used to cloud the issues. Like many others, we wanted to see Mr. Connor defeated, and to this end we endured postponement after postponement. Having aided in this community need, we felt that our direct-action program could be delayed no longer.

You may well ask, "Why direct action? Why sit-ins, marches, and so 10 forth? Isn't negotiation a better path?" You are quite right in calling for negotiation. Indeed, this is the very purpose of direct action. Nonviolent direct action seeks so to create such a crisis and foster such tension that a community which has constantly refused to negotiate is forced to confront the issue. It seeks to dramatize the issue that it can no longer be ignored. My citing the creation of tension as part of the work of the nonviolent-resister may sound rather shocking. But I must confess that I am not afraid of the word "tension." I have earnestly opposed violent tension, but there is a type of constructive, nonviolent tension which is necessary for growth. Just as Socrates felt that it was necessary to create a tension in the mind so that individuals could rise from the bondage of myths and half-truths to the unfettered realm of creative analysis and objective appraisal, so must we see the need for nonviolent gadflies[2] to create the kind of tension in society that will help men rise from the dark depths of prejudice and racism to the majestic heights of understanding and brotherhood.

The purpose of our direct-action program is to create a situation so crisis-packed that it will inevitably open the door to negotiation. I therefore concur with you in your call for negotiation. Too long has our beloved Southland been bogged down in a tragic effort to live in monologue rather than dialogue.

One of the basic points in your statement is that the action that I and my associates have taken in Birmingham is untimely. Some have asked: "Why didn't you give the new city administration time to act?" The only answer that I can give to this query is that the new Birmingham administration must be prodded about as much as the outgoing one, before it will act. We are sadly mistaken if we feel that the election of Albert Boutwell as mayor will bring the millennium to Birmingham. While Mr. Boutwell is a much more gentle person than Mr. Connor, they are both segregationists, dedicated to maintenance of the status quo. I have hoped that Mr. Boutwell will be reasonable enough to see the futility of massive resistance to desegregation. But he will not see this without pressure from devotees of civil rights. My friends, I must say to you that we have not made a single gain in civil rights without determined legal and nonviolent pressure. Lamentably, it is an historical fact that privileged groups seldom give up their privileges voluntarily. Individuals may see the moral light and voluntarily give up their unjust posture; but, as Reinhold Niebuhr has reminded us, groups tend to be more immoral than individuals.

We know through painful experience that freedom is never voluntarily given by the oppressor; it must be demanded by the oppressed. Frankly, I have yet to engage in a direct-action campaign that was "well timed" in the view of those who have not suffered unduly from the disease of segregation. For years now I have heard the word "Wait!" It rings in the ear of every Negro with piercing familiarity. This "Wait" has almost always meant "Never." We must come to see, with one of our distinguished jurists, that "justice too long delayed is justice denied."

---

2   *gadflies*   Reference to Plato's *Apology*, an account of the trial of the ancient Athenian philosopher Socrates, who was condemned to death for his philosophical pursuits. As part of his defense, Socrates describes himself as a "gadfly" who helps Athenians by provoking them into alertness as a biting fly irritates a horse into action.

We have waited for more than 340 years for our constitutional and God-given rights. The nations of Asia and Africa are moving with jetlike speed toward gaining political independence, but we still creep at horse-and-buggy pace toward gaining a cup of coffee at a lunch counter. Perhaps it is easy for those who have never felt the stinging darts of segregation to say, "Wait." But when you have seen vicious mobs lynch* your mothers and fathers at will and drown your sisters and brothers at whim; when you have seen hate-filled policemen curse, kick, and even kill your black brothers and sisters; when you see the vast majority of your twenty million Negro brothers smothering in an airtight cage of poverty in the midst of an affluent society; when you suddenly find your tongue twisted and your speech stammering as you seek to explain to your six-year-old daughter why she can't go to the public amusement park that has just been advertised on television, and see tears welling up in her eyes when she is told that Funtown is closed to colored children, and see ominous clouds of inferiority beginning to form in her little mental sky, and see her beginning to distort her personality by developing an unconscious bitterness toward white people; when you have to concoct an answer for a five-year-old son who is asking, "Daddy, why do white people treat colored people so mean?"; when you take a cross-country drive and find it necessary to sleep night after night in the uncomfortable corners of your automobile because no motel will accept you; when you are humiliated day in and day out by nagging signs reading "white" and "colored"; when your first name becomes "nigger," your middle name becomes "boy" (however old you are) and your last name becomes "John," and your wife and mother are never given the respected title "Mrs."; when you are harried by day and haunted by night by the fact that you are a Negro, living constantly at tiptoe stance, never quite knowing what to expect next, and are plagued with inner fears and outer resentments; when you are forever fighting a degenerating sense of "nobodiness"—then you will understand why we find it difficult to wait. There comes a time when the cup of endurance runs over, and men are no longer willing to be plunged into the abyss of despair. I hope, sirs, you can understand our legitimate and unavoidable impatience.

You express a great deal of anxiety over our willingness to break laws. 15
This is certainly a legitimate concern. Since we so diligently urge people to obey the Supreme Court's decision of 1954[3] outlawing segregation in the public schools, at first glance it may seem rather paradoxical for us consciously to break laws. One may well ask: "How can you advocate breaking some laws

---

3   *Supreme Court's decision of 1954*   Brown v. Board of Education, a landmark 1954 Supreme Court case that declared the segregation of schoolchildren on the basis of race to be unconstitutional.

and obeying others?" The answer lies in the fact that there are two types of laws: just and unjust. I would be the first to advocate obeying just laws. One has not only a legal but a moral responsibility to obey just laws. Conversely, one has a moral responsibility to disobey unjust laws. I would agree with St. Augustine[4] that "an unjust law is no law at all."

Now, what is the difference between the two? How does one determine whether a law is just or unjust? A just law is a man-made code that squares with the moral law or the law of God. An unjust law is a code that is out of harmony with the moral law. To put it in the terms of St. Thomas Aquinas: An unjust law is a human law that is not rooted in eternal law and natural law.[5] Any law that uplifts human personality is just. Any law that degrades human personality is unjust. All segregation statutes are unjust because segregation distorts the soul and damages the personality. It gives the segregator a false sense of superiority and the segregated a false sense of inferiority. Segregation, to use the terminology of the Jewish philosopher Martin Buber, substitutes an "I-it" relationship for an "I-thou" relationship and ends up relegating persons to the status of things.[6] Hence segregation is not only politically, economically, and sociologically unsound, it is morally wrong and sinful. Paul Tillich[7] has said that sin is separation. Is not segregation an existential expression of man's tragic separation, his awful estrangement, his terrible sinfulness? Thus it is that I can urge men to obey the 1954 decision of the Supreme Court, for it is morally right; and I can urge them to disobey segregation ordinances, for they are morally wrong.

Let us consider a more concrete example of just and unjust laws. An unjust law is a code that a numerical or power majority group compels a minority group to obey but does not make binding on itself. This is *difference* made legal. By the same token, a just law is a code that a majority compels a minority to follow and that it is willing to follow itself. This is *sameness* made legal.

Let me give another explanation. A law is unjust if it is inflicted on a minority that, as a result of being denied the right to vote, had no part in enacting or

---

4   *St. Augustine*   Early Christian theologian (354–430).

5   *St. Thomas Aquinas*   Medieval Italian philosopher and theologian (1225–74); *eternal law* Law decreed by God; *natural law* Law whose inherent justice can be shown through human reason.

6   *substitutes ... of things*   In his book *I and Thou* (1923), Buber distinguishes between two ways of being: in the "I-it" mode, we encounter others as objects we experience, fully distinct from ourselves, while in the "I-thou" mode we encounter others as whole beings with whom we share relationship.

7   *Paul Tillich*   German-American philosopher and theologian (1886–1965).

devising the law. Who can say that the legislature of Alabama which set up that state's segregation laws was democratically elected? Throughout Alabama all sorts of devious methods are used to prevent Negroes from becoming registered voters, and there are some counties in which, even though Negroes constitute a majority of the population, not a single Negro is registered. Can any law enacted under such circumstances be considered democratically structured?

Sometimes a law is just on its face and unjust in its application. For instance, I have been arrested on a charge of parading without a permit. Now, there is nothing wrong in having an ordinance which requires a permit for a parade. But such an ordinance becomes unjust when it is used to maintain segregation and to deny citizens the First-Amendment privilege* of peaceful assembly and protest.

I hope you are able to see the distinction I am trying to point out. In no sense   20
do I advocate evading or defying the law, as would the rabid segregationist. That would lead to anarchy. One who breaks an unjust law must do so openly, lovingly, and with a willingness to accept the penalty. I submit that an individual who breaks a law that conscience tells him is unjust, and who willingly accepts the penalty of imprisonment in order to arouse the conscience of the community over its injustice, is in reality expressing the highest respect for law.

Of course, there is nothing new about this kind of civil disobedience. It was evidenced sublimely in the refusal of Shadrach, Meshach, and Abednego[8] to obey the laws of Nebuchadnezzar, on the ground that a higher moral law was at stake. It was practiced superbly by the early Christians, who were willing to face hungry lions and the excruciating pain of chopping blocks rather than submit to certain unjust laws of the Roman Empire.[9] To a degree, academic freedom is a reality today because Socrates practiced civil disobedience. In our own nation, the Boston Tea Party[10] represented a massive act of civil disobedience.

We should never forget that everything Adolf Hitler did in Germany was "legal" and everything the Hungarian freedom fighters[11] did in Hungary was "illegal." It was "illegal" to aid and comfort a Jew in Hitler's Germany. Even

---

8   *Shadrach, Meshach, and Abednego*   In Daniel 3.12, three Jews who refused to worship the image of Babylonian King Nebuchadnezzar.

9   *early Christians ... Roman Empire*   The Roman Empire became Christianized under the Emperor Constantine (272–337); before that time Roman authorities frequently persecuted Christians.

10   *Boston Tea Party*   Political demonstration in Boston, Massachusetts, in which protestors destroyed a shipment of tea in defiance of Britain's Tea Act of 1773. The protest is considered a major event in the beginnings of the American Revolution.

11   *Hungarian freedom fighters*   The Hungarian Rebellion in 1956 against an oppressive government was brutally suppressed with the help of the Soviet army.

so, I am sure that, had I lived in Germany at the time, I would have aided and comforted my Jewish brothers. If today I lived in a Communist country where certain principles dear to the Christian faith are suppressed, I would openly advocate disobeying that country's anti-religious laws.

I must make two honest confessions to you, my Christian and Jewish brothers. First, I must confess that over the past few years I have been gravely disappointed with the white moderate. I have almost reached the regrettable conclusion that the Negro's great stumbling block in his stride toward freedom is not the White Citizen's Counciler[12] or the Ku Klux Klanner,* but the white moderate, who is more devoted to "order" than to justice; who prefers a negative peace which is the absence of tension to a positive peace which is the presence of justice; who constantly says, "I agree with you in the goal you seek, but I cannot agree with your methods of direct action"; who paternalistically believes he can set the timetable for another man's freedom; who lives by a mythical concept of time and who constantly advises the Negro to wait for a "more convenient season." Shallow understanding from people of good will is more frustrating than absolute misunderstanding from people of ill will. Lukewarm acceptance is much more bewildering than outright rejection.

I had hoped that the white moderate would understand that law and order exist for the purpose of establishing justice and that when they fail in this purpose they become the dangerously structured dams that block the flow of social progress. I had hoped that the white moderate would understand that the present tension in the South is a necessary phase of the transition from an obnoxious negative peace, in which the Negro passively accepted his unjust plight, to a substantive and positive peace, in which all men will respect the dignity and worth of human personality. Actually, we who engage in nonviolent direct action are not the creators of tension. We merely bring to the surface the hidden tension that is already alive. We bring it out in the open, where it can be seen and dealt with. Like a boil that can never be cured so long as it is covered up but must be opened with all its ugliness to the natural medicines of air and light, injustice must be exposed, with all the tension its exposure creates, to the light of human conscience and the air of national opinion, before it can be cured.

25   In your statement you assert that our actions, even though peaceful, must be condemned because they precipitate violence. But is this a logical assertion? Isn't this like condemning a robbed man because his possession of money precipitated the evil act of robbery? Isn't this like condemning Socrates because his

---

12 *White Citizen's Counciler* Member of the White Citizens' Council, a white supremacist organization that fought desegregation during the mid-twentieth century.

unswerving commitment to truth and his philosophical inquiries precipitated the act by the misguided populace in which they made him drink hemlock? Isn't this like condemning Jesus because his unique God-consciousness and never-ceasing devotion to God's will precipitated the evil act of crucifixion? We must come to see that, as the federal courts have consistently affirmed, it is wrong to urge an individual to cease his efforts to gain his basic constitutional rights because the quest may precipitate violence. Society must protect the robbed and punish the robber.

I had also hoped that the white moderate would reject the myth concerning time in relation to the struggle for freedom. I have just received a letter from a white brother in Texas. He writes: "All Christians know that the colored people will receive equal rights eventually, but it is possible that you are in too great a religious hurry. It has taken Christianity almost two thousand years to accomplish what it has. The teachings of Christ take time to come to earth." Such an attitude stems from a tragic misconception of time, from the strangely irrational notion that there is something in the very flow of time that will inevitably cure all ills. Actually, time itself is neutral; it can be used either destructively or constructively. More and more I feel that the people of ill will have used time much more effectively than have the people of good will. We will have to repent in this generation not merely for the hateful words and actions of the bad people, but for the appalling silence of the good people. Human progress never rolls in on wheels of inevitability; it comes through the tireless efforts of men willing to be co-workers with God, and without this hard work, time itself becomes an ally of the forces of social stagnation. We must use time creatively, in the knowledge that the time is always ripe to do right. Now is the time to make real the promise of democracy and transform our pending national elegy into a creative psalm of brotherhood. Now is the time to lift our national policy from the quicksand of racial injustice to the solid rock of human dignity.

You speak of our activity in Birmingham as extreme. At first I was rather disappointed that fellow clergymen would see my nonviolent efforts as those of an extremist. I began thinking about the fact that I stand in the middle of two opposing forces in the Negro community. One is a force of complacency, made up in part of Negroes who, as a result of long years of oppression, are so drained of self-respect and a sense of "somebodiness" that they have adjusted to segregation; and in part of a few middle-class Negroes who, because of a degree of academic and economic security and because in some ways they profit by segregation, have become insensitive to the problems of the masses. The other force is one of bitterness and hatred, and it comes perilously close to advocating violence. It is expressed in the various black nationalist groups that are springing up across the nation, the largest and best-known being Elijah Muhammad's Muslim movement.[13] Nourished by the Negro's frustration over the continued existence of racial discrimination, this movement is made up of people who have lost faith in America, who have absolutely repudiated Christianity, and who have concluded that the white man is an incorrigible "devil."

I have tried to stand between these two forces, saying that we need emulate neither the "do-nothingism" of the complacent nor the hatred and despair of the black nationalist. For there is the more excellent way of love and nonviolent protest. I am grateful to God that, through the influence of the Negro church, the way of nonviolence became an integral part of our struggle.

If this philosophy had not emerged, by now many streets of the South would, I am convinced, be flowing with blood. And I am further convinced that if our white brothers dismiss as "rabblerousers" and "outside agitators" those of us who employ nonviolent direct action, and if they refuse to support our nonviolent efforts, millions of Negroes will, out of frustration and despair, seek solace and security in black-nationalist ideologies—a development that would inevitably lead to a frightening racial nightmare.

30 Oppressed people cannot remain oppressed forever. The yearning for freedom eventually manifests itself, and that is what has happened to the American Negro. Something within has reminded him of his birthright of freedom, and something without has reminded him that it can be gained. Consciously or unconsciously, he has been caught up by the *Zeitgeist*,* and with his black brothers of Africa and his brown and yellow brothers of Asia, South America, and the Caribbean, the United States Negro is moving with a sense of great urgency toward the promised land of racial justice. If one recognizes this vital urge that has engulfed the Negro community, one should readily understand why public demonstrations are taking place. The Negro has many pent-up resentments and latent frustrations, and he must release them. So let him march; let him make prayer pilgrimages to the city hall; let him go on freedom rides—and try to understand why he must do so. If his repressed emotions are not released in nonviolent ways, they will seek expression through violence; this is not a threat but a fact of history. So I have not said to my people, "Get rid of your discontent." Rather, I have tried to say that this normal and healthy discontent can be channeled into the creative outlet of nonviolent direct action. And now this approach is being termed extremist.

---

13 *Elijah Muhammad's Muslim Movement* From 1934 to 1975, Elijah Muhammad was the leader of the Nation of Islam, a religious and political movement that sought to improve conditions for African Americans and argued that Black people were best served by separation from white people.

But though I was initially disappointed at being categorized as an extremist, as I continued to think about the matter I gradually gained a measure of satisfaction from the label. Was not Jesus an extremist for love: "Love your enemies, bless them that curse you, do good to them that hate you, and pray for them which despitefully use you, and persecute you." Was not Amos[14] an extremist for justice: "Let justice roll down like waters and righteousness like an ever-flowing stream." Was not Paul an extremist for the Christian gospel: "I bear in my body the marks of the Lord Jesus." Was not Martin Luther[15] an extremist: "Here I stand; I cannot do otherwise, so help me God." And John Bunyan:[16] "I will stay in jail to the end of my days before I make a butchery of my conscience." And Abraham Lincoln:* "This nation cannot survive half slave and half free." And Thomas Jefferson:* "We hold these truths to be self-evident, that all men are created equal...."* So the question is not whether we will be extremists, but what kind of extremists we will be. Will we be extremists for hate or for love? Will we be extremists for the preservation of injustice or for the extension of justice? In that dramatic scene on Calvary's hill[17] three men were crucified. We must never forget that all three were crucified for the same crime—the crime of extremism. Two were extremists for immorality, and thus fell below their environment. The other, Jesus Christ, was an extremist for love, truth, and goodness, and thereby rose above his environment. Perhaps the South, the nation, and the world are in dire need of creative extremists.

I had hoped that the white moderate would see this need. Perhaps I was too optimistic; perhaps I expected too much. I suppose I should have realized that few members of the oppressor race can understand the deep groans and passionate yearnings of the oppressed race, and still fewer have the vision to see that injustice must be rooted out by strong, persistent, and determined action. I am thankful, however, that some of our white brothers in the South have grasped the meaning of this social revolution and committed themselves to it. They are still all too few in quantity, but they are big in quality. Some—such as Ralph McGill, Lillian Smith, Harry Golden, James McBridge Dabbs, Ann Braden, and Sarah Patton Boyle—have written about our struggle in eloquent and prophetic terms. Others have marched with us down nameless streets of the South. They have languished in filthy, roach-infested jails, suffering the abuse and brutality of policemen who view them as "dirty nigger-lovers." Unlike so

---

14 *Amos* Biblical prophet; the quotation is from the Book of Amos 5.24.

15 *Martin Luther* German theologian (1483–1546) who instigated the Protestant Reformation.

16 *John Bunyan* English preacher and writer (1628–88) who was imprisoned for his preaching.

17 *Calvary's hill* Site of the Crucifixion of Jesus.

many of their moderate brothers and sisters, they have recognized the urgency of the moment and sensed the need for powerful "action" antidotes to combat the disease of segregation.

Let me take note of my other major disappointment. I have been so greatly disappointed with the white church and its leadership. Of course, there are some notable exceptions. I am not unmindful of the fact that each of you has taken some significant stands on this issue. I commend you, Reverend Stallings, for your Christian stand on this past Sunday, in welcoming Negroes to your worship service on a nonsegregated basis. I commend the Catholic leaders of this state for integrating Spring Hill College several years ago.

But despite these notable exceptions, I must honestly reiterate that I have been disappointed with the church. I do not say this as one of those negative critics who can always find something wrong with the church. I say this as a minister of the gospel, who loves the church; who was nurtured in its bosom; who has been sustained by its spiritual blessings and who will remain true to it as long as the cord of life shall lengthen.

35   When I was suddenly catapulted into the leadership of the bus protest in Montgomery, Alabama,[18] a few years ago, I felt we would be supported by the white church. I felt that the white ministers, priests, and rabbis of the South would be among our strongest allies. Instead, some have been outright opponents, refusing to understand the freedom movement and misrepresenting its leaders; all too many others have been more cautious than courageous and have remained silent behind the anesthetizing security of stained glass windows.

In spite of my shattered dreams, I came to Birmingham with the hope that the white religious leadership of this community would see the justice of our cause and, with deep moral concern, would serve as the channel through which our just grievances could reach the power structure. I had hoped that each of you would understand. But again I have been disappointed.

I have heard numerous southern religious leaders admonish their worshippers to comply with a desegregation decision because it is the law, but I have longed to hear white ministers declare: "Follow this decree because integration is morally right and because the Negro is your brother." In the midst of blatant injustices inflicted upon the Negro, I have watched white churchmen stand on the sideline and mouth pious irrelevancies and sanctimonious trivialities. In the midst of a mighty struggle to rid our nation of racial and economic injustice, I have heard many ministers say: "Those are social issues, with which the gospel

---

18   *bus protest in Montgomery, Alabama* In December 1955, Rosa Lee Parks, a 42-year-old Civil Rights activist, refused to give her seat on a local bus to a white man, sparking a year-long boycott by African-Americans of the Montgomery buses.

has no real concern." And I have watched many churches commit themselves to a completely otherworldly religion which makes a strange un-Biblical distinction between the body and soul, between the sacred and the secular.

I have traveled the length and breadth of Alabama, Mississippi, and all the other southern states. On sweltering summer days and crisp autumn mornings I have looked at the South's beautiful churches with their lofty spires pointing heavenward. I have beheld the impressive outlines of her massive religious-education buildings. Over and over I have found myself asking: "What kind of people worship here? Who is their God? Where were their voices when the lips of Governor Barnett dripped with words of interposition and nullification? Where were they when Governor Wallace gave a clarion call for defiance and hatred? Where were their voices of support when bruised and weary Negro men and women decided to rise from the dark dungeons of complacency to the bright hills of creative protest?"

Yes, these questions are still in my mind. In deep disappointment I have wept over the laxity of the church. But be assured that my tears have been tears of love. There can be no deep disappointment where there is not deep love. Yes, I love the church. How could I do otherwise? I am in the rather unique position of being the son, the grandson, and the great-grandson of preachers. Yes, I see the church as the body of Christ. But, oh! How we have blemished and scarred that body through social neglect and through fear of being nonconformists.

There was a time when the church was very powerful—in the time when 40
the early Christians rejoiced at being deemed worthy to suffer for what they believed. In those days the church was not merely a thermometer that recorded the ideas and principles of popular opinion; it was a thermostat that transformed the mores of society. Whenever the early Christians entered a town, the people in power became disturbed and immediately sought to convict the Christians of being "disturbers of the peace" and "outside agitators." But the Christians pressed on, in the conviction that they were "a colony of heaven," called to obey God rather than man. Small in number, they were big in commitment. They were too God-intoxicated to be "astronomically intimidated." By their effort and example they brought an end to such ancient evils as infanticide and gladiatorial contests.

Things are different now. So often the contemporary church is a weak, ineffectual voice with an uncertain sound. So often it is an arch-defender of the status quo. Far from being disturbed by the presence of the church, the power structure of the average community is consoled by the church's silent—and often even vocal—sanction of things as they are.

But the judgment of God is upon the church as never before. If today's church does not recapture the sacrificial spirit of the early church, it will lose its authenticity, forfeit the loyalty of millions, and be dismissed as an irrelevant social club with no meaning for the twentieth century. Every day I meet young people whose disappointment with the church has turned into outright disgust.

Perhaps I have once again been too optimistic. Is organized religion too inextricably bound to the status quo to save our nation and the world? Perhaps I must turn my faith to the inner spiritual church, the church within the church, as the true *ekklesia*[19] and the hope of the world. But again I am thankful to God that some noble souls from the ranks of organized religion have broken loose from the paralyzing chains of conformity and joined us as active partners in the struggle for freedom. They have left their secure congregations and walked the streets of Albany, Georgia, with us. They have gone down the highways of the South on tortuous rides for freedom. Yes, they have gone to jail with us. Some have been dismissed from their churches, have lost the support of their bishops and fellow ministers. But they have acted in the faith that right defeated is stronger than evil triumphant. Their witness has been the spiritual salt that has preserved the true meaning of the gospel in these troubled times. They have carved a tunnel of hope through the dark mountain of disappointment.

I hope the church as a whole will meet the challenge of this decisive hour. But even if the church does not come to the aid of justice, I have no despair about the future. I have no fear about the outcome of our struggle in Birmingham, even if our motives are at present misunderstood. We will reach the goal of freedom in Birmingham and all over the nation, because the goal of America is freedom. Abused and scorned though we may be, our destiny is tied up with America's destiny. Before the pilgrims landed at Plymouth,* we were here. Before the pen of Jefferson etched the majestic words of the Declaration of Independence across the pages of history, we were here. For more than two centuries our forebears labored in this country without wages; they made cotton king;* they built the homes of their masters while suffering gross injustice and shameful humiliation—and yet out of a bottomless vitality they continued to thrive and develop. If the inexpressible cruelties of slavery could not stop us, the opposition we now face will surely fail. We will win our freedom because the sacred heritage of our nation and the eternal will of God are embodied in our echoing demands.

45   Before closing I feel impelled to mention one other point in your statement that has troubled me profoundly. You warmly commended the Birmingham police for keeping "order" and "preventing violence." I doubt that you would have so warmly commended the police force if you had seen its dogs sinking their teeth into unarmed, nonviolent Negroes. I doubt that you would so quickly

---

19   *ekklesia*   Latin: Christian church, especially when understood as an abstract entity made up of all Christians throughout time, rather than as a specific worldly organization.

commend the policemen if you were to observe their ugly and inhumane treatment of Negroes here in the city jail; if you were to watch them push and curse old Negro women and young Negro girls; if you were to see them slap and kick old Negro men and young boys; if you were to observe them, as they did on two occasions, refuse to give us food because we wanted to sing our grace together. I cannot join you in your praise of the Birmingham police department.

It is true that the police have exercised a degree of discipline in handling the demonstrators. In this sense they have conducted themselves rather "nonviolently" in public. But for what purpose? To preserve the evil system of segregation. Over the past few years I have consistently preached that nonviolence demands that the means we use must be as pure as the ends we seek. I have tried to make clear that it is wrong to use immoral means to attain moral ends. But now I must affirm that it is just as wrong, or perhaps even more so, to use moral means to preserve immoral ends. Perhaps Mr. Connor and his policemen have been rather nonviolent in public, as was Chief Pritchett[20] in Albany, Georgia, but they have used moral means of nonviolence to maintain the immoral end of racial injustice. As T.S. Eliot has said, "The last temptation is the greatest treason: To do the right deed for the wrong reason."[21]

I wish you had commended the Negro sit-inners and demonstrators of Birmingham for their sublime courage, their willingness to suffer, and their amazing discipline in the midst of great provocation. One day the South will recognize its real heroes. They will be the James Merediths,[22] with the noble sense of purpose that enables them to face jeering and hostile mobs, and with the agonizing loneliness that characterizes the life of the pioneer. They will be old, oppressed, battered Negro women, symbolized in a seventy-two-year-old woman in Montgomery, Alabama, who rose up with a sense of dignity and with her people decided not to ride segregated buses,[23] and who responded with ungrammatical profundity to one who inquired about her weariness: "My feets is tired, but my soul is at rest." They will be the young high school and college students, the young ministers of the gospel and a host of their elders, courageously and nonviolently sitting in at lunch counters and willingly going to jail for conscience' sake. One day the South will know that when these

---

20 *Chief Pritchett* Laurie Pritchett (1926–2000), police chief who prevented his forces from using violence against Civil Rights protesters in Albany. His refusal to create a public spectacle undercut the effectiveness of the protests in the city.

21 *The last ... wrong reason* These lines are part of the response of St. Thomas à Becket to the fourth tempter in T.S. Eliot's play *Murder in the Cathedral*.

22 *James Merediths* In 1962 James H. Meredith became the first African American student at the University of Mississippi.

23 *seventy-two-year-old ... segregated buses* Mother Pollard, who was a participant in the Montgomery Bus Protest.

disinherited children of God sat down at lunch counters, they were in reality standing up for what is best in the American dream and for the most sacred values in our Judaeo-Christian heritage, thereby bringing our nation back to those great wells of democracy which were dug deep by the founding fathers in their formulation of the Constitution and the Declaration of Independence.

Never before have I written such a long letter. I'm afraid it is much too long to take your precious time. I can assure you that it would have been much shorter if I had been writing from a comfortable desk, but what else can one do when he is alone in a narrow jail cell, other than write long letters, think long thoughts, and pray long prayers?

If I have said anything in this letter that overstates the truth and indicates an unreasonable impatience, I beg you to forgive me. If I have said anything that understates the truth and indicates my having a patience that allows me to settle for anything less than brotherhood, I beg God to forgive me.

50   I hope this letter finds you strong in the faith. I also hope that circumstances will soon make it possible for me to meet each of you, not as an integrationist or a civil-rights leader but as a fellow clergyman and a Christian brother. Let us all hope that the dark clouds of racial prejudice will soon pass away and the deep fog of misunderstanding will be lifted from our fear-drenched communities, and in some not too distant tomorrow the radiant stars of love and brotherhood will shine over our great nation with all their scintillating beauty.

Yours for the cause of Peace and Brotherhood,

Martin Luther King Jr.

(1963)

Questions

1. In paragraph 26, King discusses time in relation to the ethical issues involved in the Civil Rights struggle. Are there ways in which time may appropriately be thought of as influencing moral questions?

2. Summarize the various reasons King gives, first of all for the Birmingham protest, and second for the means through which the protest is pursued.

3. To what extent is it ever desirable—or possible—to separate ethical from political questions?

4. Find at least three examples of parallel structure in King's writing, involving words, phrases, or clauses.

5. What is the significance of King writing the letter from jail? How do conditions under which the letter was written and disseminated influence its message?

6. What does King mean when he says that "there are two types of laws: just and unjust"? What does this indicate about King's interpretation of justice? In his view, is justice a human creation, determined by laws and legislation? Or does justice derive from something universal?

7. Who is "the white moderate," and why is King addressing this audience in his letter? What is King's message to them? How, in his view, has the white moderate gone wrong?

8. How does King respond to the accusation that his movement's actions in Birmingham are "extreme"?

MALCOLM X WITH ALEX HALEY

from THE AUTOBIOGRAPHY OF MALCOLM X

After beginning life in poverty and crime, Malcolm X became an inspirational African American political-religious leader. Though he later disowned the group, Malcolm X would rise to prominence as a leading figure of the Nation of Islam, a religious and political movement that sought to improve conditions for African Americans and argued that Black people were best served by separation from white people.

Malcolm X's 1965 autobiography was the result of a collaboration between Malcolm X himself and Alex Haley (later to become famous for the historical novel and television mini-series Roots*); Haley drafted the text out of material provided by Malcolm X in a series of interviews. These interviews were conducted while Malcolm X was facing threats against his life by the Nation of Islam, which he had by then repudiated; he was assassinated a few months before the book was published.* The Autobiography of Malcolm X *was originally contracted to be published by Doubleday, a mainstream publishing house, but after his death the publisher backed out, citing fears for the safety of its editors. The independent and politically left-of-center Grove Press instead became the publisher of a book that has now sold more than ten million copies.*

Malcolm X's biography begins with his very difficult childhood, rendered traumatic by profound loss, racism, and racist violence against his family; his young adulthood was spent making a living through crime in Harlem and Boston. The excerpts included here begin after he was arrested in Boston for a house burglary. In prison, he experienced a religious and political conversion, becoming a follower of Elijah Muhammad (1897–1975), leader of the Nation of Islam. The following selection begins as Malcolm X begins to accept "'the true knowledge of the black man' that was possessed by the followers of the Honorable Elijah Muhammad"; the excerpt concludes with the beginnings of his work as a minister and social activist in Detroit in the early 1950s.

℮

CHAPTER 10
SATAN

"The true knowledge," reconstructed much more briefly than I received it, was that history had been "whitened" in the white man's history books, and that the black man had been "brainwashed for hundreds of years." Original Man was black, in the continent called Africa where the human race had emerged on the planet Earth.

The black man, original man, built great empires and civilizations and cultures while the white man was still living on all fours in caves. "The devil white man," down through history, out of his devilish nature, had pillaged, murdered, raped, and exploited every race of man not white.

Human history's greatest crime was the traffic in black flesh when the devil white man went into Africa and murdered and kidnapped to bring to the West in chains, in slave ships, millions of black men, women, and children, who were worked and beaten and tortured as slaves.

The devil white man cut these black people off from all knowledge of their own kind, and cut them off from any knowledge of their own language, religion, and past culture, until the black man in Africa was the earth's only race of people who had absolutely no knowledge of his true identity.

In one generation, the black slave women in America had been raped by the slavemaster white man until there had begun to emerge a homemade, hand-made, brainwashed race that was no longer even of its true color, that no longer even knew its true family names. The slavemaster forced his family name upon the rape-mixed race, which the slavemaster began to call "the Negro." 5

This "Negro" was taught of his native Africa that it was peopled by hea-then, black savages, swinging like monkeys from trees. This "Negro" accepted this along with every other teaching of the slavemaster that was designed to make him accept and obey and worship the white man.

And where the religion of every other people on earth taught its believ-ers of a God with whom they could identify, a God who at least looked like one of their own kind, the slavemaster injected his Christian religion into this "Negro." This "Negro" was taught to worship an alien God having the same blond hair, pale skin, and blue eyes as the slavemaster.

This religion taught the "Negro" that black was a curse. It taught him to hate everything black, including himself. It taught him that everything white was good, to be admired, respected, and loved. It brainwashed this "Negro" to think he was superior if his complexion showed more of the white pollu-tion of the slavemaster. This white man's Christian religion further deceived and brainwashed this "Negro" to always turn the other cheek,* and grin, and scrape, and bow, and be humble, and to sing, and to pray, and to take whatever was dished out by the devilish white man; and to look for his pie in the sky,[1] and for his heaven in the hereafter, while right here on earth the slavemaster white man enjoyed *his* heaven.

Many a time, I have looked back, trying to assess, just for myself, my first reactions to all this. Every instinct of the ghetto jungle streets, every hustling fox and criminal wolf instinct in me, which would have scoffed at and rejected anything else, was struck numb. It was as though all of that life merely was back there, without any remaining effect, or influence. I remember how, some time later, reading the Bible in the Norfolk Prison Colony[2] library, I came upon, then I read, over and over, how Paul[3] on the road to Damascus, upon hearing the voice of Christ, was so smitten that he was knocked off his horse, in a daze. I do not now, and I did not then, liken myself to Paul. But I do understand his experience.

I have since learned—helping me to understand what then began to happen within me—that the truth can be quickly received, or received at all, only by the sinner who knows and admits that he is guilty of having sinned much. Stated another way: only guilt admitted accepts truth. The Bible again: the one people whom Jesus could not help were the Pharisees;[4] they didn't feel they needed any help.

The very enormity of my previous life's guilt prepared me to accept the truth.

Not for weeks yet would I deal with the direct, personal application to myself, as a black man, of the truth. It still was like a blinding light.

---

1   *pie in the sky*   Line from "The Preacher and the Slave," a 1911 song by Joe Hill. The song is a parody of "In the Sweet By-and-By," the Salvation Army's hymn, which promises earthly fulfillment after death. "The Preacher and the Slave" ridicules this position of Christian resignation: "You will eat, by and bye, / In that glorious land above the sky; / Work and pray, live on hay, / You'll get a pie in the sky when you die."

2   *Norfolk Prison Colony*   In 1948 Malcolm X was transferred from Charlestown State Prison to the Norfolk Prison Colony—a transfer he had requested because of the latter's innovative inmate educational programs. The prisoners at Norfolk had a developed intellectual culture, and Malcolm X participated in weekly debates, honing his public speaking skills.

3   *Paul*   Apostle who was dedicated to the persecution of Christians before Christ appeared to him in a vision; the conversion is described in several places in the New Testament, including Acts 9.1–9.

4   *Pharisees*   Members of a Jewish sect with which Jesus comes into conflict frequently in the New Testament.

THE AUTOBIOGRAPHY OF MALCOLM X | 155

Reginald[5] left Boston and went back to Detroit. I would sit in my room and stare. At the dining-room table, I would hardly eat, only drink the water. I nearly starved. Fellow inmates, concerned, and guards, apprehensive, asked what was wrong with me. It was suggested that I visit the doctor, and I didn't. The doctor, advised, visited me. I don't know what his diagnosis was, probably that I was working on some act.

I was going through the hardest thing, also the greatest thing, for any human being to do; to accept that which is already within you, and around you....

CHAPTER 11
SAVED

I did write to Elijah Muhammad. He lived in Chicago at that time, at 6116   15
South Michigan Avenue. At least twenty-five times I must have written that first one page letter to him, over and over. I was trying to make it both legible and understandable. I practically couldn't read my handwriting myself; it shames even to remember it. My spelling and my grammar were as bad, if not worse. Anyway, as well as I could express it, I said I had been told about him by my brothers and sisters, and I apologized for my poor letter.

Mr. Muhammad sent me a typed reply. It had an all but electrical effect on me to see the signature of the "Messenger of Allah." After he welcomed me into the "true knowledge," he gave me something to think about. The black prisoner, he said, symbolized white society's crime of keeping black men oppressed and deprived and ignorant, and unable to get decent jobs, turning them into criminals.

He told me to have courage. He even enclosed some money for me, a five-dollar bill. Mr. Muhammad sends money all over the country to prison inmates who write to him, probably to this day.

Regularly my family wrote to me, "Turn to Allah ... pray to the East."

The hardest test I ever faced in my life was praying. You understand. My comprehending, my believing the teachings of Mr. Muhammad had only required my mind's saying to me, "That's right!" or "I never thought of that."

But bending my knees to pray—that *act*—well, that took me a week.   20

You know what my life has been. Picking a lock to rob someone's house was the only way my knees had ever been bent before.

I had to force myself to bend my knees. And waves of shame and embarrassment would force me back up.

---

5   *Reginald* Brother with whom Malcolm X had a very close relationship, and who was the first to prompt him to join the Nation of Islam.

For evil to bend its knees, admitting its guilt, to implore the forgiveness of God, is the hardest thing in the world. It's easy for me to see and to say that now. But then, when I was the personification of evil, I was going through it. Again, again, I would force myself back down into the praying-to-Allah posture. When finally I was able to make myself stay down—I didn't know what to say to Allah.

For the next years, I was the nearest thing to a hermit in the Norfolk Prison Colony. I never have been more busy in my life. I still marvel at how swiftly my previous life's thinking pattern slid away from me, like snow off a roof....

CHAPTER 12
SAVIOR

25   I don't know if Mr. Muhammad suggested it or if our Temple One Minister Lemuel Hassan on his own decision encouraged me to address our assembled brothers and sisters. I know that I testified to what Mr. Muhammad's teachings had done for me: "If I told you the life I have lived, you would find it hard to believe me.... When I say something about the white man, I am not talking about someone I don't know...."

Soon after that, Minister Lemuel Hassan urged me to address the brothers and sisters with an extemporaneous lecture. I was uncertain, and hesitant—but at least I had debated in prison, and I tried my best. (Of course, I can't remember exactly what I said, but I do know that in my beginning efforts my favorite subject was Christianity and the horrors of slavery, where I felt well-equipped from so much reading in prison.)

"My brothers and sisters, our white slavemaster's Christian religion has taught us black people here in the wilderness of North America that we will sprout wings when we die and fly up into the sky where God will have for us a special place called heaven. This is white man's Christian religion used to *brainwash* us black people! We have *accepted* it! We have *embraced* it! We have *believed* it! We have *practiced* it! And while we are doing all of that, for himself, this blue-eyed devil has *twisted* his Christianity, to keep his foot on our backs ... to keep our eyes fixed on the pie in the sky and heaven in the hereafter ... while *he* enjoys *his* heaven right *here* ... on *this* earth ... in *this* life."

Today when thousands of Muslims and others have been audiences out before me, when audiences of millions have been beyond radio and television microphones, I'm sure I rarely feel as much electricity as was then generated in me by the upturned faces of those seventy-five or a hundred Muslims, plus other curious visitors, sitting there in our storefront temple with the squealing of pigs filtering in from the slaughterhouse just outside....

(1965)

Questions

1. In everyday speech the word "myth" is often used in a pejorative sense to refer to stories or ideas that are mistakenly believed to be true. But the word "myth" can also refer to something quite different: a narrative that helps establish a set of beliefs and values for a culture or group. (This second sense carries no implications as to whether a given myth could be considered objectively true or false.) In this second sense of the word, how (if at all) does Elijah Muhammad's "true knowledge" function as a myth of Black history?

2. How are white people characterized in Elijah Muhammad's "true knowledge"? To what extent (if at all) do you agree with this characterization? Explain your view.

3. How, for Malcolm X, is the political understanding he reaches through Muhammad's teaching related to his personal and spiritual development?

4. Read Martin Luther King Jr.'s "Letter from Birmingham Jail," also reprinted in this anthology, and compare King's and Malcolm X's approach with respect to the following:

   a. Religion

   b. Attitudes regarding white people

   c. Self-improvement as a component of activism

   d. Rhetorical style as a reflection of intended audience

5. When a set of ideas such as those put forward in paragraphs 1–8 is "framed" by a surrounding personal narrative, that framing lends a different tone to the ideas presented. How does the autobiographical framing here make the presentation of ideas more (or less) persuasive, interesting, or accessible than they would have been if presented on their own?

6. There is a long history of African American biographical "success stories," often published for reasons of racial uplift, as emblems of hope and examples of achievement through education and industry. Read, as an example of this genre, the selections from Pauline Hopkins's biography of Frederick Douglass that are included elsewhere in this anthology, and compare them with the selections from Malcolm X's book reprinted here. What is different, and what is similar, about these two narratives—and about the visions of Black life they offer?

BAYARD RUSTIN

"BLACK POWER" AND COALITION POLITICS

Often thought of as a moment of triumph for the Civil Rights movement, the mid-1960s saw the passage of the Civil Rights Acts of 1964, which made it illegal to discriminate on the basis of race and other specific categories, and the Voting Rights Act of 1965, which banned discriminatory practices that prevented Black Americans from exercising their right to vote in public elections. But these legal measures were of little comfort to many Black Americans who had been denied a good education, had few prospects of employment, and often lived in ghettos. It was in that context that various rifts began to open in what had, through most of the 1950s and early 60s, been a relatively unified front among Black civil rights leaders. Mainstream leaders of the African American community—Martin Luther King Jr. chief among them—pushed to achieve change within the existing political framework by building coalitions with white politicians of various stripes. Another group of mostly younger leaders—among whom Stokely Carmichael became the best known—took a more confrontational "Black Power" approach. In this article, first published in the September 1966 issue of Commentary *(at that time, a current affairs magazine known for its progressive politics), a leading activist explores the background of this divide, and considers which of the two divergent approaches offers better prospects for future change.*

There are two Americas—black and white—and nothing has more clearly revealed the divisions between them than the debate currently raging around the slogan of "black power." Despite—or perhaps because of—the fact that this slogan lacks any clear definition, it has succeeded in galvanizing emotions on all sides, with many whites seeing it as the expression of a new racism and many Negroes taking it as a warning to white people that Negroes will no longer tolerate brutality and violence. But even within the Negro

158

community itself, "black power" has touched off a major debate—the most bitter the community has experienced since the days of Booker T. Washington and W.E.B. Du Bois,[1] and one which threatens to ravage the entire civil-rights movement. Indeed, a serious split has already developed between advocates of "black power" like Floyd McKissick of CORE and Stokely Carmichael of SNCC on the one hand, and Dr. Martin Luther King of SCLC, Roy Wilkins of the NAACP, and Whitney Young[2] of the Urban League on the other.

There is no question, then, that great passions are involved in the debate over the idea of "black power"; nor, as we shall see, is there any question that these passions have their roots in the psychological and political frustrations of the Negro community. Nevertheless, I would contend that "black power" not only lacks any real value for the civil-rights movement, but that its propagation is positively harmful. It diverts the movement from a meaningful debate over strategy and tactics, it isolates the Negro community, and it encourages the growth of anti-Negro forces.

In its simplest and most innocent guise, "black power" merely means the effort to elect Negroes to office in proportion to Negro strength within the population. There is, of course, nothing wrong with such an objective in itself, and nothing inherently radical in the idea of pursuing it. But in Stokely Carmichael's extravagant rhetoric about "taking over" in districts of the South where Negroes are in the majority, it is important to recognize that Southern Negroes are only in a position to win a maximum of two congressional seats

---

1   *the days .... Du Bois*   Activists W.E.B. Du Bois and Booker T. Washington are often considered representative of two divergent movements in early twentieth-century Black activism: Washington advocated compromise with whites on issues of voting rights and desegregation, instead concentrating on economic advancement; Du Bois argued against this compromise approach. See Washington's speech reprinted in this anthology, as well as the selections from Du Bois's essay "Of Mr. Booker T. Washington and Others," also included in this volume.

2   *Floyd McKissick*   Under McKissick's leadership, the formerly nonviolent Congress Of Racial Equality (CORE) embraced direct action and mobilization of the Black community to effect change;   *Stokely Carmichael*   Activist who led the Student Nonviolent Coordinating Committee (SNCC) and went on to become a prominent member of the militant Black Panther Party;   *Dr. Martin Luther King*   Civil rights leader who advocated the use of civil disobedience and nonviolent protest as the best means to effect change. He was the first president of the Southern Christian Leadership Conference (SCLC), which organized many nonviolent actions for civil rights, including the 1963 March on Washington;   *Roy Wilkins*   Wilkins became executive director of the National Association for the Advancement of Colored People (NAACP) in 1964 and worked to enact legislation to protect rights won in the Civil Rights Movement;   *Whitney Young*   Young's activism emphasized expanding economic opportunities for Black workers, and he worked with prominent white businesspeople and politicians to achieve those goals.

and control of eighty local counties.[3] (Carmichael, incidentally, is in the paradoxical position of screaming at liberals—wanting only to "get whitey off my
back"—and simultaneously needing their support: after all, he can talk about
Negroes taking over Lowndes County[4] only because there is a fairly liberal
federal government to protect him should Governor Wallace decide to eliminate this pocket of black power.) Now there might be a certain value in having
two Negro congressmen from the South, but obviously they could do nothing
by themselves to reconstruct the face of America. Eighty sheriffs, eighty tax
assessors, and eighty school-board members might ease the tension for a while
in their communities, but they alone could not create jobs and build low-cost
housing; they alone could not supply quality integrated education.

The relevant question, moreover, is not whether a politician is black or
white, but what forces he represents.... [I]f a politician is elected because he
is black and is deemed to be entitled to a "slice of the pie,"* he will behave in
one way; if he is elected by a constituency pressing for social reform, he will,
whether he is white or black, behave in another way.

5 ... SNCC's Black Panther perspective is simultaneously utopian and reaction-
ary—the former for the by now obvious reason that one-tenth of the population
cannot accomplish much by itself, the latter because such a party would remove
Negroes from the main area of political struggle in this country (particularly in
the one-party South, where the decisive battles are fought out in Democratic
primaries[5]), and would give priority to the issue of race precisely at a time
when the fundamental questions facing the Negro and American society alike
are economic and social....

... While I myself would prefer Negro machines[6] to a situation in which
Negroes have no power at all, it seems to me that there is a better alternative
today—a liberal-labor-civil rights coalition which would work to make the
Democratic party truly responsive to the aspirations of the poor, and which

---

3   [Rustin's note]   See "The Negroes Enter Southern Politics" by Pat Watters, *Dissent*,
July–August 1966.

4   *Lowndes County*   Black-majority county in Alabama where, in the mid-1960s,
Carmichael organized a voter registration drive that was met with violent opposition from
white supremacists.

5   *the one-party ... primaries*   Though in recent decades Southern states have
predominantly elected Republicans, the Democratic party dominated the South for much
of the twentieth century; the party gradually lost its footing there in the second half of the
century.

6   *Negro machines*   A "political machine" is a long-standing organization that can
reliably obtain enough votes to get its candidate elected. The phrase often suggests
corruption and the consolidation of power through backroom dealing rather than legitimate
democracy.

would develop support for programs (specifically those outlined in A. Philip Randolph's $100 billion Freedom Budget[7]) aimed at the reconstruction of American society in the interests of greater social justice. The advocates of "black power" have no such programs in mind; what they are in fact arguing for (perhaps unconsciously) is the creation of a *new black establishment.*

Nor, it might be added, are they leading the Negro people along the same road which they imagine immigrant groups traveled so successfully in the past. Proponents of "black power"—accepting a historical myth perpetrated by moderates—like to say that the Irish and the Jews and the Italians, by sticking together and demanding their share, finally won enough power to overcome their initial disabilities. But the truth is that it was through alliances with other groups (in political machines or as part of the trade-union movement) that the Irish and the Jews and the Italians acquired the power to win their rightful place in American society. They did not "pull themselves up by their own bootstraps"*—no group in American society has ever done so; and they most certainly did not make isolation their primary tactic.

In some quarters, "black power" connotes not an effort to increase the number of Negroes in elective office but rather a repudiation of nonviolence in favor of Negro "self-defense." Actually this is a false issue, since no one has ever argued that Negroes should not defend themselves as individuals from attack.[8] Non-violence has been advocated as a tactic for organized demonstrations in a society where Negroes are a minority and where the majority controls the police. Proponents of non-violence do not, for example, deny that James Meredith[9] has the right to carry a gun for protection when he visits his mother in Mississippi; what they question is the wisdom of his carrying a gun while participating in a demonstration.

---

7   *A. Philip Randolph's ... Budget*   Randolph (1889–1979) was a leader in the Civil Rights movement. In 1966 he, Rustin, and King together created the Freedom Budget, a plan to abolish poverty, ensure employment for all, and provide a minimum basic income for those unable to work.

8   [Rustin's note]   As far back as 1934, A. Philip Randolph, Walter White, then executive secretary of the NAACP, Lester Granger, then executive director of the Urban League, and I joined a committee to try to save the life of Odell Waller. Waller, a sharecropper, had murdered his white boss in self-defense.

9   *James Meredith*   In 1966 Meredith, a civil rights activist and writer, planned a March Against Fear from Memphis, Tennessee, to Jackson, Mississippi, to encourage African Americans to register to vote. According to his own report, he contemplated carrying a gun with him but chose to carry a Bible instead. He was shot by a white man on the second day, near Coldwater, Mississippi, but survived, and by the time he returned to the March it was 15,000 strong, the largest march in Mississippi history.

There is, as well, a tactical side to the new emphasis on "self-defense" and the suggestion that non-violence be abandoned. The reasoning here is that turning the other cheek* is not the way to win respect, and that only if the Negro succeeds in frightening the white man will the white man begin taking him seriously. The trouble with this reasoning is that it fails to recognize that fear is more likely to bring hostility to the surface than respect; and far from prodding the "white power structure" into action, the new militant leadership, by raising the slogan of black power and lowering the banner of non-violence, has obscured the moral issue facing this nation, and permitted the President and Vice President to lecture us about "racism in reverse" instead of proposing more meaningful programs for dealing with the problems of unemployment, housing, and education.

10   "Black power" is, of course, a somewhat nationalistic slogan and its sudden rise to popularity among Negroes signifies a concomitant rise in nationalist sentiment (Malcolm X's[10] autobiography is quoted nowadays in Grenada, Mississippi as well as in Harlem*). We have seen such nationalistic turns and withdrawals back into the ghetto before, and when we look at the conditions which brought them about, we find that they have much in common with the conditions of Negro life at the present moment: conditions which lead to despair over the goal of integration and to the belief that the ghetto will last forever.

It may, in the light of the many juridical and legislative victories which have been achieved in the past few years, seem strange that despair should be so widespread among Negroes today. But anyone to whom it seems strange should reflect on the fact that despite these victories *Negroes today are in worse economic shape, live in worse slums, and attend more highly segregated schools than in 1954.*[11] Thus—to recite the appalling, and appallingly familiar, statistical litany once again—more Negroes are unemployed today than in 1954; the gap between the wages of the Negro worker and the white worker is wider; while the unemployment rate among white youths is decreasing, the rate among Negro youths has increased to *32 per cent* (and among Negro girls the rise is even more startling). Even the one gain which has been registered, a decrease in the unemployment rate among Negro adults, is deceptive, for it represents men who have been called back to work after a period of being laid off. In any event, unemployment among Negro men is still twice that of whites, and no new jobs have been created.

---

10   *Malcolm X* Influential Muslim leader and Black nationalist activist (1925–65). His autobiography (1965, written with Alex Haley) is excerpted elsewhere in this anthology.

11   *1954* Date of the *Brown v. Board of Education* Supreme Court ruling against school segregation.

So too with housing, which is deteriorating in the North (and yet the housing provisions of the 1966 civil-rights bill[12] are weaker than the antidiscrimination laws in several states which contain the worst ghettos even with these laws on their books). And so too with schools: according to figures issued recently by the Department of Health, Education and Welfare, 65 per cent of first-grade Negro students in this country attend schools that are from 90 to 100 per cent black. (If in 1954, when the Supreme Court handed down the desegregation decision, you had been the Negro parent of a first-grade child, the chances are that this past June you would have attended that child's graduation from a segregated high school.)

To put all this in the simplest and most concrete terms: the day-to-day lot of the ghetto Negro has not been improved by the various judicial and legislative measures of the past decade.

Negroes are thus in a situation similar to that of the turn of the century, when Booker T. Washington advised them to "cast down their buckets"[13] (that is to say, accommodate to segregation and disenfranchisement) and when even his leading opponent, W.E.B. Du Bois, was forced to advocate the development of a group economy in place of the direct-action boycotts, general strikes, and protest techniques which had been used in the 1880s, before the enactment of the Jim-Crow* laws. For all their differences, both Washington and Du Bois then found it impossible to believe that Negroes could ever be integrated into American society, and each in his own way therefore counseled withdrawal into the ghetto, self-help, and economic self-determination.

World War I aroused new hope in Negroes that the rights removed at the turn of the century would be restored. More than 360,000 Negroes entered military service and went overseas; many left the South seeking the good life in the North and hoping to share in the temporary prosperity created by the war. But all these hopes were quickly smashed at the end of the fighting. In the first year following the war, more than seventy Negroes were lynched,* and during the last six months of that year, there were some twenty-four riots throughout America. White mobs took over whole cities, flogging, burning, shooting, and torturing at will, and when Negroes tried to defend themselves, the violence only increased. Along with this, Negroes

15

---

12 *1966 civil-rights bill* The Civil Rights Act of 1966 would have outlawed racial discrimination in the sale and rental of housing, as well as in the selection of jurors. It encountered Republican resistance in the Senate and did not pass.

13 *"cast down their buckets"* Reference to Booker T. Washington's famous exhortation to African Americans to "cast down your bucket where you are"; see his speech reprinted in this anthology.

were excluded from unions and pushed out of jobs they had won during the war, including federal jobs.

In the course of this period of dashed hope and spreading segregation—the same period, incidentally, when a reorganized Ku Klux Klan* was achieving a membership which was to reach into the millions—the largest mass movement ever to take root among working-class Negroes, Marcus Garvey's "Back to Africa" movement,[14] was born. "Buy Black" became a slogan in the ghettos; faith in integration was virtually snuffed out in the Negro community until the 1930s.... No sooner did jobs begin to open up and Negroes begin to be welcomed into mainstream organizations than "Buy Black" campaigns gave way to "Don't Buy Where You Can't Work" movements.... Altogether, World War II was a period of hope for Negroes, and the economic progress they made through wartime industry continued steadily until about 1948 and remained stable for a time. Meanwhile, the non-violent movement of the 1950s and 60s achieved the desegregation of public accommodations and established the right to vote.

Yet at the end of this long fight, the Southern Negro is too poor to use those integrated facilities and too intimidated and disorganized to use the vote to maximum advantage, while the economic position of the Northern Negro deteriorates rapidly.

The promise of meaningful work and decent wages once held out by the anti-poverty programs has not been fulfilled. Because there has been a lack of the necessary funds, the program has in many cases been reduced to wrangling for positions on boards or for lucrative staff jobs. Negro professionals working for the program have earned handsome salaries—ranging from $14 to $25,000—while young boys have been asked to plant trees at $1.25 an hour....

Then there is the war in Vietnam,[15] which poses many ironies for the Negro community. On the one hand, Negroes are bitterly aware of the fact that more and more money is being spent on the war, while the anti-poverty program is being cut; on the other hand, Negro youths are enlisting in great numbers, as though to say that it is worth the risk of being killed to learn a trade, to leave a dead-end situation, and to join the only institution in this society which seems really to be integrated.

---

14 *Marcus Garvey ... movement* Black nationalist Marcus Garvey (1887–1940) launched a shipping company, Black Star, to improve transatlantic economic connections between Blacks and to return African Americans to their ancestral homes in Africa.

15 *war in Vietnam* The American war in Vietnam lasted from 1955 to 1975.

The youths who rioted in Watts, Cleveland, Omaha, Chicago, and   20
Portland[16] are the members of a truly hopeless and lost generation. They can
see the alien world of affluence unfold before them on the TV screen. But they
have already failed in their inferior segregated schools. Their grandfathers
were sharecroppers,[17] their grandmothers were domestics, and their mothers
are domestics too. Many have never met their fathers. Mistreated by the local
storekeeper, suspected by the policeman on the beat, disliked by their teachers,
they cannot stand more failures and would rather retreat into the world of heroin
than risk looking for a job downtown or having their friends see them push a
rack in the garment district. Floyd McKissick and Stokely Carmichael may
accuse Roy Wilkins of being out of touch with the Negro ghetto, but nothing
more clearly demonstrates their own alienation from ghetto youth than their
repeated exhortations to these young men to oppose the Vietnam war when
so many of them tragically see it as their only way out. Yet there is no need to
labor the significance of the fact that the rice fields of Vietnam and the Green
Berets[18] have more to offer a Negro boy than the streets of Mississippi or the
towns of Alabama or 125th Street in New York.

The Vietnam war is also partly responsible for the growing disillusion
with non-violence among Negroes. The ghetto Negro does not in general ask
whether the United States is right or wrong to be in Southeast Asia. He does,
however, wonder why he is exhorted to non-violence when the United States
has been waging a fantastically brutal war, and it puzzles him to be told that he
must turn the other cheek in our own South while we must fight for freedom in
South Vietnam.

Thus, as in roughly similar circumstances in the past—circumstances, I
repeat, which in the aggregate foster the belief that the ghetto is destined to last
forever—Negroes are once again turning to nationalistic slogans, with "black
power" affording the same emotional release as "Back to Africa" and "Buy
Black" did in earlier periods of frustration and hopelessness. This is not only
the case with the ordinary Negro in the ghetto; it is also the case with leaders

---

16   *rioted in Watts ... Portland*   Riots had erupted in predominantly Black neighborhoods
in these cities in the summer of 1966 (Watts is a neighborhood in Los Angeles). The riots
were caused by deteriorating living conditions, segregated schools, and ever-increasing
poverty and unemployment, though most were also specifically triggered by white police
violence against Black victims.

17   *sharecroppers*   Farmers who give a portion of their crops to landlords as rent
for the land they work. This system of labor largely replaced slavery in the South after
Emancipation. While Black sharecroppers had some autonomy under this system, they
were often placed in a situation of increasing debt to the white landowners.

18   *Green Berets*   Special forces in the United States army that are recognizable by their
distinctive green hats.

like McKissick and Carmichael, neither of whom began as a nationalist or was at first cynical about the possibilities of integration.[19] It took countless beatings and 24 jailings—that, and the absence of strong and continual support from the liberal community—to persuade Carmichael that his earlier faith in coalition politics was mistaken, that nothing was to be gained from working with whites, and that an alliance with the black nationalists was desirable. In the areas of the South where SNCC has been working so nobly, implementation of the Civil Rights Acts of 1964 and 1965 has been slow and ineffective. Negroes in many rural areas cannot walk into the courthouse and register to vote. Despite the voting-rights bill, they must file complaints and the Justice Department must be called to send federal registrars. Nor do children attend integrated schools as a matter of course. There, too, complaints must be filed and the Department of Health, Education and Welfare must be notified. Neither department has been doing an effective job of enforcing the bills. The feeling of isolation increases among SNCC workers as each legislative victory turns out to be only a token victory—significant on the national level, but not affecting the day-to-day lives of Negroes. Carmichael and his colleagues are wrong in refusing to support the 1966 bill, but one can understand why they feel as they do.

It is, in short, the growing conviction that the Negroes cannot win—a conviction with much grounding in experience—which accounts for the new popularity of "black power." So far as the ghetto Negro is concerned, this conviction expresses itself in hostility first toward the people closest to him who have held out the most promise and failed to deliver (Martin Luther King, Roy Wilkins, etc.), then toward those who have proclaimed themselves his friends (the liberals and the labor movement), and finally toward the only oppressors he can see (the local storekeeper and the policeman on the corner). On the leadership level, the conviction that the Negroes cannot win takes other forms, principally the adoption of what I have called a "no-win" policy. Why bother with programs when their enactment results only in "sham"? Why concern ourselves with the image of the movement when nothing significant has been gained...? Why compromise with reluctant white allies when nothing of consequence can be achieved anyway? Why indeed have anything to do with whites at all?

On this last point, it is extremely important for white liberals to understand— as, one gathers from their references to "racism in reverse," the President and the Vice President of the United States do not—that there is all the difference in the world between saying, "If you don't want me, I don't want you" (which

---

19 [original note] On Carmichael's background, see "Two for SNCC" by Robert Penn Warren in the April 1965 *Commentary*—ED.

is what some proponents of "black power" have in effect been saying) and the statement, "Whatever you do, I don't want you" (which is what racism declares). It is, in other words, both absurd and immoral to equate the despairing response of the victim with the contemptuous assertion of the oppressor. It would, moreover, be tragic if white liberals allowed verbal hostility on the part of Negroes to drive them out of the movement or to curtail their support for civil rights. The issue was injustice before "black power" became popular, and the issue is still injustice.

In any event, even if "black power" had not emerged as the slogan, problems would have arisen in the relation between whites and Negroes in the civil-rights movement. In the North, it was inevitable that Negroes would eventually wish to run their own movement and would rebel against the presence of whites in positions of leadership as yet another sign of white supremacy. In the South, the well-intentioned white volunteer had the cards stacked against him from the beginning. Not only could he leave the struggle anytime he chose to do so, but a higher value was set on his safety by the press and government—apparent in the differing degrees of excitement generated by the imprisonment or murder of whites and Negroes. The white person's importance to the movement in the South was thus an ironic outgrowth of racism and was therefore bound to create resentment.

But again: however understandable all this may be as a response to objective conditions and to the seeming irrelevance of so many hard-won victories to the day-to-day life of the mass of Negroes, the fact remains that the quasi-nationalist sentiments and "no-win" policy lying behind the slogan of "black power" do no service to the Negro. Some nationalist emotion is, of course, inevitable, and "black power" must be seen as part of the psychological rejection of white supremacy, part of the rebellion against the stereotypes which have been ascribed to Negroes for three hundred years. Nevertheless, pride, confidence, and a new identity cannot be won by glorifying blackness or attacking whites; they can only come from meaningful action, from good jobs, and from real victories such as were achieved on the streets of Montgomery, Birmingham, and Selma.[20] When SNCC and CORE went into the South, they awakened the country, but now they emerge isolated and demoralized, shouting a slogan that may afford a momentary satisfaction but that is calculated to destroy them and their movement. Already their frustrated call is being answered with counter-demands for law and order and with opposition to

20 *real victories ... Selma* Locations of civil rights actions that led to the legislative victories of 1964 and 1965: the Montgomery Bus Boycott of 1955–56; the Birmingham Campaign of 1963, which included marches, sit-ins, and other nonviolent methods of protest; and the 1963 voting rights protests in Selma, Alabama.

police-review boards. Already they have diverted the entire civil-rights movement from the hard task of developing strategies to realign the major parties of
this country, and embroiled it in a debate that can only lead more and more to
politics by frustration.

On the other side, however—the more important side, let it be said—it
is the business of those who reject the negative aspects of "black power" not
to preach but to act. Some weeks ago President Johnson, speaking at Fort
Campbell, Kentucky, asserted that riots impeded reform, created fear, and
antagonized the Negro's traditional friends. Mr. Johnson, according to the New
York *Times*, expressed sympathy for the plight of the poor, the jobless, and
the ill-housed. The government, he noted, has been working to relieve their
circumstances, but "all this takes time."

One cannot argue with the President's position that riots are destructive
or that they frighten away allies. Nor can one find fault with his sympathy for
the plight of the poor; surely the poor need sympathy. But one can question
whether the government has been working seriously enough to eliminate the
conditions which lead to frustration-politics and riots. The President's very
words, "all this takes time," will be understood by the poor for precisely what
they are—an excuse instead of a real program, a cover-up for the failure to
establish real priorities, and an indication that the administration has no real
commitment to create new jobs, better housing, and integrated schools.

For the truth is that it need only take ten years to eliminate poverty—ten years
and the $100 billion Freedom Budget recently proposed by A. Philip Randolph.
In his introduction to the budget (which was drawn up in consultation with the
nation's leading economists, and which will be published later this month),
Mr. Randolph points out: "The programs urged in the Freedom Budget attack
all of the major causes of poverty—unemployment and underemployment,
substandard pay, inadequate social insurance and welfare payments to those
who cannot or should not be employed; bad housing; deficiencies in health
services, education, and training; and fiscal and monetary policies which tend
to redistribute income regressively rather than progressively. The Freedom
Budget leaves no room for discrimination in any form because its programs are
addressed to all who need more opportunity and improved incomes and living
standards, not to just some of them."

30 The legislative precedent Mr. Randolph has in mind is the 1945 Full
Employment bill. This bill—conceived in its original form by Roosevelt to
prevent a postwar depression—would have made it public policy for the government to step in if the private economy could not provide enough employment. As passed finally by Congress in 1946, with many of its teeth removed,
the bill had the result of preventing the Negro worker, who had finally reached

the pay level about 55 per cent that of the white wage, from making any further progress in closing that discriminatory gap; and instead, he was pushed back by the chronically high unemployment rates of the 50s. Had the original bill been passed, the public sector of our economy would have been able to insure fair and full employment. Today, with the spiraling thrust of automation, it is even more imperative that we had a legally binding commitment to this goal.

Let me interject a word here to those who say that Negroes are asking for another handout and are refusing to help themselves. From the end of the 19th century up to the last generation, the United States absorbed and provided economic opportunity for tens of millions of immigrants. These people were usually uneducated and a good many could not speak English. They had nothing but their hard work to offer and they labored long hours, often in miserable sweatshops and unsafe mines. Yet in a burgeoning economy with a need for unskilled labor, they were able to find jobs, and as industrialization proceeded, they were gradually able to move up the ladder to greater skills. Negroes who have been driven off the farm into a city life for which they are not prepared and who have entered an economy in which there is less and less need for unskilled labor, cannot be compared with these immigrants of old. The tenements which were jammed by newcomers were way-stations of hope; the ghettos of today have become dead-ends of despair. Yet just as the older generation of immigrants—in its most decisive act of self-help—organized the trade-union movement and then in alliance with many middle-class elements went on to improve its own lot and the condition of American society generally, so the Negro of today is struggling to go beyond the gains of the past and, in alliance with liberals and labor, to guarantee full and fair employment to all Americans.

Mr. Randolph's Freedom Budget not only rests on the Employment Act of 1946,[21] but on the precedent set by Harry Truman when he believed freedom was threatened in Europe. In 1947, the Marshall Plan was put into effect and 3 per cent of the gross national product was spent in foreign aid. If we were to allocate a similar proportion of our GNP to destroy the economic and social consequences of racism and poverty at home today, it might mean spending more than 20 billion dollars a year, although I think it's quite possible that we can fulfill these goals with a much smaller sum. It would be intolerable, however, if our plan for domestic social reform were less audacious and less far-reaching than our international programs of a generation ago.

We must see, therefore, in the current debate over "black power," a fantastic challenge to American society to live up to its proclaimed principles in the

---

21 *Employment Act of 1946*   Watered-down version of the 1945 Full Employment Bill discussed above. The 1946 bill was the one that was passed; its failure to insist on "full" employment meant that it was ineffective, more a list of goals than actual policy.

area of race by transforming itself so that all men may live equally and under justice. We must see to it that in rejecting "black power," we do not also reject the principle of Negro equality. Those people who would use the current debate and/or the riots to abandon the civil-rights movement leave us no choice but to question their original motivation.

If anything, the next period will be more serious and more difficult than the preceding ones. It is much easier to establish the Negro's right to sit at a Woolworth's counter[22] than to fight for an integrated community. It takes very little imagination to understand that the Negro should have the right to vote, but it demands more creativity, patience, and political stamina to plan, develop, and implement programs and priorities. It is one thing to organize sentiment behind laws that do not disturb consensus politics, and quite another to win battles for the redistribution of wealth. Many people who marched in Selma are not prepared to support a bill for a $2.00 minimum wage, to say nothing of supporting a redefinition of work or guaranteed annual income.

35 It is here that we who advocate coalitions and integration and to object to the "black-power" concept have a massive job to do. We must see to it that the liberal-labor-civil rights coalition is maintained and, indeed, strengthened so that it can fight effectively for a Freedom Budget. We are responsible for the growth of the "black-power" concept because we have not used our own power to ensure the full implementation of the bills whose passage we were strong enough to win, and we have not mounted the necessary campaign for winning a decent minimum wage and extended benefits. "Black power" is a slogan directed primarily against liberals by those who once counted liberals among their closest friends. It is up to the next liberal movement to prove that coalition and integration are better alternatives.

(1966)

Questions

1. Locate, in the first two paragraphs, the thesis of Rustin's argument. To what extent does the article as a whole succeed in persuading you of the truth of this thesis?

2. Compare the slogan "Black Power" at the time Rustin was writing with the slogan "Black Lives Matter" in the second decade of the twenty-first century. In what ways are the two similar? In what ways are they different?

---

22 *Woolworth's counter* As part of the nonviolent Greensboro sit-in protests, four Black college students, when refused service at a segregated Woolworth's restaurant on 1 February 1960, refused to comply and remained at their seats.

3. What clues can you find in this piece about the nature of the audience Rustin was writing for? (Rich or poor? University educated or not? More male or female? More young or old? Mostly white? Largely Black?)

4. Rustin discusses tensions between more and less militant segments of the Black community, and between Black activists and white liberals.

   a. To what extent do tensions between more and less militant Black activists still exist today? To what extent do Rustin's statements about this tension still apply?

   b. Choose an article from this book that was published in the twenty-first century. (Consider the articles by Obama, McKenzie, Coates, or Staples.) How (if at all) does the article you chose reflect one (or both) of the tensions named above?

5. What, according to Rustin, are "frustration-politics"? Do you agree with this characterization?

6. The mythos of the American dream is premised on the idea of the "self-made" person who achieves prosperity with hard work and determination. Why, according to Rustin, was this dream achievable for immigrants in the early twentieth-century, but not for African Americans in Northern urban ghettos in the 1960s? To what extent (if at all) do Rustin's statements apply to Black Americans living in poverty now?

7. Read the selections from Howard Zinn's *A People's History of the United States* that are reprinted in this anthology.

   a. Summarize Zinn's evaluation of the relative contributions of the more militant activism associated with Black Power as opposed to the nonviolent activism associated with King.

   b. How (if at all) does Zinn's view differ from Rustin's? Which view do you find more compelling, and why?

8. Read Ta-Nehisi Coates's essay "The Case for Reparations," also printed in this anthology.

   a. Compare Coates's economic vision with Rustin's. How are they similar? How different?

   b. What political positions motivate these two economic proposals?

   c. What political-economic approach should serve as the basis for policy now—Rustin's, Coates's, or something else? Argue for the superiority of Rustin's or Coates's approach, or outline a different approach and explain why it should be adopted.

SHIRLEY CHISHOLM

EQUAL RIGHTS FOR WOMEN

In 1923, suffragist and feminist leader Alice Paul proposed to Congress the Equal Rights Amendment (ERA), which stated that "Equality of rights under the law shall not be denied or abridged by the United States or by any State on account of sex." The amendment was introduced in Congress every year for forty years, until it was finally passed in 1972, with a seven-year deadline for ratification. Three quarters of the States were required to ratify the ERA, and, by the extended deadline of 1982, only 35 States had done so (three short of the required number). The Amendment is still not ratified, more than 90 years since its introduction to Congress.

Resistance to the ERA in many States, particularly in the South, was spearheaded by working-class women who feared that certain special rights accorded to women would be taken away should the ERA pass (shorter working hours, for example, or limits to how much weight a woman could be asked to lift). Conservative women, too, opposed the amendment. They worried that the ERA would erode special rights granted to homemakers (alimony, for example, or custody rights to children in case of divorce); they also resisted the idea of women serving in the military, and particularly of women being conscripted. Black women were generally in favor of the ERA, as were the NAACP (National Association for the Advancement of Colored People) and The National Black Feminist Organization. Black and Latina women suffered an even more unequal pay scale than white women; for them, the ERA held some promise of protection, at least in terms of the law.

In 1969, the first Black congresswoman, Shirley Chisholm, introduced the ERA to Congress. Her speech, printed below, outlines her reasons for supporting the amendment.

ADDRESS TO THE UNITED STATES HOUSE OF REPRESENTATIVES,
WASHINGTON, DC:
MAY 21, 1969

Mr. Speaker, when a young woman graduates from college and starts looking for a job, she is likely to have a frustrating and even demeaning experience ahead of her. If she walks into an office for an interview, the first question she will be asked is, "Do you type?"

There is a calculated system of prejudice that lies unspoken behind that question. Why is it acceptable for women to be secretaries, librarians, and teachers, but totally unacceptable for them to be managers, administrators, doctors, lawyers, and Members of Congress?

The unspoken assumption is that women are different. They do not have executive ability, orderly minds, stability, leadership skills, and they are too emotional.

It has been observed before, that society for a long time discriminated against another minority, the blacks, on the same basis—that they were different and inferior. The happy little homemaker and the contented "old darkey" on the plantation were both produced by prejudice.

As a black person, I am no stranger to race prejudice. But the truth is that in the political world I have been far oftener discriminated against because I am a woman than because I am black.

Prejudice against blacks is becoming unacceptable although it will take years to eliminate it. But it is doomed because, slowly, white America is beginning to admit that it exists. Prejudice against women is still acceptable. There is very little understanding yet of the immorality involved in double pay scales and the classification of most of the better jobs as "for men only."

More than half of the population of the United States is female. But women occupy only 2 percent of the managerial positions. They have not even reached the level of tokenism[1] yet. No women sit on the AFL-CIO[2] council or Supreme Court. There have been only two women who have held Cabinet rank, and at present there are none. Only two women now hold ambassadorial rank in the diplomatic corps. In Congress, we are down to one Senator and 10 Representatives.

Considering that there are about 3 1/2 million more women in the United States than men, this situation is outrageous.

---

1   *tokenism*   Practice of making a slight (token) effort to conciliate a minority group.

2   *AFL-CIO*   American Federation of Labor and Congress of Industrial Organizations.

It is true that part of the problem has been that women have not been aggressive in demanding their rights. This was also true of the black population for many years. They submitted to oppression and even cooperated with it. Women have done the same thing. But now there is an awareness of this situation particularly among the younger segment of the population.

As in the field of equal rights for blacks, Spanish-Americans, the Indians, and other groups, laws will not change such deep-seated problems overnight. But they can be used to provide protection for those who are most abused, and to begin the process of evolutionary change by compelling the insensitive majority to reexamine its unconscious attitudes.

It is for this reason that I wish to introduce today a proposal that has been before every Congress for the last 40 years and that sooner or later must become part of the basic law of the land—the equal rights amendment.

Let me note and try to refute two of the commonest arguments that are offered against this amendment. One is that women are already protected under the law and do not need legislation. Existing laws are not adequate to secure equal rights for women. Sufficient proof of this is the concentration of women in lower paying, menial, unrewarding jobs and their incredible scarcity in the upper level jobs. If women are already equal, why is it such an event whenever one happens to be elected to Congress?

It is obvious that discrimination exists. Women do not have the opportunities that men do. And women that do not conform to the system, who try to break with the accepted patterns, are stigmatized as "odd" and "unfeminine." The fact is that a woman who aspires to be chairman of the board, or a Member of the House, does so for exactly the same reasons as any man. Basically, these are that she thinks she can do the job and she wants to try.

A second argument often heard against the equal rights amendment is that it would eliminate legislation that many States and the Federal Government have enacted giving special protection to women and that it would throw the marriage and divorce laws into chaos.

As for the marriage laws, they are due for a sweeping reform, and an excellent beginning would be to wipe the existing ones off the books. Regarding special protection for working women, I cannot understand why it should be needed. Women need no protection that men do not need. What we need are laws to protect working people, to guarantee them fair pay, safe working conditions, protection against sickness and layoffs, and provision for dignified, comfortable retirement. Men and women need these things equally. That one sex needs protection more than the other is a male supremacist myth as ridiculous and unworthy of respect as the white supremacist myths that society is trying to cure itself of at this time.

(1969)

Questions

1. How does Chisholm address the concern held by many working-class women that the ERA would eliminate laws providing special protections for women in the workplace? In your view, does she address these concerns adequately?

2. How does Chisholm address the concern held especially by many conservative women that the ERA would eliminate special protections given to them by the marriage laws of the time? In your view, does she address these concerns adequately?

3. What role, according to Chisholm, can the law play in ending discrimination? Do you agree with her?

4. Do some research to determine what activism is currently underway in regard to the ERA. Summarize your findings.

5. Do you think the ERA should be ratified? Why or why not?

6. As a Black woman working in politics in the late 1960s, Chisholm experienced prejudice on account of both her race and her gender. Which form of prejudice does she describe as affecting her life more? Does this surprise you? Why or why not?

7. Cite examples from the text in which Chisholm draws a comparison between sexism and racism. How does she view the two as similar? How, for her, are they different?

8. To what extent do the claims Chisholm makes in this speech apply in the present day? What, if anything, has changed? What, if anything, remains the same?

ALICE WALKER

IN SEARCH OF OUR MOTHERS' GARDENS: THE CREATIVITY OF BLACK WOMEN IN THE SOUTH

The following is the title essay of African American novelist and activist Alice Walker's collection In Search of Our Mothers' Gardens: Womanist Prose *(1983). Walker coined the term "womanist" as an alternative to "feminist," partly in reaction to the racism Black women encountered within the white-dominated feminist movement, and also to define her own gender politics. According to the definition Walker gives in her essay collection, a womanist is "A black feminist or feminist of color. From the black folk expression of mothers to female children, 'you acting womanish,' i.e., like a woman. Usually referring to outrageous, audacious, courageous, or wilful behaviour.... Also: A woman who loves other women, sexually and/or nonsexually. Appreciates and prefers women's culture, women's emotional flexibility ... and women's strength. Sometimes loves individual men, sexually and/or nonsexually. Committed to survival and wholeness of entire people, male and female."*

"In Search of Our Mothers' Gardens" appears here as it did when it was first published, in 1974 in Ms. *magazine, an influential feminist magazine with a wide popular readership. Alice Walker was a contributing editor of* Ms. *until the mid-1980s, when she resigned because she found that the magazine underrepresented people of color.*

I described her own nature and temperament. Told how they needed a larger life for their expression.... I pointed out that in lieu of proper channels, her emotions had overflowed into paths that dissipated them. I talked, beautifully I thought, about an art that would be born, an art that would open the way for women the likes of her. I asked her to hope, and build up an inner life against the coming of that day.... I sang, with a strange quiver in my voice, a promise song.
—"Avey," Jean Toomer, *Cane*[1]

The poet speaking to a prostitute who falls asleep while he's talking—

When the poet Jean Toomer walked through the South in the early twenties, he discovered a curious thing: Black women whose spirituality was so intense, so deep, so unconscious, that they were themselves unaware of the richness they held. They stumbled blindly through their lives: creatures so abused and mutilated in body, so dimmed and confused by pain, that they considered themselves unworthy even of hope. In the selfless abstractions their bodies became to the men who used them, they became more than "sexual objects," more even than mere women: they became Saints. Instead of being perceived as whole persons, their bodies became shrines: what was thought to be their minds became temples suitable for worship. These crazy "Saints" stared out at the world, wildly, like lunatics—or quietly, like suicides; and the "God" that was in their gaze was as mute as a great stone.

Who were these "Saints"? These crazy, loony, pitiful women?

Some of them, without a doubt, were our mothers and grandmothers.

In the still heat of the post-Reconstruction[2] South, this is how they seemed to Jean Toomer: exquisite butterflies trapped in an evil honey, toiling away their lives in an era, a century, that did not acknowledge them, except as "the mule of the world."[3] They dreamed dreams that no one knew—not even themselves, in any coherent fashion—and saw visions no one could understand.

5

---

1   *Cane*   Harlem Renaissance author Jean Toomer's 1923 novel explores African American experiences in the United States using various writing genres. In the quoted passage, the narrator is speaking to a woman whom he has desired for many years, and who has become a prostitute; he hopes to seduce her, but she falls asleep.

2   *post-Reconstruction*   The Reconstruction era (1865–77), which immediately followed the Civil War, was a time of some hopeful progress for African Americans; it was followed by a period during which living conditions for African Americans again worsened, especially in the South, where many states imposed segregation and undermined the voting rights of African Americans.

3   *"the mule of the world"*   Reference to Zora Neale Hurston's 1937 novel *Their Eyes Were Watching God*: "De nigger woman is de mule uh de world so fur as Ah can see."

They wandered or sat about the countryside crooning lullabies to ghosts, and drawing the mother of Christ in charcoal on courthouse walls.[4]

They forced their minds to desert their bodies and their striving spirits sought to rise, like frail whirlwinds from the hard red clay. And when those frail whirlwinds fell, in scattered particles, upon the ground, no one mourned. Instead, men lit candles to celebrate the emptiness that remained, as people do who enter a beautiful but vacant space to resurrect a God.

Our mothers and grandmothers, some of them: moving to music not yet written. And they waited.

They waited for a day when the unknown thing that was in them would be made known; but guessed, somehow in their darkness, that on the day of their revelation they would be long dead. Therefore to Toomer they walked, and even ran, in slow motion. For they were going nowhere immediate, and the future was not yet within their grasp. And men took our mothers and grandmothers, "but got no pleasure from it."[5] So complex was their passion and their calm.

To Toomer, they lay vacant and fallow as autumn fields with harvest time never in sight: and he saw them enter loveless marriages, without joy; and become prostitutes, without resistance; and become mothers of children, without fulfillment.

10   For these grandmothers and mothers of ours were not "Saints," but Artists; driven to a numb and bleeding madness by the springs of creativity in them for which there was no release. They were Creators, who lived lives of spiritual waste, because they were so rich in spirituality—which is the basis of Art—that the strain of enduring their unused and unwanted talent drove them insane. Throwing away this spirituality was their pathetic attempt to lighten the soul to a weight their work-worn, sexually abused bodies could bear.

What did it mean for a Black woman to be an artist in our grandmothers' time? It is a question with an answer cruel enough to stop the blood.

Did you have a genius of a great-great-grandmother who died under some ignorant and depraved white overseer's lash? Or was she required to bake biscuits for a lazy backwater tramp,* when she cried out in her soul to paint watercolors of sunsets, or the rain falling on the green and peaceful pasturelands? Or was her body broken and forced to bear children (who were more often than not sold away from her)—eight, ten, fifteen, twenty children—when her one joy was the thought of modeling heroic figures of Rebellion, in stone or clay?

---

4   *drawing ... walls* In *Cane*, "an inspired Negress, of wide reputation for being sanctified, drew a portrait of a black Madonna on the courthouse wall."

5   *And men ... from it* Cf. *Cane*: "Fern's eyes said to [men] that she was easy. When she was young, a few men took her but got no joy from it."

How was the creativity of the Black woman kept alive, year after year and century after century, when for most of the years Black people have been in America, it was a punishable crime for a Black person to read or write? And the freedom to paint, to sculpt, to expand the mind with action did not exist. Consider, if you can bear to imagine it, what might have been the result if singing, too, had been forbidden by law. Listen to the voices of Bessie Smith, Billie Holiday, Nina Simone, Roberta Flack, and Aretha Franklin,[6] among others, and imagine those voices muzzled for life. Then you may begin to comprehend the lives of our "crazy," "Sainted" mothers and grandmothers. The agony of the lives of women who might have been Poets, Novelists, Essayists, and Short Story Writers, who died with their real gifts stifled within them.

And if this were the end of the story, we would have cause to cry out in my paraphrase of Okot p'Bitek's[7] great poem:

O, my clanswomen
Let us all cry together!
Come,
Let us mourn the death of our mother,
The death of a Queen
The ash that was produced
By a great fire,
O this homestead is utterly dead
Close the gates
With lacari thorns,
For our mother
The creator of the
Stool[8] is lost!
And all the young women
Have perished in the wilderness!

But this is not the end of the story, for all the young women—our mothers and grandmothers, ourselves—have not perished in the wilderness. And if we ask ourselves why, and search for and find the answer, we will know beyond

15

---

6   *Bessie Smith ... Aretha Franklin*   Acclaimed and influential Black women singers, songwriters, and musicians of the twentieth century.

7   *Okot p'Bitek*   Internationally prominent Ugandan poet (1931–82); Walker adapts a passage from his best-known work, the narrative poem *Song of Lawino* (1966): "O, my clansmen, / Let us all cry together! / Come, / Let us mourn the death of my husband, / The death of a Prince / The Ash that was produced / By a great Fire! / O, this homestead is utterly dead, / Close the gates / With lacari thorns, / For the Prince / The heir to the Stool is lost! / And all the young men / Have perished in the wilderness!"

8   *Stool*   I.e., throne.

all efforts to erase it from our minds, just exactly who, and of what, we Black American women are.

One example, perhaps the most pathetic, most misunderstood one, can provide a backdrop: Phillis Wheatley,[9] a slave in the 1700s.

Virginia Woolf, in her book, *A Room of One's Own*, wrote that in order for a woman to write fiction she must have two things, certainly: a room of her own (with key and lock) and enough money to support herself.

What then are we to make of Phillis Wheatley, a slave, who owned not even herself? This sickly, frail, Black girl who required a servant of her own at times—her health was so precarious—and who, had she been white would have been easily considered the intellectual superior of all the women and most of the men in the society of her day.

Virginia Woolf wrote further, speaking of course not of our Phillis, that "any woman born with a great gift in the sixteenth century [insert eighteenth century, insert Black woman, insert born or made a slave] would certainly have gone crazed, shot herself, or ended her days in some lonely cottage outside the village, half witch, half wizard [insert Saint], feared and mocked at. For it needs little skill and psychology to be sure that a highly gifted girl who had tried to use her gift for poetry would have been so thwarted and hindered by contrary instincts [add chains, guns, the lash, the ownership of one's body by someone else, submission to an alien religion], that she must have lost her health and sanity to a certainty."

20   The key words, as they relate to Phillis, are "contrary instincts." For when we read the poetry of Phillis Wheatley—as when we read the novels of Nella Larsen or the oddly false-sounding autobiography of that freest of all Black women writers, Zora Hurston[10]—evidence of "contrary instincts" is everywhere. Her loyalties were completely divided, as was, without question, her mind.

But how could this be otherwise? Captured at seven, a slave of wealthy, doting whites who instilled in her the "savagery" of the Africa they "rescued" her from ... one wonders if she was even able to remember her homeland as she had known it, or as it really was.

Yet, because she did try to use her gift for poetry in a world that made her a slave, she was "so thwarted and hindered by ... contrary instincts, that she

---

9   *Phillis Wheatley*   Wheatley was the first Black person to publish a book of poetry in English.

10   *Nella Larsen*   African American novelist and short story writer (1891–1964);   *Zora Hurston*   Zora Neale Hurston, African American writer best known for her novel *Their Eyes Were Watching God*; the autobiography Walker refers to is *Dust Tracks on the Road* (1942).

... lost her health...." In the last years of her brief life, burdened not only with the need to express her gift but also with a penniless, friendless "freedom" and several small children for whom she was forced to do strenuous work to feed, she lost her health. Suffering from malnutrition and neglect and who knows what mental agonies, Phillis Wheatley died.

So torn by "contrary instincts" was Black, kidnapped, enslaved Phillis that her description of "the Goddess"—as she poetically called the liberty she did not have—is ironically, cruelly humorous. And, in fact, has held Phillis up to ridicule for more than a century. It is usually read prior to hanging Phillis's memory as that of a fool. She wrote:

> The Goddess comes, she moves divinely fair,
> Olive and laurel binds her *golden* hair.
> Wherever shines this native of the skies
> Unnumber'd charms and recent graces rise.

(Emphasis mine)

It is obvious that Phillis, the slave, combed the "Goddess's" hair every morning; prior, perhaps to bringing in the milk, or fixing her mistress's lunch. She took her imagery from the one thing she saw elevated above all others.

With the benefit of hindsight we ask "How could she?"

25

But at last, Phillis, we understand. No more snickering when your stiff, struggling ambivalent lines are forced on us. We know now that you were not an idiot nor a traitor; only a sickly little Black girl, snatched from your home and country and made a slave; a woman who still struggled to sing the song that was your gift, although in a land of barbarians who praised you for your bewildered tongue. It is not so much what you sang, as that you kept alive, in so many of our ancestors, the notion of song.

Black women are called, in the folklore that so aptly identifies one's status in society, "the mule of the world," because we have been handed the burdens that everyone else—everyone else—refused to carry. We have also been called "Matriarchs," "Superwomen," and "Mean and Evil Bitches." Not to mention "Castraters" and "Sapphire's Mama."[11] When we have pleaded for understanding, our character has been distorted; when we have asked for simple caring, we have been handed empty inspirational appellations, then stuck in a far corner. When we have asked for love, we have been given children. In short, even our plainer gifts, our labors of fidelity and love, have been knocked down

---

11 *Sapphire's Mama* Character in *Amos 'n' Andy*, a mid-twentieth-century American radio show and then TV sitcom set in Harlem. Sapphire's Mama, one of many stereotypical Black characters on the show, is presented as a difficult, overbearing, critical, and undesirable woman.

our throats. To be an artist, and a Black woman, even today, lowers our status in many respects, rather than raises it: and yet, artists we will be.

Therefore we must fearlessly pull out of ourselves and look at and identify with our lives the living creativity some of our great-grandmothers knew, even without "knowing" it, the reality of their spirituality, even if they didn't recognize it beyond what happened in the singing at church—and they never had any intention of giving it up.

How they did it—those millions of Black women who were not Phillis Wheatley, or Lucy Terry or Frances Harper or Zora Hurston or Nella Larsen or Bessie Smith—nor Elizabeth Catlett, nor Katherine Dunham,[12] either—brings me to the title of this essay, "In Search of Our Mothers' Gardens," which is a personal account that is yet shared, by all of us. I found, while thinking about the far-reaching world of the creative Black woman, that often the truest answer to a question that really matters can be found very close. So I was not surprised when my own mother popped into my mind.

30　　　In the late 1920s my mother ran away from home to marry my father. Marriage, if not running away, was expected of 17-year-old girls. By the time she was 20, she had two children and was pregnant with a third. Five children later, I was born. And this is how I came to know my mother: she seemed a large, soft, loving-eyed woman who was rarely impatient in our home. Her quick, violent temper was on view only a few times a year when she battled with the white landlord who had the misfortune to suggest to her that her children did not need to go to school.

She made all the clothes we wore, even my brothers' overalls. She made all the towels and sheets we used. She spent the summers canning vegetables and fruits. She spent the winter evenings making quilts enough to cover all our beds.

During the "working" day, she labored beside—not behind—my father in the fields. Her day began before sunup, and did not end until late at night. There was never a moment for her to sit down, undisturbed, to unravel her own private thoughts; never a time free from interruption—by work or the noisy inquiries of her many children. And yet, it is to my mother—and all our mothers who were not famous—that I went in search of the secret of what has fed that muzzled and often mutilated, but vibrant, creative spirit that the Black woman has inherited, and that pops out in wild and unlikely places to this day.

12　*Lucy Terry*　Former slave (c. 1730–1821) whose "Bars Fight" is considered the oldest known literary work by an African American;　*Frances Harper*　African American poet, author, abolitionist, and suffragist (1825–1911);　*Elizabeth Catlett*　African American sculptor and graphic artist (1915–2012);　*Katherine Dunham*　African American choreographer, dancer, author, and social activist (1909–2006).

But when, you will ask, did my overworked mother have time to know or care about feeding the creative spirit?

The answer is so simple that many of us have spent years discovering it. We have constantly looked high, when we should have looked high-and-low.

For example: in the Smithsonian Institution in Washington, D.C., there hangs a quilt unlike any other in the world. In fanciful, inspired, and yet simple and identifiable figures, it portrays the story of the Crucifixion. It is considered rare, beyond price. Though it follows no known pattern of quilt-making, and though it is made of bits and pieces of worthless rags, it is obviously the work of a person of powerful imagination and deep spiritual feeling. Below this quilt I saw a note that says it was made by "an anonymous Black woman in Alabama, a hundred years ago."

35

If we could locate this "anonymous" Black woman from Alabama, she would turn out to be one of our grandmothers—an artist who left her mark in the only materials she could afford, and in the only medium her position in society allowed her to use.

As Virginia Woolf wrote further, in *A Room of One's Own*:

> Yet genius of a sort must have existed among women as it must have existed among the working class. [Change this to slaves and the wives and daughters of sharecroppers.] Now and again an Emily Brontë or a Robert Burns [change this to a Zora Hurston or a Richard Wright[13]] blazes out and proves its presence. But certainly it never got itself on to paper. When, however, one reads of a witch being ducked,[14] of a woman possessed by devils [or Sainthood], of a wise woman selling herbs [our rootworkers[15]], or even a very remarkable man who had a mother, then I think we are on the track of a lost novelist, a suppressed poet, of some mute and inglorious Jane Austen.... Indeed, I would venture to guess that Anon,* who wrote so many poems without signing them, was often a woman....

And so our mothers and grandmothers have, more often than not anonymously, handed on the creative spark, the seed of the flower they themselves never hoped to see: or like a sealed letter they could not plainly read.

---

13 *Emily Brontë* English novelist (1818–48) from a middle-class family; *Robert Burns* Scottish poet and lyricist (1759–96), who was the son of a tenant farmer; *Richard Wright* African American poet and author (1908–60).

14 *ducked* Ducking is a method of interrogation and punishment, often used during witch trials, whereby the victim was tied hand and foot and thrown in the water; floating was an indication of guilt, while sinking (and death) indicated innocence.

15 *rootworkers* Practitioners of rootwork (also called Hoodoo), an African American folk magic tradition.

And so it is, certainly, with my own mother. Unlike "Ma" Rainey's[16] songs, which retained their creator's name even while blasting forth from Bessie Smith's mouth, no song or poem will bear my mother's name. Yet so many of the stories that I write, that we all write, are my mother's stories. Only recently did I fully realize this: that through years of listening to my mother's stories of her life, I have absorbed not only the stories themselves, but something of the manner in which she spoke, something of the urgency that involves the knowledge that her stories—like her life—must be recorded. It is probably for this reason that so much of what I have written is about characters whose counterparts in real life are so much older than I am.

40   But the telling of these stories, which came from my mother's lips as naturally as breathing, was not the only way my mother showed herself as an artist. For stories, too, were subject to being distracted, to dying without conclusion. Dinners must be started, and cotton must be gathered before the big rains. The artist that was and is my mother showed itself to me only after many years. This is what I finally noticed:

Like Mem, a character in *The Third Life of Grange Copeland*,[17] my mother adorned with flowers whatever shabby house we were forced to live in. And not just your typical straggly country stand of zinnias, either. She planted ambitious gardens—and still does—with over 50 different varieties of plants that bloom profusely from early March until late November. Before she left home for the fields, she watered her flowers, chopped up the grass, and laid out new beds. When she returned from the fields she might divide clumps of bulbs, dig a cold pit, uproot and replant roses, or prune branches from her taller bushes or trees—until it was too dark to see.

Whatever she planted grew as if by magic, and her fame as a grower of flowers spread over three counties. Because of her creativity with her flowers, even my memories of poverty are seen through a screen of blooms—sunflowers, petunias, roses, dahlias, forsythia, spirea, delphiniums, verbena ... and on and on.

And I remember people coming to my mother's yard to be given cuttings from her flowers; I hear again the praise showered on her because whatever rocky soil she landed on, she turned into a garden. A garden so brilliant with colors, so original in its design, so magnificent with life and creativity, that to this day people drive by our house in Georgia—perfect strangers and imperfect strangers—and ask to stand or walk among my mother's art.

---

16 *"Ma" Rainey*   African American blues singer (1886–1939) known as the "Mother of the Blues."

17 *The Third Life of Grange Copeland*   Alice Walker's first novel, published in 1970.

I notice that it is only when my mother is working in her flowers that she is radiant, almost to the point of being invisible except as Creator: hand and eye. She is involved in work her soul must have. Ordering the universe in the image of her personal conception of Beauty.

Her face, as she prepares the Art that is her gift, is a legacy of respect she leaves to me, for all that illuminates and cherishes life. She had handed down respect for the possibilities—and the will to grasp them. 45

For her, so hindered and intruded upon in so many ways, being an artist has still been a daily part of her life. This ability to hold on, even in very simple ways, is work Black women have done for a very long time.

This poem is not enough, but it is something, for the woman who literally covered the holes in our walls with sunflowers:

They were women then
My mama's generation
Husky of voice—Stout of Step
With fists as well as
Hands
How they battered down
Doors
And ironed
Starched white
Shirts
How they led
Armies
Headragged Generals
Across mined
Fields
Booby-trapped
Ditches
To discover books
Desks
A place for us
How they knew what we
Must know
Without knowing a page
Of it
Themselves.

Guided by my heritage of a love of beauty and a respect for strength—in search of my mother's garden, I found my own.

And perhaps in Africa over 200 years ago, there was just such a mother; perhaps she painted vivid and daring decorations in oranges and yellows and greens on the walls of her hut; perhaps she sang in a voice like Roberta Flack's—sweetly over the compounds of her village; perhaps she wove the most stunning mats or told the most ingenious stories of all the village story-tellers. Perhaps she was herself a poet—though only her daughter's name is signed to the poems that we know.

50   Perhaps Phillis Wheatley's mother was also an artist.

Perhaps in more than Phillis Wheatley's biological life is her mother's signature made clear.

(1974)

Questions

1. Writing in 1974, Walker imagines the fate of Black women artists in the generations that preceded hers. Read the selections from Harriet Jacobs's *Incidents in the Life of Slave Girl* that are reprinted in this anthology. To what extent does Jacobs's account of her life accord with Walker's imagining of Black women's lives in nineteenth-century America?

2. Consider the symbol of the garden, both in its wider historical and mythological contexts and as it appears in this essay.

   a. How does Walker characterize her mother's garden? What do these characteristics mean in the context of the full essay?

   b. What connotations or cultural meanings do gardens carry—in Christian tradition, for example, or in literary traditions? Brainstorm as many as you can think of; which, if any, are reflected in Walker's essay, and how?

   c. Walker has continued to be drawn to the symbol of the garden (her website address, for example, is alicewalkersgarden.com). Why might the garden be a fitting symbol to associate with wom-anism? How does this symbol help Walker express her vision of Black women's creativity?

3. For Walker, what role does spirituality play for the artist?

4. Virginia Woolf's *A Room of One's Own* is an important intertext in this piece. How does Walker use this white woman's feminist essay to elucidate her argument about the history and legacy of Black women artists?

5. Walker writes that in "the oddly false-sounding autobiography of that freest of all Black women writers, Zora Hurston[,] ... evidence of 'contrary instincts' is everywhere" (paragraph 20). Read Hurston's autobiographical essay reprinted in this anthology, "How It Feels to Be Colored Me." To what extent (if at all) do you find "evidence of 'contrary instincts'" in this essay?

6. The work of ancestors is foundational to Walker's own creativity. Research another contemporary Black woman artist. How (if at all) does her work relate to the past? To her heritage?

7. One of the artworks reproduced in this anthology's color insert is a quilt made by an ex-slave, Harriet Powers, in the late eighteenth century. What (if anything) does Walker's essay add to your understanding of the quilt—of its importance, its meaning, and/or the context in which it was created?

AUDRE LORDE

THE TRANSFORMATION OF SILENCE INTO LANGUAGE AND ACTION

"I am defined as other in every group I'm part of," wrote Black lesbian feminist Audre Lorde. "The outsider, both strength and weakness. Yet without community there is no liberation." Lorde's work in poetry and critical theory combats patriarchy, racism, heterosexism, and classism, and has been particularly influential in its insistence that social justice movements must appreciate the differences among women and among people of color: "Certainly there are very real differences between us of race, age, and sex. But it is not those differences between us that are separating us. It is rather our refusal to recognize those differences." The following piece was initially a paper Lorde delivered at the Modern Language Association's "Lesbians and Literature Panel" in 1977; it was then published in Sinister Wisdom, *a lesbian literary and art journal. It is reprinted below as it appeared in Lorde's nonfiction collection* Sister Outsider *(1984).*

I have come to believe over and over again that what is most important to me must be spoken, made verbal and shared, even at the risk of having it bruised or misunderstood. That the speaking profits me, beyond any other effect. I am standing here as a Black lesbian poet, and the meaning of all that waits upon the fact that I am still alive, and might not have been. Less than two months ago I was told by two doctors, one female and one male, that I would have to have breast surgery, and that there was a 60 to 80 percent chance that the tumor was malignant. Between that telling and the actual surgery, there was a three week period of the agony of an involuntary reorganization of my entire life. The surgery was completed, and the growth was benign.

But within those three weeks, I was forced to look upon myself and my living with a harsh and urgent clarity that has left me still shaken but much stronger. This is a situation faced by many women, by some of you here today. Some of what I experienced during that time has helped elucidate for me much of what I feel concerning the transformation of silence into language and action.

In becoming forcibly and essentially aware of my mortality, and of what I wished and wanted for my life, however short it might be, priorities and omissions became strongly etched in a merciless light, and what I most regretted were my silences. Of what had I *ever* been afraid? To question or to speak as I believed could have meant pain, or death. But we all hurt in so many different ways, all the time, and pain will either change, or end. Death, on the other hand, is the final silence. And that might be coming quickly, now, without regard for whether I had ever spoken what needed to be said, or had only betrayed myself into small silences, while I planned someday to speak, or waited for someone else's words. And I began to recognize a source of power within myself that comes from the knowledge that while it is most desirable not to be afraid, learning to put fear into a perspective gave me great strength.

I was going to die, if not sooner then later, whether or not I had ever spoken myself. My silences had not protected me. Your silence will not protect you. But for every real word spoken, for every attempt I had ever made to speak those truths for which I am still seeking, I had made contact with other women while we examined the words to fit a world in which we all believed, bridging our differences. And it was the concern and caring of all those women which gave me strength and enabled me to scrutinize the essentials of my living.

The women who sustained me through that period were Black and white, old and young, lesbian, bisexual, and heterosexual, and we all shared a war against the tyrannies of silence. They all gave me a strength and concern without which I could not have survived intact. Within those weeks of acute fear came the knowledge—within the war we are all waging with the forces of death, subtle and otherwise, conscious or not, I am not only a casualty, I am also a warrior. 5

What are the words you do not yet have? What do you need to say? What are the tyrannies you swallow day by day and attempt to make your own, until you will sicken and die of them, still in silence? Perhaps for some of you here today, I am the face of one of your fears. Because I am woman, because I am Black, because I am lesbian, because I am myself a Black woman warrior poet doing my work, come to ask you, are you doing yours?

And, of course, I am afraid—you can hear it in my voice—because the transformation of silence into language and action is an act of self-revelation and that always seems fraught with danger. But my daughter, when I told her of our topic and my difficulty with it, said, "Tell them about how you're never really a whole person if you remain silent, because there's always that one little piece inside of you that wants to be spoken out, and if you keep ignoring it, it gets madder and madder and hotter and hotter, and if you don't speak it out one day it will just up and punch you in the mouth from the inside."

In the cause of silence, each one of us draws the face of her own fear—fear of contempt, of censure, or some judgment, or recognition, of challenge, of annihilation. But most of all, I think, we fear the very visibility without which we also cannot truly live. Within this country where racial difference creates a constant, if unspoken, distortion of vision, Black women have on one hand always being highly visible, and so, on the other hand, have been rendered invisible through the depersonalization of racism. Even within the women's movement, we have had to fight and still do, for that very visibility which also renders us most vulnerable, our Blackness. For to survive in the mouth of this dragon we call america, we have had to learn this first and most vital lesson—that we were never meant to survive. Not as human beings. And neither were most of you here today, Black or not. And that visibility which makes us most vulnerable is that which also is the source of our greatest strength. Because the machine will try to grind you into dust anyway, whether or not we speak. We can sit in our corners mute forever while our sisters and our selves are wasted, while our children are distorted and destroyed, while our earth is poisoned, we can sit in our safe corners mute as bottles, and we still will be no less afraid.

In my house this year we are celebrating the feast of Kwanza, the African-American festival of harvest which begins the day after Christmas and lasts for seven days. There are seven principles of Kwanza, one for each day. The first principle is Umoja, which means unity, the decision to strive for and maintain unity in self and community. The principle for yesterday, the second day, was Kujichagulia—self-determination—the decision to define ourselves, name ourselves, and speak for ourselves, instead of being defined and spoken for by others. Today is the third day of Kwanza, and the principle for today is Ujima—collective work and responsibility—the decision to build and maintain ourselves and our communities together and to recognize and solve our problems together.

10   Each of us is here now because in one way or another we share a commitment to language and to the power of language, and to the reclaiming of that language which has been made to work against us. In the transformation of silence into language and action, it is vitally necessary for each one of us to establish or examine her function in that transformation, and to recognize her role as vital within that transformation.

For those of us who write, it is necessary to scrutinize not only the truth of what we speak, but the truth of that language by which we speak it. For others, it is to share and spread also those words that are meaningful to us. But primarily for us all, it is necessary to teach by living and speaking those truths which we believe and know beyond understanding. Because in this way alone we can survive, by taking part in a process of life that is creative and continuing, that is growth.

And it is never without fear; of visibility, of the harsh light of scrutiny and perhaps judgment, of pain, of death. But we have lived through all of those already, in silence, except death. And I remind myself all the time now, that if I were to have been born mute, and had maintained an oath of silence my whole life long for safety, I would still have suffered, and I would still die. It is very good for establishing perspective.

And where the words of women are crying to be heard, we must each of us recognize our responsibility to seek those words out, to read them and share them and examine them in their pertinence to our lives. That we not hide behind the mockeries of separations that have been imposed upon us and which so often we accept as our own: for instance, "I can't possibly teach Black women's writings—their experience is so different from mine," yet how many years have you spent teaching Plato and Shakespeare and Proust? Or another: "She's a white woman and what could she possibly have to say to me?" Or "She's a lesbian, what would my husband say, or my chairman?" Or again, "This woman writes of her sons and I have no children." And all the other endless ways in which we rob ourselves of ourselves and each other.

We can learn to work and speak when we are afraid in the same way we have learned to work and speak when we are tired. For we have been socialized to respect fear more than our own needs for language and definition, and while we wait in silence for that final luxury of fearlessness, the weight of that silence will choke us.

The fact that we are here and that I speak now these words is an attempt to break that silence and bridge some of those differences between us, for it is not difference which immobilizes us, but silence. And there are so many silences to be broken.

15

(1977, 1978, 1984)

Questions

1. In this paper, how does Lorde characterize the relationship between the personal and the political?

2. Why, according to Lorde, is visibility important for Black women? Why is it frightening?

3. Read Lorde's "Uses of Anger," also reprinted in this anthology. To what extent do these essays share common underlying ideas?

4. Read Mia McKenzie's "White Silence," also reprinted in this anthology. Whose silence is discussed in each piece? To what extent is there overlap between the causes of silence noted in each piece?

5. Lorde poses the following questions: "What are the words you do not yet have? What do you need to say? What are the tyrannies you swallow day by day and attempt to make your own, until you will sicken and die of them, still in silence?" Write a private reflection on your own answers to these questions; then, based on that reflection, write a statement to share with your class.

6. Listen to Lorde's speech online in the Lesbian Herstory Archives ("'Lesbians and Literature Panel Discussion at MLA Conference,'" http://herstories.prattinfoschool.nyc/omeka/document/54; Lorde's speech begins about 40 minutes into the recording). How does the writing in this piece reflect its initial form as a speech? How (if at all) does the rhetorical impact of the recording differ from that of the written text?

USES OF ANGER: WOMEN RESPONDING TO RACISM

The theme of the 1981 National Women's Studies Association Conference, where Lorde delivered the following keynote address, was "Women Respond to Racism." The conference, which was predominantly white—about 300 women of color attended, out of about 1400 participants—offered a series of consciousness-raising groups for people of shared background: an extensive range of choices for white women, from "white/immigrant" to "white/working-class," and only one group for all women of color. There was a great deal of tension regarding the failure both of the conference and of mainstream feminism in general to adequately address racial differences and the relationship between racial and patriarchal oppression. With this keynote address, Lorde, among other things, calls for a more nuanced understanding of womanhood and offers several ways of understanding how anger functions.

☙

R acism. The belief in the inherent superiority of one race over all others and thereby the right to dominance, manifest and implied.

Women respond to racism. My response to racism is anger. I have lived with that anger, on that anger, ignoring it, feeding upon it, learning to use it before it laid my visions to waste, for most of my life. Once I did it in silence, afraid of the weight. My fear of that anger taught me nothing. Your fear of that anger will teach you nothing, also.

Women responding to racism means women responding to anger, the anger of exclusion, of unquestioned privilege, of racial distortions, of silence, ill-use, stereotyping, defensiveness, misnaming, betrayal, and co-optation.*

My anger is a response to racist attitudes and to the actions and presumptions that arise out of those attitudes. If your dealings with other women reflect those attitudes, then my anger and your attendant fears are spotlights that can be used for growth in the same way I have used learning to express anger for my growth. But for corrective surgery, not guilt. Guilt and defensiveness are bricks in a wall against which we all flounder; they serve none of our futures.

Because I do not want this to become a theoretical discussion, I am going to give a few examples of interchanges between women that illustrate these points. In the interest of time, I am going to cut them short. I want you to know that there were many more.   5

For example:

• I speak out of a direct and particular anger at a particular academic conference, and a white woman says, "Tell me how you feel but don't say it too harshly or I cannot hear you." But is it my manner that keeps her from hearing, or the threat of a message that her life may change?

• The Women's Studies Program of a southern university invites a Black woman to read following a week-long forum on Black and white women. "What has this week given to you?" I ask. The most vocal white woman says, "I think I've gotten a lot. I feel Black women really understand me a lot better now; they have a better idea of where I'm coming from." As if understanding her lay at the core of the racist problem.

• After fifteen years of a women's movement which professes to address the life concerns and possible futures of all women, I still hear, on campus after campus, "How can we address the issues of racism? No women of Color attended." Or, the other side of that statement, "We have no one in our department equipped to teach their work." In other words, racism is a Black women's problem, a problem of women of Color, and only we can discuss it.

• After I have read from my work entitled "Poems for Women in Rage"[1]   10
a white woman asks me, "Are you going to do anything with how we can deal

---

1   [Lorde's note]   *Poems for Women in Rage*   One poem from this series is included in *Chosen Poems: Old and New* (W.W. Norton and Company, New York, 1978), pp. 105–108.

directly with *our* anger? I feel it's so important." I ask, "How do you use *your* rage?" And then I have to turn away from the blank look in her eyes, before she can invite me to participate in her own annihilation. I do not exist to feel her anger for her.

• White women are beginning to examine their relationships to Black women, yet often I hear them wanting only to deal with the little colored children across the roads of childhood, the beloved nursemaid, the occasional second-grade classmate—those tender memories of what was once mysterious and intriguing or neutral. You avoid the childhood assumptions formed by the raucous laughter at Rastus and Alfalfa,[2] the acute message of your mommy's handkerchief spread upon the park bench because I had just been sitting there, the indelible and dehumanizing portraits of Amos 'n Andy[3] and your daddy's humorous bedtime stories.

I wheel my two-year-old daughter in a shopping cart through a supermarket in Eastchester[4] in 1967, and a little white girl riding past in her mother's cart calls out excitedly, "Oh look, Mommy, a baby maid!" And your mother shushes you, but she does not correct you. And so fifteen years later, at a conference on racism, you can still find that story humorous. But I hear your laughter is full of terror and dis-ease.

• A white academic welcomes the appearance of a collection by non-Black women of Color.[5] "It allows me to deal with racism without dealing with the harshness of Black women," she says to me.

• At an international cultural gathering of women, a well-known white american woman poet interrupts the reading of the work of women of Color to read her own poem, and then dashes off to an "important panel."

15   If women in the academy truly want a dialogue about racism, it will require recognizing the needs and the living contexts of other women. When

---

2   *Rastus* Stock character of a cheerful African American man that appeared in minstrel shows and other racist works of popular culture in the late nineteenth and early twentieth centuries; *Alfalfa* Character in the series of films *Our Gang* (1922–44), which were later shown as the television series *Little Rascals*. Alfalfa was white, but the show was groundbreaking in its portrayal of African American and white children playing together. It has also, however, been heavily criticized for stereotypical treatment of its African American characters.

3   *Amos 'n Andy* Mid-twentieth-century radio show that also became a television series. On the radio, the show's white creators, Freeman Gosden and Charles Correll, voiced most of the characters, including the two African American main characters.

4   *Eastchester* Town in Westchester County on Long Island in the state of New York.

5   [Lorde's note] *This Bridge Called My Back: Writings by Radical Women of Color* edited by Cherríe Moraga and Gloria E. Anzaldúa (Kitchen Table: Women of Color Press, New York, 1984), first published in 1981.

an academic woman says, "I can't afford it," she may mean she is making a choice about how to spend her available money. But when a woman on welfare says, "I can't afford it," she means she is surviving on an amount of money that was barely subsistence in 1972, and she often does not have enough to eat. Yet the National Women's Studies Association here in 1981 holds a conference in which it commits itself to responding to racism, yet refuses to waive the registration fee for poor women and women of Color who wished to present and conduct workshops. This has made it impossible for many women of Color—for instance, Wilmette Brown, of Black Women for Wages for Housework—to participate in this conference. Is this to be merely another case of the academy discussing life within the closed circuits of the academy?

To the white women present who recognize these attitudes as familiar, but most of all, to all my sisters of Color who live and survive thousands of such encounters—to my sisters of Color who like me still tremble their rage under harness, or who sometimes question the expression of our rage as useless and disruptive (the two most popular accusations)—I want to speak about anger, my anger, and what I have learned from my travels through its dominions.

Everything can be used / except what is wasteful / (you will need / to remember this when you are accused of destruction.)[6]

Every woman has a well-stocked arsenal of anger potentially useful against those oppressions, personal and institutional, which brought that anger into being. Focused with precision it can become a powerful source of energy serving progress and change. And when I speak of change, I do not mean a simple switch of positions or a temporary lessening of tensions, nor the ability to smile or feel good. I am speaking of a basic and radical alteration in all those assumptions underlining our lives.

I have seen situations where white women hear a racist remark, resent what has been said, become filled with fury, and remain silent because they are afraid. That unexpressed anger lies within them like an undetonated device, usually to be hurled at the first woman of Color who talks about racism.

But anger expressed and translated into action in the service of our vision and our future is a liberating and strengthening act of clarification, for it is in the painful process of this translation that we identify who are our allies with whom we have grave differences, and who are our genuine enemies.

Anger is loaded with information and energy. When I speak of women of Color, I do not only mean Black women. The woman of Color who is not Black and who charges me with rendering her invisible by assuming that her

20

6　[Lorde's note]　From "For Each of You," first published in *From a Land Where Other People Live* (Broadside Press, Detroit, 1973), and collected in *Chosen Poems: Old and New* (W.W. Norton and Company, New York, 1982), p. 42.

struggles with racism are identical with my own has something to tell me that I had better learn from, lest we both waste ourselves fighting the truths between us. If I participate, knowingly or otherwise, in my sister's oppression and she calls me on it, to answer her anger with my own only blankets the substance of our exchange with reaction. It wastes energy. And yes, it is very difficult to stand still and to listen to another woman's voice delineate an agony I do not share, or even one to which I myself have participated.

In this place we speak removed from the more blatant reminders of our embattlement as women. This need not blind us to the size and complexities of the forces mounting against us and all that is most human within our environment. We are not here as women examining racism in a political and social vacuum. We operate in the teeth of a system for which racism and sexism are primary, established, and necessary props of profit. Women responding to racism is a topic so dangerous that when the local media attempt to discredit this conference they choose to focus upon the provision of lesbian housing as a diversionary device[7]—as if the Hartford *Courant* dare not mention the topic chosen for discussion here, racism, lest it become apparent that women are in fact attempting to examine and to alter all the repressive conditions of our lives.

Mainstream communication does not want women, particularly white women, responding to racism. It wants racism to be accepted as an immutable given in the fabric of your existence, like eveningtime or the common cold.

So we are working in a context of opposition and threat, the cause of which is certainly not the angers which lie between us, but rather that virulent hatred leveled against all women, people of Color, lesbians and gay men, poor people—against all of us who are seeking to examine the particulars of our lives as we resist our oppressions, moving toward coalition and effective action.

25   Any discussion among women about racism must include the recognition and the use of anger. It must be direct and creative because it is crucial. We cannot allow our fear of anger to deflect us nor seduce us into settling for anything less than the hard work of excavating honesty; we must be quite serious about the choice of this topic and the angers entwined within it because, rest assured, our opponents are quite serious about their hatred of us and of what we are trying to do here.

And while we scrutinize the often painful face of each other's anger, please remember that it is not our anger which makes me caution you to lock your doors at night and not to wander the streets of Hartford alone. It is the hatred which lurks in those streets, that urge to destroy us all if we truly work for change rather than merely indulge in our academic rhetoric.

---

7   *the provision ... device*   A 19 May 1981 article in the *Hartford Courant* discussed the conference; its headline was "Lesbian Housing Available for Women's Conference at UConn."

This hatred and our anger are very different. Hatred is the fury of those who do not share our goals, and its object is death and destruction. Anger is the grief of distortions between peers, and its object is change. But our time is getting shorter. We have been raised to view any difference other than sex as a reason for destruction, and for Black women and white women to face each other's angers without denial or immobility or silence or guilt is in itself a heretical and generative* idea. It implies peers meeting upon a common basis to examine difference, and to alter those distortions which history has created around our difference. For it is those distortions which separate us. And we must ask ourselves: Who profits from all this?

Women of Color in america have grown up within a symphony of anger, at being silenced, at being unchosen, at knowing that when we survive, it is in spite of a world that takes for granted our lack of humanness, and which hates our very existence outside of its service. And I say symphony rather than cacophony because we have had to learn to orchestrate those furies so that they do not tear us apart. We have had to learn to move through them and use them for strength and force and insight within our daily lives. Those of us who did not learn this difficult lesson did not survive. And part of my anger is always libation* for my fallen sisters.

Anger is an appropriate reaction to racist attitudes, as is fury when the actions arising from those attitudes do not change. To those women here who fear the anger of women of Color more than their own unscrutinized racist attitudes, I ask: Is the anger of women of Color more threatening than the woman-hatred that tinges all aspects of our lives?

It is not the anger of other women that will destroy us but our refusals to stand still, to listen to its rhythms, to learn within it, to move beyond the manner of presentation to the substance, to tap that anger as an important source of empowerment.

I cannot hide my anger to spare you guilt, nor hurt feelings, nor answering anger; for to do so insults and trivializes all our efforts. Guilt is not a response to anger; it is a response to one's own actions or lack of action. If it leads to change then it can be useful, since it is then no longer guilt but the beginning of knowledge. Yet all too often, guilt is just another name for impotence, for defensiveness destructive of communication; it becomes a device to protect ignorance and the continuation of things the way they are, the ultimate protection for changelessness.

Most women have not developed tools for facing anger constructively. CR[8] groups in the past, largely white, dealt with how to express anger, usually at the world of men. And these groups were made up of white women

---

8   *CR*   Consciousness-raising.

who shared the terms of their oppressions. There was usually little attempt to articulate the genuine differences between women, such as those of race, color, age, class, and sexual identity. There was no apparent need at that time to examine the contradictions of self, woman as oppressor. There was work on expressing anger, but very little on anger directed against each other. No tools were developed to deal with other women's anger except to avoid it, deflect it, or flee from it under a blanket of guilt.

I have no creative use for guilt, yours or my own. Guilt is only another way of avoiding informed action, of buying time out of the pressing need to make clear choices, out of the approaching storm that can feed the earth as well as bend the trees. If I speak to you in anger, at least I have spoken to you: I have not put a gun to your head and shot you down in the street; I have not looked at your bleeding sister's body and asked, "What did she do to deserve it?" This was the reaction of two white women to Mary Church Terrell's[9] telling of the lynching* of a pregnant Black woman whose baby was then torn from her body. That was in 1921, and Alice Paul had just refused to publicly endorse the enforcement of the Nineteenth Amendment for all women—by refusing to endorse the inclusion of women of Color, although we had worked to help bring about that amendment.[10]

The angers between women will not kill us if we can articulate them with precision, if we listen to the content of what is said with at least as much intensity as we defend ourselves from the manner of saying. When we turn from anger we turn from insight, saying we will accept only the designs already known, those deadly and safely familiar. I have tried to learn my anger's usefulness to me, as well as its limitations.

35   For women raised to fear, too often anger threatens annihilation. In the male construct of brute force, we were taught that our lives depended upon the good will of patriarchal power. The anger of others was to be avoided at

---

9   *Mary Church Terrell*   Journalist, educator, and activist for civil rights and women's rights (1863–1954). She was a founding member of the National Association for the Advancement of Colored People and the first African American woman to serve on a city schoolboard.

10   *Alice Paul*   Women's rights activist (1885–1977) and leader of the campaign that resulted in the Nineteenth Amendment (1920), which gave women the right to vote;   *I have not ... amendment*   Terrell asked Paul to make a statement in favor of enforcing the Nineteenth Amendment universally; many measures had been taken in Southern states to make it more difficult for African American women to vote. Paul refused to do so, and Terrell then made a speech to the Resolutions Committee of the Woman's Party requesting backing; in the course of this speech she described the lynching of a pregnant woman. When one white woman asked why the lynching had occurred, another added "She [the victim] did something, of course."

all costs because there was nothing to be learned from it but pain, a judgment that we had been bad girls, come up lacking, not done what we were supposed to do. And if we accept our powerlessness, then of course any anger can destroy us.

But the strength of women lies in recognizing differences between us as creative, and in standing to those distortions which we inherited without blame, but which are now ours to alter. The angers of women can transform difference through insight into power. For anger between peers births change, not destruction, and the discomfort and sense of loss it often causes is not fatal, but a sign of growth.

My response to racism is anger. That anger has eaten clefts into my living only when it remained unspoken, useless to anyone. It has also served me in classrooms without light or learning, where the work and history of Black women was less than a vapor. It has served me as fire in the ice zone of uncomprehending eyes of white women who see in my experience and the experience of my people only new reasons for fear or guilt. And my anger is no excuse for not dealing with your blindness, no reason to withdraw from the results of your own actions.

When women of Color speak out of the anger that laces so many of our contacts with white women, we are often told that we are "creating a mood of hopelessness," "preventing white women from getting past guilt," or "standing in the way of trusting communication and action." All these quotes come directly from letters to me from members of this organization within the last two years. One woman wrote, "Because you are Black and Lesbian, you seem to speak with the moral authority of suffering."[11] Yes, I am Black and Lesbian, and what you hear in my voice is fury, not suffering. Anger, not moral authority. There is a difference.

To turn aside from the anger of Black women with excuses or the pretexts of intimidation is to award no one power—it is merely another way of preserving racial blindness, the power of unaddressed privilege, unbreached, intact. Guilt is only another form of objectification. Oppressed peoples are always being asked to stretch a little more, to bridge the gap between blindness and humanity. Black women are expected to use our anger only in the service of other people's salvation or learning. But that time is over. My anger has meant pain to me but it has also meant survival, and before I give it

---

11 *Because ... suffering* Lorde quotes from a letter she received from the organizers of a 1979 conference in which she had participated. In Lorde's view, the conference had failed to adequately address matters of race, class, and sexual orientation, and she had pointed this out in a now-famous speech, "The Master's Tools Will Never Dismantle the Master's House," made during the conference.

up I'm going to be sure that there is something at least as powerful to replace it on the road to clarity.

40   What woman here is so enamored of her own oppression that she cannot see her heelprint upon another woman's face? What woman's terms of oppression have become precious and necessary to her as a ticket into the fold of the righteous, away from the cold winds of self-scrutiny?

I am a lesbian woman of Color whose children eat regularly because I work in a university. If their full bellies make me fail to recognize my commonality with a woman of Color whose children do not eat because she cannot find work, or who has no children because her insides are rotted from home abortions and sterilization; if I fail to recognize the lesbian who chooses not to have children, the woman who remains closeted because her homophobic community is her only life support, the woman who chooses silence instead of another death, the woman who is terrified lest my anger trigger the explosion of hers; if I fail to recognize them as other faces of myself, then I am contributing not only to each of their oppressions but also to my own, and the anger which stands between us then must be used for clarity and mutual empowerment, not for evasion by guilt or for further separation. I am not free while any woman is unfree, even when her shackles are very different from my own. And I am not free as long as one person of Color remains chained. Nor is any one of you.

I speak here as a woman of Color who is not bent upon destruction, but upon survival. No woman is responsible for altering the psyche of her oppressor, even when that psyche is embodied in another woman. I have suckled the wolf's lip of anger and I have used it for illumination, laughter, protection, fire in places where there was no light, no food, no sisters, no quarter.* We are not goddesses or matriarchs or edifices of divine forgiveness; we are not fiery fingers of judgment or instruments of flagellation; we are women forced back always upon our woman's power. We have learned to use anger as we have learned to use the dead flesh of animals, and bruised, battered, and changing, we have survived and grown and, in Angela Wilson's words, we *are* moving on. With or without uncolored women. We use whatever strengths we have fought for, including anger, to help define and fashion a world where all our sisters can grow, where our children can love, and where the power of touching and meeting another woman's difference and wonder will eventually transcend the need for destruction.

For it is not the anger of Black women which is dripping down over this globe like a diseased liquid. It is not my anger that launches rockets, spends over sixty thousand dollars a second on missiles and other agents of war and death, slaughters children in cities, stockpiles nerve gas and chemical bombs, sodomizes our daughters and our earth. It is not the anger of Black women which corrodes into blind, dehumanizing power, bent upon the annihilation of us all unless we meet it with what we have, our power to examine and to redefine the terms upon which we will live and work; our power to envision and to reconstruct, anger by painful anger, stone upon heavy stone, a future of pollinating difference and the earth to support our choices.

We welcome all women who can meet us, face to face, beyond objectification and beyond guilt.

(1981, revised 1984)

Questions

1. This essay was first delivered as a speech to an academic women's studies conference, where more than three-quarters of the attendees were white women. How (if at all) does the content of Lorde's speech reflect its audience?

2. How, according to Lorde, can anger be useful?

3. Lorde's speech includes a listing of examples of racism she encountered within academia and/or the feminist movement. Give an example of racism in your own academic experience.

4. What issues of injustice cause you to experience the most anger? To what extent do you find this anger productive?

5. In paragraph 15, Lorde says "If women in the academy truly want a dialogue about racism, it will require recognizing the needs and the living contexts of other women." When Lorde points to living contexts, what does she mean? Why might understanding difference be important?

HOWARD ZINN

from A PEOPLE'S HISTORY OF THE UNITED STATES

In the 1970s a great many American history textbooks—at both the high-school and the post-secondary levels—displayed notably right-wing biases; they often taught students, for example, that the Civil War had been fought mainly over "the principle of states' rights" rather than over slavery, and they tended to say little or nothing of the viciousness with which Black Americans had continued to be oppressed over more than a century of post-Civil War American history. Textbooks also tended to downplay or ignore the contributions made throughout American history by those who had resisted oppression—whether it be oppression of African Americans, of Native Americans, of women, or of labor organizers, anti-war crusaders, and other activists. In the late 1970s white historian and political scientist Howard Zinn, who had himself been active in the civil rights struggle since the mid 1950s, set out to write a corrective—a history that would be, in the words of Eric Foner, "about ordinary Americans' struggles for justice, equality, and power." The first edition of Zinn's A People's History of the United States *was published in 1980. Since then the book has sold more than 2,000,000 copies; widely used as a textbook, it has also been widely read by members of the general public. The excerpts included here are from a chapter focused on the Civil Rights Movement in the mid-twentieth century.*

CHAPTER 17: "OR DOES IT EXPLODE?"

The black revolt of the 1950s and 1960s—North and South—came as a sur- prise. But perhaps it should not have. The memory of oppressed people is one thing that cannot be taken away, and for such people, with such memories, revolt is always an inch below the surface. For blacks in the United States, there was the memory of slavery, and after that of segregation, lynching,* humiliation. And it was not just a memory but a living presence—part of the daily lives of blacks in generation after generation....

... The black militant mood, flashing here and there in the thirties, was reduced to a subsurface simmering during World War II, when the nation on the one hand denounced racism, and on the other hand maintained segregation in the armed forces and kept blacks in low-paying jobs. When the war ended, a new element entered the racial balance in the United States—the enormous, unprecedented upsurge of black and yellow people in Africa and Asia.

President Harry Truman had to reckon with this, especially as the cold war rivalry with the Soviet Union began, and the dark-skinned revolt of former colonies all over the world threatened to take Marxist[1] form. Action on the race question was needed, not just to calm a black population at home emboldened by war promises, frustrated by the basic sameness of their condition. It was needed to present to the world a United States that could counter the continuous Communist thrust at the most flagrant failure of American society—the race question. What Du Bois[2] had said long ago, unnoticed, now loomed large in 1945: "The problem of the 20th century is the problem of the color line."

President Harry Truman, in late 1946, appointed a Committee on Civil Rights, which recommended that the civil rights section of the Department of Justice be expanded, that there be a permanent Commission on Civil Rights, that Congress pass laws against lynching and to stop voting discrimination, and suggested new laws to end racial discrimination in jobs.

Truman's Committee was blunt about its motivation in making these recommendations. Yes, it said, there was "moral reason": a matter of conscience. But there was also an "economic reason"—discrimination was costly to the country, wasteful of its talent. And, perhaps most important, there was an international reason:

> ... We cannot escape the fact that our civil rights record has been an issue in world politics. The world's press and radio are full of it.... The United States is not so strong, the final triumph of the democratic ideal is not so inevitable that we can ignore what the world thinks of us or our record.

5

---

1   *dark-skinned revolt ... the world*   In the twenty years following 1945, more than twenty former colonies were granted or declared independence; these included, in Asia, India and Pakistan and, in Africa, Ghana, Nigeria, Kenya, and the Democratic Republic of the Congo;   *Marxist*   Informed by the philosophy of Karl Marx (1818–83), who interpreted history predominantly in terms of struggle between economic classes and predicted the replacement of capitalism with communism.

2   *Du Bois*   W.E.B. Du Bois (1868–1963), a prominent and enormously influential African American writer and activist; the quoted statement is from his influential book *The Souls of Black Folk* (1903).

... And so the United States went ahead to take small actions, hoping they would have large effects. Congress did not move to enact the legislation asked for by the Committee on Civil Rights. But Truman—four months before the presidential election of 1948, and challenged from the left in that election by Progressive party[3] candidate Henry Wallace—issued an executive order asking that the armed forces, segregated in World War II, institute policies of racial equality "as rapidly as possible." The order may have been prompted not only by the election but by the need to maintain black morale in the armed forces, as the possibility of war grew. It took over a decade to complete the desegregation in the military....

Meanwhile, the Supreme Court was taking steps—ninety years after the Constitution had been amended to establish racial equality—to move toward that end. During the war it ruled that the "white primary" used to exclude blacks from voting in the Democratic party primaries—which in the South were really the elections[4]—was unconstitutional.

In 1954, the Court finally struck down the "separate but equal" doctrine that it had defended since the 1890s. The NAACP* brought a series of cases before the Court to challenge segregation in the public schools, and now in *Brown v. Board of Education*[5] the Court said the separation of schoolchildren "generates a feeling of inferiority ... that may affect their hearts and minds in a way unlikely ever to be undone." In the field of public education, it said, "the doctrine of 'separate but equal' has no place." The Court did not insist on immediate change: a year later it said that segregated facilities should be integrated "with all deliberate speed." By 1965, ten years after the "all deliberate speed" guideline, more than 75 percent of the school districts in the South remained segregated.

Still, it was a dramatic decision—and the message went around the world in 1954 that the American government had outlawed segregation. In the United States too, for those not thinking about the customary gap between word and fact, it was an exhilarating sign of change.

10   What to others seemed rapid progress to blacks was apparently not enough....

---

3   *Progressive party*   American political party established for the purpose of Wallace's campaign; its platform included desegregation and socialist approaches to welfare and health care. The party never attracted a significant share of the popular vote, in large part because the public associated it with communism, and it collapsed altogether in 1955.

4   *which in the South ... elections*   Though in recent decades Southern states have predominantly elected Republicans, the Democratic party dominated the South for the first half of the twentieth century; the party gradually lost its footing there in the second half of the century.

5   *Brown v. Board of Education*   Landmark 1954 Supreme Court case, which declared the segregation of schoolchildren on the basis of race to be unconstitutional.

For such a people, with such a memory, and such daily recapitulation of history, revolt was always minutes away, in a timing mechanism which no one had set, but which might go off with some unpredictable set of events. Those events came, at the end of 1955, in the capital city of Alabama—Montgomery.

Three months after her arrest, Mrs. Rosa Parks,[6] a forty-three-year-old seamstress, explained why she refused to obey the Montgomery law providing for segregation on city buses, why she decided to sit down in the "white" section of the bus:

> Well, in the first place, I had been working all day on the job. I was quite tired after spending a full day working. I handle and work on clothing that white people wear. That didn't come in my mind but this is what I wanted to know: when and how would we ever determine our rights as human beings? ... It just happened that the driver made a demand and I just didn't feel like obeying his demand. He called a policeman and I was arrested and placed in jail....

Montgomery blacks called a mass meeting. A powerful force in the community was F.D. Nixon, a veteran trade unionist and experienced organizer. There was a vote to boycott all city buses. Car pools were organized to take Negroes to work; most people walked. The city retaliated by indicting one hundred leaders of the boycott, and sent many to jail. White segregationists turned to violence. Bombs exploded in four Negro churches. A shotgun blast was fired through the front door of the home of Dr. Martin Luther King, Jr.,* the twenty-seven-year-old Atlanta-born minister who was one of the leaders of the boycott. King's home was bombed. But the black people of Montgomery persisted, and in November 1956, the Supreme Court outlawed segregation on local bus lines.

Montgomery was the beginning. It forecast the style and mood of the vast protest movement that would sweep the South in the next ten years: emotional church meetings, Christian hymns adapted to current battles, references to lost American ideals, the commitment to nonviolence, the willingness to struggle and sacrifice....

[At a mass meeting in Montgomery during the boycott] Martin Luther King gave a preview of the oratory that would soon inspire millions of people to demand racial justice. He said the protest was not merely over buses but over things that "go deep down into the archives of history": 15

---

6   *Rosa Parks*   African American activist (1913–2005) whose refusal in 1955 to give up her seat on the portion of a bus reserved for white passengers was a key moment in the Civil Rights Movement.

We have known humiliation, we have known abusive language, we have been plunged into the abyss of oppression. And we decided to raise up only with the weapon of protest. It is one of the greatest glories of America that we have the right of protest.

If we are arrested every day, if we are exploited every day, if we are trampled over every day, don't ever let anyone pull you so low as to hate them. We must use the weapon of love. We must have compassion and understanding for those who hate us. We must realize so many people are taught to hate us that they are not totally responsible for their hate. But we stand in life at midnight, we are always on the threshold of a new dawn.

King's stress on love and nonviolence was powerfully effective in building a sympathetic following throughout the nation, among whites as well as blacks. But there were blacks who thought the message naive, that while there were misguided people who might be won over by love, there were others who would have to be bitterly fought, and not always with nonviolence....

Still, in the years that followed, southern blacks [continued to stress] nonviolence. On February 1, 1960, four freshmen at a Negro college in Greensboro, North Carolina, decided to sit down at the Woolworth's lunch counter downtown, where only whites ate. They were refused service, and when they would not leave, the lunch counter was closed for the day. The next day they returned, and then, day after day, other Negroes came to sit silently.

In the next two weeks, sit-ins spread to fifteen cities in five southern states....

There was violence against the sit-inners. But the idea of taking the initiative against segregation took hold. In the next twelve months, more than fifty thousand people, mostly black, some white, participated in demonstrations of one kind or another in a hundred cities, and over 3,600 people were put in jail. But by the end of 1960, lunch counters were open to blacks in Greensboro and many other places.

20   A year after the Greensboro incident, a northern-based group dedicated to racial equality—CORE (Congress of Racial Equality)—organized "Freedom Rides" in which blacks and whites traveled together on buses going through the South, to try to break the segregation pattern in interstate travel. Such segregation had long been illegal, but the federal government never enforced the law in the South; the President now was John F. Kennedy, but he too seemed cautious about the race question, concerned about the support of southern white leaders of the Democratic Party.

The two buses that left Washington, D.C., on May 4, 1963, headed for New Orleans, never got there. In South Carolina, riders were beaten. In Alabama, a bus was set afire. Freedom Riders were attacked with fists and iron bars. The southern police did not interfere with any of this violence, nor did the federal government. FBI agents watched, took notes, did nothing.

At this point, veterans of the sit-ins, who had recently formed the Student Nonviolent Coordinating Committee (SNCC), dedicated to nonviolent but militant action for equal rights, organized another Freedom Ride, from Nashville to Birmingham....

The racially mixed SNCC Freedom Riders were arrested in Birmingham, Alabama, spent a night in jail, were taken to the Tennessee border by police, made their way back to Birmingham, took a bus to Montgomery, and there were attacked by whites with fists and clubs, in a bloody scene. They resumed their trip, to Jackson, Mississippi.

By this time the Freedom Riders were in the news all over the world, and the government was anxious to prevent further violence. Attorney General Robert Kennedy, instead of insisting on their right to travel without being arrested, agreed to the Freedom Riders' being arrested in Jackson, in return for Mississippi police protection against possible mob violence....

There is no way of measuring the effect of that southern movement on the sensibilities of a whole generation of young black people, or of tracing the process by which some of them became activists and leaders....

In Birmingham in 1963, thousands of blacks went into the streets, facing police clubs, tear gas, dogs, high-powered water hoses. And meanwhile, all over the deep South, the young people of SNCC, mostly black, a few white, were moving into communities in Georgia, Alabama, Mississippi, Arkansas. Joined by local black people, they were organizing, to register people to vote, to protest against racism, to build up courage against violence. The Department of Justice recorded 1412 demonstrations in three months of 1963. Imprisonment became commonplace, beatings became frequent....

As the summer of 1964 approached, SNCC and other civil rights groups working together in Mississippi, and facing increasing violence, decided to call upon young people from other parts of the country for help. They hoped that would bring attention to the situation in Mississippi. Again and again in Mississippi and elsewhere, the FBI had stood by, lawyers for the Justice Department had stood by, while civil rights workers were beaten and jailed, while federal laws were violated.

On the eve of the Mississippi Summer,[7] in early June 1964, the civil rights movement rented a theater near the White House, and a busload of black Mississippians traveled to Washington to testify publicly about the

25

---

7   *Mississippi Summer*   Also called the Freedom Summer, an intensive civil rights campaign that focused on registering Black voters in Mississippi in the summer of 1964.

daily violence, the dangers facing the volunteers coming into Mississippi. Constitutional lawyers testified that the national government had the legal power to give protection against such violence. The transcript of this testimony was given to President Johnson and Attorney General Kennedy, accompanied by a request for a protective federal presence during the Mississippi Summer. There was no response.

Twelve days after the public hearing, three civil rights workers, James Chaney, a young black Mississippian, and two white volunteers, Andrew Goodman and Michael Schwerner, were arrested in Philadelphia, Mississippi, released from jail late at night, then seized, beaten with chains, and shot to death. Ultimately, an informer's testimony led to jail sentences for the sheriff and deputy sheriff and others. That came too late. The Mississippi murders had taken place after the repeated refusal of the national government, under Kennedy or Johnson, or any other President, to defend blacks against violence.

30   Dissatisfaction with the national government intensified. Later that summer, during the Democratic National Convention in Washington, Mississippi, blacks asked to be seated as part of the state delegation to represent the 40 percent of the state's population who were black. They were turned down by the liberal Democratic leadership, including vice-presidential candidate Hubert Humphrey.

Congress began reacting to the black revolt, the turmoil, the world publicity. Civil rights laws [had been] passed in 1957, 1960, and 1964. They promised much, on voting equality, on employment equality, but were enforced poorly or ignored. In 1965, President Johnson sponsored and Congress passed an even stronger Voting Rights Law, this time ensuring on-the-spot federal protection of the right to register and vote. The effect on Negro voting in the South was dramatic. In 1952, a million southern blacks (20 percent of those eligible) registered to vote. In 1964 the number was 2 million—40 percent. By 1968, it was 3 million, 60 percent—the same percentage as white voters.

The federal government was trying—without making fundamental changes—to control an explosive situation, to channel anger into the traditional cooling mechanism of the ballot box, the polite petition, the officially endorsed quiet gathering. When black civil rights leaders planned a huge march on Washington in the summer of 1963 to protest the failure of the nation to solve the race problem, it was quickly embraced by President Kennedy and other national leaders, and turned into a friendly assemblage.

Martin Luther King's speech there thrilled 200,000 black and white Americans—"I have a dream ..." It was magnificent oratory, but without the anger that many blacks felt. When John Lewis, a young Alabama-born SNCC leader, much arrested, much beaten, tried to introduce a stronger note of outrage at the meeting, he was censored by the leaders of the march, who insisted he omit certain sentences critical of the national government and urging militant action.

Eighteen days after the Washington gathering, almost as if in deliberate contempt for its moderation, a bomb exploded in the basement of a black church in Birmingham and four girls attending a Sunday school class were killed. President Kennedy had praised the "deep fervor and quiet dignity" of the march, but the black militant Malcolm X* was probably closer to the mood of the black community. In Detroit, two months after the march on Washington and the Birmingham bombing, Malcolm X spoke in his powerful, icy-clear, rhythmic style:

> ... This is what [the Kennedy administration] did with the march on Washington. They joined it ... became part of it, took it over. And as they took it over, it lost its militancy. It ceased to be angry, it ceased to be hot, it ceased to be uncompromising. Why, it even ceased to be a march. It became a picnic, a circus. Nothing but a circus, with clowns and all....
>
> No, it was a sellout. It was a takeover....

The accuracy of Malcolm X's caustic description of the march on Washington is corroborated in the description from the other side—from the Establishment, by White House adviser Arthur Schlesinger, in his book *A Thousand Days*. He tells how Kennedy met with the civil rights leaders and said the march would "create an atmosphere of intimidation" just when Congress was considering civil rights bills. A. Philip Randolph replied: "The Negroes are already in the streets. It is very likely impossible to get them off...." Schlesinger says: "The conference with the President did persuade the civil rights leaders that they should not lay siege to Capitol Hill." Schlesinger describes the Washington march admiringly and then concludes: "So in 1963 Kennedy moved to incorporate the Negro revolution into the democratic coalition...."

But it did not work. The blacks could not be easily brought into "the democratic coalition" when bombs kept exploding in churches, when new "civil rights" laws did not change the root condition of black people. In the spring of 1963, the rate of unemployment for whites was 4.8 percent. For nonwhites it was 12.1 percent. According to government estimates, one-fifth of the white population was below the poverty line, and one-half of the black population was below that line. The civil rights bills emphasized voting, but voting was not a fundamental solution to racism or poverty. In Harlem,* blacks who had voted for years still lived in rat-infested slums.

In precisely those years when civil rights legislation coming out of Congress reached its peak, 1964 and 1965, there were black outbreaks in every part of the country: in Florida, set off by the killing of a Negro woman and a bomb threat against a Negro high school; in Cleveland, set off by the killing of a white minister who sat in the path of a bulldozer to protest discrimination against blacks in construction work; in New York, set off by the fatal shooting of a fifteen-year-old Negro boy during a fight with an off-duty policeman. There were riots also in Rochester, Jersey City, Chicago, Philadelphia.

In August 1965, just as Lyndon Johnson was signing into law the strong Voting Rights Act, providing for federal registration of black voters to ensure their protection, the black ghetto in Watts, Los Angeles, erupted in the most violent urban outbreak since World War II. It was provoked by the forcible arrest of a young Negro driver, the clubbing of a bystander by police, the seizure of a young black woman falsely accused of spitting on the police. There was rioting in the streets, looting and firebombing of stores. Police and National Guardsmen were called in; they used their guns. Thirty-four people were killed, most of them black, hundreds injured, four thousand arrested. Robert Conot, a West Coast journalist, wrote of the riot in his *Rivers of Blood, Years of Darkness*: "In Los Angeles the Negro was going on record that he would no longer turn the other cheek. That, frustrated and goaded, he would strike back, whether the response of violence was an appropriate one or no."

In the summer of 1966, there were more outbreaks, with rock throwing, looting, and fire bombing by Chicago blacks and wild shootings by the National Guard; three blacks were killed, one a thirteen-year-old boy, another a fourteen-year-old pregnant girl....

40 It seemed clear by now that the nonviolence of the southern movement, perhaps tactically necessary in the southern atmosphere, and effective because it could be used to appeal to national opinion against the segregationist South, was not enough to deal with the entrenched problems of poverty in the black ghetto. In 1910, 90 percent of Negroes lived in the South. But by 1965, mechanical cotton pickers harvested 81 percent of Mississippi Delta cotton. Between 1940 and 1970, 4 million blacks left the country for the city. By 1965, 80 percent of blacks lived in cities and 50 percent of the black people lived in the North....

In 1967, in the black ghettos of the country, came the greatest urban riots of American history. According to the report of the National Advisory Committee on Urban Disorders, they "involved Negroes acting against local symbols of white American society," symbols of authority and property in the black neighborhoods—rather than purely against white persons....

The "typical rioter," according to the Commission, was a young, high school dropout but "nevertheless, somewhat better educated than his non-rioting Negro neighbor" and "usually underemployed or employed in a menial job." He was "proud of his race, extremely hostile to both whites and middle-class Negroes and, although informed about politics, highly distrustful of the political system."

The report blamed "white racism" for the disorders, and identified the ingredients of the "explosive mixture which has been accumulating in our cities since the end of World War II":

> Pervasive discrimination and segregation in employment, education, and housing ... growing concentrations of impoverished Negroes in our major cities, creating a growing crisis of deteriorating facilities and services and unmet human needs....
>
> A new mood has sprung up among Negroes, particularly the young, in which self-esteem and enhanced racial pride are replacing apathy and submission to the "system."

... "Black Power" was the new slogan—an expression of distrust of any "progress" given or conceded by whites, a rejection of paternalism.... Also, a pride in race, an insistence on black independence, and often, on black separation to achieve this independence. Malcolm X was the most eloquent spokesman for this. After he was assassinated as he spoke on a public platform in February 1965, in a plan whose origins are still obscure, he became the martyr of this movement. Hundreds of thousands read his *Autobiography*. He was more influential in death than during his lifetime.

Martin Luther King, though still respected, was being replaced now by new heroes: Huey Newton of the Black Panthers,[8] for instance. The Panthers had guns; they said blacks should defend themselves.

Malcolm X in late 1964 had spoken to black students from Mississippi visiting Harlem:*

> You'll get freedom by letting your enemy know that you'll do anything to get your freedom; then you'll get it. It's the only way you'll get it. When you get that kind of attitude, they'll label you as a "crazy Negro," or they'll call you a "crazy nigger"—they don't say Negro. Or they'll call you an extremist or a subversive, or seditious, or a red or a radical. But when you stay radical long enough and get enough people to be like you, you'll get your freedom.

Congress responded to the riots of 1967 by passing the Civil Rights Act of 1968. Presumably it would make stronger the laws prohibiting violence against blacks; it increased the penalties against those depriving people of their

45

---

8   *Black Panthers*   Black nationalist organization active from the 1960s to the 1980s. Among other efforts, Black Panthers developed community by providing such services as medical clinics and feeding programs.

civil rights. However, it said: "The provisions of this section shall not apply to acts or omissions on the part of law enforcement officers, members of the National Guard ... or members of the Armed Forces of the United States, who are engaged in suppressing a riot or civil disturbance...."

Furthermore, it added a section—agreed to by liberal members of Congress in order to get the whole bill passed—that provided up to five years in prison for anyone traveling interstate or using interstate facilities (including mail and telephone) "to organize, promote, encourage, participate in, or carry on a riot." It defined a riot as an action by three or more people involving threats of violence. The first person prosecuted under the Civil Rights Act of 1968 was a young black leader of SNCC, H. Rap Brown, who had made a militant, angry speech in Maryland, just before a racial disturbance there. (Later the Act would be used against antiwar demonstrators in Chicago—the Chicago Eight.)

Martin Luther King himself became more and more concerned about problems untouched by civil rights laws—problems coming out of poverty. In the spring of 1968, he began speaking out, against the advice of some Negro leaders who feared losing friends in Washington, against the war in Vietnam. He connected war and poverty:

> ... it's inevitable that we've got to bring out the question of the tragic mix-up in priorities. We are spending all of this money for death and destruction, and not nearly enough money for life and constructive development ... when the guns of war become a national obsession, social needs inevitably suffer.

50   King now became a chief target of the FBI, which tapped his private phone conversations, sent him fake letters, threatened him, blackmailed him, and even suggested once in an anonymous letter that he commit suicide. FBI internal memos discussed finding a black leader to replace King. As a Senate report on the FBI said in 1976, the FBI tried "to destroy Dr. Martin Luther King."

King was turning his attention to troublesome questions. He still insisted on nonviolence. Riots were self-defeating, he thought. But they did express a deep feeling that could not be ignored. And so, nonviolence, he said, "must be militant, massive non-violence." He planned a "Poor People's Encampment" in Washington, this time not with the paternal approval of the President. And he went to Memphis, Tennessee, to support a strike of garbage workers in that city. There, standing on a balcony outside his hotel room, he was shot to death by an unseen marksman. The Poor People's Encampment went on, and then it was broken up by police action....

The killing of King brought new urban outbreaks all over the country, in which thirty-nine people were killed, thirty-five of them black. Evidence was piling up that even with all of the civil rights laws now on the books, the courts would not protect blacks against violence and injustice:

1. In the 1967 riots in Detroit, three black teen-agers were killed in the Algiers Motel. Three Detroit policemen and a black private guard were tried for this triple murder. The defense conceded, a UPI dispatch said, that the four men had shot two of the blacks. A jury exonerated them.

2. In Jackson, Mississippi, in the spring of 1970, on the campus of Jackson State College, a Negro college, police laid down a 28-second barrage of gunfire, using shotguns, rifles, and a submachine gun. Four hundred bullets or pieces of buckshot struck the girls' dormitory and two black students were killed. A local grand jury found the attack "justified" and U.S. District Court Judge Harold Cox (a Kennedy appointee) declared that students who engage in civil disorders "must expect to be injured or killed." ...

These were "normal" cases, endlessly repeated in the history of the country, coming randomly but persistently out of a racism deep in the institutions, the mind of the country. But there was something else—a planned pattern of violence against militant black organizers, carried on by the police and the Federal Bureau of Investigation. On December 4, 1969, a little before five in the morning, a squad of Chicago police, armed with a submachine gun and shotguns, raided an apartment where Black Panthers lived. They fired at least eighty-two and perhaps two hundred rounds into the apartment, killing twenty-one-year-old Black Panther leader Fred Hampton as he lay in his bed, and another Black Panther, Mark Clark. Years later, it was discovered in a court proceeding that the FBI had an informer among the Panthers, and that they had given the police a floor plan of the apartment, including a sketch of where Fred Hampton slept.

Was the government turning to murder and terror because the concessions—the legislation, the speeches, the intonation of the civil rights hymn "We Shall Overcome" by President Lyndon Johnson—were not working? It was discovered later that the government in all the years of the civil rights movement, while making concessions through Congress, was acting through the FBI to harass and break up black militant groups.... Was there fear that blacks would turn their attention from the controllable field of voting to the more dangerous arena of wealth and poverty—of class conflict? In 1966, seventy poor black people in Greenville, Mississippi, occupied an unused air force barracks, until they were evicted by the military. A local woman, Mrs. Unita Blackwell, said:

214 | Howard Zinn

... We the poor people of Mississippi is tired. We're tired of it so we're going to build for ourselves, because we don't have a government that represents us.

55   Out of the 1967 riots in Detroit came an organization devoted to organizing black workers for revolutionary change. This was the League of Revolutionary Black Workers, which lasted until 1971 and influenced thousands of black workers in Detroit during its period of activity.

The new emphasis was more dangerous than civil rights, because it created the possibility of blacks and whites uniting on the issue of class exploitation. Back in November 1963, A. Philip Randolph had spoken to an AFL-CIO[9] convention about the civil rights movement, and foreseen its direction: "The Negro's protest today is but the first rumbling of the 'under-class.' As the Negro has taken to the streets, so will the unemployed of all races take to the streets."

Attempts began to do with blacks what had been done historically with whites—to lure a small number into the system with economic enticements....

Chase Manhattan Bank and the Rockefeller family (controllers of Chase) took a special interest in developing "black capitalism." The Rockefellers had always been financial patrons of the Urban League, and a strong influence in black education through their support of Negro colleges in the South. David Rockefeller tried to persuade his fellow capitalists that while helping black businessmen with money might not be fruitful in the short run, it was necessary "to shape an environment in which the business can continue earning a profit four or five or ten years from now." With all of this, black business remained infinitesimally small. The largest black corporation (Motown Industries) had sales in 1974 of $45 million, while Exxon Corporation had sales of $42 billion....

There was a small amount of change and a lot of publicity. There were more black faces in the newspapers and on television, creating an impression of change—and siphoning off into the mainstream a small but significant number of black leaders.

60   Some new black voices spoke [out]....

A black woman, Patricia Robinson, in a pamphlet distributed in Boston in 1970 (*Poor Black Woman*), tied male supremacy to capitalism and said the black woman "allies herself with the have-nots in the wider world and their revolutionary struggles." She said the poor black woman did not in the past "question the social and economic system" but now she must, and in fact, "she has begun to question aggressive male domination and the class society which enforces it, capitalism." ...

---

9   *AFL-CIO* American Federation of Labor and Congress of Industrial Organizations.

The system was working hard, by the late sixties and early seventies, to contain the frightening explosiveness of the black upsurge. Blacks were voting in large numbers in the South, and in the 1968 Democratic-Convention three blacks were admitted into the Mississippi delegation. By 1977, more than two thousand blacks held office in eleven southern states (in 1965 the number was seventy-two).... But blacks, with 20 percent of the South's population, still held less than 3 percent of the elective offices. A *New York Times* reporter, analyzing the new situation in 1977, pointed out that even where blacks held important city offices: "Whites almost always retain economic power." After Maynard Jackson, a black, became mayor of Atlanta, "the white business establishment continued to exert its influence."

Those blacks in the South who could afford to go to downtown restaurants and hotels were no longer barred because of their race. More blacks could go to colleges and universities, to law schools and medical schools. Northern cities were busing children back and forth in an attempt to create racially mixed schools, despite the racial segregation in housing. None of this, however, was halting what Frances Piven and Richard Cloward (*Poor People's Movements*) called "the destruction of the black lower class"—the unemployment, the deterioration of the ghetto, the rising crime, drug addiction, violence.

In the summer of 1977, the Department of Labor reported that the rate of unemployment among black youths was 34.8 percent. A small new black middle class had been created, and it raised the overall statistics for black income—but there was a great disparity between the newly risen middle-class black and the poor left behind. Despite the new opportunities for a small number of blacks, the median black family income of 1977 was only about 60 percent that of whites; blacks were twice as likely to die of diabetes; seven times as likely to be victims of homicidal violence rising out of the poverty and despair of the ghetto.

A *New York Times* report in early 1978 said: "... the places that experienced urban riots in the 1960's have, with a few exceptions, changed little, and the conditions of poverty have spread in most cities." [65]

Statistics did not tell the whole story. Racism, always a national fact, not just a southern one, emerged in northern cities, as the federal government made concessions to poor blacks in a way that pitted them against poor whites for resources made scarce by the system. Blacks, freed from slavery to take their place under capitalism, had long been forced into conflict with whites for scarce jobs. Now, with desegregation in housing, blacks tried to move into neighborhoods where whites, themselves poor, crowded, troubled, could find in them a target for their anger....

In Boston, the busing of black children to white schools, and whites to black schools, set off a wave of white neighborhood violence. The use of busing to integrate schools—sponsored by the government and the courts in response to the black movement—was an ingenious concession to protest. It had the effect of pushing poor whites and poor blacks into competition for the miserable inadequate schools which the system provided for all the poor.

Was the black population—hemmed into the ghetto, divided by the growth of a middle class, decimated by poverty, attacked by the government, driven into conflict with whites—under control? Surely, in the mid-seventies, there was no great black movement under way. Yet, a new black consciousness had been born and was still alive. Also, whites and blacks were crossing racial lines in the South to unite as a class against employers. In 1971, two thousand woodworkers in Mississippi, black and white, joined together to protest a new method of measuring wood that led to lower wages. In the textile mills of J.P. Stevens, where 44,000 workers were employed in eighty-five plants, mostly in the South, blacks and whites were working together in union activity. In Tifton, Georgia, and Milledgeville, Georgia, in 1977, blacks and whites served together on the union committees of their plants.

Would a new black movement go beyond the limits of the civil rights actions of the sixties, beyond the spontaneous urban riots of the seventies, beyond separatism to a coalition of white and black in a historic new alliance? There was no way of knowing this in 1978. In 1978, 6 million black people were unemployed. As Langston Hughes [had asked decades earlier], what happens to a dream deferred? Does it dry up, or does it explode?[10] ...

(1980)

Questions

1. Zinn quotes Malcolm X's characterization of the March on Washington as "a sellout" taken over by the Kennedy administration (paragraph 34). Considering the information provided by Zinn as well as your own outside knowledge, do you agree with this assessment? How (if at all) can activists work with governments without "selling out"?

2. What motivations does Zinn ascribe to politicians who made progressive changes in response to the Civil Rights Movement? To what extent (if at all) do you think similar motivations could be ascribed to politicians today?

---

10 *Langston Hughes ... explode* The reference is to Hughes' poem "Harlem," which appeared in his 1951 book-length collection of related poems, *Montage of a Dream Deferred*.

3. Zinn distinguishes between the nonviolent activism associated with Martin Luther King Jr. and the "militant" activism associated with Malcolm X and the Black Panthers. How (and to what extent) did each form of activism contribute to the achievements of the Civil Rights Movement?

4. If you attended secondary school in the United States, how does Zinn's history of civil rights in the mid-twentieth century compare with the history of this subject you received in school? If you did not attend secondary school in the United States, does the country where you attended school have any history of race- or ethnicity-based oppression? If so, how effectively was this history addressed in your education?

5. In "Undue Certainty," an article in *American Educator*, education professor Sam Wineburg expresses concerns about the use of *A People's History of the United States* as a textbook, arguing, among other things, that the text overuses "[a]necdotes as [e]vidence" and avoids using qualifying language even where the historical record is unclear such that "the seams of history are concealed by the presence of an author who speaks with thunderous certainty."

    a. What rhetorical goals do you think motivated *A People's History of the United States*? How might writing choices such as the incorporation of anecdotes and the use of direct, unqualified language reflect these rhetorical goals?

    b. Find an example of the use of an anecdote as evidence in this selection. In your view, is the anecdote appropriately used?

    c. Are there any places in the text where the addition of qualifying words (such as "might," "probably," or "mostly") would improve the accuracy of the text? If so, identify three such places and explain how you would revise them; if not, explain why no such revision is needed.

    d. Overall, how reliable do you think this selection from *A People's History of the United States* is? Explain your assessment.

COMING TO CLASS CONSCIOUSNESS
[from *WHERE WE STAND*]

An important critical theorist known for her writing on the intersections of race, sex, and class, bell hooks in this essay considers her journey through college and university as a working-class black woman. "Coming to Class Consciousness" first appeared as the second chapter in hooks's Where We Stand: Class Matters, *published in 2000; the book as a whole takes class in America as its primary focus, combining autobiographical essays with more general critiques of systemic inequality.*

As a child I often wanted things money could buy that my parents could not afford and would not get. Rather than tell us we did not get some material thing because money was lacking, mama would frequently manipulate us in an effort to make the desire go away. Sometimes she would belittle and shame us about the object of our desire. That's what I remember most. That lovely yellow dress I wanted would become in her storytelling mouth a really ugly mammy-made* thing that no girl who cared about her looks would desire. My desires were often made to seem worthless and stupid. I learned to mistrust and silence them. I learned that the more clearly I named my desires, the more unlikely those desires would ever be fulfilled.

I learned that my inner life was more peaceful if I did not think about money, or allow myself to indulge in any fantasy of desire. I learned the art of sublimation and repression.[1] I learned it was better to make do with acceptable material desires than to articulate the unacceptable. Before I knew money mattered, I had often chosen objects to desire that were costly, things a girl of my class would not ordinarily desire. But then I was still a girl who was unaware of

---

1   *sublimation* According to early twentieth-century psychoanalyst Sigmund Freud, sublimation transforms an instinctual impulse into a more socially acceptable interest;   *repression* In psychoanalysis, the action of keeping unacceptable ideas out of the conscious mind.

class, who did not think my desires were stupid and wrong. And when I found they were I let them go. I concentrated on survival, on making do.

When I was choosing a college to attend, the issue of money surfaced and had to be talked about. While I would seek loans and scholarships, even if everything related to school was paid for, there would still be transportation to pay for, books, and a host of other hidden costs. Letting me know that there was no extra money to be had, mama urged me to attend any college nearby that would offer financial aid. My first year of college I went to a school close to home. A plain-looking white woman recruiter had sat in our living room and explained to my parents that everything would be taken care of, that I would be awarded a full academic scholarship, that they would have to pay nothing. They knew better. They knew there was still transportation, clothes, all the hidden costs. Still they found this school acceptable. They could drive me there and pick me up. I would not need to come home for holidays. I could make do.

After my parents dropped me at the predominately white women's college, I saw the terror in my roommate's face that she was going to be housed with someone black, and I requested a change. She had no doubt also voiced her concern. I was given a tiny single room by the stairs—a room usually denied a first-year student—but I was a first-year black student, a scholarship girl who could never in a million years have afforded to pay her way or absorb the cost of a single room. My fellow students kept their distance from me. I ate in the cafeteria and did not have to worry about who would pay for pizza and drinks in the world outside. I kept my desires to myself, my lacks and my loneliness; I made do.

I rarely shopped. Boxes came from home with brand-new clothes mama   5
had purchased. Even though it was never spoken she did not want me to feel ashamed among privileged white girls. I was the only black girl in my dorm. There was no room in me for shame. I felt contempt and disinterest. With their giggles and their obsession to marry, the white girls at the women's college were aliens. We did not reside on the same planet. I lived in the world of books. The one white woman who became my close friend found me there reading. I was hiding under the shadows of a tree with huge branches, the kinds of trees that just seemed to grow effortlessly on well-to-do college campuses. I sat on the "perfect" grass reading poetry, wondering how the grass around me could be so lovely and yet when daddy had tried to grow grass in the front yard of Mr. Porter's house it always turned yellow or brown and then died. Endlessly, the yard defeated him, until finally he gave up. The outside of the house looked good but the yard always hinted at the possibility of endless neglect. The yard looked poor.

Foliage and trees on the college grounds flourished. Greens were lush and deep. From my place in the shadows I saw a fellow student sitting alone weeping. Her sadness had to do with all the trivia that haunted our day's class-work, the fear of not being smart enough, of losing financial aid (like me she had loans and scholarships, though her family paid some), and boys. Coming from an Illinois family of Czechoslovakian immigrants she understood class.

When she talked about the other girls who flaunted their wealth and family background there was a hard edge of contempt, anger, and envy in her voice. Envy was always something I pushed away from my psyche. Kept too close for comfort envy could lead to infatuation and on to desire. I desired nothing that they had. She desired everything, speaking her desires openly without shame. Growing up in the kind of community where there was constant competition to see who could buy the bigger better whatever, in a world of organized labor, of unions and strikes, she understood a world of bosses and workers, of haves and have-nots.

White friends I had known in high school wore their class privilege mod-estly. Raised, like myself, in church traditions that taught us to identify only with the poor, we knew that there was evil in excess. We knew rich people were rarely allowed into heaven.[2] God had given them a paradise of bounty on earth and they had not shared. The rare ones, the rich people who shared, were the only ones able to meet the divine in paradise, and even then it was harder for them to find their way. According to the high school friends we knew, flaunting wealth was frowned upon in our world, frowned upon by God and community.

The few women I befriended my first year in college were not wealthy. They were the ones who shared with me stories of the other girls flaunting the fact that they could buy anything expensive—clothes, food, vacations. There were not many of us from working class backgrounds; we knew who we were. Most girls from poor backgrounds tried to blend in, or fought back by triumphing over wealth with beauty or style or some combination of the above. Being black made me an automatic outsider. Holding their world in contempt pushed me further to the edge. One of the fun* things the "in" girls did was choose someone and trash their room. Like so much else deemed cute by insiders, I dreaded the thought of strangers entering my space and going through my things. Being outside the in crowd made me an unlikely target. Being contemptuous made me first on the list. I did not understand. And when my room was trashed it unleashed my rage and deep grief over not being able to protect my space from violation and invasion. I hated that girls who had so much, took so much for granted, never considered that those of us who did not

---

2   *We knew ... into heaven*   See Matthew 19.24: "And again I say unto you, it is easier for a camel to go through the eye of a needle, than for a rich man to enter into the kingdom of God."

have mad money would not be able to replace broken things, perfume poured out, or talcum powder spread everywhere—that we did not know everything could be taken care of at the dry cleaner's because we never took our clothes there. My rage fueled by contempt was deep, strong, and long lasting. Daily it stood as a challenge to their fun, to their habits of being.

Nothing they did to win me over worked. It came as a great surprise. They had always believed black girls wanted to be white girls, wanted to possess their world. My stoney gaze, silence, and absolute refusal to cross the threshold of their world was total mystery; it was for them a violation they needed to avenge. After trashing my room, they tried to win me over with apologies and urges to talk and understand. There was nothing about me I wanted them to understand. Everything about their world was overexposed, on the surface.

One of my English professors had attended Stanford University. She felt that was the place for me to go—a place where intellect was valued over foolish fun and games and dress up, and finding a husband did not overshadow academic work. She had gone to Stanford. I had never thought about the state of California. Getting my parents to agree to my leaving Kentucky to attend a college in a nearby state had been hard enough. They had accepted a college they could reach by car, but a college thousands of miles away was beyond their imagination. Even I had difficulty grasping going that far away from home. The lure for me was the promise of journeying and arriving at a destination where I would be accepted and understood.

All the barely articulated understandings of class privilege that I had learned my first year of college had not hipped me[3] to the reality of class shame. It still had not dawned on me that my parents, especially mama, resolutely refused to acknowledge any difficulties with money because her sense of shame around class was deep and intense. And when this shame was coupled with her need to feel that she had risen above the low-class backwoods culture of her family, it was impossible for her to talk in a straightforward manner about the strains it would put on the family for me to attend Stanford.

All I knew then was that, as with all my desires, I was told that this desire was impossible to fulfill. At first it was not talked about in relation to money, it was talked about in relation to sin. California was an evil place, a modern-day Babylon[4] where souls were easily seduced away from the path of righteousness. It was not a place for an innocent young girl to go on her own. Mama brought the message back that my father had absolutely refused to give permission.

I expressed my disappointment through ongoing unrelenting grief. I explained to mama that other parents wanted their children to go to good

10

---

3   *hipped me*   Made me "hip," that is, well-informed.
4   *Babylon*   Proverbially decadent or sinful large city.

schools. It still had not dawned on me that my parents knew nothing about "good" schools. Even though I knew mama had not graduated from high school I still held her in awe. Mama and daddy were awesome authority figures—family fascists[5] of a very high order. As children we knew that it was better not to doubt their word or their knowledge. We blindly trusted them.

15   A crucial aspect of our family fascism was that we were not allowed much contact with other families. We were rarely allowed to go to someone's house. We knew better than to speak about our family in other people's homes. While we caught glimpses of different habits of being, different ways of doing things in other families, we knew that to speak of those ways at our home, to try to use them to influence or change our parents, was to risk further confinement.

Our dad had traveled to foreign countries as a soldier but he did not speak of these experiences. Safety, we had been religiously taught in our household, was always to be found close to home. We were not a family who went on vacations, who went exploring. When relatives from large cities would encourage mama to let us children go back with them, their overtures were almost always politely refused. Once mama agreed that I could go to Chicago to visit an elderly cousin, Schuyler[6]—a name strange and beautiful on our lips.

Retired Cousin Schuyler lived a solitary life in a basement flat of the brownstone he shared with Lovie, his wife of many years. Vocationally a painter, he did still lifes and nudes. When they came to visit us, Mama had shown them the painting I had done that won a school prize. It was a portrait of a poor lonely boy with sad eyes. Despite our class background all of us took art classes in school. By high school the disinterested had forgotten about art and only those of us who were committed to doing art, to staying close to an artistic environment, remained. For some that closeness was just a kindly voyeurism. They had talent but were simply not sufficiently interested to use it. Then there were folks like me, full of passion and talent, but without the material resources to do art. Making art was for people with money.

I understood this when my parents adamantly refused to have my painting framed. Only framed work could be in the show. My art teacher, an Italian immigrant who always wore black, showed me how to make a frame from pieces of wood found in the trash. Like my granddaddy he was a lover of found objects. Both of them were men without resources who managed to love beauty and survive. In high school art classes we talked about beauty—about

5   *fascists* Fascism is a nationalistic, totalitarian form of government that enforces conformity and oppresses those who disagree. The term is most frequently used in reference to political movements in Italy, Germany, and other European countries after World War I.

6   *Schuyler* Often pronounced "sky-lar" by American speakers, this Dutch name for "shelter" or "hiding place" also means "scholar" in German.

aesthetics. But it was after class that I told the teacher how I had learned these things already from my grandmother.

Each year students would choose an artist and study their work and then do work in that same tradition. I chose abstract expressionism[7] and the work of Willem de Kooning. Choosing to paint a house in autumn, the kind of house I imagined living in, with swirls of color—red, yellow, brown—I worked for hours after class, trying to give this house the loneliness I felt inside. This painting was my favorite. I showed it to Cousin Schuyler along with the image of the lonely boy.

It remains a mystery how Schuyler and Lovie convinced mama that it would be fine to let me spend some time with them in Chicago—my first big city. Traveling to Chicago was my first sojourn out of the apartheid south.* It was my first time in a world where I saw black people working at all types of jobs. They worked at the post office delivering mail, in factories, driving buses, collecting garbage—black people with good jobs. This new world was awesome. It was a world where black people had power. I worked in a little store owned by a black male friend of my aunt. The wife of this friend had her own beauty parlor but no children. They had money.   20

Lovie talked to me about class. There were low-class folks one should not bother with. She insisted one should aim high. These were big city ideas. In our small town community we had been taught to see everyone as worthy. Mama especially preached that you should never see yourself as better than anyone, that no matter anyone's lot in life they deserved respect. Mama preached this even though she aimed high. These messages confused me. The big city was too awesome[8] and left me afraid.

Yet it also changed my perspective, for it had shown me a world where black people could be artists. And what I saw was that artists barely survived. No one in my family wanted me to pursue art; they wanted me to get a good job, to be a teacher. Painting was something to do when real work was done. Once, maybe twice even, I expressed my desire to be an artist. That became an occasion for dire warning and laughter, since like so many desires it was foolish, hence the laughter. Since foolish girls are likely to do foolish things dire warnings had to come after the laughter. Black folks could not make a living as artists. They pointed to the one example—the only grown-up black artist they knew, Cousin Schuyler, living in a dark basement like some kind of mole or rat.

---

7   *abstract expressionism* Fine art form using abstraction to convey powerful feeling. First used to describe the painting style of Wassily Kandinsky, the term also applies to a mid-century American art movement including painters such as Jackson Pollock, Mark Rothko, and Willem de Kooning.

8   *awesome* Awe-inspiring.

Like everything else the choice to be an artist was talked about in terms of race, not class. The substance of the warnings was always to do with the untalked-about reality of class in America. I did not think about being an artist anymore. I struggled with the more immediate question of where to continue college, of how to find a place where I would not feel like such an alien.

When my parents refused to permit me to attend Stanford, I accepted the verdict for awhile. Overwhelmed by grief, I could barely speak for weeks. Mama intervened and tried to change my father's mind as folks she respected in the outside world told her what a privilege it was for me to have this opportunity, that Stanford University was a good school for a smart girl. Without their permission I decided I would go. And even though she did not give her approval mama was willing to help.

25   My decision made conversations about money necessary. Mama explained that California was too far away, that it would always "cost" to get there, that if something went wrong they would not be able to come and rescue me, that I would not be able to come home for holidays. I heard all this but its meaning did not sink in. I was just relieved I would not be returning to the women's college, to the place where I had truly been an outsider.

There were other black students at Stanford. There was even a dormitory where many black students lived. I did not know I could choose to live there. I went where I was assigned. Going to Stanford was the first time I flew somewhere. Only mama stood and waved farewell as I left to take the bus to the airport. I left with a heavy heart, feeling both excitement and dread. I knew nothing about the world I was journeying to. Not knowing made me afraid but my fear of staying in place was greater.

Since we do not talk about class in this society and since information is never shared or talked about freely in a fascist family, I had no idea what was ahead of me. In small ways I was ignorant. I had never been on an escalator, a city bus, an airplane, or a subway. I arrived in San Francisco with no understanding that Palo Alto was a long drive away—that it would take money to find transportation there. I decided to take the city bus. With all my cheap overpacked bags I must have seemed like just another innocent immigrant when I struggled to board the bus.

This was a city bus with no racks for luggage. It was filled with immigrants. English was not spoken. I felt lost and afraid. Without words the strangers surrounding me understood the universal language of need and distress. They reached for my bags, holding and helping. In return I told them my story—that I had left my village in the South to come to Stanford University, that like them my family were workers, they worked the land—they worked in the world. They were workers. They understood workers. I would go to college and learn how to make a world where they would not have to work so hard.

When I arrived at my destination, the grown-ups in charge cautioned me about trusting strangers, telling me what I already knew, that I was no longer in my town, that nothing was the same. On arriving I called home. Before I could speak, I began to weep as I heard the far-away sound of mama's voice. I tried to find the words, to slow down, to tell her how it felt to be a stranger, to speak my uncertainty and longing. She told me this is the lot I had chosen. I must live with it. After her words there was only silence. She had hung up on me—let me go into this world where I am a stranger still.

Stanford University was a place where one could learn about class from the ground up. Built by a man who believed in hard work, it was to have been a place where students of all classes would come, women and men, to work together and learn. It was to be a place of equality and communalism. His vision was seen by many as almost communist.[9] The fact that he was rich made it all less threatening. Perhaps no one really believed the vision could be realized. The university was named after his son who had died young, a son who had carried his name but who had no future money could buy. No amount of money can keep death away. But it could keep memory alive. And so we work and learn in buildings that remind us of a young son carried away by death too soon, of a father's unrelenting grief remembered.

Everything in the landscape of my new world fascinated me, the plants brought from a rich man's travels all over the world back to this place of water and clay. At Stanford University adobe buildings blend with Japanese plum trees and leaves of kumquat.[10] On my way to study medieval literature, I ate my first kumquat. Surrounded by flowering cactus and a South American shrub bougainvillea[11] of such trailing beauty it took my breath away, I was in a landscape of dreams, full of hope and possibility. If nothing else would hold me, I would not remain a stranger to the earth. The ground I stood on would know me.

Class was talked about behind the scenes. The sons and daughters from rich, famous, or notorious families were identified. The grownups in charge of us were always looking out for a family who might give their millions to the college. At Stanford my classmates wanted to know me, thought it hip, cute, and downright exciting to have a black friend. They invited me on the expensive vacations and ski trips I could not afford. They offered to pay. I never went. Along with other students who were not from privileged families,

30

---

9   *communist*   Embodying the ideals of communism, a political doctrine advocating collective ownership, revolution to end capitalism, and the establishment of a classless society.

10   *kumquat*   Small orange citrus fruit originating in southern China and Malaysia.

11   *bougainvillea*   Tropical plants with large leaves that nearly cover their flowers.

I searched for places to go during the holiday times when the dormitory was closed. We got together and talked about the assumption that everyone had money to travel and would necessarily be leaving. The staff would be on holiday as well, so all students had to leave. Now and then the staff did not leave and we were allowed to stick around. Once, I went home with one of the women who cleaned for the college.

Now and then when she wanted to make extra money mama would work as a maid. Her decision to work outside the home was seen as an act of treason by our father. At Stanford I was stunned to find that there were maids who came by regularly to vacuum and tidy our rooms. No one had ever cleaned up behind me and I did not want them to. At first I roomed with another girl from a working-class background—a beautiful white girl from Orange County who looked like pictures I had seen on the cover of *Seventeen*[12] magazine. Her mother had died of cancer during her high school years and she had since been raised by her father. She had been asked by the college officials if she would find it problematic to have a black roommate. A scholarship student like myself, she knew her preferences did not matter and as she kept telling me, she did not really care.

Like my friend during freshman year she shared the understanding of what it was like to be a have-not in a world of haves. But unlike me she was determined to become one of them. If it meant she had to steal nice clothes to look the same as they did, she had no problem taking these risks. If it meant having a privileged boyfriend who left bruises on her body now and then, it was worth the risk. Cheating was worth it. She believed the world the privileged had created was all unfair—all one big cheat; to get ahead one had to play the game. To her I was truly an innocent, a lamb being led to the slaughter. It did not surprise her one bit when I began to crack under the pressure of contradictory values and longings.

35   Like all students who did not have seniority, I had to see the school psychiatrists to be given permission to live off campus. Unaccustomed to being around strangers, especially strangers who did not share or understand my values, I found the experience of living in the dorms difficult. Indeed, almost everyone around me believed working-class folks had no values. At the university where the founder, Leland Stanford, had imagined different classes meeting on common ground, I learned how deeply individuals with class privilege feared and hated the working classes. Hearing classmates express contempt and hatred toward people who did not come from the right backgrounds shocked me. Naively, I believed them to be so young to hold those views, so devoid of life experiences that would serve to uphold or make sense

---

12 *Seventeen* Magazine for teenage girls; beauty and fashion tips are its primary focus.

of these thoughts. I had always worked. Working-class people had always encouraged and supported me.

To survive in this new world of divided classes, this world where I was also encountering for the first time a black bourgeois elite that was as contemptuous of working people as their white counterparts were, I had to take a stand, to get clear my own class affiliations. This was the most difficult truth to face. Having been taught all my life to believe that black people were inextricably bound in solidarity by our struggles to end racism, I did not know how to respond to elitist black people who were full of contempt for anyone who did not share their class, their way of life.

At Stanford I encountered for the first time a black diaspora.[13] Of the few black professors present, the vast majority were from African or Caribbean backgrounds. Elites themselves, they were only interested in teaching other elites. Poor folks like myself, with no background to speak of, were invisible. We were not seen by them or anyone else. Initially, I went to all meetings welcoming black students, but when I found no one to connect with I retreated. In the shadows I had time and books to teach me about the nature of class—about the ways black people were divided from themselves.

Despite this rude awakening, my disappointment at finding myself estranged from the group of students I thought would understand, I still looked for connections. I met an older black male graduate student who also came from a working-class background. Even though he had gone to the right high school, a California school for gifted students, and then to Princeton as an undergraduate, he understood intimately the intersections of race and class. Good in sports and in the classroom, he had been slotted early on to go far, to go where other black males had not gone. He understood the system. Academically, he fit. Had he wanted to, he could have been among the elite but he chose to be on the margins, to hang with an intellectual artistic avant garde.[14] He wanted to live in a world of the mind where there was no race or class. He wanted to worship at the throne of art and knowledge. He became my mentor, comrade, and companion.

When we were not devoting ourselves to books and to poetry we confronted a real world where we were in need of jobs. Even though I taught an occasional class, I worked in the world of the mundane. I worked at a bookstore, cooked at a club, worked for the telephone company. My way out of being a maid,

---

13 *diaspora* Group of people who have dispersed from their original or traditional homeland. The term "African diaspora" or "Black diaspora" refers to the movement of African people out of Africa over the past centuries—with a particular emphasis on enforced movement via the slave trade.

14 *avant garde* Literally, the front line of an advancing army, though the term is most often used to describe intellectual innovators.

of doing the dirty work of cleaning someone else's house, was to become a schoolteacher. The thought terrified me. From grade school on I feared and hated the classroom. In my imagination it was still the ultimate place of inclusion and exclusion, discipline and punishment—worse than the fascist family because there was no connection of blood to keep in check impulses to search and destroy.

40   Now and then a committed college professor opened my mind to the reality that the classroom could be a place of passion and possibility, but, in general, at the various colleges I attended it was the place where the social order was kept in place. Throughout my graduate student years, I was told again and again that I lacked the proper decorum of a graduate student, that I did not understand my place. Slowly I began to understand fully that there was no place in academe for folks from working-class backgrounds who did not wish to leave the past behind. That was the price of the ticket. Poor students would be welcome at the best institutions of higher learning only if they were willing to surrender memory, to forget the past and claim the assimilated present as the only worthwhile and meaningful reality.

Students from nonprivileged backgrounds who did not want to forget often had nervous breakdowns. They could not bear the weight of all the contradictions they had to confront. They were crushed. More often than not they dropped out with no trace of their inner anguish recorded, no institutional record of the myriad ways their take on the world was assaulted by an elite vision of class and privilege. The records merely indicated that even after receiving financial aid and other support, these students simply could not make it, simply were not good enough.

At no time in my years as a student did I march in a graduation ceremony. I was not proud to hold degrees from institutions where I had been constantly scorned and shamed. I wanted to forget these experiences, to erase them from my consciousness. Like a prisoner set free I did not want to remember my years on the inside. When I finished my doctorate I felt too much uncertainty about who I had become. Uncertain about whether I had managed to make it through without giving up the best of myself, the best of the values I had been raised to believe in—hard work, honesty, and respect for everyone no matter their class—I finished my education with my allegiance to the working class intact. Even so, I had planted my feet on the path leading in the direction of class privilege. There would always be contradictions to face. There would always be confrontations around the issue of class. I would always have to reexamine where I stand.

(2000)

Questions

1. "I was in a landscape of dreams, full of hope and possibility. If nothing else would hold me, I would not remain a stranger to the earth. The ground I stood on would know me." Explain the significance of this passage.

2. What role does geography play in this essay?

3. "My way out of being a maid, of doing the dirty work of cleaning someone else's house, was to become a schoolteacher. The thought terrified me. From grade school on I feared and hated the classroom. In my imagination it was still the ultimate place of inclusion and exclusion, discipline and punishment—worse than the fascist family because there was no connection of blood to keep in check impulses to search and destroy." Explain what hooks means in this passage. Why would hooks feel this way? How often have you felt this way?

4. "Mama especially preached that you should never see yourself as better than anyone, that no matter anyone's lot in life they deserved respect. Mama preached this even though she aimed high. These messages confused me. The big city was too awesome and left me afraid." Explain the contradiction young hooks sees here.

5. "Without their permission I decided I would go. And even though she did not give her approval mama was willing to help." Describe hooks's relationship with her mother here and elsewhere in the chapter. To what extent does hooks receive support from her mother, and what does she learn from her?

6. hooks details points about class in her work. How does she bring in conversations about race and gender? How are race, class, and gender interrelated in her essay?

MALCOLM GLADWELL

NONE OF THE ABOVE: WHAT I.Q. DOESN'T TELL YOU ABOUT RACE

Malcolm Gladwell is a journalist and staff writer at the New Yorker.
*His work often examines research findings in the social sciences
and interprets them for a broader audience. In the following article
Gladwell reviews* What Is Intelligence? *(2007), by the scholar
James Flynn, delving into the debate among psychologists and
geneticists surrounding IQ and its relationship to race, class, and
culture. "None of the Above" was first published in the* New Yorker
in 2007.

O ne Saturday in November of 1984, James Flynn, a social scientist at the
University of Otago, in New Zealand, received a large package in the mail.
It was from a colleague in Utrecht, and it contained the results of I.Q. tests*
given to two generations of Dutch eighteen-year-olds. When Flynn looked
through the data, he found something puzzling. The Dutch eighteen-year-olds
from the nineteen-eighties scored better than those who took the same tests in
the nineteen-fifties—and not just slightly better, *much* better.

Curious, Flynn sent out some letters. He collected intelligence-test results
from Europe, from North America, from Asia, and from the developing world,
until he had data for almost thirty countries. In every case, the story was pretty
much the same. I.Q.s around the world appeared to be rising by 0.3 points per
year, or three points per decade, for as far back as the tests had been administered. For some reason, human beings seemed to be getting smarter.

Flynn has been writing about the implications of his findings—now known
as the Flynn effect—for almost twenty-five years. His books consist of a series
of plainly stated statistical observations, in support of deceptively modest
conclusions, and the evidence in support of his original observation is now
so overwhelming that the Flynn effect has moved from theory to fact. What
remains uncertain is how to make sense of the Flynn effect. If an American born
in the nineteen-thirties has an I.Q. of 100, the Flynn effect says that his children
will have I.Q.s of 108, and his grandchildren I.Q.s of close to 120—more than

a standard deviation higher. If we work in the opposite direction, the typical teen-ager of today, with an I.Q. of 100, would have had grandparents with average I.Q.s of 82—seemingly below the threshold necessary to graduate from high school. And, if we go back even farther, the Flynn effect puts the average I.Q.s of the schoolchildren of 1900 at around 70, which is to suggest, bizarrely, that a century ago the United States was populated largely by people who today would be considered mentally retarded.

For almost as long as there have been I.Q. tests, there have been I.Q. fundamentalists. H.H. Goddard, in the early years of the past century, established the idea that intelligence could be measured along a single, linear scale. One of his particular contributions was to coin the word "moron." "The people who are doing the drudgery are, as a rule, in their proper places," he wrote. Goddard was followed by Lewis Terman, in the nineteen-twenties, who rounded up the California children with the highest I.Q.s, and confidently predicted that they would sit at the top of every profession. In 1969, the psychometrician Arthur Jensen argued that programs like Head Start, which tried to boost the academic performance of minority children, were doomed to failure, because I.Q. was so heavily genetic; and in 1994 Richard Herrnstein and Charles Murray, in "The Bell Curve," notoriously proposed that Americans with the lowest I.Q.s be sequestered in a "high-tech" version of an Indian reservation,* "while the rest of America tries to go about its business."[1] To the I.Q. fundamentalist, two things are beyond dispute: first, that I.Q. tests measure some hard and identifiable trait that predicts the quality of our thinking; and, second, that this trait is stable—that is, it is determined by our genes and largely impervious to environmental influences.

This is what James Watson, the co-discoverer of DNA, meant when he told an English newspaper recently that he was "inherently gloomy" about the prospects for Africa. From the perspective of an I.Q. fundamentalist, the fact that Africans score lower than Europeans on I.Q. tests suggests an ineradicable cognitive disability. In the controversy that followed, Watson was defended by the journalist William Saletan, in a three-part series for the online magazine *Slate*. Drawing heavily on the work of J. Philippe Rushton—a psychologist who specializes in comparing the circumference of what he calls the Negroid brain with the length of the Negroid penis—Saletan took the fundamentalist position to its logical conclusion. To erase the difference between blacks and whites, Saletan wrote, would probably require vigorous interbreeding between the races, or some kind of corrective genetic engineering aimed at upgrading

5

---

1   *in 1994 ... business*   *The New Yorker* posted the following correction to this statement: "In fact, Herrnstein and Murray deplored the prospect of such 'custodialism' and recommended that steps be taken to avert it. We regret the error."

African stock.* "Economic and cultural theories have failed to explain most of the pattern," Saletan declared, claiming to have been "soaking [his] head in each side's computations and arguments." One argument that Saletan never soaked his head in, however, was Flynn's, because what Flynn discovered in his mailbox upsets the certainties upon which I.Q. fundamentalism rests. If whatever the thing is that I.Q. tests measure can jump so much in a generation, it can't be all that immutable and it doesn't look all that innate.

The very fact that average I.Q.s shift over time ought to create a "crisis of confidence," Flynn writes in "What Is Intelligence?," his latest attempt to puzzle through the implications of his discovery. "How could such huge gains be intelligence gains? Either the children of today were far brighter than their parents or, at least in some circumstances, I.Q. tests were not good measures of intelligence."

The best way to understand why I.Q.s rise, Flynn argues, is to look at one of the most widely used I.Q. tests, the so-called WISC (for Wechsler Intelligence Scale for Children). The WISC is composed of ten subtests, each of which measures a different aspect of I.Q. Flynn points out that scores in some of the categories—those measuring general knowledge, say, or vocabulary or the ability to do basic arithmetic—have risen only modestly over time. The big gains on the WISC are largely in the category known as "similarities," where you get questions such as "In what way are 'dogs' and 'rabbits' alike?" Today, we tend to give what, for the purposes of I.Q. tests, is the right answer: dogs and rabbits are both mammals. A nineteenth-century American would have said that "you use dogs to hunt rabbits."

"If the everyday world is your cognitive home, it is not natural to detach abstractions and logic and the hypothetical from their concrete referents," Flynn writes. Our great-grandparents may have been perfectly intelligent. But they would have done poorly on I.Q. tests because they did not participate in the twentieth century's great cognitive revolution, in which we learned to sort experience according to a new set of abstract categories. In Flynn's phrase, we have now had to put on "scientific spectacles," which enable us to make sense of the WISC questions about similarities. To say that Dutch I.Q. scores rose substantially between 1952 and 1982 was another way of saying that the Netherlands in 1982 was, in at least certain respects, much more cognitively demanding than the Netherlands in 1952. An I.Q., in other words, measures not so much how smart we are as how *modern* we are.

This is a critical distinction. When the children of Southern Italian immigrants were given I.Q. tests in the early part of the past century,* for example, they recorded median scores in the high seventies and low eighties, a full standard deviation below their American and Western European counterparts. Southern Italians did as poorly on I.Q. tests as Hispanics and blacks did. As you can imagine, there was much concerned talk at the time about the genetic inferiority of Italian stock, of the inadvisability of letting so many second-class immigrants into the United States, and of the squalor that seemed endemic to Italian urban neighborhoods.* Sound familiar? These days, when talk turns to the supposed genetic differences in the intelligence of certain races, Southern Italians have disappeared from the discussion. "Did their genes begin to mutate somewhere in the 1930s?" the psychologists Seymour Sarason and John Doris ask, in their account of the Italian experience. "Or is it possible that somewhere in the 1920s, if not earlier, the sociocultural history of Italo-Americans took a turn from the blacks and the Spanish Americans which permitted their assimilation into the general undifferentiated mass of Americans?"

The psychologist Michael Cole and some colleagues once gave members 10 of the Kpelle tribe, in Liberia, a version of the WISC similarities test: they took a basket of food, tools, containers, and clothing and asked the tribesmen to sort them into appropriate categories. To the frustration of the researchers, the Kpelle chose functional pairings. They put a potato and a knife together because a knife is used to cut a potato. "A wise man could only do such-and-such," they explained. Finally, the researchers asked, "How would a fool do it?" The tribesmen immediately re-sorted the items into the "right" categories. It can be argued that taxonomical categories are a developmental improvement—that is, that the Kpelle would be more likely to advance, technologically and scientifically, if they started to see the world that way. But to label them less intelligent than Westerners, on the basis of their performance on that test, is merely to state that they have different cognitive preferences and habits. And if I.Q. varies with habits of mind, which can be adopted or discarded in a generation, what, exactly, is all the fuss about?

When I was growing up, my family would sometimes play Twenty Questions* on long car trips. My father was one of those people who insist that the standard categories of animal, vegetable, and mineral be supplemented with a fourth category: "abstract." Abstract could mean something like "whatever it was that was going through my mind when we drove past the water tower fifty miles back." That abstract category sounds absurdly difficult, but it wasn't: it merely required that we ask a slightly different set of questions and grasp a slightly different set of conventions, and, after two or three rounds of practice, guessing the contents of someone's mind fifty miles ago becomes as easy as guessing Winston Churchill.* (There is one exception. That was the trip on which my old roommate Tom Connell chose, as an abstraction, "the Unknown Soldier"*—which allowed him legitimately and gleefully to answer "I have no idea" to almost every question. There were four of us playing. We gave up after an hour.) Flynn would say that my father was teaching his three sons how to put on scientific spectacles, and that extra practice probably bumped up all of our I.Q.s a few notches. But let's be clear about what this means. There's a world of difference between an I.Q. advantage that's genetic and one that depends on extended car time with Graham Gladwell.

Flynn is a cautious and careful writer. Unlike many others in the I.Q. debates, he resists grand philosophizing. He comes back again and again to the fact that I.Q. scores are generated by paper-and-pencil tests—and making sense of those scores, he tells us, is a messy and complicated business that requires something closer to the skills of an accountant than to those of a philosopher.

For instance, Flynn shows what happens when we recognize that I.Q. is not a freestanding number but a value attached to a specific time and a specific test. When an I.Q. test is created, he reminds us, it is calibrated or "normed" so that the test-takers in the fiftieth percentile—those exactly at the median—are assigned a score of 100. But since I.Q.s are always rising, the only way to keep that hundred-point benchmark is periodically to make the tests more difficult—to "renorm" them. The original WISC was normed in the late nineteen-forties. It was then renormed in the early nineteen-seventies, as the WISC-R; renormed a third time in the late eighties, as the WISC III; and renormed again a few years ago, as the WISC IV—with each version just a little harder than its predecessor. The notion that anyone "has" an I.Q. of a certain number, then, is meaningless unless you know which WISC he took, and when he took it, since there's a substantial difference between getting a 130 on the WISC IV and getting a 130 on the much easier WISC.

This is not a trivial issue. I.Q. tests are used to diagnose people as mentally retarded, with a score of 70 generally taken to be the cutoff. You can imagine how the Flynn effect plays havoc with that system. In the nineteen-seventies and eighties, most states used the WISC-R to make their mental-retardation diagnoses. But since kids—even kids with disabilities—score a little higher every year, the number of children whose scores fell below 70 declined steadily through the end of the eighties. Then, in 1991, the WISC III was introduced, and suddenly the percentage of kids labeled retarded went up. The psychologists Tomoe Kanaya, Matthew Scullin, and Stephen Ceci estimated that, if every state had switched to the WISC III right away, the number of Americans labeled mentally retarded should have doubled.

15   That is an extraordinary number. The diagnosis of mental disability is one of the most stigmatizing of all educational and occupational classifications— and yet, apparently, the chances of being burdened with that label are in no small degree a function of the point, in the life cycle of the WISC, at which a child happens to sit for his evaluation. "As far as I can determine, no clinical or school psychologists using the WISC over the relevant 25 years noticed that its criterion of mental retardation became more lenient over time," Flynn wrote, in a 2000 paper. "Yet no one drew the obvious moral about psychologists in

the field: They simply were not making any systematic assessment of the I.Q. criterion for mental retardation."

Flynn brings a similar precision to the question of whether Asians have a genetic advantage in I.Q., a possibility that has led to great excitement among I.Q. fundamentalists in recent years. Data showing that the Japanese had higher I.Q.s than people of European descent, for example, prompted the British psychometrician and eugenicist Richard Lynn to concoct an elaborate evolutionary explanation involving the Himalayas, really cold weather, premodern hunting practices, brain size, and specialized vowel sounds. The fact that the I.Q.s of Chinese-Americans also seemed to be elevated has led I.Q. fundamentalists to posit the existence of an international I.Q. pyramid, with Asians at the top, European whites next, and Hispanics and blacks at the bottom.

Here was a question tailor-made for James Flynn's accounting skills. He looked first at Lynn's data, and realized that the comparison was skewed. Lynn was comparing American I.Q. estimates based on a representative sample of schoolchildren with Japanese estimates based on an upper-income, heavily urban sample. Recalculated, the Japanese average came in not at 106.6 but at 99.2. Then Flynn turned his attention to the Chinese-American estimates. They turned out to be based on a 1975 study in San Francisco's Chinatown using something called the Lorge-Thorndike Intelligence Test. But the Lorge-Thorndike test was normed in the nineteen-fifties. For children in the nineteen-seventies, it would have been a piece of cake. When the Chinese-American scores were reassessed using up-to-date intelligence metrics, Flynn found, they came in at 97 verbal and 100 nonverbal. Chinese-Americans had slightly lower I.Q.s than white Americans.

The Asian-American success story had suddenly been turned on its head. The numbers now suggested, Flynn said, that they had succeeded not because of their *higher* I.Q.s but despite their *lower* I.Q.s. Asians were overachievers. In a nifty piece of statistical analysis, Flynn then worked out just how great that overachievement was. Among whites, virtually everyone who joins the ranks of the managerial, professional, and technical occupations has an I.Q. of 97 or above. Among Chinese-Americans, that threshold is 90. A Chinese-American with an I.Q. of 90, it would appear, does as much with it as a white American with an I.Q. of 97.

There should be no great mystery about Asian achievement. It has to do with hard work and dedication to higher education, and belonging to a culture that stresses professional success. But Flynn makes one more observation. The children of that first successful wave of Asian-Americans really did have I.Q.s that were higher than everyone else's—coming in somewhere around 103. Having worked their way into the upper reaches of the occupational scale, and taken note of how much the professions value abstract thinking,

Asian-American parents have evidently made sure that their own children wore scientific spectacles. "Chinese Americans are an ethnic group for whom high achievement preceded high I.Q. rather than the reverse," Flynn concludes, reminding us that in our discussions of the relationship between I.Q. and success we often confuse causes and effects. "It is not easy to view the history of their achievements without emotion," he writes. That is exactly right. To ascribe Asian success to some abstract number is to trivialize it.

20   Two weeks ago, Flynn came to Manhattan to debate Charles Murray at a forum sponsored by the Manhattan Institute. Their subject was the black-white I.Q. gap in America. During the twenty-five years after the Second World War, that gap closed considerably. The I.Q.s of white Americans rose, as part of the general worldwide Flynn effect, but the I.Q.s of black Americans rose faster. Then, for about a period of twenty-five years, that trend stalled—and the question was why.

Murray showed a series of PowerPoint slides, each representing different statistical formulations of the I.Q. gap. He appeared to be pessimistic that the racial difference would narrow in the future. "By the nineteen-seventies, you had gotten most of the juice out of the environment that you were going to get," he said. That gap, he seemed to think, reflected some inherent difference between the races. "Starting in the nineteen-seventies, to put it very crudely, you had a higher proportion of black kids being born to really dumb mothers," he said. When the debate's moderator, Jane Waldfogel, informed him that the most recent data showed that the race gap had begun to close again, Murray seemed unimpressed, as if the possibility that blacks could ever make further progress was inconceivable.

Flynn took a different approach. The black-white gap, he pointed out, differs dramatically by age. He noted that the tests we have for measuring the cognitive functioning of infants, though admittedly crude, show the races to be almost the same. By age four, the average black I.Q. is 95.4—only four and a half points behind the average white I.Q. Then the real gap emerges: from age four through twenty-four, blacks lose six-tenths of a point a year, until their scores settle at 83.4.

That steady decline, Flynn said, did not resemble the usual pattern of genetic influence. Instead, it was exactly what you would expect, given the disparate cognitive environments that whites and blacks encounter as they grow older. Black children are more likely to be raised in single-parent homes than are white children—and single-parent homes are less cognitively complex than two-parent homes. The average I.Q. of first-grade students in schools that blacks attend is 95, which means that "kids who want to be above average don't have to aim as high." There were possibly adverse differences between black teen-age culture and white teen-age culture, and an enormous number of young black men are in jail—which is hardly the kind of environment in which someone would learn to put on scientific spectacles.

Flynn then talked about what we've learned from studies of adoption and mixed-race children—and that evidence didn't fit a genetic model, either. If I.Q. is innate, it shouldn't make a difference whether it's a mixed-race child's mother or father who is black. But it does: children with a white mother and a black father have an eight-point I.Q. advantage over those with a black mother and a white father. And it shouldn't make much of a difference where a mixed-race child is born. But, again, it does: the children fathered by black American G.I.s in postwar Germany and brought up by their German mothers have the same I.Q.s as the children of white American G.I.s and German mothers. The difference, in that case, was not the fact of the children's blackness, as a fundamentalist would say. It was the fact of their *Germanness*—of their being brought up in a different culture, under different circumstances. "The mind is much more like a muscle than we've ever realized," Flynn said. "It needs to get cognitive exercise. It's not some piece of clay on which you put an indelible mark." The lesson to be drawn from black and white differences was the same as the lesson from the Netherlands years ago: I.Q. measures not just the quality of a person's mind but the quality of the world that person lives in.

(2007)

Questions

1. According to Gladwell, what does IQ tell us about race?

2. Does Gladwell give us enough information to evaluate for ourselves whether Flynn's interpretation of the statistics is superior to the other interpretations he mentions? If so, how do we know? If not, what information is missing?

3. Gladwell says that making generalizations based on I.Q. scores "requires something closer to the skills of an accountant than to those of a philosopher." What does this mean? What differentiates Flynn's interpretation of the numbers from those of the "I.Q. fundamentalists" Gladwell cites?

4. What are some real world implications of how society defines and interprets I.Q.? Draw examples from Gladwell's article and/or your own experience.

5. In your own words, summarize Gladwell's thesis. What evidence does he give to support his argument?

6.   What does I.Q. actually measure? How important do you think this measurement is?

7.   Considering the information given in this article, do you think that I.Q. should be used in the diagnosis of mental disability? If so, why? If not, why not, and what method would be better?

8.   In part, I.Q. tests measure one's ability to apply abstract taxonomical categories. Gladwell writes that "it can be argued" that the ability to apply these categories is "a developmental improvement" because it can lead to technological and scientific advancement. Do you agree? Is it good for I.Q. tests to emphasize the importance of this mode of thinking?

A MORE PERFECT UNION

This speech on unity, race relations, and then-Senator Barack Obama's personal story was considered a turning point in his 2008 presidential campaign. The speech was delivered on March 18, 2008 in Philadelphia; Obama was in the midst of campaigning against Hillary Clinton and other Democratic Party candidates for their party's presidential nomination.

"We the people, in order to form a more perfect union."

Two hundred and twenty one years ago, in a hall that still stands across the street, a group of men gathered and, with these simple words, launched America's improbable experiment in democracy. Farmers and scholars; statesmen and patriots who had traveled across an ocean to escape tyranny and persecution finally made real their declaration of independence at a Philadelphia convention that lasted through the spring of 1787.

The document they produced was eventually signed but ultimately unfinished. It was stained by this nation's original sin of slavery, a question that divided the colonies and brought the convention to a stalemate until the founders chose to allow the slave trade to continue for at least twenty more years, and to leave any final resolution to future generations.

Of course, the answer to the slavery question was already embedded within our Constitution—a Constitution that had at is very core the ideal of equal citizenship under the law; a Constitution that promised its people liberty, and justice, and a union that could be and should be perfected over time.

And yet words on a parchment would not be enough to deliver slaves from bondage, or provide men and women of every color and creed their full rights and obligations as citizens of the United States. What would be needed were Americans in successive generations who were willing to do their part—through protests and struggle, on the streets and in the courts, through a civil war and civil disobedience and always at great risk—to narrow that gap between the promise of our ideals and the reality of their time.

5

This was one of the tasks we set forth at the beginning of this campaign—to continue the long march of those who came before us, a march for a more just, more equal, more free, more caring and more prosperous America. I chose to run for the presidency at this moment in history because I believe deeply that we cannot solve the challenges of our time unless we solve them together—unless we perfect our union by understanding that we may have different stories, but we hold common hopes; that we may not look the same and we may not have come from the same place, but we all want to move in the same direction—towards a better future for our children and our grandchildren.

This belief comes from my unyielding faith in the decency and generosity of the American people. But it also comes from my own American story.

I am the son of a black man from Kenya and a white woman from Kansas. I was raised with the help of a white grandfather who survived a Depression to serve in Patton's Army during World War II and a white grandmother who worked on a bomber assembly line at Fort Leavenworth while he was overseas. I've gone to some of the best schools in America and lived in one of the world's poorest nations. I am married to a black American who carries within her the blood of slaves and slaveowners—an inheritance we pass on to our two precious daughters. I have brothers, sisters, nieces, nephews, uncles and cousins, of every race and every hue, scattered across three continents, and for as long as I live, I will never forget that in no other country on Earth is my story even possible.

It's a story that hasn't made me the most conventional candidate. But it is a story that has seared into my genetic makeup the idea that this nation is more than the sum of its parts—that out of many, we are truly one.

Throughout the first year of this campaign, against all predictions to the contrary, we saw how hungry the American people were for this message of unity. Despite the temptation to view my candidacy through a purely racial lens, we won commanding victories in states with some of the whitest populations in the country. In South Carolina, where the Confederate Flag still flies, we built a powerful coalition of African Americans and white Americans.

This is not to say that race has not been an issue in the campaign. At various stages in the campaign, some commentators have deemed me either "too black" or "not black enough." We saw racial tensions bubble to the surface during the week before the South Carolina primary. The press has scoured every exit poll for the latest evidence of racial polarization, not just in terms of white and black, but black and brown as well.

And yet, it has only been in the last couple of weeks that the discussion of race in this campaign has taken a particularly divisive turn.

On one end of the spectrum, we've heard the implication that my candidacy is somehow an exercise in affirmative action; that it's based solely on the desire of wide-eyed liberals to purchase racial reconciliation on the cheap. On the other end, we've heard my former pastor, Reverend Jeremiah Wright, use incendiary language to express views that have the potential not only to widen the racial divide, but views that denigrate both the greatness and the goodness of our nation; that rightly offend white and black alike.

I have already condemned, in unequivocal terms, the statements of Reverend Wright that have caused such controversy.[1] For some, nagging questions remain. Did I know him to be an occasionally fierce critic of American domestic and foreign policy? Of course. Did I ever hear him make remarks that could be considered controversial while I sat in church? Yes. Did I strongly disagree with many of his political views? Absolutely—just as I'm sure many of you have heard remarks from your pastors, priests, or rabbis with which you strongly disagreed.

But the remarks that have caused this recent firestorm weren't simply controversial. They weren't simply a religious leader's effort to speak out against perceived injustice. Instead, they expressed a profoundly distorted view of this country—a view that sees white racism as endemic, and that elevates what is wrong with America above all that we know is right with America; a view that sees the conflicts in the Middle East as rooted primarily in the actions of stalwart allies like Israel, instead of emanating from the perverse and hateful ideologies of radical Islam.

As such, Reverend Wright's comments were not only wrong but divisive, divisive at a time when we need unity; racially charged at a time when we need to come together to solve a set of monumental problems—two wars, a terrorist threat, a falling economy, a chronic health care crisis and potentially devastating climate change; problems that are neither black or white or Latino or Asian, but rather problems that confront us all.

Given my background, my politics, and my professed values and ideals, there will no doubt be those for whom my statements of condemnation are not enough. Why associate myself with Reverend Wright in the first place, they may ask? Why not join another church? And I confess that if all that I knew of Reverend Wright were the snippets of those sermons that have run in an endless loop on the television and YouTube, or if Trinity United Church of Christ

15

---

1   *statements of … such controversy*   At the time this speech was delivered, there was a major controversy in the media over statements that Obama's pastor Jeremiah Wright had made during sermons, including an assertion that the American government had "failed" Black people.

conformed to the caricatures being peddled by some commentators, there is no doubt that I would react in much the same way.

But the truth is, that isn't all that I know of the man. The man I met more than twenty years ago is a man who helped introduce me to my Christian faith, a man who spoke to me about our obligations to love one another; to care for the sick and lift up the poor. He is a man who served his country as a US Marine; who has studied and lectured at some of the finest universities and seminaries in the country, and who for over thirty years led a church that serves the community by doing God's work here on Earth—by housing the homeless, ministering to the needy, providing day care services and scholarships and prison ministries, and reaching out to those suffering from HIV/AIDS.

In my first book, *Dreams from My Father*, I described the experience of my first service at Trinity:

20 "People began to shout, to rise from their seats and clap and cry out, a forceful wind carrying the reverend's voice up into the rafters.... And in that single note—hope!—I heard something else; at the foot of that cross, inside the thousands of churches across the city, I imagined the stories of ordinary black people merging with the stories of David and Goliath, Moses and Pharaoh, the Christians in the lion's den, Ezekiel's field of dry bones. Those stories—of survival, and freedom, and hope—became our story, my story; the blood that had spilled was our blood, the tears our tears; until this black church, on this bright day, seemed once more a vessel carrying the story of a people into future generations and into a larger world. Our trials and triumphs became at once unique and universal, black and more than black; in chronicling our journey, the stories and songs gave us a means to reclaim memories that we didn't need to feel shame about ... memories that all people might study and cherish—and with which we could start to rebuild."

That has been my experience at Trinity. Like other predominantly black churches across the country, Trinity embodies the black community in its entirety—the doctor and the welfare mom, the model student and the former gang-banger. Like other black churches, Trinity's services are full of raucous laughter and sometimes bawdy humor. They are full of dancing, clapping, screaming and shouting that may seem jarring to the untrained ear. The church contains in full the kindness and cruelty, the fierce intelligence and the shocking ignorance, the struggles and successes, the love and yes, the bitterness and bias that make up the black experience in America.

And this helps explain, perhaps, my relationship with Reverend Wright. As imperfect as he may be, he has been like family to me. He strengthened my faith, officiated my wedding, and baptized my children. Not once in my conversations with him have I heard him talk about any ethnic group in derogatory terms, or treat whites with whom he interacted with anything but courtesy and respect. He contains within him the contradictions—the good and the bad—of the community that he has served diligently for so many years.

I can no more disown him than I can disown the black community. I can no more disown him than I can my white grandmother—a woman who helped raise me, a woman who sacrificed again and again for me, a woman who loves me as much as she loves anything in this world, but a woman who once confessed her fear of black men who passed by her on the street, and who on more than one occasion has uttered racial or ethnic stereotypes that made me cringe.

These people are a part of me. And they are a part of America, this country that I love.

Some will see this as an attempt to justify or excuse comments that are   25
simply inexcusable. I can assure you it is not. I suppose the politically safe thing would be to move on from this episode and just hope that it fades into the woodwork. We can dismiss Reverend Wright as a crank or a demagogue, just as some have dismissed Geraldine Ferraro, in the aftermath of her recent statements, as harboring some deep-seated racial bias.

But race is an issue that I believe this nation cannot afford to ignore right now. We would be making the same mistake that Reverend Wright made in his offending sermons about America—to simplify and stereotype and amplify the negative to the point that it distorts reality.

The fact is that the comments that have been made and the issues that have surfaced over the last few weeks reflect the complexities of race in this country that we've never really worked through—a part of our union that we have yet to perfect. And if we walk away now, if we simply retreat into our respective corners, we will never be able to come together and solve challenges like health care, or education, or the need to find good jobs for every American.

Understanding this reality requires a reminder of how we arrived at this point. As William Faulkner once wrote, "The past isn't dead and buried. In fact, it isn't even past." We do not need to recite here the history of racial injustice in this country. But we do need to remind ourselves that so many of the disparities that exist in the African-American community today can be directly traced to inequalities passed on from an earlier generation that suffered under the brutal legacy of slavery and Jim Crow.*

Segregated schools were, and are, inferior schools; we still haven't fixed them, fifty years after Brown v. Board of Education, and the inferior education they provided, then and now, helps explain the pervasive achievement gap between today's black and white students.

Legalized discrimination—where blacks were prevented, often through   30
violence, from owning property, or loans were not granted to African-American

business owners, or black homeowners could not access FHA mortgages, or blacks were excluded from unions, or the police force, or fire departments—meant that black families could not amass any meaningful wealth to bequeath to future generations. That history helps explain the wealth and income gap between black and white, and the concentrated pockets of poverty that persists in so many of today's urban and rural communities.

A lack of economic opportunity among black men, and the shame and frustration that came from not being able to provide for one's family, contributed to the erosion of black families—a problem that welfare policies for many years may have worsened. And the lack of basic services in so many urban black neighborhoods—parks for kids to play in, police walking the beat, regular garbage pick-up and building code enforcement—all helped create a cycle of violence, blight and neglect that continue to haunt us.

This is the reality in which Reverend Wright and other African-Americans of his generation grew up. They came of age in the late fifties and early sixties, a time when segregation was still the law of the land and opportunity was systematically constricted. What's remarkable is not how many failed in the face of discrimination, but rather how many men and women overcame the odds; how many were able to make a way out of no way for those like me who would come after them.

But for all those who scratched and clawed their way to get a piece of the American Dream, there were many who didn't make it—those who were ultimately defeated, in one way or another, by discrimination. That legacy of defeat was passed on to future generations—those young men and increasingly young women who we see standing on street corners or languishing in our prisons, without hope or prospects for the future. Even for those blacks who did make it, questions of race, and racism, continue to define their world-view in fundamental ways. For the men and women of Reverend Wright's generation, the memories of humiliation and doubt and fear have not gone away; nor has the anger and the bitterness of those years. That anger may not get expressed in public, in front of white co-workers or white friends. But it does find voice in the barbershop or around the kitchen table. At times, that anger is exploited by politicians, to gin up votes along racial lines, or to make up for a politician's own failings.

And occasionally it finds voice in the church on Sunday morning, in the pulpit and in the pews. The fact that so many people are surprised to hear that anger in some of Reverend Wright's sermons simply reminds us of the old truism that the most segregated hour in American life occurs on Sunday morning. That anger is not always productive; indeed, all too often it distracts attention from solving real problems; it keeps us from squarely facing our own complicity in our condition, and prevents the African-American community from forging the alliances it needs to bring about real change. But the anger is real; it is powerful; and to simply wish it away, to condemn it without understanding its roots, only serves to widen the chasm of misunderstanding that exists between the races.

In fact, a similar anger exists within segments of the white community. Most working- and middle-class white Americans don't feel that they have been particularly privileged by their race. Their experience is the immigrant experience—as far as they're concerned, no one's handed them anything, they've built it from scratch. They've worked hard all their lives, many times only to see their jobs shipped overseas or their pension dumped after a lifetime of labor. They are anxious about their futures, and feel their dreams slipping away; in an era of stagnant wages and global competition, opportunity comes to be seen as a zero sum game, in which your dreams come at my expense. So when they are told to bus their children to a school across town; when they hear that an African American is getting an advantage in landing a good job or a spot in a good college because of an injustice that they themselves never committed; when they're told that their fears about crime in urban neighborhoods are somehow prejudiced, resentment builds over time.

Like the anger within the black community, these resentments aren't always expressed in polite company. But they have helped shape the political landscape for at least a generation. Anger over welfare and affirmative action helped forge the Reagan Coalition. Politicians routinely exploited fears of crime for their own electoral ends. Talk show hosts and conservative commentators built entire careers unmasking bogus claims of racism while dismissing legitimate discussions of racial injustice and inequality as mere political correctness or reverse racism.

Just as black anger often proved counterproductive, so have these white resentments distracted attention from the real culprits of the middle class squeeze—a corporate culture rife with inside dealing, questionable accounting practices, and short-term greed; a Washington dominated by lobbyists and special interests; economic policies that favor the few over the many. And yet, to wish away the resentments of white Americans, to label them as misguided or even racist, without recognizing they are grounded in legitimate concerns—this too widens the racial divide, and blocks the path to understanding.

This is where we are right now. It's a racial stalemate we've been stuck in for years. Contrary to the claims of some of my critics, black and white, I have never been so naïve as to believe that we can get beyond our racial divisions in a single election cycle, or with a single candidacy—particularly a candidacy as imperfect as my own.

But I have asserted a firm conviction—a conviction rooted in my faith in God and my faith in the American people—that working together we can move beyond some of our old racial wounds, and that in fact we have no choice if we are to continue on the path of a more perfect union.

40   For the African-American community, that path means embracing the burdens of our past without becoming victims of our past. It means continuing to insist on a full measure of justice in every aspect of American life. But it also means binding our particular grievances—for better health care, and better schools, and better jobs—to the larger aspirations of all Americans—the white woman struggling to break the glass ceiling, the white man who's been laid off, the immigrant trying to feed his family. And it means taking full responsibility for our own lives—by demanding more from our fathers, and spending more time with our children, and reading to them, and teaching them that while they may face challenges and discrimination in their own lives, they must never succumb to despair or cynicism; they must always believe that they can write their own destiny.

Ironically, this quintessentially American—and yes, conservative—notion of self-help found frequent expression in Reverend Wright's sermons. But what my former pastor too often failed to understand is that embarking on a program of self-help also requires a belief that society can change.

The profound mistake of Reverend Wright's sermons is not that he spoke about racism in our society. It's that he spoke as if our society was static; as if no progress has been made; as if this country—a country that has made it possible for one of his own members to run for the highest office in the land and build a coalition of white and black; Latino and Asian, rich and poor, young and old—is still irrevocably bound to a tragic past. But what we know—what we have seen—is that America can change. That is the true genius of this nation. What we have already achieved gives us hope—the audacity to hope—for what we can and must achieve tomorrow.

In the white community, the path to a more perfect union means acknowledging that what ails the African-American community does not just exist in the minds of black people; that the legacy of discrimination—and current incidents of discrimination, while less overt than in the past—are real and must be addressed. Not just with words, but with deeds—by investing in our schools and our communities; by enforcing our civil rights laws and ensuring fairness in our criminal justice system; by providing this generation with ladders of opportunity that were unavailable for previous generations. It requires all Americans to realize that your dreams do not have to come at the expense of my dreams; that investing in the health, welfare, and education of black and brown and white children will ultimately help all of America prosper.

In the end, then, what is called for is nothing more, and nothing less, than what all the world's great religions demand—that we do unto others as we would have them do unto us. Let us be our brother's keeper, Scripture tells us. Let us be our sister's keeper. Let us find that common stake we all have in one another, and let our politics reflect that spirit as well.

For we have a choice in this country. We can accept a politics that breeds 45 division, and conflict, and cynicism. We can tackle race only as spectacle—as we did in the OJ trial—or in the wake of tragedy, as we did in the aftermath of Katrina—or as fodder for the nightly news. We can play Reverend Wright's sermons on every channel, every day and talk about them from now until the election, and make the only question in this campaign whether or not the American people think that I somehow believe or sympathize with his most offensive words. We can pounce on some gaffe by a Hillary supporter as evidence that she's playing the race card, or we can speculate on whether white men will all flock to John McCain in the general election regardless of his policies.

We can do that.

But if we do, I can tell you that in the next election, we'll be talking about some other distraction. And then another one. And then another one. And nothing will change.

That is one option. Or, at this moment, in this election, we can come together and say, "Not this time." This time we want to talk about the crumbling schools that are stealing the future of black children and white children and Asian children and Hispanic children and Native American children. This time we want to reject the cynicism that tells us that these kids can't learn; that those kids who don't look like us are somebody else's problem. The children of America are not those kids, they are our kids, and we will not let them fall behind in a 21st-century economy. Not this time.

This time we want to talk about how the lines in the Emergency Room 50 are filled with whites and blacks and Hispanics who do not have health care; who don't have the power on their own to overcome the special interests in Washington, but who can take them on if we do it together.

This time we want to talk about the shuttered mills that once provided a decent life for men and women of every race, and the homes for sale that once belonged to Americans from every religion, every region, every walk of life. This time we want to talk about the fact that the real problem is not that someone who doesn't look like you might take your job; it's that the corporation you work for will ship it overseas for nothing more than a profit.

This time we want to talk about the men and women of every color and creed who serve together, and fight together, and bleed together under the same proud flag. We want to talk about how to bring them home from a war that never should've been authorized and never should've been waged, and we want to talk about how we'll show our patriotism by caring for them, and their families, and giving them the benefits they have earned.

I would not be running for President if I didn't believe with all my heart that this is what the vast majority of Americans want for this country. This union may never be perfect, but generation after generation has shown that it can always be perfected. And today, whenever I find myself feeling doubtful or cynical about this possibility, what gives me the most hope is the next generation—the young people whose attitudes and beliefs and openness to change have already made history in this election.

There is one story in particularly that I'd like to leave you with today—a story I told when I had the great honor of speaking on Dr. King's birthday at his home church, Ebenezer Baptist, in Atlanta.

There is a young, twenty-three year old white woman named Ashley Baia who organized for our campaign in Florence, South Carolina. She had been working to organize a mostly African-American community since the beginning of this campaign, and one day she was at a roundtable discussion where everyone went around telling their story and why they were there.

55   And Ashley said that when she was nine years old, her mother got cancer. And because she had to miss days of work, she was let go and lost her health care. They had to file for bankruptcy, and that's when Ashley decided that she had to do something to help her mom.

She knew that food was one of their most expensive costs, and so Ashley convinced her mother that what she really liked and really wanted to eat more than anything else was mustard and relish sandwiches. Because that was the cheapest way to eat.

She did this for a year until her mom got better, and she told everyone at the roundtable that the reason she joined our campaign was so that she could help the millions of other children in the country who want and need to help their parents too.

Now Ashley might have made a different choice. Perhaps somebody told her along the way that the source of her mother's problems were blacks who were on welfare and too lazy to work, or Hispanics who were coming into the country illegally. But she didn't. She sought out allies in her fight against injustice.

Anyway, Ashley finishes her story and then goes around the room and asks everyone else why they're supporting the campaign. They all have different stories and reasons. Many bring up a specific issue. And finally they come to this elderly black man who's been sitting there quietly the entire time. And Ashley asks him why he's there. And he does not bring up a specific issue. He does not say health care or the economy. He does not say education or the war. He does not say that he was there because of Barack Obama. He simply says to everyone in the room, "I am here because of Ashley."

"I'm here because of Ashley." By itself, that single moment of recognition between that young white girl and that old black man is not enough. It is not enough to give health care to the sick, or jobs to the jobless, or education to our children.   60

But it is where we start. It is where our union grows stronger. And as so many generations have come to realize over the course of the two-hundred and twenty one years since a band of patriots signed that document in Philadelphia, that is where the perfection begins.

(2008)

Questions

1. In the opening to this speech, Senator Obama talks about slavery as sin. How has slavery shaped how we understand the United States?

2. How does Senator Obama relate his personal experience to the American political situation?

3. Comment on the role of the words "perfect," "perfected," and "perfectable" in this speech.

4. Although Obama's chief campaign speechwriter, Jonathan Favreau, did some work on this speech, Obama wrote the majority of it himself. This was contrary to Obama's usual speechwriting practice of discussing ideas with Favreau, then editing Favreau's rough draft—and even this usual practice represents more involvement in the speechwriting process than is typical of contemporary politicians. To what extent does it matter whether a politician writes her speeches herself, or only approves their content? Discuss in the context of this speech.

5. Consider Obama's presidential portrait, reproduced in this volume's color insert. What impression of Obama is conveyed in the portrait? How does that impression corroborate—or contradict—the way Obama represents himself in this speech?

CHIMAMANDA NGOZI ADICHIE

THE COLOR OF AN AWKWARD
CONVERSATION

*Chimamanda Ngozi Adichie is a Nigerian writer whose work
not only has won international acclaim and prestigious awards,
including a MacArthur Foundation Genius Grant, but also has had
significant mainstream impact. The video of her TEDx talk "We
Should All Be Feminists" was viewed more than 3 million times,
and it was sampled by Beyoncé in her 2013 song "Flawless."*

*When Adichie was 19, she moved to America to attend Drexel
University; she now divides her time between Nigeria and the
United States. The following essay appeared in the* Washington Post
Opinion section in June 2008.

I was annoyed the first time an African American man called me "sister." It
was in a Brooklyn store, and I had recently arrived from Nigeria, a country
where, thanks to the mosquitoes that kept British colonizers from settling,
my skin color did not determine my identity, did not limit my dreams or my
confidence. And so, although I grew up reading books about the baffling places
where black people were treated badly for being black, race remained an exotic
abstraction: It was Kunta Kinte.[1]

Until that day in Brooklyn. To be called "sister" was to be black, and
blackness was the very bottom of America's pecking order. I did not want to
be black.

In college I babysat for a Jewish family, and once I went to pick up first-
grader Stephen from his play date's home. The lovely house had an American
flag hanging from a colonnade. The mother of Stephen's play date greeted me
warmly. Stephen hugged me and went to look for his shoes. His play date ran

---

1   *Kunta Kinte*   Major character in *Roots: The Saga of an American Family* (1976), a
popular American historical work by Alex Haley that was made into a TV series in 1977
(and again in 2016). In the book, which traces the genealogy of Haley's own family from
the eighteenth century to the twentieth, Kunta Kinte, Haley's ancestor, is captured from his
home in Gambia, enslaved, and sold to a Virginia plantation owner.

down the stairs and stopped halfway. "She's black," he said to his mother and stared silently at me before going back upstairs. I laughed stupidly, perhaps to deflate the tension, but I was angry.

I was angry that this child did not merely think that black was different but had been taught that black was not a good thing. I was angry that his behavior left Stephen bewildered, and for a long time I half-expected something similar to happen in other homes that displayed American flags.

"That kid's mother is so ignorant," one friend said. "Ignorant" suggested 5 that an affluent, educated American living in a Philadelphia suburb in 1999 did not realize that black people are human beings. "It was just a kid being a kid. It wasn't racist," another said. "Racist" suggested it was no big deal, since neither the child nor his mother had burned a cross in my yard. I called the first friend a Diminisher and the second a Denier and came to discover that both represented how mainstream America talks about blackness.

Diminishers have a subtle intellectual superiority and depend on the word "ignorant." They believe that black people still encounter unpleasantness related to blackness but in benign forms and from unhappy people or crazy people or people with good intentions that are bungled in execution. Diminishers think that people can be "ignorant" but not "racist" because these people have black friends, supported the civil rights movements or had abolitionist forebears.

Deniers believe that black people stopped encountering unpleasantness related to their blackness when Martin Luther King Jr. died. They are "color-blind" and use expressions like "white, black or purple, we're all the same"—as though race were a biological rather than a social identity. Incidents that black people attribute to blackness are really about other factors, such as having too many children or driving too fast, but if deniers are compelled to accept that an incident was indeed about blackness, they launch into stories of Irish or Native American oppression, as though to deny the legitimacy of one story by generalizing about others. Deniers use "racist" as one would use "dinosaur," to refer to a phenomenon that no longer exists.

Although the way that blackness manifests itself in America has changed since 1965, the way that it is talked about has not. I have a great and compli-cated affection for this country—America is like my distant uncle who does not always remember my name but occasionally gives me pocket money—and what I admire most is its ability to create enduring myths. The myth of black-ness is this: "Once upon a time, black towns were destroyed, black Americans were massacred and barred from voting, etc. All this happened because of racists. Today, these things no longer happen, and therefore racists no longer exist."

The word "racist" should be banned. It is like a sweater wrung completely out of shape; it has lost its usefulness. It makes honest debate impossible, whether about small realities such as little boys who won't say hello to black babysitters or large realities such as who is more likely to get the death penalty. In place of "racist," descriptive, albeit unwieldy, expressions might be used, such as "incidents that negatively affect black people, which, although possibly complicated by class and other factors, would not have occurred if the affected people were not black." Perhaps qualifiers would be added: "These incidents do not implicate all non-black people."

10   There are many stories like mine of Africans discovering blackness in America; of people who are consequently amused, resentful or puzzled by Americans being afraid of them or assuming they play sports or reacting to their intelligence with surprise. Still, what is most striking to me are the strange ways in which blackness is talked about. Ten years after first being called a "sister," I think of Don Cheadle[2] as a talented brother, but I have never stopped being aware of the relative privilege of having had those West African mosquitoes.

(2008)

Questions

1. What does Adichie mean when she says that, having grown up in Nigeria, "race remained an exotic abstraction"?

2. Consider Adichie's description of the house where she picked Stephen up from his playdate: "The lovely house had an American flag hanging from a colonnade." How are the architectural details significant? What does this house represent for the young Adichie?

3. What, for Adichie, characterizes the attitudes of "diminishers" and "deniers"? Do you agree that these attitudes predominate in the way white people talk about Blackness?

4. What are Adichie's objections to the way the word "racist" is used in American discourse? Do you agree with her suggestion that the word has "lost its usefulness"?

5. Ten years after Adichie's move to America, has race remained an "abstraction" for her? Why or why not?

6. In what senses is Adichie privileged in the United States? In what senses is she not privileged?

7. Who are the targets of humor in this essay? How, if at all, does humor affect the rhetorical impact of the essay?

---

2   *Don Cheadle*   Award-winning African American actor, writer, director, and activist.

MICHELLE ALEXANDER

from THE NEW JIM CROW*

Through the 1990s and the first decade of this century there was much talk of how the American socioeconomic, legal, and "correctional" systems discriminated in particular against young Black men, who were consigned to prison at alarmingly high rates. But not until the 2010 publication of Michelle Alexander's The New Jim Crow: Mass Incarceration in the Age of Colorblindness *was there a book that connected all the dots—that showed in thorough and persuasive fashion how various twenty-first century forms of systemic discrimination could, in aggregate, have an effect comparable in its oppressiveness to the systemic discriminations of the notorious Jim Crow era.*

Alexander is trained both as a lawyer and as an academic. For this book, though, she was writing with a broader audience in mind: one that included the general public as well as scholars, such that her work would (in the words of reviewer Darryl Pinkney) "educate social commentators, policymakers, and politicians." The book won several awards, and has indeed helped to change the opinions of many policy makers as well as many members of the general public.

The excerpts included here are from the heart of the book—Chapter 5, which bears the same title as the book itself: "The New Jim Crow."

... Hundreds of thousands of black men are unable to be good fathers for their children, not because of a lack of commitment or desire but because they are warehoused in prisons, locked in cages. They did not walk out on their families voluntarily; they were taken away in handcuffs, often due to the massive federal program known as the War on Drugs.[1]

---

1   *War on Drugs*   Term for a collection of government policies that began in the 1970s; it involves American participation in armed combat against drug producers in Mexico and South America, as well as the imprisonment of drug users within the United States.

More African American adults are under correctional control today—in prison or jail, on probation or parole—than were enslaved in 1850, a decade before the Civil War began.[7] The mass incarceration of people of color is a big part of the reason that a black child born today is less likely to be raised by both parents than a black child born during slavery.[8] The absence of black fathers from families across America is not simply a function of laziness, immaturity, or too much time watching Sports Center. Thousands of black men have disappeared into prisons and jails, locked away for drug crimes that are largely ignored when committed by whites.

The clock has been turned back on racial progress in America, though scarcely anyone seems to notice. All eyes are fixed on people like Barack Obama and Oprah Winfrey, who have defied the odds and risen to power, fame, and fortune. For those left behind, especially those within prison walls, the celebration of racial triumph in America must seem a tad premature. More black men are imprisoned today than at any other moment in our nation's history. More are disenfranchised today than in 1870, the year the Fifteenth Amendment was ratified prohibiting laws that explicitly deny the right to vote on the basis of race.[9] Young black men today may be just as likely to suffer discrimination in employment, housing, public benefits, and jury service as a black man in the Jim Crow era—discrimination that is perfectly legal, because it is based on one's criminal record.

This is the new normal, the new racial equilibrium.

The launching of the War on Drugs and the initial construction of the new system required the expenditure of tremendous political initiative and resources. Media campaigns were waged; politicians blasted "soft" judges and enacted harsh sentencing laws, poor people of color were vilified. The system now, however, requires very little maintenance or justification. In fact, if you are white and middle class, you might not even realize the drug war is still going on. Most high school and college students today have no recollection of the political and media frenzy surrounding the drug war in the early years. They were young children when the war was declared, or not even born yet. Crack is out; terrorism is in.

Today, the political fanfare and the vehement, racialized rhetoric regarding crime and drugs are no longer necessary. Mass incarceration has been normalized, and all of the racial stereotypes and assumptions that gave rise to the system are now embraced (or at least internalized) by people of all colors, from all walks of life, and in every major political party. We may

---

NB **Explanatory footnotes are indicated by superscript numbers in this anthology; numbers that refer to the author's list of references are indicated by subscript numbers.**

wonder aloud "where have the black men gone?" but deep down we already know. It is simply taken for granted that, in cities like Baltimore and Chicago, the vast majority of young black men are currently under the control of the criminal justice system or branded criminals for life. This extraordinary circumstance—unheard of in the rest of the world—is treated here in America as a basic fact of life, as normal as separate water fountains were just a half century ago.

STATES OF DENIAL

... Much has been written about the ways in which people manage to deny, even to themselves, that extraordinary atrocities, racial oppression, and other forms of human suffering have occurred or are occurring. Criminologist Stanley Cohen wrote perhaps the most important book on the subject, *States of Denial*. The book examines how individuals and institutions—victims, perpetrators, and bystanders—know about yet deny the occurrence of oppressive acts. They see only what they want to see and wear blinders to avoid seeing the rest. This has been true about slavery, genocide, torture, and every form of systemic oppression.

Cohen emphasizes that denial, though deplorable, is complicated. It is not simply a matter of refusing to acknowledge an obvious, though uncomfortable truth. Many people "know" and "not-know" the truth about human suffering at the same time. In his words, "Denial may be neither a matter of telling the truth nor intentionally telling a lie. There seem to be states of mind, or even whole cultures, in which we know and don't know at the same time."[10]

Today, most Americans know and don't know the truth about mass incarceration. For more than three decades, images of black men in handcuffs have been a regular staple of the evening news. We know that large numbers of black men have been locked in cages. In fact, it is precisely because we know that black and brown people are far more likely to be imprisoned that we, as a nation, have not cared too much about it. We tell ourselves they "deserve" their fate, even though we know—and don't know—that whites are just as likely to commit many crimes, especially drug crimes. We know that people released from prison face a lifetime of discrimination, scorn, and exclusion, and yet we claim not to know that an undercaste exists. We know and we don't know at the same time.

Upon reflection, it is relatively easy to understand how Americans come to deny the evils of mass incarceration. Denial is facilitated by persistent racial segregation in housing and schools, by political demagoguery, by racialized media imagery, and by the ease of changing one's perception of reality simply by changing television channels. There is little reason to doubt the prevailing

10

"common sense" that black and brown men have been locked up en masse merely in response to crime rates, when one's sources of information are mainstream media outlets. In many respects, the reality of mass incarceration is easier to avoid knowing than the injustices and sufferings associated with slavery or Jim Crow. Those confined to prisons are out of sight and out of mind; once released, they are typically confined in ghettos. Most Americans only come to "know" about the people cycling in and out of prisons through fictional police dramas, music videos, gangsta rap, and "true" accounts of ghetto experience on the evening news. These racialized narratives tend to confirm and reinforce the prevailing public consensus that we need not care about "those people"; they deserve what they get.

Of all the reasons that we fail to know the truth about mass incarceration though, one stands out: a profound misunderstanding regarding how racial oppression actually works. If someone were to visit the United States from another country (or another planet) and ask: Is the U.S. criminal justice system some kind of tool of racial control? Most Americans would swiftly deny it. Numerous reasons would leap to mind why that could not possibly be the case. The visitor would be told that crime rates, black culture, or bad schools were to blame. "The system is not run by a bunch of racists," the apologist would explain. "It's run by people who are trying to fight crime." That response is predictable because most people assume that racism, and racial systems generally, are fundamentally a function of attitudes. Because mass incarceration is officially colorblind, it seems inconceivable that the system could function much like a racial caste system. The widespread and mistaken belief that racial animus[2] is necessary for the creation and maintenance of racialized systems of social control is the most important reason that we, as a nation, have remained in deep denial.

The misunderstanding is not surprising. As a society, our collective understanding of racism has been powerfully influenced by the shocking images of the Jim Crow era and the struggle for civil rights. When we think of racism we think of Governor Wallace of Alabama blocking the schoolhouse door;[3] we think of water hoses, lynchings,* racial epithets, and "whites only" signs.* These images make it easy to forget that many wonderful, good-hearted white people who were generous to others, respectful of their neighbors, and even kind to their black maids, gardeners, or shoe shiners—and wished them

---

2   *racial animus*   Hostility based on race.
3   *Governor Wallace ... door*   In 1963, Governor George Wallace made a symbolic protest against desegregation by standing in the doorway to an auditorium to prevent two Black students, Vivian Malone and James Hood, from completing their registration at the University of Alabama.

well—nevertheless went to the polls and voted for racial segregation. Many whites who supported Jim Crow justified it on a paternalist grounds, actually believing they were doing blacks a favor or believing the time was not yet "right" for equality. The disturbing images from the Jim Crow era also make it easy to forget that many African Americans were complicit in the Jim Crow system, profiting from it directly or indirectly or keeping their objections quiet out of fear of the repercussions. Our understanding of racism is therefore shaped by the most extreme expressions of individual bigotry, not by the way in which it functions naturally, almost invisibly (and sometimes with genuinely benign intent), when it is embedded in the structure of a social system.

The unfortunate reality we must face is that racism manifests itself not only in individual attitudes and stereotypes, but also in the basic structure of society. Academics have developed complicated theories and obscure jargon in an effort to describe what is now referred to as *structural racism*, yet the concept is fairly straightforward. One theorist, Iris Marion Young, relying on a famous "birdcage" metaphor, explains it this way: If one thinks about racism by examining only one wire of the cage, or one form of disadvantage, it is difficult to understand how and why the bird is trapped. Only a large number of wires arranged in a specific way, and connected to one another, serve to enclose the bird and to ensure that it cannot escape.[11]

What is particularly important to keep in mind is that any given wire of the cage may or may not be specifically developed for the purpose of trapping the bird, yet it still operates (together with the other wires) to restrict its freedom. By the same token, not every aspect of a racial caste system needs to be developed for the specific purpose of controlling black people in order for it to operate (together with other laws, institutions, and practices) to trap them at the bottom of a racial hierarchy. In the system of mass incarceration, a wide variety of laws, institutions, and practices—ranging from racial profiling to biased sentencing policies, political disenfranchisement, and legalized employment discrimination—trap African Americans in a virtual (and literal) cage.

Fortunately, as Marilyn Frye has noted, every birdcage has a door, and every birdcage can be broken and can corrode.[12] What is most concerning about the new racial caste system, however, is that it may prove to be more durable than its predecessors. Because this new system is not explicitly based on race, it is easier to defend on seemingly neutral grounds. And while all previous methods of control have blamed the victim in one way or another, the current system invites observers to imagine that those who are trapped in the system were free to avoid second-class status or permanent banishment from society simply by choosing not to commit crimes. It is far more convenient to imagine that a majority of young African American men in urban areas freely chose a

15

life of crime than to accept the real possibility that their lives were structured in a way that virtually guaranteed their early admission into a system from which they can never escape. Most people are willing to acknowledge the existence of the cage but insist that a door has been left open.

One way of understanding our current system of mass incarceration is to think of it as a birdcage with a locked door. It is a set of structural arrangements that locks a racially distinct group into a subordinate political, social, and economic position, effectively creating a second-class citizenship. Those trapped within the system are not merely disadvantaged, in the sense that they are competing on an unequal playing field or face additional hurdles to political or economic success; rather, the system itself is structured to lock them into a subordinate position.

How It Works

... This, in brief, is how the system works: The War on Drugs is the vehicle through which extraordinary numbers of black men are forced into the cage. The entrapment occurs in three distinct phases, each of which has been explored earlier, but a brief review is useful here. The first stage is the roundup. Vast numbers of people are swept into the criminal justice system by the police, who conduct drug operations primarily in poor communities of color. They are rewarded in cash—through drug forfeiture laws and federal grant programs— for rounding up as many people as possible, and they operate unconstrained by constitutional rules of procedure that once were considered inviolate. Police can stop, interrogate, and search anyone they choose for drug investigations, provided they get "consent." Because there is no meaningful check on the exercise of police discretion, racial biases are granted free rein. In fact, police are allowed to rely on race as a factor in selecting whom to stop and search (even though people of color are no more likely to be guilty of drug crimes than whites)—effectively guaranteeing that those who are swept into the system are primarily black and brown.

The conviction marks the beginning of the second phase: the period of formal control. Once arrested, defendants are generally denied meaningful legal representation and pressured to plead guilty whether they are or not. Prosecutors are free to "load up" defendants with extra charges, and their decisions cannot be challenged for racial bias. Once convicted, due to the drug war's harsh sentencing laws, drug offenders in the United States spend more time under the criminal justice system's formal control—in jail or prison, on probation or parole—than drug offenders anywhere else in the world. While under formal control, virtually every aspect of one's life is regulated and monitored by the system, and any form of resistance or disobedience is subject to swift sanction. This period of control may last a lifetime, even for those convicted of extremely minor, nonviolent offenses, but the vast majority of those swept into the system are eventually released. They are transferred from their prison cells to a much larger, invisible cage.

The final stage has been dubbed by some advocates as the period of invisible punishment.[13] This term, first coined by Jeremy Travis, is meant to describe the unique set of criminal sanctions that are imposed on individuals after they step outside the prison gates, a form of punishment that operates largely outside of public view and takes effect outside the traditional sentencing framework. These sanctions ... operate collectively to ensure that the vast majority of convicted offenders will never integrate into mainstream, white society. They will be discriminated against, legally, for the rest of their lives—denied employment, housing, education, and public benefits. Unable to surmount these obstacles, most will eventually return to prison and then be released again, caught in a closed circuit of perpetual marginality....

NOTHING NEW

... In Chicago, like the rest of the country, the War on Drugs is the engine of mass incarceration, as well as the primary cause of gross racial disparities in the criminal justice system and in the ex-offender population. About 90 percent of those sentenced to prison for a drug offense in Illinois are African American.[18] White drug offenders are rarely arrested, and when they are, they are treated more favorably at every stage of the criminal justice process, including plea bargaining and sentencing.[19] Whites are consistently more likely to avoid prison and felony charges, even when they are repeat offenders.[20] Black offenders, by contrast, are routinely labeled felons and released into a permanent racial undercaste.

The total population of black males in Chicago with a felony record (including both current and ex-felons) is equivalent to 55 percent of the black adult male population and an astonishing 80 percent of the adult black male workforce in the Chicago area.[21] This stunning development reflects the dramatic increase in the number and race of those sent to prison for drug crimes. From the Chicago region alone, the number of those annually sent to prison for drug crimes increased almost 2,000 percent, from 469 in 1985 to 8,755 in 2005.[22] That figure, of course, does not include the thousands who avoid prison but are arrested, convicted, and sentenced to jail or probation. They, too, have criminal records that will follow them for life. More than 70 percent of all criminal cases in the Chicago area involve a class D felony drug possession charge, the lowest-level felony charge.[23] Those who do go to prison find little freedom upon release.

20

When people are released from Illinois prisons, they are given as little as $10 in "gate money" and a bus ticket to anywhere in the United States. Most return to the impoverished neighborhoods in the Chicago area, bringing few resources and bearing the stigma of their prison record.[24] In Chicago, as in most cities across the country, ex-offenders are banned or severely restricted from employment in a large number of professions, job categories, and fields by professional licensing statutes, rules, and practices....

MAPPING THE PARALLELS

... [F]or black men, the stigma of being a "criminal" in the era of mass incarceration is fundamentally a *racial* stigma. This is not to say stigma is absent for white criminals; it is present and powerful. Rather, the point is that the stigma of criminality for white offenders if different—it is a nonracial stigma.

An experiment may help to illustrate how and why this is the case. Say the following to nearly anyone and watch the reaction: "We really need to do something about the problem of white crime." Laughter is a likely response. The term *white crime* is nonsensical in the era of mass incarceration, unless one is really referring to white-collar crime,* in which case the term is understood to mean the types of crimes that seemingly respectable white people commit in the comfort of fancy offices. Because the term *white crime* lacks social meaning, the term *white criminal* is also perplexing. In that formulation, *white* seems to qualify the term *criminal*—as if to say, "he's a criminal but not *that* kind of criminal." Or, he's not a *real* criminal—i.e., not what we mean by *criminal* today.

25   In the era of mass incarceration, what it means to be a criminal in our collective consciousness has become conflated with what it means to be black, so the term *white criminal* is confounding, while the term *black criminal* is nearly redundant. Recall the study discussed in chapter 3 [not included here] that revealed that when survey respondents were asked to picture a drug criminal, nearly everyone pictured someone who was black. This phenomenon helps to explain why studies indicate that white ex-offenders may actually have an easier time gaining employment than African Americans *without* a criminal record.[53] To be a black man is to be thought of as a criminal, and to be a black criminal is to be despicable—a social pariah. To be a white criminal is not easy, by any means, but as a white criminal you are not a *racial* outcast, though you may face many forms of social and economic exclusion. Whiteness mitigates crime, whereas blackness defines the criminal.

... [T]he conflation of blackness with crime did not happen organically; rather, it was constructed by political and media elites as part of the broad project known as the War on Drugs. This conflation served to provide a legitimate outlet to the expression of antiblack resentment and animus—a convenient release valve now that explicit forms of racial bias are strictly condemned. In the era of colorblindness, it is no longer permissible to hate blacks, but we can hate criminals. Indeed, we are encouraged to do so. As writer John Edgar Wideman points out, "it's respectable to tar and feather criminals, to advocate locking them up and throwing away the key. It's not racist to be against crime, even though the archetypal criminal in the media and the public imagination almost always wears Willie Horton's[4] face."[54]

It is precisely because our criminal justice system provides a vehicle for the expression of conscious and unconscious antiblack sentiment that the prison label is experienced as a racial stigma. The stigma exists whether or not one has been formally branded a criminal, yet another parallel to Jim Crow. Just as African Americans in the North were stigmatized by the Jim Crow system even if they were not subject to its formal control, black men today are stigmatized by mass incarceration—and the social construction of the "criminalblackman"—whether they have ever been to prison or not. For those who have been branded, the branding serves to intensify and deepen the racial stigma, as they are constantly reminded in virtually every contact they have with public agencies, as well as with private employers and landlords, that they are the new "untouchables."

In this way, the stigma of race has become the stigma of criminality. Throughout the criminal justice system, as well as in our schools and public spaces, young + black + male is equated with reasonable suspicion, justifying the arrest, interrogation, search, and detention of thousands of African Americans every year, as well as their exclusion from employment and housing and the denial of educational opportunity....

(2010)

References[5]

7. One in eleven black adults was under correctional supervision at year end 2007, or approximately 2.4 million people. See Pew Center on the States, *One in 31: The Long Reach of American Corrections* (Washington, DC: Pew Charitable Trusts, 2009). According to the 1850 Census, approximately 1.7 million adults (ages 15 and older) were slaves.

---

4 *Willie Horton* African American man who, in 1987 while serving a life sentence for murder, failed to return to prison after a weekend leave and committed armed robbery, assault, and rape before being recaptured.

5 *References* References have been excerpted to reflect only those noted in the portion of Alexander's text reprinted here.

8. See Andrew J. Cherlin, *Marriage, Divorce, Remarriage*, rev. ed. (Cambridge, MA: Harvard University Press, 1992), 110.

9. See Glenn C. Loury, *Race, Incarceration, and American Values* (Cambridge, MA: MIT Press, 2008), commentary by Pam Karlan.

10. Stanley Cohen, *States of Denial: Knowing About Atrocities and Suffering* (Cambridge, UK: Polity, 2001), 4–5.

11. Iris Marilyn Young, *Inclusion and Democracy* (New York: Oxford University Press, 2000), 92–99.

12. Marilyn Frye, "Oppression," in *The Politics of Reality* (Trumansburg, NY: Crossing Press, 1983).

13. See Marc Mauer and Meda Chesney-Lind, eds., *Invisible Punishment: The Collateral Consequences of Mass Imprisonment* (New York: The New Press, 2002); and Jeremy Travis, *But They All Come Back: Facing the Challenges of Prisoner Reentry* (Washington, DC: Urban Institute Press, 2005).

18. [Paul] Street, [*The*] *Vicious Circle*[*: Race, Prison, Jobs, and Community in Chicago, Illinois, and the Nation* (Chicago: Chicago Urban League, Department of Research and Planning, 2002)], 3.

19. Alden Loury, "Black Offenders Face Stiffest Drug Sentences," *Chicago Reporter*, Sept. 12, 2007.

20. Ibid.

21. Street, *Vicious Circle*, 15.

22. Donald G. Lubin et al., *Chicago Metropolis 2020: 2006 Crime and Justice Index*, (Washington, DC: Pew Center on the States, 2006), 5, www.pewcenteronthestates.org/report_detail.aspx?id=33022.

23. Report of the Illinois Disproportionate Justice Impact Study Commission, Dec. 2010, available at www.centerforhealthandjustice.org/DJIS_ExecSumm_FINAL.pdf.

24. Lubin et al., *Chicago Metropolis 2020*, 37.

53. Devah Pager, *Marked: Race, Crime, and Finding Work in an Era of Mass Incarceration* (Chicago: University of Chicago Press, 2007), 90–91, 146–47.

54. John Edgar Wideman, "Doing Time, Marking Race," *The Nation*, Oct. 30 1995.

Questions

1. What is the "widespread and mistaken belief" regarding racial systems that, according to Alexander, makes it difficult to recognize the American justice system as a "tool of racial control" (paragraph 11)? Give another example of this "mistaken belief" being expressed (for example, in a comment made by a politician or journalist, or in your own experience).

2. Alexander suggests that one widely held view is that America's prison system is not racially oppressive because "those who are trapped in the system were free to avoid second-class status or permanent banishment from society simply by choosing not to commit crimes."

Why does Alexander object to this view? Do you think she is right to do so?

3. Alexander claims that "[p]olice can stop, interrogate, and search any-one they choose for drug investigations, provided they get 'consent.'" What does she suggest is wrong with this approach? Why does she place "consent" in quotation marks?

4. Based on your reading of this article, what (if any) aspects of the American justice system should be changed? Consider changes affecting any or all of the "three distinct phases" of entrapment that Alexander describes in paragraphs 17 to 19.

5. Research the prison abolition movement. What alternatives to America's current prison system have prison abolitionists suggested? What do you think is the best of these alternatives—and should it, in your view, replace the current system?

6. Alexander writes that "[w]hiteness mitigates crime, whereas black-ness defines the criminal" (paragraph 25). Find a news report of a recent crime with a Black or a white perpetrator, and examine the role the race of the perpetrator plays in the report. How (if at all) does the report reflect Alexander's claims regarding the racialization of criminals in paragraphs 23–28?

7. Find an example of the use of statistics in this article and evaluate it. What makes your example an effective or ineffective use of statistics?

8. *The New Jim Crow* is written in a style appropriate to a popular audi-ence. In a style suitable for publication in an academic article, write an abstract summarizing this material.

ADILIFU NAMA

from SUPER BLACK: AMERICAN POP CULTURE AND BLACK SUPERHEROES

A scholar of African American studies with a focus on popular culture, Adilifu Nama has published books such as Black Space: Imagining Race in Science Fiction Film *(2008) and* Race on the QT: Blackness and the Films of Quentin Tarantino *(2015). The following selection is from the introduction to his book* Super Black: American Pop Culture and Black Superheroes *(2011). In the book, Nama examines characters from DC and Marvel, including Black Panther, Black Lightning, Storm, Luke Cage, Blade, the Falcon, and Nubia. He argues that "Black superheroes are not the disposable refuse of American pop culture, but serve as a source of potent racial meaning that has substance and resonance far beyond their function and anticipated shelf life."*

My problem ... and I'll speak as a writer now ... with writing a black character in either the Marvel or DC universe is that he is not a man. He is a symbol.

—DWAYNE MCDUFFIE, *Comics Journal*

Circa 1975, when I was five or six, my father took me to a toy store. I went straight to the section where all the superhero action figures were on display, enclosed in window-boxed packaging. They were eight-inch toys made by the now defunct Mego Corporation. Prior to this moment, superheroes inhabited the television reruns of Filmation's *The Superman/Aquaman Hour of Adventure* (1967–1968) and the few comic books I had tucked in the corner of my room. Now I was poised to have a handful of superheroes of my very own and I would be able to dictate the terms, times, and types of superhero adventures I could enjoy. I mentally pleaded with my bladder to stop distracting me long enough to concentrate on prioritizing which superhero figure to choose. I wanted to grab them all right then and there. Since I could not, I examined them all and mentally separated various superhero figures into two groups: my

264

must-haves and my want-to-haves. I made sure to point to the Falcon superhero first, and after he was firmly in my grasp I asked my pops* if I could get a few more. His "yes" gave me the go-ahead to scrutinize several other superhero figures and pick the ones I thought looked best. Aquaman, Captain America, and Spider-Man made the cut. Over time I would later acquire Batman, Hulk, Iron Man, Thor, and the Human Torch, but it was the Falcon that captured my imagination most and cemented my attachment to virtually all things superhero. Why? He was a black man that could fly.

With the Falcon I was able to imagine myself as a superhero, rising above my socioeconomic environment, beating the neighborhood bullies, commanding respect from my male peers, and enjoying approval from all of the pretty girls that made me feel so nervous. I later became captivated by another "flying" black man, the legendary Dr. J (Julius Erving), a basketball player known for defying gravity and for dunking the basketball right in his opponents' faces. Although I dutifully tried to imitate the "moves" I had seen Dr. J perform and dedicated virtually all of my free time to watching, playing, and practicing basketball, I never forgot about the Falcon. The Falcon was my first and my favorite flying black superhero.

The image of a black man gliding through the air, compelling attention, awe, and respect, made a lasting impact on my imagination. The Falcon also operated on a broader social level. The image of the Falcon gliding across an urban skyline symbolized the unprecedented access and upward social mobility many African Americans were experiencing in education and professional positions in the wake of hard-earned antidiscrimination laws and affirmative action. In this sense, black superheroes like the Falcon are not only fantastic representations of our dreams, desires, and idealized projections of ourselves, they are also a symbolic extension of America's shifting political ethos and racial landscape.$_1$

Even though I am, in the popular parlance of the black barbershop, a "grownass man," I still enjoy seeing superheroes save the day in comics, films, live-action television shows, cartoons, and video games. My enjoyment of superheroes as a mature adult, however, does not take place without some degree of trepidation. When parents see me gleefully poking around a local comic book store alongside their children, or catch me dragging my wife into the latest superhero film, I often detect their scornful glances that betray feelings ranging from mild annoyance to awkward disdain for what they probably perceive as an adult still stuck in adolescence. Nonetheless, I am not deterred

---

NB Explanatory footnotes are indicated by superscript numbers in this anthology; numbers that refer to the author's list of references are indicated by subscript numbers.

by their embarrassment for me because I know that the imaginative realms and representational schemes that black superheroes occupy in comics, cartoons, television, and film express powerful visuals, compelling narratives, and multiple meanings around a range of racial ideas and beliefs circulating in American culture.

5   Despite the symbolic significance of black superheroes in American popular culture, the topic remains, for the most part, unexamined. Admittedly, there are a few scholarly studies concerning black superheroes, but they are topical or truncated glimpses of the fascinating racial complexity black superheroes articulate. For example, Fredrik Stromberg's *Black Images in the Comics: A Visual History* (2003) includes only a handful of black superheroes alongside a wide-ranging pictorial documentation of black comic figures. Richard Reynolds's *Super Heroes: A Modern Mythology* (1992) contains just a few paragraphs about black superheroes and even boasts that black superheroes have very little to offer in the way of ideological meaning.[2] In contrast, Bradford W. Wright's definitive text *Comic Book Nation: The Transformation of Youth Culture in America* (2003) addresses the importance of superhero comic books to American culture and aptly touches on race. Yet Wright's discussion of black superheroes and their cultural significance is subsumed under broader social themes. Consequently, his analysis flattens distinguishing features between black superheroes and has very little to say about what black superheroes articulate concerning the cultural politics of race and blackness in America.

      Even the most definitive text to date on the topic, Jeffrey A. Brown's *Black Superheroes, Milestone Comics, and Their Fans* (2001), devotes scant attention and analysis to the cultural work, symbolism, and sociological significance of the mainstream black superheroes that populate DC and Marvel comics. Instead, Brown invests virtually all his analytic efforts in covering the significance of black comic-book company Milestone Comics, negotiating the fickle terrain of a predominantly white comic-book culture, and discussing how racialized notions of hypermasculinity are a signature feature of black superheroes. As a result, the broad scope and social significance of black superheroes across the Marvel and DC Comics universes and in their television and film incarnations is severely diminished. In addition, the full range of cultural work that black superheroes have performed across several decades is completely ignored. In short, the bulk of analysis concerning black superheroes has come to obvious conclusions, is embarrassingly reductive, and neglects to draw deeper connections across significant cultural dynamics, social trends, and historical events. Most often the topic of blackness in the superhero genre compels discussions over the difficulty white audiences might experience identifying with black superheroes or knee-jerk criticisms that frame the genre as racially biased.[3]

Certainly, comic books featuring heroes like Tarzan, the beneficent white jungle-savior, presented black characters as stereotypically subservient, primitive, or savage. Moreover, such examples make easy fodder for critique and open up a Pandora's box* of vexing sociopsychological questions about racial projection and reader identification with superhero characters that promote racially insensitive images and ideas. Yet by using these issues as a point of analytical departure, the dynamic and rich source of racial meaning presented in the superhero universes of DC Comics, Marvel Comics, television, and film becomes buried beneath a mound of superficial critiques. Either black superheroes are critiqued as updated racial stereotypes from America's comic-book past, or they are uncritically affixed to the blaxploitation film[1] craze as negative representations of blackness.$_4$ What emerges from such nearsighted analysis is an incomplete description of the fascinating and complex ideological give and take that black superheroes have with American culture. In stark contrast, *Super Black* calls attention to black superheroes as a fascinating racial phenomenon and a powerful source of racial meaning, narrative, and imagination in American society that expresses a myriad of racial assumptions, political perspectives, and fantastic (re)imaginings of black identity.

The superhero archetype is heavily steeped in affirming a division between right and wrong, thus superheroes operate within a moral framework. Moreover, virtually all superheroes are victorious, not because of superior strength or weaponry, but because of moral determination demonstrated by concern for others and notions of justice.$_5$ Accordingly, black superheroes are not merely figures that defeat costumed supervillains: they symbolize American racial morality and ethics. They overtly represent or implicitly signify social discourse and accepted wisdom concerning notions of racial reciprocity, racial equality, racial forgiveness, and, ultimately, racial justice. But black superheroes are not only representative of what is racially right. They are also ripe metaphors for race relations in America, and are often reflective of escalating and declining racial unrest. In this sense, black superheroes in American comic books and, to a lesser extent, in Hollywood films and television are cultural ciphers for accepted wisdom regarding racial justice and the shifting politics of black racial formation in America....

... My approach employs an eclectic synthesis of cultural criticism, historical and cultural contextualization, and a hearty dash of textual analysis intent on yielding information, insights, and connections between text, ideas, and important moments in the cultural history of black superheroes and black racial formation. Most importantly, this book [*Super Black*] adopts a self-conscious

---

1   *blaxploitation film*   Film genre whose primary characteristics were low budgets, violent action scenes, and predominantly Black casts with Black actors playing lead roles.

critically celebratory perspective for examining the various expressions of superhero blackness. In other words, the purpose of this book is to reclaim black superheroes from the easily perceived, easily argued, and clichéd assumptions used to examine them that diminish their sociocultural significance and view the cultural work they perform as tired tropes about blackness primarily written by white men. The point is not to uncritically embrace these figures. Rather the mission of my analysis is to steer the discussion away from theoretical dead ends or conversations that lead only in one direction to one conclusion: black superheroes are negative stereotypes....

(2011)

References[2]

1. See Richard Reynolds, *Super Heroes: A Modern Mythology* (Jackson: University Press of Mississippi, 1994), and Danny Fingeroth, *Superman on the Couch: What Superheroes Really Tell Us About Ourselves and Our Society* (New York: Continuum, 2004).
2. Reynolds, *Super Heroes*, 77.
3. See Anna Beatrice Scott, "Superpower vs Supernatural: Black Superheroes and the Quest for a Mutant Reality," *Journal of Visual Culture* 5, no. 3 (December 2006): 295–314; Marc Singer, "'Black Skins' and White Masks: Comic Books and the Secret of Race," *African American Review* 36, no. 1 (Spring 2002): 107–119; Jeffery Brown, *Black Superheroes, Milestone Comics, and Their Fans* (Jackson: University Press of Mississippi, 2000).
4. See Christian Davenport, "Black Is the Color of My Comic Book Character: An Examination of Ethnic Stereotypes," *Inks: Cartoon and Comic Art Studies* 4, no. 1 (1997): 20–28; Trina Robbins, *The Great Women Superheroes* (New York: Kitchen Sink Press, 1996), 148; Ora C. McWilliams, "Not Just Another Racist Honkey: A History of Racial Representation in Captain America and Related Publications," in *Captain America and the Struggle of the Superhero: Critical Essays*, ed., Robert G. Weiner, 66–78 (Jefferson, NC: McFarland, 2009); Darius James's opening salvo, "Straight-up Real Nigga," in the graphic comic *Cage* (New York: Marvel Comics, 2003), by Brian Azzarello, Richard Corben, and Jose Villarubia.
5. Reynolds, *Super Heroes*, 41.

---

2   *References*   References have been excerpted to reflect only those noted in the portion of Nama's text reprinted here.

Questions

1. Consider the quotation from Dwayne McDuffie that opens this introduction. To what extent (if at all) does Nama endorse McDuffie's view? To what extent (if at all) does he contradict McDuffie?

2. What does Nama mean by a *"critically celebratory"* approach to examining comics? Does this strike you as a productive approach? Why or why not?

3. Nama suggests that, in most scholarly analysis, "the dynamic and rich source of racial meaning presented in the superhero universes of DC Comics, Marvel Comics, television, and film becomes buried beneath a mound of superficial critiques" (paragraph 7). Read Gateward and Jennings's introduction to *The Blacker the Ink*, also reprinted in this anthology. To what extent (if at all) does Nama's critique apply to Gateward and Jennings's piece?

4. Examine a recent DC or Marvel work that features a Black hero (see, for example, the Marvel film *Black Panther* [2018]; an episode of the Marvel TV series *Luke Cage* [2016–] or the DC TV series *Black Lightning* [2018–]; an issue of Ta-Nehisi Coates's *Black Panther* comic [2016–]; or the video game *Marvel: Future Fight* [2015; you may wish to focus on one playable character, such as Luke Cage, Storm, Falcon, Blade, or Black Panther]). Discuss the work you chose with Nama's argument in mind; what (if anything) does the work suggest about "American racial morality and ethics"?

Mia McKenzie

White Silence

In addition to her work as a fiction writer and activist, Mia McKenzie is the founder and editor-in-chief of Black Girl Dangerous, *a website created in 2011 to "amplif[y] the voices of queer and trans people of color." The following post appeared there in 2012, and created a stir on social media. It was later reprinted in McKenzie's collection* Black Girl Dangerous on Race, Queerness, Class and Gender *(2014).*

I've noticed a trend. When I post to my Facebook page about gay cats, or my friend Sacha (a boy) trying out for the Denver Broncos cheerleaders, or bacon, my Facebook friends respond with comments and likes all across the board. That is to say, the friends who respond are all across the board—black, brown, white, queer, straight, all genders. There is no specific category of friends that responds more or less than any other, when it comes to pretty much anything I post on Facebook.

Except, as it turns out, when I post anything about race.

When I post anything about race, there's a shift in who responds. Suddenly, my white friends are silent. Almost all of them. Every time.

And it's starting to piss me off.

5 Most of the stuff I post about race is in the form of articles about things going on in the country and in the world, having to do with racism. Most recently, I've been posting links to news and articles about Trayvon Martin, the 17-year-old boy who was murdered last month in Florida while walking home with a bag of skittles. He was shot by a self-appointed neighborhood watch captain who thought he looked "suspicious" and followed him, accosted him, and shot him in the chest. Anyone who knows about this story, I would think, would be outraged. Scratch that. I know enough to know that there are many people who would not be outraged, many, many people who would not and do not give a shit. But I am not Facebook friends with those people. Or, at least, I didn't think I was.

I am careful about who I friend on Facebook. I keep my friends around 150 or so, because I don't think it's possible to really know more people than that, and I like my bubble, I like to be surrounded by people who share most of my politics. I'm okay with that. I'm almost 36, and I have learned that I don't really need to "appreciate everyone's point of view." I mean, you can have politics that are opposed to mine. Fine. But if you do, we are not going to be friends. I think that's reasonable. So, I think my Facebook friends pretty much fall into the category of "people who share my politics," with very few exceptions. This includes the white folks on my friends list. My white Facebook friends are mostly liberal democrat/independent types, queer or ally, feminist, etc. And yet, whenever I post about race, they are silent.

Why?

They are people I like, so I want to give them the benefit of the doubt. Maybe they are silent because they don't know what to say. Maybe they feel uncomfortable about chiming in on a subject that is so touchy. Maybe. But a simple "like" doesn't require any comment. A simple "like" would show that you at least read the article, that you at least gave enough of a fuck to follow the link and get informed.

Or maybe they think they don't have a right to comment because they are white and it's not their place. That it's for black people to discuss issues of racism, that they'd be overstepping by commenting. This answer only makes sense if they don't see racism as their problem. If they don't see the oppression of racialized people as part of the history and present of their own country. If they don't know that their involvement in these discussions is necessary, even if it's scary, even if it's hard. Which maybe they don't.

And I guess I shouldn't be surprised, but I am. Again, these are not random white folks. These are my "friends." These are people I like, and who like me. Some of them I even love. I imagine that some of them love me. And yet, when yet another black person is murdered in cold blood, for the crime of being black, or locked up for "stealing" an education for their kid,[1] they don't seem to see that it could have been my brother or my mother. They don't seem to know that it could have been me.

Because it is me. I have had the experience of being racially profiled a thousand times. I have had a white person characterize me as "violent" for no other reason than a look I gave them, for something they "saw in my eyes." I live in a world where I am believed to be dangerous because a white person says I am. Case closed. I have never committed a crime, but I am terrified of the police. Because I know that if one day they decide I did something,

10

---

1   *locked up ... their kid*   Reference to the high-profile case of Tanya McDowell, a homeless Black woman who was arrested for theft because she enrolled her son in kindergarten in Norwalk, Connecticut, a wealthier district than the location of her last permanent address.

whether I did it or not, my life could be over. Just like that. And this is not just true of me. It is true of every black person you know, regardless of gender or age or education level or artistic talents or any other factor. And yet my white "friends" don't seem to know that. They don't seem to understand. They don't seem to want to.

White privilege is a hell of a thing. It makes it possible for my white "friends" to look the other way when a tragedy of as much magnitude as the Trayvon Martin killing happens. If it's too much, they can just choose not to read it, not to think about it. But we don't all have that option.

So, I want to say this to my white friends: I need you to care about this. And I need you to show that you do, by commenting, by sharing, by making noise about this. I need you to be OUTRAGED. Because otherwise, I can't trust you. Otherwise, you are part of the problem. Otherwise, we are not really friends at all.

(2012)

Questions

1. How, according to McKenzie, is white silence in the face of events such as the shooting of Trayvon Martin a manifestation of white privilege?

2. What are individual white people obligated to do in response to racial oppression?

3. McKenzie wrote a piece titled "White Silence: A Follow-Up," in which she made the following clarifying statement:

   > I am not calling for "commentary" from my white friends about issues of race. I am not calling for my white friends to tell me that they understand what it is like for folks of color in this country and in this world. I am not calling for my white friends to suddenly start acting like experts on these issues, or, God forbid, to stop listening in order to start talking.

   Why would these be unhelpful or damaging ways for white people to speak about racial oppression? What ways of speaking would be more helpful?

4. Who is the intended audience of this piece? How can you tell?

5. How would you describe the tone of "White Silence"? How does it influence the persuasiveness of the piece?

ALISHA KNIGHT

from "TO AID IN EVERYWAY POSSIBLE IN UPLIFTING THE COLORED PEOPLE OF AMERICA": HOPKINS'S REVISIONARY DEFINITION OF AFRICAN AMERICAN SUCCESS

How do biographies—brief biographical sketches as well as full-length volumes—shape our sense of history, and our sense of ourselves? That is, at least in part, the question literary scholar Alisha Knight addresses in her 2012 book Pauline Hopkins and the American Dream: An African American Writer's (Re)Visionary Gospel of Success *(Knoxville: University of Tennessee Press, 2012). In her examination of this question, Knight focuses on the work of the prominent African American writer and editor Pauline Hopkins (1859–1930). Knight's book addresses not only Hopkins's fiction (in which, as Knights puts it, the novelist "depicted heroes who fail to achieve success or must leave the United States to do so"), but also the many brief profiles of admirable African Americans that Hopkins published in the* Colored American *magazine—one of which, her profile of Frederick Douglass, is included elsewhere in this volume. The first chapter of Knights's study, "To Aid in Everyway Possible in Uplifting the Colored People of America': Hopkins's Revisionary Definition of African American Success," is excerpted below.*

During the late nineteenth and early twentieth centuries, the phrase "self-made man" invoked the image of an autonomous male who became wealthy and powerful through his ambition, hard work, and shrewd judgment. According to Richard Weiss, "Tradition has it that every American child receives, as part of his birthright, the freedom to mold his own life.... The belief that all men, in accordance with certain rules, but exclusively by their own efforts, can make of their lives what they will has been widely popularized for well over a century."₁ This tradition, generally referred to as the "American Dream" or the "gospel of success," has deep roots in American culture, and there is an entire body of what I call "success literature"—self-improvement guides, biographical dictionaries, autobiographical narratives, and novels— that prescribes and perpetuates this belief system. The figure of the self-made man is a common trope in fictional and nonfictional "rags-to-riches" or, more accurately, "rags-to-respectability" narratives, where a young hero moves from the country to the city, or from the gutter to the penthouse, searching for em- ployment opportunities and a better quality of life. Once he secures entry-level employment, he incrementally works his way up through the ranks from a me- nial laborer to become an office manager, corporate executive, or entrepreneur.

Although success literature and the self-made man are not unique to American culture, the origins of the American rendering of the gospel of success have been traced back to Puritan[1] advice guides that instructed early settlers how to conduct themselves in a proper Christian manner.... Puritans believed that everyone's personal calling should service and help others, should not be sinful, and should be compatible with his personality. A Christian should perform his job well and not be "Slothful in Business."₃ He should conduct his business affairs with diligence, discretion, honesty, contentment, and piety. Pursuing this personal calling should not be done at the expense of the general calling; hence, Christians were instructed to pray every day and not to conduct business on Sunday. From this type of advice grew the Protestant work ethic* in which success was tied to religious duty and dutiful Christians sought mate- rial success in the name of God....

By the late 1700s, the gospel of success became increasingly secular.... Benjamin Franklin* is often considered the archetype of the self-made man in the United States. One of Franklin's most popular texts, *The Way to Wealth*, links seventeenth- and eighteenth-century assumptions about the meaning of success and how to achieve it. *The Way to Wealth* promotes the virtues of industry and frugality and discourages idleness and extravagance. It includes practical quotations of Franklin's Poor Richard[2] persona, including: "God

---

NB Explanatory footnotes are indicated by superscript numbers in this anthology; numbers that refer to the author's list of references are indicated by subscript numbers.

1   *Puritan*   Protestant Christian sect that criticized the Church of England for retaining certain Catholic practices; many Puritans migrated to New England in the early seventeenth century to seek freedom of religion.

2   *Poor Richard*   Pseudonym under which Franklin published a series of almanacs featuring clever aphorisms.

helps them that help themselves," "Sloth makes all things difficult, but industry all easy," "Early to bed, and early to rise, makes a man healthy, wealthy, and wise," ...

... As time progressed, writers who produced success literature continued to justify acquiring wealth as a means of helping others, and readers were reminded that wealth was not an end* in itself. Yet, by the end of the nineteenth century, "the dominant concept of success was one of opulent materialism competitively won."[11] The original, religious ideal did not become completely obsolete, however. The rapid geographical expansion and technological changes of the period created a sense of conflict between economic advancement and traditional social and religious mores.* As a result, American culture experienced some anxiety and felt uncertain about the meaning of individuals' lives and personal moral duties. Hence many Americans clung to the religious prescription for success.

Sketches of poor young boys striving to become successful businessmen   5
were read by working- and middle-class adults and children not only for inspiration to better themselves, but also to escape the realities of economic hardship. Indeed, the American success myth and the trope of the self-made man served dual purposes in late nineteenth- and early twentieth-century society. On the one hand, they provided models for working- and middle-class citizens to aspire to. Although post-Civil War technological advancements like the telegraph and the transcontinental railroad contributed to the rapid development of the nation's major cities and to a shift from an agrarian to an industrial economy and culture, as Paulette Kilmer notes, "frequently, progress intensified the misery of the poor, even while raising their standard of living."[12] ...

Success literature at the turn of the twentieth century assumed the guise of popular literature that targeted a broad, mass reading audience whose education and reading tastes varied but would not be considered erudite. A number of scholars have assumed that no one produced any popular literature, and by extension, success literature, specifically for turn-of-the-century black readers. For example, Weiss has observed that mainstream success literature targeted native-born, Protestant, middle-class whites and that there was a "nativist bias" in these texts.[21] Yet, other sources indicate the black working and middle-class communities were just as hungry for success literature as whites, perhaps even more so.... African Americans were an ideal audience for success literature because of their intense desire to rise up and overcome racial segregation and discrimination. August Meier's *Negro Thought in America, 1880–1915*, discusses the specific requirements for progress in the black middle class: "thrift, industry, frugality, morality, land ownership and the acquisition of wealth."[24] Meier traces these values back to the Reconstruction* period, when blacks "focused their attention upon becoming full-fledged citizens. The franchise,[3] education, guarantees for civil rights, the acquisition of property and wealth, and the cultivation of morality were all designed to elevate Negroes and achieve their integration into American society."[25] Post-Reconstruction black leaders believed economic success achieved through racial solidarity and self-help would earn the black masses the respect of whites and the full benefits of United States citizenship. This belief "was based upon the assumption that by the acquisition of wealth and morality—attained largely by their own efforts—Negroes would gain the respect of white men and thus be accorded their rights as citizens."[26] In short, the American gospel of success was as much a part of the black cultural ethos as it was of white culture. After Reconstruction, blacks increasingly viewed wealth as a sign of success and they adopted "the ideas of the gospel of wealth and Social Darwinism and applied them to their own racial situation."[27]

African Americans have a history of producing and reading success literature, either in the form of autobiographical narratives or biographical dictionaries and collected sketches of prominent individuals. One can readily identify African American texts that manifest the black community's preoccupation with both individual success and race progress, although twenty-first-century readers might not typically use the term "self-help" or "success literature" when referring to these works. Slave narratives, for example, which served to advocate the abolition of slavery, not only established the black author's humanity but also contributed to the discourse on the American Dream.* James Olney's study of the slave narrative's literary conventions has made it clear that slave narratives possessed "very specific motives, intentions, and uses," which were "to reveal the truth of slavery and so to bring about its abolition."[28] But the literary conventions that we are accustomed to identifying with the slave narrative can also be mapped to the typical success narrative. For example, when Frederick Douglass[4] provides a limited account of his parentage in *Narrative of the Life of Frederick Douglass* (1845), and when he describes the plantation system in which he and other enslaved blacks were deprived of adequate food and clothing and were subjected to dehumanizing physical abuse, he establishes himself as the lone hero determined to overcome his "humble beginnings" to achieve not only freedom, but also dignity and respectability. Douglass's observations of freedom in the North provide opportunities for him to comment on the gospel of success. When he recounts his impressions of New Bedford, Massachusetts, upon his arrival, he describes signs of

---

3   *franchise*   I.e., the right to vote.
4   *Frederick Douglass*   Selections from Hopkins's piece on Douglass are reprinted elsewhere in this anthology.

a community that is prosperous without being dependent upon slave labor, and he is awed that "Every man appeared to understand his work, and went at it with a sober, yet cheerful earnestness, which betokened the deep interest which he felt in what he was doing, as well as a sense of his own dignity as a man."[29] At the conclusion of his narrative, he reflects on his own means of employment, which "was new, dirty, and hard work for me; but I went at it with a glad heart and a willing hand. I was now my own master.... It was the first work, the reward of which was to be entirely my own."[30] Here Douglass is showing how he has adopted an appreciation for the dignity of labor that he did not have when he was enslaved. This work ethic would later earn him wealth and influence, which he would describe in two subsequent autobiographies, *My Bondage and My Freedom* (1855) and *The Life and Times of Frederick Douglass* (1881, 1892), and which others, including Pauline Hopkins, would describe in their tributes to him.

In addition to autobiographical texts, a number of biographical dictionaries were produced in the nineteenth century that targeted an African American reading audience. Abigail Field Mott's *Biographical Sketches and Interesting Anecdotes of Persons of Color* (1837), which was intended to be used as a textbook in New York's "African Free Schools,"[5] presents sketches of Ignatius Sancho, Phillis Wheatley, Gustavus Vassa (Olaudah Equiano), and Toussaint L'Ouverture,[6] along with sketches of local blacks, "to encourage virtue and morality in the different classes of society; and by bringing into view the effects which a system of slavery has on the human mind."[31] Mott's collection illustrates that early discourses about African American success focused more on Christian morality and less on material gain. Furthermore, antebellum[7] literature defined African American success in terms of *physical freedom* as well as spiritual salvation....

---

5   *African Free Schools*   New York-based schools for Black students; they provided a basic education to both free and enslaved children. The first African Free School was established in the late eighteenth century.

6   *Ignatius Sancho ... L'Ouverture*   Prominent Black writers and political figures of the eighteenth century, all of whom were slaves before making major contributions to literature and/or politics; *Ignatius Sancho*   British public figure (1729–80) known especially for his published letters; *Phillis Wheatley*   Prominent West African-born poet (1753–84); *Olaudah Equiano*   Abolitionist activist and writer best known for his important autobiography, *The Interesting Narrative of the Life of Olaudah Equiano, Or Gustavus Vassa, The African* (1789); *Touissant L'Ouverture*   Prominent military and political leader (1743–1803) of the Haitian Revolution, a successful slave uprising; he governed Haiti for a few years, though full and permanent independence was not achieved until after his death.

7   *antebellum*   I.e., before the Civil War.

Once slavery was abolished, the black community turned its focus on achieving further progress, and success literature of the postbellum[8] period reflected this shift in focus. For example, two of Booker T. Washington's[9] post-Reconstruction autobiographies, *The Story of My Life and Work* (1900) and *Up From Slavery* (1901), revisit and revise a number of conventions of the ante-bellum slave narrative.... [I]t is worth noting that the story of [Washington's] rise "up from slavery" through hard work, industry, and thrift to become the head of a successful educational institution and race leader is a self-conscious rendering of the gospel of success. Both white and black writers, including Washington, produced "conduct guides" for African American readers at the turn of the century. These lengthy books contained moral and ethical lessons on etiquette, health and hygiene, household management, and personal finance. They typically included elaborate engravings and were marketed door-to-door by traveling sales agents for the subscription publishing trade. *The College of Life, or Practical Self-Educator* is one example that contains sketches of prominent African American men but does not claim to be a simple biographi-cal dictionary. Instead, according to its subtitle, it was offered as "A Manual of Self-Improvement for the Colored Race." This collaboration between Henry Davenport Northrop, Joseph R. Gay, and Irving Garland Penn was first published by the Chicago Publication and Lithograph Company in 1895.... Northrop, a prolific white author, was already familiar to his contemporary readers, and Penn's name would have been readily recognized by anyone who knew of *The Afro-American Press and Its Editors*, which he published in 1891.

10 ... *College of Life* illustrates the increasing secularization of the success gospel at the turn of the twentieth century. In the introduction, the authors explain their desire to "advise, encourage and educate the many young people of the race and to inspire them with a desire to better their condition in life by Self-Improvement."[34] The profiles of notable black men and women included in the book provide "sketches of their achievements in life ... as examples of what may be accomplished through education, patience, perseverance and integrity of character."[35] Conduct guides for African Americans presented black models for readers to emulate, but they typically did not radically politicize success. In this sense, *College of Life*'s objectives were very similar to Samuel Smiles's *Self-Help* (1859), an immensely popular book that was originally published in England and pirated numerous times abroad, including in the United States.

---

8   *postbellum*   I.e., after the Civil War.
9   *Booker T. Washington*   Influential African American political figure and writer (1856–1915) who was born into slavery. As an advocate of educational and economic advancement (as opposed to advancement in legal rights), he played a very significant role in shaping African American activism in the decades following the Civil War.

According to Smiles, his book's "chief object unquestionably is to stimulate youths to apply themselves diligently to right pursuits ... and to rely upon their own efforts in life, rather than depend upon the help or patronage of others."[36] ... Not only did post-Reconstruction success literature for African Americans tend to depoliticize success, but it also tended to place the onus for overcoming the past disadvantages of slavery into the hands of the black community, as they were given the charge of becoming upstanding American citizens. For example, the authors of *College of Life* seem particularly preoccupied with teaching their reading audience to be "the most useful members of society. We should be guided by right principles and prove ourselves worthy of the liberty granted us by emancipation."[39]

Pauline Hopkins was one turn-of-the-century black intellectual who was less concerned with proving that blacks were worthy of emancipation. While the authors of *College of Life* presented biographical sketches as evidence of the African American race's potential to succeed, Hopkins employed sketches of noteworthy blacks as evidence of the race's past and *ongoing* achievement. A close analysis of Hopkins's articles in the *Colored American Magazine* and *New Era Magazine* reveals that she realized the traditional gospel of success did not reflect the political, social, and economic conditions of the majority of African Americans, nor did it factor in the impact of discrimination or racism on a black person's ability to follow the common proscription for success. Her project took on visionary characteristics when she discussed African American success in a manner that was much more politicized than her contemporaries. Furthermore, the thematic content of her nonfiction is notable because of its sustained adaptation of the American success myth to the unique social circumstances of the black middle-class community.

"Famous Men of the Negro Race" is a series of twelve articles that recounts the accomplishments of historical and contemporary black men. While individual biographical pieces like Daniel Murray's "Cyrus Field Adams" and John Livinston Wright's "Charles W. Chesnutt" were dispersed throughout the volumes of the *Colored American Magazine*, "Famous Men" may well have been the first *series* of its kind to appear in a black monthly periodical with a national audience. Compared with the sketches in *College of Life*, Hopkins's "Famous Men" installments are more thorough; yet, what makes her treatment of these figures distinctive is the political commentary she weaves into them. Whereas the tone of *College of Life* and similar works implies that white culture and models of success are the most superior, Hopkins's writing is grounded on the premise that white models are flawed.

Consider, for example, the difference between Hopkins's depiction of Toussaint L'Ouverture and those of her contemporaries. In *College of Life*, the authors qualify their discussion of L'Ouverture, one example of "brilliant military genius," by reassuring their audience that blacks as a whole are not a violent people who seek "military glory."$_{40}$ L'Ouverture is characterized as a leader who assumed command of the Haitian revolution to achieve peace, not to conquer the French. The description of his noble character warrants quoting: "By the sheer force of his native ability and integrity he rose to the highest position among his people, and it is not too much to say that no nobler leader ever marshaled an army or struggled for independence. Not merely great military genius, not merely great ability as a statesman appeared in his marvelous career, but above all his exalted character shone resplendently, and he was too honest to be bribed, too courageous to surrender, and too devoted to the welfare [of] his race to count his life dear to him."$_{41}$ Here, this martyr's virtuous character is celebrated more than his military achievements. His instruction to his son to "forget that France murdered your father" is repeated twice in this very short sketch as if to emphasize his lack of bitterness or desire for vengeance against his French captors.$_{42}$ Hopkins begins her piece by signifying on previous depictions of L'Ouverture, like the one included in *College of Life*, by arguing in the head note that his "extraordinary fortunes ... bespeak for him more than the passing interest of a dry biography."$_{43}$ She presents a more thorough treatment of her subject by including a geography lesson and history of slavery in Haiti in order to establish a context for the installment. Hopkins challenges the lowly position assigned to black people and their "supposed inferiority" by seeking "the ray of light in history that reveals the God in man; the divine attribute that must exist in the Negro as well as in other races, or he sinks to the level of the brute creation" (10). For Hopkins, L'Ouverture exemplifies how black people are just as intelligent, capable, and honorable as whites (if not more so), and that they have a history that accounts for these virtues. Hopkins does regret that L'Ouverture was profoundly loyal to France as she explains "the ruin of Toussaint was due in great measure to his loyalty to France and his filial feeling for Bonaparte"[10] (16). Yet his dedication to a higher, more moral cause shows the breadth and depth of his discipline and self-control, for "It is no small evidence of Toussaint's greatness, then, that he enforced during such times such a principle as *no retaliation*." (17). Whereas Northrop, Gay, and Penn simply call L'Ouverture "the Napoleon Bonaparte of his race," Hopkins takes this comparison one step further and refers to him as "Napoleon's black

---

10 *Bonaparte* Napoleon Bonaparte, military and political leader of France from 1799 to 1814. Touissant took a somewhat conciliatory approach to relations with Napoleon, attempting to govern Haiti as an autonomous colony without declaring independence from France. Napoleon, however, renewed military efforts to regain control of the island and had Touissant captured and brought to France, where he died in prison.

shadow," which connotes his powerful leadership.$_{44}$ In essence, she crafts this portrait in a manner that motivates blacks and at the same time advocates in favor of the recognition she believed they deserved.

C.K. Doreski has analyzed the manner in which Hopkins used "Famous Men of the Negro Race" to reshape race history. Doreski observes that the *Colored American Magazine*, of which Hopkins was an instrumental contributor, "schooled its readers in arts and manners, hoping to provide that surface of success expected in the emerging middle class. But it also advanced a politically charged, cultural agenda in its challenge to the status quo and its commitment to the discovery and preservation of African American history."$_{45}$ While I do agree with Doreski's assessment of Hopkins as a historian and biographer, I want to emphasize how Hopkins's biographies did more than serve "a larger historical project" or were "a means of shaping race history"$_{46}$; they were also conduits to promote her vision of African American success in the present and future.... [W]hen Hopkins quotes Smiles in her exposé of the New York subway system and writes, "All nations have been made what they are by the thinking and working of many generations of men. Patient and persevering laborers in all ranks and conditions of life ... all have contributed towards the grand result, one generation building upon another's labors, and carrying them forward to still higher stages," she revisits the issue of human progress but places it in a social context that Smiles fails to do, reminding readers at the end of the article that racial inequality continues to persist in spite of the city's technological achievements ("New York Subway," 605).

Hopkins's journalism, particularly the two series "Famous Men of the Negro Race" in the *Colored American Magazine* and "Men of Vision" in *New Era Magazine*, spoke to the black community's need for successful male role models and promoted her definitions of African American success and the black success archetype. "Famous Men of the Negro Race" consists of sketches of abolitionists, attorneys, politicians, educators, and other men who had a positive impact on the black community.... Throughout both series and a number of other articles, Hopkins maintained her commitment to provide her audience with models of success. For example, in "Men of Vision: No. 2. Rev. Leonard Andrew Grimes," she argues that the life story she is offering to the reader "is a splendid example of successful individual effort working for the uplift of others are well as of self" (99). Individuals who were successful helped make the race successful in three ways. First, successful men served as role models for black youth. Throughout the "Famous Men" series, Hopkins comments on the potential her subject's life story has for motivating others. For example, in "Hon. Frederick Douglass," she writes, "He presents to us in his life an example of possibilities which may be within the reach of many young

15

men of the rising generation" (132). In Lewis Hayden's biography, Hopkins argues that "The deeds of men of a past generation are the beacon lights along the shore for the youth of today" (476). Furthermore, of Robert Morris, she writes, "His life is a rich legacy to point the young Negro to the heights of manhood" (342). Second, these men helped uplift the race by using their power and influence to help those less fortunate than they were. For example, after recounting how Mark Rene Demortie used his influence to secure higher wages for black soldiers during the Civil War, Hopkins concludes, "So ends the record of an active life of love for humanity" (39). Third, the accomplishments of successful black men proved to whites they had already earned their place among the other United States citizens.... Hopkins linked the individual and the race's successes in response to the debate over whether or not blacks could "catch up" to other races on the hierarchal chain of civilization.... For Hopkins and other black intellectuals of this period, the black man's success had already ... indicated that the entire race [had] earned and deserved its citizenship. In the following mission statement for the "Famous Men" series, Hopkins explains:

> We delight to honor the great men of our race because the lives of these noble Negroes are tongues of living flame[11] speaking in the powerful silence of example, and sent to baptize the race with heaven's holy fire into the noble heritage of perfected manhood. The contemplation of the life-work of these men is about all that we have to cheer and encourage us in our strivings after high ideals, and to appease our longings for the perfect day of our true emancipation—the black man's sweet but ever-vanishing vision of the Holy Grail.* ("Robert Morris" 337)

Again, not only were these articles intended as examples of black achievement for white readers; they were also motivators for black readers.

At the turn of the century, African Americans realized whites often judged the entire black race by the actions of a few individuals. Meier explains, "If whites believed Negroes to be inferior, then Negroes must show themselves the equals of whites—by publicizing their past achievements, by successfully running the race of Social Darwinist[12] competition with the whites, and by cultivating a vigorous racial pride to offset the Anglo-Saxon consciousness of

---

11 *tongues of living flame* More commonly "tongues of fire," manifestations of the Holy Spirit that appear on Christ's apostles in Acts 2.3–4.

12 *Social Darwinist* According to Social Darwinism, human societies are improved through competition for survival such that only the "fittest" members of the society are able to reproduce; such theories have typically been invoked in an attempt to justify the suffering of oppressed groups.

kind."$_{50}$ Following in the tradition of Thomas Carlyle, Ralph Waldo Emerson,[13] and Samuel Smiles, Hopkins wrote of the achievements of a select group of men, but she did this to remind her white and black readers of the role blacks have played in shaping American history and to provide models for her young black readers to emulate....

... Although Hopkins deemphasized the importance of wealth, fame was a key factor in her version of success. Hopkins wrote about black men whose notoriety may not have been recognized in the white press but who were famous in the black community. Often their fame was achieved by working to uplift the race in some manner.... Frederick Douglass was a successful individual whose personal fame had a positive impact on the black community, and "An honored name is his bequest to the Negro of the United States" (132). William Wells Brown was "widely known both at home and abroad" (232). Hopkins notes that as an abolitionist and author, "Doctor Brown was the recipient of many congratulations on his work as an author, and the British press vied with their American brothers in doing honor to this new star in the world of letters" (233)....

In addition to fame, another indication that a black man had achieved success was the extent to which he was socially accepted and could use his acquired power to influence others. Although all blacks suffered from segregation and Jim Crow laws,* all of Hopkins's self-made men were socially accepted in some way that transcended these barriers. For Hopkins, self-made men like Robert Elliott and Edwin Garrison Walker were noteworthy because they used their influence with whites to improve sociopolitical conditions for the African American community. ... Frederick Douglass's skill as a lecturer gave him power: "White men and black men had spoken on slavery but never like Frederick Douglas.... He made his audiences weep, laugh, swear. He opened the hearts of thousands to mercy and pity for the slave by his eloquence and pathos. Many kept away from his lectures lest they be converted against their will" (124). Furthermore, Douglass was also successful because he was respected by both blacks and whites: "As a freeman and a citizen the respect of mankind has been heaped upon his head, and trusts of great honor have been laid in his lap by a great nation" (130)....

As noted above, ... some increase in financial status is part of the traditional [success] model. For Hopkins, wealth was not key to African American success, the way social acceptance and influence were. Interestingly, Hopkins

---

13 *Thomas Carlyle*   British writer and theorist whose book *On Heroes, Hero-Worship, and The Heroic in History* (1841) discusses the lives of "Great Men" and their historical impact;   *Ralph Waldo Emerson*   American essayist and poet whose book *Representative Men* (1850) discusses "great men" and their virtues.

rarely comments on her subjects' financial status, and when she does, it is often in passing, for the purpose of showing how the individual sacrifices personal gain for the benefit of the black community, or it is tied to some other element of success like social acceptance. For example, Frederick Douglass's opulent Washington, D.C., home was formerly owned by a white man: "His villa was one of the finest and most desirable in the Republic, whose original proprietor stipulated in the deed of transfer that the property should never be owned by a descendant of the African race" (131). Yet, the deed was transferred to Douglass, one assumes, because of his fame and social stature. Hopkins informs her audience that Lewis Hayden used his wealth to help John Brown:[14] "He might have been wealthy, for he possessed the faculty of making money, but he scattered it broadcast to help those poorer than himself" (476)....

20   Instead of being judged by the amount of money they make, Hopkins's successful men on the whole were esteemed for their social contributions, especially for their efforts to uplift the race. Six of the sixteen men were abolitionists, or at least helped fugitive slaves escape their captors. L'Ouverture, Douglass, Wells Brown, Hayden, Remond, and Grimes all helped the slave population in varying degrees—from leading a slave rebellion to saving fugitive slaves from mob violence. Robert Brown Elliott was noted for helping establish the first public school system in South Carolina. Lewis Hayden's social contributions extended beyond providing a safe haven for the fugitive slaves William and Ellen Crafts; according to Hopkins, "Lewis Hayden's greatness came from his love of his race and the sacrifices he made of money, of time and of physical comfort for the redemption of a people from chattel bondage" (474). Robert Morris personally fought discrimination and northern segregation in Boston public schools, the railroad system, theaters, churches "and other public places" (341). He lobbied for black officers and equal pay for black troops during the Civil War. Morris risked his life to save a fugitive slave from imprisonment by rescuing him from the courtroom and helping him on his way to Canada. Mark Demortie, like Robert Morris, also worked to desegregate Boston's public school system. His long list of racial uplift activities includes helping to get the ethnic designation "colored" removed from voting lists, working to get equal pay for black Civil War troops, establishing more black schools in Virginia, and lobbying to get anti-lynching* legislation introduced to Congress. Hopkins emphasized these individuals' community service years before white success writers are willing to give more credence to the self-made man's social contributions to society....

---

14 *Lewis Hayden*   Escaped slave, business owner, and abolitionist activist (1811–89) best known for the assistance he gave to other fugitive slaves; *John Brown*   Abolitionist (1800–59) best known for coordinating an attempted slave uprising in West Virginia.

Corresponding with her definition of success, the virtues of Hopkins's self-made man share some characteristics with the traditional archetype, but Hopkins added specific traits to give racial significance to these characteristics and to highlight the special political and social circumstances blacks face in the United States. Like the traditional success model, Hopkins's self-made men possessed natural intelligence, high ethical and moral standards, honor, determination, and self-reliance. Unlike the white model, Hopkins's model also had a strong commitment to racial uplift.

... Racial uplift through personal social contributions is key to African American success. Hopkins's self-made men were active in the black community, charitable, and had a propensity for performing unselfish acts to benefit the race. According to Cawelti, during the late nineteenth century many Americans believed that the personal "pursuit of economic advancement is not only to the individual's advantage, but the best way to help others" because economic expansion created more income opportunities for the general public.[59] For Hopkins, blacks directly helping each other was more advantageous for the black community than waiting for whites to accept what she perceived to be their responsibility to provide assistance to blacks. Though the traditional model includes charity work, most successful whites were politically conservative, giving money only to certain causes, and they did not express the same level of personal responsibility to their communities as blacks. Furthermore, during the late nineteenth century most people thought poverty was the result of sloth. People did not intervene on behalf of the poor unless they earned it: "In fact, many people believed, to qualify for financial assistance, a beneficiary had to earn respect and thus indicate loyalty, courage, and parity of spirit."[60] Here is one particular area where Hopkins redefined the archetype, making the participation in racial uplift a key characteristic of the self-made man. Robert Morris personally fought discrimination and segregation in Massachusetts by allowing himself to be thrown out of public places and then suing in court. Hopkins adds that "The most heroic proof of his devotion to his race, was given during the trying time of the operation of the fugitive slave law"[15] when Morris risked his own life to rescue African Americans who were being remanded back to slavery (341)....

(2012)

---

15 *fugitive slave law*   Enacted by U.S. Congress in 1850, the Fugitive Slave Act mandated increased efforts to hunt down and arrest fugitive slaves, while also imposing fines and jail time on anyone who assisted a fugitive slave. Since the Act also made it almost impossible for accused fugitives to defend themselves in court, it placed both free and fugitive Black people at greater risk of enslavement.

References[16]

1. [Richard] Weiss, *The American Myth of Success*[: *From Horatio Alger to Norman Vincent Peale* (New York: Basic Books, 1969)], 3.
3. Cotton Mather, *A Christian at His Calling* . . ., in *The American Gospel of Success: Individualism and Beyond*, ed. Moses Rischin (Chicago: Quadrangle Books, 1965), 25.
11. [Rex] Burns, *Success in America*[: *The Yeoman Dream and the Industrial Revolution* (Amherst: U of Massachussets P, 1976)], 167.
12. [Paulette D.] Kilmer, [*The*] *Fear of Sinking*[: *The American Success Formula in the Gilded Age* (Knoxville: U of Tennessee P, 1996)], 4.
21. Weiss, *American Myth of Success*, 116.
24. August Meier, *Negro Thought in America, 1880–1915: Radical Ideologies in the Age of Booker T. Washington* (Ann Arbor: U of Michigan P, 1963), 10.
25. Ibid., 15.
26. Ibid., 42.
27. Ibid., 23–24.
28. James Olney, "'I was Born': Slave Narratives, Their Status as Autobiography and as Literature," in *The Slave's Narrative*, ed. Charles T. Davis and Henry Louis Gates Jr. (Oxford: Oxford UP, 1985), 154.
29. Frederick Douglass, *Narrative of the Life of Frederick Douglass, an American Slave* (New York: Penguin, 1982), 148.
30. Ibid., 150.
31. A[bigail] Mott, compiler, *Biographical Sketches and Interesting Anecdotes of Persons of Color to which is Added, a Selection of Pieces of Poetry* (New York: Mahlon Day, 1837), n.p.
34. Henry Davenport Northrop, Joseph R. Gay, and I. Garland Penn, *The College of Life, or Practical Self-Educator* (n.p.: Horace C. Fry, 1900), iv.
35. Ibid.
36. Samuel Smiles, *Self-Help, with Illustrations of Character, Conduct, and Perseverance*, ed. Peter W. Sinnema (Oxford: Oxford UP, 2002), 3.
39. [Northrop, Gay, and Penn, *College of Life*], 111.
40. Ibid., 74.
41. Ibid., 75.
42. Ibid., 75, 77.
43. Pauline Hopkins, "Toussaint L'Overture," *Colored American Magazine* 2.1 (Nov. 1900): 9.
44. Northrop, Gay, and Penn, *College of Life*, 74; Hopkins, "Toussaint L'Overture," 11. Subsequent references to Hopkins's periodical publications will be made parenthetically within the text. See bibliography below.
45. C.K. Doreski, "Inherited Rhetoric and Authentic History: Pauline Hopkins at the *Colored American Magazine*," in *The Unruly Voice: Rediscovering Pauline Elizabeth Hopkins*, ed. John Cullen Gruesser (Urbana: U of Illinois P, 1996), 72.
46. Ibid., 72, 73.

---

16 *References*   References have been excerpted to reflect only those noted in the portion of Knight's text reprinted here.

50. Meier, *Negro Thought*, 24.
59. [John G.] Cawelti, *Apostles of the Self-Made Man* [(Chicago: U of Chicago P, 1965)], 46.
60. Kilmer, *Fear of Sinking*, 10.

Bibliography[17]

[Hopkins, Pauline E.] "Famous Men of the Negro Race: Lewis Hayden." *Colored American Magazine* 2.6 (Apr. 1901): 473–77.
———. "Famous Men of the Negro Race: Robert Morris." *Colored American Magazine* 3.5 (Sept. 1901): 337–42.
———. "Hon. Frederick Douglass." *Colored American Magazine* 2.2 (Dec. 1900): 121–32.
———. "Men of Vision No. 1. Mark Rene Demortie." *New Era Magazine* 7.3 (Mar. 1904): 151–60.
———. "Men of Vision No. 2. Rev. Leonard Andrew Grimes." *New Era Magazine* (Mar. 1916): 99–105.
———. "The New York Subway." *The Voice of the Negro* (Dec. 1904): 20–26.
———. "William Wells Brown." *Colored American Magazine* 2.3 (Jan. 1901): 232–36.

Questions

1. Find in your institution's library or online a copy of one of the success narratives by a writer other than Hopkins that Knight summarizes and comments on. Write a brief comparison of your own between some aspect of that success narrative and one of Hopkins's.

2. Read a profile from Hopkins's "Famous Men of the Negro Race" series or her subsequent "Famous Women of the Negro Race" series. (Her profile of Douglass is reprinted in this anthology, while other entries in the series can be found in digital issues of *The Colored American Magazine*, available at http://coloredamerican.org.) Citing specific passages, discuss the extent to which Knights's ideas about Hopkins's approach apply (or do not apply) to the profile you have chosen.

3. This piece is taken from a scholarly monograph. What is there about the piece that might suggest that it was written with an academic audience in mind?

4. What, in your opinion, is the purpose of biographies, both in terms of individual readers and of communities? Do we still have "success narratives" today?

---

17 *Bibliography*   The bibliography has been excerpted to show only the pieces cited in the material included here

BETTINA LOVE

from HIP HOP'S LI'L SISTAS SPEAK: NEGOTIATING HIP HOP IDENTITIES AND POLITICS IN THE NEW SOUTH

In her introduction to Hip Hop's Li'l Sistas Speak, *Bettina Love reflects on her experience growing up in the 1980s and links her personal development to the political and cultural forces that shaped that decade: "The phenomenon of Hip Hop emerged in the decade of Reaganomics—President Ronald Reagan's attack on the poor and disadvantaged. By manipulating Americans with fear slogans like 'War on Crime,' 'War on Drugs,' 'welfare queens,' and 'gang wars,'" Reagan helped "cultivate the brash, gritty, often rebellious sound and culture of Hip Hop." Her ethnographical study focuses on six young women negotiating twenty-first century Hip-Hop culture in Atlanta, Georgia, but Love continually supplements their accounts with reflections on her own experiences as a consumer of Hip Hop culture, as a Black educator, as a woman, and as a lesbian. The excerpts included here are from the final two chapters of the book.*

CHAPTER SEVEN: THE BEAT OF HEGEMONY

The driving force of Hip Hop is its sound, the beat of the music that pulls you in as a listener. Every rapper knows that in order to have a hit record, the beat of the song must be audibly gratifying for the listener.... Hip Hop historians (Forman & Neal, 2004; George, 1999; Rose, 1994) write that the contemporary sound of Hip Hop started in New York City with the arrival of a Jamaican immigrant by the name of Clive Campbell, better known in the Hip Hop world as DJ Kool Herc. Herc grew up with the musical influence of reggae, which infused aspects of African and slave-era music with infectious rhythmic beats (Perkins, 1996). Rose states, "Time suspension via rhythmic breaks—points at which the bass lines are isolated and suspended—are important clues in explaining sources of pleasure in black music" (p. 67). The rhythmic patterns of Hip Hop are powerful, soulful, endearing, and rebellious all at the same time.

The beat of Hip Hop can be both freeing and repressive. For example, in 2005 one of the most hypersexual and misogynistic songs I have ever heard—and liked—was "Wait" by the Ying Yang Twins, an Atlanta-based group. Here is just a small fraction of the foul language within the song: "Fuck a bitch on da counter.... Fuck that bend over imma give you the dick.... Ay bitch! Wait 'til you see my dick.... Beat da pussy up" (Ying Yang Twins, 2005). I was not the only person fond of this song. In 2005, "Wait" reached number two on the *Billboard* charts in the rap category. The video for the song followed the sexist storyline of the record. At one point in the video, there are over twenty half-clothed women laying on top of and around the Ying Yang Twins as they sing "Beat da pussy up." Although I detested the lyrics of the song, the beat was controlling and influential and seemed to paralyze my ability to critically examine the song as it took over my body. Every time I heard the song on the radio or in the club, I thought to myself, "This record is so demeaning to both men and women." However, I was reluctant to turn the song off in my car because I was alone and not visually accountable to anyone for finding pleasure in a song that I knew was misogynistic. This is the contradictory space of Hip Hop feminism, as I was ideologically split by my love for Hip Hop music and culture and my desire to challenge patriarchy. So in an effort to reconcile my divided position as a Hip Hop feminist, I did sit down when the song was played at clubs I attended. This action, in some respect, made me feel both powerful and fake. I took a stand when people were watching, as my social politics were on display, but when I was alone I blasted the song, in love with the beat. Thus, no matter how uncomfortable I felt with the content of the song, the beat kept me drawn to it, and at times I ignored the lyrics. My noncritical position relating to the song, which stopped me from taking personal action to resist it, was common among many of my friends, both male and female. As a collective group, we all knew the song was misogynistic but found it enjoyable.

The teens in the study were no different than my friends and me in regard to enjoying misogynistic rap music. However, as a first-year doctoral student at the time, I was learning to understand rap as a "discourse"—a production of knowledge—and not just as a genre that I found entertaining (Foucault, 1980). Thus, using the words of Foucault and Hall, I began to view rap music and culture as representations that formed issues of power and knowledge and the question of the subject (Hall, 1997). Within rap, the subjects are the rappers and women of color who appear in rap videos, or the women who are cited in rap songs as bitches. Yet, according to Foucault, subjects are not autonomous and stable entities; subjects are produced within the "regime of truth," which operates by creating truths that are discursive, which in turn regulates social practices and what is deemed as knowledge and power (Foucault, 1980). For example, there is much discourse surrounding same-sex parents' inability to effectively parent. There is no evidence that this assumption is accurate. On the contrary, there are a good number of studies that contend that same-sex parents are effective parents (Pruett & Pruett, 2009). Nonetheless, the common discourse penalizes same-sex parents and gives power to heterosexual parents.... McLaren (1994) defines hegemony as "a struggle in which the powerful win the consent of those who are oppressed, with the oppressed unknowingly participating in their own oppression.... Within the hegemonic process, established meanings are often laundered of contradiction, contestation, and ambiguity" (pp. 182–183). By way of Foucault and Hall, I was learning how to be media literate....

But I was twenty-five years old with two degrees and working toward a third before I understood hegemony and its fluidity regarding Black popular culture. I never learned in high school that Hip Hop music and culture had been co-opted to create music and sounds that only highlighted the most demeaning notions of Blackness. As a youngster and young adult, I unknowingly consented to hypersexual, degrading, and misogynistic lyrics of rap. My consent often led to contradictory thinking, as I opposed the same music whose beat I enjoyed. My experience was no different than the girls in the study. Sad to say, it took a Ph.D. program to teach me media literacy.

THE BEAT GOES ON ...

5   Similar to my experiences with the beat of rap, the problematic lyrics and images of rap music were secondary to the beat of the music for the girls, even as the girls critiqued the music for its derogatory content.... In "Keepin' It Real: Black Youth, Hip-Hop Culture, and Black Identity," Clay (2003) recognized that "in conversations, many of the youth said that it was the 'beats,' not the lyrics, that are important to them about hip-hop" (p. 1346). Many of the teens in this study echoed Clay's findings that the beat drove them to listen to and accept degrading lyrics.

> They [male rappers] call us the "H" stuff and you get kind of offended, but I don't know why. We still listen and dance because we like the beat. (Star, Interview, 2007)

> When I first heard it [Plies, "Shawty"], I listened to the whole song. Then I just start laughing. I was like, he nasty. And like now ... I didn't listen to it, I listen to the beat. (Nicole, Interview, 2007)

You listen to it and if a boy come up to me and I like the song, and I can turn it off. (Lisa, Interview, 2007)

The teens referred to the beat for enjoyment, disregarding the messages, which is problematic because the music's messages take on a latent, secondary meaning in juxtaposition to the primacy of the beat. As the girls found pleasure in rap music because of the beat, they consented to degrading diatribes about Black culture and Black identity even as they brilliantly critiqued it. I read their consent to the misogynistic and sexually explicit lyrics as revealing a hege-monic structure at play within rap music and Black popular culture. Although the girls denounced the sexist lyrics by attempting to ignore them, they still danced and listened to the songs. Furthermore, the girls created methods of reconciling the contradictory space because they knew listening to the songs sent a message to their male counterparts regarding sex, which was a mes-sage the girls wanted to control. However, the beat of the songs made the girls disregard their better judgment.

For example, Lisa admitted that she would not listen to degrading songs if a male was present; this is insightful. Lisa feared that males would think she was promiscuous, which could have social ramifications.... Lisa knew that males would label her a freak or a ho, much like the women in videos. Nevertheless, by listening to the song, Lisa consented to the message. Maxine too realized that male rappers degraded Black women in rap songs. Just like Lisa, however, she listened to the songs because of the beat. Nicole stated that she does not even listen to the lyrics of "Shawty" by Plies—she just listened to the beat of the song. "Shawty" is one of Plies's hit records, and the title track topped the *Billboard* charts for rap tracks. In the song, Plies states, "I told her I don't usually do this, I don't fuck on the first night, 'cause after I beat ya baby I'm liable to fuck up ya whole life. I gotta train her, now she suck me with ice" (Plies, 2007). Nicole knew that the song was vulgar, so she only listened for the beat. Nicole was not alone; Dee and Maxine also admitted that they did not know the song lyrics and at times only knew the chorus but enjoyed the beat.

So you don't think about it at all, just the beat. (Dee, Interview, 2007)

I don't like it, I just. I don't like it, I like the beat. I just don't like the fact that he's talking about it and all that. Like Soulja Boy—I like Soulja Boy—The real version is not good. I don't like it because it's talking about sex ... um, degrading women. (Maxine, Interview, 2007)

Dee admitted that she does not think about the degrading lyrics because she knows how damaging the lyrics are. Her love of the beat superseded her position that the music was problematic. Above, Maxine referenced Soulja

Boy's hit song "Crank Dat." In the song Soulja Boy states, "Super soak that hoe. I'm too fresh off in this bitch.... And superman that bitch." "Crank Dat" is yet another song with an infectious beat and a memorable chorus but problematic lyrics. To "superman" a woman is to masturbate and then ejaculate on the back of a female. Maxine understood the coded language of the record, so she preferred to listen to the song for the beguiling beat.

All the girls liked to dance. Because it was a community center that focused on homework help, the environment restricted much of the music to their personal mp3 players or iPods. Therefore, the girls would pass around their mp3 players so everyone could hear the latest dance songs. Maxine spoke passionately about her dislike of rap music because of how it degrades women. When I asked her if she liked Soulja Boy's song "Crank Dat," she repeated the phrase, "I don't like it." Maxine tried to resist rap's message when the songs degraded women. At times during our interviews, Maxine told me that she refused to listen to music by Soulja Boy that was sexually explicit. According to my observations, though, Maxine's resistance was not consistent, much like mine as I enjoyed the Ying Yang Twins.

> Maxine loves to dance. She and Star know all the latest dances including the Soulja Boy, who has become extremely popular. Even though Maxine has stated she does not like Soulja Boy, she and Star dance to the song every time one of the students has it on their mp3 players. (Field notes, B. Love, 1/08)

10 My field notes and observations addressed many of the students' conflicted and contradictory ideological stances. Maxine wanted rap music to change. She stated that she did not like rap music that degrades women and is sexually explicit, but she continued to use Soulja Boy as a medium for social engagement.... Maxine's and the rest of the girls' consent to find enjoyment in some of rap's most debasing messages is an example of hegemony, as the girls, a marginalized group, consented to their own oppression. Storey (1998) stated that the relationship between popular culture and hegemony is the "site of struggle between the forces of 'resistance' of subordinate groups in society, and the forces of 'incorporation' of dominant groups in society" (p. 14).

The girls stated that they found the lyrics of rap music explicit and vulgar; however, their cell phone ring tones were the same songs they detested.... Each Internet music site provided the beat to the music in which they escaped while doing their homework or searching the Internet.

Some of my field notes address the beat of the music as a vital part of their day at the center.

> Dee and Lisa did their homework while listening to music today. They
> would bob their heads while doing their homework humming the beat
> of the song. They would smile at certain parts of the song and some-
> times smile at each other. (Field notes, B. Love, 2007)

The beat served as the background for many of their daily activities, especially homework. I observed students' dancing at times with no music playing,
just the beat they carried in their heads....

The beat influenced a resounding number of comments, which led the
youth to consent blindly to the messages. Even when the youth expressed their
dislike for the lyrics, the beat of the music kept them listening.

> It's just they cute. Like I don't know, I listen to the songs because I
> think how cute they is but they've got some songs on there that's nice,
> they're nice. I like the beat and stuff. (Lara, Interview, 2007)

> Yeah, but I don't like the words, I like the beat.... Sometimes you don't
> understand what they be saying, so fast. (Maxine, Interview, 2007)

Obviously, the teens maintained that the beat of a song was the driving   15
force behind why they listened to the song. Yet, they acknowledged the presence of the lyrics. They explained that they did not know many of the words
to a particular song and may not have liked the particular rapper but enjoyed
the beat. Adams and Fuller (2006) argued, "It is imperative that we as a society
move beyond the beat and seriously consider the effect that negative imagery
produced in misogynistic rap can have on the African American community
and society at large" (p. 955). The beat of the song masks the explicit lyrics of
rap music and the negative imagery consumed by youth who enjoy the songs.
Because the youth engaged with the beat, their ability to evaluate the lyrics was
challenged.

NOBODY WANTS TO BE LAME

The girls in the study were at the age where being accepted by their peers
was extremely important. Hip Hop music and culture were precursors to their
peers' accepting them. The girls believed there were social ramifications for
not liking the rap music of their peers or taking a stand against music they
found to be demeaning. The girls conceptualized rap's vulgar language as a
permanent fixture within rap and feared being seen as lame or as someone who
thought otherwise. When I asked Dee why she listened to music she thought
was belittling to women she stated, "What can I do, it's everywhere you go"
(Dee, informal interview, 2008). Dee is right; in Atlanta music that has a sexual

message can be heard just about everywhere. Moreover, if the lyrics cannot be heard, the beat is in the background. To be clear, I am not an advocate of censoring music that has sexual messages; I support the need for girls and boys to learn the tools to unpack sexual and degrading messages regarding women and hyper-macho stereotypes of masculinity....

Young girls need a space where they feel comfortable resisting demeaning notions of womanhood. They also need teachers who expose popular culture for its contrived messages built on stereotypes but do not demoralize youth choices to consume Hip Hop or any form of popular culture; this is a hard pedagogical technique but is needed, according to the experiences of the girls. For example, Lisa commented on the social repercussions associated with attempts to take action against the music when I asked her why she does not turn off songs she believes degrade women. Lisa stated, "If you say turn it off, then you lame" (Lisa, informal interview, 2008). Previously, Lisa had stated that she does not listen to sexually explicit music around males; however, here she has a fear of being viewed as uncool by her peers for turning off the music. Lisa wants to live above the peer pressure, but does not know how, which is evident by her words. Lisa is at odds because she is trying to fit in and take a stance in spaces that are overwhelmed with the music she is trying to challenge. Nicole passionately speculated, "Everyone dances to the music, how would it look if you don't dance"? (Nicole, informal interview, 2008). None of the girls ever tried resisting rap's misogynistic and sexually explicit lyrics by participating in some type of social action....

The pressure to confirm to what society and rap music say Black men and women should be like is quite powerful and hegemonic. The girls ... feared the risk of being uncool—or to use Lisa's term, lame—if we rejected misogynistic rap music. Therefore, we enjoyed the beat and ignored our better judgment because of the fear of being an outcast. Fear was the driving force of our conformity; we wanted to fit in and be seen as cool. Learning the latest dance and listening to the most popular rap song were the cool things to do, and none of the girls, including myself years ago, felt powerful enough to resist Hip Hop's misogynistic messages....

CHAPTER EIGHT: BLACK GIRLS RESISTING WHEN NO ONE IS LISTENING

Intuitively, the girls resisted Hip Hop's more pugnacious messages. A fundamental part of consuming popular culture is resisting popular culture. Hall (1981) argued, "Popular culture is one of the sites where this struggle for and against culture of the powerful is engaged: it is also the stake to be won or lost in the struggle. It is the arena of consent and resistance" (p. 65). I, however, argue that their resistance was undermined by rap's hegemonic force, which can be a normal outcome in today's mass media built on hegemonic race, class, gender, and political ideologies. Collins (2004) writes:

> All women engage an ideology that deems middle-class, heterosexual, White femininity as normative. In this context, Black femininity as a subordinated gender identity becomes constructed not just in relation to White women, but also in relation to multiple others, namely, all men, sexual outlaws (prostitutes and lesbians), unmarried women, and girls. These benchmarks construct a discourse of a hegemonic (White) femininity that becomes a normative yardstick for all femininities in which Black women typically are relegated to the bottom of the gender hierarchy. (p. 193)

The girls' resistance was never nurtured in classrooms, where conversations that problematize and critique rap in nonjudgmental disclosures took place, which are vital to their development. Their voices and experiences with rap were disregarded in classrooms and pushed to the margins. The complex issues of race, sexuality, class, and gender that are embedded within the music are dismissed by school officials as immature youth culture and music not worthy of classroom time. When I began to ask the girls to critique Hip Hop, their intellectual prowess was evident. The girls understood that the music did not always represent Black folks in constructive ways, specifically Black men, and that the messages within rap were problematic.

20

> Like they need to change what they talking about. They [rappers] probably not like that for real but they know that young people don't do that and want to sing it and stuff because of the beat and stuff and they doing it mostly because of money.... Future kids that doing drugs, so they're sending out future things so what the police and the government and the President is doing, building more jailhouses than schools and after school because people are going to drop out, they know people are going to drop out and go to jail. (Maxine, Interview, 2007)

> Like violence. Like they [rappers] be talking about how they got guns and then you know a teenager might think they can have guns, they [rappers] go get a gun to feel protected. They [rappers] talk about they might want to go to jail then come rap about how they was in jail. You know, like they be some of them songs have negative impact on children because they want to be just like the rappers. (Lisa, Interview, 2007)

> Yeah, talking about killing people and stuff (Lara, Interview, 2007)

These comments make it apparent that the girls had the ability to negotiate not only rap but also social issues around the music and urban life. Maxine's notions that rap needs to change and her understandings of the social issues that plague the Black community were insightful in that she used contemporary politics to address some of the current sociopolitical issues Black America faces. The fact that Maxine thought in regard to future generations showed her keen intellect and concern for others. Maxine also understood the masked racism of the prison industrial complex. Moreover, the girls' comments about violence represented their ideological perspectives concerning rappers and gun use. Lisa linked rappers' gun use to the belief that rappers carrying guns may influence other youth to follow their example. Dyson (2007) stated, "There's a preoccupation with the gun because the gun is the central part of the iconography of the ghetto" (p. 91). Black youth's obsession with guns and violence, according to Dyson, is a staple of urban life. Lisa linked guns and violence to rap music and rappers. She spoke to the perpetual violence that takes place in urban communities because of the belief that males need a gun to be viewed as fully masculine. Lisa understood the large-scale significance of rap music.

When I asked the girls why they thought rappers rhymed about guns and violence, they all stated in some fashion that rappers do not care about the youth who listen to their music.

> It is all about money basically. They [rappers] really don't care. Oh, they're [rappers] sending a bad message. (Lara, Interview, 2008)

> They don't care about us. They care about the money. (Star, Interview, 2008)

> They do it for money. (Nicole, Interview, 2008)

The girls state that rappers take on hardcore and hypersexual facades for financial gain. Their critique of rap speaks to the materialistic, bling-bling* culture of the music that glorifies conspicuous consumption above social issues that many scholars have unpacked (Basu, 2005; Love, 2010). A ... concrete example surrounding the girls' thoughts regarding rappers and their motives lies in their opinions of Atlanta-based rapper T.I. (Clifford Joseph Harris, Jr.) and his hardcore image. During the study, the police arrested T.I. on federal gun charges....

> Not T.I., he got locked up. T.I., I like him but he is a bad influence so that's it. Because he's in jail. And what he did wasn't called for. Like he shouldn't have did it.... And he got everybody disappointed, all his fans and stuff.... Now what he's going to do time because he's in jail, he gone be there a while. (Star, Interview, 2008)

Something wrong with that boy; he think he tough. (Dee, Interview, 2008)

He actin' like that for the money. (Lara, Interview, 2008)

... Star looked upon T.I.'s message of violence and criminal activity as discreditable, and the fact that the rapper's stage persona became a reality disappointed her. Lara suggested that money was the primary reason for T.I.'s hardcore image. In an interview with Lisa, she accused T.I. of pretending to be dangerous and nefarious to sell records.

Lisa: He actin' like that to sell records.

Tina: Actin' like what?

Lisa: Like he a gangsta. Actin' hard. (Interview, 2008)

... The girls critically examined the authenticity of T.I. and his music. These examinations of T.I., and Hip Hop music and culture in general, are important to the overall growth and well-being of Black girls and all youth. The dialogue that these girls engaged in created a space for them to resist rap's monolithic image of Black males.

However, conversations surrounding Black women did not produce the same outcome. When I asked the girls to examine Black women with a more critical lens, they relied heavily on how black women react to the position of Black males. For example, Maxine felt that Black women dressed scantily in rap videos because they were attempting to gain the attention of males. Lisa, Dee, and Lara had views parallel to those of Maxine. The girls felt that Black women's choices were a reaction to what Black males wanted, as well as poor decision making in general. Conversely, the teens saw rap through multiple lenses of Black expression. In some cases the teens challenged rap's hegemonic messages, but in other cases the teens understood rap as essentialized[1] notions of Blackness and were unable to reject its images and sounds...

... When asked about what they thought it meant to be Black, all the youth stated that to be Black is to be beautiful, smart, athletic, and have the ability to dance. They essentialized their ideas of what it means to be Black on multiple levels depending on the question. The data showed that the teens contradicted themselves as they struggled to make meaning of images of Blackness that they understood as authentic, even when those images glorified degrading women. The teens resisted labeling the Black race as violent, but they accepted

---

1   *essentialized* I.e., based on the idea that the characteristics of Blackness are fundamental and unchanging (rather than being shaped by historical events, culture, and, therefore, changeable).

Black women who appeared in rap videos as hos and freaks.* The postmodern condition allows these fluid and contradictory ideas because of the hybridizations of culture and the contradictory nature of Black popular culture (Hall, 1983). Their conclusions regarding the choices of Black women ... illustrate why Black girls need a space to question what it means to be a Black woman in conjunction with how Hip Hop, issues of class, race, politics, and body influence Black womanhood.

The data expressed within this book show that girls are engaging in the complicated and contradictory work of negotiating the space of Hip Hop music and culture but are doing the work alone. The girls were able to deconstruct Hip Hop's violent images in profound ways and question the lyrical content of rappers as juxtaposed to their own lives. Also, through questioning rappers' authenticity, the girls interrogated the monolithic image of male rappers as hardcore. Their critiques are insightful and have the power to become the foundation of revolutionary change and paradigm shifts in youth culture; however, these teens found no educational support to explore further rap's contrived and stereotypical messages....

(2012)

References[2]

Adams, T.M., & Fuller, D.B. (2006). The words have changed but the ideology remains the same: Misogynistic lyrics in rap music. *Journal of Black Studies*, 36(6), 938–957.

Basu, D. (2005). A critical examination of the political economy of the hip-hop industry. In C. Cecilia, J. Whitehead, P. Mason, & J. Stewart (Eds.), *African Americans in the US economy* (pp. 290–305). Lanham, MD: Rowman and Littlefield.

Clay, A. (2003). Keepin' it real: Black youth, hip-hop culture, and black identity. *American Behavioral Scientist*, 46(10), 1346.

Collins, P.H. (2004). *Black sexual politics: African Americans, gender, and the new racism*. New York: Routledge.

Dyson, M.E. (2007). *Know what I mean?: Reflections on hip hop*. New York: Basic Civitas Books.

Emdin, C. (2006). Affiliation and alienation: Hip-hop, rap, and urban science education. *Journal of Curriculum Studies*, 42(1), 1–25.

Forman, M., & Neal, M.A. (2004). *That's the joint!: The hip-hop studies reader*. New York: Routledge.

Foucault, M. (1980). *Power/Knowledge: Selected interviews and other writings, 1972–1977*. New York: Pantheon.

---

2   *References*   References have been excerpted to reflect only those noted in the portion of Love's text reprinted here.

George, N. (1999). *Hip hop America*. New York: Penguin.

Hall, S. (1981). Notes on deconstructing the popular. *People's History and Socialist Theory, 233*, 227–240.

Hall, S. (1983). What is this black in black popular culture. In M. Wallace (Ed.), *Black popular culture*. Boston, MA: Beacon Press.

Hall, S. (1997). *Representation: Cultural representations and signifying practices*. London: Sage Publications.

Love, B.L. (2010). Commercial hip hop: The sounds and images of a racial project. In D. Alridge, J.B. Stewart, & V.P. Franklin (Eds.), *Message in the music: Hip hop, history, and pedagogy* (pp. 55–67). Washington, D.C.: Association for the Study of African American Life and History Press.

McLaren, P. (1994). Life in schools. *An introduction to critical pedagogy in the foundations of education*. Chicago: Addison-Wesley.

Perkins, W.E. (1996). *Droppin' science: Critical essays on rap music and hip hop culture*. Philadelphia, PA: Temple University Press.

Plies. (2007). Shawty. On *The real testament*. Big Gates/Slip-n-Slide Records.

Pruett, K., & Pruett, M. (2009). *Partnership parenting: How men and women parent differently—why it helps your kids and can strengthen your marriage*. New York: Da Capo Lifelong Books.

Rose, T. (1994). *Black noise: Rap music and black culture in contemporary America*. Hanover, NH, and London: Wesleyan University Press.

Storey, J. (1998). *An introduction to cultural theory and popular culture*. Athens, GA: University of Georgia Press.

Ying Yang Twins (2005). Wait (The whisper song). On *United State of Atlanta*. TVT Records.

Questions

1. Love's book incorporates primary research in the form of interviews. What role does this research play in the argument she advances here?

2. Love critiques commercial rap as "only highlight[ing] the most demeaning notions of Blackness" and as "hypersexual, degrading, and misogynistic" (paragraph 4). To what extent is this an accurate characterization of commercial rap? To what extent is it unfairly reductive?

3. Love writes that "Maxine's and the rest of the girls' consent to find enjoyment in some of rap's most debasing messages is an example of hegemony, as the girls, a marginalized group, consented to their own oppression" (paragraph 10). Is this how you would interpret the interviews Love quotes in this selection? Why or why not?

4. Find a recent popular song by a Black male rapper. To what extent (if at all) does Love's critique of Hip Hop in general apply to the song you chose?

5. Find a recent popular song by a Black female rapper. To what extent (if at all) does Love's critique of Hip Hop in general apply to the song you chose?

Darnell L. Moore

Black, LGBT, American: A Search for Sanctuaries

The following article appeared in The Advocate, *a prominent news and opinion magazine focused on issues likely to be of interest to LGBTQ* people. This piece, by activist and writer Darnell L. Moore, was part of a 2013 issue titled "Black, LGBT, American" that featured a series of articles and interviews from Black LGBTQ writers and celebrities. Since then, Moore has addressed his experiences more fully in his 2018 memoir,* No Ashes in the Fire: Coming of Age Black and Free in America.

On May 17, Mark Carson, a 32-year-old black gay man in New York City, was murdered in gay-friendly Greenwich Village by homophobes wielding a 38-caliber revolver. I did not know Carson, but I feel I have encountered him on countless occasions. I encounter him when I speak with the young, mostly black and brown people we serve at the Hetrick-Martin Institute[1] where I work. I encounter him when I look in the mirror. My life, like his, like that of many of the kids I work with, has been shaped by the multiple identities that mark me. I am black, but rendered invisible within most mainstream LGBT movements. I am gay and have been ostracized by the homophobia of other black people. I am male and realize that my privileges are not granted to black lesbian and trans women. Like Carson, my personal experiences are often missing from narratives of gay progress.

Hundreds attended a march on May 20 in Carson's memory. While I was moved by the solidarity, I knew that if Carson hadn't been gay, 1,500 (mostly white) LGBT-supporting people would not have been out on the street protesting a black man's murder. I don't even know if I would have been standing at a busy intersection in Greenwich Village, where a makeshift memorial now stands. I stood in front of the memorial and remembered my own experience on the same block several months ago. I remembered the fact that in most

---

1   *Hetrick-Martin Institute*   Support and advocacy organization for LGBTQ youth.

gay spaces my blackness is pronounced, in some black spaces my queerness is animated, and in both spaces I have experienced a lack of safety.

BLACK IN A GAY SPACE

There was nothing remarkable about the cramped bar and grill where I often partied on Thursday nights. It was decorated with the kind of faux-leather lounge couches and tiny cocktail tables that look better at night under the glare of tinted lights. It was an unspectacular space, except that on Thursday nights it teemed with a crowd of mostly black gay men downing cocktails, chatting, and flirting with each other over a hot mix of hip-hop beats in the heart of mostly white and queer-friendly Greenwich Village.

The red-lit lounge was, appropriately enough, named Desire. And, despite its short distance from the iconic Stonewall Bar,[2] the weekly event there was one of the few spaces that attracted black gay men in a city with few social outlets that cater to black and brown queer and trans people. Desire attracted me, a 37-year-old black gay Brooklynite who often feels underrepresented in New York's gay bars. I was ecstatic to have another weekday party option.

But the last time I attended Desire's Thursday night mixer, in March, was the last time anyone attended it; that night it was shut down by a horde of New York City police officers. They were all white, an important detail in a bar full of black gay men. In such a place, a dozen white cops are bound to inspire an array of responses, including fear. Gay or straight, we're all too well-versed in how the justice system encounters us.

My stomach clenched at the sight of the NYPD storming through the entrance that night, but I have become jaded by my frequent encounters with the law. The memory of a black police officer in Camden, N.J., who many years ago mistook me for a "lookout boy"—the boy whose job it was to holler "Po-Po" as a signal to the neighborhood dealers that a cop car was approaching—still angers me. The officer grabbed me without warning, twisted my arms behind my back, pushed me into the back seat of his police cruiser, and sped off without reading me my Miranda rights.[3] I was an honors student, more interested in the dealers than the deals.

Those of us gathered in Desire that Thursday night weren't doing anything wrong, but before long, the music stopped and conversations turned to whispers. We were commanded to leave while several cops patrolled the area outside.

---

2 *Stonewall Bar* Site of the instigation of the historic 1969 Stonewall riots, a key moment in the formation of the modern gay liberation movement. During the period of the riots, people of color constituted the majority of the Stonewall's patrons.

3 *Miranda rights* Warning police officers are required to give suspects in custody prior to questioning.

They had followed a black trans woman from another location—watched as they apprehended and arrested her a few feet from the bar. The melee was messy enough to bring more cops and an ambulance.

Asking a gay man to leave a party at the very moment it is getting good is inviting trouble. Privileged with a clean record, my friend and I weren't afraid to demand a reason for our expulsion. One of the officers shoved my friend by the arm in response, so we asked for badge numbers. A few of the cops quickly covered them up.

A precarious situation was in the making. We knew it and left, watching in disgust as the lounge finally cleared out. I felt anger and I felt shame, because I realized that once again, this black queer had been denied an opportunity to be present in the queerest space in all of New York City.

GAY IN A BLACK SPACE

Whether they are the dark, asphalt-paved roadways of large urban landscapes like New York City or dirt-lined thoroughfares of unfamiliar towns, streets carry the traces of so many of our black queer encounters in a mostly white and straight America.

Seventeen-year-old Wauynee Wallace, a black gay teen who grew up in Camden, N.J., was shot dead in the summer of 2012 on the very streets where I had played as a youth. Tragically, Wallace was shot in the back of the head while walking with his friends one night. Whether or not he was killed because of his perceived sexuality and gender non-conforming expression, the case is an eerie and tragic reminder of the ways that queer and trans people are placed under surveillance, policed, attacked, and killed throughout the United States, even in this post-Matthew Shepard and James Byrd, Jr. Hate Crimes Prevention Act[4] moment.

Yet Wallace, like 15-year-old black lesbian Sakia Gunn, who was stabbed in the heart by a black man in Newark in 2003, did not entirely match the profile of HCPA's namesakes, white gay Matthew Shepard or black straight James Byrd Jr., who was brutalized because of his race. Gunn, a young black girl, did not entirely match the image of any of the male victims. Indeed, Wallace, like Gunn—like me—existed within a crossing where sexual identities, gender expressions, and racial markers not only meet but are thoroughly entangled.

Wallace and Gunn existed in a complicated intersection of identities. And crossings can be precarious spaces to occupy for those who must dodge multiple arrows of racism, homophobia, sexism, and so much else daily. I know

10

---

4   *Matthew Shepard ... Act*   2009 Act of Congress that expands federal hate-crime law in several ways, including the addition of gender, sexual orientation, and disability as categories protected against hate crimes.

what it feels like to be multiply marked: I was brutally attacked on a street not too far from Wallace's home when I was 14. The Whitman Park section of Camden, or "Polacktown," as it is called, is a distressed area of an underprivileged 16-square-mile slice of urban America. The neighborhood is lined with small-porched row houses, vacant lots, and some trash-lined streets. And yes, the media calls it the "hood," but it was my home.

The close proximity of our living quarters made community-building easy. It is difficult to disengage those whose conversations you can overhear on connected porches or through walls of closely attached homes. Like Wallace, I was a peculiar black boy who preferred to hang out with the neighborhood girls. I was a good dancer and enjoyed the arts. My difference made for a series of intriguing conversations and rumors on my block. There were whispers. The news of my perceived queerness traveled quickly in a densely populated neighborhood where it is impossible to be invisible. And even though I desired to be undetectable and unmarked, I was often targeted by neighbors and strangers alike.

15 Several boys coming from the grocery store one day during my eighth grade year surrounded me. A few of the "hard" boys on my block were my classmates, and one happened to live next door. After some words were exchanged while walking down the street, I heard the word "faggot." Then, one of the boys, whose nickname was OB, uncovered a gallon of kerosene, taken from the small yellow moped given me by my uncle as a gift, which had been stolen several days prior. I was actually relieved when it disappeared, because I was too scared to take it for a ride.

Kerosene in hand in a tightly closed milk jug, OB uncoiled the plastic cap and emptied the gallon on my head. The liquid enveloped my body. I could barely see. My eyes were glazed and throbbing. I felt hands—many hands,—violently hammering my body. Then I heard a match. It flickered several times. The wind, however, seemed, instinctively, to put out each fire.

My aunt, returning home from work, saw the assault and quickly intervened. She is a woman with a small frame, but a lot of courage. She gathered my things and quickly walked me to West Jersey Hospital, about 10 minutes away from our home. She held my hand as I moved about embarrassedly, with kerosene in my eyes and on my skin. I cried uncontrollably when they covered my eyes with nozzles spewing water to cleanse them.

OB was determined to burn me alive that day. I still don't understand what would provoke him to set me afire. What made him so angry that he would want to dispose of me, his peer? I knew little about his family and personal life, but I knew enough. I knew that the immense poverty he and his siblings encountered and the violence that had become mundane in our neighborhood had begun to shape him in the same ways that they had started to shape me.

Maybe OB and I were more alike than I wanted to believe. For instance, I shed fewer and fewer tears every time I was told that another young person had been murdered in my neighborhood. The real tragedy of living with gun violence is often the way it deadens emotions. I can still feel the sensation that moved through my body when one of my friends stayed over at my house. He was a black teen, like me. But unlike me, he was a drug dealer and fighter. He lay opposite me on my grandparents' couch, where I would try to sleep every night. He smirked, moved his leg under the covers, and placed his foot on my crotch. I was aroused and he knew it. He smirked again. A few months later, he was dead, shot while walking. I can still see his grin and feel his touch. The memories haunt me. I cannot begin to imagine the memories of the many dead friends that troubled OB so much so that he was no longer able to see life in me.

We were all black boys living in the same black neighborhood, but it was clear that day that some of us were different. Some of us were gay. I was gay. And the streets in Camden remember my queer encounter in that black space in the same way that they now contain the ghostly imprint of Wallace's blood.

LACK OF SPACE

Why the telling of these particular and personal stories in response to the larger question of what it might mean to be black and gay in an American moment of supposed progress? My narrative is just one of a number of stories of black LGBT life in America, after all.

On April 29, Jason Collins made history when he publicly disclosed that he was a black gay man, the first active male professional athlete in a major North American team sport to come out. Several days before Collins' announcement, Brittney Griner, the three-time All-American women's college basketball player and the Phoenix Mercury's first overall pick in the 2013 draft, disclosed that she was a lesbian. Griner is also black. Collins' and Griner's announcements occurred a year after black musician Frank Ocean's public release of a letter detailing his love for another man. Ocean, like comedian Wanda Sykes, who disclosed her sexual identity in 2008, received words of support from black celebrities like Beyoncé, Jay-Z, and Russell Simmons. In 2011, Janet Mock, the former staff editor of People magazine's website, came out as transgender in an article published in *Marie Claire*.

In the wake of Ocean, Lewis, and Griner, many people are asking if the tides have changed for those who are black and queer in today's seemingly progressive America. But one must ask: Which type of black queer person figures as the central character in this narrative of progress? Whose narrative matters? And who is afforded safe space to exist as black and queer?

The structural forces that impede or advance our lives will always shape the many ways that one exists as black or gay—whether he (or she) is praised by the president, shot to death by a stranger, lauded by celebrities, or doused with a gallon of kerosene. There is no single way to be black and gay in America, but it is clear that there are too few spaces for most black gay men to exist safely. And if that is true, there are even fewer sanctuaries for black queer youth, lesbians, and trans people to exist in their entirety as well.

(2013)

Questions

1. Moore refers to "gay spaces" and "black spaces" in this article. To what extent are these presented as geographical spaces, and to what extent are they presented as psychological spaces? How are these spaces constructed?

2. What is the significance of the encounter with police at Desire that Moore describes in this essay?

3. How would you characterize Moore's attitude toward the boys who victimized him in the neighborhood of his youth?

4. Discuss the following questions posed by Moore: "Which type of black queer person figures as the central character in [America's] narrative of progress [for those who are black and queer]? Whose narrative matters? And who is afforded safe space to exist as black and queer?" (paragraph 23).

5. This article appeared in *The Advocate*, a news and opinion magazine that targets an LGBTQ audience. How (if at all) does this piece reflect the intended audience? What about this piece might the intended audience have found challenging or affirming?

6. Read Shanita Hubbard's op-ed "Russell Simmons, R. Kelly, and Why Black Women Can't Say #MeToo," also reprinted in this anthology. Compare Hubbard's treatment of intersectional oppression with Moore's.

THE CASE FOR REPARATIONS

Ta-Nehisi Coates, whose bestselling Between the World and Me *won the National Book Award for Non-fiction in 2015, came into prominence the previous year with this long essay, published in the June 2014 issue of* The Atlantic. *The essay helped to inspire the Black Lives Matter movement—and helped as well to change many minds on the issue of whether or not reparations for slavery would be appropriate. (Coates had himself changed his mind on the issue—as he recounted in a May 22 online background piece for* The Atlantic, *"The Case for Reparations: An Intellectual Autopsy.")*

And if thy brother, a Hebrew man, or a Hebrew woman, be sold unto thee, and serve thee six years; then in the seventh year thou shalt let him go free from thee. And when thou sendest him out free from thee, thou shalt not let him go away empty: thou shalt furnish him liberally out of thy flock, and out of thy floor, and out of thy winepress: of that wherewith the LORD thy God hath blessed thee thou shalt give unto him. And thou shalt remember that thou wast a bondman in the land of Egypt, and the LORD thy God redeemed thee: therefore I command thee this thing today.—Deuteronomy 15: 12–15

Besides the crime which consists in violating the law, and varying from the right rule of reason, whereby a man so far becomes degenerate, and declares himself to quit the principles of human nature, and to be a noxious creature, there is commonly injury done to some person or other, and some other man receives damage by his transgression: in which case he who hath received any damage, has, besides the right of punishment common to him with other men, a particular right to seek reparation.—John Locke, "Second Treatise"

By our unpaid labor and suffering, we have earned the right to the soil, many times over and over, and now we are determined to have it.—Anonymous, 1861

C lyde Ross was born in 1923, the seventh of 13 children, near Clarksdale, Mississippi, the home of the blues.* Ross's parents owned and farmed a 40-acre tract of land, flush with cows, hogs, and mules. Ross's mother would drive to Clarksdale to do her shopping in a horse and buggy, in which she invested all the pride one might place in a Cadillac. The family owned another horse, with a red coat, which they gave to Clyde. The Ross family wanted for little, save that which all black families in the Deep South then desperately desired—the protection of the law.

In the 1920s, Jim Crow Mississippi[1] was, in all facets of society, a kleptocracy.[2] The majority of the people in the state were perpetually robbed of the vote—a hijacking engineered through the trickery of the poll tax and the muscle of the lynch mob.* Between 1882 and 1968, more black people were lynched in Mississippi than in any other state. "You and I know what's the best way to keep the nigger from voting," blustered Theodore Bilbo, a Mississippi senator and a proud Klansman.* "You do it the night before the election."

The state's regime partnered robbery of the franchise with robbery of the purse. Many of Mississippi's black farmers lived in debt peonage,[3] under the sway of cotton kings who were at once their landlords, their employers, and their primary merchants. Tools and necessities were advanced against the return on the crop, which was determined by the employer. When farmers were deemed to be in debt—and they often were—the negative balance was then carried over to the next season. A man or woman who protested this arrangement did so at the risk of grave injury or death. Refusing to work meant arrest under vagrancy laws and forced labor under the state's penal system.

Well into the 20th century, black people spoke of their flight from Mississippi in much the same manner as their runagate[4] ancestors had. In her 2010 book, *The Warmth of Other Suns*, Isabel Wilkerson tells the story of Eddie Earvin, a spinach picker who fled Mississippi in 1963, after being made to work at gunpoint. "You didn't talk about it or tell nobody," Earvin said. "You had to sneak away."

5   When Clyde Ross was still a child, Mississippi authorities claimed his father owed $3,000 in back taxes. The elder Ross could not read. He did not have a lawyer. He did not know anyone at the local courthouse. He could not expect the police to be impartial. Effectively, the Ross family had no way to contest the claim and no protection under the law. The authorities seized the

---

1   *Jim Crow Mississippi* Mississippi under the Jim Crow laws, which enforced segregation.

2   *kleptocracy* Jurisdiction in which theft is central to the operation of society.

3   *debt peonage* Forced servitude to one's creditors.

4   *runagate* Runaway, especially one who has broken the law.

land. They seized the buggy. They took the cows, hogs, and mules. And so for the upkeep of separate but equal, the entire Ross family was reduced to sharecropping.*

This was hardly unusual. In 2001, the Associated Press published a three-part investigation into the theft of black-owned land stretching back to the antebellum period.* The series documented some 406 victims and 24,000 acres of land valued at tens of millions of dollars. The land was taken through means ranging from legal chicanery to terrorism. "Some of the land taken from black families has become a country club in Virginia," the AP reported, as well as "oil fields in Mississippi" and "a baseball spring training facility in Florida."

Clyde Ross was a smart child. His teacher thought he should attend a more challenging school. There was very little support for educating black people in Mississippi. But Julius Rosenwald, a part owner of Sears, Roebuck, had begun an ambitious effort to build schools for black children throughout the South. Ross's teacher believed he should attend the local Rosenwald school. It was too far for Ross to walk and get back in time to work in the fields. Local white children had a school bus. Clyde Ross did not, and thus lost the chance to better his education.

Then, when Ross was 10 years old, a group of white men demanded his only childhood possession—the horse with the red coat. "You can't have this horse. We want it," one of the white men said. They gave Ross's father $17.

"I did everything for that horse," Ross told me. "Everything. And they took him. Put him on the racetrack. I never did know what happened to him after that, but I know they didn't bring him back. So that's just one of my losses."

The losses mounted. As sharecroppers, the Ross family saw their wages treated as the landlord's slush fund. Landowners were supposed to split the profits from the cotton fields with sharecroppers. But bales would often disappear during the count, or the split might be altered on a whim. If cotton was selling for 50 cents a pound, the Ross family might get 15 cents, or only five. One year Ross's mother promised to buy him a $7 suit for a summer program at their church. She ordered the suit by mail. But that year Ross's family was paid only five cents a pound for cotton. The mailman arrived with the suit. The Rosses could not pay. The suit was sent back. Clyde Ross did not go to the church program.

It was in these early years that Ross began to understand himself as an American—he did not live under the blind decree of justice, but under the heel of a regime that elevated armed robbery to a governing principle. He thought about fighting. "Just be quiet," his father told him. "Because they'll come and kill us all."

Clyde Ross grew. He was drafted into the Army. The draft officials offered him an exemption if he stayed home and worked. He preferred to take his chances with war. He was stationed in California. He found that he could go into stores without being bothered. He could walk the streets without being harassed. He could go into a restaurant and receive service.

Ross was shipped off to Guam. He fought in World War II to save the world from tyranny. But when he returned to Clarksdale, he found that tyranny had followed him home. This was 1947, eight years before Mississippi lynched Emmett Till[5] and tossed his broken body into the Tallahatchie River. The Great Migration,* a mass exodus of 6 million African Americans that spanned most of the 20th century, was now in its second wave. The black pilgrims did not journey north simply seeking better wages and work, or bright lights and big adventures. They were fleeing the acquisitive warlords of the South. They were seeking the protection of the law.

Clyde Ross was among them. He came to Chicago in 1947 and took a job as a taster at Campbell's Soup. He made a stable wage. He married. He had children. His paycheck was his own. No Klansmen stripped him of the vote. When he walked down the street, he did not have to move because a white man was walking past. He did not have to take off his hat or avert his gaze. His journey from peonage to full citizenship seemed near-complete. Only one item was missing—a home, that final badge of entry into the sacred order of the American middle class of the Eisenhower years.*

15   In 1961, Ross and his wife bought a house in North Lawndale, a bustling community on Chicago's West Side. North Lawndale had long been a predominantly Jewish neighborhood, but a handful of middle-class African Americans had lived there starting in the '40s. The community was anchored by the sprawling Sears, Roebuck headquarters. North Lawndale's Jewish People's Institute actively encouraged blacks to move into the neighborhood, seeking to make it a "pilot community for interracial living." In the battle for integration then being fought around the country, North Lawndale seemed to offer promising terrain. But out in the tall grass, highwaymen,* nefarious as any Clarksdale kleptocrat, were lying in wait.

Three months after Clyde Ross moved into his house, the boiler blew out. This would normally be a homeowner's responsibility, but in fact, Ross was not really a homeowner. His payments were made to the seller, not the bank. And Ross had not signed a normal mortgage. He'd bought "on contract": a predatory agreement that combined all the responsibilities of homeownership with all the disadvantages of renting—while offering the benefits of neither. Ross had bought his house for $27,500. The seller, not the previous homeowner but a new kind of middleman, had bought it for only $12,000 six months before selling it to Ross. In a contract sale, the seller kept the deed

---

5   *Emmett Till*   14-year-old boy whose murder became emblematic of racial injustice.

until the contract was paid in full—and, unlike with a normal mortgage, Ross would acquire no equity in the meantime. If he missed a single payment, he would immediately forfeit his $1,000 down payment, all his monthly payments, and the property itself.

The men who peddled contracts in North Lawndale would sell homes at inflated prices and then evict families who could not pay—taking their down payment and their monthly installments as profit. Then they'd bring in another black family, rinse, and repeat. "He loads them up with payments they can't meet," an office secretary told *The Chicago Daily News* of her boss, the speculator Lou Fushanis, in 1963. "Then he takes the property away from them. He's sold some of the buildings three or four times."

Ross had tried to get a legitimate mortgage in another neighborhood, but was told by a loan officer that there was no financing available. The truth was that there was no financing for people like Clyde Ross. From the 1930s through the 1960s, black people across the country were largely cut out of the legitimate home-mortgage market through means both legal and extralegal. Chicago whites employed every measure, from "restrictive covenants"[6] to bombings, to keep their neighborhoods segregated.

Their efforts were buttressed by the federal government. In 1934, Congress created the Federal Housing Administration. The FHA insured private mortgages, causing a drop in interest rates and a decline in the size of the down payment required to buy a house. But an insured mortgage was not a possibility for Clyde Ross. The FHA had adopted a system of maps that rated neighborhoods according to their perceived stability. On the maps, green areas, rated "A," indicated "in demand" neighborhoods that, as one appraiser put it, lacked "a single foreigner or Negro." These neighborhoods were considered excellent prospects for insurance. Neighborhoods where black people lived were rated "D" and were usually considered ineligible for FHA backing. They were colored in red. Neither the percentage of black people living there nor their social class mattered. Black people were viewed as a contagion. Redlining[7] went beyond FHA-backed loans and spread to the entire mortgage industry, which was already rife with racism, excluding black people from most legitimate means of obtaining a mortgage.

"A government offering such bounty to builders and lenders could have 20 required compliance with a nondiscrimination policy," Charles Abrams, the

---

6 *"restrictive covenants"* Clauses in property owners' deeds or leases that limit how a given property can be used. In the cases mentioned here, covenants often permitted the sale of homes only to white buyers.

7 *Redlining* Withholding services to people because of the racial or ethnic makeup of the neighborhoods they live in.

urban-studies expert who helped create the New York City Housing Authority, wrote in 1955. "Instead, the FHA adopted a racial policy that could well have been culled from the Nuremberg laws."[8]

The devastating effects are cogently outlined by Melvin L. Oliver and Thomas M. Shapiro in their 1995 book, *Black Wealth/White Wealth*:

> Locked out of the greatest mass-based opportunity for wealth accumulation in American history, African Americans who desired and were able to afford home ownership found themselves consigned to central-city communities where their investments were affected by the "self-fulfilling prophecies" of the FHA appraisers: cut off from sources of new investment[,] their homes and communities deteriorated and lost value in comparison to those homes and communities that FHA appraisers deemed desirable.

In Chicago and across the country, whites looking to achieve the American dream could rely on a legitimate credit system backed by the government. Blacks were herded into the sights of unscrupulous lenders who took them for money and for sport. "It was like people who like to go out and shoot lions in Africa. It was the same thrill," a housing attorney told the historian Beryl Satter in her 2009 book, *Family Properties*. "The thrill of the chase and the kill."

The kill was profitable. At the time of his death, Lou Fushanis owned more than 600 properties, many of them in North Lawndale, and his estate was estimated to be worth $3 million. He'd made much of this money by exploiting the frustrated hopes of black migrants like Clyde Ross. During this period, according to one estimate, 85 percent of all black home buyers who bought in Chicago bought on contract. "If anybody who is well established in this business in Chicago doesn't earn $100,000 a year," a contract seller told *The Saturday Evening Post* in 1962, "he is loafing."

Contract sellers became rich. North Lawndale became a ghetto.

25   Clyde Ross still lives there. He still owns his home. He is 91, and the emblems of survival are all around him—awards for service in his community, pictures of his children in cap and gown. But when I asked him about his home in North Lawndale, I heard only anarchy.

"We were ashamed. We did not want anyone to know that we were that ignorant," Ross told me. He was sitting at his dining-room table. His glasses were as thick as his Clarksdale drawl. "I'd come out of Mississippi where there was one mess, and come up here and got in another mess. So how dumb am I? I didn't want anyone to know how dumb I was.

---

8   *Nuremberg laws* Laws that governed policies regarding "racial purity" in Nazi Germany.

"When I found myself caught up in it, I said, 'How? I just left this mess. I just left no laws. And no regard. And then I come here and get cheated wide open.' I would probably want to do some harm to some people, you know, if I had been violent like some of us. I thought, 'Man, I got caught up in this stuff. I can't even take care of my kids.' I didn't have enough for my kids. You could fall through the cracks easy fighting these white people. And no law."

But fight Clyde Ross did. In 1968 he joined the newly formed Contract Buyers League—a collection of black homeowners on Chicago's South and West Sides, all of whom had been locked into the same system of predation. There was Howell Collins, whose contract called for him to pay $25,500 for a house that a speculator had bought for $14,500. There was Ruth Wells, who'd managed to pay out half her contract, expecting a mortgage, only to suddenly see an insurance bill materialize out of thin air—a requirement the seller had added without Wells's knowledge. Contract sellers used every tool at their disposal to pilfer from their clients. They scared white residents into selling low. They lied about properties' compliance with building codes, then left the buyer responsible when city inspectors arrived. They presented themselves as real-estate brokers, when in fact they were the owners. They guided their clients to lawyers who were in on the scheme.

The Contract Buyers League fought back. Members—who would eventually number more than 500—went out to the posh suburbs where the speculators lived and embarrassed them by knocking on their neighbors' doors and informing them of the details of the contract-lending trade. They refused to pay their installments, instead holding monthly payments in an escrow account. Then they brought a suit against the contract sellers, accusing them of buying properties and reselling in such a manner "to reap from members of the Negro race large and unjust profits."

THE STORY OF CLYDE ROSS AND THE CONTRACT BUYERS LEAGUE

In return for the "deprivations of their rights and privileges under the Thirteenth and Fourteenth Amendments,"* the league demanded "prayers for relief"—payback of all moneys paid on contracts and all moneys paid for structural improvement of properties, at 6 percent interest minus a "fair, non-discriminatory" rental price for time of occupation. Moreover, the league asked the court to adjudge that the defendants had "acted willfully and maliciously and that malice is the gist of this action."

Ross and the Contract Buyers League were no longer appealing to the government simply for equality. They were no longer fleeing in hopes of a better deal elsewhere. They were charging society with a crime against their community. They wanted the crime publicly ruled as such. They wanted the crime's executors declared to be offensive to society. And they wanted restitution for the great injury brought upon them by said offenders. In 1968, Clyde Ross and the Contract Buyers League were no longer simply seeking the protection of the law. They were seeking reparations.

According to the most-recent statistics, North Lawndale is now on the wrong end of virtually every socioeconomic indicator. In 1930 its population was 112,000. Today it is 36,000. The halcyon talk of "interracial living" is dead. The neighborhood is 92 percent black. Its homicide rate is 45 per 100,000—triple the rate of the city as a whole. The infant-mortality rate is 14 per 1,000—more than twice the national average. Forty-three percent of the people in North Lawndale live below the poverty line—double Chicago's overall rate. Forty-five percent of all households are on food stamps—nearly three times the rate of the city at large. Sears, Roebuck left the neighborhood in 1987, taking 1,800 jobs with it. Kids in North Lawndale need not be confused about their prospects: Cook County's Juvenile Temporary Detention Center sits directly adjacent to the neighborhood.

North Lawndale is an extreme portrait of the trends that ail black Chicago. Such is the magnitude of these ailments that it can be said that blacks and whites do not inhabit the same city. The average per capita income of Chicago's white neighborhoods is almost three times that of its black neighborhoods. When the Harvard sociologist Robert J. Sampson examined incarceration rates in Chicago in his 2012 book, *Great American City*, he found that a black neighborhood with one of the highest incarceration rates (West Garfield Park) had a rate more than 40 times as high as the white neighborhood with the highest rate (Clearing). "This is a staggering differential, even for community-level comparisons," Sampson writes. "A difference of kind, not degree."

In other words, Chicago's impoverished black neighborhoods—characterized by high unemployment and households headed by single parents—are not simply poor; they are "ecologically distinct." This "is not simply the same thing as low economic status," writes Sampson. "In this pattern Chicago is not alone."

35   The lives of black Americans are better than they were half a century ago. The humiliation of Whites Only signs are gone. Rates of black poverty have decreased. Black teen-pregnancy rates are at record lows—and the gap between black and white teen-pregnancy rates has shrunk significantly. But such progress rests on a shaky foundation, and fault lines are everywhere. The income gap between black and white households is roughly the same today as it was in 1970. Patrick Sharkey, a sociologist at New York University, studied children born from 1955 through 1970 and found that 4 percent of whites and 62 percent of blacks across America had been raised in poor neighborhoods. A generation later, the same study showed, virtually nothing had changed. And

whereas whites born into affluent neighborhoods tended to remain in affluent neighborhoods, blacks tended to fall out of them.

This is not surprising. Black families, regardless of income, are significantly less wealthy than white families. The Pew Research Center estimates that white households are worth roughly 20 times as much as black households, and that whereas only 15 percent of whites have zero or negative wealth, more than a third of blacks do. Effectively, the black family in America is working without a safety net. When financial calamity strikes—a medical emergency, divorce, job loss—the fall is precipitous.

And just as black families of all incomes remain handicapped by a lack of wealth, so too do they remain handicapped by their restricted choice of neighborhood. Black people with upper-middle-class incomes do not generally live in upper-middle-class neighborhoods. Sharkey's research shows that black families making $100,000 typically live in the kinds of neighborhoods inhabited by white families making $30,000. "Blacks and whites inhabit such different neighborhoods," Sharkey writes, "that it is not possible to compare the economic outcomes of black and white children."

The implications are chilling. As a rule, poor black people do not work their way out of the ghetto—and those who do often face the horror of watching their children and grandchildren tumble back.

Even seeming evidence of progress withers under harsh light. In 2012, the Manhattan Institute cheerily noted that segregation had declined since the 1960s. And yet African Americans still remained—by far—the most segregated ethnic group in the country.

With segregation, with the isolation of the injured and the robbed, comes   40
the concentration of disadvantage. An unsegregated America might see poverty, and all its effects, spread across the country with no particular bias toward skin color. Instead, the concentration of poverty has been paired with a concentration of melanin.[9] The resulting conflagration has been devastating.

· One thread of thinking in the African American community holds that these depressing numbers partially stem from cultural pathologies that can be altered through individual grit and exceptionally good behavior. (In 2011, Philadelphia Mayor Michael Nutter, responding to violence among young black males, put the blame on the family: "Too many men making too many babies they don't want to take care of, and then we end up dealing with your children." Nutter turned to those presumably fatherless babies: "Pull your pants up and buy a belt, because no one wants to see your underwear or the crack of your butt.") The thread is as old as black politics itself. It is also wrong. The kind of trenchant racism to which black people have persistently been subjected can never be defeated by making

---

9   *melanin*   Pigment in skin (darker shades are produced by more melanin).

its victims more respectable. The essence of American racism is disrespect. And in the wake of the grim numbers, we see the grim inheritance.

The Contract Buyers League's suit brought by Clyde Ross and his allies took direct aim at this inheritance. The suit was rooted in Chicago's long history of segregation, which had created two housing markets—one legitimate and backed by the government, the other lawless and patrolled by predators. The suit dragged on until 1976, when the league lost a jury trial. Securing the equal protection of the law proved hard; securing reparations proved impossible. If there were any doubts about the mood of the jury, the foreman removed them by saying, when asked about the verdict, that he hoped it would help end "the mess Earl Warren made with *Brown v. Board of Education*[10] and all that nonsense."

The Supreme Court seems to share that sentiment. The past two decades have witnessed a rollback of the progressive legislation of the 1960s. Liberals have found themselves on the defensive. In 2008, when Barack Obama was a candidate for president, he was asked whether his daughters—Malia and Sasha—should benefit from affirmative action.* He answered in the negative.

The exchange rested upon an erroneous comparison of the average American white family and the exceptional first family. In the contest of upward mobility, Barack and Michelle Obama have won. But they've won by being twice as good—and enduring twice as much. Malia and Sasha Obama enjoy privileges beyond the average white child's dreams. But that comparison is incomplete. The more telling question is how they compare with Jenna and Barbara Bush—the products of many generations of privilege, not just one. Whatever the Obama children achieve, it will be evidence of their family's singular perseverance, not of broad equality.

45 In 1783, the freedwoman* Belinda Royall petitioned the commonwealth of Massachusetts for reparations. Belinda had been born in modern-day Ghana. She was kidnapped as a child and sold into slavery. She endured the Middle Passage and 50 years of enslavement at the hands of Isaac Royall and his son. But the junior Royall, a British loyalist, fled the country during the Revolution.* Belinda, now free after half a century of labor, beseeched the nascent Massachusetts legislature:

> The face of your Petitioner, is now marked with the furrows of time, and her frame bending under the oppression of years, while she, by the Laws of the Land, is denied the employment of one morsel of that immense wealth, apart whereof hath been accumilated by her own industry, and the whole augmented by her servitude.

---

10 *Brown v. Board of Education*   Landmark 1954 decision in which the Supreme Court decreed segregation in schools to be unconstitutional.

WHEREFORE, casting herself at your feet if your honours, as to a body of men, formed for the extirpation of vassalage, for the reward of Virtue, and the just return of honest industry—she prays, that such allowance may be made her out of the Estate of Colonel Royall, as will prevent her, and her more infirm daughter, from misery in the greatest extreme, and scatter comfort over the short and downward path of their lives.

Belinda Royall was granted a pension of 15 pounds and 12 shillings, to be paid out of the estate of Isaac Royall—one of the earliest successful attempts to petition for reparations. At the time, black people in America had endured more than 150 years of enslavement, and the idea that they might be owed something in return was, if not the national consensus, at least not outrageous.

"A heavy account lies against us as a civil society for oppressions committed against people who did not injure us," wrote the Quaker* John Woolman in 1769, "and that if the particular case of many individuals were fairly stated, it would appear that there was considerable due to them."

As the historian Roy E. Finkenbine has documented, at the dawn of this country, black reparations were actively considered and often effected. Quakers in New York, New England, and Baltimore went so far as to make "membership contingent upon compensating one's former slaves." In 1782, the Quaker Robert Pleasants emancipated his 78 slaves, granted them 350 acres, and later built a school on their property and provided for their education. "The doing of this justice to the injured Africans," wrote Pleasants, "would be an acceptable offering to him who 'Rules in the kingdom of men.'"

Edward Coles, a protégé of Thomas Jefferson* who became a slaveholder through inheritance, took many of his slaves north and granted them a plot of land in Illinois. John Randolph, a cousin of Jefferson's, willed that all his slaves be emancipated upon his death, and that all those older than 40 be given 10 acres of land. "I give and bequeath to all my slaves their freedom," Randolph wrote, "heartily regretting that I have been the owner of one."

In his book *Forever Free*, Eric Foner recounts the story of a disgruntled 50 planter reprimanding a freedman loafing on the job:

Planter: "You lazy nigger, I am losing a whole day's labor by you."
Freedman: "Massa, how many days' labor have I lost by you?"

In the 20th century, the cause of reparations was taken up by a diverse cast that included the Confederate veteran Walter R. Vaughan, who believed that reparations would be a stimulus for the South; the black activist Callie House; black-nationalist* leaders like "Queen Mother" Audley Moore; and the civil-rights activist James Forman. The movement coalesced in 1987 under an umbrella organization called the National Coalition of Blacks for Reparations in America (N'COBRA). The NAACP* endorsed reparations in 1993. Charles J. Ogletree Jr., a professor at Harvard Law School, has pursued reparations claims in court.

But while the people advocating reparations have changed over time, the response from the country has remained virtually the same. "They have been taught to labor," the *Chicago Tribune* editorialized in 1891. "They have been taught Christian civilization, and to speak the noble English language instead of some African gibberish. The account is square with the ex-slaves."

Not exactly. Having been enslaved for 250 years, black people were not left to their own devices. They were terrorized. In the Deep South, a second slavery ruled.* In the North, legislatures, mayors, civic associations, banks, and citizens all colluded to pin black people into ghettos, where they were overcrowded, overcharged, and undereducated. Businesses discriminated against them, awarding them the worst jobs and the worst wages. Police brutalized them in the streets. And the notion that black lives, black bodies, and black wealth were rightful targets remained deeply rooted in the broader society. Now we have half-stepped away from our long centuries of despoilment, promising, "Never again." But still we are haunted. It is as though we have run up a credit-card bill and, having pledged to charge no more, remain befuddled that the balance does not disappear. The effects of that balance, interest accruing daily, are all around us.

Broach the topic of reparations today and a barrage of questions inevitably follows: Who will be paid? How much will they be paid? Who will pay? But if the practicalities, not the justice, of reparations are the true sticking point, there has for some time been the beginnings of a solution. For the past 25 years, Congressman John Conyers Jr., who represents the Detroit area, has marked every session of Congress by introducing a bill calling for a congressional study of slavery and its lingering effects as well as recommendations for "appropriate remedies."

55 A country curious about how reparations might actually work has an easy solution in Conyers's bill, now called HR 40, the Commission to Study Reparation Proposals for African Americans Act. We would support this bill, submit the question to study, and then assess the possible solutions. But we are not interested.

"It's because it's black folks making the claim," Nkechi Taifa, who helped found N'COBRA, says. "People who talk about reparations are considered left lunatics. But all we are talking about is studying [reparations]. As John Conyers has said, we study everything. We study the water, the air. We can't even study the issue? This bill does not authorize one red cent to anyone."

That HR 40 has never—under either Democrats or Republicans—made it to the House floor suggests our concerns are rooted not in the impracticality of reparations but in something more existential. If we conclude that the conditions in North Lawndale and black America are not inexplicable but are instead precisely what you'd expect of a community that for centuries has lived in America's crosshairs, then what are we to make of the world's oldest democracy?

One cannot escape the question by hand-waving at the past, disavowing the acts of one's ancestors, nor by citing a recent date of ancestral immigration. The last slaveholder has been dead for a very long time. The last soldier to endure Valley Forge[11] has been dead much longer. To proudly claim the veteran and disown the slaveholder is patriotism à la carte.* A nation outlives its generations. We were not there when Washington crossed the Delaware,* but Emanuel Gottlieb Leutze's rendering[12] has meaning to us. We were not there when Woodrow Wilson took us into World War I, but we are still paying out the pensions. If Thomas Jefferson's genius matters, then so does his taking of Sally Hemings's[13] body. If George Washington crossing the Delaware matters, so must his ruthless pursuit of the runagate Oney Judge.[14]

In 1909, President William Howard Taft told the country that "intelligent" white southerners were ready to see blacks as "useful members of the community." A week later Joseph Gordon, a black man, was lynched outside Greenwood, Mississippi. The high point of the lynching era has passed. But the memories of those robbed of their lives still live on in the lingering effects. Indeed, in America there is a strange and powerful belief that if you stab a black person 10 times, the bleeding stops and the healing begins the moment the assailant drops the knife. We believe white dominance to be a fact of the inert past, a delinquent debt that can be made to disappear if only we don't look.

There has always been another way. "It is in vain to allege, that *our ancestors* brought them hither, and not we," Yale President Timothy Dwight said in 1810.

60

> We inherit our ample patrimony with all its incumbrances; and are bound to pay the debts of our ancestors. *This* debt, particularly, we are bound to discharge: and, when the righteous Judge of the Universe comes to reckon with his servants, he will rigidly exact the payment at

---

11 *Valley Forge* Site of a Revolutionary War-era military camp where American forces spent the winter of 1777 with inadequate provisions; thousands died.

12 *Emanuel ... rendering* Emanuel Gottlieb Leutze's 1857 painting *Washington Crosssing the Delaware* is an iconic image of the event.

13 *Sally Hemings* Hemings (1773–1835) was a slave of Thomas Jefferson with whom he had a long-term sexual relationship.

14 *Oney Judge* Judge (c. 1773–1848) was a slave of George Washington who escaped; Washington tried repeatedly to secure her return.

our hands. To give them liberty, and stop here, is to entail upon them a curse.

America begins in black plunder and white democracy, two features that are not contradictory but complementary. "The men who came together to found the independent United States, dedicated to freedom and equality, either held slaves or were willing to join hands with those who did," the historian Edmund S. Morgan wrote. "None of them felt entirely comfortable about the fact, but neither did they feel responsible for it. Most of them had inherited both their slaves and their attachment to freedom from an earlier generation, and they knew the two were not unconnected."

When enslaved Africans, plundered of their bodies, plundered of their families, and plundered of their labor, were brought to the colony of Virginia* in 1619, they did not initially endure the naked racism that would engulf their progeny. Some of them were freed. Some of them intermarried. Still others escaped with the white indentured servants who had suffered as they had. Some even rebelled together, allying under Nathaniel Bacon to torch Jamestown in 1676.

One hundred years later, the idea of slaves and poor whites joining forces would shock the senses, but in the early days of the English colonies, the two groups had much in common. English visitors to Virginia found that its masters "abuse their servantes with intollerable oppression and hard usage." White servants were flogged, tricked into serving beyond their contracts, and traded in much the same manner as slaves.

This "hard usage" originated in a simple fact of the New World—land was boundless but cheap labor was limited. As life spans increased in the colony, the Virginia planters found in the enslaved Africans an even more efficient source of cheap labor. Whereas indentured servants were still legal subjects of the English crown and thus entitled to certain protections, African slaves entered the colonies as aliens. Exempted from the protections of the crown, they became early America's indispensable working class—fit for maximum exploitation, capable of only minimal resistance.

For the next 250 years, American law worked to reduce black people to a class of untouchables[15] and raise all white men to the level of citizens. In 1650, Virginia mandated that "all persons except Negroes" were to carry arms. In 1664, Maryland mandated that any Englishwoman who married a slave must live as a slave of her husband's master. In 1705, the Virginia assembly passed a law allowing for the dismemberment of unruly slaves—but forbidding masters from whipping "a Christian white servant naked, without an order from a justice of the peace." In that same law, the colony mandated that "all horses, cattle, and hogs, now belonging, or that hereafter shall belong to any slave" be

---

15 *untouchables* Lowest members in India's elaborate class hierarchy.

seized and sold off by the local church, the profits used to support "the poor of the said parish." At that time, there would have still been people alive who could remember blacks and whites joining to burn down Jamestown only 29 years before. But at the beginning of the 18th century, two primary classes were enshrined in America.

"The two great divisions of society are not the rich and poor, but white and black," John C. Calhoun, South Carolina's senior senator, declared on the Senate floor in 1848. "And all the former, the poor as well as the rich, belong to the upper class, and are respected and treated as equals." 65

In 1860, the majority of people living in South Carolina and Mississippi, almost half of those living in Georgia, and about one-third of all Southerners were on the wrong side of Calhoun's line. The state with the largest number of enslaved Americans was Virginia, where in certain counties some 70 percent of all people labored in chains. Nearly one-fourth of all white Southerners owned slaves, and upon their backs the economic basis of America—and much of the Atlantic world—was erected. In the seven cotton states, one-third of all white income was derived from slavery. By 1840, cotton produced by slave labor constituted 59 percent of the country's exports. The web of this slave society extended north to the looms of New England,* and across the Atlantic to Great Britain, where it powered a great economic transformation and altered the trajectory of world history. "Whoever says Industrial Revolution," wrote the historian Eric J. Hobsbawm, "says cotton."

The wealth accorded America by slavery was not just in what the slaves pulled from the land but in the slaves themselves. "In 1860, slaves as an asset were worth more than all of America's manufacturing, all of the railroads, all of the productive capacity of the United States put together," the Yale historian David W. Blight has noted. "Slaves were the single largest, by far, financial asset of property in the entire American economy." The sale of these slaves—"in whose bodies that money congealed," writes Walter Johnson, a Harvard historian—generated even more ancillary wealth. Loans were taken out for purchase, to be repaid with interest. Insurance policies were drafted against the untimely death of a slave and the loss of potential profits. Slave sales were taxed and notarized. The vending of the black body and the sundering of the black family became an economy unto themselves, estimated to have brought in tens of millions of dollars to antebellum America. In 1860 there were more millionaires per capita in the Mississippi Valley than anywhere else in the country.

Beneath the cold numbers lay lives divided. "I had a constant dread that Mrs. Moore, her mistress, would be in want of money and sell my dear wife," a freedman wrote, reflecting on his time in slavery. "We constantly dreaded a final separation. Our affection for each was very strong, and this made us always apprehensive of a cruel parting."

Forced partings were common in the antebellum South. A slave in some parts of the region stood a 30 percent chance of being sold in his or her lifetime. Twenty-five percent of interstate trades destroyed a first marriage and half of them destroyed a nuclear family.

70   When the wife and children of Henry Brown, a slave in Richmond, Virginia, were to be sold away, Brown searched for a white master who might buy his wife and children to keep the family together. He failed:

> The next day, I stationed myself by the side of the road, along which the slaves, amounting to three hundred and fifty, were to pass. The purchaser of my wife was a Methodist minister, who was about starting for North Carolina. Pretty soon five waggon-loads of little children passed, and looking at the foremost one, what should I see but a little child, pointing its tiny hand towards me, exclaiming, "There's my father; I knew he would come and bid me good-bye." It was my eldest child! Soon the gang approached in which my wife was chained. I looked, and beheld her familiar face; but O, reader, that glance of agony! may God spare me ever again enduring the excruciating horror of that moment! She passed, and came near to where I stood. I seized hold of her hand, intending to bid her farewell; but words failed me; the gift of utterance had fled, and I remained speechless. I followed her for some distance, with her hand grasped in mine, as if to save her from her fate, but I could not speak, and I was obliged to turn away in silence.

In a time when telecommunications were primitive and blacks lacked freedom of movement, the parting of black families was a kind of murder. Here we find the roots of American wealth and democracy—in the for-profit destruction of the most important asset available to any people, the family. The destruction was not incidental to America's rise; it facilitated that rise. By erecting a slave society, America created the economic foundation for its great experiment in democracy. The labor strife that seeded Bacon's rebellion was suppressed. America's indispensable working class existed as property beyond the realm of politics, leaving white Americans free to trumpet their love of freedom and democratic values. Assessing antebellum democracy in Virginia, a visitor from England observed that the state's natives "can profess an unbounded love of liberty and of democracy in consequence of the mass of the people, who in other countries might become mobs, being there nearly altogether composed of their own Negro slaves."

The consequences of 250 years of enslavement, of war upon black families and black people, were profound. Like homeownership today, slave ownership was aspirational, attracting not just those who owned slaves but those who wished to. Much as homeowners today might discuss the addition of a patio or the painting of a living room, slaveholders traded tips on the best methods for breeding workers, exacting labor, and doling out punishment. Just as a home-owner today might subscribe to a magazine like *This Old House*, slaveholders had journals such as *De Bow's Review*, which recommended the best practices for wringing profits from slaves. By the dawn of the Civil War, the enslavement of black America was thought to be so foundational to the country that those who sought to end it were branded heretics worthy of death. Imagine what would happen if a president today came out in favor of taking all American homes from their owners: the reaction might well be violent.

"This country was formed for the *white*, not for the black man," John Wilkes Booth wrote, before killing Abraham Lincoln. "And looking upon *African slavery* from the same standpoint held by those noble framers of our Constitution, I for one have ever considered it one of the greatest blessings (both for themselves and us) that God ever bestowed upon a favored nation."

In the aftermath of the Civil War, Radical Republicans attempted to reconstruct the country upon something resembling universal equality—but they were beaten back by a campaign of "Redemption," led by White Liners, Red Shirts,[16] and Klansmen bent on upholding a society "formed for the *white*, not for the black man." A wave of terrorism roiled the South. In his massive history *Reconstruction*, Eric Foner recounts incidents of black people being attacked for not removing their hats; for refusing to hand over a whiskey flask; for disobeying church procedures; for "using insolent language"; for disputing labor contracts; for refusing to be "tied like a slave." Sometimes the attacks were intended simply to "thin out the niggers a little."

Terrorism carried the day. Federal troops withdrew from the South in 1877. The dream of Reconstruction* died. For the next century, political violence was visited upon blacks wantonly, with special treatment meted out toward black people of ambition. Black schools and churches were burned to the ground. Black voters and the political candidates who attempted to rally them were intimidated, and some were murdered. At the end of World War I, black veterans returning to their homes were assaulted for daring to wear the American uniform. The demobilization of soldiers after the war, which put white and black veterans into competition for scarce jobs, produced the Red Summer of 1919: a succession of racist pogroms against dozens of cities ranging from Longview, Texas, to Chicago to Washington, D.C. Organized white violence against blacks continued into the 1920s—in 1921 a white mob leveled Tulsa's "Black Wall Street,"* and in 1923 another one razed the black town of Rosewood, Florida—and virtually no one was punished.

75

---

16   *White Liners, Red Shirts*   Groups of white supremacists.

The work of mobs was a rabid and violent rendition of prejudices that extended even into the upper reaches of American government. The New Deal* is today remembered as a model for what progressive government should do—cast a broad social safety net that protects the poor and the afflicted while building the middle class. When progressives wish to express their disappointment with Barack Obama, they point to the accomplishments of Franklin Roosevelt. But these progressives rarely note that Roosevelt's New Deal, much like the democracy that produced it, rested on the foundation of Jim Crow.

"The Jim Crow South," writes Ira Katznelson, a history and political-science professor at Columbia, "was the one collaborator America's democracy could not do without." The marks of that collaboration are all over the New Deal. The omnibus programs passed under the Social Security Act in 1935 were crafted in such a way as to protect the southern way of life. Old-age insurance (Social Security proper) and unemployment insurance excluded farmworkers and domestics—jobs heavily occupied by blacks. When President Roosevelt signed Social Security into law in 1935, 65 percent of African Americans nationally and between 70 and 80 percent in the South were ineligible. The NAACP protested, calling the new American safety net "a sieve with holes just big enough for the majority of Negroes to fall through."

The oft-celebrated G.I. Bill* similarly failed black Americans, by mirroring the broader country's insistence on a racist housing policy. Though ostensibly color-blind, Title III of the bill, which aimed to give veterans access to low-interest home loans, left black veterans to tangle with white officials at their local Veterans Administration as well as with the same banks that had, for years, refused to grant mortgages to blacks. The historian Kathleen J. Frydl observes in her 2009 book, *The GI Bill*, that so many blacks were disqualified from receiving Title III benefits "that it is more accurate simply to say that blacks could not use this particular title."

In Cold War America,* homeownership was seen as a means of instilling patriotism, and as a civilizing and anti-radical force. "No man who owns his own house and lot can be a Communist," claimed William Levitt, who pioneered the modern suburb with the development of the various Levittowns, his famous planned communities. "He has too much to do."

But the Levittowns were, with Levitt's willing acquiescence, segregated throughout their early years. Daisy and Bill Myers, the first black family to move into Levittown, Pennsylvania, were greeted with protests and a burning cross.* A neighbor who opposed the family said that Bill Myers was "probably a nice guy, but every time I look at him I see $2,000 drop off the value of my house."

The neighbor had good reason to be afraid. Bill and Daisy Myers were from the other side of John C. Calhoun's dual society. If they moved next door,

80

housing policy almost guaranteed that their neighbors' property values would decline.

Whereas shortly before the New Deal, a typical mortgage required a large down payment and full repayment within about 10 years, the creation of the Home Owners' Loan Corporation in 1933 and then the Federal Housing Administration the following year allowed banks to offer loans requiring no more than 10 percent down, amortized over 20 to 30 years. "Without federal intervention in the housing market, massive suburbanization would have been impossible," writes Thomas J. Sugrue, a historian at the University of Pennsylvania. "In 1930, only 30 percent of Americans owned their own homes; by 1960, more than 60 percent were home owners. Home ownership became an emblem of American citizenship."

That emblem was not to be awarded to blacks. The American real-estate industry believed segregation to be a moral principle. As late as 1950, the National Association of Real Estate Boards' code of ethics warned that "a Realtor should never be instrumental in introducing into a neighborhood ... any race or nationality, or any individuals whose presence will clearly be detrimental to property values." A 1943 brochure specified that such potential undesirables might include madams, bootleggers, gangsters—and "a colored man of means who was giving his children a college education and thought they were entitled to live among whites."

The federal government concurred. It was the Home Owners' Loan Corporation, not a private trade association, that pioneered the practice of redlining, selectively granting loans and insisting that any property it insured be covered by a restrictive covenant—a clause in the deed forbidding the sale of the property to anyone other than whites. Millions of dollars flowed from tax coffers into segregated white neighborhoods.

"For perhaps the first time, the federal government embraced the discrimi- 85 natory attitudes of the marketplace," the historian Kenneth T. Jackson wrote in his 1985 book, *Crabgrass Frontier*, a history of suburbanization. "Previously, prejudices were personalized and individualized; FHA exhorted segregation and enshrined it as public policy. Whole areas of cities were declared ineligible for loan guarantees." Redlining was not officially outlawed until 1968, by the Fair Housing Act. By then the damage was done—and reports of redlining by banks have continued.

The federal government is premised on equal fealty from all its citizens, who in return are to receive equal treatment. But as late as the mid-20th century, this bargain was not granted to black people, who repeatedly paid a higher price for citizenship and received less in return. Plunder had been the essential feature of slavery, of the society described by Calhoun. But practically a full century after the end of the Civil War and the abolition of slavery, the plunder—quiet, systemic, submerged—continued even amidst the aims and achievements of New Deal liberals.

Today Chicago is one of the most segregated cities in the country, a fact that reflects assiduous planning. In the effort to uphold white supremacy at every level down to the neighborhood, Chicago—a city founded by the black fur trader Jean Baptiste Point du Sable—has long been a pioneer. The efforts began in earnest in 1917, when the Chicago Real Estate Board, horrified by the influx of southern blacks, lobbied to zone the entire city by race. But after the Supreme Court ruled against explicit racial zoning that year, the city was forced to pursue its agenda by more-discreet means.

Like the Home Owners' Loan Corporation, the Federal Housing Administration initially insisted on restrictive covenants, which helped bar blacks and other ethnic undesirables from receiving federally backed home loans. By the 1940s, Chicago led the nation in the use of these restrictive covenants, and about half of all residential neighborhoods in the city were effectively off-limits to blacks.

It is common today to become misty-eyed about the old black ghetto, where doctors and lawyers lived next door to meatpackers and steelworkers, who themselves lived next door to prostitutes and the unemployed. This segregationist nostalgia ignores the actual conditions endured by the people living there—vermin and arson, for instance—and ignores the fact that the old ghetto was premised on denying black people privileges enjoyed by white Americans.

90

In 1948, when the Supreme Court ruled that restrictive covenants, while permissible, were not enforceable by judicial action, Chicago had other weapons at the ready. The Illinois state legislature had already given Chicago's city council the right to approve—and thus to veto—any public housing in the city's wards. This came in handy in 1949, when a new federal housing act sent millions of tax dollars into Chicago and other cities around the country. Beginning in 1950, site selection for public housing proceeded entirely on the grounds of segregation. By the 1960s, the city had created with its vast housing projects what the historian Arnold R. Hirsch calls a "second ghetto," one larger than the old Black Belt but just as impermeable. More than 98 percent of all the family public-housing units built in Chicago between 1950 and the mid-1960s were built in all-black neighborhoods.

Governmental embrace of segregation was driven by the virulent racism of Chicago's white citizens. White neighborhoods vulnerable to black encroachment formed block associations for the sole purpose of enforcing segregation. They lobbied fellow whites not to sell. They lobbied those blacks who did manage to buy to sell back. In 1949, a group of Englewood Catholics formed block associations intended to "keep up the neighborhood." Translation: keep black people out. And when civic engagement was not enough, when government failed, when private banks could no longer hold the line, Chicago turned to an old tool in the American repertoire—racial violence. "The pattern of terrorism is easily discernible," concluded a Chicago civic group in the 1940s. "It is at the seams of the black ghetto in all directions." On July 1 and 2 of 1946, a mob of thousands assembled in Chicago's Park Manor neighborhood, hoping to eject a black doctor who'd recently moved in. The mob pelted the house with rocks and set the garage on fire. The doctor moved away.

In 1947, after a few black veterans moved into the Fernwood section of Chicago, three nights of rioting broke out; gangs of whites yanked blacks off streetcars and beat them. Two years later, when a union meeting attended by blacks in Englewood triggered rumors that a home was being "sold to niggers," blacks (and whites thought to be sympathetic to them) were beaten in the streets. In 1951, thousands of whites in Cicero, 20 minutes or so west of downtown Chicago, attacked an apartment building that housed a single black family, throwing bricks and firebombs through the windows and setting the apartment on fire. A Cook County grand jury declined to charge the rioters—and instead indicted the family's NAACP attorney, the apartment's white owner, and the owner's attorney and rental agent, charging them with conspiring to lower property values. Two years after that, whites picketed and planted explosives in South Deering, about 30 minutes from downtown Chicago, to force blacks out.

When terrorism ultimately failed, white homeowners simply fled the neighborhood. The traditional terminology, white flight, implies a kind of natural expression of preference. In fact, *white flight* was a triumph of social engineering, orchestrated by the shared racist presumptions of America's public and private sectors. For should any nonracist white families decide that integration might not be so bad as a matter of principle or practicality, they still had to contend with the hard facts of American housing policy: When the mid-20th-century white homeowner claimed that the presence of a Bill and Daisy Myers decreased his property value, he was not merely engaging in racist dogma—he was accurately observing the impact of federal policy on market prices. Redlining destroyed the possibility of investment wherever black people lived.

Speculators in North Lawndale, and at the edge of the black ghettos, knew there was money to be made off white panic. They resorted to "block-busting"—spooking whites into selling cheap before the neighborhood became black. They would hire a black woman to walk up and down the street with a stroller. Or they'd hire someone to call a number in the neighborhood looking for "Johnny Mae."* Then they'd cajole whites into selling at low prices, informing them that the more blacks who moved in, the more the value of their homes would decline, so better to sell now. With these white-fled homes in hand, speculators then turned to the masses of black people who had streamed northward as part of the Great Migration, or who were desperate to escape the ghettos: the speculators would take the houses they'd just bought cheap through block-busting and sell them to blacks on contract.

95   To keep up with his payments and keep his heat on, Clyde Ross took a second job at the post office and then a third job delivering pizza. His wife took a job working at Marshall Field.* He had to take some of his children out of private school. He was not able to be at home to supervise his children or help them with their homework. Money and time that Ross wanted to give his children went instead to enrich white speculators.

"The problem was the money," Ross told me. "Without the money, you can't move. You can't educate your kids. You can't give them the right kind of food. Can't make the house look good. They think this neighborhood is where they supposed to be. It changes their outlook. My kids were going to the best schools in this neighborhood, and I couldn't keep them in there."

Mattie Lewis came to Chicago from her native Alabama in the mid-'40s, when she was 21, persuaded by a friend who told her she could get a job as a hairdresser. Instead she was hired by Western Electric, where she worked for 41 years. I met Lewis in the home of her neighbor Ethel Weatherspoon. Both had owned homes in North Lawndale for more than 50 years. Both had bought their houses on contract. Both had been active with Clyde Ross in the Contract Buyers League's effort to garner restitution from contract sellers who'd operated in North Lawndale, banks who'd backed the scheme, and even the Federal Housing Administration. We were joined by Jack Macnamara, who'd been an organizing force in the Contract Buyers League when it was founded, in 1968. Our gathering had the feel of a reunion, because the writer James Alan McPherson had profiled the Contract Buyers League for *The Atlantic* back in 1972.

Weatherspoon bought her home in 1957. "Most of the whites started moving out," she told me. "'The blacks are coming. The blacks are coming.' They actually said that. They had signs up: Don't sell to blacks."

Before moving to North Lawndale, Lewis and her husband tried moving to Cicero after seeing a house advertised for sale there. "Sorry, I just sold it today," the Realtor told Lewis's husband. "I told him, 'You know they don't want you in Cicero,'" Lewis recalls. "'They ain't going to let nobody black in Cicero.'"

100   In 1958, the couple bought a home in North Lawndale on contract. They were not blind to the unfairness. But Lewis, born in the teeth of Jim Crow, considered American piracy—black people keep on making it, white people keep on taking it—a fact of nature. "All I wanted was a house. And that was the

only way I could get it. They weren't giving black people loans at that time," she said. "We thought, 'This is the way it is. We going to do it till we die, and they ain't never going to accept us. That's just the way it is.'

"The only way you were going to buy a home was to do it the way they wanted," she continued. "And I was determined to get me a house. If everybody else can have one, I want one too. I had worked for white people in the South. And I saw how these white people were living in the North and I thought, 'One day I'm going to live just like them.' I wanted cabinets and all these things these other people have."

Whenever she visited white co-workers at their homes, she saw the difference. "I could see we were just getting ripped off," she said. "I would see things and I would say, 'I'd like to do this at my house.' And they would say, 'Do it,' but I would think, 'I can't, because it costs us so much more.'"

I asked Lewis and Weatherspoon how they kept up on payments.

"You paid it and kept working," Lewis said of the contract. "When that payment came up, you knew you had to pay it."

"You cut down on the light bill. Cut down on your food bill," Weatherspoon interjected.

"You cut down on things for your child, that was the main thing," said Lewis. "My oldest wanted to be an artist and my other wanted to be a dancer and my other wanted to take music."

Lewis and Weatherspoon, like Ross, were able to keep their homes. The suit did not win them any remuneration. But it forced contract sellers to the table, where they allowed some members of the Contract Buyers League to move into regular mortgages or simply take over their houses outright. By then they'd been bilked for thousands. In talking with Lewis and Weatherspoon, I was seeing only part of the picture—the tiny minority who'd managed to hold on to their homes. But for all our exceptional ones, for every Barack and Michelle Obama, for every Ethel Weatherspoon or Clyde Ross, for every black survivor, there are so many thousands gone.

"A lot of people fell by the way," Lewis told me. "One woman asked me if I would keep all her china. She said, 'They ain't going to set you out.'"

On a recent spring afternoon in North Lawndale, I visited Billy Lamar Brooks Sr. Brooks has been an activist since his youth in the Black Panther Party,* when he aided the Contract Buyers League. I met him in his office at the Better Boys Foundation, a staple of North Lawndale whose mission is to direct local kids off the streets and into jobs and college. Brooks's work is personal. On June 14, 1991, his 19-year-old son, Billy Jr., was shot and killed. "These guys tried to stick him up," Brooks told me. "I suspect he could have been involved in some things ... He's always on my mind. Every day."

110   Brooks was not raised in the streets, though in such a neighborhood it is impossible to avoid the influence. "I was in church three or four times a week. That's where the girls were," he said, laughing. "The stark reality is still there. There's no shield from life. You got to go to school. I lived here. I went to Marshall High School. Over here were the Egyptian Cobras. Over there were the Vice Lords."[17]

    Brooks has since moved away from Chicago's West Side. But he is still working in North Lawndale. If "you got a nice house, you live in a nice neighborhood, then you are less prone to violence, because your space is not deprived," Brooks said. "You got a security point. You don't need no protection." But if "you grow up in a place like this, housing sucks. When they tore down the projects here, they left the high-rises and came to the neighborhood with that gang mentality. You don't have nothing, so you going to take something, even if it's not real. You don't have no street, but in your mind it's yours."

    We walked over to a window behind his desk. A group of young black men were hanging out in front of a giant mural memorializing two black men: In Lovin Memory Quentin aka "Q," July 18, 1974 ❤ March 2, 2012. The name and face of the other man had been spray-painted over by a rival group. The men drank beer. Occasionally a car would cruise past, slow to a crawl, then stop. One of the men would approach the car and make an exchange, then the car would drive off. Brooks had known all of these young men as boys.

    "That's their corner," he said.

    We watched another car roll through, pause briefly, then drive off. "No respect, no shame," Brooks said. "That's what they do. From that alley to that corner. They don't go no farther than that. See the big brother there? He almost died a couple of years ago. The one drinking the beer back there ... I know all of them. And the reason they feel safe here is cause of this building, and because they too chickenshit to go anywhere. But that's their mentality. That's their block."

115   Brooks showed me a picture of a Little League team he had coached. He went down the row of kids, pointing out which ones were in jail, which ones were dead, and which ones were doing all right. And then he pointed out his son—"That's my boy, Billy," Brooks said. Then he wondered aloud if keeping his son with him while working in North Lawndale had hastened his death. "It's a definite connection, because he was part of what I did here. And I think maybe I shouldn't have exposed him. But then, I had to," he said, "because I wanted him with me."

    From the White House on down, the myth holds that fatherhood is the great antidote to all that ails black people. But Billy Brooks Jr. had a father.

---

17   *Egyptian Cobras ... Vice Lords*   Gang names.

Trayvon Martin had a father. Jordan Davis[18] had a father. Adhering to middle-class norms is what made Ethel Weatherspoon a lucrative target for rapacious speculators. Contract sellers did not target the very poor. They targeted black people who had worked hard enough to save a down payment and dreamed of the emblem of American citizenship—homeownership. It was not a tangle of pathology that put a target on Clyde Ross's back. It was not a culture of poverty that singled out Mattie Lewis for "the thrill of the chase and the kill." Some black people always will be twice as good. But they generally find white predation to be thrice as fast.

Liberals today mostly view racism not as an active, distinct evil but as a relative of white poverty and inequality. They ignore the long tradition of this country actively punishing black success—and the elevation of that punishment, in the mid-20th century, to federal policy. President Lyndon Johnson may have noted in his historic civil-rights speech at Howard University in 1965 that "Negro poverty is not white poverty." But his advisers and their successors were, and still are, loath to craft any policy that recognizes the difference.

After his speech, Johnson convened a group of civil-rights leaders, including the esteemed A. Philip Randolph and Bayard Rustin, to address the "ancient brutality." In a strategy paper, they agreed with the president that "Negro poverty is a special, and particularly destructive, form of American poverty." But when it came to specifically addressing the "particularly destructive," Rustin's group demurred, preferring to advance programs that addressed "all the poor, black and white."

The urge to use the moral force of the black struggle to address broader inequalities originates in both compassion and pragmatism. But it makes for ambiguous policy. Affirmative action's precise aims, for instance, have always proved elusive. Is it meant to make amends for the crimes heaped upon black people? Not according to the Supreme Court. In its 1978 ruling in *Regents of the University of California v. Bakke*, the Court rejected "societal discrimination" as "an amorphous concept of injury that may be ageless in its reach into the past." Is affirmative action meant to increase "diversity"? If so, it only tangentially relates to the specific problems of black people—the problem of what America has taken from them over several centuries.

This confusion about affirmative action's aims, along with our inability to face up to the particular history of white-imposed black disadvantage, dates back to the policy's origins. "There is no fixed and firm definition of affirmative action," an appointee in Johnson's Department of Labor declared. "Affirmative

120

---

18 *Trayvon Martin ... Jordan Davis*   Martin and Davis were both African American teens who were shot and killed in 2012 by civilians while breaking no law.

action is anything that you have to do to get results. But this does not necessarily include preferential treatment."

Yet America was built on the preferential treatment of white people—395 years of it. Vaguely endorsing a cuddly, feel-good diversity does very little to redress this.

Today, progressives are loath to invoke white supremacy as an explanation for anything. On a practical level, the hesitation comes from the dim view the Supreme Court has taken of the reforms of the 1960s. The Voting Rights Act has been gutted. The Fair Housing Act might well be next. Affirmative action is on its last legs. In substituting a broad class struggle for an anti-racist struggle, progressives hope to assemble a coalition by changing the subject.

The politics of racial evasion are seductive. But the record is mixed. Aid to Families With Dependent Children was originally written largely to exclude blacks—yet by the 1990s it was perceived as a giveaway to blacks. The Affordable Care Act* makes no mention of race, but this did not keep Rush Limbaugh* from denouncing it as reparations. Moreover, the act's expansion of Medicaid was effectively made optional, meaning that many poor blacks in the former Confederate states do not benefit from it. The Affordable Care Act, like Social Security, will eventually expand its reach to those left out; in the meantime, black people will be injured.

"All that it would take to sink a new WPA program[19] would be some skillfully packaged footage of black men leaning on shovels smoking cigarettes," the sociologist Douglas S. Massey writes. "Papering over the issue of race makes for bad social theory, bad research, and bad public policy." To ignore the fact that one of the oldest republics in the world was erected on a foundation of white supremacy, to pretend that the problems of a dual society are the same as the problems of unregulated capitalism, is to cover the sin of national plunder with the sin of national lying. The lie ignores the fact that reducing American poverty and ending white supremacy are not the same. The lie ignores the fact that closing the "achievement gap" will do nothing to close the "injury gap," in which black college graduates still suffer higher unemployment rates than white college graduates, and black job applicants without criminal records enjoy roughly the same chance of getting hired as white applicants *with* criminal records.

125   Chicago, like the country at large, embraced policies that placed black America's most energetic, ambitious, and thrifty countrymen beyond the pale of society and marked them as rightful targets for legal theft. The effects

---

19 *WPA program* Works Progress Administration program, a part of the New Deal in which unemployed workers were given employment building schools, roads, and other public works.

reverberate beyond the families who were robbed to the community that beholds the spectacle. Don't just picture Clyde Ross working three jobs so he could hold on to his home. Think of his North Lawndale neighbors—their children, their nephews and nieces—and consider how watching this affects them. Imagine yourself as a young black child watching your elders play by all the rules only to have their possessions tossed out in the street and to have their most sacred possession—their home—taken from them.

The message the young black boy receives from his country, Billy Brooks says, is "'You ain't shit. You not no good. The only thing you are worth is working for us. You will never own anything. You not going to get an education. We are sending your ass to the penitentiary.' They're telling you no matter how hard you struggle, no matter what you put down, you ain't shit. 'We're going to take what you got. You will never own anything, nigger.'"

When Clyde Ross was a child, his older brother Winter had a seizure. He was picked up by the authorities and delivered to Parchman Farm, a 20,000-acre state prison in the Mississippi Delta region.*

"He was a gentle person," Clyde Ross says of his brother. "You know, he was good to everybody. And he started having spells, and he couldn't control himself. And they had him picked up, because they thought he was dangerous."

Built at the turn of the century, Parchman was supposed to be a progressive and reformist response to the problem of "Negro crime." In fact it was the gulag[20] of Mississippi, an object of terror to African Americans in the Delta. In the early years of the 20th century, Mississippi Governor James K. Vardaman used to amuse himself by releasing black convicts into the surrounding wilderness and hunting them down with bloodhounds. "Throughout the American South," writes David M. Oshinsky in his book *Worse Than Slavery*, "Parchman Farm is synonymous with punishment and brutality, as well it should be ... Parchman is the quintessential penal farm, the closest thing to slavery that survived the Civil War."

When the Ross family went to retrieve Winter, the authorities told them   130
that Winter had died. When the Ross family asked for his body, the authorities at Parchman said they had buried him. The family never saw Winter's body.

And this was just one of their losses.

Scholars have long discussed methods by which America might make reparations to those on whose labor and exclusion the country was built. In the 1970s, the Yale Law professor Boris Bittker argued in *The Case for Black*

---

20   *gulag*   In the former Soviet Union, gulags were prisons to which political dissidents were sent. Such prisons were known for brutally harsh conditions; many prisoners died before the end of their sentence.

Reparations that a rough price tag for reparations could be determined by multiplying the number of African Americans in the population by the difference in white and black per capita income. That number—$34 billion in 1973, when Bittker wrote his book—could be added to a reparations program each year for a decade or two. Today Charles Ogletree, the Harvard Law School professor, argues for something broader: a program of job training and public works that takes racial justice as its mission but includes the poor of all races.

Perhaps no statistic better illustrates the enduring legacy of our country's shameful history of treating black people as sub-citizens, sub-Americans, and sub-humans than the wealth gap. Reparations would seek to close this chasm. But as surely as the creation of the wealth gap required the cooperation of every aspect of the society, bridging it will require the same.

Perhaps after a serious discussion and debate—the kind that HR 40 proposes—we may find that the country can never fully repay African Americans. But we stand to discover much about ourselves in such a discussion—and that is perhaps what scares us. The idea of reparations is frightening not simply because we might lack the ability to pay. The idea of reparations threatens something much deeper—America's heritage, history, and standing in the world.

135 The early American economy was built on slave labor. The Capitol and the White House were built by slaves. President James K. Polk traded slaves from the Oval Office. The laments about "black pathology,"[21] the criticism of black family structures by pundits and intellectuals, ring hollow in a country whose existence was predicated on the torture of black fathers, on the rape of black mothers, on the sale of black children. An honest assessment of America's relationship to the black family reveals the country to be not its nurturer but its destroyer.

And this destruction did not end with slavery. Discriminatory laws joined the equal burden of citizenship to unequal distribution of its bounty. These laws reached their apex in the mid-20th century, when the federal government—through housing policies—engineered the wealth gap, which remains with us to this day. When we think of white supremacy, we picture COLORED ONLY signs,* but we should picture pirate flags.

On some level, we have always grasped this.

"Negro poverty is not white poverty," President Johnson said in his historic civil-rights speech.

> Many of its causes and many of its cures are the same. But there are differences—deep, corrosive, obstinate differences—radiating painful

---

21 *black pathology*   Allegedly diseased nature of African American culture.

roots into the community and into the family, and the nature of the individual. These differences are not racial differences. They are solely and simply the consequence of ancient brutality, past injustice, and present prejudice.

We invoke the words of Jefferson and Lincoln because they say something about our legacy and our traditions. We do this because we recognize our links to the past—at least when they flatter us. But black history does not flatter American democracy; it chastens it. The popular mocking of reparations as a harebrained scheme authored by wild-eyed lefties and intellectually unserious black nationalists is fear masquerading as laughter. Black nationalists have always perceived something unmentionable about America that integrationists dare not acknowledge—that white supremacy is not merely the work of hotheaded demagogues, or a matter of false consciousness, but a force so fundamental to America that it is difficult to imagine the country without it.

And so we must imagine a new country. Reparations—by which I mean the full acceptance of our collective biography and its consequences—is the price we must pay to see ourselves squarely. The recovering alcoholic may well have to live with his illness for the rest of his life. But at least he is not living a drunken lie. Reparations beckons us to reject the intoxication of hubris and see America as it is—the work of fallible humans. 140

Won't reparations divide us? Not any more than we are already divided. The wealth gap merely puts a number on something we feel but cannot say— that American prosperity was ill-gotten and selective in its distribution. What is needed is an airing of family secrets, a settling with old ghosts. What is needed is a healing of the American psyche and the banishment of white guilt.

What I'm talking about is more than recompense for past injustices—more than a handout, a payoff, hush money, or a reluctant bribe. What I'm talking about is a national reckoning that would lead to spiritual renewal. Reparations would mean the end of scarfing hot dogs on the Fourth of July while denying the facts of our heritage. Reparations would mean the end of yelling "patriotism" while waving a Confederate flag. Reparations would mean a revolution of the American consciousness, a reconciling of our self-image as the great democratizer with the facts of our history.

We are not the first to be summoned to such a challenge.

In 1952, when West Germany began the process of making amends for the Holocaust, it did so under conditions that should be instructive to us. Resistance was violent. Very few Germans believed that Jews were entitled to anything. Only 5 percent of West Germans surveyed reported feeling guilty about the

Holocaust, and only 29 percent believed that Jews were owed restitution from the German people.

145   "The rest," the historian Tony Judt wrote in his 2005 book, *Postwar*, "were divided between those (some two-fifths of respondents) who thought that only people 'who really committed something' were responsible and should pay, and those (21 percent) who thought 'that the Jews themselves were partly responsible for what happened to them during the Third Reich.'"

Germany's unwillingness to squarely face its history went beyond polls. Movies that suggested a societal responsibility for the Holocaust beyond Hitler were banned. "The German soldier fought bravely and honorably for his homeland," claimed President Eisenhower, endorsing the Teutonic national myth. Judt wrote, "Throughout the fifties West German officialdom encouraged a comfortable view of the German past in which the Wehrmacht[22] was heroic, while Nazis were in a minority and properly punished."

Konrad Adenauer, the postwar German chancellor, was in favor of reparations, but his own party was divided, and he was able to get an agreement passed only with the votes of the Social Democratic opposition.

Among the Jews of Israel, reparations provoked violent and venomous reactions ranging from denunciation to assassination plots. On January 7, 1952, as the Knesset—the Israeli parliament—convened to discuss the prospect of a reparations agreement with West Germany, Menachem Begin, the future prime minister of Israel, stood in front of a large crowd, inveighing against the country that had plundered the lives, labor, and property of his people. Begin claimed that all Germans were Nazis and guilty of murder. His condemnations then spread to his own young state. He urged the crowd to stop paying taxes and claimed that the nascent Israeli nation characterized the fight over whether or not to accept reparations as a "war to the death." When alerted that the police watching the gathering were carrying tear gas, allegedly of German manufacture, Begin yelled, "The same gases that asphyxiated our parents!"

Begin then led the crowd in an oath to never forget the victims of the Shoah,[23] lest "my right hand lose its cunning" and "my tongue cleave to the roof of my mouth." He took the crowd through the streets toward the Knesset. From the rooftops, police repelled the crowd with tear gas and smoke bombs. But the wind shifted, and the gas blew back toward the Knesset, billowing through windows shattered by rocks. In the chaos, Begin and Prime Minister David Ben-Gurion exchanged insults. Two hundred civilians and 140 police officers were wounded. Nearly 400 people were arrested. Knesset business was halted.

---

22 *Wehrmacht*   Term for the armed forces in Nazi Germany.
23 *Shoah*   Hebrew term for the Holocaust.

Begin then addressed the chamber with a fiery speech condemning the   150
actions the legislature was about to take. "Today you arrested hundreds," he
said. "Tomorrow you may arrest thousands. No matter, they will go, they will
sit in prison. We will sit there with them. If necessary, we will be killed with
them. But there will be no 'reparations' from Germany."

Survivors of the Holocaust feared laundering the reputation of Germany
with money, and mortgaging the memory of their dead. Beyond that, there was
a taste for revenge. "My soul would be at rest if I knew there would be 6 million German dead to match the 6 million Jews," said Meir Dworzecki, who'd
survived the concentration camps of Estonia.

Ben-Gurion countered this sentiment, not by repudiating vengeance but
with cold calculation: "If I could take German property without sitting down
with them for even a minute but go in with jeeps and machine guns to the
warehouses and take it, I would do that—if, for instance, we had the ability to
send a hundred divisions and tell them, 'Take it.' But we can't do that."

The reparations conversation set off a wave of bomb attempts by Israeli
militants. One was aimed at the foreign ministry in Tel Aviv. Another was aimed
at Chancellor Adenauer himself. And one was aimed at the port of Haifa, where
the goods bought with reparations money were arriving. West Germany ultimately agreed to pay Israel 3.45 billion deutsche marks, or more than $7 billion
in today's dollars. Individual reparations claims followed—for psychological
trauma, for offense to Jewish honor, for halting law careers, for life insurance,
for time spent in concentration camps. Seventeen percent of funds went toward
purchasing ships. "By the end of 1961, these reparations vessels constituted
two-thirds of the Israeli merchant fleet," writes the Israeli historian Tom Segev
in his book *The Seventh Million*. "From 1953 to 1963, the reparations money
funded about a third of the total investment in Israel's electrical system, which
tripled its capacity, and nearly half the total investment in the railways."

Israel's GNP tripled during the 12 years of the agreement. The Bank of
Israel attributed 15 percent of this growth, along with 45,000 jobs, to invest-
ments made with reparations money. But Segev argues that the impact went
far beyond that. Reparations "had indisputable psychological and political
importance," he writes.

Reparations could not make up for the murder perpetrated by the Nazis.   155
But they did launch Germany's reckoning with itself, and perhaps provided a
road map for how a great civilization might make itself worthy of the name.

Assessing the reparations agreement, David Ben-Gurion said:

For the first time in the history of relations between people, a precedent has been created by which a great State, as a result of moral
pressure alone, takes it upon itself to pay compensation to the victims

338 | TA-NEHISI COATES

of the government that preceded it. For the first time in the history of a people that has been persecuted, oppressed, plundered and despoiled for hundreds of years in the countries of Europe, a persecutor and despoiler has been obliged to return part of his spoils and has even undertaken to make collective reparation as partial compensation for material losses.

Something more than moral pressure calls America to reparations. We cannot escape our history. All of our solutions to the great problems of health care, education, housing, and economic inequality are troubled by what must go unspoken. "The reason black people are so far behind now is not because of now," Clyde Ross told me. "It's because of then." In the early 2000s, Charles Ogletree went to Tulsa, Oklahoma, to meet with the survivors of the 1921 race riot that had devastated "Black Wall Street." The past was not the past to them. "It was amazing seeing these black women and men who were crippled, blind, in wheelchairs," Ogletree told me. "I had no idea who they were and why they wanted to see me. They said, 'We want you to represent us in this lawsuit.'"

A commission authorized by the Oklahoma legislature produced a report affirming that the riot, the knowledge of which had been suppressed for years, had happened. But the lawsuit ultimately failed, in 2004. Similar suits pushed against corporations such as Aetna (which insured slaves) and Lehman Brothers (whose co-founding partner owned them) also have thus far failed. These results are dispiriting, but the crime with which reparations activists charge the country implicates more than just a few towns or corporations. The crime indicts the American people themselves, at every level, and in nearly every configuration. A crime that implicates the entire American people deserves its hearing in the legislative body that represents them.

John Conyers's HR 40 is the vehicle for that hearing. No one can know what would come out of such a debate. Perhaps no number can fully capture the multi-century plunder of black people in America. Perhaps the number is so large that it can't be imagined, let alone calculated and dispensed. But I believe that wrestling publicly with these questions matters as much as—if not more than—the specific answers that might be produced. An America that asks what it owes its most vulnerable citizens is improved and humane. An America that looks away is ignoring not just the sins of the past but the sins of the present and the certain sins of the future. More important than any single check cut to any African American, the payment of reparations would represent America's maturation out of the childhood myth of its innocence into a wisdom worthy of its founders.

In 2010, Jacob S. Rugh, then a doctoral candidate at Princeton, and the soci-   160
ologist Douglas S. Massey published a study of the recent foreclosure crisis.*
Among its drivers, they found an old foe: segregation. Black home buyers—
even after controlling for factors like creditworthiness—were still more likely
than white home buyers to be steered toward subprime loans.* Decades of
racist housing policies by the American government, along with decades of
racist housing practices by American businesses, had conspired to concentrate
African Americans in the same neighborhoods. As in North Lawndale half a
century earlier, these neighborhoods were filled with people who had been cut
off from mainstream financial institutions. When subprime lenders went looking for prey, they found black people waiting like ducks in a pen.

"High levels of segregation create a natural market for subprime lending,"
Rugh and Massey write, "and cause riskier mortgages, and thus foreclosures,
to accumulate disproportionately in racially segregated cities' minority
neighborhoods."

Plunder in the past made plunder in the present efficient. The banks of
America understood this. In 2005, Wells Fargo promoted a series of Wealth
Building Strategies seminars. Dubbing itself "the nation's leading originator
of home loans to ethnic minority customers," the bank enrolled black public
figures in an ostensible effort to educate blacks on building "generational
wealth." But the "wealth building" seminars were a front for wealth theft. In
2010, the Justice Department filed a discrimination suit against Wells Fargo
alleging that the bank had shunted blacks into predatory loans regardless of
their creditworthiness. This was not magic or coincidence or misfortune. It
was racism reifying itself. According to *The New York Times*, affidavits found
loan officers referring to their black customers as "mud people" and to their
subprime products as "ghetto loans."

"We just went right after them," Beth Jacobson, a former Wells Fargo loan
officer, told *The Times*. "Wells Fargo mortgage had an emerging-markets unit
that specifically targeted black churches because it figured church leaders had
a lot of influence and could convince congregants to take out subprime loans."

In 2011, Bank of America agreed to pay $355 million to settle charges of
discrimination against its Countrywide unit. The following year, Wells Fargo
settled its discrimination suit for more than $175 million. But the damage had
been done. In 2009, half the properties in Baltimore whose owners had been
granted loans by Wells Fargo between 2005 and 2008 were vacant; 71 percent
of these properties were in predominantly black neighborhoods.

(2014)

Questions

1. In Chicago, how did contract sellers profit from Black migrants look-
    ing to buy a home? How were neighborhoods kept segregated? What
    part did the government play?

2. What are the present-day results of the history of segregation delin-
    eated here by Coates?

3. How was the issue of reparations viewed in the eighteenth century?
    Are efforts being made to claim reparations now? What is HR 40, and
    why has it not been sufficiently supported?

4. How did the New Deal affect African Americans?

5. What are some of the practical suggestions that have been made to
    make reparations possible? What historical precedents are there? If
    the United States were to pursue reparations for African Americans,
    what do you think would be the best way to do so?

6. How do the three epigraphs for this essay begin the argument for
    reparations? Who wrote them? Why is their authorship significant?

7. What means did white people use to steal land from African
    Americans?

8. What did Clyde Ross find when he was stationed in California? What
    did he find in Mississippi when he returned after World War II?

9. What is redlining?

10. What was the Contract Buyers League? How did they seek justice?
    Were they successful?

11. How is slavery the basis of American democracy and wealth?

12. Anne-Marie Slaughter wrote a response to this essay in a Facebook
    post, 22 November 2015. She said: "I started reading Ta-Nehisi
    Coates' article ... firmly convinced that I was opposed to reparations
    ... I finished it convinced that he was right." What was your experi-
    ence reading this essay? Were you convinced by the arguments?

13. What are some of the reasons for resistance to reparations? What
    impact—positive and/or negative—would reparations have on
    American society?

from THE FIRST WHITE PRESIDENT

As the causes of Donald Trump's 2016 victory came to be explored in the months following the election, some observers pointed to how voting patterns for the candidates had differed on the basis of gender or education level. Many others pointed to various sorts of disaffection with educated coastal elites—disaffection that found expression among members of the white working class, the white middle class, and the white population of the "rustbelt" states in Middle America. The Coates essay below, which was published in late 2017, elucidates another cause: the degree to which whiteness itself was a common denominator for Trump supporters—and the degree to which Trump himself had based his appeal to voters on his whiteness.

The essay appeared almost simultaneously as the final piece in Coates's book We Were Eight Years in Power: An American Tragedy, *and as an article in the October 2017 issue of* The Atlantic. *There are numerous slight differences between the two versions; it is the book version that is reprinted here.*

It is insufficient to state the obvious of Donald Trump: that he is a white man who would not be president were it not for this fact. With one immediate exception, Trump's predecessors made their way to high office through the passive power of whiteness—that bloody heirloom which cannot ensure mastery of all events but can conjure a tailwind for most of them. Land theft and human plunder cleared the grounds for Trump's forefathers and barred others from it. Once upon the field, these men became soldiers, statesmen, and scholars; held court in Paris; presided at Princeton; advanced into the Wilderness and then into the White House. Their individual triumphs made this exclusive party seem above America's founding sins, and it was forgotten that the former was in fact bound to the latter, that all their victories had transpired on cleared grounds. No such elegant detachment can be attributed to Donald Trump—a president who, more than any other, has made the awful inheritance explicit.

His political career began in advocacy of birtherism,[1] that modern recasting of the old American precept that black people are not fit to be citizens of the

---

1   *birtherism*   Belief that Barack Obama is not a natural-born U.S. citizen and is therefore ineligible to hold the office of President. Obama released his birth certificate in 2008, but in 2011 was forced to release further evidence, including his long-form birth certificate, to combat continuing unfounded doubt.

country they built. But long before birtherism, Trump had made his worldview clear. He fought to keep blacks out of his buildings, according to the U.S. government; called for the death penalty for the eventually exonerated Central Park Five;[2] and railed against "lazy" black employees. "Black guys counting my money! I hate it," Trump was once quoted as saying. "The only kind of people I want counting my money are short guys that wear yarmulkes every day." After his cabal of conspiracy theorists forced Barack Obama to present his birth certificate, Trump demanded the president's college grades (offering $5 million in exchange for them), insisting that Obama was not intelligent enough to have gone to an Ivy League school, and that his acclaimed memoir, *Dreams from My Father*, had been ghostwritten by a white man, Bill Ayers.

It is often said that Trump has no real ideology, which is not true—his ideology is white supremacy, in all its truculent and sanctimonious power. Trump inaugurated his campaign by casting himself as the defender of white maidenhood against Mexican "rapists," only to be later alleged by multiple accusers, and by his own proud words, to be a sexual violator himself. White supremacy has always had a perverse sexual tint. Trump's rise was shepherded by Steve Bannon, a man who mocks his white male critics as "cucks." The word, derived from *cuckold*, is specifically meant to debase by fear and fantasy—the target is so weak that he would submit to the humiliation of having his white wife lie with black men. That the slur *cuck* casts white men as victims aligns with the dicta of whiteness, which seek to alchemize one's profligate sins into virtue. So it was with Virginia slaveholders claiming that Britain sought to make slaves of them. So it was with marauding Klansmen* organized against alleged rapes and other outrages. So it was with a candidate who called for a foreign power to hack his opponent's email and who now, as president, is claiming to be the victim of "the single greatest witch hunt of a politician in American history."

In Trump, white supremacists see one of their own. Only grudgingly did Trump denounce the Ku Klux Klan and David Duke, one of its former grand wizards*—and after the clashes between white supremacists and counterprotesters in Charlottesville, Virginia, in August, Duke in turn praised Trump's contentious claim that "both sides" were responsible for the violence.

5   To Trump, whiteness is neither notional nor symbolic but is the very core of his power. In this, Trump is not singular. But whereas his forebears carried whiteness like an ancestral talisman, Trump cracked the glowing amulet open, releasing its eldritch[3] energies. The repercussions are striking: Trump is the first

---

2   *Central Park Five*   Five teenagers—four African American and one Hispanic—who were wrongfully convicted of the violent assault and rape of a jogger in New York's Central Park in 1989.

3   *eldritch*   Sinister and supernatural.

president to have served in no public capacity before ascending to his perch. But more telling, Trump is also the first president to have publicly affirmed that his daughter is a "piece of ass." The mind seizes trying to imagine a black man extolling the virtues of sexual assault on tape ("When you're a star, they let you do it"), fending off multiple accusations of such assaults, immersed in multiple lawsuits for allegedly fraudulent business dealings, exhorting his followers to violence, and then strolling into the White House. But that is the point of white supremacy—to ensure that that which all others achieve with maximal effort, white people (particularly white men) achieve with minimal qualification. Barack Obama delivered to black people the hoary message that if they work twice as hard as white people, anything is possible. But Trump's counter is persuasive: Work half as hard as black people, and even more is possible.

For Trump, it almost seems that the fact of Obama, the fact of a black president, insulted him personally. The insult intensified when Obama and Seth Meyers publicly humiliated him at the White House Correspondents' Dinner in 2011.[4] But the bloody heirloom ensures the last laugh. Replacing Obama is not enough—Trump has made the negation of Obama's legacy the foundation of his own. And this too is whiteness. "Race is an idea, not a fact," the historian Nell Irvin Painter has written, and essential to the construct of a "white race" is the idea of not being a nigger. Before Barack Obama, niggers could be manufactured out of Sister Souljahs, Willie Hortons, and Dusky Sallys.[5] But Donald Trump arrived in the wake of something more potent—an entire nigger presidency with nigger health care, nigger climate accords, and nigger justice reform, all of which could be targeted for destruction or redemption, thus reifying the idea of being white. Trump truly is something new—the first president whose entire political existence hinges on the fact of a black president. And so it will not suffice to say that Trump is a white man like all the others who rose to become president. He must be called by his rightful honorific—America's first white president.

---

4 *Obama and ... 2011* At the White House Correspondents' Dinner—an event that usually incorporates a political comedy performance—comedian Seth Meyers openly mocked Trump's birtherism and his unsuitability as a presidential candidate. Obama also made jokes about birtherism.

5 *Sister Souljah* Black American author and activist (b. 1964) who became a subject of controversy when she made statements some interpreted as endorsing the killing of white people; *Willie Horton* African American who, in 1987 while serving a life sentence for murder, failed to return to prison after a weekend leave and committed armed robbery, assault, and rape before being recaptured; *Dusky Sally* Sally Hemings (1773–1835), a slave owned by President Thomas Jefferson, who was the father of her six children

The scope of Trump's commitment to whiteness is matched only by the depth of popular disbelief in the power of whiteness. We are now being told that support for Trump's "Muslim ban," his scapegoating of immigrants, his defenses of police brutality are somehow the natural outgrowth of the cultural and economic gap between Lena Dunham's America and Jeff Foxworthy's.[6] The collective verdict holds that the Democratic Party lost its way when it abandoned everyday economic issues like job creation for the softer fare of social justice. The indictment continues: To their neoliberal economics, Democrats and liberals have married a condescending elitist affect that sneers at blue-collar culture and mocks the white man as history's greatest monster and prime-time television's biggest doofus. In this rendition, Donald Trump is not the product of white supremacy so much as the product of a backlash against contempt for white working-class people.

"We so obviously despise them, we so obviously condescend to them," the conservative social scientist Charles Murray, who co-wrote *The Bell Curve*, recently told *The New Yorker*, speaking of the white working class. "The only slur you can use at a dinner party and get away with is to call somebody a redneck—that won't give you any problems in Manhattan."

"The utter contempt with which privileged Eastern liberals such as myself discuss red-state, gun-country, working-class America as ridiculous and morons and rubes," charged the celebrity chef Anthony Bourdain, "is largely responsible for the upswell of rage and contempt and desire to pull down the temple that we're seeing now."

10 That black people, who have lived for centuries under such derision and condescension, have not yet been driven into the arms of Trump does not trouble these theoreticians. After all, in this analysis, Trump's racism and the racism of his supporters are incidental to his rise. Indeed, the alleged glee with which liberals call out Trump's bigotry is assigned even more power than the bigotry itself. Ostensibly assaulted by campus protests, battered by arguments about intersectionality, and oppressed by new bathroom rights,[7] a blameless white working class did the only thing any reasonable polity might: elect an orcish* reality-television star who insists on taking his intelligence briefings in picture-book form.

Asserting that Trump's rise was primarily powered by cultural resentment and economic reversal has become de rigueur among white pundits and thought

6   *Lena Dunham*   White American actor, writer, and director (b. 1986) associated with the liberal elite;   *Jeff Foxworthy*   White American comedian (b. 1958) known as a self-described "redneck."

7   *bathroom rights*   Especially in 2016 and 2017, an intense controversy has surrounded the question of whether transgender people should be permitted to use the public bathrooms appropriate to their gender.

leaders. But evidence for this is, at best, mixed. In a study of preelection polling data, the Gallup researchers Jonathan Rothwell and Pablo Diego-Rosell
found that "people living in areas with diminished economic opportunity" were
"somewhat more likely to support Trump." But the researchers also found that
voters in their study who supported Trump generally had a higher mean household income ($81,898) than those who did not ($77,046). Those who approved
of Trump were "less likely to be unemployed and less likely to be employed
part-time" than those who did not. They also tended to be from areas that were
very white: "The racial and ethnic isolation of whites at the zip code* level is
one of the strongest predictors of Trump support."

An analysis of exit polls conducted during the presidential primaries estimated the median household income of Trump supporters to be about $72,000.
But even this lower number is almost double the median household income of
African Americans, and $15,000 above the American median. Trump's white
support was not determined by income. According to Edison Research, Trump
won whites making less than $50,000 by 20 points, whites making $50,000
to $99,999 by 28 points, and whites making $100,000 or more by 14 points.
This shows that Trump assembled a broad white coalition that ran the gamut
from Joe the Dishwasher to Joe the Plumber[8] to Joe the Banker. So when white
pundits cast the elevation of Trump as the handiwork of an inscrutable white
working class, they are being too modest, declining to claim credit for their
own economic class. Trump's dominance among whites across class lines is
of a piece with his larger dominance across nearly every white demographic.
Trump won white women (+9) and white men (+31). He won white people with
college degrees (+3) and white people without them (+37). He won whites ages
18–29 (+4), 30–44 (+17), 45–64 (+28), and 65 and older (+19). Trump won
whites in midwestern Illinois (+11), whites in mid-Atlantic New Jersey (+12),
and whites in the Sun Belt's New Mexico (+5). In no state that Edison polled
did Trump's white support dip below 40 percent. Hillary Clinton's did, in states
as disparate as Florida, Utah, Indiana, and Kentucky. From the beer track to
the wine track, from soccer moms to NASCAR dads, Trump's performance
among whites was dominant. According to *Mother Jones*, based on preelection
polling data, if you tallied the popular vote of only white America to derive
2016 electoral votes, Trump would have defeated Clinton 389 to 81, with the
remaining 68 votes either a toss-up or unknown.

Part of Trump's dominance among whites resulted from his running as
a Republican, the party that has long cultivated white voters. Trump's share

---

8   *Joe the Plumber*   Activist Samuel Joseph Wurzelbacher (b. 1973) became famous as
"Joe the Plumber" during the 2008 presidential campaign, when he appeared frequently in
support of the Republican candidate.

of the white vote was similar to Mitt Romney's in 2012. But unlike Romney, Trump secured this support by running against his party's leadership, against accepted campaign orthodoxy, and against all notions of decency. By his sixth month in office, embroiled in scandal after scandal, a Pew Research Center poll found Trump's approval rating underwater with every single demographic group. Every demographic group, that is, except one: people who identified as white.

The focus on one subsector of Trump voters—the white working class—is puzzling, given the breadth of his white coalition. Indeed, there is a kind of theater at work in which Trump's presidency is pawned off as a product of the white working class as opposed to a product of an entire whiteness that includes the very authors doing the pawning. The motive is clear: escapism. To accept that the bloody heirloom remains potent even now, some five decades after Martin Luther King Jr. was gunned down on a Memphis balcony—even after a black president; indeed, strengthened by the fact of that black president—is to accept that racism remains, as it has since 1776, at the heart of this country's political life. The idea of acceptance frustrates the left. The left would much rather have a discussion about class struggles, which might entice the white working masses, instead of about the racist struggles that those same masses have historically been the agents and beneficiaries of. Moreover, to accept that whiteness brought us Donald Trump is to accept whiteness as an existential danger to the country and the world. But if the broad and remarkable white support for Donald Trump can be reduced to the righteous anger of a noble class of smallville firefighters and evangelicals, mocked by Brooklyn hipsters and womanist professors into voting against their interests, then the threat of racism and whiteness, the threat of the heirloom, can be dismissed. Consciences can be eased; no deeper existential reckoning is required....

15   When David Duke, the former grand wizard of the Ku Klux Klan, shocked the country in 1990 by almost winning one of Louisiana's seats in the U.S. Senate, the apologists came out once again. They elided the obvious—that Duke had appealed to the racist instincts of a state whose schools are, at this very moment, still desegregating—and instead decided that something else was afoot. "There is a tremendous amount of anger and frustration among working-class whites, particularly where there is an economic downturn," a researcher told the *Los Angeles Times*. "These people feel left out; they feel government is not responsive to them." By this logic, postwar America—with its booming economy and low unemployment—should have been an egalitarian utopia and not the violently segregated country it actually was.

But this was the past made present. It was not important to the apologists that a large swath of Louisiana's white population thought it was a good idea to send a white supremacist who once fronted a terrorist organization to the nation's capital. Nor was it important that blacks in Louisiana had long felt left out. What was important was the fraying of an ancient bargain, and the potential degradation of white workers to the level of "negers."[9] "A viable left must find a way to differentiate itself strongly from such analysis," David Roediger, the University of Kansas professor, has written.

That challenge of differentiation has largely been ignored. Instead, an imagined white working class remains central to our politics and to our cultural understanding of those politics, not simply when it comes to addressing broad economic issues but also when it comes to addressing racism. At its most sympathetic, this belief holds that most Americans—regardless of race—are exploited by an unfettered capitalist economy. The key, then, is to address those broader patterns that afflict the masses of all races; the people who suffer from those patterns more than others (blacks, for instance) will benefit disproportionately from that which benefits everyone. "These days, what ails working-class and middle-class blacks and Latinos is not fundamentally different from what ails their white counterparts," Senator Barack Obama wrote in 2006:

> Downsizing, outsourcing, automation, wage stagnation, the dismantling of employer-based health-care and pension plans, and schools that fail to teach young people the skills they need to compete in a global economy.

Obama allowed that "blacks in particular have been vulnerable to these trends"—but less because of racism than for reasons of geography and job-sector distribution. This notion—raceless antiracism—marks the modern left, from the New Democrat Bill Clinton to the socialist Bernie Sanders. Few national liberal politicians have shown any recognition that there is something systemic and particular in the relationship between black people and their country that might require specific policy solutions.

In 2016, Hillary Clinton acknowledged the existence of systemic racism more explicitly than any of her modern Democratic predecessors. She had to—black voters remembered too well the previous Clinton administration, as well as her previous campaign. While her husband's administration had touted the rising-tide theory of economic growth, it did so while slashing welfare and getting "tough on crime," a phrase that stood for specific policies but also served as rhetorical bait for white voters. One is tempted to excuse Hillary Clinton from

---

9   *negers*   Reference to an earlier portion of the article not excerpted here, in which Coates suggests that eighteenth-century white workers were motivated by a fear of "'being mistaken for slaves, or "negers" or "negurs."'" ("Neger" is a word used in reference to Black people in several languages, including Dutch and German; its degree of offensiveness varies depending on the language, context, and culture in which it is shared.)

having to answer for the sins of her husband. But in her 2008 campaign, she evoked the old dichotomy between white workers and loafing blacks, claiming to be the representative of "hardworking Americans, white Americans." By the end of the 2008 primary campaign against Barack Obama, her advisers were hoping someone would uncover an apocryphal "whitey tape," in which an angry Michelle Obama was alleged to have used the slur. During Bill Clinton's presidential-reelection campaign in the mid-1990s, Hillary Clinton herself had endorsed the "super-predator" theory of William J. Bennett, John P. Walters, and John J. DiIulio Jr. This theory cast "inner-city" children of that era as "almost completely unmoralized" and the font of "a new generation of street criminals ... the youngest, biggest and baddest generation any society has ever known." The "baddest generation" did not become super-predators. But by 2016, they were young adults, many of whom judged Hillary Clinton's newfound consciousness to be lacking.

It's worth asking why the country has not been treated to a raft of sympathetic portraits of this "forgotten" young black electorate, forsaken by a Washington bought off by Davos[10] elites and special interests. The unemployment rate for young blacks (20.6 percent) in July 2016 was double that of young whites (9.9 percent). And since the late 1970s, William Julius Wilson and other social scientists following in his wake have noted the disproportionate effect that the decline in manufacturing jobs has had on African American communities. If anyone should be angered by the devastation wreaked by the financial sector and a government that declined to prosecute the perpetrators, it is African Americans—the housing crisis was one of the primary drivers in the past 20 years of the wealth gap between black families and the rest of the country. But the cultural condescension toward and economic anxiety of black people is not news. Toiling blacks are in their proper state; toiling whites raise the specter of white slavery.

20   Moreover, a narrative of long-neglected working-class black voters, injured by globalization and the financial crisis, forsaken by out-of-touch politicians, and rightfully suspicious of a return of Clintonism, does not serve to cleanse the conscience of white people for having elected Donald Trump. Only the idea of a long-suffering white working class can do that. And though much has been written about the distance between elites and "Real America," the existence of a class-transcending, mutually dependent tribe of white people is evident.

Joe Biden, then the vice president, last year:

"They're all the people I grew up with ... And they're not racist. They're not sexist."

---

10 *Davos* Town in Switzerland that hosts the World Economic Forum, an annual meeting attended by people who possess economic or political power on a global scale.

Bernie Sanders, senator and former candidate for president, last year:

"I come from the white working class, and I am deeply humiliated that the Democratic Party cannot talk to the people where I came from."

Nicholas Kristof, the *New York Times* columnist, in February of this year:

My hometown, Yamhill, Ore., a farming community, is Trump country, and I have many friends who voted for Trump. I think they're profoundly wrong, but please don't dismiss them as hateful bigots.

... Certainly not every Trump voter is a white supremacist, just as not every white person in the Jim Crow South* was a white supremacist. But every Trump voter felt it acceptable to hand the fate of the country over to one.

One can, to some extent, understand politicians' embracing a self-serving 25 identity politics. Candidates for high office, such as Sanders, have to cobble together a coalition. The white working class is seen, understandably, as a large cache of potential votes, and capturing these votes requires eliding uncomfortable truths. But journalists have no such excuse. Again and again in the past year, Nicholas Kristof could be found pleading with his fellow liberals not to dismiss his old comrades in the white working class as bigots—even when their bigotry was evidenced in his own reporting. A visit to Tulsa, Oklahoma, finds Kristof wondering why Trump voters support a president who threatens to cut the programs they depend on. But the problem, according to Kristof's interviewees, isn't Trump's attack on benefits so much as an attack on *their* benefits. "There's a lot of wasteful spending, so cut other places," one man tells Kristof. When Kristof pushes his subjects to identify that wasteful spending, a fascinating target is revealed: "Obama phones," the products of a fevered conspiracy theory that turned a long-standing government program into a scheme through which the then-president gave away free cellphones to undeserving blacks....

... [A]ny empirical evaluation of the relationship between Trump and the white working class would reveal that one adjective in that phrase is doing more work than the other. In 2016, Trump enjoyed majority or plurality support among every economic branch of whites. It is true that his strongest support among whites came from those making $50,000 to $99,999. This would be something more than working-class in many nonwhite neighborhoods, but even if one accepts that branch as the working class, the difference between how various groups in this income bracket voted is revealing. Sixty-one percent of whites in this "working class" supported Trump. Only 24 percent of Hispanics and 11 percent of blacks did. Indeed, the plurality of all voters making less than $100,000 and the majority making less than $50,000 voted for the Democratic candidate. So when Packer laments the fact that "Democrats can no longer really claim to be the party of working people—not white ones, anyway," he commits a kind of category error. The real problem is that Democrats aren't the party of white people—working or otherwise. White workers are not divided by the fact of labor from other white demographics; they are divided from all other laborers by the fact of their whiteness....

The dent of racism is not hard to detect in West Virginia. In the 2008 Democratic primary there, 95 percent of the voters were white. Twenty percent of those—one in five—openly admitted that race was influencing their vote, and more than 80 percent voted for Hillary Clinton over Barack Obama. Four years later, the incumbent Obama lost the primary in 10 counties to Keith Judd, a white felon incarcerated in a federal prison; Judd racked up more than 40 percent of the Democratic-primary vote in the state. A simple thought experiment: Can one imagine a black felon in a federal prison running in a primary against an incumbent white president doing so well? ...

The triumph of Trump's campaign of bigotry presented the problematic spectacle of an American president succeeding at best in spite of his racism and possibly because of it. Trump moved racism from the euphemistic and plausibly deniable to the overt and freely claimed. This presented the country's thinking class with a dilemma. Hillary Clinton simply could not be correct when she asserted that a large group of Americans was endorsing a candidate because of bigotry. The implications—that systemic bigotry is still central to our politics; that the country is susceptible to such bigotry; that the salt-of-the-earth Americans whom we lionize in our culture and politics are not so different from those same Americans who grin back at us in lynching* photos; that Calhoun's aim of a pan-Caucasian embrace between workers and capitalists[11] still endures—were just too dark. Leftists would have to cope with the failure, yet again, of class unity in the face of racism. Incorporating all of this into an analysis of America and the path forward proved too much to ask. Instead, the response has largely been an argument aimed at emotion—the summoning of the white working class, emblem of America's hardscrabble roots, inheritor of its pioneer spirit, as a shield against the horrific and empirical evidence of trenchant bigotry....

When Barack Obama came into office, in 2009, he believed that he could work with "sensible" conservatives by embracing aspects of their policy as his own. Instead he found that his very imprimatur made that impossible. Senate

---

11   *Calhoun's ... capitalists*   In an earlier portion of the essay not excerpted here, Coates quotes an 1848 statement by Senator John C. Calhoun that "[w]ith [America] the two great divisions of society are not the rich and poor, but white and black; and all the former, the poor as well as the rich, belong to the upper class, and are respected and treated as equals."

Minority Leader Mitch McConnell announced that the GOP's[12] primary goal was not to find common ground but to make Obama a "one-term president." A health-care plan inspired by Romneycare[13] was, when proposed by Obama, suddenly considered socialist and, not coincidentally, a form of reparations. The first black president found that he was personally toxic to the GOP base. An entire political party was organized around the explicit aim of negating one man. It was thought by Obama and some of his allies that this toxicity was the result of a relentless assault waged by Fox News and right-wing talk radio. Trump's genius was to see that it was something more, that it was a hunger for revanche[14] so strong that a political novice and accused rapist could topple the leadership of one major party and throttle the heavily favored nominee of the other.

"I could stand in the middle of Fifth Avenue and shoot somebody and I wouldn't lose any voters," Trump bragged in January 2016. This statement should be met with only a modicum of skepticism. Trump has mocked the disabled, withstood multiple accusations of sexual violence (all of which he has denied), fired an FBI director, sent his minions to mislead the public about his motives, personally exposed those lies by boldly stating his aim to scuttle an investigation into his possible collusion with a foreign power, then bragged about that same obstruction to representatives of that same foreign power. It is utterly impossible to conjure a black facsimile of Donald Trump—to imagine Obama, say, implicating an opponent's father in the assassination of an American president or comparing his physical endowment with that of another candidate and then successfully capturing the presidency. Trump, more than any other politician, understood the valence of the bloody heirloom and the great power in not being a nigger....

... Before the election, Obama found no takers among Republicans for a bipartisan response, and Obama himself, underestimating Trump and thus underestimating the power of whiteness, believed the Republican nominee too objectionable to actually win. In this Obama was, tragically, wrong. And so the most powerful country in the world has handed over all its affairs—the prosperity of its entire economy; the security of its 300 million citizens; the purity of its water, the viability of its air, the safety of its food; the future of its vast system of education; the soundness of its national highways, airways, and railways; the apocalyptic potential of its nuclear arsenal—to a carnival barker

30

---

12 *GOP* Acronym that is used to refer to the Republican party.
13 *Romneycare* Health care reform law passed in Massachusetts while Republican Mitt Romney was governor of the state.
14 *revanche* Attempt to recover lost territory.

who introduced the phrase *grab 'em by the pussy*[15] into the national lexicon. It is as if the white tribe united in demonstration to say, "If a black man can be president, then any white man—no matter how fallen—can be president." ...

The American tragedy now being wrought is larger than most imagine and will not end with Trump. In recent times, whiteness as an overt political tactic has been restrained by a kind of cordiality that held that its overt invocation would scare off "moderate" whites. This has proved to be only half true at best. Trump's legacy will be exposing the patina of decency for what it is and revealing just how much a demagogue can get away with. It does not take much to imagine another politician, wiser in the ways of Washington and better schooled in the methodology of governance—and now liberated from the pretense of antiracist civility—doing a much more effective job than Trump.

It has long been an axiom among certain black writers and thinkers that while whiteness endangers the bodies of black people in the immediate sense, the larger threat is to white people themselves, the shared country, and even the whole world. There is an impulse to blanch at this sort of grandiosity. When W.E.B. Du Bois claims that slavery was "singularly disastrous for modern civilization" or James Baldwin claims that whites "have brought humanity to the edge of oblivion: because they think they are white,"[16] the instinct is to cry exaggeration. But there really is no other way to read the presidency of Donald Trump. The first white president in American history is also the most dangerous president—and he is made more dangerous still by the fact that those charged with analyzing him cannot name his essential nature, because they too are implicated in it.

(2017)

Questions

1. Coates makes frequent reference in this essay to the metaphor of the "bloody heirloom." What is it? What does this metaphor imply?

---

15 *grab 'em by the pussy* A month before the 2016 presidential election, a video was released in which Trump described sexually assaulting women, saying, "Grab them by the pussy. You can do anything."

16 *singularly ... civilization* From W.E.B. Du Bois, *Black Reconstruction in America* (1935); *"have brought ... are white"* From James Baldwin, "On Being White and Other Lies" (1984). Both Baldwin and Du Bois were prominent Black intellectuals, and their writing appears elsewhere in this anthology.

2.   What does Coates mean when he calls Trump "America's first white president"? In your view, is he right to distinguish Trump from all other white presidents in this way?

3.   How does Coates critique the common assertion that Trump's election is "the product of a backlash against contempt for white working-class people"? After considering Coates's critique, do you think there is any merit to this assertion?

4.   Why, according to Coates, does the white liberal left want to believe that Trump's election was not a result of widespread racism?

5.   Coates claims that "[i]t is utterly impossible to conjure a black facsimile of Donald Trump" (paragraph 30). Choose a few of Trump's actions or attributes and discuss how the electorate likely would have perceived them in a Black candidate.

6.   In paragraph 12, Coates incorporates a large number of statistics. Evaluate the rhetorical effectiveness of this approach.

7.   Coates summarizes the narrative suggesting Trump's election is the result of white working-class disillusionment:

     Ostensibly assaulted by campus protests, battered by arguments about intersectionality, and oppressed by new bathroom rights, a blameless white working class did the only thing any reasonable polity might: elect an orcish reality-television star who insists on taking his intelligence briefings in picture-book form (paragraph 10).

     Evaluate this as a persuasive sentence. Is the argument fair and accurate? What (if any) rhetorical strategies does it employ, and how effective are they?

ROXANE GAY

THE POLITICS OF RESPECTABILITY

Writer, editor, and academic Roxane Gay is known primarily for her acclaimed fiction and memoir, her opinion pieces appearing regularly in publications such as the New York Times, *and her bestselling 2014 essay collection* Bad Feminist. *The essays in* Bad Feminist *draw on critical theory and on her personal experience as a bisexual Haitian American woman, examining issues such as abortion rights and racism together with elements of popular culture as diverse as the films of Quentin Tarantino, the hit song "Blurred Lines," and the world of competitive Scrabble. The following essay addresses the subject of respectability politics.*

When a black person behaves in a way that doesn't fit the dominant cultural ideal of how a black person should be, there is all kinds of trouble. The authenticity of his or her blackness is immediately called into question. We should be black but not too black, neither too ratchet nor too bougie.[1] There are all manner of unspoken rules of how a black person should think and act and behave, and the rules are ever changing.

We hold all people to unspoken rules about who and how they should be, how they should think, and what they should say. We say we hate stereotypes but take issue when people deviate from those stereotypes. Men don't cry. Feminists don't shave their legs. Southerners are racist. Everyone is, by virtue of being human, some kind of rule breaker, and my goodness, do we hate when the rules are broken.

Black people often seem to be held to a particularly unreasonable standard. Prominent figures have a troubling habit of coming forward with maxims about

---

1   *ratchet* Slang: displaying characteristics that are generally unrefined or lacking structure; *bougie* Slang: displaying characteristics associated with affluence, especially when pretending to be from a wealthier class than one actually is.

how black people should be and behave. One such person is Bill Cosby.[2] In an op-ed for the *New York Post*, Cosby identified apathy as one of the black community's biggest problems. If we just care enough about ourselves and our communities, we will reach a hallowed place where we will no longer suffer the effects of racism. Most of Cosby's commentary on race, in recent years, might be summarized as such: if we act right, we will finally be good enough for white people to love us.

CNN anchor Don Lemon offered five suggestions for the black community to overcome racism: black people should stop using the N-word, black people should respect their communities by not littering, black people should stay in school, black people should have fewer children out of wedlock, and, most inexplicably, young black men should pull their pants up. Lemon also offered anecdotal evidence that he rarely sees people litter in white communities. He then played on the assumption of homophobia, explaining, with regard to sagging pants, that "in fact, it comes from prison. When they take away belts from prisoners so they can't make a weapon. And then it evolved into which role each prisoner would have during male-on-male prison sex." Implicit in Lemon's argument was that the white, heterosexual man is the cultural ideal toward which we should all aspire—curious thinking from Lemon.[3]

Cosby, Lemon, and others who espouse similar ideas are, I would like to believe, coming from a good place. Their suggestions are, on one level, reasonable, mostly grounded in common sense, but these leaders traffic in respectability politics—the idea that if black (or other marginalized) people simply behave in "culturally approved" ways, if we mimic the dominant culture, it will be more difficult to suffer the effects of racism. Respectability politics completely overlook institutional racism and the ways in which the education system, the social welfare system, and the justice system only reinforce many of the problems the black community faces.

We are having an ongoing and critical conversation about race in America. The question on many minds, the question that is certainly on my mind, is how do we prevent racial injustices from happening? How do we protect young black children? How do we overcome so many of the institutional barriers that exacerbate racism and poverty?

₅

---

2   *Bill Cosby*   Black comedian and actor (b. 1937) known for his positive representations of Black Americans; he has made controversial public statements chastising Black people for perceived failures in parenting and moral responsibility. This essay was published before Cosby's reputation as a moralist was significantly altered by the emergence of accusations that he had drugged and raped or sexually assaulted more than fifty women.

3   *curious thinking from Lemon*   Lemon came out as gay in 2011.

It's a nice idea that we could simply follow a prescribed set of rules and make the world a better place for all. It's a nice idea that racism is a finite problem for which there is a finite solution, and that respectability, perhaps, could have saved all the people who have lost their lives to the effects of racism.

But we don't live in that world and it's dangerous to suggest that the targets of oppression are wholly responsible for ending that oppression. Respectability politics suggest that there's a way for us to all be model (read: like white) citizens. We can always be better, but will we ever be ideal? Do we even want to be ideal or is there a way for us to become more comfortably human?

Take, for example, someone like Don Lemon. He is a black man, raised by a single mother, and now he is a successful news anchor for a major news network. His outlook seems driven by the notion that if he can make it, anyone can. This is the ethos espoused by people who believe in respectability politics. Because they have achieved success, because they have transcended, in some way, the effects of racism or other forms of discrimination, all people should be able to do the same.

In truth, they have climbed a ladder and shattered a glass ceiling but are seemingly uninterested in extending that ladder as far as it needs to reach so that others may climb. They are uninterested in providing a detailed blueprint for how they achieved their success. They are unwilling to consider that until the institutional problems are solved, no blueprint for success can possibly exist. For real progress to be made, leaders like Lemon and Cosby need to at least acknowledge reality.

Respectability politics are not the answer to ending racism. Racism doesn't care about respectability, wealth, education, or status. Oprah Winfrey, one of the wealthiest people in the world and certainly the wealthiest black woman in the world, openly discusses the racism she continues to encounter in her daily life. In July 2013, while in Zurich to attend Tina Turner's wedding, Winfrey was informed by a store clerk at the Trois Pommes boutique that the purse she was interested in was too expensive for her. We don't need to cry for Oprah, prevented from buying an obscenely overpriced purse, but we can recognize the incident as one more reminder that racism is so pervasive and pernicious that we will never be respectable enough to outrun racism, not here in the United States, not anywhere in the world.

We must stop pointing to the exceptions—these bright shining stars who transcend circumstance. We must look at how we can best support the least among us, not spend all our time blindly revering and trying to mimic the greatest without demanding systemic change.

In July 2013, President Obama made a historic speech about race. His remarks were, by far, the most explicit remarks the president has made on the subject. In addition to sharing his own experiences with racism, he offered suggestions about how we might improve race relations in the United States—ending racial profiling, reexamining state and local laws that might contribute to tragedies like Trayvon Martin's[4] murder, and finding more effective ways to support black boys. These suggestions are a bit vague (and black girls seem to be forgotten, as if they too don't need support), but at least Obama's ideas place the responsibility for change on all of us. We are, after all, supposed to be one nation indivisible. Only if we act as such, might we begin to truly effect change.

(2014)

Questions

1. Gay begins the essay by noting the following:

    When a black person behaves in a way that doesn't fit the dominant cultural ideal of how a black person should be, there is all kinds of trouble. The authenticity of his or her blackness is immediately called into question. We should be black but not too black, neither too ratchet nor too bougie. There are all manner of unspoken rules of how a black person should think and act and behave, and the rules are ever changing.

    Who makes the "rules" that Gay speaks about here?

2. What are "respectability politics"? What, according to Gay, is wrong with this way of thinking?

3. Find and explain a recent example of respectability politics being enacted or resisted in politics or popular culture.

4. In his essay "Lifting as We Climb" (*Harper's Magazine*, 2015), Randall Kennedy offers "[a] progressive defense of respectability politics." Consider the following passage from Kennedy's essay:

    [There] is an oft-heard critique of the politics of respectability: that it wrongly shifts attention from illegitimate social conditions to the perceived deficiencies of those victimized by those conditions. We err, however, in forcing a Manichaean [i.e., binary]

---

4   *Trayvon Martin*   Seventeen-year-old Black teenager who was fatally shot without cause by a neighborhood watch coordinator in Florida in 2012.

choice between outward-facing protest and inward-facing character building.... In demanding more of African Americans, most proponents of black respectability politics are not "letting the oppressor off the hook." They are being realistic in telling blacks that the support or at least the acceptance of many whites is necessary to enact policies that will bring about substantial positive change.

To what extent (if at all) does the argument advanced in this paragraph effectively challenge Gay's claims? What, if any, place should respectability politics have in the pursuit of social justice for Black Americans?

5. Read one of the following pieces also included in this anthology: Olaudah Equiano's *The Interesting Narrative of the Life of Olaudah Equiano*, Pauline Hopkins's "Hon. Frederick Douglass," Booker T. Washington's "Speech Delivered at the Cotton States and International Exposition," Martin Luther King Jr.'s "Letter from Birmingham Jail" Barack Obama's "A More Perfect Union," or Bettina Love's *Hip Hop's Li'l Sistas Speak*.

   a. To what extent (if at all) does the piece you chose engage in respectability politics as described by Gay?

   b. How does the choice to engage in—or to resist—respectability politics affect the persuasive impact of the piece you chose?

I SELL THE SHADOW TO SUPPORT THE
SUBSTANCE.

SOJOURNER TRUTH.

Photograph of Sojourner Truth, 1864. Sojourner Truth sold souvenir photographs such as these, known as *cartes de visite*, as a means of financing her speaking tours. Usually, photographers held copyright over the portraits they took, but Truth obtained copyright over her own images, to which she attached the caption "I sell the shadow to support the substance." *Cartes de visite* were typically very small; the original image reproduced here is about 3.25 inches high.

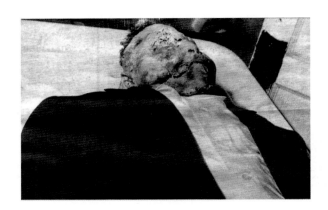

(Left) Photograph of Emmett Till taken by his mother; and (above) photograph of the body of Emmett Till before his funeral, from *The Chicago Defender*, 1955. Emmett Till was fourteen years old in 1955, when he was murdered and mutilated by a white mob after a white woman falsely accused him of attempting to flirt with her. Till became an icon of the Civil Rights Movement when his mother, Mamie Till-Mobley, held a public open-casket funeral to display the brutality of the violence committed against him: as she later explained, "The whole nation had to bear witness to this." Tens of thousands of people viewed Till's body, and photographs showing his mutilation were printed in *The American Negro: A Magazine of Protest*, *Jet* magazine, and the *Chicago Defender*, all publications with a predominantly Black readership. (No publications with a predominantly white readership printed images of Till's body.) The photographs prompted many African Americans to take a more active role in the Civil Rights Movement.

Gordon Parks, *Ondria Tanner and Her Grandmother Window-shopping, Mobile, Alabama, 1956*. This photograph was taken by African American photographer and filmmaker Gordon Parks while on assignment for *Life* magazine, which had sent him to document segregation in the South.

Kehinde Wiley, portrait of Barack Obama, 2018. This painting, Obama's official presidential portrait, is held by the Smithsonian's National Portrait Gallery.

Amy Sherald, portrait of Michelle LaVaughn Robinson Obama, 2018. This painting, the official portrait of the former first lady, is held by the Smithsonian's National Portrait Gallery.

Whitney Curtis, *Rashaad Davis, 23, backs away slowly as St. Louis County police officers approach him with guns drawn and eventually arrest him on Monday, Aug. 11, 2014, at the corner of Canfield Drive and West Florissant Avenue in Ferguson, Missouri*. This photograph, which originally appeared in *The New York Times*, was taken during the weeks of protest that followed the killing of Michael Brown, an unarmed Black teenager, by a police officer who shot him at least six times.

Jonathan Bachman, *Police arrest Leshia Evans at a protest over the police shooting death of Alton Sterling in Baton Rouge on July 9, 2016*. This photograph, depicting the arrest of New York City nurse Leshia Evans in a protest against police brutality, has become an iconic image of the Black Lives Matter movement.

Harriet Powers, *Pictorial Quilt*, 1895–98. Harriet Powers, born into slavery in 1837, is considered one of the most accomplished quilters in the nineteenth-century American Southern tradition. This quilt—one of her two known surviving works—depicts a series of biblical and historical events. Powers's own descriptions of the panels can be found on the website of the Boston Museum of Fine Arts, where the quilt is displayed.

from CITIZEN: AN AMERICAN LYRIC

In 2014, for the first time in the history of the National Book Critics Circle Awards, the same book was nominated in two different categories: Claudia Rankine's Citizen, *a short, heavily illustrated book exploring various aspects of African American experience in unconventional ways, was a finalist in the Criticism category, and the winner in the Poetry category.*

The excerpt included here is the second of the book's seven, unnamed chapters.

Hennessy Youngman aka Jayson Musson, whose *Art Thoughtz* take the form of tutorials on YouTube, educates viewers on contemporary art issues. In one of his many videos, he addresses how to become a successful black artist, wryly suggesting black people's anger is marketable. He advises black artists to cultivate "an angry nigger exterior"* by watching, among other things, the Rodney King video[1] while working.

Youngman's suggestions are meant to expose expectations for blackness as well as to underscore the difficulty inherent in any attempt by black artists to metabolize real rage. The commodified anger his video advocates rests lightly on the surface for spectacle's sake. It can be engaged or played like the race card* and is tied solely to the performance of blackness and not to the emotional state of particular individuals in particular situations.

On the bridge between this sellable anger and "the artist" resides, at times, an actual anger. Youngman in his video doesn't address this type of anger: the anger built up through experience and the quotidian struggles against dehumanization every brown or black person lives simply because of skin color. This other kind of anger in time can prevent, rather than sponsor, the production of anything except loneliness.

---

1   *the Rodney King video*   Video footage from 3 March 1991 showed the violent beating of African American taxi driver Rodney King (1965–2012) by four white Los Angeles police officers. The event heightened awareness of racism in law enforcement, and the subsequent acquittal of the police officers prompted the 1992 Los Angeles Riots.

You begin to think, maybe erroneously, that this other kind of anger is really a type of knowledge: the type that both clarifies and disappoints. It responds to insult and attempted erasure simply by asserting presence, and the energy required to present, to react, to assert is accompanied by visceral disappointment: a disappointment in the sense that no amount of visibility will alter the ways in which one is perceived.

5   Recognition of this lack might break you apart. Or recognition might illuminate the erasure the attempted erasure triggers. Whether such discerning creates a healthier, if more isolated self, you can't know. In any case, Youngman doesn't speak to this kind of anger. He doesn't say that witnessing the expression of this more ordinary and daily anger might make the witness believe that a person is "insane."

And insane is what you think, one Sunday afternoon, drinking an Arnold Palmer,* watching the 2009 Women's US Open semifinal, when brought to full attention by the suddenly explosive behavior of Serena Williams.[2] Serena in HD before your eyes becomes overcome by a rage you recognize and have been taught to hold at a distance for your own good. Serena's behavior, on this particular Sunday afternoon, suggests that all the injustice she has played through all the years of her illustrious career flashes before her and she decides finally to respond to all of it with a string of invectives. Nothing, not even the repetition of negations ("no, no, no") she employed in a similar situation years before as a younger player at the 2004 US Open, prepares you for this. Oh my God, she's gone crazy, you say to no one.

What does a victorious or defeated black woman's body in a historically white space look like? Serena and her big sister Venus Williams brought to mind Zora Neale Hurston's[3] "I feel most colored when I am thrown against a sharp white background." This appropriated line, stenciled on canvas by Glenn Ligon, who used plastic letter stencils, smudging oil sticks, and graphite to transform the words into abstractions, seemed to be ad copy[4] for some aspect of life for all black bodies.

Hurston's statement has been played out on the big screen by Serena and Venus: they win sometimes, they lose sometimes, they've been injured, they've been happy, they've been sad, ignored, booed mightily (see Indian

---

2   *US Open* One of the four most important annual tennis tournaments, which together comprise the Grand Slam; *Serena Williams* African American tennis player (b. 1981), often considered the best female tennis player of all time.

3   *Zora Neale Hurston* African American writer (1891–1960), best known for her novel *Their Eyes Were Watching God* (1937). The quotation here appears in her essay "How It Feels to Be Colored Me," also included in this anthology.

4   *Glenn Ligon* African American artist (b. 1960); *ad copy* Text of an advertisement.

Wells,[5] which both sisters have boycotted for more than a decade), they've been cheered, and through it all and evident to all were those people who are enraged they are there at all—graphite against a sharp white background.

For years you attribute to Serena Williams a kind of resilience appropriate only for those who exist in celluloid. Neither her father nor her mother nor her sister nor Jehovah her God nor NIKE camp could shield her ultimately from people who felt her black body didn't belong on their court, in their world. From the start many made it clear Serena would have done better struggling to survive in the two-dimensionality of a Millet painting, rather than on their tennis court—better to put all that strength to work in their fantasy of her working the land, rather than be caught up in the turbulence of our ancient dramas, like a ship fighting a storm in a Turner[6] seascape.

The most notorious of Serena's detractors takes the form of Mariana Alves, the distinguished tennis chair umpire.[7] In 2004 Alves was excused from officiating any more matches on the final day of the US Open after she made five bad calls against Serena in her quarterfinal matchup against fellow American Jennifer Capriati. The serves and returns Alves called out were landing, stunningly unreturned by Capriati, inside the lines, no discerning eyesight needed. Commentators, spectators, television viewers, line judges, everyone could see the balls were good, everyone, apparently, except Alves. No one could understand what was happening. Serena, in her denim skirt, black sneaker boots, and dark mascara, began wagging her finger and saying "no, no, no," as if by negating the moment she could propel us back into a legible world. Tennis superstar John McEnroe,[8] given his own keen eye for injustice during his professional career, was shocked that Serena was able to hold it together after losing the match.

Though no one was saying anything explicitly about Serena's black body, you are not the only viewer who thought it was getting in the way of Alves's sight line. One commentator said he hoped he wasn't being unkind when he stated, "Capriati wins it with the help of the umpires and the line judges." A

10

5   *Indian Wells*   Tennis tournament held annually in Indian Wells, California. In 2001, the Williams sisters and their father Richard Williams were booed, and some in the crowd shouted racial slurs.

6   *Millet*   Jean-François Millet (1815–75), French painter best known for works depicting peasant farmers;   *Turner*   J.M.W. Turner (1775–1851), English painter known for his evocative landscapes. (Rankine includes reproductions of his painting *Slave Ship* and of a detail from the painting as the final images in *Citizen*.)

7   *chair umpire*   In tennis, person who holds final authority to decide questions and disputes during a match.

8   *John McEnroe*   American tennis player (b. 1959), often considered one of the all-time best players.

year later that match would be credited for demonstrating the need for the speedy installation of Hawk-Eye, the line-calling technology that took the seeing away from the beholder. Now the umpire's call can be challenged by a replay; however, back then after the match Serena said, "I'm very angry and bitter right now. I felt cheated. Shall I go on? I just feel robbed." And though you felt outrage for Serena after that 2004 US Open, as the years go by, she seems to put Alves, and a lengthening list of other curious calls and oversights, against both her and her sister, behind her as they happen.

Yes, and the body has memory. The physical carriage hauls more than its weight. The body is the threshold across which each objectionable call passes into consciousness—all the unintimidated, unblinking, and unflappable resilience does not erase the moments lived through, even as we are eternally stupid or everlastingly optimistic, so ready to be inside, among, a part of the games.

And here Serena is, five years after Alves, back at the US Open, again in a semifinal match, this time against Belgium's Kim Clijsters. Serena is not playing well and loses the first set. In response she smashes her racket on the court. Now McEnroe isn't stunned by her ability to hold herself together and is moved to say, "That's as angry as I've ever seen her." The umpire gives her a warning; another violation will mean a point penalty.

She is in the second set at the critical moment of 5–6 in Clijsters's favor, serving to stay in the match, at match point. The line judge employed by the US Open to watch Serena's body, its every move, says Serena stepped on the line while serving. What? (The Hawk-Eye cameras don't cover the feet, only the ball, apparently.) What! Are you serious? She is serious; she has seen a foot fault, one no one else is able to locate despite the numerous replays. "No foot fault, you definitely do not see a foot fault there," says McEnroe. "That's overofficiating for certain," says another commentator. Even the ESPN tennis commentator, who seems predictable in her readiness to find fault with the Williams sisters, says, "Her foot fault call was way off." Yes, and even if there had been a foot fault, despite the rule, they are rarely ever called at critical moments in a Grand Slam match because "You don't make a call," tennis official Carol Cox says, "that can decide a match unless it's flagrant."

15 As you look at the affable Kim Clijsters, you try to entertain the thought that this scenario could have played itself out the other way. And as Serena turns to the lineswoman and says, "I swear to God I'm fucking going to take this fucking ball and shove it down your fucking throat, you hear that? I swear to God!" As offensive as her outburst is, it is difficult not to applaud her for reacting immediately to being thrown against a sharp white background. It is difficult not to applaud her for existing in the moment, for fighting crazily against the so-called wrongness of her body's positioning at the service line.

She says in 2009, belatedly, the words that should have been said to the umpire in 2004, the words that might have snapped Alves back into focus, a focus that would have acknowledged what actually was happening on the court. Now Serena's reaction is read as insane. And her punishment for this moment of manumission[9] is the threatened point penalty resulting in the loss of the match, an $82,500 fine, plus a two-year probationary period by the Grand Slam Committee.

Perhaps the committee's decision is only about context, though context is not meaning. It is a public event being watched in homes across the world. In any case, it is difficult not to think that if Serena lost context by abandoning all rules of civility, it could be because her body, trapped in a racial imaginary, trapped in disbelief—code for being black in America—is being governed not by the tennis match she is participating in but by a collapsed relationship that had promised to play by the rules. Perhaps this is how racism feels no matter the context—randomly the rules everyone else gets to play by no longer apply to you, and to call this out by calling out "I swear to God!" is to be called insane, crass, crazy. Bad sportsmanship.

Two years later, September 11, 2011, Serena is playing the Australian Sam Stosur in the US Open final. She is expected to win, having just beaten the number-one player, the Dane Caroline Wozniacki, in the semifinal the night before. Some speculate Serena especially wants to win this Grand Slam because it is the tenth anniversary of the attack on the Twin Towers.[10] It's believed that by winning she will prove her red-blooded American patriotism and will once and for all become beloved by the tennis world (think Arthur Ashe[11] after his death). All the bad calls, the boos, the criticisms that she has made ugly the game of tennis—through her looks as well as her behavior—that entire cluster of betrayals will be wiped clean with this win.

One imagines her wanting to say what her sister would say a year later after being diagnosed with Sjögren's syndrome[12] and losing her match to shouts of "Let's go, Venus!" in Arthur Ashe Stadium: "I know this is not proper tennis etiquette, but this is the first time I've ever played here that the crowd has been

---

9 *manumission* Release from slavery.

10 *tenth anniversary ... Twin Towers* In the terrorist attacks by al-Qaeda on September 11, 2001, the Twin Towers of the World Trade Center in New York were destroyed; almost 3000 people died.

11 *Arthur Ashe* American tennis player (1943–93), winner of three Grand Slam tournaments. An African American, Ashe was often the target of racism during his lifetime, but he became almost universally revered after his death.

12 *Sjögren's syndrome* Autoimmune disorder which typically causes dry mouth, dry eyes, joint pain, and fatigue, as well as often being the cause of other complications.

behind me like that. Today I felt American, you know, for the first time at the US Open. So I've waited my whole career to have this moment and here it is."

20   It is all too exhausting and Serena's exhaustion shows in her playing; she is losing, a set and a game down. Yes, and finally she hits a great shot, a big forehand, and before the ball is safely past Sam Stosur's hitting zone, Serena yells, "Come on!" thinking she has hit an irretrievable winner. The umpire, Eva Asderaki, rules correctly that Serena, by shouting, interfered with Stosur's concentration. Subsequently, a ball that Stosur seemingly would not have been able to return becomes Stosur's point. Serena's reply is to ask the umpire if she is trying to screw her again. She remembers the umpire doing this to her before. As a viewer, you too, along with John McEnroe, begin to wonder if this is the same umpire from 2004 or 2009. It isn't—in 2004 it was Mariana Alves and in 2009 it was Sharon Wright; however, the use of the word "again" by Serena returns her viewers to other times calling her body out.

Again Serena's frustrations, her disappointments, exist within a system you understand not to try to understand in any fair-minded way because to do so is to understand the erasure of the self as systemic, as ordinary. For Serena, the daily diminishment is a low flame, a constant drip. Every look, every comment, every bad call blossoms out of history, through her, onto you. To understand is to see Serena as hemmed in as any other black body thrown against our American background. "Aren't you the one that screwed me over last time here?" she asks umpire Asderaki. "Yeah, you are. Don't look at me. Really, don't even look at me. Don't look my way. Don't look my way," she repeats, because it is that simple.

Yes, and who can turn away? Serena is not running out of breath. Despite all her understanding, she continues to serve up aces while smashing rackets and fraying hems. In the 2012 Olympics she brought home two of the three gold medals the Americans would win in tennis. After her three-second celebratory dance on center court at the All England Club, the American media reported, "And there was Serena ... Crip-Walking[13] all over the most lily-white place in the world.... You couldn't help but shake your head.... What Serena did was akin to cracking a tasteless, X-rated* joke inside a church.... What she did was immature and classless."

Before making the video *How to Be a Successful Black Artist*, Hennessy Youngman uploaded to YouTube *How to Be a Successful Artist*. While putting forward the argument that one needs to be white to be truly successful, he adds, in an aside, that this might not work for blacks because if "a nigger paints a

---

13 *Crip-Walking*   Dance move originated by the Los Angeles Crip gang in the 1970s.

flower it becomes a slavery flower, flower de *Amistad*,"[14] thereby intimating that any relationship between the white viewer and the black artist immediately becomes one between white persons and black property, which was the legal state of things once upon a time,* as Patricia Williams has pointed out in *The Alchemy of Race and Rights*: "The cold game of equality staring makes me feel like a thin sheet of glass.... I could force my presence, the real me contained in those eyes, upon them, but I would be smashed in the process."

Interviewed by the Brit Piers Morgan after her 2012 Olympic victory, Serena is informed by Morgan that he was planning on calling her victory dance "the Serena Shuffle"; however, he has learned from the American press that it is a Crip Walk, a gangster dance. Serena responds incredulously by asking if she looks like a gangster to him. Yes, he answers. All in a day's fun, perhaps, and in spite and despite it all, Serena Williams blossoms again into Serena Williams. When asked if she is confident she can win her upcoming matches, her answer remains, "At the end of the day, I am very happy with me and I'm very happy with my results."

Serena would go on to win every match she played between the US Open   25
and the year-end 2012 championship tournament, and because tennis is a game of adjustments, she would do this without any reaction to a number of questionable calls. More than one commentator would remark on her ability to hold it together during these matches. She is a woman in love, one suggests. She has grown up, another decides, as if responding to the injustice of racism is childish and her previous demonstration of emotion was free-floating and detached from any external actions by others. Some others theorize she is developing the admirable "calm and measured logic" of an Arthur Ashe, who the sportswriter Bruce Jenkins felt was "dignified" and "courageous" in his ability to confront injustice without making a scene. Jenkins, perhaps inspired by Serena's new comportment, felt moved to argue that her continued boycott of Indian Wells in 2013, where she felt traumatized by the aggression of racist slurs hurled at her in 2001, was lacking in "dignity" and "integrity" and demonstrated "only stubbornness and a grudge." (Serena lifted her boycott in 2015, though Venus continues to boycott Indian Wells.)

Watching this newly contained Serena, you begin to wonder if she finally has given up wanting better from her peers or if she too has come across Hennessy's *Art Thoughtz* and is channeling his assertion that the less that is communicated the better. Be ambiguous. This type of ambiguity could also be diagnosed as dissociation and would support Serena's claim that she has had to split herself off from herself and create different personae.

---

14   *Amistad*   The reference is to *La Amistad*, a nineteenth-century schooner on which a slave revolt occurred in 1839.

Now that there is no calling out of injustice, no yelling, no cursing, no finger wagging or head shaking, the media decides to take up the mantle when on December 12, 2012, two weeks after Serena is named WTA[15] Player of the Year, the Dane Caroline Wozniacki, a former number-one player, imitates Serena by stuffing towels in her top and shorts, all in good fun, at an exhibition match. Racist? CNN* wants to know if outrage is the proper response.

It's then that Hennessy's suggestions about "how to be a successful artist" return to you: be ambiguous, be white. Wozniacki, it becomes clear, has finally enacted what was desired by many of Serena's detractors, consciously or unconsciously, the moment the Compton[16] girl first stepped on court. Wozniacki (though there are a number of ways to interpret her actions—playful mocking of a peer, imitation of the mimicking antics of the tennis player known as the joker, Novak Djokovic) finally gives the people what they have wanted all along by embodying Serena's attributes while leaving Serena's "angry nigger exterior" behind. At last, in this real, and unreal, moment, we have Wozniacki's image of smiling blond goodness posing as the best female tennis player of all time.

(2014)

Questions

1. Rankine frequently writes in the second person, referring to a "you" who observes and reflects upon Williams and her games. What purpose do these asides serve? Who is the "you" of whom she speaks?

2. How appropriate is the word "lyrical" as a descriptor of Rankine's style?

3. Rankine discusses two types of anger at the beginning of the essay. How would you characterize them, and how are they different? What does Rankine say about anger and the body?

4. How does Rankine interpret Serena Williams's response during the 2009 US Open? How does she use the tennis match as a metaphor to make a larger argument?

5. The book from which this essay was drawn was a finalist for the National Book Award in two categories, Poetry and Criticism. What (if any) characteristics make it a work of criticism? Does this piece accomplish or communicate anything that neither poetry nor criticism could on their own?

---

15 *WTA* Women's Tennis Association.
16 *Compton* City in California, south of Los Angeles.

BRYAN STEVENSON

from JUST MERCY

Just Mercy *is an autobiographical account of the work of Bryan Stevenson, an African American lawyer who has received numerous prestigious awards and grants for his work defending those who have been disproportionately harmed by the American criminal justice system, including child convicts and people who have been wrongly sentenced to death. Stevenson is the founder and Executive Director of the Equal Justice Initiative, an organization "committed to ending mass incarceration and excessive punishment in the United States, to challenging racial and economic injustice, and to protecting basic human rights for the most vulnerable people in American society."*

Just Mercy *incorporates analysis of the causes of systemic injustice alongside the stories of individuals whose lives are impacted. One thread throughout the book is a case that influenced Stevenson early in his career—that of Walter McMillian, a Black man who, through an egregiously mishandled investigation and trial, was convicted of murder on the basis of a false testimony and despite significant evidence suggesting his innocence. Another important case in the book is that of Joe Sullivan, a teen with intellectual disabilities and Multiple Sclerosis who, after receiving an inadequate defense, was sentenced to life without parole for a sexual assault he was alleged to have committed at the age of thirteen. Stevenson took Sullivan's case to the Supreme Court to challenge the constitutionality of imposing life without parole on children found guilty of crimes other than murder.*

The final chapter of Stevenson's Just Mercy *appears here.*

The Stonecatchers' Song of Sorrow

On May 17, 2010, I was sitting in my office waiting anxiously when the U.S. Supreme Court announced its decision: Life imprisonment without parole sentences imposed on children convicted of non-homicide crimes is cruel and unusual punishment and constitutionally impermissible. My staff and I jumped up and down in celebration. Moments later we were inundated with a flood of calls from media, clients, families, and children's rights advocates. It was the first time the Court had issued a categorical ban on a punishment other than the death penalty. Joe Sullivan was entitled to relief. Scores of people, including Antonio Nuñez and Ian Manuel,[1] were entitled to reduced sentences that would give them a "meaningful opportunity for release."

Two years later, in June 2012, we won a constitutional ban on mandatory life-without-parole sentences imposed on children convicted of homicides. The Supreme Court had agreed to review Evan Miller's case and the case of our client from Arkansas, Kuntrell Jackson.[2] I argued both cases in March of that year and waited anxiously until we won a favorable ruling. The Court's decision meant that no child accused of any crime could ever again be automatically sentenced to die in prison. Over two thousand condemned people sentenced to life imprisonment without parole for crimes when they were children were now potentially eligible for relief and reduced sentences. Some states changed their statutes to create more hopeful sentences for child offenders. Prosecutors in many places resisted retroactive application of the Court's decision in *Miller v. Alabama*, but everyone now had new hope, including Ashley Jones and Trina Garnett.[3]

---

1   *Antonio Nuñez*   Californian who was sentenced to life without parole for an incident that occurred when he was fourteen. California law did not allow this sentence to be given to people under sixteen who are found guilty of murder, but one of Nuñez's charges was aggravated kidnapping, to which the restriction did not apply;   *Ian Manuel*   Floridian who was given a life without parole sentence at thirteen and was kept in solitary confinement in an adult facility for eighteen years. Both Nuñez's and Manuel's cases are discussed in an earlier chapter of *Just Mercy* not reprinted here.

2   *Evan Miller*   Alabaman sentenced to life without parole for capital murder committed at the age of fourteen;   *Kuntrell Jackson*   Arkansan sentenced to life without parole for a gun murder committed during a robbery he participated in at the age of fourteen (his accomplice was the shooter). Both Miller's and Jackson's cases were considered in a 2012 Supreme Court ruling, *Miller v. Alabama*, which stated that it was unconstitutional for laws to impose mandatory sentences of life without parole for minors seventeen and younger. The case is discussed elsewhere in *Just Mercy*.

3   *Ashley Jones*   Alabaman convicted of killing two of her family members at the age of fourteen as she attempted to flee from an abusive household. She was sentenced to life without the possibility of parole;   *Trina Garnett*   Intellectually disabled Pennsylvanian

We continued our work on issues involving children by pursuing more cases. I believe there should be a total ban on housing children under the age of eighteen with adults in jails or prisons. We filed cases seeking to stop the practice. I am also convinced that very young children should never be tried in adult court. They're vulnerable to all sorts of problems that increase the risk of a wrongful conviction. No child of twelve, thirteen, or fourteen can defend him or herself in the adult criminal justice system. Wrongful convictions and illegal trials involving young children are very common.

A few years earlier, we won the release of Phillip Shaw, who was fourteen when he was improperly convicted and sentenced to life imprisonment without parole in Missouri. His jury was illegally selected, excluding African Americans. I argued two cases at the Mississippi Supreme Court in which the Court ruled that the convictions and sentences of young children were illegal. Demarious Banyard was a thirteen-year-old who had been bullied into participating in a robbery that resulted in a fatal shooting in Jackson, Mississippi. He was given a mandatory death-in-prison sentence after his jury was illegally told that he had to prove his innocence beyond a reasonable doubt and the State introduced impermissible evidence. He was resentenced to a finite term of years and now has hope for release.

Dante Evans was a fourteen-year-old child living in a FEMA trailer* with his abusive father in Gulfport, Mississippi, after Hurricane Katrina. His dad, who had twice before nearly killed Dante's mother, was shot by Dante while he slept in a chair. Dante had repeatedly told school officials about his father's abuse, but no one ever intervened. I discussed Dante's prior diagnosis of post-traumatic stress disorder following the attempted murder of his mother in my oral argument before the Mississippi Supreme Court. The Court emphasized the trial court's refusal to permit introduction of this evidence and granted Dante a new trial.

Our death penalty work had also taken a hopeful turn. The number of death row prisoners in Alabama for whom we'd won relief reached one hundred. We had created a new community of formerly condemned prisoners in Alabama who had been illegally convicted or sentenced and received new trials or sentencing hearings. Most never returned to death row. Starting in 2012, we had eighteen months with no executions in Alabama. Continued litigation about lethal injection protocols and other questions about the reliability of the death

5

who at age fourteen received a mandatory sentence of life without parole for two deaths relating to arson. At the time of the book's publication in 2014, she had been in prison for thirty-eight years. Both Jones's and Garnett's cases are mentioned earlier in Stevenson's book.

penalty slowed the execution rate in Alabama dramatically. In 2013, Alabama recorded the lowest number of new death sentences since the resumption of capital punishment in the mid-1970s. These were very hopeful developments.

Of course, there were still challenges. I was losing sleep over another man on Alabama's death row, a man who was clearly innocent. Anthony Ray Hinton was on death row when Walter McMillian arrived in the 1980s. Mr. Hinton was wrongly convicted of two robbery murders outside Birmingham after state forensic employees mistakenly concluded that a gun recovered from his mother's home had been used in the crimes. Mr. Hinton's appointed defense lawyer got only $500 from the court to retain a gun expert to confront the state's case, so he ended up with a mechanical engineer who was blind in one eye and who had almost no experience testifying as a gun expert.

The State's primary evidence against Mr. Hinton involved a third crime where a witness identified him as the assailant. But we found a half-dozen people and security records that proved that Mr. Hinton was locked inside a secure supermarket warehouse working as a night laborer fifteen miles away at the time of the crime. We got some of the nation's best experts to review the gun evidence, and they concluded the Hinton weapon could not be matched to the murders. I had hopes that the State might reopen the case. Instead they persisted in moving toward execution. The media was not interested in the story, citing "innocence fatigue." "We've done that story before," we heard again and again. We kept getting very close decisions from appellate courts denying relief, and Mr. Hinton remained on death row facing execution. It would soon be thirty years. He was always upbeat and encouraging when I met with him, but I was increasingly desperate to find a way to get his case overturned.

I was encouraged by the fact that nationwide the rate of mass incarceration had finally slowed. For the first time in close to forty years, the country's prison population did not increase in 2011. In 2012, the United States saw the first decline in its prison population in decades. I spent a lot of time in California that year supporting ballot initiatives and was encouraged that voters decided, by a huge margin, to end the state's "three strikes" law that imposed mandatory sentences on non-violent offenders. The initiative won majority support in every county in the state. California voters also came very close to banning the death penalty; the ballot initiative lost by only a couple of percentage points. Almost banning the death penalty through a popular referendum in an American state would have been unimaginable just a few years earlier.

10   We were able to finally launch the race and poverty initiative I'd long been hoping to start at EJI.[4] For years I wanted to implement a project to change the way we talk about racial history and contextualize contemporary race issues.

---

4   *EJI*   Equal Justice Initiative.

We published a racial history calendar for 2013 and 2014. We started working with poor children and families in Black Belt[5] counties across the South. We brought hundreds of high school students to our office for supplemental education and discussion about rights and justice. Also, we worked on reports and materials that seek to deepen the national conversation about the legacy of slavery and lynching* and our nation's history of racial injustice.

I found the new race and poverty work extremely energizing. It closely connected to our work on criminal justice issues; I believe that so much of our worst thinking about justice is steeped in the myths of racial difference that still plague us. I believe that there are four institutions in American history that have shaped our approach to race and justice but remain poorly understood. The first, of course, is slavery. This was followed by the reign of terror that shaped the lives of people of color following the collapse of Reconstruction* until World War II. Older people of color in the South would occasionally come up to me after speeches to complain about how antagonized they feel when they hear news commentators talking about how we were dealing with domestic terrorism for the first time in the United States after the 9/11 attacks.

An older African American man once said to me, "You make them stop saying that! We grew up with terrorism all the time. The police, the clan,* anybody who was white can terrorize you. We had to worry about bombings and lynchings, racial violence of all kinds."

The racial terrorism of lynching in many ways created the modern death penalty. America's embrace of speedy executions was, in part, an attempt to redirect the violent energies of lynching while assuring white Southerners that black men would still pay the ultimate price.

Convict leasing[6] was introduced at the end of the nineteenth century to criminalize former slaves and convict them of nonsensical offenses so that freed men, women, and children could be "leased" to businesses and effectively forced back into slave labor. Private industries throughout the country made millions of dollars with free convict labor, while thousands of African Americans died in horrific working conditions. The practice of re-enslavement was so widespread in some states that it was characterized in the Pulitzer Prize-winning book by Douglas Blackmon as *Slavery by Another Name*. But the practice is not well-known to most Americans.

---

5   *Black Belt*   Region of the Southern U.S. characterized by rich, black soil favored for growing cotton; the name "Black Belt" initially reflected the color of the soil, but now also evokes the area's large Black population, comprised mostly of descendants of slaves forced there to work the cotton fields.

6   *Convict leasing*   Practice of hiring out prisoners to labor for private businesses, such as plantations, at a very low cost.

15   During the terror era there were hundreds of ways in which people of color could commit a social transgression or offend someone that might cost them their lives. Racial terror and the constant threats created by violently enforced racial hierarchy were profoundly traumatizing for African Americans. Absorbing these psychosocial realities created all kinds of distortions and difficulties that manifest themselves today in multiple ways.

The third institution, "Jim Crow," is the legalized racial segregation and suppression of basic rights that defined the American apartheid era. It is more recent and is recognized in our national consciousness, but it is still not well understood. It seems to me that we've been quick to celebrate the achievements of the Civil Rights Movement and slow to recognize the damage done in that era. We have been unwilling to commit to a process of truth and reconciliation in which people are allowed to give voice to the difficulties created by racial segregation, racial subordination, and marginalization. Because I was born during the time when the stigma of racial hierarchy and Jim Crow had real consequences for the ways my elders had to act or react to a variety of indignations, I was mindful of the way that the daily humiliations and insults accumulated.

The legacy of racial profiling carries many of the same complications. Working on all of these juvenile cases across the country meant that I was frequently in courtrooms and communities where I'd never been before. Once I was preparing to do a hearing in a trial court in the Midwest and was sitting at counsel table in an empty courtroom before the hearing. I was wearing a dark suit, white shirt, and tie. The judge and the prosecutor entered through a door in the back of the courtroom laughing about something.

When the judge saw me sitting at the defense table, he said to me harshly, "Hey, you shouldn't be in here without counsel. Go back outside and wait in the hallway until your lawyer arrives."

I stood up and smiled broadly. I said, "Oh, I'm sorry, Your Honor, we haven't met. My name is Bryan Stevenson, I am the lawyer on the case set for hearing this morning."

20   The judge laughed at his mistake, and the prosecutor joined in. I forced myself to laugh because I didn't want my young client, a white child who had been prosecuted as an adult, to be disadvantaged by a conflict I had created with the judge before the hearing. But I was disheartened by the experience. Of course innocent mistakes occur, but the accumulated insults and indignations caused by racial presumptions are destructive in ways that are hard to measure. Constantly being suspected, accused, watched, doubted, distrusted, presumed guilty, and even feared is a burden borne by people of color that can't be understood or confronted without a deeper conversation about our history of racial injustice.

The fourth institution is mass incarceration. Going into any prison is deeply confusing if you know anything about the racial demographics of America. The extreme overrepresentation of people of color, the disproportionate sentencing of racial minorities, the targeted prosecution of drug crimes in poor communities, the criminalization of new immigrants and undocumented people, the collateral consequences of voter disenfranchisement, and the barriers to re-entry can only be fully understood through the lens of our racial history.

It was gratifying to be able, finally, to address some of these issues through our new project and to articulate the challenges created by racial history and structural poverty. The materials we developed were generating positive feedback, and I became hopeful that we might be able to push back against the suppression of this difficult history of racial injustice.

I was also encouraged by our new staff. We were now attracting young, gifted lawyers from all over the country who are extremely skilled. We started a program for college graduates to work at EJI as Justice Fellows. Having a bigger staff with very talented people made meeting the new challenges created by our much broader docket seem possible.

A bigger staff, bigger cases, and a bigger docket also sometimes meant bigger problems. While exciting and very gratifying, the Supreme Court rulings on juveniles created all sorts of new challenges for us. Hundreds of people were now entitled to pursue new sentences, and most were in states where they have no clear right to counsel. In states like Louisiana, Alabama, Mississippi, and Arkansas, there were hundreds of people whose cases were affected by the recent decisions, but no lawyers were available to assist these condemned juvenile lifers. We ended up taking on almost one hundred new cases following the court's ban on life imprisonment without parole for kids convicted of non-homicide offenses. We then took on another hundred new cases after the decision banning mandatory life without parole for juveniles. In addition to the dozens of cases already on our juvenile docket, we were quickly overwhelmed.

The total ban on life-without-parole sentences for children convicted of non-homicides should have been the easiest decision to implement, but enforcing the Supreme Court's ruling was proving much more difficult than I had hoped. I was spending more and more time in Louisiana, Florida, and Virginia, which together had close to 90 percent of the non-homicide cases. The trial courts were often less sophisticated in thinking about the differences between children and adults than we had hoped, and we would often have to relitigate the basic unfairness of treating kids like adults that the Supreme Court had already recognized.

Some judges seemed to want to get as close to life expectancy or natural death as possible before they would create release opportunities for child

25

offenders. Antonio Nuñez's judge in Orange County, California, replaced his sentence of life imprisonment without parole with a sentence of 175 years. I had to go back to an appellate court in California and argue to get that sentence replaced with a reasonable sentence. We met resistance in Joe Sullivan's and Ian Manuel's cases as well. Ultimately, we were able to get sentences that meant they could both be released after serving a few more years.

In some cases, clients had already been in prison for decades and had very few, if any, support systems to help them re-enter society. We decided to create a re-entry program to assist these clients. EJI's program was specifically developed for people who have spent many years in prison after being incarcerated when they were children. We were committed to providing services, housing, job training, life skills, counseling, and anything else people coming out of prison needed to succeed. We told the judges and parole boards we were committed to providing the assistance our clients required.

In particular, the Louisiana clients serving life without parole for non-homicides faced many challenges. We undertook representation of all sixty of those eligible for relief in Louisiana. Almost all of them were at Angola, a notoriously difficult place to do time, especially in the 1970s and 1980s when many had first arrived. For many years, violence was so bad at Angola that it was almost impossible to be incarcerated and not get disciplinaries—additional punishments or time tacked onto your sentence—due to conflicts with another inmate or staff. Prisoners were required to do manual labor in very difficult work environments or face solitary confinement or other disciplinary action. It was not uncommon for inmates to be seriously injured, losing fingers or limbs, after working long hours in brutal and dangerous conditions.

For years, Angola—a slave plantation before the end of the Civil War—forced inmates to work in the fields picking cotton. Prisoners who refused would receive "write-ups" that went into their files and face months of solitary confinement. The horrible conditions of confinement and their constantly being told that they would die in prison no matter how well they behaved meant that most of our clients had long lists of disciplinaries. At the resentencing hearings we were preparing, state lawyers were using these prior disciplinaries to argue against favorable new sentences.

30   Remarkably, several former juvenile lifers had developed outstanding institutional histories with very few disciplinaries, even though they did their time with no hope of ever being released or having their institutional history reviewed. Some became trustees, mentors, and advocates against violence among inmates. Others had become law librarians, journalists, and gardeners. Angola evolved over time to have some excellent programs for incarcerated people who stayed out of trouble, and many of our clients took full advantage.

We decided to prioritize resentencing hearings in Louisiana for the "old-timers," juvenile lifers who had been there for decades. Joshua Carter and Robert Caston were the first two cases we decided to litigate. In 1963, when he was sixteen, Joshua Carter was accused of a rape in New Orleans and quickly given the death penalty. A condemned black child awaiting execution in those days had little reason to hope for relief. But to coerce a confession from him, police officers had beaten Joshua so brutally that even in 1965 the Louisiana Supreme Court felt the need to overturn his conviction. Mr. Carter was resentenced to life imprisonment without parole and sent to Angola. After struggling for years, he became a model prisoner and trustee. In the 1990s, he developed glaucoma and didn't get the medical care he needed, and he soon lost his sight in both eyes. We tried to persuade New Orleans prosecutors that Mr. Carter, blind and in his sixties, should be released after nearly fifty years in prison.

Robert Caston had been at Angola for forty-five years. He lost several fingers working in a prison factory and was now disabled as a result of his forced labor at Angola.

I traveled back and forth between the trial courts in Orleans Parish quite a bit on the Carter and Caston cases. The Orleans Parish courthouse is a massive structure with intimidating architecture. There are multiple courtrooms aligned down an enormous hallway with grand marble floors and high ceilings. Hundreds of people crowded the hallways, bustling between the various courtrooms each day. Hearings in the vast courthouse are never reliably scheduled. Frequently, there would be a date and time for the Carter and Caston resentencings, but it seemed to mean very little to anyone. I would arrive in court, and there would always be a stack of cases, and clients with lawyers gathered in an overcrowded courtroom, all waiting to be heard at the time of our hearings. Overwhelmed judges tried to manage the proceedings with bench meetings while dozens of young men—most of whom were black—sat handcuffed in standard jail-issued orange jumpsuits in the front of the court. Lawyers consulted with clients and family members scattered around the chaotic courtroom.

After three trips to New Orleans for sentencing hearings, we still did not have a new sentence for Mr. Carter or Mr. Caston. We met with the district attorney, filed papers with the judge, and consulted with a variety of local officials in an effort to achieve a new, constitutionally acceptable sentence. Because Mr. Carter and Mr. Caston had both been in prison for nearly fifty years, we wanted their immediate release.

A couple of weeks before Christmas, I was back in court for the fourth time trying to win the release of the two men. There were two different judges and courtrooms involved, but we felt if we won release for one it might then become easier to win release for the other. We were working with the Juvenile Justice Project of Louisiana, and their lawyer Carol Kolinchak had agreed to be our local counsel in all of the Louisiana cases. At this fourth hearing, Carol and I were busily trying to process papers and resolve the endless issues that had emerged to keep Mr. Carter and Mr. Caston incarcerated.

Mr. Carter had a large family that had maintained a close relationship with him despite the passage of time. In the aftermath of Hurricane Katrina, many family members had fled New Orleans and were now living hundreds of miles away. But a dozen or so family members would dutifully show up at each hearing, some traveling from as far away as California. Mr. Carter's mother was nearly a hundred years old. She had vowed to Mr. Carter for decades that she wouldn't die until he came home from prison.

Finally, it seemed like we were close to success. We got things resolved so that the Court could grant our motion and resentence Mr. Caston so that he would immediately be released from prison. The State usually wouldn't bring inmates from Angola to New Orleans for hearings but instead had them view proceedings on a video hookup at the prison. After I made our arguments in the noisy, frenetic courtroom, the judge granted our motion. She recited the facts about the date of Mr. Caston's conviction, and then something quite unexpected happened. As the judge spoke about Mr. Caston's decades in prison, the courtroom, for the first time in my multiple trips there, became completely silent. The lawyers stopped conferring, the prosecutors awaiting other cases paid attention, and family members ceased their chatter. Even the handcuffed inmates awaiting their cases had stopped talking and were listening intently. The judge detailed Mr. Caston's forty-five years at Angola for a non-homicide crime when he was sixteen. She noted that Caston had been sent to Angola in the 1960s. Then the judge pronounced a new sentence that meant Mr. Caston would immediately be released from prison.

I looked at Carol and smiled. Then the people in the silent courtroom did something I'd never seen before: They erupted in applause. The defense lawyers, prosecutors, family members, and deputy sheriffs applauded. Even the inmates applauded in their handcuffs.

Carol was wiping tears from her eyes. Even the judge, who usually tolerated no disruptions, seemed to embrace the drama of the moment. A number of my former students now worked with the public defender's office in New Orleans, and they, too, had come to court and were cheering. I had to speak with Mr. Caston by phone and explain what had happened, since he couldn't see everything from the video monitor. He was overjoyed. He became the first person to be released as a result of the Supreme Court's ban on death-in-prison sentences for juvenile lifers.

We went down the hall to Mr. Carter's courtroom and had another success, winning a new sentence that meant that he, too, would be released immediately. Mr. Carter's family was ecstatic. There were hugs and promises of home-cooked meals for me and the staff of EJI. Carol and I busily began making arrangements for Mr. Caston's and Mr. Carter's releases, which would take place that evening. The protocol at Angola was to release prisoners at midnight and give them bus fare to New Orleans or a city of their choice in Louisiana. We dispatched staff to Angola, which was several hours away, to meet the men when they were released, sparing them the midnight bus trip.

Exhausted, I wandered the halls of the courthouse while we waited for one more piece of paper to be faxed and approved to clear the way for the release of Mr. Caston and Mr. Carter. An older black woman sat on the marble steps in the massive courthouse hallway. She looked tired and wore what my sister and I used to call a "church meeting hat." She had smooth dark skin, and I recognized her as someone who had been in the courtroom when Mr. Carter was resentenced. In fact, I thought I'd seen her each time I'd come to the courthouse in New Orleans. I assumed that she was related or connected to one of the clients, although I didn't remember the other family members ever mentioning her. I must have been staring because she saw me looking and waved at me, gesturing for me to come to her.

When I walked over to her she smiled at me. "I'm tired and I'm not going to get up, so you're going to have to lean over for me to give you a hug." She had a sweet voice that crackled.

I smiled back at her. "Well, yes, ma'am. I love hugs, thank you." She wrapped her arms around my neck.

"Sit, sit. I want to talk to you," she said.

I sat down beside her on the steps. "I've seen you here several times, are you related to Mr. Caston or Mr. Carter?" I asked. 45

"No, no, no, I'm not related to nobody here. Not that I know of, anyway." She had a kind smile, and she looked at me intensely. "I just come here to help people. This is a place full of pain, so people need plenty of help around here."

"Well, that's really kind of you."

"No, it's what I'm supposed to do, so I do it." She looked away before locking eyes with me again. "My sixteen-year-old grandson was murdered fifteen years ago," she said, "and I loved that boy more than life itself."

I wasn't expecting that response and was instantly sobered. The woman grabbed my hand.

"I grieved and grieved and grieved. I asked the Lord why he let someone 50 take my child like that. He was killed by some other boys. I came to this courtroom for the first time for their trials and sat in there and cried every day for nearly two weeks. None of it made any sense. Those boys were found guilty for killing my grandson, and the judge sent them away to prison forever. I thought it would make me feel better but it actually made me feel worse."

She continued, "I sat in the courtroom after they were sentenced and just cried and cried. A lady came over to me and gave me a hug and let me lean on her. She asked me if the boys who got sentenced were my children, and I told her no. I told her the boy they killed was my child." She hesitated. "I think she sat with me for almost two hours. For well over an hour, we didn't neither one of us say a word. It felt good to finally have someone to lean on at that trial, and I've never forgotten that woman. I don't know who she was, but she made a difference."

"I'm so sorry about your grandson," I murmured. It was all I could think of to say.

"Well, you never fully recover, but you carry on, you carry on. I didn't know what to do with myself after those trials, so about a year later I started coming down here. I don't really know why. I guess I just felt like maybe I could be someone, you know, that somebody hurting could lean on." She looped her arm with mine.

I smiled at her. "That's really wonderful."

"It has been wonderful. What's your name again?"

"It's Bryan."

"It has been wonderful, Bryan. When I first came, I'd look for people who had lost someone to murder or some violent crime. Then it got to the point where some of the ones grieving the most were the one whose children or parents were on trial, so I just started letting anybody lean on me who needed it. All these young children being sent to prison forever, all this grief and violence. Those judges throwing people away like they're not even human, people shooting each other, hurting each other, like they don't care. I don't know, it's a lot of pain. I decided that I was supposed to be here to catch some of the stones people cast at each other."

I chuckled when she said it. During the McMillian hearings, a local minister had held a regional church meeting about the case and had asked me to come speak. There were a few people in the African American community whose support of Walter was muted, not because they thought he was guilty but because he had had an extramarital affair and wasn't active in the church. At the church meeting, I spoke mostly about Walter's case, but I also reminded people that when the woman accused of adultery was brought to Jesus, he told the accusers who wanted to stone her to death, "Let he who is without sin cast the first stone." The woman's accusers retreated, and Jesus forgave her and urged her to sin no more.[7] But today, our self-righteousness, our fear, and our anger have caused even the Christians to hurl stones at the people who fall down, even when we know we should forgive or show compassion. I told the

---

7   *the woman ... no more*   See John 8.7–11.

congregation that we can't simply watch that happen. I told them we have to be stonecatchers.

When I chuckled at the older woman's invocation of the parable, she laughed, too. "I heard you in that courtroom today. I've even seen you here a couple of times before. I know you's a stonecatcher, too."

I laughed even more. "Well, I guess I try to be." 60

She took my hands and rubbed my palms. "Well, it hurts to catch all them stones people throw." She kept stroking my hands, and I couldn't think of anything to say. I felt unusually comforted by this woman. It would take me nearly five hours to drive back to Montgomery once I got things settled for Mr. Caston and Mr. Carter. I needed to keep moving, but it felt nice sitting there with the woman now earnestly massaging my palms in a way that was so sweet, even though it seemed strange, too.

"Are you trying to make me cry?" I asked. I tried to smile.

She put her arm around me and smiled back. "No, you done good today. I was so happy when that judge said that man was going home. It gave me goose bumps. Fifty years in prison, he can't even see no more. No, I was grateful to God when I heard that. You don't have anything to cry about. I'm just gonna let you lean on me a bit, because I know a few things about stonecatching."

She squeezed me a bit and then said, "Now, you keep this up and you're gonna end up like me, singing some sad songs. Ain't no way to do what we do and not learn how to appreciate a good sorrow song.

"I've been singing sad songs my whole life. Had to. When you catch 65 stones, even happy songs can make you sad." She paused and grew silent. I heard her chuckle before she continued. "But you keep singing. Your songs will make you strong. They might even make you happy."

People buzzed down the busy corridors of the courthouse while we sat silently.

"Well, you're very good at what you do," I finally said. "I feel much better."

She slapped my arm playfully. "Oh, don't you try to charm me, young man. You felt just fine before you saw me. Them men are going home and you were fine walking around here. I just do what I do, nothing more."

When I finally excused myself, giving her a kiss on the cheek and telling her I needed to sign the prisoners' release papers, she stopped me. "Oh, wait." She dug around in her purse until she found a piece of wrapped peppermint candy. "Here, take this."

The gesture made me happy in a way that I can't fully explain. 70

"Well, thank you." I smiled and leaned down to give her another kiss on the cheek.

She waved at me, smiling. "Go on, go on."

(2014)

Questions

1. Much of the work Stevenson describes involves the defense of children who have been sentenced to life without parole. Why does Stevenson object to this sentence being given to children? In your view, under what circumstances—if any—should a person who commits a crime while still a minor be sentenced to life without parole?

2. Stevenson mentions his work in obtaining relief for death row inmates. When—if ever—do you think the death penalty should be used as a punishment? Consider Stevenson's commentary on the legal system in giving your answer.

3. What is a "stonecatcher"? Explain this metaphor and its role in the article.

4. This selection concludes with Stevenson's account of a conversation with an "older black woman" he meets after concluding a court case. What is the effect of this conclusion?

5. The following questions relate to this article and to the selection from *The New Jim Crow* that is also reprinted in this anthology:

    a. Alexander writes that "[w]hiteness mitigates crime, whereas blackness defines the criminal" (paragraph 25). How (if at all) is the racialization of the criminal as discussed by Alexander reflected in the injustices described by Stevenson?

    b. Stevenson writes that the realities of mass incarceration "can only be fully understood through the lens of our racial history" (paragraph 21). How is mass incarceration linked to the history of Black oppression in the United States? Answer with reference to both Stevenson and Alexander.

    c. This portion of Stevenson's book employs numerous anecdotes in service of its argument, while the selection from Alexander's employs more statistics. Which approach do you find more persuasive? Why?

Nikole Hannah-Jones

School Segregation: The Continuing Tragedy of Ferguson

The 9 August 2014 shooting by police officer Darren Wilson of unarmed teenager Michael Brown in Ferguson, Missouri (a suburb of St. Louis) became a cause célèbre when no charges were filed against the officer responsible. Protests carried on for many weeks, and the incident prompted many to ask fresh questions about race relations in America. Nikole Hannah-Jones' article was originally published 19 December 2014 in the online magazine ProPublica*; an abridged version was later published in* The New York Times.

O n August 1, five black students in satiny green and red robes and mortar boards* waited inside an elementary school classroom, listening for their names to be called as graduates of Normandy High School. The ceremony was held months after the school's main graduation for students who had been short of credits or had opted not to participate earlier.

One of those graduating that day was Michael Brown. He was 18, his mother's oldest son. He was headed to college in the fall.

Eight days later, Brown was dead—killed in the streets of nearby Ferguson, Mo., by a white police officer in a shooting that ignited angry protests and another round of painful national debate about race, policing, and the often elusive matter of justice.

News reports in the days and weeks after Brown's death often noted his recent graduation and college ambitions, the clear implication that the teen's school achievements only deepened the sorrow over his loss.

But if Brown's educational experience was a success story, it was a damn-   5
ing one.

The Normandy school district from which Brown graduated is among the poorest and most segregated in Missouri. It ranks last in overall academic performance. Its rating on an annual state assessment was so dismal that by the time Brown graduated the district had lost its accreditation.

About half of black male students at Normandy High never graduate. Just one in four graduates enters a four-year college. The college where Brown was headed is a troubled for-profit trade-school that a U.S. Senate report said targeted students for their "vulnerabilities," and that at one time advertised itself to what it internally called the area's "Unemployed, Underpaid, Unsatisfied, Unskilled, Unprepared, Unsupported, Unmotivated, Unhappy, Underserved!"

A mere five miles down the road from Normandy is the wealthy county seat where a grand jury recently decided not to indict[1] Darren Wilson, the officer who killed Brown. Success there looks drastically different. The Clayton Public Schools are predominantly white, with almost no poverty to speak of. The district is regularly ranked among the top 10 percent in the state. More than 96 percent of students graduate. Fully 84 percent of graduates head to four-year universities.

Brown's tragedy, then, is not limited to his individual potential cut brutally short. His schooling also reveals a more subtle, ongoing racial injustice: the vast disparity in resources and expectations for black children in America's stubbornly segregated educational system.

10 As ProPublica has documented in a series of stories on the resegregation of America's schools, hundreds of school districts across the nation have been released from court-enforced integration* over the past 15 years. Over that same time period, the number of so-called apartheid schools—schools whose white population is 1 percent or less—has shot up. The achievement gap, greatly narrowed during the height of school desegregation, has widened.

"American schools are disturbingly racially segregated, period," Catherine Lhamon, head of the U.S. Education Department's civil rights office, said in an October speech. "We are reserving our expectations for our highest rigor level of courses, the courses we know our kids need to be able to be full and productive members of society, but we are reserving them for a class of kids who are white and who are wealthier."

According to data compiled by the Education Department, black and Latino children are the least likely to be taught by a qualified, experienced teacher, to get access to courses such as chemistry and calculus, and to have access to technology.

The inequalities along racial lines are so profound nationally that in October the department's Office for Civil Rights issued a 37-page letter to school district superintendents warning that the disparities may be unconstitutional.

---

1   *indict*   Formally charge with a serious crime.

Few places better reflect the rise and fall of attempts to integrate U.S. schools than St. Louis and its suburbs.

Decades of public and private housing discrimination made St. Louis one of the most racially segregated metropolitan areas in the country. Out of that grew a network of school district boundaries that to this day have divided large numbers of black students in racially separate schools as effectively as any Jim Crow law.* 15

In 1983, under federal court order, St. Louis and some of its suburbs embarked on what would become the grandest and most successful interdistrict school desegregation program in the land, one that, at least for a time, broke the grim grip of ZIP codes for tens of thousands of black students. As an elementary school student, under this order, Michael Brown's mother rode the bus from St. Louis to affluent Ladue.

But like so many other desegregation efforts across the country, the St. Louis plan proved short-lived, largely abandoned after several years by politicians and others who complained that it was too costly. Jay Nixon, Missouri's current governor, whose response to Brown's killing has come under intense scrutiny in recent months, helped lead the effort that brought the court order to a close.

Since their retreat from desegregation initiatives, many St. Louis County schools have returned to the world of separate and unequal that existed before the U.S. Supreme Court's landmark decision in Brown v. Board of Education.[2]

It could be said that the Normandy school district, where Michael Brown spent the last year and a half of high school, never left. Excluded from the court-ordered integration plan that transformed other school systems in the St. Louis area, Normandy's fiscally and academically disadvantaged schools have essentially been in freefall since the 1980s.

Throughout the region, the educational divide between black children and white children is stark. In St. Louis County, 44 percent of black children attend schools in districts the state says perform so poorly that it has stripped them of full accreditation. Just 4 percent of white students do. 20

Yet state education officials say there is little political will to change that.

Instead, they have promised to work to make segregated school districts equal, the very doctrine the Supreme Court struck down in the Brown decision.

"We are failing to properly educate the black child," said Michael Jones, vice president of the Missouri State Board of Education. "Individually, any one person can overcome anything. But we've got masses of children with bad starts in life. They can't win. We ought to be ashamed of that."

---

2 *Brown v. Board of Education* This ruling established that state laws allowing separate public schools for Black and white students were unconstitutional.

384 | NIKOLE HANNAH-JONES

Since Aug. 9, the day Michael Brown's lifeless body lay for hours under a hot summer sun, St. Louis County has become synonymous with the country's racial fault lines when it comes to police conduct and the criminalization of black youth. But most black youth will not die at the hands of police.

25   They will face the future that Brown would have faced if he had lived. That is, to have the outcome of their lives deeply circumscribed by what they learn and experience in their segregated, inferior schools.

DRED SCOTT, DESEGREGATION AND A DEARTH OF PROGRESS

Missouri is what the locals like to call a Southern state with Northern exposure. It entered the Union through a compromise that determined how much of the country would permit slavery, and wound up a slave state surrounded on three sides by free states.

It was in a St. Louis case in 1857 that the U.S. Supreme Court handed down one of its most infamous opinions. The court, in ruling against the enslaved Dred Scott, affirmed that black people were not citizens and "had no rights that the white man was bound to respect."

The spirit of the ruling reverberated for generations in St. Louis, which in the years after the Civil War became the destination for large numbers of former slaves. Indeed, the Mississippi River town became a national leader in how to contain what white real estate agents called the "Negro invasion."

In 1916, after a successful campaign that included placards urging, "Save Your Home! Vote for Segregation!," the city's residents passed a measure requiring that black and white residents live on separate, designated blocks. In doing so, St. Louis became the first city in the country to require housing segregation by popular ballot. The tactic eventually fell to a legal challenge, but white residents found other ways to keep themselves, and their schools, protected from black residents.

30   One way was to write segregation into the sales contracts of houses. The clauses, known as real estate covenants, ensured the whiteness of neighborhoods by barring the sale of homes to black homebuyers—ever, and across entire sectors of the city. These practices quickly created a clear dividing line in St. Louis that endures to this day: Black people north of Delmar Boulevard; white people south.

In 1948, another landmark St. Louis case led to the U.S. Supreme Court striking down the enforcement of real estate covenants anywhere in the country. The case involved a black resident named J.D. Shelley, who bought a home with a deed restriction and then was sued by a white homeowner, Louis Kraemer, trying to block him from moving into the subdivision.

With legal discrimination under attack in the courts, white residents began abandoning St. Louis altogether. From 1950 to 1970, the city lost nearly 60 percent of its white population. This white flight was partly underwritten by the federal government, which secured loans reserved only for white homebuyers.

Town after town sprung up along the northern edge of St. Louis, some no larger than a single subdivision. Immediately, many forbade rentals and required homes to be built on large, more expensive lots. These devices helped keep neighborhoods white because black residents tended to be poorer and had difficulty getting home loans after decades of workplace, lending, and housing discrimination. Even today, 77 percent of white St. Louis area residents own their homes, compared to 45 percent of black residents, the U.S. Census shows.

Some of the tactics employed by St. Louis suburbs, including zoning, also were knocked down by courts.

But court victories, in the end, mattered little. A century of white effort   35
had lastingly etched the county map: a struggling, heavily black urban core surrounded by a constellation of 90 segregated little towns.

"St. Louis yielded some of the starkest racial dividing lines in any American city, North or South," said Colin Gordon, a University of Iowa professor who traces this history in his book *Mapping Decline: St. Louis and the Fate of the American City.* "I like to think of St. Louis not as an outlier, but one in which all the things we're talking about are just more visible."

A SEGREGATION SUCCESS, QUICKLY ABANDONED

One legal fight breached—at least temporarily—the St. Louis area's stark boundaries of home and property, and with them the 24 segregated school districts covering those 90 segregated little towns.

In 1954, the year of the Brown v. Board of Education Supreme Court decision, St. Louis ran the second-largest segregated school district in the country.

In the face of the ruling, school officials promised to integrate voluntarily. But they redrew school district lines around distinctly black and white neighborhoods to preserve their segregated schools. Even so, many white families still left, avoiding the chance of integration by simply moving across municipal lines. By 1980, 90 percent of black children in St. Louis still attended predominantly black schools.

With few white students left, it was clear that a desegregation plan that did   40
not include the white suburbs would be futile. In 1981, a federal judge called for a plan to bus black St. Louis children to white suburban schools.

White suburban residents, and their school leaders, revolted. They filed motions in court and penned angry letters to the local newspaper. The judge,

William Hungate, responded by threatening to do the one thing the white suburbs feared more than the bussing plan: Dissolve the carefully constructed school district boundaries and merge all 24 of the discrete districts into a single metro-wide one.

The opposition to the plan to bus children out of St. Louis collapsed. In 1983, St. Louis and its suburbs enacted the largest and most expensive interdistrict school desegregation program in the country.

At its peak, some 15,000 St. Louis public school students a year went to school in 16 heavily white suburban districts. Another 1,300 white students headed the opposite direction to new, integrated magnet schools in St. Louis.

The program had its flaws—chief among them, that it left another 15,000 of St. Louis's black students in segregated, inferior schools. And the transition of black urban students into white suburban schools was not always smooth.

45 But for the transfer students who rode buses out of the city, the plan successfully broke the deeply entrenched connection between race, ZIP code, and opportunity. Test scores for 8th and 10th grade transfer students rose. The transfer students were more likely to graduate and go on to college.

In surveys, white students overwhelmingly said they'd benefited from the opportunity to be educated alongside black students. In short order, St. Louis's was heralded by researchers and educators as the nation's most successful metro-wide desegregation program.

But from the moment it started, the St. Louis effort was under assault. It was never popular among the area's white residents. Politicians, Republicans and Democrats alike, vowed to end the program.

Then-state Attorney General John Ashcroft tried first, appealing St. Louis' school desegregation case all the way to the Supreme Court. He was succeeded by Jay Nixon, a Democrat who matched Ashcroft's fervor in seeking to end the program.

"Nixon came from a rural area. His position on school desegregation was more of a Southern Democrat, and it came pretty close to massive resistance," said William Freivogel, director of Southern Illinois University's School of Journalism, who covered the Supreme Court for the St. Louis Post-Dispatch during the 1980s and early 1990s. "I once wrote that Nixon behaved like a Southern politician standing in the schoolhouse door."

50 Nixon never expressly opposed the idea of integration. His argument centered on what he considered the astronomical costs of the desegregation plan. The price tag, initially in the hundreds of millions of dollars, would reach $1.7 billion.

Nixon, who would not be interviewed for this article, launched a number of legal challenges and prevailed in 1999 when supporters of the desegregation plan ultimately agreed to make the program voluntary. Nixon had successfully challenged Kansas City's desegregation plan before the U.S. Supreme Court, and some feared he would be similarly successful if the St. Louis case came before the court.

Districts soon began to drop out of the program, and the number of students participating steadily dwindled. Today, the voluntary program remains in place, still the largest of just eight interdistrict desegregation programs in the country. But it is a shadow of what it once was. Some 4,800 students get to escape the troubles of the St. Louis public schools, but each year, the program receives seven times as many applicants as open spaces.

Amy Stuart Wells is a Columbia's Teachers College professor who co-authored a book, *Stepping Over the Color Line: African-American Students in White Suburban Schools*, on the impact of the St. Louis plan on transfer students.

"I don't think many people realized how far ahead St. Louis really was," she said. "There are hundreds of thousands of people in the St. Louis metro area who were affected by this plan, but (the suburbs) did it because they had to and nobody said, 'Look, we're a national model for our country.' There were seeds sown that could have been so much more.

"This was the epicenter of where people tried to grapple with race, and failed miserably."   55

FEARS, FLIGHT AND A SUDDENLY BLACK SUBURB LEFT TO CRUMBLE

The white flight out of St. Louis left behind a trail of decay, as it did in many large Northern cities. City services lapsed when more affluent residents left. Businesses and jobs migrated as well. The schools in particular suffered.

Not surprisingly, black residents who could afford it looked for a way out, too. They looked to older North St. Louis suburbs, including Normandy. Incorporated in 1945 and covering fewer than two square miles, Normandy became a destination for the city's fleeing white working class.

Nedra Martin's family was among the black strivers who began to make their way to Normandy. Martin, who lives in Normandy today and works for Wal-Mart, said her parents first came to the town in 1975. They both worked government jobs—her dad was a welder for the city, her mom an aide in a state group home.

"My parents raised us to know that we are as good as anybody else," Martin said.

But as black families like the Martins moved in, "For Sale" signs went   60
up. White families started moving out, often to emerging outposts even farther from the heart of St. Louis.

After 1970, black enrollment in the Normandy schools exploded, more than doubling within eight years to 6,200. By 1978, only St. Louis enrolled more black students than Normandy.

Yet Normandy was left out of the metro-wide desegregation order that produced those few years of brighter outcomes for black students between 1983 and 1999. The order capped black enrollment at suburban districts at 25 percent, and Normandy and six other North St. Louis suburbs were already too black.

Instead, the Normandy schools buckled under their swift demographic shift, beginning a steep decline. Many of the best teachers followed the white and middle-class exodus. Instruction fell off. The district suffered from a revolving door of leadership, with principals and superintendents seldom sticking around more than a couple of years. Unable to meet minimum requirements for student achievement, the district clung to provisional accreditation for 15 years.

But black families had less freedom to simply move away to better school districts than even their poorer white neighbors. Housing discrimination continues to keep black families out of communities with quality schools, according to a 2013 St. Louis housing study.

65   The most affluent black families in Normandy, then, often opted out of the local school system, paying to send their children to private school. As a result, Normandy's schools ended up considerably poorer and more racially segregated than the communities they serve.

For years, the Normandy school system walked an academic tightrope. Then, in 2009, the state made matters worse.

New Education Commissioner Chris Nicastro decided that it was time to move on segregated districts that consistently failed their students. The state shuttered Wellston, a desperately poor, 500-student district next to Normandy that held the distinction of being Missouri's only 100 percent-black school system.

One state official had called conditions in Wellston's schools "deplorable" and "academically abusive."

The issue for state officials was what to do next with Wellston's students.

70   One thing was clear: The students were not going to be absorbed into any of the high-performing, mostly white districts nearby. Jones, the state board of education official, was blunt about why: "You'd have had a civil war."

Officials then turned to Normandy, which already enrolled almost 5,000 students. Merging two impoverished, struggling systems made sense to almost no one, especially the officials in charge of Normandy's schools.

The state went forward with it anyway.

"If you are strictly doing what's best for all kids, you don't merge those two districts," Stanton Lawrence, Normandy's superintendent at the time, said in a recent interview. "Why would you do that? They had written those kids off."

"It Was All Corrupt Politics"

By the time Michael Brown reached his junior year in high school, he had bounced between local districts and spent most of his career in racially segregated and economically disadvantaged schools. Behind in credits, he enrolled at Normandy High in the spring of 2013.

If he had dreams of academic success, he could not have wound up in a more challenging place to realize them.   75

The state's 2014 assessment report on Normandy's schools was spectacularly bleak: Zero points awarded for academic achievement in English. Zero for math, for social studies, for science. Zero for students headed to college. Zero for attendance. Zero for the percent of students who graduate. Its total score: 10 out of 140.

Out of 520 districts in the state, Normandy, where 98 percent of students are black and 9 of 10 were poor in 2013, is marooned at the very bottom.

Decades of research show that segregated, high-poverty schools are simply toxic for students of all races and backgrounds. Just last month, the University of North Carolina at Chapel Hill released a study showing that black first-graders in segregated schools performed worse than black students with the same backgrounds (meaning poverty, parental education and other factors) who attend integrated schools.

But for a moment prior to the start of Brown's senior year, the Normandy district's students were thrown an unlikely lifeline.

Just two years after the merger with Wellston, Normandy's schools were performing so poorly that the state stripped Normandy of its accreditation altogether. That triggered a state law requiring that any student there be allowed to transfer to an accredited district nearby. The law had been challenged by suburban districts uninterested in absorbing kids from failing schools, but in 2013 the Missouri State Supreme Court upheld it.   80

For Nedra Martin, whose honors student daughter, Mah'Ria, was stuck in Normandy's failing schools, the development was the miracle she had prayed for. Martin could not afford private schools, and her attempts to enroll her daughter in neighboring white districts had been rebuffed.

Just like that, the court's decision erased the invisible, impenetrable lines of segregation that had trapped her child.

"I was elated," Martin said. "Just elated."

Parents in the school districts that would have to take Normandy's students were not. Normandy had chosen to provide transportation for its transfers to attend Francis Howell, which was 85 percent white at the time and some 26 miles away.

When Francis Howell officials held a public forum to address community concerns, more than 2,500 parents packed into the high school gymnasium.

Would the district install metal detectors? What about the violence their children would be subjected to, an elementary school parent asked. Wouldn't test scores plummet? The issue wasn't about race, one parent said, "but trash."

Mah'Ria Martin was sitting in the audience that night with her mother. One of the few brown faces in the audience, the rising 8th grader said she wiped away tears.

"It made me heartbroken because they were putting us in a box," said Mah'Ria, soft spoken but firm, in recalling the episode. "I was sitting there thinking, 'Would you want some other parents talking about your kid that way?'"

In the fall of 2013, nearly 1,000 Normandy students—about a quarter of the district's enrollment—fled to schools in accredited districts. More than 400, including Mah'Ria, headed to Francis Howell.

Mah'Ria said that she was, in fact, welcomed by students and teachers at her new middle school. It was the first time in her life that she'd attended a district that had the full approval of the state.

She thrived. And she was not alone.

Despite the fears, recently released state data shows that, with the exception of one district, test scores in the transfer schools did not drop.

But the success came with a perverse twist. The state required failing districts whose students were allowed to transfer to pay the costs of the children's education in the adjoining districts. For the whiter, more affluent districts, it was a replay of what had happened during the court-ordered desegregation plan, when transfer students were referred to as "black gold": students the districts had to educate but who cost them nothing.

The millions of dollars in payments to other districts drained Normandy's finances. Within months, the district shuttered an elementary school and laid off 40 percent of its staff. Already deeply troubled, the Normandy schools were headed to insolvency.

"In order to save the district, they killed the district," said John Wright, a longtime St. Louis educator who spent stints as superintendent in both St. Louis and Normandy.

Recognizing the problem of student transfers, the state engineered their end.

This June, when students were on summer break, the state announced that it was taking over the Normandy Public Schools district and reconstituting it as the Normandy Schools Collaborative. As a new educational entity, state officials said, the district got a clean slate. It no longer was unaccredited but operated under a newly created status as a "state oversight district."

The transfer program, the state claimed, no longer applied. One by one, transfer districts announced that Normandy children were no longer welcome.

Martin and her daughter were devastated. "I honestly felt they were black-listing our children," Martin said.

Martin and other parents sued, asserting the state had no legal authority to act as it had. St. Louis lawyer Josh Schindler represented the parents. 100

"These are just families who want their kids to have a good education. Decent, hard-working people who want their kids to have a chance," he said in an interview. "This has been a decades-long battle. How are we going to remedy the situation?"

On August 15, after the new school year had begun in some districts, a state judge granted a temporary injunction that allowed the plaintiffs to enroll their children in the transfer districts.

"Every day a student attends an unaccredited school," the judge wrote, the child "could suffer harm that cannot be repaired."

The ruling brought a rush of relief to many parents.

"I cried and just held onto my kid," said Janine Crawford, whose son was able return to the Pattonville School District. "It meant that he was going to get a decent education. And it meant that I could take a deep breath." 105

The state is still fighting the ruling, and Francis Howell required all transfer students to obtain court orders to return.

Martin briefly returned Mah'Ria to the Normandy schools after they came under state oversight but found them little improved and has since sent her back to Francis Howell. The entire situation has only reinforced her cynicism and despair, she said.

"What about your neighbor? Is it so hard to embrace the children who clearly need your help right now?" she asked. "The whole way this was handled by the state on down was sheisty[3] and underhanded. They were not thinking about the children."

The state's top education officials admit that the way they've dealt with Normandy has laid bare racial divisions in St. Louis County and beyond. In an interview, Nicastro, the state superintendent, called it a "low point" in her career, a "blight and commentary about Missouri."

---

3   *sheisty*   Untrustworthy or dishonest (a slang term).

110   When asked whether black children in Missouri were receiving an equal education, she paused, then inhaled deeply. "Do I think black children in Missouri are getting in all cases the same education as their white counterparts?" Nicastro said. "I'd have to say no."

LITTLE HOPE AND A TELLING BURIAL

On a cold, clear morning in November, with the grand jury still assessing the killing of Michael Brown, a group of black leaders and concerned citizens gathered in a classroom at Harris-Stowe State University in downtown St. Louis. The school was founded in 1829 to train black teachers.

The gathering produced a recommitment to the solution to segregation floated 30 years before: A single, unified school district for St. Louis and its suburbs.

But there was recognition that the answer would require a long and uphill fight.

"We know what would have been best educationally for these kids—we always know what the best thing to do is. What we lack is the moral courage and political will to do it," said Jones, of the state Board of Education. "If we had treated the civil rights movement the way we've treated the education of black children, we'd still be drinking out of colored drinking fountains."

115   Separate but equal has not worked, Jones said. Not in St. Louis. Not anywhere else. The school lines that advantage some and deprive others, he said, must be toppled.

Students who spend their careers in segregated schools can look forward to a life on the margins, according to a 2014 study on the long-term impacts of school desegregation by University of California, Berkeley economist Rucker Johnson. They are more likely to be poor. They are more likely to go to jail. They are less likely to graduate from high school, to go to college, and to finish if they go. They are more likely to live in segregated neighborhoods as adults.

Their children are more likely to also attend segregated schools, repeating the cycle.

Even in the fog of her grief, Michael Brown's mother spoke to this struggle. With her son's body laying on the concrete behind police tape, Lesley McSpadden cried, "Do you know how hard it was for me to get him to stay in school and graduate?

"You know how many black men graduate?" she implored. "Not many."

120   With a diploma from a district that one report called "catastrophically underperforming," her oldest son had been headed to nearby Vatterott College.

Schools like Vatterott enroll a disproportionate percentage of black students. Those who attend are often saddled with debt they cannot pay back.

In 2013, a jury awarded more than $13 million to a single mother who sued Vatterott for misleading enrollment practices.

An executive with Vatterott Educational Centers, Inc. said the company's problems were in the past, and that it had reformed its admissions practices.

Brown never made it to Vatterott. Maybe he would have bucked the odds and found a way to master a trade and make a career.

Today, Brown is buried in the old St. Peter's Cemetery. Right next to Normandy High School.

(2015)

Questions

1. How segregated have the schools that you have attended been when you think of your teachers? fellow students? staff? administrators? How, do you believe, has segregation affected your education?

2. How does the history of segregation in St. Louis, and in Normandy in particular, illuminate the state of its schools today? Why is St. Louis "the epicenter of where people tried to grapple with race, and failed miserably"?

3. Does this article have a central argument or thesis? If so, what is it?

4. How does Hannah-Jones's analysis of Michael Brown's education deepen and complicate the tragedy of his death?

5. What is an "apartheid school"? Why are there more now than in the recent past?

6. In the final paragraph of this article, Hannah-Jones mentions the proximity of St. Peter's Cemetery to Normandy High School. What is she suggesting here about the fate of Black students in Normandy? Is this true in other parts of America?

7. How does Hannah-Jones describe segregation through a conversation about housing?

8. How does Darren Wilson's acquittal play into conversations about apartheid?

TEJU COLE

A TRUE PICTURE OF BLACK SKIN

Teju Cole is an acclaimed novelist, essayist, photographer, and commentator on politics and art. The following piece is part of his monthly column "On Photography," appearing in The New York Times Magazine. *Its subject is the photographer Roy DeCarava, whose artistic achievement and influence are widely acknowledged; he was the first African American photographer to receive a Guggenheim Fellowship. In 2006 DeCarava received a National Medal of Arts for work that "[i]n the midst of the Civil Rights movement ... seized the attention of our Nation while displaying the dignity and determination of his subjects."*

What comes to mind when we think of photography and the civil rights movement? Direct, viscerally affecting images with familiar subjects: huge rallies, impassioned speakers, people carrying placards ("I Am a Man"), dogs and fire hoses turned on innocent protesters. These photos, as well as the portraits of national leaders like Martin Luther King Jr.* and Malcolm X,* are explicit about the subject at hand. They tell us what is happening and make a case for why things must change. Our present moment, a time of vigorous demand for equal treatment, evokes those years of sadness and hope in black American life and renews the relevance of those photos. But there are other, less expected images from the civil rights years that are also worth thinking about: images that are forceful but less illustrative.

One such image left me short of breath the first time I saw it. It's of a young woman whose face is at once relaxed and intense. She is apparently in bright sunshine, but both her face and the rest of the picture give off a feeling of modulated darkness; we can see her beautiful features, but they are under-lit somehow. Only later did I learn the picture's title, "Mississippi Freedom Marcher, Washington, D.C., 1963" which helps explain the young woman's serene and resolute expression. It is an expression suitable for the event she's attending, the most famous civil rights march of them all. The title also confirms the sense that she's standing in a great crowd, even though we see only half of one other person's face (a boy's, indistinct in the foreground) and, behind the young woman, the barest suggestion of two other bodies.

The picture was taken by Roy DeCarava, one of the most intriguing and poetic of American photographers. The power of this picture is in the loveliness of its dark areas. His work was, in fact, an exploration of just how much could be seen in the shadowed parts of a photograph, or how much could be imagined into those shadows. He resisted being too explicit in his work, a reticence that expresses itself in his choice of subjects as well as in the way he presented them.

DeCarava, a lifelong New Yorker, came of age in the generation after the Harlem Renaissance[1] and took part in a flowering in the visual arts that followed that largely literary movement. By the time he died in 2009, at 89, he was celebrated for his melancholy and understated scenes, most of which were shot in New York City: streets, subways, jazz clubs, the interiors of houses, the people who lived in them. His pictures all share a visual grammar of decorous mystery: a young woman in a white graduation dress in the empty valley of a lot, a pair of silhouetted dancers reading each other's bodies in a cavernous hall, a solitary hand and its cuff-linked wrist emerging from the midday gloom of a taxi window. DeCarava took photographs of white people tenderly but seldom. Black life was his greater love and steadier commitment. With his camera he tried to think through the peculiar challenge of shooting black subjects at a time when black appearance, in both senses (the way black people looked and the very presence of black people), was under question.

All technology arises out of specific social circumstances. In our time, as in previous generations, cameras and the mechanical tools of photography have rarely made it easy to photograph black skin. The dynamic range of film emulsions, for example, were generally calibrated for white skin and had limited sensitivity to brown, red or yellow skin tones. Light meters had similar limitations, with a tendency to underexpose dark skin. And for many years, beginning in the mid-1940s, the smaller film-developing units manufactured by Kodak came with Shirley cards, so-named after the white model who was featured on them and whose whiteness was marked on the cards as "normal." Some of these instruments improved with time. In the age of digital photography, for instance, Shirley cards are hardly used anymore. But even now, there are reminders that photographic technology is neither value-free nor ethnically neutral. In 2009, the face-recognition technology on HP webcams had difficulty recognizing black faces, suggesting, again, that the process of calibration had favored lighter skin.

5

---

1   *Harlem Renaissance*   Social and artistic movement of the early twentieth century characterized by a flourishing of African American culture.

An artist tries to elicit from unfriendly tools the best they can manage. A black photographer of black skin can adjust his or her light meters; or make the necessary exposure compensations while shooting; or correct the image at the printing stage. These small adjustments would have been necessary for most photographers who worked with black subjects, from James Van Der Zee at the beginning of the century to DeCarava's best-known contemporary, Gordon Parks, who was on the staff of *Life* magazine. Parks's work, like DeCarava's, was concerned with human dignity, specifically as it was expressed in black communities. Unlike DeCarava, and like most other photographers, he aimed for and achieved a certain clarity and technical finish in his photo essays. The highlights were high, the shadows were dark, the mid-tones well-judged. This was work without exaggeration; perhaps for this reason it sometimes lacked a smoldering fire even though it was never less than soulful.

DeCarava, on the other hand, insisted on finding a way into the inner life of his scenes. He worked without assistants and did his own developing, and almost all his work bore the mark of his idiosyncrasies. The chiaroscuro effects[2] came from technical choices: a combination of underexposure, darkroom virtuosity and occasionally printing on soft paper. And yet there's also a sense that he gave the pictures what they wanted, instead of imposing an agenda on them. In "Mississippi Freedom Marcher," for example, even the whites of the shirts have been pulled down, into a range of soft, dreamy grays, so that the tonalities of the photograph agree with the young woman's strong, quiet expression. This exploration of the possibilities of dark gray would be interesting in any photographer, but DeCarava did it time and again specifically as a photographer of black skin. Instead of trying to brighten blackness, he went against expectation and darkened it further. What is dark is neither blank nor empty. It is in fact full of wise light which, with patient seeing, can open out into glories.

This confidence in "playing in the dark" (to borrow a phrase of Toni Morrison's) intensified the emotional content of DeCarava's pictures. The viewer's eye might at first protest, seeking more conventional contrasts, wanting more obvious lighting. But, gradually, there comes an acceptance of the photograph and its subtle implications: that there's more there than we might think at first glance, but also that when we are looking at others, we might come to the understanding that they don't have to give themselves up to us. They are allowed to stay in the shadows if they wish.

Thinking about DeCarava's work in this way reminds me of the philosopher Édouard Glissant, who was born in Martinique, educated at the Sorbonne

---

2   *chiaroscuro effects*   In visual art, effects created by the variation of light and dark tones.

and profoundly involved in anticolonial movements of the '50s and '60s. One of Glissant's main projects was an exploration of the word "opacity." Glissant defined it as a right to not have to be understood on others' terms, a right to be misunderstood if need be. The argument was rooted in linguistic consider-ations: It was a stance against certain expectations of transparency embedded in the French language. Glissant sought to defend the opacity, obscurity and inscrutability of Caribbean blacks and other marginalized peoples. External pressures insisted on everything being illuminated, simplified and explained. Glissant's response: No. And this gentle refusal, this suggestion that there is another way, a deeper way, holds true for DeCarava, too.

DeCarava's thoughtfulness and grace influenced a whole generation of black photographers, though few of them went on to work as consistently in the shadows as he did. But when I see luxuriantly crepuscular[3] images like Eli Reed's photograph of the Boys' Choir of Tallahassee (2004), or those in Carrie Mae Weems's "Kitchen Table Series" (1990), I see them as extensions of the DeCarava line. One of the most gifted cinematographers currently at work, Bradford Young, seems to have inherited DeCarava's approach even more directly. Young shot Dee Rees's "Pariah" (2011) and Andrew Dosunmu's "Restless City" (2012) and "Mother of George" (2013), as well as Ava DuVernay's "Selma" (2014). He works in color, and with moving rather than still images, but his visual language is cognate with DeCarava's: Both are keeping faith with the power of shadows.

The leading actors in the films Young has shot are not only black but also tend to be dark-skinned: Danai Gurira as Adenike in "Mother of George," for instance, and David Oyelowo as Martin Luther King Jr., in "Selma." Under Young's lenses, they become darker yet and serve as the brooding centers of these overwhelmingly beautiful films. Black skin, full of unexpected gradations of blue, purple or ocher, set a tone for the narrative: Adenike lost in thought on her wedding day, King on an evening telephone call to his wife or in discussion in a jail cell with other civil rights leaders. In a larger culture that tends to value black people for their abilities to jump, dance or otherwise entertain, these moments of inwardness open up a different space of encounter.

These images pose a challenge to another bias in mainstream culture: that to make something darker is to make it more dubious. There have been instances when a black face was darkened on the cover of a magazine or in a political ad to cast a literal pall of suspicion over it, just as there have been times when a black face was lightened after a photo shoot with the apparent goal of making it more appealing. What could a response to this form of contempt look like? One answer is in Young's films, in which an intensified darkness makes the actors

10

---

3   *crepuscular*   Dimly or inconsistently lit.

seem more private, more self-contained and at the same time more dramatic. In "Selma," the effect is strengthened by the many scenes in which King and the other protagonists are filmed from behind or turned away from us. We are tuned into the eloquence of shoulders, and we hear what the hint of a profile or the fragment of a silhouette has to say.

I think of another photograph by Roy DeCarava that is similar to "Mississippi Freedom Marcher," but this other photograph, "Five Men, 1964," has quite a different mood. We see one man, on the left, who faces forward and takes up almost half the picture plane. His face is sober and tense, his expression that of someone whose mind is elsewhere. Behind him is a man in glasses. This second man's face is in three-quarter profile and almost wholly visible except for where the first man's shoulder covers his chin and jawline. Behind these are two others, whose faces are more than half concealed by the men in front of them. And finally there's a small segment of a head at the bottom right of the photograph. The men's varying heights could mean they are standing on steps. The heads are close together, and none seem to look in the same direction: The effect is like a sheet of studies made by a Renaissance master. In an interview DeCarava gave in 1990 in the magazine *Callaloo*, he said of this picture: "This moment occurred during a memorial service for the children killed in a church in Birmingham, Ala., in 1964. The photograph shows men coming out of the service at a church in Harlem." He went on to say that the "men were coming out of the church with faces so serious and so intense that I responded, and the image was made."

The adjectives that trail the work of DeCarava and Young as well as the philosophy of Glissant—opaque, dark, shadowed, obscure—are metaphorical when we apply them to language. But in photography, they are literal, and only after they are seen as physical facts do they become metaphorical again, visual stories about the hard-won, worth-keeping reticence of black life itself. These pictures make a case for how indirect images guarantee our sense of the human. It is as if the world, in its careless way, had been saying, "You people are simply too dark," and these artists, intent on obliterating this absurd way of thinking, had quietly responded, "But you have no idea how dark we yet may be, nor what that darkness may contain."

(2015)

Questions

1. Near the end of this essay, Cole introduces another image by DeCarava, "Five Men, 1964." What role does the discussion of this image play in the context of his essay?

2. What does Cole mean when he says that "indirect images guarantee our sense of the human"? How do DeCarava's photographs demonstrate this?

3. In the opening of this essay, Cole draws a distinction between photographs that directly "tell us what is happening and make a case for why things must change" and photographs such as DeCarava's "that are forceful but less illustrative." How (if at all) do these types of photographs differ in their political impact—and in their artistic impact?

4. Cole observes that "cameras and the mechanical tools of photography have rarely made it easy to photograph black skin" (paragraph 5). Give an example of a contemporary tool or technology that, like camera technology, "is neither value-free nor ethnically neutral."

5. Consult Cole's list in paragraph 10 and find one of the photographs or a still from one of the films listed; then find one of the DeCarava photographs he mentions. In the style of Cole's article, write a short piece comparing the images you chose.

FRANCES GATEWARD AND JOHN JENNINGS

from THE BLACKER THE INK: CONSTRUCTIONS OF BLACK IDENTITY IN COMICS AND SEQUENTIAL ART

This co-authored piece serves as an introduction to The Blacker the Ink: Constructions of Black Identity in Comics and Sequential Art, *a collection of academic essays edited by Gateward and Jennings (both of whom are scholars in the field of visual and media studies). The volume as a whole, in the words of Michelle Burnaby, who reviewed it in Cinema Journal, provides a "theoretical framework for thinking through questions of Blackness in comics." Gateward and Jennings' introduction, however, is not heavily theoretical; it provides an accessible overview of the field.*

INTRODUCTION: THE SWEETER THE CHRISTMAS

If you are an avid reader of superhero comics, then you most likely smiled or chuckled at the reference in the title of this introduction to *Luke Cage, Powerman*'s signature "expletive" of shock used in the Marvel Comics character's early adventures. Luke Cage, like many other of his contemporaries, was an attempt to capitalize on the Blaxploitation film[1] boom of the 1970s. He was the first African American superhero to be featured in his own monthly comic book. Cage's "Sweet Christmas!" catchphrase was his equivalent to Superman's "Great Scott!" or The Mighty Thor's "By Odin's beard!" or Robin's "Holy ——, Batman!" It was also an attempt of a white writer to create authentic street slang for a character that was born and raised in a space where [the writer] had most likely never visited. Even though the words were echoing from a pair of Black lips, a Black man's voice was not being heard. In reality, many of the Christmases the character would have experienced

---

1   *Blaxploitation film*   Film genre whose primary characteristics were low budgets, violent action scenes, and predominantly Black casts with Black actors playing lead roles.

in the inner city would have been something far less "sweet" and far more foreboding. It was very difficult to negotiate the contrast between what was supposed to be an urban crime fighter and his costume of a steel tiara and steel wristbands with matching chain-link belt, accessorized with a bright yellow butterfly-collared shirt and boots. The shirt, by the way, was either always opened to expose his Black body or perpetually ripped to shreds each issue. Luke Cage is unremarkable insofar as many of the characters created in this era can be seen, in retrospect and most likely at the time, as being at the very least problematic. Jonathan Gayles's groundbreaking documentary from California Newsreel, *White Scripts and Black Supermen: Black Masculinities in Comic Books* (2012), deals with these issues head-on with interviews from Black male creators and scholars. Many of the men in the film openly express their love/ hate relationship not only with Cage but also with The Black Panther, The Falcon, Black Lightning, and other Black male superheroes. So even though the catchphrase "Sweet Christmas" is now looked on as a well-intentioned faux pas, it and other racially centered missteps bring forth extremely interesting opportunities to explore the various modes and nuances of the representation of an underrepresented people via a historically misrepresented medium.

... The genre of the superhero is very much a white-male-dominated power fantasy that is itself very much based in ideas around physical performance and power in relation to the negotiation of identity. Because the Black body has historically been linked to physicality and not intelligence, the depictions of Black superheroes already have inherent issues built into the very conventions of the genre. It is very hard for white men to see Black people as heroic outside the sports arena.

... [W]hen in the fall of 2011 DC Comics decided to relaunch its entire line of monthly comics, it did so by ending over seventy years of continuity and beginning the entire roster of characters over with fifty-two new books under the general heading "The New 52." To put things into perspective, DC Comics is second only to Marvel as the largest publisher of comics in the United States. It is owned by Warner Bros., and its superheroes include some of the most rec-ognizable in the industry. This list of characters includes Batman, Superman, Wonder Woman, Green Lantern, The Flash, and Aquaman. The relaunch was an attempt to secure the future of the publisher by supplying it with fresh read-ers. Much to the chagrin of comics retailers, "The New 52" planned to capture the interest of younger readers by simultaneously selling the online versions. Five of the fifty-two comics featured a Black character in the titular role: *Batwing, Static Shock, Mister Terrific, Voodoo*, and *The Fury of Firestorm: The Nuclear Men*. Three of these titles—*Fury of the Firestorm, Static Shock*, and *Mr. Terrific*—were canceled after just eight issues due to low sales. Some few months later, *Voodoo* followed suit. No "replacement" series featured a Black superhero. Only *Batwing* is still making his presence felt, with twenty-five issues as of this writing.[2] However, *Batwing*, whose alter ego is a former child solider from the Democratic Republic of Congo, is basically "The Batman of Africa" and works under Batman's supervision. The other books in "The New 52" were in some ways more problematic. *Firestorm* is about two high-school teens, one Black and one white, who join together in one body. That body is racially coded as white. *Static Shock* was a remnant of Milestone Media, the first multicultural comics imprint featuring diverse characters. *Voodoo* is the story of an exotic dancer of mixed-race heritage who is also part alien and turns into a dragon-like monster. *Voodoo* was bought from Jim Lee, formerly of Image Comics and now publisher of DC Comics. *Mister Terrific* was the most progressive of these offerings, about an Olympics-level athlete whose primary superpower is his incredible intellect, which he showcases via his fourteen PhDs in various fields. However, despite the fact that only 10 percent of "The New 52" featured Black superheroes, it is fair to say that Black images in the comics have come a long way.

The first images of Black people in comics were loosely based on the stereotypes generated in blackface minstrelsy,[3] stereotypes mired in the notion of fixity. These images dominated the mid-1930s until the mid-1940s. Characters such as Whitewash and Ebony White depicted Black Americans as dim-witted ·buffoons who needed the white male either to save them or to guide them in their lives. Whitewash appeared in the *Young Allies* comics from Marvel in the first half of the 1940s. He was a friend of Bucky Barnes, the spunky sidekick of Captain America. Whitewash's "superpower" seemed to be centered on speaking broken English and having the constant capacity for being captured and subsequently tied to various types of explosive devices. He was in constant need of rescue. Ebony White, the sidekick to The Spirit, created by Will Eisner, was a collection of stereotypes reified in a sometimes childish and animalistic form.

5   Such depictions were challenged by alternative works. In 1947, Orrin C. Evans, a Black news reporter from Philadelphia, along with his brothers, created *All-Negro Comics*, the first comics anthology featuring Black characters. Even during this time, Black creators were playing around with the various modes of representation afforded via the comics medium. The collection featured action, romance, and comedy within its first issue. A subsequent issue

---

2   *Only Batwing ... this writing*   In August 2014, *Batwing* was canceled after 34 issues.

3   *blackface minstrelsy* In minstrel shows of the nineteenth and early twentieth centuries, white actors donned "blackface"—makeup used to create cartoonishly exaggerated Black features—and enacted profoundly racist stereotypes in performances incorporating song and dance.

was never to be. Once suppliers learned what Evans was doing, they refused to sell paper and ink to the newsman. Nevertheless, *All-Negro Comics* demonstrates what Black writers and artists can produce when allowed agency, access, and freedom of expression. Even within this first collection of comics, Black people were attempting not only to show the potential of comics but also to destabilize Blackness as an identity....

In 1993, a Chicago-born surrealist artist and cartoonist named Turtel Onli posed a question relating to the "ages" of comics. The Golden Age of American comics runs from the 1930s into the late 1940s; the Silver Age goes from about 1956 to 1970; the Bronze Age of Comics is from 1970 to 1985; the Modern Age runs from 1985 to the present day. Onli's question was a simple one: "Where does the Black Age of Comics fall?" From that one query, an entire movement was spawned. Onli began to seek out comics created by Black people that featured Black characters. Once he found titles such as *Brotherman* (1990, from Black-owned Big City Comics out of Irving, Texas), *Heru, Son of Ausar* (published in 1993 by ANIA, a consortium of four small Black presses), and a handful of others, Onli began to distribute these books around the country from the trunk of his car, much as the independent filmmaker/novelist Oscar Micheaux did with his books and films decades before, during the period of the "race film." Onli used his position as an art teacher in Chicago's Kenwood Academy to launch the first Black Age of Comics Convention, turning the trunk of his car into a space of resistance. Now, on the eve of the twentieth anniversary of the Black Age of Comics, you can see the results of Orrin C. Evans's vision that started more than sixty years ago. Black images in comics now have an entire subculture and community connected to them. They have their own conventions, their own heroes and villains, their own superstar creators, their own awards ceremonies, and their own history. There are hundreds of Black creators of comics operating outside of the mainstream, making their own stories and their own futures with this amazing medium. However, even with all of this innovation and history, the notions of a Black superhero, a Black-comics publisher, and a Black-comics collector are still foreign concepts to many people....

So, what of *Luke Cage, Powerman* and his yuletide battle cry? Today, Cage enjoys a more modern-day vocabulary, mission, and appearance. He has become one of Marvel Comics' A-list characters and has even led an incarnation of *The Avengers*, Marvel's multimillion-dollar superhero team. In fact, Cage is now set to lead *The Mighty Avengers*. This is Marvel/Disney's new attempt to diversify its offerings by putting together an Avengers team that is composed almost solely of persons of color. The first Black superhero to have his own title has also been reimagined in other alternative titles such as *Earth X* and *Cage: Noir*, in which he becomes more like the legend of Stagger Lee.[4] He has even survived a "thugged out" gangsta version of himself written by Brian Azarello and illustrated by the comics legend Richard Corben. The character was once *the* representative of the Black American in the superhero genre. He has now become something much more. Like Blackness, Luke Cage has seen fit to become flexible despite his superpowered, steel-hard skin. His exploits are now global, important, nuanced, relevant, and yes, sweet....

(2015)

Questions

1. After reading Gateward and Jennings's work, reflect on the early history of Black people in comics. How does this history add to your understanding of the genre and how it has evolved?

2. Look online or in a library and find a cover image or interior page from the 1970s Luke Cage comics series. What (if anything) about it might be described as, in Gateward and Jennings's words, "at the very least problematic" (paragraph 1)? Why might Black comics creators and scholars have a "love/hate relationship" with this character (paragraph 1)?

3. Gateward and Jennings point out that (like many Black superheroes) Luke Cage was developed by a white writer: "Even though the words were echoing from a pair of Black lips, a Black man's voice was not being heard" (paragraph 1). Should writers and artists who are not Black be permitted to work on comics with Black protagonists? Explain your view.

4. Compare this selection with that from Adilifu Nama's *Super Black*, also reprinted in this anthology.

   a. To what extent do these academics endorse similar views of the history of Black representation in mainstream comics? To what extent do their positions differ?

   b. To the extent that they differ, is one piece stronger than the other? Explain your reasoning.

5. In the final paragraph of this selection, Gateward and Jennings describe more recent portrayals of Luke Cage in positive terms. Find

---

4   *Stagger Lee*   Lee Shelton (1865–1912), a Black pimp who became a folk figure after he purportedly murdered a friend for taking his hat.

a relatively recent portrayal of the character and evaluate it in terms of racial politics. Consider, for example, an episode of Marvel's *Luke Cage* (2016–) or *The Defenders* (2017), a recent issue of the Marvel comic *Luke Cage* (2017–), or the video game *Marvel: Future Fight* (2015; Cage is a playable character).

DAWN MARIE DOW

THE DEADLY CHALLENGES OF RAISING AFRICAN AMERICAN BOYS: NAVIGATING THE CONTROLLING IMAGE OF THE "THUG"

The following article by sociologist Dawn Marie Dow appeared in the April 2016 issue of the academic journal Gender and Society; *it had been published online on the journal's website earlier that year.*

ABSTRACT

Through 60 in-depth interviews with African American middle- and upper-middle-class mothers, this article examines how the controlling image of the "thug"* influences the concerns these mothers have for their sons and how they parent their sons in light of those concerns. Participants were principally concerned with preventing their sons from being perceived as criminals, protecting their sons' physical safety, and ensuring they did not enact the "thug," a form of subordinate masculinity. Although this image is associated with strength and toughness, participants believed it made their sons vulnerable in various social contexts. They used four strategies to navigate the challenges they and their sons confronted related to the thug image. Two of these strategies—experience and environment management—were directed at managing characteristics of their sons' regular social interactions—and two—image and emotion management—were directed at managing their sons' appearance. By examining parenting practices, this research illuminates the strategies mothers use to prepare their sons to address gendered racism through managing the expression of their masculinity, racial identity, and class status.

I interviewed Karin, a married mother, in her apartment while she nursed her only child. Karin let out a deep sigh before describing how she felt when she learned the baby's gender:

> I was thrilled [the baby] wasn't a boy. I think it is hard to be a black girl and a black woman in America, but I think it is dangerous and

sometimes deadly to be a black boy and black man. Oscar Grant[1] and beyond, there are lots of dangerous interactions with police in urban areas for black men ... so I was very nervous because we thought she was a boy.... I was relieved when she wasn't. It is terrible, but it is true.

Karin's relief upon learning her child was not a boy underscores how intersections of racial identity, class, and gender influence African American middle- and upper-middle-class mothers' parenting concerns. They are aware their children will likely confront racism, often start addressing racism during their children's infant and toddler years (Feagin and Sikes 1994; Staples and Johnson 1993; Tatum 1992, 2003), and attempt to protect their children from racially charged experiences (Uttal 1999). Responding to these potential experiences of racism, parents believe giving their children the skills to address racism is an essential parenting duty (Feagin and Sikes 1994; Hill 2001; Staples and Johnson 1993; Tatum 1992, 2003). Although the participants in this research were middle- and upper-middle-class, and thus had more resources than their lower-income counterparts, they felt limited in their abilities to protect their sons from the harsh realities of being African American boys and men in America.

Research demonstrates that race and gender influence how African Americans are treated by societal institutions, including schools (Eitle and Eitle 2004; Ferguson 2000; Holland 2012; Morris 2005; Pascoe 2007; Pringle, Lyons, and Booker 2010; Strayhorn 2010), law enforcement (Brunson and Miller 2006; Hagan, Shedd, and Payne 2005; Rios 2009), and employment (Bertrand and Mullainathan 2004; Grodsky and Pager 2001; Pager 2003; Wingfield 2009, 2011). African American children also experience gendered racism (Essed 1991). African American boys face harsher discipline in school and are labeled aggressive and violent more often than whites or African American girls (Eitle and Eitle 2004; Ferguson 2000; Morris 2005, 2007; Pascoe 2007). Although African American families engage in bias preparation with their children (McHale et al. 2006), the content of that preparation and how gender and class influence it is often not researched. Anecdotal evidence depicts African American parents as compelled to provide gender- and race-specific guidance to their sons about remaining safe in various social interactions, even within

---

1 [Dow's note] On New Year's Day 2010, Johannes Mehserle, a white Bay Area Rapid Transit police officer, fatally shot Oscar Grant, an African American teenager, in Oakland. During the incident, Grant was unarmed, lying face-down on the train platform, and had been subdued by several other officers. On July 8, 2010, Mehserle was found guilty of involuntary manslaughter, not the higher charges of second-degree murder or voluntary manslaughter (McLaughlin 2014).

their own, often middle-class, neighborhoods (Graham 2014; Martinez, Elam, and Henry 2015; Washington 2012).

5   This article examines how African American middle- and upper-middle-class mothers raising young children conceptualize the challenges their sons will face and how they parent them in light of these challenges. I focus on mothers because they are often primarily responsible for socializing young children (Hays 1996), and specifically on middle- and upper-middle-class African American mothers because they typically have more resources to address discrimination than do lower-income mothers. Indeed, one might assume that these mothers' resources would enable them to protect their sons from certain challenges. African American mothers are more likely to engage in the racial socialization of younger children and to prepare children to address experiences of racism than are African American fathers (McHale et al. 2006; Thornton et al. 1990). They are also more likely to be single and, thus, principally responsible for decisions related to their children's educational, social, and cultural resources and experiences. Although there has been substantial public discourse about African American mothers' ability to teach their sons to be men, there has been little systematic analysis of their involvement in these processes (Bush 1999, 2004). Also, cultural stereotypes of uninvolved African American fathers overshadow research demonstrating their more active involvement (Coles and Green 2010; Edin, Tach, and Mincy 2009; Salem, Zimmerman, and Notaro 1998).

Although masculinity is associated with strength, participants' accounts of their parenting practices revealed their belief that the thug image made their sons vulnerable in many social interactions. Participants feared for their sons' physical safety and believed their sons would face harsher treatment and be criminalized* by teachers, police officers, and the public because of their racial identity and gender. Their accounts revealed four strategies used to navigate these challenges, which I term experience, environment, emotion, and image management.

RACED, CLASSED, AND GENDERED PARENTING CHALLENGES

Gendered Racism and Controlling Images

Scholars have examined how race, class, and gender influence African Americans' experiences in various settings (Ferguson 2000; Morris 2005, 2007; Wingfield 2007, 2009). African American boys and girls experience different levels of social integration within suburban schools (Holland 2012; Ispa-Landa 2013). Boys are viewed as "cool" and "athletic" by classmates and are provided more opportunities to participate in high-value institutional activities, while girls are viewed as aggressive and unfeminine, and are provided with fewer similar opportunities (Holland 2012; Ispa-Landa 2013). Despite having somewhat positive experiences with peers, boys' encounters with teachers and administrators are fraught, as educators often perceive them as aggressive, violent, and potential criminals (Ferguson 2000; Morris 2005; Pascoe 2007). Compared to whites and African American girls, African American boys are disciplined more severely in school (Welch and Payne 2010), and their in-school discipline is more likely to lead to criminal charges (Brunson and Miller 2006).

African American boys are also more likely to have encounters with law enforcement than are whites or African American girls, and these interactions are more likely to have negative outcomes (Brunson and Miller 2006; Quillian, Pager, and University of Wisconsin-Madison 2000) and become violent (Brunson and Miller 2006). The news provides numerous examples of fatal shootings of unarmed African American teenage boys, often by white police officers and private citizens (Alvarez and Buckley 2013; McKinley 2009; Severson 2013; Yee and Goodman 2013). Initiatives like the White House-sponsored "My Brother's Keeper" are responding to an expansive body of research that demonstrates African American boys face disproportionate challenges to their success from schools, their communities, law enforcement, the workplace, and beyond (Jarrett and Johnson 2014).

Collins (2009) theorizes how controlling images function as racialized and gendered stereotypes that justify the oppression of certain groups and naturalize existing power relations, while forcing oppressed populations to police their own behavior. Scholars studying controlling images examine how these inaccurate depictions of black sexuality, lawfulness, temperament, and financial well-being are used to justify policies that disempower women of color (Collins 2004, 2009; Gilliam 1999; Hancock 2003; Harris-Perry 2011) and impact African Americans' experiences in their workplaces, school settings, and other social contexts (Beauboeuf-Lafontant 2009; Dow 2015; Ong 2005; Wingfield 2007, 2009). These images depict African American men as hypermasculine:* revering them as superhuman or reviling them as threats to be contained (Ferber 2007; Noguera 2008). Scholars suggest that African American men enact the thug, a version of subordinate masculinity associated with violence, criminality, and toughness, because they are not permitted to attain hegemonic[2] masculinity (Schrock and Schwalbe 2009). Indeed, African American men who enact alternative versions of manhood that are associated with being educated or middle class confront challenges to their masculinity and racial authenticity (Ford 2011; Harper 2004; Harris III 2008; Noguera 2008; Young 2011).

---

2. *hegemonic* Socially and/or politically dominant.

10   Expanding on this scholarship, I examine how the thug image influences African American middle- and upper-middle-class mothers' parenting concerns and practices when raising sons. Building on Ford's view that "black manhood refers to imagined constructions of self that allow for more fluid interactions in Black and nonblack, public and private social spaces" (Ford 2011, 42), I argue that this fluidity is not just permitted but required to protect black male bodies and manage their vulnerability in different contexts. Black manhood and double consciousness (Du Bois [1903] 1994) are complementary concepts because each requires individuals to see themselves through the broader society's eyes. These concepts also illuminate how individuals who are associated with privileged identities, such as "man" or "American," confront obstacles that prevent them from benefiting from those identities' privileges.

Emotional Labor and Identity Work

Scholarship on emotional labor and identity work examines how African Americans navigate stereotypes. Hochschild (2003) argues that individuals who perform emotional labor induce or suppress the display of certain feelings to produce specific emotional states in others, thereby contributing to their subordinate position. Studying a predominately white law firm, Pierce (1995) uncovers how men, but not women, garner rewards for expressing a range of negative emotions. Summers-Effler (2002) examines how "feeling rules" become associated with particular positions in society and the members of groups generally occupying those positions. Building on Hochschild's (2003) theories, scholars demonstrate that, fearing they will affirm controlling images, African Americans believe there is a limited range of emotions they can display in the workplace without confronting negative stereotypes, and thus feel less entitled to express discontent or anger (Jackson and Wingfield 2013; Wingfield 2007, 2011, 2013).

Historically, interactions between whites and African Americans have been guided by unspoken rules of conduct that signaled different status positions and maintained and reproduced a social structure that subordinated African Americans through acts of deference (Doyle 1937). These acts included African Americans using formal greetings to signal respect to whites, while whites used less formal greetings to signal their superiority (Doyle 1937). Violations of these rules resulted in frustration, anger, and violence from whites and anxiety, fear, and submission among African Americans (Doyle 1937). Rollins's (1985) research reveals how African American women employed as domestics suppressed their emotions and physical presence in interactions with white female employers. Indeed, adhering to specific feeling rules maintains and reproduces racial, class, and gender hierarchies, even as individuals circumvent them.

As African Americans traverse different economic and social strata that are governed by different rules, scholars identify how they manage the expression of their racial identity and class through code-switching (Anderson 1990), shifting (Jones and Shorter-Gooden 2003), identity work (Carbado and Gulati 2013), and cultural flexibility[3] (Carter 2003, 2006). Carter's (2003, 2006) and Pugh's (2009) research demonstrates that African American children and families, respectively, often necessarily retain some fluency in "low-status" cultural capital,[4] even as they ascend economically. Lacy's (2007) research also suggests that some middle-class African Americans emphasize their racial identity, class identity, or racially infused class identities, depending on social context, to gain acceptance. Although these scholars examine how African American middle-class children and families negotiate race and class, gender is not central to their analysis. This article complicates their scholarship by analyzing how race, class, and gender affect how mothers encourage their sons to express their racial identity and masculinity. Schrock and Schwalbe argue, "learning how to signify a masculine self entails learning how to adjust to audiences and situations and learning how one's other identities bear on the acceptability of a performance" (Schrock and Schwalbe 2009, 282). Mothers play an important part in this gendered, classed, and racialized socialization process (Schrock and Schwalbe 2009).

METHODS

This article is based on data from a larger project that examined how African American middle- and upper-middle-class mothers approach work, family, parenting, and child care. Participants were recruited using modified snowball sampling[5] techniques. Study announcements were sent via email to African American and predominately white professional and women's organizations. Announcements were made at church services and in bulletins, and were posted at local businesses and on physical or Internet bulletin boards of community colleges, local unions, and sororities.* Announcements were also posted to list

---

3   *code-switching* Switching between linguistic styles; *shifting* In their book *The Double Lives of Black Women in America*, Jones and Shorter-Gooden suggest that Black women "shift" in a variety of ways—modifying speech and appearance, for example, as they "shift 'White' as they head to work in the morning and 'Black' as they come back home each night"; *identity work* In their research, Devon W. Carbado and Mitu Gulati explore ways in which the performance of the identities assumed, for example, in the workplace, requires work; *cultural flexibility* I.e., the flexibility to act as a part of different cultural and social groups.

4   *cultural capital* Assets that are social, not financial.

5   *snowball sampling* Method of obtaining a study sample in which study participants recruit their own acquaintances to also participate in the study.

servers catering to parents, mothers, or African American mothers. Participants who were interviewed were asked to refer others. Through these methods, 60 participants[6] were recruited to the study, of which 40 were raising sons only or sons and daughters. Aside from the opening quote describing a mother's relief upon learning she was not having a son, this analysis focuses on participants raising sons.

15 Interviews were conducted in person in a location of each participant's choosing, including her home or office, cafés or restaurants, and local parks. Interviews lasted from one hour to two and a half hours, and were conducted between 2009 and 2011. I asked participants about the families in which they were raised, becoming mothers, and their parenting concerns and practices. Before each interview, participants completed a Demographic Information Sheet that included questions about their marital status, education, total family income, and family composition. Table 1 lists participants' pseudonyms and demographic information.

All participants lived in the San Francisco Bay Area and were middle- or upper-middle-class as determined by their education and total family income. Participants attended college for at least two years, and their total annual family incomes ranged from $50,000 to $300,000. Participants' total family incomes were as follows: (1) 27 percent were between $50,000 and 99,000;

Table 1. Names and Interviewee Characteristics ($N = 60$).

Name	Age	Occupation	Degree	Marital Status	Spouse or Domestic Partner's Degree	Number of Kids
Netia	27	SAHM	SC	S	N/A	1
Jameela	26	Administrative assistant	SC	S	N/A	1
Calliope	28	Graduate Student / SAHM[7]	BA	S	N/A	1
Heather	35	Administrator and teacher / SAHM	BA	D	N/A	3
Elizabeth	40	Program manager	MA	M	BA	1
Riana	36	Analyst	MA	S	N/A	1
Rochelle	35	Clerical / SAHM	AS	M	AS	3
Tracy	35	Paralegal	BA	M	BA	5
Hana	37	Part-time consultant / SAHM	MA	M	BA	2
Nia	30	Teacher	MA	M	BA	2
Monique	28	Social worker	MA	M	BA	1
Jennifer	34	Dentist	DDS	D	N/A	1
Karin	27	Writer / SAHM	MA	M	MA	1
Sharon	44	Program manager	BA	M	BA	2
Trina	25	Part-time teacher	MA	M	MA	1
Nora	40	Educator	PhD	M	MA	2
Brandy	45	Project manager	BA	M	HS	2
Cara	48	Nurse weekends / SAHM during week	MA	D	N/A	2
Vera	45	Dentist	DDS	M	MA	2
Mary	44	Educator / SAHM	MA	M	SC	2
Kera	34	SAHM	MA	M	SC	2

(Continued)

6 [Dow's note] Sixty-five mothers were interviewed. Five were excluded because they did not meet the income and educational criteria of the study.

7 [Dow's note] She raised her nephew during his teen years with her, now deceased, husband.

TABLE 1 (continued)

	Name	Age	Occupation	Degree	Marital Status	Spouse or Domestic Partner's Degree	Number of Kids
22	Farah	32	Academic	PhD	M	SC	2
23	Maya	37	Professor	PhD	M	BA	4
24	Reagan	45	Senior manager	BA	D	N/A	1
25	Sarah	36	Graduate student / SAHM	BA	M	MA	1
26	Sydney	32	Public health administrator	MA	M	MA	1
27	Mera	32	SAHM	MA	M	MA	2
28	Tamika	41	Freelance administrator / SAHM	BA	M	BA	1
29	Robinne	40	Administrator	MA	M	BA	1
30	Ann	49	Teacher coach	MA	M	SC	2
31	Audra	37	Meeting planner	BA	M	BA	2
32	Teresa	30	Project coordinator	BA	M	BA	2
33	Ashley	44	Project manager	MA	M	SC	1
34	Asa	40	Development director	BA	M	PhD	1
35	Lakeisha	35	Marketing manager	MA	M	MA	1
36	Claudette	34	Freelance paraprofessional / merchandiser / gym teacher/ substitute teacher / SAHM	BA	M	SC	2
37	Jessica	42	Administrator	BA	D	N/A	1
38	Alana	40	Probation officer	BA	M	BA	2
39	Chandra	41	Program coordinator	MA	D	N/A	2
40	Cheryl	39	Pediatrician	MD	M	JD	1
41	Charlene	33	Attorney	JD	M	SC	1

(Continued)

TABLE 1 (continued)

	Name	Age	Occupation	Degree	Marital Status	Spouse or Domestic Partner's Degree	Number of Kids
42	Essence	37	Health educator / program manager	MA	M	SC	1
43	Christine	43	Acupuncturist	MA	S	MA	1
44	Kristen	42	Attorney	JD	M	BA	1
45	Jordana	40	Marketing program manager	MA	M	BA	2
46	Kellie	44	SAHM	AS	M	MA	4
47	Karlyn	35	Research compliance manager	MA	S	N/A	2
48	Rachel	36	Operations manager	MA	M	BA	2
49	Tammy	37	Team leader	AS	M	BA	3
50	Rebecca	40	Educator	MA	W	N/A	1 [8]
51	Charlotte	40	Self-Eeployed / SAHM	MA	M	MA	4
52	Remi	36	Nurse	MA	M	BA	6
53	Harper	37	Child psychologist	MD	M	MA	1
54	Samantha	35	Human resources director	MA	M	MA	2
55	Claire	36	SAHM	PhD	M	MA	1
56	Ava	42	Project manager	MA	M	SC	1
57	Emma	34	Public relations project manager	BA	M	BA	1
58	Grace	30	Admissions director	SC	S	N/A	1
59	Hannah	45	Training manager	BA	DP	BA	2
60	Sophia	38	Grant writer	MA	S	N/A	1

NOTE: All names are pseudonyms. Occupation: SAHM -= stay-at-home mother.[9] Degree: AS = associate's degree; BA = bachelor's degree; DDS = doctor of dental medicine; HS = high school; JD = juris doctorate; MA = master's degree; MD = doctor of medicine; PhD = doctorate; SC = some college. Marital status: S = single; M = married; D = divorced; DP = domestic partner; Sep. = separated; W = widowed.

8   [Dow's note]   She raised her nephew during his teen years with her, now deceased, husband.

9   [Dow's note]   Notably, almost half of the participants who identified as stay-at-home mothers were employed in part-time to full-time jobs.

(2) 23 percent were between $100,000 and $149,000; (3) 23 percent were between $150,000 and $199,000; and (4) 27 percent were between $200,000 and $300,000. The upper end of this income range is high by national standards; however, in the San Francisco Bay Area between 2006 and 2010, the median owner-occupied home value was $637,000 (Bay Area Census 2010). Homeownership is an important marker of middle-class status (Sullivan, Warren, and Westbrook 2000). Participants at the upper end of this income range were among the few who could easily attain that marker. Half of the participants were homeowners and half were renters. Participants' ages spanned from 25 to 49 years. The majority of participants (63 percent) earned advanced degrees such as MD, JD, PhD, or MA, with 27 percent earning college degrees and 10 percent attending some college. Three-fourths of the participants were married or in a domestic partnership, and one-fourth were divorced, never married, or widowed. All participants were raising at least one child who was 10 years old or younger, as this research focused on mothers who are raising young children. Participants' employment status included working full-time or part-time, or not working outside of the home (i.e., stay-at-home mothers).

Using grounded theory[10] (Glaser and Strauss 1967) and the procedures and techniques described by Strauss and Corbin (1998), I transcribed interviews and coded them to identify and differentiate recurring concepts and categories. A key concept that emerged was the controlling image of the "thug," a version of subordinate masculinity identified in masculinity and black feminist scholarship. Some participants used the term "thug" or "thuggish." Others used language that referred to components of the thug, such as criminality, violence, and toughness. Outliers[11] within the data were examined to determine how they challenged or could be reconciled with emerging themes. My focus here on the accounts of mothers precluded a direct analysis of fathers' views, but fathers were involved in these strategies. This focus also precluded an analysis of how African boys and teenagers navigated these challenges themselves.

As a middle-class African American mother, I shared traits with my participants. These characteristics, in some ways, positioned me as an insider with participants and facilitated building rapport and their willingness to share information about their lives. This status also required that I refrain from assuming I understood a participant's meanings. I balanced building rapport with guarding

10 *grounded theory* Before Glaser and Strauss's 1967 book *The Discovery of Grounded Theory*, sociological theory was often developed in the abstract—without any data having been collected and analyzed; only after theories had been developed would they be tested against empirical evidence. The Glaser and Strauss approach advocated linking data collection and analysis to theory development throughout the process—in other words, grounding theory in evidence even as the theory is being developed.

11 *Outliers* Pieces of evidence that do not follow the pattern of the main body of data.

against making assumptions by probing for additional clarification when a participant suggested I understood something based on our shared background.

PROTECTING SONS FROM BABY RACISM AND CRIMINALIZATION

Although participants described parenting concerns that transcended gender and related to fostering other aspects of their children's identity, this article examines their specific concerns about raising sons. Participants' concerns included ensuring the physical safety of their sons in interactions with police officers, educators, and the public, and preventing their sons from being criminalized by these same groups.

Gender, Racial Identity, and Parenting

Generally, middle-class children are thought to live in realms of safety, characterized by good schools, an abundance of educational resources, and protection from harsh treatment from police, teachers, and the public. However, numerous scholars have demonstrated that despite the expansion of the African American middle class, its members face economic, social, residential, and educational opportunities that are substantively different from those of middle-class whites (Feagin and Sikes 1994; Lacy 2007; Pattillo 1999). Middle-class African Americans continue to face discrimination in lending, housing (Massey and Denton 1993; Oliver and Shapiro 1995; Sharkey 2014), and employment (Pager 2003). African American middle-class children often attend schools that are poorly funded, lack adequate infrastructure, and are characterized by lower academic achievement than their white counterparts (Pattillo 1999, 2007). These children are also more likely to grow up in neighborhoods with higher levels of crime and inferior community services as compared to their white counterparts (Oliver and Shapiro 1995; Pattillo 1999). Although participants recognized that their middle-class status afforded them additional resources, they believed that their sons' access to middle-class realms of safety were destabilized and diminished because of their racial identity and gender.

Charlotte, a married mother of four sons, who lived in an elite and predominately white neighborhood, held back tears as she described her fears about how others would respond to them:

> I look at the president.* I see how he is treated and it scares me. I want people to look at my sons and see them for the beautiful, intelligent, gifted, wonderful creatures that they are and nothing else. I do not want them to look at my sons and say, "There goes that Black guy," or hold onto their purse.

20

Similarly, Nia, a married mother of two sons, who lived in an economically diverse, predominantly African American neighborhood, described interactions with other families at local children's activities that she called "baby racism":

> From the time our first son was a baby and we would go [to different children's activities]. Our son would go and hug a kid and a parent would grab their child and be like, "Oh, he's going to attack him!" And it was just, like, "Really? Are you serious?" He was actually going to hug him. You see, like little "baby racism." ... I have even written to local parents' listservs to ask, "Am I imagining this ... ?" And the response was interesting. Almost all the black mothers wrote in, "You're not imagining this, this is real. You're going to have to spend the rest of your life fighting for your child." And all the white mothers said, "You're imagining it. It's not like that. You're misinterpreting it." And it was like, okay, so I'm not imagining this.

Charlotte and Nia, like other participants, believed that when African American boys participated in activities that were engaged in by predominantly white and middle-class families, their behavior faced greater scrutiny. Race and gender trumped class;* poverty and crime were associated with being an African American boy. Participants believed the process of criminalizing their sons' behaviors began at an early age, and was not confined to educational settings but was pervasive. Although participants had no way of knowing how others were thinking about their sons, numerous studies support their belief that African American boys' actions are interpreted differently in a range of settings (Ferguson 2000; Morris 2005; Pascoe 2007).

Participants also saw teachers and educators as potential threats to their sons' development. Karlyn, a single mother of a son and daughter, described her son's experience of being harshly disciplined at school:

> A teacher was yelling at my son because some girls reported that he cheated in Four Square.[12] ... I had to let her know "don't ever pull my son out of class for a Four Square game again.... And don't ever yell at my child unless he has done something horrible." ... I told the principal, "You know, she may not think she is racist but what would make her yell at a little black boy over a stupid Four Square game?" ... He said, "Oh my God, I am just so glad that you have the amount of restraint that you did because I would have been really upset." I said, "As the mother of a black son, I am always concerned about how he is treated by people."

---

12 *Four Square* Game played on school grounds.

Like Karlyn, others relayed stories of educators having disproportionately negative responses to their sons' behavior, describing them as aggressive or scary, when similar behavior in white boys was described as more benign. Karlyn, and others, continuously monitored their sons' schools to ensure they received fair treatment. Ferguson's (2000) and Noguera's (2008) research supports their assessment, identifying a tendency among educators to criminalize the behavior of African American boys. Participants' middle-class status did not protect their sons from these experiences.

Mary, a married mother of a son and daughter, also believed her son faced distinct challenges related to his racial identity, class, and gender and sought out an African American middle- and upper-middle-class mothers' group to get support from mothers who were negotiating similar challenges. Mary described a conversation that regularly occurred in her mothers' group, revealing her worries about adequately preparing her son to navigate interactions with teachers and police officers:

> With our sons, we talk about how can we prepare them or teach them about how to deal with a society, especially in a community like Oakland, where black men are held to a different standard than others, and not necessarily a better one.... When you are a black man and you get stopped by the policeman, you can't do the same things a white person would do because they might already have some preconceived notions, and that might get you into a heap more trouble.... We talk about our sons who are a little younger and starting kindergarten. What do we have to do to make sure teachers don't have preconceived ideas that stop our sons from learning because they believe little brown boys are rambunctious, or little brown boys are hitting more than Caucasian boys?

It is worth emphasizing that although these participants were middle- and upper-middle-class African American mothers with more resources than lower-income mothers, these resources did not protect their sons from gendered racism. Also, middle-class mothers are depicted as viewing educators as resources (Lareau 2011), but these participants viewed educators as potential threats. They believed their sons' racial identity marked them as poor, uneducated, violent, and criminal, and they would have to actively and continuously challenge that marking and assert their middle-class status in mainstream white society—a version of the politics of respectability (Collins 2004). Some participants attended workshops aimed at helping them teach their sons to safely engage with teachers, police officers, and the public. Like the parents described by Lareau and McNamara (1999), some used race-conscious strategies and others used color-blind strategies to address concerns about gendered racism.

25

Although most participants believed their sons faced challenges related to the thug, a few did not. These participants attributed their lack of concern to their sons' racially ambiguous appearance. Kera, a married mother of two sons, said, "The way they look, they're like me. They could be damn near anything depending on how they put their hair.... I don't think they'll have the full repercussions of being a black man like my brothers or my husband." Kera's comments echo research suggesting that skin color differences impact African Americans' experiences in employment, school, and relationships (Hunter 2007).

Participants also believed their sons faced pressure to perform specific versions of African American masculinity that conformed to existing raced, classed, and gendered hierarchies. Nora, a married mother of a son and daughter, said, "There is a lot of pressure for black boys to assume a more 'thuggish' identity. There aren't enough different identity spaces for black boys in schools ... and so I want my kids to have choices. And if that's the choice, I might cringe ... but I would want it to be among a menu of choices." Elements of the thug, such as criminality, aggression, and low academic performance, recurred in participants' accounts as something they and their sons navigated. Scholars (Ong 2005; Wingfield 2007) have identified how African American adults negotiate controlling images, but Nora's comments underscore that these negotiations begin at a young age.

Given these pressures to perform specific versions of African American masculinity associated with poverty and criminality, participants tried to protect their sons from early experiences of subtle and explicit racism because of the potential impact on their identity formation. Sharon, a married mother of a son and daughter, captured a sentiment shared by many participants when she stated,

> Each time a black boy has a racially charged interaction with a police officer, a teacher, or a shop owner, those experiences will gradually start to eat at his self-worth and damage his spirit. He might become so damaged that he starts to believe and enact the person he is expected to be, rather than who he truly is as a person.

Participants believed their sons were bombarded by negative messages about African American manhood from the broader white society and, at times, the African American community. Participants worried about the toll these messages might take on their sons' self-perception as they transitioned to manhood. They steered their sons away from enacting the thug, but also observed an absence of other viable expressions of racially authentic middle-class masculinity.

Strategies to Navigate the Thug

Legal scholar Krieger (1995) argues that the law has a flawed understanding of   30
racial prejudice and that, rather than being an active and explicit set of beliefs,
racism operates by shaping our perceptions of behaviors. A loud white boy is
viewed as animated and outgoing; a loud black boy is viewed as aggressive
and disruptive (Ferguson 2000). Similar to the interracial interactions in the
South that Doyle (1937) describes, participants believed that whites expected
African American boys to adjust their behavior depending on the racial identity
of the person with whom they were interacting. Participants walked a tightrope
between preparing their sons to overcome the gendered racism they might confront and ensuring they did not internalize these views or use them as excuses
to fail. Christine, who was engaged to be married and the mother of a son,
explained that in teaching her son what it means to be an African American
man, she wanted to ensure that he did not grow up "with that black man chip
on the shoulder. Feeling we are weak. Whites have done something to us and
we can't do something because of white people." Christine wanted her son to
understand how some viewed him, but she tried to foster a version of double
consciousness that emphasized his agency and discouraged him from feeling
bitter toward whites, disempowered, or constrained by others' views.

Next, I outline the strategies participants used to navigate the thug image
and teach their sons how to modulate their expression of masculinity, race, and
class. Participants often preferred one strategy but they may have used other
strategies, or a combination of strategies, during different periods of their sons'
lives.

Experience and Environment Management

Participants used two explicitly race-, class-, and gender-conscious strategies
to manage their sons' regular social interactions: experience and environment
management. Experience management focused on seeking out opportunities
for sons to engage in activities to gain fluency in different experiences—both
empowering and challenging—of being African American boys and men.
Environment management focused on monitoring their sons' regular social
environment, such as their school or neighborhood, with the aim of excluding
sources of discrimination. These environments were often primarily middle-
class but diverse in terms of racial identity, religion, and sexual orientation.
Participants often used environment management when children were pre-
school age to avoid early experiences of discrimination. Despite having additional resources, participants navigated a landscape of institutionalized child
care, which they believed included racially insensitive providers.

Participants using experience management tried to help their sons acquire what they viewed as an essential life skill: the ability to seamlessly shift from communities that differed by race, class, and gender. Experience management involved shuttling sons to activities, such as Little League baseball, basketball, or music lessons, in a variety of neighborhoods comprising African Americans from different economic backgrounds. Participants also exposed sons to African American culture and history and African American men, including fathers, uncles, cousins, coaches, or friends, whom they believed expressed healthy versions of masculinity. Karlyn said, "I worry about my son because he is not growing up with the kind of 'hood' mentality* that me and his father had, but he will have to interact with those people." Karlyn's son was not completely ensconced within the safety of a middle-class community. She believed as her son traveled through his day—to school, riding on buses, walking down the street, going in and out of stores, and interacting with police officers and the public—he would be perceived in a range of different and primarily negative ways. Karlyn believed her son would have to adjust the expression of his masculinity, racial identity, and class to successfully interact with people from that "hood mentality"—a version of subordinate masculinity and people from other racial and class backgrounds. She believed that lacking regular experiences in settings like the one she grew up in put her son at a disadvantage in these situations. Karlyn sought out experiences to help her son learn to navigate a world that she believed viewed him primarily as an African American boy and potential troublemaker, rather than a good middle-class kid. She ensured that her son had regular contact with his father and other African American men. She also regularly discussed examples of clashes between African American men and the police with her son.

Maya, a married mother of four, also used experience management. She described how she and her husband exposed their son to alternative and, in her view, more positive ideals of masculinity:

> With our son, we definitely have a heightened level of concern, especially around public schools, about what it means to be a black male in this society.... [My] husband does stuff with him that is very much male socializing stuff.... But, it is worrisome to think about sending him into the world where he is such a potential target.... I know how to make a kid that does well in school and can navigate academic environments. My husband knows how to help young people—black young people—understand their position, how the world sees them and how they might see themselves in a different and much more positive way.

Through these experiences, out of necessity, participants aimed to help their sons develop a double consciousness—"a sense of always looking at one's self through the eyes of others" (Du Bois [1903] 1994, 5). Maya and her husband did this by teaching their son how others might perceive him while rejecting prevailing images of African American masculinity and crafting alternatives.

Environment management involved managing sons' daily social interactions by excluding specific kinds of exposures. Rachel, a married mother of a son and daughter, said, "My son thinks he is street-smart but he is used to being in an environment in which he is known. No one thinks of my son as a black boy, they think of him as my son, but when he goes out into the real world people will make assumptions about him." Rachel lived in a predominately white neighborhood with few other African American families. She believed her neighbors did not view her family as "the African American family," but simply as a family, and this protected her son from challenges associated with being an African American male in the broader society where he might be assumed to be part of the urban underclass. Charlotte, mentioned earlier, described her efforts to find a neighborhood with the right kind of community:

> When we lived in [a different predominately white suburb], none of the mothers spoke to me. Maybe they would wave but I was really taken aback by how shunned I felt. We were the only black family in the school and no one spoke [to us].... Here [another predominately white area], over the summer, people knew my name and I didn't know their name.... There was a feeling of welcome and friendliness from the group.... You know, I just worry so much for them. I want them to be accepted, and not judged, and not looked at like a black kid. I want people to look at them as "that is a good young man or a good boy." ... Maybe if they know my sons and me and my husband, it won't be "Oh, there are the black kids"; it will be "There is us."

Charlotte wanted her sons to have access to better resources and schools, and that translated to living in primarily white neighborhoods. Nonetheless, revealing the diversity in white settings, she looked for white neighborhoods where she believed her sons would not face discrimination. Charlotte hoped to transform her sons from "anonymous" African American boys, assumed to be up to no good, to "the kid next door." Being African American was accompanied by assumptions about lower-class status and criminality that participants sought to overcome. Charlotte's experience underscores how intersections of race, gender, and class are used to value individuals and the challenges her sons confronted to be seen as both African American and "good middle-class kids."

Participants living in economically diverse predominantly African American communities with higher crime rates faced particular challenges when using environment management. Jameela, a single mother of a son, explained, "I live in Richmond because it is more affordable, but I don't see a lot of parents like me. I keep a tight leash on my son because of where we live. I don't want him to get involved with the wrong element." Jameela, and participants living in similar environments, often did not let their sons play with neighborhood children. Her experiences highlight class divisions within African American communities and the intensive peer group monitoring parents engaged in when their residential choices were limited. These children's regular environment did not include their immediate neighborhood but was confined to controlled spaces, including their school, church, or other settings that were diverse, free of racial discrimination, and often primarily middle class.

Experience and environment management both focus on social interactions but with different aims. Experience management aims to inform sons through regular controlled activities about the challenges they may face as African American boys and men and teach them how to modify the expression of their masculinity, class, and racial identity. Environment management aims to reduce or eliminate the challenges of being an African American male so they are not the defining features of their sons' lives. These mothers tried to find or create bias-free environments that would not limit their sons' expression of their masculinity but worried about their sons' treatment outside of these "safe havens."

Image and Emotion Management

Participants also used image and emotion management to reduce the vulnerability they believed their sons experienced related to the thug image and to prevent them from being associated with poor urban African Americans. These strategies were also explicitly race, gender, and class conscious and focused on their sons' emotional expressions and physical appearance. Sons were encouraged to restrain their expressions of anger, frustration, or excitement lest others view them as aggressive or violent. Participants also counseled their sons to strictly monitor their dress and appearance so they would be viewed not as criminals but as middle-class kids.

40   Karlyn engaged in something she called "prepping for life" with her son. She said, "I talk to [my son] constantly. We do scenarios and we talk about stuff. I'll pose a situation, like say, if you are ever kidnapped, what do you do? If the police ever pull you over, how do you need to react? So we do scenarios for all of that, it's just prepping for life." It would not be unreasonable for a parent to instruct their child to view police officers as sources of help. What is striking about Karlyn's examples is that she viewed child predators and police officers as equally dangerous to her son. She used emotion management with the hope

that preparing her son for these scenarios would give him some agency* in his response in the moment.

Some participants looked for places where their sons could safely express "normal boy" behaviors while gaining control over those behaviors. Heather, a divorced mother of a son and two daughters described her plan to help her son control his emotions at school: "I'm hoping to get [my son] into enough relaxation-type yoga classes so he is a little bit calmer when he does go to school. I want to make sure he lets it all out in the play yard and activities after school." Through activities like yoga, karate, and meditation, these participants hoped their sons would learn to restrain their emotions, and that this ability would translate to their interactions with teachers, police officers, peers, and the public. Participants emphasized that there were appropriate times to express feelings and advised their sons to refrain from responding to discrimination in the moment, instead taking their time to determine the best approach. This often meant reframing race-related grievances in nonracial terms so they would be better received by white teachers and administrators. Although masculinity is associated with strength, participants believed their sons were vulnerable and did not have the freedom to exhibit certain feelings or behaviors.

Participants also encouraged their sons to engage in image management to avoid being viewed as thugs. Rebecca, a widow with one son who also raised her nephew in his teenage years, recounted discussions during which she counseled her nephew about how people interpreted his clothing:

> Things like him wearing his hoodie and the assumption that he is up to no good. I tried to explain that to him because he didn't understand. He said, "I am just wearing my hoodie." "But baby, I understand what you are doing, and there is nothing wrong with that, but if you walk through the [poor, primarily African American and high-crime] neighborhood near my school, we see something different." You know, just having to protect him and trying to shelter him from unnecessary stress and trauma.... You know, the sagging pants and all the things that teenage boys do that don't necessarily mean they are doing anything wrong..... Is it fair? No. Is it reality? Yes.

Rebecca's comments illustrate a parenting paradox. Even as Rebecca challenged the double standards that she believed were used to evaluate her nephew's and son's behavior and appearance, as a practical matter, she felt compelled to educate them about these different standards. At times, she counseled them to adhere to those standards for their own safety. Given the recurring news stories of unarmed African American boys shot by police officers and private citizens, Rebecca's approach seems reasonable. Participants believed their sons might be labeled thugs because of their attire, thus leaving them vulnerable to attacks from others. Participants could not prevent these interactions from happening, but wanted their sons to survive them.

CONCLUSION

This research was bookended* by two shooting deaths of unarmed African American males. The first, Oscar Grant, was shot in the back by Officer Johannes Mehserle while lying face-down on a Bay Area Rapid Transit platform (McLaughlin 2014). The second, Trayvon Martin, was pursued, shot, and killed by George Zimmerman, a neighborhood watch coordinator, while walking home in his father's "safe," middle-class, gated community (Alvarez and Buckley 2013). Despite being a child from that community, it was not safe for Mr. Martin. He was not viewed as a good middle-class kid, but was instead interpreted as a threat. Since these incidents, African American parents are increasingly sharing the concerns they have for their sons' safety. Associated Press writer Jesse Washington (2012) wrote a heart-wrenching but matter-of-fact editorial describing how he advises his son to behave in affluent neighborhoods and in interactions with police and others. These instructions may have damaged his son's spirit but increased his chance of remaining alive. Incidents like these reminded participants that their sons have different experiences with the public than do white boys and men.

Initiatives like My Brother's Keeper focus on heightening African American male youths' agency in their lives, often paying less attention to the societal constraints they face. Some might suggest that recent videos of unarmed African American boys and men being shot by officers are shedding light on those constraints and are compelling the US government to take a closer look at law enforcement's interactions with African American boys and men. These incidents draw attention to contradictions between American ideals and practices, underscoring the fact that solving these challenges is not just a matter of changing behavior or increasing resources. These concerns about safety and vulnerability transcend class and are produced by societal forces.

45   Although the practices of fathers were not directly examined, it is clear from participants' statements that they helped to execute these strategies. Nonetheless, given that African American fathers' parenting practices at times differ from those of mothers (McHale et al. 2006), future research might directly examine their concerns and strategies. Researchers might also examine how different intersections of race, class, and gender produce different forms of vulnerability and protection.

Existing research suggests that having a male body and access to masculinity confers privileges and protections that serve as a symbolic asset in social interactions. However, my research demonstrates that depending on its racialization, the male body can be a "symbolic liability." The thug image derives its power and strength from intimidation and is used to justify attacks on African American boys' and men's bodies and minds. Participants' additional labor to protect their sons and its raced, classed, and gendered nature is largely invisible to the people it is meant to make more comfortable. Despite having additional resources, participants and their sons were not immune to a social system that required them to police their behaviors, emotions, and appearance to signal to others that they were respectable and safe middle-class African American males. Ironically, by feeling compelled to engage in strategies that encouraged their sons to conform to stricter standards and engage in acts of deference, participants contributed to reproducing a social structure that subordinates African Americans. Their accounts show a continuing need for African Americans to have a double consciousness through which they understand how society views them. Their actions also suggest a tension between individual strategies of survival and strategies that challenge and transform existing gendered, classed, and raced hierarchies.

(2016)

NOTES

Author's Note: I am greatly indebted and grateful to Raka Ray, Barrie Thorne, Evelyn Nakano Glenn, Katie Hasson, Jennifer Carlson, Katherine Mason, Oluwakemi Balogun, Kimberly Hoang, Sarah Anne Minkin, Nazanin Shahrokni, Abigail Andrews, Jordana Matlon, and the members of Raka Ray's Gender Working Group for their guidance, encouragement, and incisive suggestions on previous drafts of this manuscript. I would also like to thank David Minkus, Deborah Lustig and Christine Trost, who served as the program directors for the Graduate Fellows Program at the Institute for the Study of Societal Issues during my fellowship period, and my cohort of graduate fellows for their contributions to improving an early version of this manuscript. I am also thankful to Joya Misra, Adia Harvey Wingfield, and the anonymous reviewers at *Gender & Society* for their insightful feedback and comments on this manuscript. An earlier version of this paper was presented at the 2015 American Sociological Association Annual Meeting.

References

Alvarez Lizzett, Buckley Cara. 2013. Zimmerman is acquitted in Trayvon Martin killing. *The New York Times*, 13 July.

Anderson Elijah. 1990. *Streetwise: Race, class, and change in an urban community*. Chicago: University of Chicago Press.

Bay Area Census. 2010. http://www.bayareacensus.ca.gov/counties/alamedacounty.htm.

Beauboeuf-Lafontant Tamara. 2009. Behind the mask of the strong black woman: Voice and the embodiment of a costly performance. Philadelphia: Temple University Press.

Bertrand Marianne, Mullainathan Sendhil. 2004. Are Emily and Greg more employable than Lakisha and Jamal? A field experiment on labor market discrimination. *American Economic Review* 94:991–1013.

Brunson Rod K., Miller Jody. 2006. Gender, race, and urban policing: The experience of African American youths. *Gender & Society* 20:531–52.

Bush Lawson. 1999. *Can black mothers raise our sons?* 1st ed. Chicago: African American Images.

Bush Lawson. 2004. How black mothers participate in the development of manhood and masculinity: What do we know about black mothers and their sons? *Journal of Negro Education* 73:381–91.

Carbado Devon W., Gulati Mitu. 2013. *Acting white? Rethinking race in post-racial America*. New York: Oxford University Press.

Carter Prudence L. 2003. "Black" cultural capital, status positioning, and schooling conflicts for low-income African American youth. *Social Problems* 50:136–55.

Carter Prudence L. 2006. Straddling boundaries: Identity, culture, and school. *Sociology of Education* 79:304–28.

Coles Roberta L., Green Charles. 2010. *The myth of the missing black father*. New York: Columbia University Press.

Collins Patricia Hill. 2004. *Black sexual politics: African Americans, gender, and the new racism*. New York: Routledge.

Collins Patricia Hill. 2009. *Black feminist thought: Knowledge, consciousness, and the politics of empowerment*, 2nd ed., Routledge classics. New York: Routledge.

Dow Dawn. 2015. Negotiating "The Welfare Queen" and "The Strong Black Woman": African American middle-class mothers' work and family perspectives. *Sociological Perspectives* 58:36–55.

Doyle Bertram Wilbur. 1937. *The etiquette of race relations in the South: A study in social control*. Chicago: University of Chicago Press.

Du Bois William Edward Burghardt. (1903) 1994. *The souls of black folks*. New York: Gramercy Books.

Edin Kathryn, Tach Laura, Mincy Ronald. 2009. Claiming fatherhood: Race and the dynamics of paternal involvement among unmarried men. *Annals of the American Academy of Political and Social Science* 621:149–77.

Eitle Tamela McNulty, Eitle David James. 2004. Inequality, segregation, and the overrepresentation of African Americans in school suspensions. *Sociological Perspectives* 47:269–87.

Essed Philomena. 1991. *Understanding everyday racism*. New York: Russell Sage.

Feagin Joseph R., Sikes Melvin P. 1994. *Living with racism: The black middle-class experience*. Boston: Beacon Press.

Ferber Abby L. 2007. The construction of black masculinity: White supremacy now and then. *Journal of Sport & Social Issues* 31:11–24.

Ferguson Ann Arnett. 2000. *Bad boys: Public schools in the making of black masculinity, law, meaning, and violence*. Ann Arbor: University of Michigan Press.

Ford Kristie A. 2011. Doing fake masculinity, being real men: Present and future constructions of self among black college men. *Symbolic Interaction* 34:38–62.

Gilliam Franklin D. Jr.. 1999. The "Welfare Queen" experiment. *Nieman Reports* 53:49–52.

Glaser Barney G., Strauss Anselm L. 1967. *The discovery of grounded theory: Strategies for qualitative research, observations*. Chicago: Aldine.

Graham Lawrence O. 2014. I taught my black kids that their elite upbringing would protect them from discrimination. I was wrong. *The Washington Post*, 6 November.

Grodsky Eric, Pager Devah. 2001. The structure of disadvantage: Individual and occupational determinants of the black-white wage gap. *American Sociological Review* 66:542–67.

Hagan John, Shedd Carla, Payne Monique R. 2005. Race, ethnicity, and youth perceptions of criminal injustice. *American Sociological Review* 70:381–407.

Hancock Ange-Marie. 2003. Contemporary welfare reform and the public identity of the "Welfare Queen." *Race, Gender & Class* 10:31–59.

Harper Shaun R. 2004. The measure of a man: Conceptualizations of masculinity among high-achieving African American male college students. *Berkeley Journal of Sociology* 48:89–107.

Harris Frank III. 2008. Deconstructing masculinity: A qualitative study of college men's masculine conceptualizations and gender performance. *NASPA Journal* 45:453–74.

Harris-Perry Melissa V. 2011. *Sister citizen: Shame, stereotypes, and black women in America*. New Haven, CT: Yale University Press.

Hays Sharon. 1996. *The cultural contradictions of motherhood*. New Haven, CT: Yale University Press.

Hill Shirley A. 2001. Class, race, and gender dimensions of child rearing in African American families. *Journal of Black Studies* 31:494–508.

Hochschild Arlie Russell. 2003. *The managed heart: Commercialization of human feeling, 20th anniversary ed.* Berkeley: University of California Press.

Holland Megan M. 2012. Only here for the day: The social integration of minority students at a majority white high school. *Sociology of Education* 85:101–20.

Hunter Margaret. 2007. The persistent problem of colorism: Skin tone, status, and inequality. *Sociology Compass* 1:237–54.

Ispa-Landa Simone. 2013. Gender, race, and justifications for group exclusion: Urban black students bused to affluent suburban schools. *Sociology of Education* 86:218–33.

Jackson Brandon A., Wingfield Adia Harvey. 2013. Getting angry to get ahead: Black college men, emotional performance, and encouraging respectable masculinity. *Symbolic Interaction* 36:275–92.

Jarrett Valeria, Johnson Broderick. 2014. My brother's keeper: A new White House initiative to empower boys and young men of color. The White House Blog, 27 Feburary. https://www.whitehouse.gov/blog/2014/02/27/my-brother-s-keeper-new-white-house-initiative-empower-boys-and-young-men-of-color.

Jones Charisse, Shorter-Gooden Kumea. 2003. *Shifting: The double lives of black women in America*. New York: HarperCollins.

Krieger Linda Hamilton. 1995. The content of our categories: A cognitive bias approach to discrimination and equal employment opportunity. *Stanford Law Review* 47:1161–1248.

Lacy Karyn R. 2007. *Blue-chip black: Race, class, and status in the new black middle class*. Berkeley: University of California Press.

Lareau Annette. 2011. *Unequal childhoods: Class, race, and family life*, 2nd ed. Berkeley: University of California Press.

Lareau Annette, McNamara Horvat Erin. 1999. Moments of social inclusion and exclusion: Race, class, and cultural capital in family-school relationships. *Sociology of Education* 72:37–53.

Martinez Michael, Elam Stephanie, Henry Eric. 2015. Within black families, hard truths told to sons amid Ferguson unrest. *CNN*, 5 February. http://www.cnn.com/2014/08/15/living/parenting-black-sons-ferguson-missouri.

Massey Douglas S., Denton Nancy A. 1993. *American apartheid: Segregation and the making of the underclass.* Cambridge, MA: Harvard University Press.

McHale Susan M., Crouter Ann C., Ji-Yeon Kim, Burton Linda M., Davis Kelly D., Dotterer Aryn M., Swanson Dena P. 2006. Mothers' and fathers' racial socialization in African American families: Implications for youth. *Child Development* 77:1387–1402.

McKinley Jesse. 2009. In California, protests after man dies at hands of transit police. *The New York Times*, 8 January.

McLaughlin Michael. 2014. Ex-transit officer who killed Oscar Grant, unarmed black man, wins lawsuit. *Huffington Post*, 1 February. http://www.huffingtonpost.com/2014/07/01/oscar-grant-lawsuit-bart-officer_n_5548719.html.

Morris Edward W. 2005. "Tuck in that shirt!": Race, class, gender, and discipline in an urban school. *Sociological Perspectives* 48:25–48.

Morris Edward W. 2007. "Ladies" or "loudies"?: Perceptions and experiences of black girls in classrooms. *Youth & Society* 38:490–515.

Noguera Pedro. 2008. *The trouble with black boys: And other reflections on race, equity, and the future of public education.* San Francisco: Jossey-Bass.

Oliver Melvin L., Shapiro Thomas M. 1995. *Black wealth/white wealth: A new perspective on racial inequality.* New York: Routledge.

Ong Maria. 2005. Body projects of young women of color in physics: Intersections of gender, race, and science. *Social Problems* 52:593–617.

Pager Devah. 2003. The mark of a criminal record. *American Journal of Sociology* 108:937–75.

Pascoe C. J. 2007. *Dude, you're a fag: Masculinity and sexuality in high school.* Berkeley: University of California Press.

Pattillo Mary E. 1999. *Black picket fences: Privilege and peril among the black middle class.* Chicago: University of Chicago Press.

Pattillo Mary E. 2007. *Black on the block: The politics of race and class in the city.* Chicago: University of Chicago Press.

Pierce Jennifer L. 1995. *Gender trials: Emotional lives in contemporary law firms.* Berkeley: University of California Press.

Pringle Beverley E., Lyons James E., Booker Keonya C. 2010. Perceptions of teacher expectations by African American high school students. *Journal of Negro Education* 79:33–40.

Pugh Allison J. 2009. *Longing and belonging: Parents, children, and consumer culture.* Berkeley: University of California Press.

Quillian Lincoln Grey, Pager Devah, University of Wisconsin-Madison. 2000. Black neighbors, higher crime? The role of racial stereotypes in evaluations of neighborhood crime. CDE working paper. Madison: Center for Demography and Ecology, University of Wisconsin-Madison.

Rios Victor M. 2009. The consequences of the criminal justice pipeline on black and Latino masculinity. *Annals of the American Academy of Political and Social Science* 623:150–62.

Rollins Judith. 1985. *Between women: Domestics and their employers, labor and social change.* Philadelphia: Temple University Press.

Salem Deborah A., Zimmerman Marc A., Notaro Paul C. 1998. Effects of family structure, family process, and father involvement on psychosocial outcomes among African

American adolescents. *Family Relations* 117:331–41.

Schrock Douglas, Schwalbe Michael. 2009. Men, masculinity, and manhood acts. *Annual Review of Sociology* 35:277–95.

Severson Kim. 2013. Asking for help, then killed by an officer's barrage. *The New York Times*, 16 September.

Sharkey Patrick. 2014. Spatial segmentation and the black middle class. *American Journal of Sociology* 119:903–54.

Staples Robert, Johnson Leanor Boulin. 1993. *Black families at the crossroads: Challenges and prospects*. San Francisco: Jossey-Bass.

Strauss Anselm L., Corbin Juliet M. 1998. *Basics of qualitative research: Techniques and procedures for developing grounded theory*. Thousand Oaks, CA: Sage.

Strayhorn Terrell L. 2010. When race and gender collide: Social and cultural capital's influence on the academic achievement of African American and Latino males. *Review of Higher Education* 33:307–32.

Sullivan Teresa A., Warren Elizabeth, Westbrook Jay Lawrence. 2000. *The fragile middle class: Americans in debt*. New Haven, CT: Yale University Press.

Summers-Effler Erika. 2002. The micro potential for social change: Emotion, consciousness, and social movement formation. *Sociological Theory* 20:41–60.

Tatum Beverly Daniel. 1992. *Assimilation blues: Black families in a white community*, 1st ed. Northampton, MA: Hazel-Maxwell.

Tatum Beverly Daniel. 2003. *"Why are all the black kids sitting together in the cafeteria?" And other conversations about race*. New York: Basic Books.

Thornton Michael C., Chatters Linda M., Taylor Robert Joseph, Allen Walter R. 1990. Sociodemographic and environmental correlates of racial socialization by black parents. *Child Development* 61:401–09.

Uttal Lynet. 1999. Using kin for child care: Embedment in the socioeconomic networks of extended families. *Journal of Marriage and the Family* 61:845–57.

Washington Jesse. 2012. Trayvon Martin, my son, and the "black male code." *Huffington Post*, 24 March. http://www.huffingtonpost.com/2012/03/24/trayvon-martin-my-son-and_1_n_1377003.html.

Welch Kelly, Payne Allison Ann. 2010. Racial threat and punitive school discipline. *Social Problems* 57:25–48.

Wingfield Adia Harvey. 2007. The modern mammy and the angry black man: African American professionals' experiences with gendered racism in the workplace. *Race, Gender & Class* 14:196–212.

Wingfield Adia Harvey. 2009. Racializing the glass escalator: Reconsidering men's experiences with women's work. *Gender & Society* 23:5–26.

Wingfield Adia Harvey. 2011. *Changing times for black professionals*, 1st edition, Framing 21st-century social issues. New York: Routledge.

Wingfield Adia Harvey. 2013. *No more invisible man: Race and gender in men's work*. Philadelphia: Temple University Press.

Yee Vivian, Goodman J. David. 2013. Teenager is shot and killed by officer on foot patrol in the Bronx. *The New York Times*, 4 August.

Young Alford A. Jr.. 2011. The black masculinities of Barack Obama: Some implications for African American men. *Daedalus* 140:206–14.

Questions

1. What would be the benefits—and what would be the drawbacks—of widening the criteria for participants in this study to include Black men or other women of color? What might be gleaned from exploring the dangers for Black girls as well as Black boys?

2. How could the American government do more to address the security of African American males?

3. What is "image management"? How can the male body be a "symbolic liability"?

4. What are "feeling rules" and why are they important?

5. Describe one way in which the author's research could be applied to improve the experience of young African American males at the community level.

6. Dow is a sociologist, and this article is addressed to an academic audience and written using extensive citation and jargon. How does this rhetorical context affect the article's accessibility? Its credibility?

BRENT STAPLES

THE MOVIE *GET OUT* IS A STRONG ANTIDOTE TO THE MYTH OF "POSTRACIAL" AMERICA

This New York Times *editorial discusses the acclaimed horror film* Get Out *(2017), written and directed by Jordan Peele.*

The touchstone scene in the new horror film *Get Out* depicts a 20-something white woman named Rose appraising the sculpted torsos of black athletes on a laptop as she sits in her bedroom sipping milk through a straw. In another context—say, in the popular HBO television series *Girls*[1]—this would be an unremarkable example of a millennial catching a glimpse of beefcake on the way to bed.

In this case, the director Jordan Peele wants the audience to see Rose as what she is: the 21st-century equivalent of the plantation owner who studies the teeth and muscles of the human beings he is about to buy at a slave market. Like her antebellum predecessors, Rose—who has recently delivered her black boyfriend into the hands of her monstrous family—is on the hunt for the handsomest, buffest specimen she can find.

Get Out speaks in several voices on several themes. It subverts the horror genre itself—which has the well-documented habit of killing off black characters first. It comments on the re-emergence of white supremacy at the highest levels of American politics. It lampoons the easy listening racism that so often lies behind the liberal smile in the "postracial" United States. And it probes the systematic devaluation of black life that killed people like Trayvon Martin, Walter Scott, Tamir Rice and Eric Garner.[2]

---

1 *Girls* Television show (2012–17) in which the four main characters are all white women in their twenties.
2 *Trayvon Martin* Seventeen-year-old Black teenager who was fatally shot without cause by a neighborhood watch coordinator in Florida in 2012; *Walter Scott* Fifty-year-old Black man who was shot from behind and killed by police during an April 2015 traffic stop in South Carolina; *Tamir Rice* Twelve-year-old Black child shot and killed by Cleveland police in 2014; *Eric Garner* Forty-three-year old Black man killed by New York police in 2014 when he was arrested under suspicion of illegally selling individual cigarettes.

The film is a disquisition on the continuing impact of slavery in American life. Among other things, it argues that present-day race relations are heavily determined by the myths that were created to justify enslavement—particularly the notion that black people were never fully human.

5   The project of reconnecting this history to contemporary life is well underway. Historians have shown, for example, that slavery, once abolished under law, continued by other means, not least of all as disenfranchisement, mass incarceration and forced labor. Lynchings,* those carnivals of blood once attended by thousands of people, morphed into a sanitized, state-sanctioned death penalty that is still disproportionately used against people of color.

Novelists have followed the same line of inquiry, urged on by the desire to debunk the delusional rhetoric of "postracialism" that gained currency when the country elected its first African-American president.

This counternarrative pervades Paul Beatty's complex comic novel *The Sellout*—winner of the 2016 Man Booker Prize—whose African-American narrator attempts to resurrect slavery and segregation as a way of both deconstructing white supremacy and preventing the black community where he grew up from being erased.

Similarly, the Ben H. Winters thriller *Underground Airlines* unveils an eerily familiar America in which the Civil War never happened and the United States Marshals Service[3] cooperates with slave-holding states to track down people who have escaped to freedom.

The novelist Colson Whitehead deploys the counternarrative to great effect in *The Underground Railroad*—winner of the 2016 National Book Award—by subverting the shiny, optimistic escape-to-freedom story as it is so often told.

10   The underground railroad in this case is a real train that runs underground, not straight and true, but through dead ends and hellish catastrophes. This train travels across time as it takes the bondswoman from one destination to another, exposing her to unspeakable violence and the evolving versions of white supremacy that formed the actual journey from slavery to freedom.

Despite its comic elements, *Get Out* is cut from the same cloth. Indeed, the affluent white community into which Rose introduces her African-American boyfriend, Chris, has the flavor of the Stepford[4] stop on Mr. Whitehead's dystopian railroad.

---

3   *United States Marshals Service*   Under the Fugitive Slave Law of 1850 this branch of federal law enforcement was responsible for hunting down and arresting fugitive slaves.
4   *Stepford*   Reference to *The Stepford Wives* (novel 1974, films 1975 and 2004), a satirical thriller about a town in which all the women are blindly compliant and submissive homemakers.

Rose's family plays to a familiar plantation trope with black retainers who are eerily not quite right but who are represented as being almost like family. The patriarch tries to set Chris at ease, assuring him that he likes black people and "would have voted for Obama a third time" were it possible.

The faux affability heightens the sense of the sinister. Chris learns that the white people around him are coveting his body and would like nothing more than to try it on as a kind of second skin.

It would be wrong to reduce this film to an attack on white liberals who mouth racial platitudes. Mr. Peele sets out to debunk the myth of "postracialism" generally—by showing that the country is still gripped by historically conditioned preconceptions of race and blackness.

(2017)

Questions

1. Watch *Get Out*. To what extent does Staples's review accurately characterize the film? Can you think of anything worthy of comment that is not mentioned in this review?

2. Staples argues that *Get Out* is a "disquisition on the continuing impact of slavery in American life" (paragraph 4). How did Staples come to that conclusion? What examples does he provide?

3. In the style of Staples's review, write your own review of a film or other artistic work that you feel advances a praiseworthy social critique.

4. What is "postracialism"? To what extent do you think "the delusional rhetoric of 'postracialism'" holds currency in American discourse today? Offer evidence in support of your view.

5. In this film review, Staples discusses several novels that address similar concepts to those explored in *Get Out*. Why do you think he might have chosen to do this?

MITCH LANDRIEU

TRUTH: REMARKS ON THE REMOVAL OF CONFEDERATE MONUMENTS IN NEW ORLEANS

As has been the case in many cities in the American South, the prominent presence in New Orleans of memorials honoring Confederate leaders has been a continuing source of controversy. In the wake of the 2015 murder in Charleston, South Carolina, of Clementa Pinckney and eight others by a white supremacist, New Orleans Mayor Mitch Landrieu proposed the removal of four of the most prominent such memorials. His proposal was met with vigorous opposition in some quarters, but the move was approved by the New Orleans City Council, and the courts upheld its legality; in May 2017 the monuments were taken down. In order to minimize protests, the specific times at which each monument would be removed were not announced in advance; the last of the monuments (a statue of Robert E. Lee atop a pedestal in Lee Circle in central New Orleans) was removed on Friday 19 May. On the same day the Mayor delivered this speech to an invited audience at Gallier Hall (the former City Hall of New Orleans, a building dating to 1853 and steeped in history—including the history of its construction by slave laborers).

The speech was well received, and over the following week it was widely discussed and widely reprinted, including by The New York Times, The Chicago Tribune, *and* The Atlantic *magazine.*

The soul of our beloved City is deeply rooted in a history that has evolved over thousands of years; rooted in a diverse people who have been here together every step of the way—for both good and for ill.

It is a history that holds in its heart the stories of Native Americans—the Choctaw, Houma Nation, the Chitimacha. Of Hernando de Soto, Robert Cavelier, Sieur de La Salle, the Acadians, the Islenos, the enslaved people

434

from Senegambia, Free People of Color, the Haitians, the Germans, both the empires of France and Spain. The Italians, the Irish, the Cubans, the south and central Americans, the Vietnamese and so many more. New Orleans is truly a city of many nations, a melting pot, a bubbling cauldron of many cultures. There is no other place that so eloquently exemplifies the uniquely American motto: *E pluribus unum*—out of many we are one.

But there are also other truths about our city that we must confront. New Orleans was America's largest slave market: a port where hundreds of thousands of souls were brought, sold and shipped up the Mississippi River to lives of forced labor, of misery, of rape, of torture.

America was the place where nearly 4,000 of our fellow citizens were lynched,* 540 alone in Louisiana; where the courts enshrined "separate but equal"; where Freedom riders[1] coming to New Orleans were beaten to a bloody pulp. So when people say to me that the monuments in question are history—well, what I just described is real history as well, and it is the searing truth.

And it immediately begs these questions. Why are there are no slave ship   5 monuments? No prominent markers on public land to remember the lynchings or the slave blocks? Nothing to remember this long chapter of our lives—the pain, the sacrifice, the shame—all of it happening on the soil of New Orleans. Those self-appointed defenders of history and of monuments are eerily silent on what amounts to this historical malfeasance—a lie by omission. There is a difference between remembrance of history and reverence of it.

For America and New Orleans, it has been a long, winding road, marked by great tragedy and great triumph. But we cannot be afraid of our truth. As President George W. Bush said at the dedication ceremony for the National Museum of African American History and Culture, "a great nation does not hide its history. It faces its flaws and corrects them." So today I want to speak about why we chose to remove these four monuments to the Lost Cause of the Confederacy,[2] but also how and why this process can move us towards healing and understanding of each other.

Let's start with the facts. The historical record is clear. The Robert E. Lee, Jefferson Davis, and P.G.T. Beauregard[3] statues were not erected just to honor these men; they were part of the movement which became known as The Cult of the Lost Cause. This "cult" had one goal—through monuments and

---

1   *Freedom riders*   Civil Rights activists who in the early 1960s protested the segregation of public buses.

2   *Lost Cause of the Confederacy*   Name given to the belief that the Civil War was a noble effort to protect the culture of the Southern States; believers in the "Lost Cause" tend to understate the importance of slavery to the Confederate platform.

3   *Robert E. Lee, Jefferson Davis, and P.G.T. Beauregard*   Davis was President of the Confederacy, Lee and Beauregard prominent generals in the Confederate army.

through other means—to rewrite history and to hide the truth, which is that the Confederacy was on the wrong side of humanity. First erected over 166 years after the founding of our city and 19 years after the end of the Civil War, the monuments that we took down were meant to rebrand the history of our city and the ideals of a defeated Confederacy.

It is self-evident that these men did not fight for the United States of America; they fought against it. They may have been warriors, but in this cause they were not patriots.

These statues are not just stone and metal. They are not just innocent remembrances of a benign history. These monuments purposefully celebrate a fictional, sanitized Confederacy; ignoring the death, ignoring the enslavement, and the terror that it actually stood for. After the Civil War, these statues were a part of that terrorism as much as a burning cross on someone's lawn; they were erected purposefully to send a strong message to all who walked in their shadows about who was still in charge in this city.

10   Should you have further doubt about the true goals of the Confederacy, in the very weeks before the war broke out, the Vice President of the Confederacy, Alexander Stephens, made it clear that the Confederate cause was about maintaining slavery and white supremacy. He said in his now famous "corner-stone speech" that the Confederacy's

> corner-stone rests upon the great truth, that the negro is not equal to the white man; that slavery—subordination to the superior race—is his natural and normal condition. This, our new government, is the first, in the history of the world, based upon this great physical, philosophical, and moral truth.

Now—with these shocking words still ringing in your ears—I want to try to gently peel from your hands the grip on a false narrative of our history that I think weakens us, and make straight a wrong turn we made many years ago, so we can more closely connect with integrity to the founding principles of our nation and forge a clearer and straighter path toward a better city and a more perfect union.

Last year, President Barack Obama echoed these sentiments about the need to contextualize and remember all our history. He recalled a piece of stone, a slave auction block engraved with a marker commemorating a single moment in 1830 when Andrew Jackson and Henry Clay[4] stood and spoke from it. President Obama said this:

---

4   *in 1830 ... Clay*   In 1830 Jackson had just become President; Clay, who would later become one of Jackson's most significant political opponents, was at the time out of active politics.

Consider what this artifact tells us about history ... on a stone where
day after day for years, men and women ... bound and bought and sold
and bid like cattle on a stone worn down by the tragedy of over a thousand bare feet. For a long time the only thing we considered important,
the singular thing we once chose to commemorate as history with a
plaque were the unmemorable speeches of two powerful men.

A piece of stone. One stone. Both stories were history. One story was told, one
story was forgotten or maybe even purposefully ignored.

All this is clear for me today—but for a long time I did not see it, even
though I grew up in one of New Orleans' most diverse neighborhoods, even
with my family's long proud history of fighting for civil rights[5]—I must have
passed by those monuments a million times without giving them a second
thought. So I am not judging anybody; I am not judging people. We all take our
own journey on race.

I just hope people listen like I did when my dear friend Wynton Marsalis[6]
helped me see the truth. He asked me to think about all the people who have left
New Orleans because of our exclusionary attitudes. Another friend asked me
to consider these four monuments from the perspective of an African American
mother or father trying to explain to their fifth grade daughter who Robert E.
Lee is and why he stands atop of our beautiful city.

Can you do it? Can you look into that young girl's eyes and convince her
that Robert E. Lee is there to encourage her? Do you think she will feel inspired
and hopeful by that story? Do these monuments help her see a future with
limitless potential? Have you ever thought that if her potential is limited, yours
and mine are too?

We all know the answer to these very simple questions.   15

When you look into this child's eyes is the moment when the searing truth
comes into focus for us. This is the moment when we know what is right and
what we must do. We can't walk away from this truth.

I knew that taking down these monuments was going to be tough, but
you elected me to do the right thing, not the easy thing, and this is what that
looks like.

---

5   *long proud ... civil rights*   Landrieu's father, Maurice Edwin Landrieu (known as
Moon Landrieu) was Mayor of New Orleans from 1970 to 1978; he is remembered in part
for having appointed African Americans to various positions in the city administration that
had previously been occupied only by whites.
6   *Wynton Marsalis*   One of a famous family of New Orleans musicians, Marsalis is
Artistic Director of Jazz at Lincoln Center in New York City.

Relocating these Confederate monuments[7] is not about taking something away from someone else. This is not about politics; this is not about blame or retaliation. This is not a naïve quest to solve all our problems at once.

This is, however, about showing the whole world that we as a city and as a people are able to acknowledge, understand, reconcile, and—most importantly—choose a better future for ourselves, making straight what has been crooked and making right what was wrong. Otherwise, we will continue to pay a price with discord, with division and, yes, with violence.

20   To literally put the Confederacy on a pedestal in our most prominent places of honor is an inaccurate recitation of our full past. It is an affront to our present, and it is a bad prescription for our future.

History cannot be changed. It cannot be moved like a statue. What is done is done. The Civil War is over, and the Confederacy lost and we are better for it. Surely we are far enough removed from this dark time to acknowledge that the cause of the Confederacy was wrong.

And in the second decade of the 21st century, asking African Americans—or anyone else—to drive by property that they own but that remains occupied by reverential statues of men who fought to destroy the country (and to deny the very humanity of African Americans) seems perverse and absurd.

Centuries old wounds are still raw because they never healed right in the first place. Here is the essential truth: we are better together than we are apart. Indivisibility is our essence.

Isn't this the gift that the people of New Orleans have given to the world? We radiate beauty and grace in our food, in our music, in our architecture, in our joy of life, in our celebration of death; in everything that we do. We gave the world this funky thing called jazz—the most uniquely American art form that is developed across the ages from different cultures. Think about second lines, think about Mardi Gras, think about muffaletta, think about the Saints, gumbo, red beans and rice.[8] By God, just think.

---

7   *Relocating these Confederate monuments*   The monuments themselves were placed in storage until such time as a suitable institution could be found to house them; much as the city authorities were opposed to having the monuments displayed as objects for public veneration in outdoor settings, they were not against having them displayed indoors in appropriate contexts as objects of historical significance.

In place of where the monuments stood, the city's plan was to install fountains or, in at least one case, the American flag.

8   *second lines ... red beans and rice*   Everything evoked in this list is powerfully associated with the city of New Orleans;   *second lines*   Impromptu musical celebrations that are held following the death of an individual and that involve processions along city streets;   *Mardi Gras*   In New Orleans, the "Mardi Gras" (or "Fat Tuesday") celebration before Lent is a two-week affair that attracts huge crowds from across North

All we hold dear is created by throwing everything in the pot; creating, producing something better; everything a product of our historic diversity. We are proof that out of many we are one—and better for it! Out of many we are one—and we really do love it!

And yet, we still seem to find so many excuses for not doing the right thing. Again, remember President Bush's words, "A great nation does not hide its history. It faces its flaws and corrects them." We forget, we deny how much we really depend on each other, how much we need each other. We justify our silence and inaction by manufacturing noble causes that marinate in historical detail. We still find a way to say "Wait—not so fast," but like Dr. Martin Luther King Jr. said, "this *wait* has almost always meant *never*."[9]

We can't wait any longer. We need to change. And we need to change now. No more waiting. This is not just about statues; this is about our attitudes and behavior as well. If we take these statues down and don't change to become a more open and inclusive society this would have all been in vain.

While some have driven by these monuments every day and either revered their beauty or failed to see them at all, many of our neighbors and fellow Americans see them very clearly. Many are painfully aware of the long shadows their presence casts; not only literally but figuratively. And they clearly receive the message that the Confederacy and the cult of the lost cause intended to deliver.

Earlier this week, as the cult of the lost cause statue of P.G.T. Beauregard came down, world-renowned musician Terence Blanchard stood watch, his wife Robin and their two beautiful daughters at their side. Terence went to a high school on the edge of City Park named after one of America's greatest heroes and patriots, John F. Kennedy. But to get there he had to pass by this monument to a man who fought to deny him his humanity. He said, "I've never looked at them as a source of pride ... it's always made me feel as if they were put there by people who don't respect us.... This is something I never thought I'd see in my lifetime. It's a sign that the world is changing." Yes, Terence, it is—and it is long overdue.

Now is the time to send a new message to the next generation of New Orleanians who can follow in Terence and Robin's remarkable footsteps. A message about the future, about the next 300 years and beyond; let us not miss this opportunity, New Orleans—and let us help the rest of the country do the

25

30

America; *muffaletta* Sandwich created in New Orleans by Italian immigrants; *the Saints* The New Orleans Saints football team; *gumbo, red beans and rice* Creole foods associated with New Orleans.

9 *like Dr. Martin Luther King Jr. ... meant never* See King's "Letter from Birmingham Jail" (1963).

same. Because now is the time for choosing. Now is the time to actually make this the city we always should have been, had we gotten it right in the first place.

We should stop for a moment and ask ourselves—at this point in our history—after Katrina, after Rita, after Ike, after Gustav, after the national recession, after the BP oil catastrophe and after the tornado:[10] If presented with the opportunity to build monuments that told our story or to curate these particular spaces, would these monuments be what we want the world to see? Is this really our story?

We have not erased history; we are becoming part of the city's history by righting the wrong image these monuments represent and crafting a better, more complete future for all our children and for future generations. And, unlike when these Confederate monuments were first erected as symbols of white supremacy, we now have a chance not only to create new symbols, but to do it together, as one people.

In our blessed land we all come to the table of democracy as equals.

We have to reaffirm our commitment to a future where each citizen is guaranteed the uniquely American gifts of life, liberty and the pursuit of happiness. That is what really makes America great and today it is more important than ever to hold fast to these values and together say as a self-evident truth that out of many we are one. That is why today we reclaim these spaces for the United States of America. Because we are one nation, not two; indivisible with liberty and justice for all, not just for some. We all are part of one nation, all pledging allegiance to one flag, the flag of the United States of America. And New Orleanians are in—all of the way. It is in this union and in this truth that real patriotism is rooted and flourishes. Instead of revering a 4-year brief historical aberration that was called the Confederacy, we can celebrate all 300 years of our rich, diverse history as a place named New Orleans, and set the tone for the next 300 years.

35   After decades of public debate, of anger, of anxiety, of anticipation, of humiliation and of frustration; after public hearings and approvals from three separate community led commissions; after two robust public hearings and a 6-1 vote by the duly elected New Orleans City Council; after review by 13 different federal and state judges, the full weight of the legislative, executive, and judicial branches of government has been brought to bear, and the monuments in accordance with the law have been removed. So now is the time to come

---

10 *Katrina ... tornado* Series of events between 2005 and 2017 that presented great challenges to the city. The most serious was the catastrophic flooding that occurred during Hurricane Katrina in 2005. When poorly constructed levees gave way, much of the city flooded and some 1,300 New Orleanians died. (Including those in other locations, total fatalities were over 1,800.)

together and heal and focus on our larger task. Not only building new symbols, but making this city a beautiful manifestation of what is possible and what we as a people can become.

Let us remember the once exiled, imprisoned and now universally loved Nelson Mandela and what he said after the fall of apartheid:

> If the pain has often been unbearable and the revelations shocking to all of us, it is because they indeed bring us the beginnings of a common understanding of what happened and a steady restoration of the nation's humanity.

Before we part, let us again state the truth clearly. The Confederacy was on the wrong side of history and humanity. It sought to tear apart our nation and subjugate our fellow Americans to slavery. This is the history we should never forget and one that we should never again put on a pedestal to be revered.

As a community, we must recognize the significance of removing New Orleans' Confederate monuments. It is our acknowledgment that now is the time to take stock of, and then move past, a painful part of our history. Anything less would render generations of courageous struggle and soul-searching a truly lost cause. Anything less would fall short of the immortal words of our greatest President Abraham Lincoln, who with an open heart and clarity of purpose calls on us today to unite as one people:

> With malice toward none, with charity for all; with firmness in the right, as God gives us to see the right; let us strive on to finish the work we are in, to bind up the nation's wounds ... to do all which may achieve and cherish—a just and lasting peace among ourselves and with all nations.[11]

(2017)

Questions

1. Landrieu says that Robert E. Lee, Jefferson Davis, and P.G.T Beauregard "did not fight for the United States of America; they fought against it." He goes on to say that these men "may have been warriors, but in this cause they were not patriots." Why, then, were statues erected in their honor? What do the statues represent and why was Landrieu encouraged to remove them?

---

11   *With malice ... with all nations*   From the Second Inaugural Address (1865).

2. Landrieu is not only calling for the removal of statues; he's suggesting a change in thinking. What does he imagine for the future of New Orleans? For the future of America?

3. What do you think about statues and buildings named after Confederate generals? How, do you believe, the history should be shared?

4. Controversies over statues and memorials have occurred frequently, both in the United States and in other countries (e.g., the removal of statues of Cecil Rhodes in Zimbabwe's main cities in 1980, the removal of a statue of Edward Cornwalis in the Canadian city of Halifax in 2018). Choose one other such controversy. In what ways are the circumstances in New Orleans similar? In what ways are they different?

CAMERON GLOVER

NO, BLACK-ONLY SAFE SPACES ARE NOT RACIST

The Nyansapo Festival, held by the Afro-feminist organization Mwasi in Paris in 2017, reserved four fifths of its event space for Black women only; a portion of the other fifth also permitted Black men, with the remaining space open to everyone. This decision was a subject of controversy—and similar controversies regarding Black-only safe spaces have arisen in America, especially surrounding the creation of safe spaces on university and college campuses. The following piece appeared on Wear Your Voice, *an intersectional feminist website "run by women and femmes of color who are trying to make more room for marginalized voices away from the white, cis-centric, heteronormative, patriarchal gaze."*

Earlier this week, news from Paris, France brought us reports that the mayor, Anne Hidalgo, had condemned a Black feminist festival as being racist for providing a section of it as a safe space for Black women only. Some international anti-racism groups even put out statements claiming that an exclusive space for Black women was racist. Why do people still interpret safe spaces as being this way?

The idea of safe spaces have been popping up quite a bit in the last few years, thanks to social justice rhetoric becoming more widely accessible and to community-focused initiatives in response to 45's[1] election. Safe spaces, or groups created to support people within a specific community, are not only becoming more popular but are necessary additions to both online and in-person spaces, as targeted violence becomes more of a reality.

But not all safe spaces are made equal.

For many, safe spaces can often carry nefarious undertones. If they are not crafted specifically to decentralize white supremacy and ... anti-Blackness, no

---

1   *45* I.e., Donald Trump, the 45th president of the United States; some people choose to use the number to avoid repeating his name.

matter how subtle, these can still be violent spaces for Black people to be in. Of course, we recognize this within safe spaces that are open to everyone, but safe spaces touted as being for "all people of color" can carry this as well.

5   Safe spaces for Black folks are not negotiable; they are necessary and vital to protect the mental health and support the multi-faceted well-being of Black people. So why is the idea of a Black-only safe space still such a taboo?

Even within the spaces that I frequent, I find that often the most amount of pushback when a Black person addresses micro-aggressions or anti-Blackness come from spaces that claim "intersectionality" in name only. I've seen this behavior happen time and time again from white people, but non-Black people of color are also not immune to this. The duality of wanting to stay within a space because it has been good for a certain part of your life (whether that's professional networking or in building community around a certain topic) often creates a deep divide within many of us, though having to rationalize survival within a space where violence occurs is an unhealthy sacrifice for Black people to make.

Don't get me wrong, having community-exclusive groups aren't perfect solutions. Black-only spaces won't completely eradicate homophobia, misogynoir,[2] ableism, and oppression from happening. However, they're still a necessary step in creating community, safety, and a feeling of visibility that Black people especially deserve to have. Whether these spaces exist online or in real life, the same rules apply.

At the same time, an important note should be made here: the creation of Black-only spaces isn't an excuse for queer Black and Indigenous people of color (BIPoC) or open-race spaces to not work on their own anti-Blackness. Black people should have the option to enter whichever kind of space they choose and not have to fear that anti-Black violence will be encountered in the group space at any moment, or that it was even something that was considered as an afterthought when creating the space.

When we fail to include dismantling oppression within the framework of a group—especially if that group lauds itself as one that is "intersectional" or "social justice" and "feminist"—these groups become the unconscious tools of upholding that oppression. And when you're creating safe spaces, this work is both necessary and non-negotiable.

10   By centering the definition of safe spaces for BIPoC in all safe spaces that we create and continue to grow, we're redefining exactly how we see these terms in ways that work best for us. How much more enjoyable would the digital work that we engage in and the community building that we center in

---

2   *misogynoir*   Misogyny directed at Black women specifically.

real life be if we knew for a fact that safe spaces would include everyone? How much more productive, joyful, and eager to engage would Black individuals be when they know that their needs and boundaries have been considered and respected?

As the need for safe spaces grows, I'm inspired by those within their communities creating the safe spaces that they wanted for themselves, but couldn't find elsewhere. These individuals, in their bravery and selflessness in filling a need, bring forward the important message that we're here, we deserve to be seen, and we matter.

(2017)

Questions

1. What distinguishes the creation of Black-only safe spaces from the type of segregation associated with the Jim Crow era*?

2. Glover shares in paragraph 6 that "[e]ven within the spaces that I frequent, I find that often the most amount of pushback when a Black person addresses micro-aggressions or anti-Blackness come from spaces that claim 'intersectionality' in name only." What is Glover's larger point here?

3. Glover refers to the "fear that anti-Black violence will be encountered in the group space at any moment" (paragraph 8). Describe the kinds of violence a Black person in a group space might fear encountering.

4. Why might some object to the creation of Black-only safe spaces? In your view, is there merit to any of these objections? How effectively does Glover's article refute them?

5. Glover references the need "to include dismantling oppression within the framework of a group" (paragraph 9). How can this be achieved?

6. There has been a recent increase in official safe spaces at American universities, including courses, dorms, and study spaces that are specifically intended for Black students. What kinds of safe spaces (if any) should American universities provide for Black students?

7. Audre Lorde's "Uses of Anger" also addresses matters of intersectionality. Read Lorde's article and compare the view of intersectional politics she advances with the view advanced in Glover's piece.

8. Consider the following comment made by activist and political com-
    mentator Van Jones at a discussion held at the University of Chicago.
    Jones argued that physical safety and protection from personally
    targeted hate speech are important, but that ideological safe spaces on
    university campuses are "a terrible idea," saying this to students:

    > I don't want you to be safe, ideologically. I don't want you to be
    > safe, emotionally. I want you to be strong. That's different.
    >
    > I'm not going to pave the jungle for you. Put on some boots,
    > and learn how to deal with adversity. I'm not going to take all the
    > weights out of the gym; that's the whole point of the gym. This is
    > the gym. You can't live on a campus where people say stuff you
    > don't like?! And these people can't fire you, they can't arrest you,
    > they can't beat you up, they can just say stuff you don't like—and
    > you get to say stuff back—and this you cannot bear?
    >
    > … I want you to be offended every single day on this campus.
    > I want you to be deeply aggrieved and offended and upset, and
    > then to learn how to speak back.

    Is this argument persuasive? To what extent (if at all) does it under-
    mine Glover's claims?

ZADIE SMITH

GETTING IN AND OUT: WHO OWNS BLACK PAIN?

British writer Zadie Smith is best known for acclaimed novels such as White Teeth *(2000) and* NW *(2012). In this essay for* Harper's Magazine, *she discusses depictions of Black suffering in the arts, including writer-director Jordon Peele's acclaimed 2017 horror film* Get Out, *an examination of race in the United States.*

Smith links her reading of this film to the controversy surrounding Dana Schutz's painting Open Casket, *which appeared in the 2017 Whitney Biennial, an influential art show held at the Whitney Museum in New York. The painting is based upon a photograph of the body of Emmett Till, a 14-year-old Black child who in 1955 was murdered and mutilated by a white mob after a white woman falsely accused him of attempting to flirt with her. Till's mother famously held an open-casket funeral to draw attention to the brutality of racist violence in Mississippi, and he became an emblematic figure of the Civil Rights Movement. Schutz's painting was condemned by those who argued that it was unacceptably exploitative for her, as a white artist, to portray the subject.*

You are white—
yet a part of me, as I am a part of you.
That's American.
Sometimes perhaps you don't want to be a part of me.
Nor do I often want to be a part of you.
But we are, that's true!
As I learn from you,
I guess you learn from me—
although you're older—and white—
and somewhat more free.
—Langston Hughes

Early on, as the opening credits roll, a woodland scene. We're upstate, viewing the forest from a passing car. Trees upon trees, lovely, dark and deep.[1] There are no people to be seen in this wood—but you get the feeling that somebody's in there somewhere. Now we switch to a different world. Still photographs, taken in the shadow of public housing: the basketball court, the abandoned lot, the street corner. Here black folk hang out on sun-warmed concrete, laughing, crying, living, surviving. The shots of the woods and those of the city both have their natural audience, people for whom such images are familiar and benign. There are those who think of Frostian[2] woods as the pastoral, as America the Beautiful,* and others who see summer in the city as, likewise, beautiful and American. One of the marvelous tricks of Jordan Peele's debut feature, *Get Out,* is to reverse these constituencies, revealing two separate planets of American fear—separate but not equal. One side can claim a long, distinguished cinematic history: Why should I fear the black man in the city? The second, though not entirely unknown (*Deliverance, The Wicker Man*[3]), is certainly more obscure: Why should I fear the white man in the woods?

A few years ago I interviewed Peele as he came to the end of a long run on the celebrated Comedy Central sketch show *Key and Peele.* On that occasion he spoke about comic reversals—"I think reversals end up being the real bread and butter of the show*"—and about finding the emotional root of a joke in order to intensify it: "What's the mythology that is funny just because people know it's not true?" *Get Out* is structured around such inversions and reversals, although here "funny" has been replaced, more often than not, with "scary," and a further question has been posed: Which mythology? Or, more precisely: Whose? Instead of the familiar, terrified white man, robbed at gunpoint by a black man on a city street, we meet a black man walking in the leafy white suburbs, stalked by a white man in a slow-moving vehicle from whose stereo issues perhaps the whitest song in the world: "Run, rabbit, run, rabbit, run run run..."

Get Out flips the script, offering a compendium of black fears about white folk. White women who date black men. Waspy* families. Waspy family garden parties. Ukuleles. Crazy younger brothers. Crazy younger brothers who

---

1   *lovely, dark and deep*   Reference to American poet Robert Frost's famous poem "Stopping by Woods on a Snowy Evening" (1923).

2   *Frostian*   In the vein of Robert Frost, whose poetry frequently addresses nature and country life.

3   *Deliverance*   1972 film in which a group of friends from the city venture into the wilderness, where they are attacked by local white people;   *The Wicker Man*   1973 film in which a police officer travels to a remote Scottish island, where he is sacrificed in a pagan ritual.

play ukuleles. Sexual psychopaths, hunting, guns, cannibalism, mind control, well-meaning conversations about Obama. The police. Well-meaning conversations about basketball. Spontaneous roughhousing, spontaneous touching of one's biceps or hair. Lifestyle cults, actual cults. Houses with no other houses anywhere near them. Fondness for woods. The game bingo. Servile household staff, sexual enslavement, nostalgia for slavery—slavery itself. Every one of these reversals "lands"—just like a good joke—simultaneously describing and interpreting the situation at hand, and this, I think, is what accounts for the homogeneity of reactions to *Get Out*: It is a film that contains its own commentary.

For black viewers there is the pleasure of vindication. It's not often they have both their real and their irrational fears so thoroughly indulged. For white liberals—whom the movie purports to have in its satirical sights—there is the cringe of recognition, that queer but illuminating feeling of being suddenly "othered." (Oh, that's how *we* look to *them*?) And, I suppose, the satisfaction of being in on the joke. For example, there is the moment when the white girl, Rose (Allison Williams), and her new black boyfriend, Chris (Daniel Kaluuya), hit a deer on the way to her parents' country house. She's driving, yet when the police stop them he's the one asked for his license. Rose is sufficiently "woke" to step in front of her man and give the cop a self-righteous earful—but oblivious to the fact that only a white girl would dare assume she could do so with impunity. The audience—on both sides of the divide—groans with recognition. Chris himself—surely mindful of what happened to Sandra Bland, and Walter Scott, and Terence Crutcher, and Samuel DuBose[4]—smiles wryly but remains polite and deferential throughout. He is a photographer, those were his photographs of black city life we saw behind the credits, and that white and black Americans view the same situations through very different lenses is something he already understands.

This point is made a second time, more fiercely, in one of the final scenes. Chris is standing in those dark woods again, covered in blood; on the ground before him lies Rose, far more badly wounded. A cop car is approaching. Chris eyes it with resigned dread. As it happens, he is the victim in this gruesome tableau, but neither he nor anyone else in the cinema expects that to count

5

---

4   *Sandra Bland*   Twenty-eight-year-old Black woman who in July 2015 was found hanged in a Texas jail cell after she was arrested during a mishandled traffic stop;   *Walter Scott*   Fifty-year-old Black man who was shot from behind and killed by police during an April 2015 traffic stop in South Carolina;   *Terence Crutcher*   Forty-year-old Black man who, in September 2016, was shot and killed by Oklahoma police as he was walking to his car;   *Samuel DuBose*   Forty-three-year-old Black man who in July 2015 was shot and killed during a traffic stop by a University of Cincinnati police officer as DuBose attempted to drive away.

for a goddamned thing. ("You're really in for it now, you poor motherfucker," someone in the row behind me said. These days, a cop is apparently a more frightening prospect than a lobotomy-performing cult.) But then the car door opens and something unexpected happens: It is not the dreaded white cop after all but a concerned friend, Rod Williams (Lil Rel Howery), the charming and paranoid brother who warned Chris, at the very start, not to go stay with a load of white folks in the woods. Rod—who works for the TSA—surveys the bloody scene and does not immediately assume that Chris is the perp. A collective gasp of delight bursts over the audience, but in this final reversal the joke's on us. How, in 2017, are we still in a world where presuming a black man innocent until proven guilty is the material of comic fantasy?

These are the type of self-contained, ironic, politically charged sketches at which Peele has long excelled. But there's a deeper seam in *Get Out*, which is mined through visual symbol rather than situational comedy. I will not easily forget the lengthy close-ups of suffering black faces; suffering, but trapped behind masks, like so many cinematic analogues of the arguments of Frantz Fanon.[5] Chris himself, and the white family's maid, and the white family's groundskeeper, and the young, lobotomized beau of an old white lady—all frozen in attitudes of trauma, shock, or bland servility, or wearing chillingly fixed grins. In each case, the eyes register an internal desperation. *Get me out!* The oppressed. The cannibalized. The living dead. When a single tear or a dribble of blood runs down these masks, we are to understand this as a sign that there is still somebody in there. Somebody human. Somebody who has the potential to be whole.

As the movie progresses we learn what's going on: Black people aren't being murdered or destroyed up here in the woods, they're being used. A white grandmother's brain is now in her black maid's body. A blind old white gallerist hopes to place his brain in Chris's cranium and thus see with the young black photographer's eyes, be in his young black skin. Remnants of the black "host" remain after these operations—but not enough to make a person.

Peele has found a concrete metaphor for the ultimate unspoken fear: that to be oppressed is not so much to be hated as obscenely loved. Disgust and passion are intertwined. Our antipathies are simultaneously a record of our desires, our sublimated wishes, our deepest envies. The capacity to give birth or to make food from one's body; perceived intellectual, physical, or sexual superiority; perceived intimacy with the natural world, animals, and plants; perceived self-sufficiency in a faith or in a community. There are few qualities

---

5   *Frantz Fanon* In *Black Skin, White Masks* (1957), Martinican anti-colonial theorist Frantz Fanon argues that colonization imposes a sense of inferiority on Black individuals, prompting a desire to imitate the colonizing culture.

in others that we cannot transform into a form of fear and loathing in ourselves. In the documentary *I Am Not Your Negro* (2016), James Baldwin gets to the heart of it:

> What white people have to do is try to find out in their hearts why it was necessary for them to have a nigger in the first place. Because I am not a nigger. I'm a man.... If I'm not the nigger here, and if you invented him, you the white people invented him, then you have to find out why. And the future of the country depends on that.

But there is an important difference between the invented "nigger" of 1963 and the invented African American of 2017: The disgust has mostly fallen away. We were declared beautiful back in the Sixties, but it has only recently been discovered that we are so. In the liberal circles depicted in *Get Out,* everything that was once reviled—our eyes, our skin, our backsides, our noses, our arms, our legs, our breasts, and of course our hair—is now openly envied and celebrated and aestheticized and deployed in secondary images to sell stuff. As one character tells Chris, "black is in fashion now."

To be clear, the life of the black citizen in America is no more envied or desired today than it was back in 1963. Her schools are still avoided and her housing still substandard and her neighborhood still feared and her personal and professional outcomes disproportionately linked to her zip code.* But her physical self is no longer reviled. If she is a child and comes up for adoption, many a white family will be delighted to have her, and if she is in your social class and social circle, she is very welcome to come to the party; indeed, it's not really a party unless she does come. No one will call her the n-word on national television, least of all a black intellectual. (The Baldwin quote is from a television interview.) For liberals the word is interdicted and unsayable.

But in place of the old disgust comes a new kind of cannibalism. The white people in *Get Out* want to get inside the black experience: They want to wear it like a skin and walk around in it. The modern word for this is "appropriation." There is an argument that there are many things that are "ours" and must not be touched or even looked at sideways, including (but not limited to) our voices, our personal style, our hair, our cultural products, our history, and, perhaps more than anything else, our pain. A people from whom so much has been stolen are understandably protective of their possessions, especially the ineffable kind. In these debates my mind always turns to a line of Nabokov,[6] a writer for whom arrival in America meant the loss of pretty much everything, including

10

---

6   *Nabokov*   Vladimir Nabokov (1899–1977), a Russian-born novelist and poet, was forced by political circumstances to leave Russia. Around the time of his immigration to America in 1941, he began to write primarily in English.

a language: "Why not leave their private sorrows to people? Is sorrow not, one asks, the only thing in the world people really possess?"

Two weeks after watching *Get Out,* I stood with my children in front of *Open Casket,* Dana Schutz's painting of Emmett Till, the black teenager who, in 1955, was beaten and lynched after being accused of flirting with a white woman. My children did not know what they were looking at and were too young for me to explain. Before I came, I had read the widely circulated letter to the curators of the Whitney Biennial objecting to their inclusion of this painting:

> I am writing to ask you to remove Dana Schutz's painting *Open Casket* and with the urgent recommendation that the painting be destroyed and not entered into any market or museum ... because it is not acceptable for a white person to transmute Black suffering into profit and fun, though the practice has been normalized for a long time.

I knew, from reading about this debate, that in fact the painting had never been for sale, so I focused instead on the other prong of the argument—an artist's right to a particular subject. "The subject matter is not Schutz's; white free speech and white creative freedom have been founded on the constraint of others, and are not natural rights."

I want to follow the letter very precisely, along its own logic, in which natural rights are replaced with racial ones. I will apply it personally. If *I* were an artist, and if I could paint—could the subject matter be mine? I am biracial. I have Afro-hair, my skin is brown, I am identified, by others and by myself, as a black woman. And so, by the logic of the letter—if I understand it correctly— this question of subject matter, in my case, would not come up, as it would not come up for the author of the letter, Hannah Black, who also happens to be biracial, and brown. Neither of us is American, but the author appears to speak confidently in defense of the African-American experience, so I, like her, will assume a transnational unity. I will assume that Emmett Till, if I could paint, could be my subject too.

15   Now I want to inch a step further. I turn from the painting to my children. Their beloved father is white, I am biracial, so, by the old racial classifications of America, they are "quadroons."[7] Could *they* take black suffering as a subject of their art, should they ever make any? Their grandmother is as black as the ace of spades, as the British used to say; their mother is what the French still call café au lait. They themselves are sort of yellowy. When exactly does black suffering cease to be their concern? Their grandmother—raised on a

---

7   *quadroons* Racial classification applied to people who are one-quarter Black. Terms such as these were current during the era of slavery and remain associated with that time.

postcolonial island, in extreme poverty, descended from slaves—knew black suffering intimately. But her grandchildren look white. Are they? If they are, shouldn't white people like my children concern themselves with the suffering of Emmett Till? Is making art a form of concern? Does it matter which form the concern takes? Could they be painters of occasional black subjects? (Dana Schutz paints many subjects.) Or must their concern take a different form: civil rights law, public-school teaching? If they ignore the warnings of the letter and take black suffering as their subject in a work of art, what should be the consequence? If their painting turns out to be a not especially distinguished expression of or engagement with their supposed concern, must it be removed from wherever it hangs? Destroyed? To what purpose?

Often I look at my children and remember that quadroons—green-eyed, yellow-haired people like my children—must have been standing on those auction blocks with their café au lait mothers and dark-skinned grandmothers. And I think too of how they would have had many opportunities to "pass," to sneak out and be lost in the white majority, not visibly connected to black suffering and so able to walk through town, marry white, lighten up the race again. To be biracial in America at that time was almost always to be the issue[8] of rape. It was in a literal sense to live with the enemy within, to have your physical being exist as an embodiment of the oppression of your people. Perhaps this trace of shame and inner conflict has never entirely left the biracial experience.

To be biracial at any time is complex. Speaking for myself, I know that racially charged historical moments, like this one, can increase the ever-present torsion within my experience until it feels like something's got to give. You start to yearn for absolute clarity: personal, genetic, political. I stood in front of the painting and thought how cathartic it would be if this picture filled me with rage. But it never got that deep into me, as either representation or appropriation. I think of it as a questionably successful example of both, but the letter condemning it will not contend with its relative success or failure, the letter lives in a binary world in which the painting is either facilely celebrated as proof of the autonomy of art or condemned to the philistine art bonfire. The first option, as the letter rightly argues, is often just hoary old white privilege dressed up as aesthetic theory, but the second is—let's face it—the province of Nazis and censorious evangelicals. Art is a traffic in symbols and images, it has never been politically or historically neutral, and I do not find discussions on appropriation and representation to be in any way trivial. Each individual example has to be *thought through,* and we have every right to include such considerations in our evaluations of art (and also to point out the often dubious neutrality of supposedly pure aesthetic criteria). But when arguments of

---

8   *issue*   Offspring.

appropriation are linked to a racial essentialism no more sophisticated than antebellum miscegenation laws,[9] well, then we head quickly into absurdity. Is Hannah Black black enough to write this letter? Are my children too white to engage with black suffering? How black is black enough? Does an "octoroon"[10] still count?

When I looked at *Open Casket,* the truth is I didn't feel very much. I tried to transfer to the painting—or even to Dana Schutz—some of the cold fury that is sparked by looking at the historical photograph of Emmett Till, whose mother insisted he have an open casket, or by considering the crimes of Carolyn Bryant, the white woman who falsely accused him of harassing her, but nothing I saw in that canvas could provoke such an emotion. The painting is an abstraction without much intensity, and there's a clear caution in the brushstrokes around the eyes: Schutz has gone in only so far. Yet the anxious aporia in the upper face is countered by the area around the mouth, where the canvas roils, coming toward us three-dimensionally, like a swelling—the flesh garroted, twisted, striped—as if something is pushing from behind the death mask, trying to get out. That *did* move me.

What's harder to see is why this picture was singled out. A few floors up hung a painting by a white artist, Eric Fischl, *A Visit to?/?A Visit from?/?The Island,* in which rich white holidaymakers on a beach are juxtaposed with black boat people washed up on the sand, some dead, some half-naked, desperate, writhing, suffering. Painted in 1983, by an artist now in his late sixties, it is presumably for sale, yet it goes unmentioned in a letter whose main effect has been to divert attention from everything else in the show. Henry Taylor, Deana Lawson, Lyle Ashton Harris, and Cauleen Smith were just a few of the artists of color lighting up the Whitney in a thrilling biennial that delved deep into black experience, illuminating its joys and suffering both. Looking at their work, I found I resented the implication that black pain is so raw and unprocessed—and black art practice so vulnerable and invisible—that a single painting by a white woman can radically influence it one way or another. Nor did I need to convince myself of my own authenticity by drawing a line between somebody else's supposed fraudulence and the fears I have concerning my own (thus evincing an unfortunate tendency toward overcompensation that, it must be admitted, is not unknown among us biracial folks). No. The viewer is not a fraud. Neither is the painter. The truth is that this painting and I are simply not in profound communication.

9   *racial essentialism*   Idea that there are fundamental, unchangeable differences between races;   *antebellum miscegenation laws*   Pre-Civil War regulations prohibiting interracial marriage and, in some cases, any sexual relations between races.
10   *octoroon*   Racial classification applied to people who are one eighth Black; it is part of the same classification system as "quadroon."

This is always a risk in art. The solution remains as it has always been: Get out (of the gallery) or go deeper in (to the argument). Write a screed against it. Critique the hell out of it. Tear it to shreds in your review or paint another painting in response. But remove it? Destroy it? Instead I turned from the painting, not offended, not especially shocked or moved, not even terribly engaged by it, and walked with the children to the next room.

We have been warned not to get under one another's skin, to keep our distance. But Jordan Peele's horror-fantasy—in which we are inside one another's skin and intimately involved in one another's suffering—is neither a horror nor a fantasy. It is a fact of our experience. The real fantasy is that we can get out of one another's way, make a clean cut between black and white, a final cathartic separation between us and them. For the many of us in loving, mixed families, this is the true impossibility. There are people online who seem astounded that *Get Out* was written and directed by a man with a white wife and a white mother, a man who may soon have—depending on how the unpredictable phenotype lottery goes—a white-appearing child. But this is the history of race in America. Families can become black, then white, then black again within a few generations. And even when Americans are not genetically mixed, they live in a mixed society at the national level if no other. There is no getting out of our intertwined history.

But in this moment of resurgent black consciousness, God knows it feels good—therapeutic!—to mark a clear separation from white America, the better to speak in a collective voice. We will not be moved. We can't breathe.[11] We will not be executed for traffic violations or for the wearing of hoodies. We will no longer tolerate substandard schools, housing, health care. *Get Out*—as evidenced by its huge box office—is the right movie for this moment. It is the opposite of post-black or postracial. It reveals race as the fundamental American lens through which everything is seen. That part, to my mind, is right on the money. But the "us" and "them"? That's a cheaper gag. Whether they like it or not, Americans are one people. (And the binary of black and white is only one part of this nation's infinitely variegated racial composition.) Lobotomies are the cleanest cut; real life is messier. I can't wait for Peele— with his abundant gifts, black-nerd smarts, comprehensive cinematic fandom, and complex personal experience—to go deeper in, and out the other side.

(2017)

---

11 *We can't breathe* Reference to "I can't breathe," the last words of Eric Garner, a 43-year old Black man killed by New York police in 2014 when he was arrested under suspicion of illegally selling individual cigarettes. The phrase became a common protest chant at demonstrations against police brutality.

Questions

1. Consider the following passage:

    > Jordan Peele's horror-fantasy—in which we are inside one another's skin and intimately involved in one another's suffering—is neither a horror nor a fantasy. It is a fact of our experience. The real fantasy is that we can get out of one another's way, make a clean cut between black and white, a final cathartic separation between us and them (paragraph 21).

    What does Smith mean by this passage? How does she relate these ideas to the controversy surrounding Schutz's painting?

2. Consider the following critique of this article, advanced by Candace McDuffie on the *Ploughshares* literary blog:

    > ... [I]t is clear that [Smith] is more interested in being an ethnographer to black culture than a black woman. Although she states that she is identified by herself and others as black, she centers whiteness in an essay that was supposed to focus on black pain. She measures blackness only by its physical proximity to whiteness. While Smith acknowledges the complexities of being biracial, she doesn't probe her privilege of having light skin nor does she pay the same attention to what cultural appropriation actually is. Smith ... views it as a particular population of people guarding their culture in a malicious manner and not factoring in our justification for being so protective of it. Since black people were brought to this country, our bodies have been commodified for labor, for sexual exploitation, and even for entertainment.

    To what extent do you agree with McDuffie's critique? Explain your view.

3. Consider the photographs of Emmett Till that are reprinted in this anthology's color insert. What qualities of these photographs and their historical context make it so controversial for Schutz to use Till's image? Do you agree with those who condemn her choice?

4. Find an image of Schutz's *Open Casket* online.

    a. In your view, how well does this painting address its subject? What does it mean to address well a subject such as Till's death—or is such a thing impossible?

    b. To what extent (if at all) is the painting's quality relevant to the question of whether or not it was wrong for Schutz to use Till's image?

5. Watch *Get Out* and read Brent Staples's article "The Movie *Get Out* Is a Strong Antidote to the Myth of 'Postracial' America" (the latter is also included in this anthology). Then, write an analysis of the film that draws on the commentary of both Staples and Smith.

6. Smith uses the terms "octoroon" and "quadroon" in this essay. What is the rhetorical impact of this choice?

7. Smith was born in England to a white father and a Black mother. How, if at all, is her personal experience of race and culture reflected in this essay?

JONATHAN CAPEHART

TAKING A KNEE WITH COLIN KAEPERNICK AND STANDING WITH STEPHEN CURRY AGAINST TRUMP

Professional football player Colin Kaepernick initiated a movement when, in August 2016, as a protest against racial oppression and police brutality in the United States, he stopped standing during the national anthem. Individual players, and in some cases whole teams, gradually joined the protest through gestures such as kneeling, linking arms, or raising fists during the anthem. On 22 September 2017, President Trump responded by saying that the protesters should be "fired" from the NFL—a declaration which prompted a marked increase in the number of protests.

On the same day, Stephen Curry, widely considered one of the most skilled athletes in the NBA, publicly stated that he did not want to make the visit to the White House that his team, the Golden State Warriors, would have traditionally made as winners of the year's NBA championship. On 23 September, President Trump rescinded the invitation via tweet. The piece below appeared in the Washington Post*'s Opinion section the following day.*

If you know me, you know I'm not a big sports fan. But President Trump's deplorable attacks against the Constitution's guarantee of freedom of speech have made me a fanatic for Stephen Curry and Colin Kaepernick, the National Basketball Association and the National Football League.

By now you are well aware of Trump's attacks. His foul-mouthed hit Friday on Kaepernick's taking a knee during the national anthem to protest the treatment of African Americans at the hands of police. His juvenile disinvitation of basketball champions the Golden State Warriors because of Curry's stated disinterest in making the traditional trip to the White House.

And as outrageous as Trump's words and actions are, the reaction of the sports world is most heartening. The Golden State Warriors took the presidential diss* in stride to announce that the team would still come to Washington. But the players will do something the president refuses to do. "In lieu of a visit to the White House," the team announced Saturday, "we have decided that we'll constructively use our trip to the nation's capital in February to celebrate equality, diversity and inclusion—the values that we embrace as an organization."

NFL Commissioner Roger Goodell refused to remain silent in the face of Trump's tantrum. "The NFL and our players are at our best when we help create a sense of unity in our country and our culture," he said Saturday. "Divisive comments like these demonstrate an unfortunate lack of respect for the NFL, our great game and all of our players, and a failure to understand the overwhelming force for good our clubs and players represent in our communities." Even Robert Kraft, the Trump-supporting owner of the New England Patriots, said in a statement he was "deeply disappointed by the tone of the comments made by the president on Friday."

From London to Boston to Oakland, athletes took a knee or locked arms   5 in response to ignorant hectoring from Trump. The Pittsburgh Steelers, Seattle Seahawks and Tennessee Titans stayed in their locker rooms during the national anthem before their respective games on Sunday. Whether taking a knee or standing while putting a hand on a teammate kneeling in protest, these athletes are filling the moral chasm created by a president whose sympathy and empathy are reserved for the "very fine people" among the white supremacists, Nazis and otherwise bigoted racists marching unmasked in Charlottesville.[1]

Let's not forget why Kaepernick kicked all this off in the first place. Here's what the still-out-of-work former San Francisco 49er told the media in August 2016 when he was still playing for the team.

> I'm going to continue to stand with the people that are being oppressed. To me, this is something that has to change. When there's significant change and I feel that flag represents what it's supposed to represent, and this country is representing people the way that it's supposed to, I'll stand.
>
> This stand wasn't for me. This is because I'm seeing things happen to people that don't have a voice, people that don't have a platform to talk and have their voices heard, and effect change. So I'm in the position where I can do that and I'm going to do that for people that can't.

---

1   *Charlottesville*   In Charlottesville, Virginia, on 12 August 2017, white nationalists opposed to the removal of Confederate monuments chanted a Nazi slogan and clashed violently with counterprotesters, murdering one. Following the incident, Trump delivered a series of self-contradictory statements. In one, he indicated that the protest had involved "some very fine people on both sides" and expressed support for the position of the white nationalists regarding the removal of monuments.

It's something that can unify this team. It's something that can unify this country. If we have these real conversations that are uncomfortable for a lot of people. If we have these conversations, there's a better understanding of where both sides are coming from.

I have great respect for the men and women that have fought for this country. I have family, I have friends that have gone and fought for this country. And they fight for freedom, they fight for the people, they fight for liberty and justice, for everyone. That's not happening. People are dying in vain because this country isn't holding their end of the bargain up, as far as giving freedom and justice, liberty to everybody. That's something that's not happening. I've seen videos, I've seen circumstances where men and women that have been in the military have come back and been treated unjustly by the country they fought for, and have been murdered by the country they fought for, on our land. That's not right.

Those who argue that doing any of this plays into Trump's hands politically are flat-out wrong. That's a demand that every American remain silent as rights they revere and rely on are chipped away by the creeping normalization of the reprehensible by this president. By that logic, fighting against injustice would be never okay.

Political considerations must take a backseat when character is at stake, when matters of conscience come into play, when standing up for one's beliefs is paramount. By speaking out, by taking a knee, by not bowing or buckling to pressure from as high as the Oval Office, Kaepernick and those now joining him are showing the power of our Constitution and the promise of our nation. They neither need nor deserve lectures on patriotism. Freedom of speech and freedom of expression are what make America great.*

(2017)

Questions

1. What is Capehart's stance on the importance of character? Why does character matter, even in sports?

2. Another article included in this anthology, "The Politicization of Everything: Everybody Loses in the Trump-NFL Brawl over the National Anthem," defends a view opposing the one adopted in this piece. The following questions address both pieces:

a.   The *Wall Street Journal* article argues against "the politicization of the National Football League and the national anthem," while Capehart defends Kaepernick by saying that "[p]olitical considerations must take a backseat when character is at stake." How is each author using the concept of the "political"? To what extent do their usages overlap?

b.   Identify what you consider to be the most persuasive point in each article. Drawing on these articles and/or your own invention, come up with a counterargument one might advance against each point you identified.

c.   In response to these articles, write your own opinion piece on this topic. Your writing style should be suitable for publication in a newspaper.

3.   An extensive quotation from Kaepernick makes up almost a third of Capehart's article. What is the rhetorical impact of this?

WALL STREET JOURNAL EDITORIAL BOARD

THE POLITICIZATION OF EVERYTHING: EVERYBODY LOSES IN THE TRUMP-NFL BRAWL OVER THE NATIONAL ANTHEM

During the 2016 football season, Colin Kaepernick, a quarterback for the San Francisco 49ers, abstained from standing during the national anthem as a protest against racial oppression in the United States. Other players began to follow his example, with some kneeling and others displaying raised fists or linked arms during the anthem. The protests continued into 2017, and the following article appeared in The Wall Street Journal's *Opinion section in September of that year, two days after President Trump stated that all participants in this form of protest should be "fired" from the NFL.*

Kaepernick was not employed by any NFL team for the 2017 football season, which many suggested was a retaliation for his expression of his political views. He nonetheless continued his activism, and in early 2018 completed a "million dollar pledge" to donate a hundred thousand dollars a month for ten months to "organizations working in oppressed communities."

Healthy democracies have ample room for politics but leave a larger space for civil society and culture that unites more than divides. With the politicization of the National Football League and the national anthem, the Divided States of America are exhibiting a very unhealthy level of polarization and mistrust.

The progressive forces of identity politics started this poisoning of America's favorite spectator sport last year by making a hero of Colin Kaepernick for refusing to stand for "The Star-Spangled Banner" before games. They raised the stakes this year by turning him into a progressive martyr because no team had picked him up to play quarterback after he opted out of his contract with the San Francisco 49ers.

The NFL is a meritocracy, and maybe coaches and general managers thought he wasn't good enough for the divisions he might cause in a locker room or among fans. But the left said it was all about race and class.

All of this is cultural catnip for Donald Trump, who pounced on Friday night at a rally and on the weekend on Twitter with his familiar combination of gut political instinct, rhetorical excess, and ignorance. "Wouldn't you love to see one of these NFL owners, when somebody disrespects our flag, to say, 'Get that son of a bitch off the field right now, out, he's fired. He's fired,'" Mr. Trump said Friday.

No doubt most Americans agree with Mr. Trump that they don't want their   5
flag disrespected, especially by millionaire athletes. But Mr. Trump never stops at reasonable, and so he called for kneeling players to be fired or suspended, and if the league didn't comply for fans to "boycott" the NFL.

He also plunged into the debate over head injuries without a speck of knowledge about the latest brain science, claiming that the NFL was "ruining the game" by trying to stop dangerous physical hits. This is the kind of rant you'd hear in a lousy sports bar.

Mr. Trump has managed to unite the players and owners against him, though several owners supported him for President and donated to his inaugural.* The owners were almost obliged to defend their sport, even if their complaints that Mr. Trump was "divisive" ignored the divisive acts by Mr. Kaepernick and his media allies that injected politics into football in the first place.

Americans don't begrudge athletes their free-speech rights—see the popularity of Charles Barkley[1]—but disrespecting the national anthem puts partisanship above a symbol of nationhood that thousands have died for. Players who chose to kneel shouldn't be surprised that fans around the country booed them on Sunday. This is the patriotic sentiment that they are helping Mr. Trump exploit for what he no doubt thinks is his own political advantage.

American democracy was healthier when politics at the ballpark was limited to fans booing politicians who threw out the first ball—almost as a bipartisan obligation. This showed a healthy skepticism toward the political class. But now the players want to be politicians and use their fame to lecture other Americans, the parsons of the press corps want to make them moral spokesmen, and the President wants to run against the players.

The losers are the millions of Americans who would rather cheer for their   10
teams on Sunday as a respite from work and the other divisions of American life.

(2017)

---

1   *Charles Barkley*   African American retired college basketball player who, on the day this editorial was published, criticized Trump on the CBS program *NFL Today*.

Questions

1. Another article in this anthology, Jonathan Capehart's "Taking a Knee with Colin Kaepernick and Standing with Stephen Curry against Trump," defends a view opposing that adopted in this piece. Read that article and consider the following questions:

    a. Kaepernick's explanation of his protest is quoted in Capehart's article. In your view, does anything in Kaepernick's statement contradict the suggestion that his protest "disrespect[s] the national anthem"? Why or why not?

    b. The *Wall Street Journal* article suggests that players who kneel during the anthem "are helping Mr. Trump exploit" Americans' patriotism (paragraph 8). How does Capehart counter this point? Which view do you find most compelling?

2. The editors appear to object to the actions both of Kaepernick and of Trump. Of the two, who is more strongly condemned in this piece? How can you tell?

3. This piece criticizes Kaepernick for "inject[ing] politics into football" (paragraph 7). To what extent do you agree with the implication that football was apolitical before the controversy surrounding Kaepernick arose?

4. Identify some words and phrases in this article that signal the authors' location on the political spectrum.

AUDRA D.S. BURCH

from THE #MeToo MOMENT: AFTER ALABAMA, BLACK WOMEN WONDER, WHAT'S NEXT?

The 2017 special election in Alabama attracted a great deal of attention. In part, this was because it was the first American senate election held after Donald Trump's inauguration as president, but another factor was the personal and political history of Roy Moore, the Republican candidate. In his career as a politician and judge, Moore has made controversial statements including a condemnation of "homosexual conduct" as "a violation of the laws of nature and of nature's God," an assertion that Muslims should not be permitted to serve in Congress, and a statement that America was last "great" during the era of slavery. Moore's candidacy was also impacted by the #MeToo movement; he has been accused of sexually assaulting underage teens and of repeatedly harassing teenagers at a mall he frequented.

Alabama has historically been a solidly Republican state; in the 2016 presidential election, Donald Trump defeated Hillary Clinton in the state by almost 28 percent of the vote. Remarkably, however, in the 2017 special election, Moore lost the senate seat to his Democratic opponent, Doug Jones, by 1.5 percent. Many commentators suggested that Jones owed his victory to Black voters—especially Black women—who turned out to vote in large numbers and voted almost exclusively for Jones. In the following article from the New York Times, *Burch discusses the significance of Black women's role in the election outcome.*

In the hours after Doug Jones was declared the winner in Alabama's special Senate election and the now ubiquitous exit poll charts were splashed across television screens, Twitter churned out its latest hashtag, #BlackWomen.

By the next morning, the phrase was trending—with a seeming chorus of liberal gratitude to black women for, as the narratives goes, rescuing America from the clutches of Roy Moore. Or, as others pointed out, smartly voting their own interests.

"It was like a church revival and neighborhood block party rolled into one joyous national celebration," as the Los Angeles Times put it....

Indeed, black women, a reliably Democratic voting bloc in Alabama and across the United States, stood strong in the #MeToo era, rejecting a candidate accused of stalking malls looking for teenage girls—and sending the state's first Democrat to the Senate in a quarter century. Fully 98 percent of them voted for Doug Jones (up from 95 percent who voted to re-elect President Obama in 2012, according to exit polls back then).

5   This week's exit polls are interesting to unpack. Overall, 57 percent of Alabama women backed Mr. Jones, compared with 42 percent of men, a significant gender gap.

Among white women, 63 percent supported Mr. Moore, which at first blush suggests they were not hugely moved by the allegations of sexual misconduct.

Meanwhile 34 percent of white women voted for Mr. Jones—more than twice the percentage who cast ballots for Mr. Obama five years ago.

That's a big shift—seismic in political terms—of one demographic group voting for a member of the other party. And consider this: 72 percent of white men supported Mr. Moore, a 9-point spread between white men and white women; in 2012, the Republican candidate, Mitt Romney, got 84 percent of white men and 83 percent of white women, a statistically insignificant margin.

As a black female journalist who has written about race and its ever-present role in social, political and economic issues, I have been thinking about the lessons of this election but also listening to others who are helping to shape the conversation.

10 Yes, the black women's vote was perceived by many women on the left as a moment worth celebrating. But what's next looms larger. As Kamala Harris, the second African-American woman ever elected to the United States Senate, pointed out in a tweet.

> Kamala Harris @KamalaHarris
> #BlackWomen helped elect a Democrat to the US Senate in AL for the first time in more than 20 years. But we need to do more than congratulate them. Let's address issues that disproportionately affect Black women—like pay disparity, housing & under-representation in elected office
> 9:11 AM – Dec 13, 2017
> *671 671 Replies 11,691 Retweets 37,529 likes*

It raises questions we're only just beginning to answer: What is the cost of political loyalty? How does voting muscle translate into support for issues important to black women? Will this trigger a reckoning among the feminist movement, often accused of dismissing or ignoring the voices and work of minorities? ...

(2017)

Questions

1. In a portion of the article not reprinted here, Burch quotes strategist Symone Sanders as saying that "Black women have been showing up for years for the Democratic Party. They have long been a key voting bloc, but only recently has that power been recognized." Why do you think Black women's voting power has been recognized "only recently"? Has it been sufficiently recognized?

2. In the election discussed above, 93 per cent of Black men voted for Jones. (Black men represented 11 per cent of the voters, and Black women 17 per cent of the voters.) Why do you think Black men were not directly mentioned in the above article? Should they have been?

3. What is the significance of Burch's use of Kamala Harris's tweet? What larger questions does the tweet evoke?

4. Research Doug Jones and Roy Moore. Why do you think levels of support for these candidates in particular were so strongly affected by race and gender?

5. Do you think Black women's "voting muscle" will translate into government action on issues that matter to Black women, and to the Black community more generally? Why or why not? What factors might influence the will of the government to address these issues?

SHANITA HUBBARD

RUSSELL SIMMONS, R. KELLY,[1] AND WHY BLACK WOMEN CAN'T SAY #METOO

Black activist Tarana Burke founded the "Me Too" movement in 2007 to combat sexual violence and its effects against Black women and girls. Ten years later, white actor Alyssa Milano popularized MeToo as a hashtag, tweeting that "If all the women who have been sexually harassed or assaulted wrote 'Me too.' as a status, we might give people a sense of the magnitude of the problem." (Milano appears to have been initially unaware of the phrase's origin in Burke's campaign, and acknowledged it via twitter once it was brought to her attention.) Millions of people have since used the hashtag, leading to widespread discussion of sexual harassment and violence, especially in the workplace. Many of the most high-profile conversations have surrounded the experience of White women in Hollywood.

The following piece by Hubbard appeared in the New York Times *Opinion section in December 2017.*

There's an intersection in almost every hood that teaches young girls lessons about power, racism and sexism. In the projects, where I grew up, I had to pass it almost every day to get home from school.

This intersection is where some of the guys from the neighborhood would stand around, play music, trash-talk about which artist should hold the title

---

1   *Russell Simmons*   Co-founder of the influential music label Def Jam Recordings, Simmons is a prominent Black entrepreneur and activist. In 2017, multiple women stated that they had been raped by Simmons, with additional women speaking out about other acts of sexual violence;   *R. Kelly*   Enormously popular Black R&B artist who was first accused of sexual relationships with underage teenagers in the 1990s. He has been charged with the production of child pornography, in addition to being sued multiple times for abusive behavior toward young women.

of greatest rapper, and then, suddenly, turn into dangerous predators when young girls walked by. This is where young girls like me learned to shrink into ourselves and remain silent.

On this intersection, like so many others in the world, your body and sense of safety were both up for grabs. On a good day, if you and a girlfriend remained silent, walking past the group of "corner dudes," who were all about 15 years your senior and screaming about what they would do to your 12-year-old body, would be a short-lived experience.

On other days, especially if you were walking alone, things would escalate quickly. One of the men would grab your butt and you would pretend you didn't feel it. Fighting back would make things worse: If you resisted, they would scream at you, curse at you and, in one particular case, attempt to follow you home until you ran inside a store and waited them out. But cross this intersection enough times and such things start to feel normal.

The normalization of predatory behavior manifests itself in many forms. It's not yet clear how the black community will respond to the news that icons like Russell Simmons and Tavis Smiley[2] are among those men who have been accused of sexual misconduct. (Both deny the accusations.) Unlike when the accusations were made against Harvey Weinstein,[3] however, we have yet to see a flood of prominent figures publicly stand with the victims. What is clear is that too many of us still perform mental gymnastics, of the sort deployed during Woody Allen[4] movies, to justify attending R. Kelly concerts, despite years of reports about him victimizing young girls. For some of us, the basis for this cognitive dissonance was established at a very young age.

From my years passing through that intersection, I came to believe—wrongly—that a person can be a victim only if those committing the offenses against her had great power. By any definition, the corner guys had very little

5

---

2   *Tavis Smiley*   Prominent Black talk show host who lost his job with PBS in late 2017 because of allegations that he had pressured multiple subordinates at the company into sexual relationships.

3   *Harvey Weinstein*   White film producer who wielded an enormous degree of power in Hollywood until, in October 2017, it was revealed to the general public that he had a decades-long pattern of harassing and raping women—something that many people in the film industry already knew. By November 2017, more than a hundred women had come forward with accusations.

4   *Woody Allen*   Influential and acclaimed white filmmaker who was first accused in 1992 of molesting his adopted daughter Dylan Farrow, who was seven at the time; as an adult, Farrow has repeated the allegations multiple times in the press. Allen married another of his adopted daughters, Soon-Yi Previn, with whom he began a relationship near the time of her graduation from high school.

power—and they themselves were victims of those who did. They were victims of a type of power that drove through that same intersection, snatched people away from their families and out of the community for decades. This type of power could stop and frisk them, and return to its patrol cars and proceed with its day. On a good day, if these guys were alone and remained silent without resisting, the consequences wouldn't be as severe. A few cops would pull up, pat them down, curse at them, beat them up and scream for them to get off the corner. On other days, especially if the corner guys were in a large group, things could escalate quickly. Sometimes a corner dude wouldn't make it home that night.

This state-sanctioned abuse at the hands of police evoked, and continues to evoke, a community response that literally and figuratively calls for the protection of these young men, and rightfully so. A community is right to fight against over-policing and brutality. It *should* encourage victims of police violence to speak up and put pressure on local politicians to take a stand.

But when your community fights for those same people who terrorize you, it sends a very complicated and mixed message. Even worse, sometimes the community members fighting back consist of young women who were once the little girls walking home from school doing their best to be invisible in hopes of avoiding what nobody ever called sexual assault. This sends the message that your pain is not a priority. It tells you that perhaps you are not a victim, because those who are harming you are also being harmed and we need to focus our energy on protecting them. After all, their lives are at stake.

#MeToo is triggering memories of that corner that I've tucked away for 20 years because I've been taught there are greater needs in the community. Perhaps this is part of the reason studies indicate only one in 15 African-American women report being raped. We've seen the unchecked power of white men ravish our communities, and we carry the message of "not right now" when it comes to addressing our pain if the offender is black.

10   Maybe this is why more victims of sexual assault within the hip-hop community have not come forward. Is it possible that black women who work in hip-hop are silent victims, with pain they have been conditioned not to prioritize? I suspect this is true—but I can't say with certainty.

How can these women who live at the proverbial intersection of race and sexism, who grew up crossing that corner, ever be a part of the national #MeToo conversation when they can't be heard in their own community? The intersection of race, class, sexism and power is dangerous, and the most vulnerable women among us must navigate it alone. They are terrorized, then expected to fight for those who terrorized them because a seemingly greater predator is at large. Their faces will never grace the cover of *Time* magazine,[5] and in some cases their silence will never be broken, if they hold the same false notions of power and victimhood that I once clung to when the cognitive dissonance became too strong.

(2017)

Questions

1. How, according to Hubbard, do racial and gender-based oppression interact in Black women's experiences of sexual assault?

2. Hubbard begins this piece with a description of an intersection where sexual abuse is normalized. How does this intersection function metaphorically in the article as a whole?

3. Corinne Purtill, in her opinion piece "MeToo Hijacked Black Women's Work on Race and Gender Equality," argues that the leadership of Black women in combating sexual harassment must be acknowledged, from Tarana Burke's founding of the Me Too movement to landmark cases pursued in the 1970s and 80s by such women as Paulette Barnes, Diane Williams, and Mechelle Vinson. She goes on to say the following:

   > it's not fair, nor is it even possible, to separate gender from race and class and say, "We'll get to those later—but first let's settle this." Women of color fought the battles that brought society to this point, where even the faint hope of change seems possible. To use that work without ensuring that this broken system is replaced with one inclusive of race, in addition to gender, is not partial victory. It's complete failure.

   How does Hubbard's argument connect with Purtill's assessment? How does Purtill's point add to Hubbard's ideas?

4. Based on this article and your own knowledge, what might be some reasons beyond those suggested by Hubbard to explain "why more victims of sexual assault within the hip-hop community have not come forward"?

---

5 *Their faces ... magazine* In 2017, *Time* declared the "Silence Breakers" who contributed to the rise of the MeToo movement to be "Person of the Year." Tarana Burke was mentioned in the accompanying article, but was controversially omitted from the cover image, which depicted five women.

5. To what extent (if at all) does this article suggest that dynamics in the African American community as a whole are to blame for preventing Black women from reporting sexual violence by Black men? Is Hubbard too hard (or not hard enough) on the African American community?

6. Choose one of the accused celebrities Hubbard mentions and research how the public has responded to the allegations against him since the publication of this article. Is the response, in your view, a just one? Is the response affected by the person's race or status? Why or why not?

CARVELL WALLACE

WHY *BLACK PANTHER* IS A DEFINING MOMENT FOR BLACK AMERICA

The Marvel Cinematic Universe—a franchise that includes numerous interconnected films and television shows based on characters and storylines from Marvel comic books—has been a popular culture phenomenon since the release of its first film, Iron Man, *in 2008.* Black Panther, *released almost ten years later, was the first film in the series to feature a Black protagonist: Black Panther, who had, in 1966, also made history as the first Black superhero to appear in a Marvel comic book. Eagerly anticipated, the film garnered broad critical acclaim and was a tremendous financial success, with one of the highest-earning opening weekends in history. In the following piece from the* New York Times Magazine, *African American writer and journalist Carvell Wallace argues for the film's importance.*

The Grand Lake Theater—the kind of old-time movie house with cavernous ceilings and ornate crown moldings—is one place I take my kids to remind us that we belong to Oakland, Calif. Whenever there is a film or community event that has meaning for this town, the Grand Lake is where you go to see it. There are local film festivals, indie film festivals, erotic film festivals, congressional town halls, political fund-raisers. After Hurricane Katrina, the lobby served as a drop-off for donations. We run into friends and classmates there. On weekends we meet at the farmers' market across the street for coffee.

The last momentous community event I experienced at the Grand Lake was a weeknight viewing of *Fruitvale Station*, the 2013 film directed by the Bay Area native Ryan Coogler. It was about the real-life police shooting of Oscar Grant, 22, right here in Oakland, where Grant's killing landed less like a news story and more like the death of a friend or a child. He had worked at a popular grocery, gone to schools and summer camps with the children of acquaintances. His death—he was shot by the transit police while handcuffed, unarmed and face down on a train-station platform, early in the morning of New Year's Day 2009—sparked intense grief, outrage and sustained protest,

473

years before Black Lives Matter took shape as a movement. Coogler's telling took us slowly through the minutiae of Grant's last day alive: We saw his family and child, his struggles at work, his relationship to a gentrifying city, his attempts to make sense of a young life that felt both aimless and daunting. But the moment I remember most took place after the movie was over: A group of us, friends and strangers alike and nearly all black, stood in the cool night under the marquee, crying and holding one another. It didn't matter that we didn't know one another. We knew enough.

On a misty morning this January, I found myself standing at that same spot, having gotten out of my car to take a picture of the Grand Lake's marquee. The words *Black Panther* were on it, placed dead center. They were not in normal-size letters; the theater was using the biggest ones it had. All the other titles huddled together in another corner of the marquee. A month away from its Feb. 16 opening, *Black Panther* was, already and by a wide margin, the most important thing happening at the Grand Lake.

Marvel Comics's Black Panther was originally conceived in 1966 by Stan Lee and Jack Kirby, two Jewish New Yorkers, as a bid to offer black readers a character to identify with. The titular hero, whose real name is T'Challa, is heir apparent to the throne of Wakanda, a fictional African nation. The tiny country has, for centuries, been in nearly sole possession of vibranium, an alien element acquired from a fallen meteor. (Vibranium is powerful and nearly indestructible; it's in the special alloy Captain America's shield is made of.) Wakanda's rulers have wisely kept their homeland and its elemental riches hidden from the world, and in its isolation the nation has grown wildly powerful and technologically advanced. Its secret, of course, is inevitably discovered, and as the world's evil powers plot to extract the resources of yet another African nation, T'Challa's father is cruelly assassinated, forcing the end of Wakanda's sequestration. The young king will be forced to don the virtually indestructible vibranium Black Panther suit and face a duplicitous world on behalf of his people.

5   This is the subject of Ryan Coogler's third feature film—after *Fruitvale Station* and *Creed* (2015)—and when glimpses of the work first appeared last June, the response was frenzied. The trailer *teaser*—not even the full trailer— racked up 89 million views in 24 hours. On Jan. 10, 2018, after tickets were made available for presale, Fandango's managing editor, Erik Davis, tweeted that the movie's first 24 hours of advance ticket sales exceeded those of any other movie from the Marvel Cinematic Universe.

The black internet was, to put it mildly, exploding. Twitter reported that *Black Panther* was one of the most tweeted-about films of 2017, despite not even opening that year. There were plans for viewing parties, a fund-raiser to arrange a private screening for the Boys & Girls Club of Harlem,* hashtags like

#BlackPantherSoLit and #WelcomeToWakanda. When the date of the premiere was announced, people began posting pictures of what might be called African-Americana, a kitsch version of an older generation's pride touchstones—kente cloth du-rags, candy-colored nine-button suits, King Jaffe Joffer from *Coming to America* [1] with his lion-hide sash—alongside captions like "This is how I'ma show up to the Black Panther premiere." Someone described how they'd feel approaching the box office by simply posting a video of the Compton rapper Buddy Crip-walking[2] in front of a Moroccan hotel.

None of this is because *Black Panther* is the first major black superhero movie. Far from it. In the mid-1990s, the Damon Wayans vehicle *Blankman* and Robert Townsend's *The Meteor Man* played black-superhero premises for campy laughs. Superheroes are powerful and beloved, held in high esteem by society at large; the idea that a normal black person could experience such a thing in America was so far-fetched as to effectively constitute gallows humor.[3] *Blade*, released in 1998, featured Wesley Snipes as a Marvel vampire hunter, and *Hancock* (2008) depicted Will Smith as a slacker antihero, but in each case the actor's blackness seemed somewhat incidental.

Black Panther, by contrast, is steeped very specifically and purposefully in its blackness. "It's the first time in a very long time that we're seeing a film with centered black people, where we have a lot of agency," says Jamie Broadnax, the founder of Black Girl Nerds, a pop-culture site focused on sci-fi and comic-book fandoms. These characters, she notes, "are rulers of a kingdom, inventors and creators of advanced technology. We're not dealing with black pain, and black suffering, and black poverty"—the usual topics of acclaimed movies about the black experience.

In a video posted to Twitter in December, which has since gone viral, three young men are seen fawning over the *Black Panther* poster at a movie theater. One jokingly embraces the poster while another asks, rhetorically: "This is what white people get to feel all the time?" There is laughter before someone says, as though delivering the punch line to the most painful joke ever told: "I would love this country, too."

Ryan Coogler saw his first Black Panther comic book as a child, at an Oakland shop called Dr. Comics & Mr. Games, about a mile from the Grand Lake

10

---

1   *kente cloth*   Brightly colored woven cloth traditionally made in Ghana;   *du-rags*   Tight-fitting headwear;   *King Jaffe ... America*   1988 romantic comedy film featuring Eddie Murphy as the colorfully attired Akeem Joffer, Prince of the fictional African country Zamunda.

2   *Crip-walking*   Dance move originated by the Los Angeles Crip gang in the 1970s.

3   *gallows humor*   Ironic comedy that exploits grim subject matter; also known as "dark comedy."

Theater. When I sat down with him in early February, at the Montage Hotel in Beverly Hills, I told him about the night I saw *Fruitvale Station*, and he listened with his head down, slowly nodding. When he looked up at me, he seemed to be blinking back tears of his own.

Coogler played football in high school, and between his fitness and his humble listening poses—leaning forward, elbows propped on knees—he reminds me of what might happen if a mild-mannered athlete accidentally discovered a radioactive movie camera and was gifted with remarkable artistic vision. He's interested in questions of identity: What does it mean to be a black person or an African person? "You know, you got to have the race conversation," he told me, describing how his parents prepared him for the world. "And you can't have that without having the slavery conversation. And with the slavery conversation comes a question of, O.K., so what about before that? And then when you ask that question, they got to tell you about a place that nine times out of 10 they've never been before. So you end up hearing about Africa, but it's a skewed version of it. It's not a tactile version."

Around the time he was wrapping up *Creed*, Coogler made his first journey to the continent, visiting Kenya, South Africa and the Kingdom of Lesotho, a tiny nation in the center of the South African landmass. Tucked high amid rough mountains, Lesotho was spared much of the colonization of its neighbors, and Coogler based much of his concept of Wakanda on it. While he was there, he told me, he was being shown around by an older woman who said she'd been a lover of the South African pop star Brenda Fassie. Riding along the hills with this woman, Coogler was told that they would need to visit an even older woman in order to drop off some watermelon. During their journey, they would stop occasionally to approach a shepherd and give him a piece of watermelon; each time the shepherd would gingerly take the piece, wrap it in cloth and tuck it away as though it were a religious totem. Time passed. Another bit of travel, another shepherd, another gift of watermelon. Eventually Coogler grew frustrated: "Why are we stopping so much?" he asked. "Watermelon is sacred," he was told. "It hydrates, it nourishes and its seeds are used for offerings." When they arrived at the old woman's home, it turned out that she was, in fact, a watermelon farmer, but her crop had not yet ripened—she needed a delivery to help her last the next few weeks.

When I was a kid, I refused to eat watermelon[4] in front of white people. To this day, the word itself makes me uncomfortable. Coogler told me that in high school he and his black football teammates used to have the same rule: Never eat watermelon in front of white teammates. Centuries of demonizing

---

4   *watermelon*   Watermelon has long been associated with demeaning racist stereotypes of Black Americans.

and ridiculing blackness have, in effect, forced black people to abandon what was once sacred. When we spoke of Africa and black Americans' attempts to reconnect with what we're told is our lost home, I admitted that I sometimes wondered if we could ever fully be part of what was left behind. He dipped his head, fell briefly quiet and then looked back at me with a solemn expression. "I think we can," he said. "It's no question. It's almost as if we've been brainwashed into thinking that we can't have that connection."

Black Panther is a Hollywood movie, and Wakanda is a fictional nation. But coming when they do, from a director like Coogler, they must also function as a place for multiple generations of black Americans to store some of our most deeply held aspirations. We have for centuries sought to either find or create a promised land where we would be untroubled by the criminal horrors of our American existence. From Paul Cuffee's attempts in 1811 to repatriate blacks to Sierra Leone and Marcus Garvey's back-to-Africa Black Star shipping line to the Afrocentric movements of the '60s and '70s,[5] black people have populated the Africa of our imagination with our most yearning attempts at self-realization. In my earliest memories, the Africa of my family was a warm fever dream, seen on the record covers I stared at alone, the sun setting over glowing, haloed Afros, the smell of incense and oils at the homes of my father's friends—a beauty so pure as to make the world outside, one of car commercials and blond sitcom families, feel empty and perverse in comparison. As I grew into adolescence, I began to see these romantic visions as just another irrelevant habit of the older folks, like a folk remedy or a warning to wear a jacket on a breezy day. But by then my generation was building its own African dreamscape, populated by KRS-One, Public Enemy and Poor Righteous Teachers;[6] we were indoctrinating ourselves into a prideful militancy about our worth. By the end of the century, "Black Star" was not just the name of Garvey's shipping line but also one of the greatest hip-hop albums[7] ever made.

---

5   *Paul Cuffee's ... Leone*   Son of a Black former slave and a Native American woman, Paul Cuffee (1759–1817) was a shipping magnate who worked to assist in the resettlement of former slaves;   *Marcus Garvey's ... line*   Jamaican Black nationalist Marcus Garvey (1887–1940) launched a shipping company, Black Star, to improve transatlantic economic connections between Blacks and to return African Americans to their ancestral homes in Africa;   *Afrocentric movements ... '70s*   Movements focused on the celebration and study of African history and culture as a means of empowering people of African ancestry.
6   *KRS-One ... Poor Righteous Teachers*   Black rap and Hip Hop artists known for politically engaged work.
7   *"Black Star" ... albums*   Hip Hop duo Black Star released *Mos Def & Telib Kweli Are Black Star* in 1998.

15   Never mind that most of us had never been to Africa. The point was not verisimilitude or a precise accounting of Africa's reality. It was the envisioning of a free self. Nina Simone[8] once described freedom as the absence of fear, and as with all humans, the attempt of black Americans to picture a homeland, whether real or mythical, was an attempt to picture a place where there was no fear. This is why it doesn't matter that Wakanda was an idea from a comic book, created by two Jewish artists. No one knows colonization better than the colonized, and black folks wasted no time in recolonizing Wakanda. No genocide or takeover of land was required. Wakanda is ours now. We do with it as we please.

Until recently, most popular speculation on what the future would be like had been provided by white writers and futurists, like Isaac Asimov and Gene Roddenberry.[9] Not coincidentally, these futures tended to carry the power dynamics of the present into perpetuity. Think of the original *Star Trek*, with its peaceful, international crew, still under the charge of a white man from Iowa. At the time, the character of Lieutenant Uhura, played by Nichelle Nichols, was so vital for African-Americans—the black woman of the future as an accomplished philologist—that, as Nichols told NPR, the Rev. Dr. Martin Luther King Jr. himself persuaded her not to quit the show after the first season. It was a symbol of great progress that she was conceived as something more than a maid. But so much still stood in the way of her being conceived as a captain.

       The artistic movement called Afrofuturism, a decidedly black creation, is meant to go far beyond the limitations of the white imagination. It isn't just the idea that black people will exist in the future, will use technology and science, will travel deep into space. It is the idea that we will have won the future. There exists, somewhere within us, an image in which we are whole, in which we are home. Afrofuturism is, if nothing else, an attempt to imagine what that home would be. *Black Panther* cannot help being part of this. "Wakanda itself is a dream state," says the director Ava DuVernay, "a place that's been in the hearts and minds and spirits of black people since we were brought here in chains." She and Coogler have spent the past few months working across the hall from each other in the same editing facility, with him tending to *Black Panther* and her to her much-anticipated film of Madeleine L'Engle's *A Wrinkle in Time*. At

8   *Nina Simone*   African American composer, pianist, performer, and civil rights activist (1933–2003).

9   *Isaac Asimov*   Russian-American science fiction writer and scientist (1920–92); *Gene Roddenberry*   Film and television writer and producer (1921–91) best known as the creator of *Star Trek*.

the heart of Wakanda, she suggests, lie some of our most excruciating existen-tial questions: "What if they didn't come?" she asked me. "And what if they didn't take us? What would that have been?"

Afrofuturism, from its earliest iterations, has been an attempt to imagine an answer to these questions. The movement spans from free-jazz thinkers like Sun Ra, who wrote of an African past filled with alien technology and extraterrestrial beings, to the art of Krista Franklin and Ytasha Womack, to the writers Octavia Butler, Nnedi Okorafor and Derrick Bell, to the music of Jamila Woods and Janelle Monáe. Their work, says John I. Jennings—a media and cultural studies professor at the University of California, Riverside, and co-author of "Black Comix Returns"—is a way of upending the system, "because it jumps past the victory. Afrofuturism is like, 'We already won.'" Comic books are uniquely suited to handling this proposition. In them the laws of our familiar world are broken: Mild-mannered students become godlike creatures, mutants walk among us and untold power is, in an instant, granted to the most downtrodden. They offer an escape from reality, and who might need to escape reality more than a people kidnapped to a stolen land and treated as less-than-complete humans?

At the same time, it is notable that despite selling more than a million books and being the first science-fiction author to win a MacArthur fellowship, Octavia Butler, one of Afrofuturism's most important voices, never saw her work transferred to film, even as studios churned out adaptations of lesser works on a monthly basis. Butler's writing not only featured African-Americans as protagonists; it specifically highlighted African-American women. If projects by and about black men have a hard time getting made, projects by and about black women have a nearly impossible one. In March, Disney will release *A Wrinkle in Time*, featuring Storm Reid and Oprah Winfrey in lead roles; the excitement around this female-led film does not seem to compare, as of yet, with the explosion that came with *Black Panther*. But by focusing on a black female hero—one who indeed saves the universe—DuVernay is embodying the deepest and most powerful essence of Afrofuturism: to imagine ourselves in places where we had not been previously imagined.

Can films like these significantly change things for black people in   20 America? The expectations around *Black Panther* remind me of the way I heard the elders in my family talking about the mini-series *Roots*, which aired on ABC in 1977. A multigenerational drama based on the best-selling book in which Alex Haley traced his own family history, *Roots* told the story of an African slave kidnapped and brought to America, and traced his progeny through over 100 years of American history. It was an attempt to claim for us a home, because to be black in America is to be both with and without one: You are told that you must honor this land, that to refuse this is tantamount to hatred—but you are also told that you do not belong here, that you are a burden, an animal, a slave. Haley, through research and narrative and a fair bit of invention, was doing precisely what Afrofuturism does: imagining our blackness as a thing with meaning and with lineage, with value and place.

"The climate was very different in 1977," the actor LeVar Burton recalled to me recently. Burton was just 19 when he landed an audition, his first ever, for the lead role of young Kunta Kinte in the mini-series. "We had been through the civil rights movement, and there were visible changes as a result, like there was no more Jim Crow,"* he told me. "We felt that there were advancements that had been made, so the conversation had really sort of fallen off the table." The series, he said, was poised to reignite that conversation. "The story had never been told before from the point of view of the Africans. America, both black and white, was getting an emotional education about the costs of slavery to our common American psyche."

To say that *Roots* held the attention of a nation for its eight-consecutive-night run in January 1977 would be an understatement. Its final episode was viewed by 51.1 percent of all American homes with televisions, a kind of reach that seemed sure to bring about some change in opportunities, some new standing in American culture. "The expectation," Burton says, "was that this was going to lead to all kinds of positive portrayals of black people on the screen both big and small, and it just didn't happen. It didn't go down that way, and it's taken years."

Here in Oakland, I am doing what it seems every other black person in the country is doing: assembling my delegation to Wakanda. We bought tickets for the opening as soon as they were available—the first time in my life I've done that. Our contingent is made up of my 12-year-old daughter and her friend; my 14-year-old son and his friend; one of my oldest confidants, dating back to adolescence; and two of my closest current friends. Not everyone knows everyone else. But we all know enough. Our group will be eight black people strong.

Beyond the question of what the movie will bring to African-Americans sits what might be a more important question: What will black people bring to *Black Panther*? The film arrives as a corporate product, but we are using it for our own purposes, posting with unbridled ardor about what we're going to wear to the opening night, announcing the depths of the squads we'll be rolling with, declaring that Feb. 16, 2018, will be "the Blackest Day in History."

25   This is all part of a tradition of unrestrained celebration and joy that we have come to rely on for our spiritual survival. We know that there is no end to the reminders that our lives, our hearts, our personhoods are expendable. Yes, many nonblack people will say differently; they will declare their love for us,

they will post Martin Luther King Jr. and Nelson Mandela quotes one or two days a year. But the actions of our country and its collective society, and our experiences within it, speak unquestionably to the opposite. Love for black people isn't just *saying* Oscar Grant should not be dead. Love for black people is Oscar Grant not being dead in the first place.

This is why we love ourselves in the loud and public way we do—because we have to counter his death with the very same force with which such deaths attack our souls. The writer and academic Eve L. Ewing told me a story about her partner, a professor of economics at the University of Chicago: When it is time for graduation, he makes the walk from his office to the celebration site in his full regalia—the gown with velvet panels, full bell sleeves and golden piping, the velvet tam with gold-strand bullion tassel. And when he does it, every year, like clockwork, some older black woman or man he doesn't know will pull over, roll down their window, stop him and say, with a slow head shake and a deep, wide smile, something like: "I am just so *proud* of you!"

This is how we do with one another. We hold one another as a family because we must be a family in order to survive. Our individual successes and failures belong, in a perfectly real sense, to all of us. That can be for good or ill. But when it is good, it is very good. It is sunlight and gold on vast African mountains, it is the shining splendor of the Wakandan warriors poised and ready to fight, it is a collective soul as timeless and indestructible as vibranium. And with this love we seek to make the future ours, by making the present ours. We seek to make a place where we belong.

(2018)

Questions

1. What, according to Wallace, makes *Black Panther* different from previous movies with Black superhero protagonists?

2. What, if any, purpose(s) do works of Afrofuturism such as *Black Panther* serve that cannot be served by realist fiction?

3. Wallace notes that Black Panther was originally created by white Jewish writers. In your view, does this matter? Why or why not?

4. Wallace recounts a story Coogler tells about delivering watermelon in Lesotho (paragraph 12). What is the significance of this story in the context of Wallace's essay?

5. Wallace asks, "Can films like [*Black Panther* and *A Wrinkle in Time*] significantly change things for black people in America" (paragraph 20)? In your view, can they? If not, why not? If so, how?

6. Watch *Black Panther* and answer the following questions, supporting your answers with evidence from the film:

   a. Wallace claims that *Black Panther* "is steeped very specifically and purposefully in its blackness" (paragraph 8). What (if anything) makes the film "steeped ... in blackness," and how (if at all) can this engagement with blackness be read as "purposefu[l]"?

   b. How (if at all) does Wakanda "function as a place for multiple generations of black Americans to store some of our most deeply held aspirations" (paragraph 14)?

Biographical Notes

Adichie, Chimamanda Ngozi (1977–)
Acclaimed Nigerian writer Chimamanda Ngozi Adichie lives in the United States and Nigeria. She is the author of several award-winning novels, including *Purple Hibiscus* (2003), which received the Commonwealth Writers' Prize; *Half of a Yellow Sun* (2006), which was awarded the Orange Prize; and *Americanah* (2013), which won the National Book Critics Circle Award. She is also famous for her 2009 TED talk *The Danger of a Single Story* and the 2012 TEDx talk *We Should All Be Feminists*, both of which received millions of views online. The latter talk was published as a 2014 book, which Adichie has followed with another work of feminist nonfiction, *Dear Ijeawele, or a Feminist Manifesto in Fifteen Suggestions* (2017).

Alexander, Michelle (1967–)
African American writer, academic, and civil rights lawyer Michelle Alexander is best known for her influential first book, *The New Jim Crow: Mass Incarceration in the Age of Colorblindness* (2010). She has been director of the Racial Justice Project at the American Civil Liberties Union of Northern California, as well as of the Civil Rights Clinic at Stanford Law School, where she was also an Associate Professor of Law. As a private litigator, she has specialized in cases of race- and gender-based discrimination; her work as a freelance writer and speaker also centers on matters of racial justice.

Anderson, Jordan (1825–1907)
Jordan Anderson was a slave for over thirty years on the plantation of Colonel Patrick Anderson in Tennessee. He married Amanda McGregor, also a slave at the Anderson plantation, and they had 11 children together. Anderson and his family were freed in 1864 by the Union army, and they settled in Dayton, Ohio. While in Dayton, Anderson achieved fame with a letter he dictated in response to a request from his former master to return to the plantation; his letter became a public sensation and was published in numerous newspapers.

Baldwin, James (1924–87)
Born and raised in New York City, African American writer James Baldwin left America for Paris at the age of 24, and he remained an expatriate for most of the rest of his life. His 1955 collection of essays, *Notes of a Native Son* (now an established classic), was followed by numerous other collections of essays—notably *Nobody Knows My Name: More Notes of a Native Son* (1961) and *The Fire Next Time* (1963). His novels include *Go Tell It on the Mountain* (1953), *Giovanni's Room* (1956), and *Tell Me How Long the Train's Been Gone* (1968).

Burch, Audra D.S. (unknown)
African American writer Audra D.S. Burch is known for award-winning works of investigative journalism such as "Innocents Lost," an influential 2015 series addressing failures of the Florida Department of Children and Families. This series was co-written with Carol Marbin Miller for the *Miami Herald*, as was their 2017 series "Fight Club: Dark Secrets of Florida's Juvenile Justice System," which was a finalist for the 2018 Pulitzer Prize in Investigative Reporting. In 2017 Burch became a correspondent for *The New York Times*.

Capehart, Jonathan (1967–)
A Pulitzer Prize-winning journalist, African American writer Jonathan Capehart has served on the editorial boards for the *New York Daily News* and *The Washington Post*. He has also been a researcher for *The Today Show*, a columnist at Bloomberg News, and a speechwriter and policy advisor for Michael Bloomberg's successful 2001 campaign for mayor of New York City. Capehart also makes frequent appearances on MSNBC programs.

Chisholm, Shirley (1924–2005)
Born in Brooklyn to immigrant parents from the Caribbean, Shirley Chisholm was the first African American woman to be elected to Congress. She served from November 1968 until 1982. Throughout her career in Congress, Chisholm fought for women's rights, as well as for workers' rights and improved conditions and educational opportunities for inner-city residents. Her autobiography, *Unbought and Unbossed*, was published in 1970.

Coates, Ta-Nehisi (1975–)
African American writer and journalist Ta-Nehisi Coates is a national correspondent for *The Atlantic* magazine. He is a Distinguished Writer in Residence with New York University's Arthur L. Carter Journalism Institute, and was previously journalist-in-residence at the City University of New York, as well as Martin Luther King Visiting Professor at the Massachusetts Institute of Technology. His book *Between the World and Me* (2015), a letter to his son about the intricacies of Black life in the United States, received the National Book Award and was a finalist for the Pulitzer Prize. *We Were Eight Years in Power: An American Tragedy*, an essay collection reflecting on the presidency of Barack Obama, was published in 2017. Coates is also a writer for the Marvel comics *Black Panther* and *Captain America*.

Cole, Teju (1975–)
Nigerian-American writer Teju Cole has lived in the United States since he was 17. Author of a regular photography column for *The New York Times Magazine*, Cole is also Distinguished Writer in Residence at Bard College. His novel *Open City*

(2011) received both the PEN/Hemingway Award and the New York City Book Award. Cole's other books include *Known and Strange Things: Essays* (2016) and a collection of photography and prose, *Blind Spot* (2017).

Cooper, Anna Julia (1858–1964)
Born into slavery in Raleigh, North Carolina, Anna Julia Cooper obtained a bachelor's degree and later a master's degree in mathematics from Oberlin College. She became a teacher and then principal at the M Street High School, an institution for African American students in Washington, D.C.; while working there, she wrote her first and most famous book, *A Voice from the South: By a Black Woman of the South* (1892). In her sixties, Cooper became the fourth African American woman to receive a doctorate, which she earned from the Sorbonne.

Douglass, Frederick (1818–95)
Frederick Douglass, an escaped slave who became America's leading abolitionist, developed a reputation for inspiring oratory and powerful writing. He wrote several versions of his autobiography; *Narrative of the Life of Frederick Douglass, an American Slave* (1845) has become a classic American text.

Dow, Dawn Marie (unknown)
African American scholar Dawn Marie Dow's research examines the intersections of class, gender, and race within institutions such as the family, workplace, and school. She is an assistant professor in the sociology department of the Maxwell School of Citizenship and Public Affairs at Syracuse University.

Du Bois, W.E.B. (1868–1963)
W.E.B. Du Bois was an African American educator and historian, a founder of the Niagara Movement and of the National Association for the Advancement of Colored People (NAACP), and the editor of the NAACP journal *Crisis* from 1910 to 1934. His books include *The Philadelphia Negro* (1899) and *The Souls of Black Folk* (1903); the latter has long been recognized as a classic of American non-fiction.

Dunbar-Nelson, Alice (1875–1935)
Alice Dunbar-Nelson was a writer whose poetry, short stories, and criticism were influential in the development of the Harlem Renaissance, an African American literary, artistic, and cultural movement that flourished in the 1920s and 30s. An activist pursuing anti-lynching laws and women's suffrage, she was also a successful journalist and newspaper editor. Dunbar-Nelson is also remembered for her extensive diaries, which offer rare insight into the life of a mixed-race, bisexual woman intellectual in the late nineteenth and early twentieth centuries.

Equiano, Olaudah (1745–97)
Although his autobiography indicates that he was born in southern Nigeria, where he was captured and forced into slavery, some evidence suggests Olaudah Equiano may have been born in South Carolina. After working for more than a decade as a slave in the British navy, he was sold to a Quaker from whom he eventually purchased his freedom. Equiano settled in England, where he published his influential autobiography, *The Interesting Narrative of the Life of Olaudah Equiano* (1789), and campaigned for the abolition of slavery.

Fanon, Frantz (1925–61)
Frantz Fanon's groundbreaking works of anti-colonialism include *Black Skin, White Masks* (1952), *A Dying Colonialism* (1959), and *The Wretched of the Earth* (1961). Born in the French colony of Martinique, he served in the Free French forces during World War II; he later studied medicine and psychiatry in Lyons, moving in 1953 to Algeria, where he joined the revolutionary forces seeking independence from France. In addition to his work as a writer, philosopher, soldier, and activist, Fanon was also a practicing psychiatrist.

Gateward, Frances (unknown)
Frances Gateward is an Assistant Professor and Media Theory & Criticism Option Head at California State University, Northridge. She is the editor of such scholarly collections as *Seoul Searching: Cultural Identity and Cinema in South Korea* (2007) and *The Blacker the Ink: African Americans and Comic Books, Graphic Novels and Sequential Art* (2015, coedited with John Jennings).

Gay, Roxane (1974–)
African American intellectual Roxane Gay is an Associate Professor of English at Purdue University, an editor, and a writer of essays, reviews, short fiction, and comics. Her books include *Ayiti* (2011), the bestselling essay collection *Bad Feminist* (2014), the story collection *Difficult Women* (2017), and the memoir *Hunger* (2017). She has also contributed to numerous newspapers and both online and print magazines, among them *The Guardian*, *The New York Times*, *xoJane*, *Jezebel*, *The Nation*, and *Salon*.

Gladwell, Malcolm (1963–)
Malcolm Gladwell was born in England and raised in Canada; since 1996 he has been a staff writer for *The New Yorker* magazine. He is the bestselling author of non-fiction books such as *The Tipping Point* (2000), *Blink* (2005), *Outliers* (2008), *What the Dog Saw* (2009), and *David and Goliath: Underdogs, Misfits, and the Art of Battling Giants* (2013). Gladwell's podcast *Revisionist History* examines previously unseen facets of historical events.

Glover, Cameron (unknown)

Cameron Glover is an African American writer, podcaster, and sexuality educator whose work has appeared in *Refinery29*, *Wear Your Voice Magazine*, *Harper's Bazaar*, *Glamour*, *Ebony*, and *ThinkProgress*. She is also one of the hosts of *Nerds of Prey*, which she describes as "a nerd culture podcast hosted by four nerdy Black women to show that nerd culture is for everyone."

Hannah-Jones, Nikole (1976–)

Nikole Hannah-Jones is an African American investigative journalist whose work has focused largely on racial injustice. Her work has appeared in *The Atlantic*, *Huffington Post*, *Essence Magazine*, *Grist*, and *Politico*. She became a staff writer for *The New York Times Magazine* in 2015. Hannah-Jones is a co-founder of the Ida B. Wells Society for Investigative Reporting, a news trade organization serving journalists of color.

hooks, bell (1952–)

An award-winning African American author and social activist, Gloria Jean Watkins—writing under the name bell hooks—has written over 30 books of feminist and critical theory, social commentary, media and film theory, and poetry. Her 1981 book *Ain't I a Woman?: Black Women and Feminism* has become an important touchstone in feminist thought. hooks, who became a professor of English in 1976, has taught at such institutions as Yale, Oberlin, and The New School.

Hopkins, Pauline E. (1859–1930)

Pauline Hopkins was an African American singer, writer, and editor. She wrote politically motivated novels and plays, such as the *Slaves' Escape; or, The Underground Railroad* (1880), *Contending Forces: A Romance Illustrative of Negro Life North and South* (1900), *Hagar's Daughter: A Story of Southern Caste Prejudice* (1901–02), *Winona: A Tale of Negro Life in the South and Southwest* (1902–03), and *Of One Blood: Or, The Hidden Self* (1903). She was an editor at *The Colored American Magazine* from 1901 to 1904, writing a great number of essays and biographies for this magazine and others.

Hubbard, Shanita (unknown)

Writer, public speaker, and social justice advocate Shanita Hubbard's work focuses on juvenile justice reform. Her writing has appeared in publications including *The New York Times*, *HuffPost*, *Abernathy*, *Essence*, and *Ebony* magazine. She is also an Adjunct Professor of Criminal Justice at Pennsylvania's Northampton Community College.

Hughes, Langston (1902–67)
Langston Hughes's first poetry collection, *Weary Blues* (1926), established him as a major figure in the Harlem Renaissance, a movement of African American writers, artists, and musicians that flourished in American cities in the 1920s and 1930s. He remained a prolific figure in American literature until his death, writing in a wide range of forms, including plays, screenplays, novels, newspaper columns, and short fiction, as well as poetry.

Hurston, Zora Neale (1891–1960)
African American novelist, playwright, and folklorist Zora Neale Hurston was a significant figure in the Harlem Renaissance of the 1920s and 30s; her novel *Their Eyes Were Watching God* (1937) has come to be considered a twentieth-century classic. Hurston's other books include the novels *Jonah's Gourd Vine* (1934) and *Dust Tracks on a Road* (1942), and an anthropological study, *Mules and Men* (1935).

Jacobs, Harriet (1813–97)
Born in North Carolina, Harriet Jacobs spent her teenage years as a slave to the Norcom family, during which time she had two children. After a difficult escape, which involved seven years spent hiding in her grandmother's crawl space, she traveled to the North, where she lived under threat of re-enslavement until a friend eventually purchased her freedom. As a member of the American Anti-Slavery Society, Jacobs spoke and wrote in favor of abolition; her major work was a memoir, *Incidents in the Life of a Slave Girl*. During and after the Civil War, she undertook numerous projects to improve education, housing, and health care for Black Americans.

Jennings, John (unknown)
African American scholar and comics creator John Jennings has held positions at the University of Illinois-Urbana-Champaign, SUNY Buffalo, and Harvard University. His work as an artist includes the graphic novel *The Hole: Consumer Culture* (2008) and the 2017 graphic adaptation of Octavia Butler's novel *Kindred*. He has also co-edited the comics collections *Black Comix* (2010) and *Black Comix Returns* (2018), as well as curating numerous exhibits on comics. His scholarly works include *The Blacker the Ink: African Americans and Comic Books, Graphic Novels and Sequential Art* (2015, co-edited with Frances Gateward).

Johnson, James Weldon (1871–1938)
African American poet, novelist, songwriter, civil rights leader, educator, and diplomat, James Weldon Johnson was the head of the NAACP from 1920 to 1930. He was also a central figure in the Harlem Renaissance, both for his own

poetry—appearing in works such as *Fifty Years and Other Poems* (1917) and *God's Trombones* (1927)—and for his work collecting Black spirituals and poetry in collections such as *The Book of Negro Spirituals* (1925) and *The Book of Negro Poetry* (1931).

King, Martin Luther, Jr. (1929–68)
A Baptist minister and the leading figure of the American Civil Rights Movement in the 1950s and 1960s, Martin Luther King Jr. received the 1964 Nobel Peace Prize in recognition of his work promoting both civil rights and nonviolence. King was a charismatic speaker and bestselling author; his books include *Stride Toward Freedom* (1958), *Why We Can't Wait* (1964), and *Where Do We Go from Here: Chaos or Community?* (1967). He was assassinated in Memphis, Tennessee.

Knight, Alisha (unknown)
African American scholar Alisha Knight is an Associate Professor of English and American Studies at Washington College, where she studies African American literature and print culture in the late nineteenth and early twentieth centuries. She holds a BA from Spelman College and a PhD from Drew University; her published works include *Pauline Hopkins and the American Dream: An African American Writer's (Re)Visionary Gospel of Success* (2012).

Landrieu, Mitch (1960–)
White American politician Mitch Landrieu served in the Louisiana House of Representatives and as Lieutenant Governor of Louisiana before becoming mayor of New Orleans in 2010. His first book, *In the Shadow of Statues: A White Southerner Confronts History*, was released in 2018.

Lorde, Audre (1934–92)
African American writer, critical theorist, and activist Audre Lorde was part of the Black Arts Movement, dedicated to exploring the cultural and political foundations of African American experience. A writer who drew on all aspects of her own experience as a Black lesbian feminist, she is known for her powerful attacks on racism, sexism, and other forms of social injustice. Her books include poetry collections such as *The First Cities* (1968), *Cables to Rage* (1970), and *Coal* (1976); *The Cancer Journals* (1980) and *Zami: A New Spelling of My Name* (1982), both works of memoir; and the essay collection *Sister Outsider* (1984).

Love, Bettina (unknown)
Black scholar and educator Bettina Love is an Associate Professor of Educational Theory & Practice at the University of Georgia. Her published academic work includes numerous articles and the book *Hip Hop's Li'l Sistas Speak: Negotiating*

Hip Hop Identities and Politics in the New South (2012). In that book, she articulates a vision of Hip Hop pedagogy, a concept she has put into practice with such projects as the Hip Hop civics curriculum GET FREE and the after-school program Real Talk: Hip Hop Education for Social Justice.

Malcolm X (1925–65)

Malcolm X was a highly influential Muslim minister and human rights activist. A leading figure in the Nation of Islam, a religious and political organization advocating for African Americans, Malcolm X became disillusioned with some of its policies and left it in 1964. He then founded the Organization of Afro-American Unity, a pan-Africanist human rights group. In 1965, however, Malcolm X was assassinated by members of the Nation of Islam. His enormously influential *Autobiography*, co-written with Alex Haley, was published shortly after his death.

McKay, Claude (1889–1948)

Writer and activist Claude McKay was a central figure in the Harlem Renaissance. Born in Jamaica, he moved to the United States in 1912, where he first attended the Tuskegee Institute in South Carolina; he then moved to New York. His works include the poetry collections *Songs of Jamaica* (1912) and *Harlem Shadows* (1922), as well as the novels *Home to Harlem* (1928), *Banjo* (1929), and *Banana Bottom* (1933). He also wrote two autobiographies, *A Long Way from Home* (1937), and *My Green Hills of Jamaica* (published posthumously in 1979).

McKenzie, Mia (unknown)

Queer Black feminist writer and activist Mia McKenzie founded the website *Black Girl Dangerous*, which publishes the work of hundreds of queer and trans writers of color; selections from McKenzie's own contributions to the site are collected in her book *Black Girl Dangerous on Race, Queerness, Class and Gender* (2014). She is also a short fiction writer and the author of the Lambda Award-winning novel *The Summer We Got Free* (2013).

Moore, Darnell L. (1976–)

Darnell L. Moore is co-managing editor at the *Feminist Wire*, co-chair of the Queer Newark Oral History project, and a writer-in-residence at the Center on African American Religion, Sexual Politics and Social Justice at Columbia University. His work has been published in *Ebony*, *The Guardian*, and *The Advocate*, as well as in academic journals such as *Harvard Journal of African American Policy* and *QED: A Journal in GLBTQ World Making*. Moore's memoir *No Ashes in the Fire: Coming of Age Black and Free in America* was released in 2018.

Nama, Adilifu (1969–)
Adilifu Nama, an Associate Professor of African American Studies at Loyola Marymount University, is an African American scholar specializing in film and comics. His published works include *Black Space: Imagining Race in Science Fiction Film* (2008), *Super Black: American Pop Culture and Black Superheroes* (2011), and *Race on the QT: Blackness and the Films of Quentin Tarantino* (2015).

Obama, Barack (1961–)
The first African American President of the United States, Barack Obama was inaugurated in 2009 and served two terms as President; his signature legislative achievement was the passage of the 2009 Affordable Care Act. Obama is also known for his writing—notably his memoir *Dreams from My Father* (1995).

Rankine, Claudia (1963–)
Claudia Rankine was born in Kingston, Jamaica, and earned degrees from Williams College and Columbia University. Her published work, which straddles the boundary between poetry and non-fiction prose, includes *Nothing in Nature Is Private* (1995), *Don't Let Me Be Lonely: An American Lyric* (2004), and *Citizen: An American Lyric* (2014), which received a National Book Critics Circle Award. Rankine joined the faculty at Yale University in 2016.

Rustin, Bayard (1912–87)
Bayard Rustin was an African American civil rights organizer and gay rights activist. As an advisor to Martin Luther King Jr. in the 1950s and 60s, Rustin taught King about Gandhi's tactics of non-violent civil disobedience and played a pivotal role in organizing key protests, including the March on Washington. After Civil Rights legislation passed in 1964–65, he turned his attention to economic concerns affecting racial justice. Later in his career, he focused his activism on gay and lesbian rights.

Smith, Zadie (1975–)
The daughter of a Black Jamaican mother and a white English father, Zadie Smith was raised in North London and began her writing career while a student at Cambridge University. The great success of her first book, *White Teeth* (2000), established her reputation as an important writer of fiction; her subsequent novels include *On Beauty* (2005), *NW* (2012), and *Swing Time* (2016). In 2018 she published *Feel Free*, a collection of essays. Smith is also a professor of Creative Writing at New York University.

Sojourner Truth (1797–1883)

Sojourner Truth was born into slavery as Isabella Bomfree in rural New York, and she had several children, all of whom were sold from her, before her escape in 1827. In the following years she became a traveling evangelical preacher, then a prominent speaker and activist who achieved celebrity with her speeches on abolition and women's suffrage. Unable to read or write, she composed her widely read autobiography, *The Narrative of Sojourner Truth* (1850), by dictation. Later in her career, she contributed to the Civil War effort and, during Reconstruction, continued to work to improve the lives of African Americans.

Staples, Brent (1951–)

African American journalist Brent Staples is an editorial writer for *The New York Times*; he has also written and reported for the *New York Times Book Review* and *The Chicago Sun-Times* and contributed to the *Columbia Journalism Review* and the *Los Angeles Times*. His books include the memoir *Parallel Time: Growing Up in Black and White* (1996) and *An American Love Story* (1999).

Stevenson, Bryan (1959–)

Bryan Stevenson is an advocate for victims of racial profiling and sentencing biases in the American justice system. An African American Professor at New York University School of Law, Stevenson is the founder and Executive Director of the Equal Justice Initiative and recipient of several awards including the MacArthur Foundation "Genius" Grant. Stevenson's 2012 TED talk *We need to talk about an injustice* has been viewed over five million times, and his award-winning memoir *Just Mercy* was published in 2014.

Walker, Alice (1944–)

African American writer Alice Walker's novel *The Color Purple* (1982) won the National Book Award and the Pulitzer Prize, establishing her reputation as a major figure in American literature. Walker is also a prominent activist and womanist, advocating in particular for women of color. She continues to contribute to the world of American literature in many genres, including poetry, non-fiction, short stories, and novels.

Wallace, Carvell (unknown)

African American writer and podcaster Carvell Wallace's work has appeared in publications including *The New Yorker*, *GQ*, *The Guardian*, and *New York Times Magazine*. His podcast about race in America, *Closer Than They Appear*, debuted in 2017.

Washington, Booker T. (1846–1916)

Born into slavery, Booker T. Washington was a popular advocate for Black economic progress and education; he also served as principal of the Tuskegee Institute in Alabama from 1881 until the year of his death. Washington built relationships with many white philanthropists and politicians, and those partnerships resulted in the opening of many schools throughout the South. Washington was the author of many books, including *The Future of the American Negro* (1899) and his celebrated autobiography, *Up from Slavery* (1901).

Wells, Ida B. (1862–1931)

Born into slavery in Holly Springs, Mississippi, half a year before the Emancipation Proclamation, Ida B. Wells was an African American journalist and technical writer best known for her extended campaign against lynching. Wells (known after her marriage as Ida B. Wells-Barnett) was also a leading activist in other causes of importance to African Americans; she played a role in the foundation of the National Association for the Advancement of Colored People (NAACP), and was also the founder of the Alpha Suffrage Club, an organization that campaigned for Black women's suffrage.

Zinn, Howard (1922–2010)

Born in Brooklyn to Jewish immigrants, Howard Zinn grew up in a working-class household. After fighting in the Air Force during World War II, he attended college under the G.I. Bill, eventually earning a PhD in history from Columbia University. While teaching at Spelman College in Georgia, he became a Civil Rights activist; after being fired for supporting student protests, he moved to Boston University, where he remained teaching political science until his retirement. His books include *Vietnam: The Logic of Withdrawal* (1967) and the widely used history text *A People's History of the United States* (1980).

PERMISSIONS ACKNOWLEDGMENTS

Adichie, Chimamanda Ngozi. "The Color of an Awkward Conversation." *The Washington Post*, June 8, 2008.

Alexander, Michelle. Excerpt from *The New Jim Crow*. Copyright © 2010, 2012 by Michelle Alexander. Reprinted with the permission of The New Press, www.thenewpress.com.

Baldwin, James. "Stranger in the Village," copyright © 1955, renewed 1983, by James Baldwin. Reprinted with the permission of Beacon Press, Boston. "If Black English Isn't a Language, Then Tell Me What Is?" Copyright © 1979 by James Baldwin. Originally published in *The New York Times*; collected in *James Baldwin: Collected Essays*, published by Library of America. Used by arrangement with the James Baldwin Estate.

Burch, Audra D.S. "The #MeToo Moment: After Alabama, Black Women Wonder, What's Next?" from *The New York Times*, December 14, 2017. Copyright © 2017 The New York Times. All rights reserved. Used by permission and protected by the Copyright Laws of the United States. The printing, copying, redistribution, or retransmission of this Content without express written permission is prohibited.

Capehart, Jonathan. "Taking a Knee with Colin Kaepernick and Standing with Stephen Curry against Trump," from *The Washington Post*, September 24, 2017. Copyright © 2017 The Washington Post. All rights reserved. Used by permission and protected by the Copyright Laws of the United States. The printing, copying, redistribution, or retransmission of this Content without express written permission is prohibited.

Chisholm, Shirley. "Equal Rights for Women," Address to the United States House of Representatives, Washington, DC: May 21, 1969.

Coates, Ta-Nehisi. Excerpt from "The First White President," the Epilogue of *We Were Eight Years in Power: An American Tragedy*. Copyright © 2017 by BCP Literary, Inc. Used with the permission of One World, an imprint of Random House, a division of Penguin Random House LLC. All rights reserved. Any third party use of this material, outside of this publication, is prohibited. Interested parties must apply directly to Penguin Random House LLC for permission. "The Case for Reparations," copyright © 2014 The Atlantic Media Co., as first published in *The Atlantic Magazine*. All rights reserved. Distributed by Tribune Content Agency.

Cole, Teju. "A True Picture of Black Skin," from *The New York Times Magazine*, February 18, 2015. Copyright © 2015 The New York Times. All rights reserved. Used by permission and protected by the Copyright Laws of the United States. The printing, copying, redistribution, or retransmission of this Content without express written permission is prohibited.

Dow, Dawn Marie. "The Deadly Challenge of Raising African American Boys," from *Gender and Society* 30.2 (April 2016): 161-188. Reprinted with the permission of Sage Jounals via Copyright Clearance Center, Inc.

Dunbar-Nelson, Alice. "The Negro Woman and the Ballot," from *The Messenger* 9, April 1927. Subsequently published in *Let Nobody Turn Us Around: An African American Anthology*, edited by Manning Marable and Leith Mullings. Rowman & Littlefield Publishers, 2009.

Fanon, Frantz. Excerpt from "On Violence," from *The Wretched of the Earth*. English translation copyright © 1963 by Présence Africaine. Reprinted with the permission of Grove/Atlantic, Inc. Any third party use of this material, outside of this publication, is prohibited.

Gateward, Francis, and John Jennings. Excerpt from "The Sweeter the Christmas," Introduction to *The Blacker the Ink: Constructions of Black Identity in Comics and Sequential Art*. New Brunswick, NJ: Rutgers University Press, 2015. Copyright © 2015 by Rutgers, the State University. Reprinted with the permission of Rutgers University Press.

Gay, Roxane. "The Politics of Respectability," from *Bad Feminist*. Copyright © 2014 by Roxane Gay. Reprinted with the permission of HarperCollins Publishers.

Gladwell, Malcolm. "None of the Above: What I.Q. Doesn't Tell You About Race," from *The New Yorker*, 17 December 2007. Reprinted with the permission of Malcolm Gladwell.

Glover, Cameron. "No, Black-Only Safe Spaces Are Not Racist," from *Wear Your Voice Magazine*, May 31, 2017. Reprinted with the permission of Cameron Glover.

Hannah-Jones, Nikole. "School Segregation: The Continuing Tragedy of Ferguson," from *ProPublica*, December 19, 2014. Reprinted with the permission of ProPublica.

hooks, bell. "Coming to Class Consciousness," Chapter 2 of *Where We Stand: Class Matters*. Routledge, 2000. Reprinted with the permission of Taylor and Francis Group LLC Books via Copyright Clearance Center, Inc.

Hubbard, Shanita. "Russell Simmons, R. Kelly, and Why Black Women Can't Say #MeToo," from *The New York Times*, December 15, 2017. Copyright © 2017 The New York Times. All rights reserved. Used by permission and protected by the Copyright Laws of the United States. The printing, copying, redistribution, or retransmission of this Content without express written permission is prohibited.

Hughes, Langston. "The Negro Artist and the Racial Mountain," from *The Nation Magazine*, June 23, 1926.

Hurston, Zora Neale. "How It Feels to Be Colored Me," copyright © 1928 by Zora Neale Hurston.

King, Martin Luther Jr. "Letter from Birmingham Jail," from *Why We Can't Wait*. HarperCollins, 1963. Reprinted by arrangement with The Heirs to the Estate of Martin Luther King Jr., c/o Writers House as agent for the proprietor, New York, NY. Copyright © 1963 Dr. Martin Luther King Jr. Copyright renewed 1991 Corretta Scott King.

Knight, Alisha. Excerpt from "'To Aid in Every Way Possible in Uplifting the Colored People of America': Hopkins's Revisionary Definition of African American Success," in *Pauline Hopkins and the American Dream: An African American Writer's (Re)Visionary Gospel of Success*. Copyright © 2012 by The University of Tennessee Press. Reprinted with permission.

Landrieu, Mitch. Excerpt from "Truth: Remarks on the Removal of Confederate Monuments in New Orleans," May 19, 2017.

Lorde, Audre. "The Transformation of Silence into Language and Action," and "Uses of Anger," from *Sister Outsider*, published by Crossing Press. Copyright © 1984, 2007 by Audre Lorde. Reprinted with the permission of the Charlotte Sheedy Literary Agency.

Love, Bettina. Excerpt from Chapters 7 and 8 of *Hip Hop's Li'l Sistas Speak: Negotiating Hip Hop Identities and Politics in the New South*. New York: Peter Lang Publishing, 2012. Reprinted with the permission of Peter Lang Publishing, via Copyright Clearance Center, Inc.

McKenzie, Mia. "White Silence," from *Black Girl Dangerous: On Race, Queerness, Class and Gender*. Oakland: BGD Press, 2014. Reprinted with permission from Black Girl Dangerous Media.

Moore, Darnell L. "Black, LGBT, American: A Search for Sanctuaries," from *The Advocate*, July 13, 2013. Reprinted with the permission of Here Publishing Inc.

Nama, Adilifu. Excerpt from the Introduction to *Super Black: American Pop Culture and Black Superheroes*. Copyright © 2011 by University of Texas Press. Reprinted with the permission of the publisher.

Obama, Barack. A More Perfect Union, 2008.

Rankine, Claudia. Excerpt from Part II of *Citizen: An American Lyric*. Copyright © 2014 by Claudia Rankine. Reprinted with the permission of The Permissions Company, Inc., on behalf of Graywolf Press, www.graywolfpress.org.

Rustin, Bayard. "'Black Power' and Coalition Politics, 1966," reprinted from *Commentary*, September 1966. Used with the permission of Walter Naegle, Executor, The Estate of Bayard Rustin.

Smith, Zadie. "Getting In and Out: Who Owns Black Pain?" Published by *Harper's Magazine*, July 2017. Copyright © Zadie Smith. Reprinted with the permission of the author c/o Rogers, Coleridge & White Ltd., 20 Powis Mews, London W11 1JN.

Staples, Brent. "The Movie 'Get Out' Is a Strong Antidote to the Myth of 'Postracial' America," from *The New York Times*, March 27, 2017. Copyright © 2017 The New York Times. All rights reserved. Used by permission and protected by the Copyright Laws of the United States. The printing, copying, redistribution, or retransmission of this Content without express written permission is prohibited.

Stevenson, Bryan. "The Stonecatchers' Song of Sorrow," from *Just Mercy: A Story of Justice and Redemption*. Copyright © 2014 by Bryan Stevenson. Used by permission of Spiegel & Grau, an imprint of Random House, a division of Penguin Random House LLC. All rights reserved. Any third party use of this material, outside of this publication, is prohibited. Interested parties must apply directly to Penguin Random House LLC for permission.

Walker, Alice. "In Search of Our Mothers' Gardens: The Creativity of Black Women in the South." Copyright © *Ms. Magazine*, 2002. Reprinted with the permission of Ms. Magazine.

The Wall Street Journal Editorial Board. "The Politicization of Everything: Everybody Loses in the Trump-NFL Brawl Over the National Anthem," from *The Wall Street Journal*, Sept. 24, 2017. Copyright © 2017 Dow Jones & Company, Inc. Reprinted with permission of Dow Jones & Company, Inc. All Rights Reserved Worldwide. License number 4310940727235.

Wallace, Carvell. "Why 'Black Panther' Is a Defining Moment for Black America" from *The New York Times Magazine*, February 12, 2018. Copyright © 2018 The New York Times. All rights reserved. Used with permission and protected by the Copyright Laws of the United States. The printing, copying, redistribution, or retransmission of the Content without express written permission is prohibited.

X, Malcolm. Excerpts from "Saved," "Saviour," and "Satan," from *The Autobiography of Malcolm X*, as told to Alex Haley. Copyright © 1964 by Alex Haley and Malcolm X. Copyright © 1965 by Alex Haley and Betty Shabazz. Used by permission of Ballantine Books, an imprint of Random House, a divsion of Penguin Random House LLC. All rights reserved. Any third party use of this material, outside of this publication, is prohibitied. Interested parties must apply directly to Penguin Random House for permission.

Zinn, Howard. Excerpt from "Or Does It Explode?" Chapter 17 of *A People's History of The United States: 1492–Present*. Copyright © 1980 by Howard Zinn. Reprinted with the permission of HarperCollins Publishers.

Color Insert:

Jonathan Bachman. Police arrest Leshia Evans at a protest over the police shooting death of Alton Sterling in Baton Rouge on July 9, 2016. REUTERS/Jonathan Bachman.

Whitney Curtis. Rashaad Davis, 23, backs away slowly as St. Louis County police officers approach him with guns drawn and eventually arrest him on Monday, Aug. 11, 2014, at the corner of Canfield Drive and West Florissant Avenue in Ferguson, Missouri. Copyright © Whitney Curtis, 2014.

Photograph of Emmett Till. Bettmann/Getty Images.

The body of Emmett Till, shown before an open casket funeral, from *Chicago Defender*.

Gordon Parks. "Ondria Tanner and Her Grandmother Window-shopping, Mobile, Alabama, 1956." Courtesy of and copyright © The Gordon Parks Foundation.

Amy Sherald. Portrait of Michelle LaVaughn Robinson Obama. Oil on linen, 2018. National Portrait Gallery, Smithsonian Institution. The National Portrait Gallery is grateful to the following lead donors for their support of the Obama portraits: Kate Capshaw and Steven Spielberg; Judith Kern and Kent Whealy; Tommie L. Pegues and Donald A. Capoccia.

Kehinde Wiley. Portrait of Barack Obama. Oil on canvas, 2018. National Portrait Gallery, Smithsonian Institution. The National Portrait Gallery is grateful to the following lead donors for their support of the Obama portraits: Kate Capshaw and Steven Spielberg; Judith Kern and Kent Whealy; Tommie L. Pegues and Donald A. Capoccia. Copyright © 2018 Kehinde Wiley.

The publisher has made every attempt to locate all copyright holders of the material published in this book, and would be grateful for information that would allow correction of any errors or omissions in subsequent editions of the work.

INDEX

From the Publisher

A name never says it all, but the word "Broadview" expresses a good deal of the philosophy behind our company. We are open to a broad range of academic approaches and political viewpoints. We pay attention to the broad impact book publishing and book printing has in the wider world; for some years now we have used 100% recycled paper for most titles. Our publishing program is internationally oriented and broad-ranging. Our individual titles often appeal to a broad readership too; many are of interest as much to general readers as to academics and students.

Founded in 1985, Broadview remains a fully independent company owned by its shareholders—not an imprint or subsidiary of a larger multinational.

For the most accurate information on our books (including information on pricing, editions, and formats) please visit our website at www.broadviewpress.com. Our print books and ebooks are also available for sale on our site.

broadview press
www.broadviewpress.com

This book is made of paper from well-managed FSC® - certified forests, recycled materials, and other controlled sources.

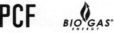